D0374456

Also by Brian Lamb:
*Booknotes: America's Finest Authors on Reading,
Writing, and the Power of Ideas*

Also by C-SPAN:
Traveling Tocqueville's America

BOOKNOTES:
LIFE STORIES

Booknotes
LIFE STORIES

Notable Biographers on the
People Who Shaped America

Brian Lamb

THREE RIVERS PRESS • NEW YORK

Copyright © 1999 by National Cable Satellite Corporation

Published by Three Rivers Press, New York, New York. Member of the
Crown Publishing Group.

Random House, Inc. New York, Toronto, London, Sydney, Auckland
www.randomhouse.com

THREE RIVERS PRESS is a registered trademark and the Three Rivers Press
colophon is a trademark of Random House, Inc.

Originally published in hardcover by Times Books, in 1999

Printed in the United States of America

Design by Robert C. Olsson

Library of Congress Cataloging-in-Publication Data
Booknotes : life stories : notable biographers on the people who shaped
America / [compiled] by Brian Lamb.
p.   cm.
Collection of essays by various biographers based on interviews originally
held on the television program Booknotes.
Includes index.
1. Biography.   I. Lamb, Brian, 1941–.   II. Booknotes (Television program)
CT104.B62 1999
920.02—dc21   98-41374
ISBN 0-8129-3339-7

10 9 8 7 6 5 4

This book is dedicated to the 114 cable television executives who have served on the C-SPAN board since the company's founding in 1978. And to six people who have had special roles since the early 1970s. They are all still close friends—of mine and the network's—today.

- *John Evans, whose commitment to C-SPAN began in 1977 over lunch at the Westpark Hotel in Arlington, Virginia, and continues to this day.*

- *Paul FitzPatrick, who put order to my lack of organization.*

- *Henry Goldberg, our attorney, who, among other things, brought us financial stability with the best satellite deal in the world.*

- *Barbara Ruger, who said the magazine column would make a difference, and it did.*

- *Bob Titsch, who took the first big chance and backed it up.*

- *Clay T. Whitehead, who truly understood how technology could offer choice, allowing many new voices to be heard.*

Foreword:
Bob Loomis on the Art and
Craft of Publishing

Bob Loomis, vice president and executive editor at Random House, is one of the best-known editors in the publishing business. For more than forty years, he has edited some of the most successful writers on the American scene—Shelby Foote, Neil Sheehan, William Styron, Maya Angelou, Daniel Boorstin, and John Toland. He edited a number of the biographies featured in this book, including Sam Tanenhaus's Whittaker Chambers *and Edmund Morris's long-awaited biography of Ronald Reagan. In September 1997, he granted C-SPAN his first-ever television interview for our* About Books *series. From that interview, we share with you some of Bob Loomis's insights on writing, editing, and the publishing business.*

The initial excitement is the best. That's when you get the manuscript, you're partway in it, and you know it's really something. There's nothing like that, because so often it's disappointing. One percent of what I read, I want to publish. So you hit that one percent, and it's quite remarkable.

The problem with this emotion is that, in publishing today, wanting to publish a book doesn't mean you get to publish it. It was never like that before. Our decision was "Can we publish it? Do we want to?" Now, if we decide to publish it, we go through an auction and a whole rigmarole of money. Since in an auction at least five to eight people are involved, it means four to seven people can't get it, no matter what. That happens over and over again. . . .

In this business you have to have a kind of catholic taste, because what the person's writing, and the way he writes it, and the effectiveness of it is what counts. In fact, we looked for books that were for the Vietnam War or had an alternative point of view because most publishers are quite liberal. Bennett [Cerf, former head of Random House] was always anxious to find someone who could write something from another point of view. We would do it if it was a good book. He felt that we had some sort of obligation, perhaps.

My politics probably have a lot to do with my initial interest in a book. But beyond that, I think that a book that can change your mind and make you see something in a different way is important. I'm a liberal Democrat; my family was Republican. My father was a Republican in a little town, Conneaut, Ohio, up on Lake Erie. When I got to college [my politics] changed.

I went to Duke for two reasons: One, there was a fellow there named Newman Ivey White, an English professor who was very well known. He was a Shelley scholar. I didn't have much interest in Shelley, but I'd heard of White. Also, they had a great football team when I was a kid. I never thought of an eastern school. It just didn't enter my mind. I wanted to get away. I wanted to go someplace different, out of Ohio. I was lucky because Duke was a remarkable place then. From a literary point of view, it was better than any other college in the United States in the late forties. Bill Styron was there. *New York Magazine* founder Clay Felker was my roommate at school. Peter Maas was there. Mac Hyman, who wrote *No Time for Sergeants,* was there. Guy Davenport was another roommate. A lot of people. Most of us came up to New York. I was very lucky that happened.

I couldn't get an editorial job at all. Then I got a job in a book-advertising agency, which I hated, writing ads for books I had never read—headlines and things. After about a year I couldn't stand it, and I was going to go back and be a teacher. I quit.

Charles Denhard, at this agency, found there was a reader's job open at Appleton-Century-Crofts, and he called me the day before I left. I shudder when I think of it. I got it. So then I was in.

I arrived at Random House in 1957. There isn't any comparison to today at all. Bennett Cerf ran it as a family. He never said anything unkind to anybody. If he went in the room and saw three people, he would leave. We had no editorial meetings, we had no lawyers. Everybody was on his own, pretty much. We went to Donald Klopfer, co-founder of Random House, or Bennett to get a book signed up. That wasn't too hard because then we only paid for what we thought the hardcover would sell. The paperback and book club revenues—everything else was extra. That made assessing the book easier. Now we figure out all of those things, and we pay that to the author as an advance. That has to be earned off by the publisher, and it usually isn't—except in enough cases to keep us afloat.

The biggest thing today is money. It's what we talk about a lot. Even in editorial meetings, money is what we have to deal with to get a book and buy it. We're used to it now, but in this business, it's also hard to evaluate things at that stage. We really don't know unless there's a track record for the author.

The bookstore situation was also entirely different when I came to Random House. Our sales force was always good, and we told stores what we wanted them to do, what titles they should take. Of course, if we were wrong, they wouldn't trust us anymore, but we were [often] right. Random House was the only one early on that could do that.

Now the stores are so powerful. In some cases you have a thousand stores—so they have a lot of clout. Dealing with a store has become much more arduous, difficult—and rewarding, too, because they have this power. Then, there are the jobbers, the middlemen, the warehouses. Ingram, a distribution company, once had only two warehouses. I think they now have eight that we have to sell to and which have to have books. That's one of the reasons returns are great. When a book stops selling—that pipeline is very big now and full, sometimes—they come back. That's a money problem, again, isn't it really?

I've been fortunate because of Random House's continuity. With authors like Shelby Foote, and Maya Angelou, and Bill Styron, and Daniel Boorstin—we published all of their books from the beginning. It is very gratifying to have that happen because now people move a lot. They don't stay where they are, mostly because of money. It's hard to turn down another thirty thousand or hundred thousand dollars from some other company just to stay. Those people are all favorite people of mine, and we've had a marvelous relationship for years.

When Shelby first signed up, it was for a one-volume short history of the Civil War. After about a year or so, he came to us and he said, "Here's your money back. I can't do it in one. It's going to be three volumes. It's going to take me years and years and years. I understand you might not want to do that." But Bennett said yes, and so began this marvelous series, which sold well, but not really well.

Shelby never got a Pulitzer Prize, never got a book award. I think when these volumes came out, to have a novelist write a serious history, academically, was out of favor. There weren't any footnotes, and there was no bibliography either. But they're impeccable.

Shelby is the most careful and meticulous man. On the last volume of *The Civil War*—we're talking about a million and a half words—I said, "Let's put the whole manuscript through to the printer without copy editing it." It had never been done before, but it worked. . . . He knew what he was doing. We've never even had to make corrections in those books. Isn't that amazing? He wrote it in a quill pen with ink, by hand, in a room where the walls were covered with faces of the Civil War people he was writing about. [A sample of Shelby Foote's manuscript is found on page xii.] When he finished it, he had postpartum depression.

From the beginning, I speak for the book. Editors do more than edit. You represent people at a house. You watch the design, the advertising. You work on the flap copy, deal with legal problems, and present the book to the sales force. I feel very strongly about it. I like our sales force a lot. It's part of what one has to do to follow up on books. If you have reservations about it, it's hard to do that well. They know it. So I've been lucky. I've been able to do mostly things that I believed in.

We know the contract calls for a satisfactory manuscript. The author morally, ethically, and by contract has the final say on what's in a book. Nothing can be changed in a book here without the author's approval. It's not

like a magazine. It's his work. He owns it. We're only licensed to publish it. It's his copyright. If it's way off, we tend to wait quite a while for it to right itself. When it doesn't, we can then turn it down. And we do, we have. That's a very awkward situation. We try to get the money back if it sells elsewhere. We should get it back right away, but, of course, the person's done a lot of work. Anyway, if you go after money from a writer who has spent time and written material, you'd have a terrible reputation. It's just something that one couldn't do, unless there were some flagrant abuses. There was one time when we had a contract with S. J. Perelman, and it had been out for years. Perelman started going around at parties saying, "I've got a contract with Random House for twenty thousand, thirty thousand dollars. I'm not gonna write it, but they'll never ask for it back. They don't do that." Bennett heard that once too often, and he went after him and got it back. That's very rare, frankly.

What does it take to be a successful writer? At writers' conferences you'll see a lot of people who want to write. Some of them write a lot, and some of them don't write very much. They write a few pages or chapters, and then they want to get published. Excuse me!

I heard Sinclair Lewis was once inveigled to go to a writers' course at his old high school or college, and he stood up and said, "How many people in this room want to be writers?" Everybody put his hand up. He said, "Why aren't you home writing?"

It's the way you learn. You write, and you read, and you write again. The problem, then, is trying to get contacts. But at the writers' conferences, I see these people saying, "Nobody gets published anymore." Not true. *Publishers Weekly* recently made one of their surveys about what was published in the last year. You know how many novels were published? Three thousand, three hundred novels—all in one year.

This is a very stimulating job. I wanted to be a teacher. My father was a teacher, my mother was a teacher. The problem with teaching is you don't learn anything after a while. You keep teaching the same thing every year. Here, I learn something new every day. But I also teach, in a way, what to do. . . . It's like being a mentor to somebody, in a professional way. Both of those things are very satisfying to me. I luckily found that out. A lot of people work at things they're not suited for.

Why did I agree to this interview? I don't think talking about writers and what they do—and I hope I haven't done it here—is anybody's business. Whether they have problems or not, that's private. Somebody else could do it, but my relationship with them is one of, I hope, confidentiality. One doesn't breach that, and one shouldn't. I never even put it into words before, but that's really what it is about.

Acknowledgments

At C-SPAN, a core team of five people made this book happen: Anne Bentzel, Susan Swain, Lea Anne Long, Carol Hellwig, and Robin Scullin. Having just finished a book on Tocqueville's travels in America for us, Anne Bentzel jumped into this book project with great enthusiasm. Her adaptability and hard work have made *Booknotes: Life Stories* possible. Another big thanks goes to C-SPAN's executive vice president, Susan Swain. If this book were a campaign, Susan would be the invaluable campaign manager.

Other members on our C-SPAN book team include Lea Anne Long and Carol Hellwig. Lea Anne, among her many other "hats" at C-SPAN, coordinated the author photos in both books. Without her help, readers would have no record of what these authors look like. Carol Hellwig spent lots of time fact-checking and line-editing this book—with unflagging good humor. Thanks also to Robin Scullin, our books producer in programming, who contributed her experience for a few weeks to help with the manuscript.

Our other executive vice president, Rob Kennedy, is an ardent supporter of the *Booknotes* program and the two books. Bruce Collins, our corporate counsel, and Barkley Kern, our business manager, helped get both books going, and I appreciate their initiative and ongoing counsel.

Our current chairman, Leo Hindery, who is the CEO of TCI cable and an enthusiastic book lover, has managed during a very busy time to do everything he can to increase C-SPAN and C-SPAN2's distribution to his cable systems. He is the twelfth C-SPAN executive committee chairman, each of whom understood the inherent public service offered through C-SPAN's programming. All played enormous roles in the growth of our network: Bob Rosencrans, John Saeman, Ed Allen, Jack Frazee, Jim Whitson, Gene Schneider, Amos Hostetter, John Evans, Jim Gray, Jim Robbins, Tom Baxter, and finally, Leo.

There are so many others to thank in the category of longtime C-SPAN supporters in this, our twentieth-anniversary year. Just a few of those names include: Bob Schmidt, Tom Wheeler, Jim Mooney, Steve Effros, and Decker Anstrom; Steve Janger and Michael Kelley; Don West, Jack Nelson, John Siegenthaler, and Pat Gushman.

My author tour for the first book would not have been a success if it had not been for ardent reader Rich Fahle, our media relations manager. Karen Jarmon designed our advertising strategy; Ivy Brown, responsible for all travel arrangements here at the network, helped organize my thirty-eight-city tour in a seemingly effortless manner.

Also at C-SPAN, Connie Brod and Nick Aretakis have been seminal to our book projects. Connie, Robin, and Nick were busy this past fall launching our new weekend series on C-SPAN2 called *Book TV.* Vice presidents Terry Murphy and Kathy Murphy have helped oversee the content and the look of our book programming. Brett Betsill, Maurice Haynes, Kevin King, Kevin Washburn, Amy Cupp, Dei Potter, and Hope Landy have been invaluable members of the *Booknotes* production team over the years. Marge Amey, in Viewer Services, processes the ideas viewers have for our book programming. Joanne Wheeler and her team in Education Relations introduce our book programming to teachers.

More recently, C-SPAN Online has created entire *Booknotes* and *Book TV* sites (at www.booknotes.org and booktv.org). Thanks to Tom Lalonde and his supervisor, Roxane Kerr, for keeping the online book information up-to-date and thorough.

At Times Books, thanks especially to Peter Bernstein, Times Books' publisher. He was tireless in his support of *"Booknotes I,"* as we now call it, and determined to make *"Booknotes II"* as successful. Our editor, Philip Turner, gently helped shape the manuscript and organize the themes of these mini-biographies. In the Times Books publicity department, our thanks to Carie Freimuth, Mary Beth Roche, and to Will Weisser—who is so enthusiastic, we almost think he likes our books.

Thanks to Jane and Garry Metcalf for their special support during my visit to take photos in Kansas City.

Our Washington, D.C.–based literary agent, Rafe Sagalyn, has been attentive to this project since the beginning. He got us going on this second book. A big thanks to Geoffrey Sonner and Suzanne Weaver at the R. R. Donnelley & Sons printing plant in Harrisonburg, Virginia. They indulged this overly curious author—the first one to visit the plant—for a whole afternoon.

Finally, a special thanks to all of the authors who have appeared on *Booknotes* over the past decade. This book is meant as a tribute to their years spent researching and writing. We hope to inspire readers of *Booknotes: Life Stories* to search out their biographies, memoirs, and studies.

Contents

Introduction

Dayton, Ohio, in July 1998 was one of the last tour stops promoting our 1997 book, *Booknotes: America's Finest Authors on Reading, Writing, and the Power of Ideas.* Laura Dempsey, a reporter for the *Dayton Daily News,* captured the scene for her readers:

> Dayton loves its C-SPAN, that much is clear. Lamb said his worst book-signing was in Dallas when six people showed up "and three of them were friends of mine." He laughed loud and long when a man from the audience quoted a friend who said, "I don't think Lamb ever reads the books (of the authors he interviews). He asks such dumb questions."

I laughed because I do read every book we discuss on *Booknotes.* And I'd heard that criticism of my questioning style before. Admittedly, my question, "Who was Abraham Lincoln?" did elicit raised eyebrows from a Lincoln historian. His answer, perhaps because the question is just too obvious for most to ask, was nonetheless interesting. My interviewing philosophy is simple: I'm not in that chair on behalf of intellectuals; my job is to ask questions on behalf of the average George and Jane, Cathy and Jim.

Booknotes celebrates its tenth anniversary in 1999. It began in April 1989 following a successful experiment the previous September when we aired a five-part interview with journalist Neil Sheehan about his Vietnam War epic, *A Bright Shining Lie.* A decade later, the series remains one of the simplest productions on television—one nonfiction book, one author, a black-curtained background, and an uninterrupted hour of conversation.

Booknotes: Life Stories is the second collection of essays based on these interviews of *Booknotes* authors. We've created brief portraits of interesting people who lived during the past three centuries, seen through the eyes of many of the nation's best-known biographers and memoirists. Reflecting C-SPAN's public affairs mission, this book focuses primarily on people in American political life.

In essence, you will read the writers in their own words. My questions are omitted so that the interviews read more like essays. The transcripts have been excerpted and those excerpts minimally edited, but they by intention retain a conversational tone. To help ensure that we were faithful to each author's original meaning, brackets and ellipses were used to indicate words added or deleted within paragraphs. Curious readers who wonder what they are missing can find complete transcripts of every interview on our website (www.booknotes.org).

A collection of biographies was an obvious sequel to our first book. Fully one third of the books discussed on *Booknotes* have been biographies. Our view is that history and issues, seen through the experiences of people who shaped them, come more fully alive. Presidential biographer Edmund Morris also reminds us that biographies serve another purpose. "In examining the lives of other people," he says, "one examines one's own."

Booknotes viewers always inquire how books are selected for our program. Many of the biographies we choose reflect my curiosity to learn more about people whose names I've heard all my life. As a broadcast journalist, I knew about Ernie Pyle and Father Charles Coughlin, yet I couldn't have supplied much detail. Reading their biographies and spending an hour with their biographers, James Tobin and the late Donald Warren, was a real education for me. You can learn why by reading our chapters on Pyle and Coughlin.

A review of the table of contents reveals this book's informal approach to history. Rather than attempting a comprehensive survey of American political lives, our selections come from recent biographies, published in the United States, about interesting people in various aspects of public life. Keeping it simple, chapters are grouped by century and subjects organized chronologically by their birth dates.

Individual chapters are brief and anecdotal; this book is intended to whet your appetite for more. And no matter how famous their names, we think you'll read some interesting new stories about our chosen subjects:

- Teddy Roosevelt gave a campaign speech with a bullet in his chest. Campaigning in Milwaukee in 1912, he was shot by an anti–third term fanatic. Biographer Nathan Miller recounts, "He'd once been told when he was in the army to [try to] cough up blood to see if he'd been wounded internally. . . . He did not cough up blood, so he knew that it was not a very serious wound. He immediately demanded to be taken to the hall . . . and stood for ninety minutes giving the speech while he had a bullet in his chest. Blood was pouring over the front of his shirt."
- Albert Einstein's brain, sought after by admiring scientists, ended up in pieces in Princeton, Philadelphia, and Japan. Einstein biographer Denis Brian devoted an entire chapter to the physicist's brain, calling the discovery of its fate "shocking news. It was exactly what he didn't want to happen."
- Paul Revere never really said "The British are coming." David Hackett Fischer, author of *Paul Revere's Ride,* noted that in 1775, the colonists "still

thought that they were British." Instead, the famous midnight rider warned his fellow Bostonians, "The regulars are out."

• General George Armstrong Custer, defeated at Little Big Horn, was a sentimental lover and an adoring husband. He regularly wrote hundred-page love letters to his wife, Libby. For her part, Libby made a career out of their union. Writer Louise Barnett reports that after Custer died, Libby went on the lecture circuit. "Being his widow did become a profession for her. . . . She became wealthy giving lectures about their life on the frontier."

• Harry and Bess Truman, after leaving the White House, decided to drive across the country by themselves. No Secret Service. No aides. Truman historian David McCullough says that Bess insisted the former president keep to the speed limit. Passing motorists were amazed. Mr. McCullough said drivers "would drop back and pass them again, just to see if their eyes were playing tricks on them."

• George Washington actually could tell a lie. Presidential biographer Richard Norton Smith says that while the first president was "profoundly honest," he was also capable of deception. Traveling extensively, dogged by admiring crowds, and tired, Washington told one group "to meet him at the hotel at eight o'clock in the morning, and at five-thirty A.M. he climbed into his coach and rode off."

• Tycoon John D. Rockefeller, Sr., had an unusual food habit. A New Age health fanatic, he chewed all his food—even liquids—ten times before swallowing. Author Ron Chernow said that people who were "absolutely thrilled to be invited to the luncheon table of the world's richest man found themselves, after twenty minutes, finished with their own food and for the next hour watching John D. finish his."

• Julia Grant was the first First Lady to secure the White House gates. "She had the gates locked so the children could play on the White House lawns; they couldn't have people staggering in there half drunk and passing out under the trees on the South Lawn," says Geoffrey Perret, author of *Ulysses S. Grant: Soldier and President.*

• During the time of Franklin and Eleanor Roosevelt, the White House was like "a residential hotel." Doris Kearns Goodwin, in *No Ordinary Time,* says "there were about seven people living there, all of whom were intimate friends of either Franklin or Eleanor."

If you notice a special interest in presidents, you're correct. From George Washington to Bill Clinton, twenty-two presidents' lives are highlighted in this book. Presidents have always been important subjects for C-SPAN, since we believe that the lives of the forty-one men who have held this office mirror the broader landscape of American history and values.

Presidents also became a personal interest for me through the *Booknotes* series, so much so that a few years back, I set out on an unusual journey—visiting all thirty-six presidential grave sites and the eleven presidential libraries. Most biographers tell me they learn through experience, too. David Hackett Fischer took riding lessons and then rode all the sections of Paul Revere's route that haven't been covered with asphalt. He also walked the old battle road used by retreating British troops.

For his John Quincy Adams biography, Paul Nagel read, more than once, all of the papers of our prolific sixth president—an estimated nine miles of microfilm.

Robert Richardson spent thirty years at the library. Using library records, he checked out every book Ralph Waldo Emerson had borrowed, reading each one several times himself. His was an intellectual biography, interpreting Emerson's life through what he read.

Carol Reardon, a professor of military history, remembers her first trip to Gettysburg—with her parents when she was in third grade. Today, she takes students there, urging them across the battlefield's stone fence, site of General Pickett's charge, to give them a feel for the conditions of battle.

I went to the stone fence at Gettysburg with Professor Reardon, too. She is one of thirty-one *Booknotes* writers who agreed to be photographed for this book. Armed with a point-and-shoot camera, I met most of these authors in their workplaces or at sites connected with their subjects: Jon Katz at the home of Thomas Paine in New Rochelle, New York; Neil Baldwin at Thomas Edison's lab in West Orange, New Jersey; Monica Crowley outside Richard Nixon's former home in Upper Saddle River, New Jersey. You'll see the results in two sections of color photographs.

Interviewing more than five hundred authors during the past decade has taught me a lot about the book business. Publishing two books of my own has nonetheless been full of learning experiences, none more interesting than my 1997–98 book tour.

We pushed hard on that tour, visiting thirty-eight cities in thirteen months, doing numerous book events and 130 radio, television, and newspaper interviews. The first stop still holds the record for attendance. Five hundred people came to the Barnes & Noble in New York's Union Square in June 1997. I'm certain it wasn't my presence that brought them; Times Books had assembled a world-class panel of writers from our first book—David Halberstam, Stanley Crouch, and Pete Hamill—to talk about the writing craft.

I was so intrigued by the book tour process that I kept a photo album of the entire thirteen months. It seemed as if nearly every stop included a surprise visitor—a distant relative, an old navy buddy, colleagues from long-ago jobs. Frequently, people brought books they hoped we'd consider for *Booknotes*. During one week in California, I acquired eleven different hardcovers.

Booknotes, airing weekly, can only accommodate fifty-two books a year, so I'm pleased to report that we've created another outlet for books. Last fall, as this book was being edited, we launched our largest book-related effort yet—*Book TV.* For forty-eight hours every weekend on C-SPAN2, we offer visits to unique libraries and bookstores, author readings, book clubs, interviews, and more. This large commitment to nonfiction books reflects our belief that reading is important and that nonfiction books play a significant role in today's political and cultural discourse. Nonfiction books are an appropriate extension of C-SPAN's public affairs mission.

All of the public affairs programming on C-SPAN's television channels, FM radio station, and internet sites, are possible because of the continuing support of the people who run the country's cable television systems. This year, C-SPAN marks its twentieth anniversary as a public affairs network. Two decades ago, seeing its value as a public service, Bob Rosencrans, who ran a cable company called UA-Columbia, wrote a check for $25,000 as seed money to start C-SPAN. Bob became our network's first chairman and his support encouraged others in the industry. By the time the U.S. House was ready to televise its sessions on March 19, 1978, our own group of "founding fathers and mothers" had helped build a satellite uplink, sign up a network of three million cable homes, and a hire staff of three.

Twenty years later, now 260 persons strong, C-SPAN can be seen in over seventy-three million U.S. homes; C-SPAN2 is available in about 55 million homes. Those who have been with us since the beginning know that building C-SPAN—a not-for-profit network that operates in an extremely competitive commercial business—has been both challenging and rewarding. Our story is one of the power of combined efforts focused on a common goal—cable operators who contribute license fees and valuable channel space for our programming; hardworking C-SPAN staffers such as Jana Fay, our first employee and today our vice president of finance; and some amazingly dedicated viewers. Together, they have nurtured the C-SPAN concept of offering ongoing televised access to the political process. C-SPAN, it's important to note, receives no government money and no government mandates for carriage on cable or satellite systems. Totally funded by affiliates fees, C-SPAN is a uniquely American story of a private industry's commitment to offering a public service.

If you have been a C-SPAN viewer for a while, thank you for keeping this unique public service alive with your viewership. If this book is your entree to C-SPAN, we welcome you to a network of people who care about history, issues, ideas, and—of course—books.

Brian Lamb
February 1999
Washington, D.C.

1700s

When you write a biography, you know more about the man than practically anybody in the world, including his wife or his best friends, because you know it from so many different sources.

—Denis Brian

George Washington

by
RICHARD NORTON SMITH

Presidential historian Richard Norton Smith appeared on Booknotes *on February 21, 1993, to discuss* Patriarch: George Washington and the New American Nation *(Houghton Mifflin, 1993). The first president of the United States (1732–99) began his military service in 1752 with the Virginia militia in the French and Indian Wars. He led the American forces through the Revolution, holding the army together during the terrible winter at Valley Forge in 1777–78. In 1789, he was unanimously elected president and was reelected in 1792.*

HE WAS BORN IN WESTMORELAND COUNTY, Virginia. People tend to think of Washington as a natural-born aristocrat, but that's not true. He was the oldest son of a second marriage. We don't know much about his father. It's interesting, there are nineteen thousand of Washington's letters that survived, and his father's name is mentioned in only two of them. He died when George was eleven. His mother is a classic example of how historical reputations rise and fall. When [writer] Parson Weems was grinding out his sugary anecdotes about the father of his country, he tended to portray Mary Ball Washington as a rather saintly figure. In our own century, she has been characterized as a shrew, as a selfish, self-centered woman whom George couldn't wait to get away from. I think the truth is somewhere in between. He owed much more to his mother than he would probably admit. A friend writing late in life said anyone who was ever around the mother would understand where Washington's air of command came from.

Washington first ran for office in his twenties. He ran for the Virginia House of Burgesses, was defeated in large part because he refused to follow the custom of the day and provide unlimited liquid refreshment to the electorate. He always, by the way, learned from defeat—a mark of a good politician, a mark of a good general. The next time he ran for the Burgesses, he didn't repeat that mistake; alcohol flowed liberally. He spent fifteen years in the House of Burgesses.

More important, he spent eight years as commanding general in the Revolution, and he was a political general. It was wonderful training for the presidency because as bad as the British were at his front, Congress, at his rear, was almost as much of an enemy. He had to deal with Congress on a day-to-day basis, and he perfected his political skills in the process. He also learned that it was not, in the end, a military war; it was a political war. It was a test of endurance and became almost guerrilla warfare. He didn't have the military resources to defeat the British head on. Never did. People are surprised: Washington only fought nine major battles during the Revolution, and he came to play the fox more often than the lion, all the while convincing himself that he was no politician. A part of his political genius was this ability to persuade everyone, beginning with himself, that he was no politician.

WASHINGTON WAS THE INEVITABLE choice [as the nation's first president]. You have to remember, the United States was not a nation in 1789. It was an idea. The Constitution was a piece of paper, not particularly popular. I think if a popular referendum had been held, the Constitution would not have been approved. It was ratified in 1789, quite narrowly in a number of states. Probably the deciding factor behind its ratification was the assumption, never made explicit, that George Washington would agree to be the first president of the United States. Washington went into office [in 1789]. . . .

He was the one thing that bound the country together. This was not a European nation. This was not a nation. This was an extraordinarily diverse society. We tend to think diversity is something we invented in the 1990s. Not so. Two hundred years ago, we were an amazingly polyglot culture. We were three separate nations. We were the eastern states, as New England was called; we were the middle states, which were the great breadbasket of the country, and we were the South, which was really a society apart. He had won the Revolution and became more than a man, more than a leader. He became the symbol of nationhood, the symbol of unity. He was the glue that held the country together. He was the one thing everyone could agree on.

ONE OF THE REAL KEYS to understanding Washington as a man and as a politician is to understand his grasp of human psychology. He was a very fine amateur psychologist. He had seen the darker side of humanity, first on the Virginia frontier, when he was having to deal with skulking militia and thieving speculators in Virginia, and then in the Revolution. He once said about democracy, "The problem with democratical states," as he put it, "is that they must feel before they can see. That is what makes their governments slow in operation, but the people, at last, will be right." He had a very healthy, very moderate view of what government could achieve and of the arduous nature of achieving it.

Because he understood human nature, he once said during the Revolution, "Anyone who thinks you can win a war on patriotism will be sadly deceived in the end. Interest is what governs." . . . The founders had a conundrum: They had to try and decide how to harmonize this society's competing interests. Washington was uniquely situated to do that because he understood interest, because his own interest had led him to amass vast land holdings, not always through the nicest of methods. The great thing about Washington was, with his grasp of psychology, over time the selfish ambitions of his youth were transformed into selfless ambitions. There were interests greater than personal interest.

[THOMAS] JEFFERSON WAS . . . ONLY eleven years younger than Washington. His contemporaries suggest, even at a fairly early age, [Washington] had a paternal quality about him. Jefferson was a very principled admirer of the French Revolution overseas, and he was a strong believer in the agrarian democracy, the ideal of states' rights here at home. Washington, he thought, sided with [Alexander] Hamilton on the opposite side of both; that is, he was much too friendly to a strong central government, to a national bank, to a national debt as a kind of national cement bonding the regions together, and overseas he thought he was too friendly to England.

From Jefferson's standpoint, his service in the cabinet [as secretary of state] was one long period of disillusionment. I think that's unfair on Jefferson's part. Quite frankly, Jefferson could be very duplicitous in his personal relations with Washington. For example, at one point, Jefferson used State Department funds to hire Philip Freneau, a fiercely partisan editor, to print a newspaper that vilified the very administration of which Jefferson was a part. On another occasion, Jefferson drafted an impeachment resolution against Hamilton, which he then submitted to one of his henchmen in the House of Representatives, who introduced it in the last days of the session.

Hamilton was secretary of the treasury, and by then Hamilton and Jefferson were bitter foes. . . . People who think of Washington as a pawn in the hands of Hamilton, or Jefferson for that matter, overlook his real accomplishment. Washington was secure enough in himself to permit these two characters to have their street brawl. Remember, his whole presidency is almost an exercise in buying time. He thought that if the United States could be preserved long enough, if he could delay factionalism and party warfare, if he could keep us out of war with England or France, then this nation might evolve a sense of nationhood. In order to do that, he had to keep both Hamilton and Jefferson within his official family as long as possible. His achievement was to do just that. Jefferson tried to quit several times before he actually left the cabinet. Hamilton also made sounds about quitting. Both of them did leave in the second term, but by that time the institutions of government had begun to take root.

HE DIDN'T WANT TO RUN for a second term, and before he was inaugurated for the first term, he had made sounds about leaving halfway through the first term once things were settled. It's interesting to speculate what the American presidency might have become had Washington, with his towering prestige, established a precedent of quitting. It might have become an almost parliamentary kind of government.

Washington appears to have wanted to treat the Senate as a kind of privy council, much as colonial governors had executive councils to advise them. He also took the Constitution very literally. He was the most strict of constructionists. He actually showed up in the Senate one day in August 1789 seeking the advice and consent of the Senate to a treaty with Georgia Indians, and a member of that body stood up and said, "This is too important to decide on the spot. Let's refer it to committee." Washington lost his legendary temper and said, "This defeats the whole purpose of my coming here." Gradually he regained his composure but eventually stalked out and was reputed to have said, "I'll be damned if I ever go back there again."

WASHINGTON WAS NOT AN ISOLATIONIST in the modern sense of the term. He was trying to buy time for this country by staying out of Europe's warfare. [One] thing that has been the most misinterpreted is this notion that Washington naïvely believed that a democracy could get along without political parties. That's not true. He knew that parties would emerge and that they would be terribly important to the democratic process. What he was warning us against [in his farewell address], and the warning is more relevant than ever, were the dangers of excessive factionalism. If you look at American society today, there are some people who see a kind of pluralism run amuck, where everyone is seated around the table and they're all bargaining for their piece of the action. I think probably President Clinton would appreciate what's in Washington's farewell address.

THERE WAS NO SECRET SERVICE and sometimes Washington got sick of the adulation. It was a bit of a bore, quite frankly, and so on occasion he would have his secretary, Tobias Lear, tell civic authorities that while the president did not wish to deny the people their chance to see him, he was anxious to get home, and could you please hold down the civic celebrations.

We tend to laugh today at the amount of time that was spent by the first Congress over seeming trifles like what would his title be and how accessible would he be, whether he would go to funerals and so forth. Many people criticized him for being inaccessible to the public. He had weekly levees, as they were known, very rigidly set pieces. He did not shake hands; he would bow. He used to wear cloth imported from Europe at five dollars a yard. He was trying constantly to strike a balance between republican simplicity and whatever prestige this new republic demanded. So, in that sense, there was nothing trifling at all about the debates that took place over how accessible the president was going to be.

HE WAS PROFOUNDLY HONEST, but he was also very capable of telling a lie, beginning with the whole notion that he was not a politician. He lived that lie and very successfully. There is a wonderful story from when he was traveling through the South in 1791. He was a little bit sick of all the attention, and he was riding in a coach. These were unpaved roads, and he had to breathe the dust coming up from the roadbed because he was surrounded by admirers— troops that would come out from a community to greet him and so forth. One day he gave them the slip. He told them to meet him at the hotel at eight o'clock in the morning, and at 5:30 A.M. he climbed into his coach and rode off. He was perfectly capable of that sort of thing.

GEORGE WASHINGTON IS MORE THAN false teeth. The false teeth were not wood; they were state-of-the-art dentures. They were carved from hippopotamus tusk. You know how he lost his teeth? He cracked Brazil nuts. He lost his first tooth when he was twenty-two, he told John Adams, and by the time he became president he had one tooth left. He had this state-of-the-art set of dentures made, and very thoughtfully, a hole was carved so it would fit over his one remaining tooth. The problem was they were terribly uncomfortable. They used to rub against the tooth. He was in agony throughout his presidency, for which he was dosed with laudanum, a derivative of opium.

WHAT I'VE TRIED TO DO is to take the reader back to his own time, in his own terms, and to recreate, as much as possible, a sense of almost day-to-day life in the 1790s so you could understand Washington within his own context. He typically once said, "It's wonderful how much we can do if we are always doing." He would characteristically rise with the sun, whether he was at Mount Vernon or in Philadelphia. He would spend a couple hours in his study working on correspondence. Then he would have breakfast, a curiously meager breakfast. He would have three biscuits smothered in honey and three cups of tea, which was a good deal less plentiful than the typical plantation breakfast, then or now. If he was in Philadelphia he would go into his office; he would look over his account books. He was a great businessman and manager. He was also rather tight. The old story about Washington throwing a dollar across the Potomac is easiest to disprove, because no man was less likely to throw a dollar away than George Washington.

He used to tell friends, "Many mickles make a muckle," and he adopted that same approach, whether in his own business or with the federal budget. He would spend the morning usually on official business and then in the afternoon would go out for exercise. He was what used to be called a man's man. At Mount Vernon, every day he would do a twenty-mile circuit of his plantations. Those who go to Mount Vernon today may not quite grasp how enormous that estate was. In Washington's day, it covered thirteen square miles. It was five separate farms with what was called a mansion house in the middle. It was, in itself, an enormous enterprise to manage. It was almost a small industrial village, and Washington was very much a hands-on manager.

IN HIS WILL, WASHINGTON made provision to free all his slaves upon the death of Martha. . . . They were indeed freed. One of the great chapters in Washington's life, illustrating this growth that I talk about, is his whole attitude towards slavery. Because he was born into a slaveholding family, he had very conventional attitudes about the subject. By the time the Revolution was being fought, he was changing his mind. He admitted free blacks to fight in the revolutionary armies, and after the war he kept dropping hints to the Virginia Assembly in hopes that they would voluntarily emancipate slaves in Virginia.

HE DIED TWO WEEKS BEFORE the end of the eighteenth century. He had made an informal promise to live to 1800; he didn't make it. He died on December 14, 1799. He was sixty-seven, and he staged his death like he staged everything else in life. He died over a period of about twenty-four hours of what was a lethally sore throat. He, in effect, strangled to death. He woke up in the middle of the night, and Martha could see he was terribly ill, unable to speak, barely able to breathe. He would not let her summon a servant or a doctor for fear that she might catch cold. During the remainder of the day and into the long night, he had this audience—the only way to put it—assembled around him, of doctors and friends. He was awesomely organized to the end. Several hours before he died, he told his secretary to go to a certain cabinet, to a certain shelf, to take two wills, to bring them back, to destroy one. He asked if all of his correspondence was in order. Just before he died, he gave instructions to the secretary. He apparently was afraid of being buried alive, which is a very human thing, so he gave instructions that his body was not to be interred in less than three days. He looked at the secretary very sharply and said, "Do you understand?" and the secretary said he did. Washington said, "All is well." He took his own pulse and he died. In control to the end.

Paul Revere

by
DAVID HACKETT FISCHER

Paul Revere (1734–1818) was a silversmith best known for his "midnight ride" to warn American citizens of British troop movements during the American Revolution. David Hackett Fischer appeared on Booknotes *on July 17, 1994, to tell the story of Paul Revere and the patriots whose cause he embraced. Fischer's book,* Paul Revere's Ride, *was published in 1994 by the Oxford University Press.*

THE QUOTATION "Listen, my children, and you shall hear of the midnight ride of Paul Revere" [is Henry Wadsworth] Longfellow's version of what happened. Longfellow is the man who made Paul Revere a national hero. He was very much a New England folk hero before that time. Longfellow was writing in 1861, and he was trying to make a point. As the Civil War was coming on and many people were in the agony of indecision, Longfellow was saying that one man alone could turn the course of history. He was trying to persuade people in the North to do as Paul Revere had done. That gave a special interpretation to . . . the event. He made it into a solitary act; Paul Revere did everything by himself. [Longfellow] had one solitary henchman for this New England night errand. Paul Revere worked his own way across the river in the poem, received the signals, and then rode by himself.

I found a very different sequence of events, much more of a collective effort. This book began with two discoveries: The first was how little had been written in a serious way about the ride. [There was] not much in the way of a full-scale history but much in the way of rhetoric, poetry, and two popular biographies. No historian had ever published a book on this subject before. The second discovery was how much there was in the way of primary material that one could work from. We have new possibilities that way. We've got computer-driven finding aids so that now we can locate the diaries that were kept on April eighteenth. From that material we began to find—I say "we"; it was my students and me, working together—that a lot of people were involved. We found that sixty other riders were out that same night. It seemed that, far from detracting from Paul Revere, they actually made his role more important in that he was more than just a messenger; he was an organizer. He was a man who would get things done. He was a great joiner. He was an associating man. Everybody seemed to know him.

PAUL REVERE . . . WAS BORN in 1734. . . . He was a silversmith. He called himself a gold and silver smith. He worked in Boston. He had many activities and many interests. He was a great joiner of organizations. He belonged to, and helped to found, Masonic organizations. He was an artisan and a member of various artisan groups.

Paul Revere's church [was] called the Cockerel Church; [it's] where he worshiped, where his mother had been a member. . . . He was very much a product of the [Boston] community . . . and there was communal effort in his purposes. He had an idea of freedom that's different from ours. For us, freedom means personal entitlement; it means individual autonomy. For Paul Revere it was that, but it was also an idea of a community running its own affairs, and that meant a sense of personal responsibility to that community. He had a balance in that idea which sometimes, I think, we've lost. That's another meaning, another message for us today.

There were about fifteen thousand people living in Boston in 1775. It had grown very little for about fifty years. It was a town that was in trouble. It was caught in the world depression that began in the early 1760s. . . . In 1765 Paul Revere himself was in court for debts he couldn't pay. That was the year when the British Parliament also imposed taxes on America. Parliament itself [was] caught in that depression.

The town was run by town meeting, and the town meeting was run partly by a group of organizations that were the first that we know of to be called caucuses. There was a North Caucus, a South and a Middle Caucus. They had all been founded by Sam Adams, and Paul Revere was a member of the North Caucus, one of many groups that he belonged to.

THIS [RIDE] WAS AN EVENT the people called the "Lexington Alarm." The alarm was the sort of event that we know very well in the twentieth century. It was like the assassination of President Kennedy—it was an event that people never forgot. They remembered everything they were doing at the moment when the news reached them. In the eighteenth century they wrote their memories down. We have their diaries, we have memoirs. . . . Altogether, [there are] hundreds of these accounts of the event.

[BRITISH] GENERAL [THOMAS] GAGE was the first to use the word *democracy* in something like its modern meaning, applying it to the institutions of New England. He persuaded Parliament to pass a set of acts that they called the Coercive Acts. The Americans called them the Intolerable Acts. Two of them transformed the government of Massachusetts and one of them came very close to abolishing town meetings. General Gage was actually trying to shut down town meetings except as administrative bodies, so there was really a head-on collision between these men over ideas of representative government.

One beginning point leading up to [Paul Revere's ride] would be in the fall of 1774 when General Gage was trying to do another part of his program, which was to disarm the people of New England. He thought that the way to do that was probably to seize their gunpowder. They could not manufacture their own gunpowder in quantity in 1774. In September, [Gage] seized the largest supply in Massachusetts. This caused something that was called the "Powder Alarm." It was another event that people always remembered. The Massachusetts towns were horrified that their right of resistance would be threatened in that way, and that galvanized many people, among them Paul Revere. He organized a kind of intelligence organization, a voluntary association composed mainly of his fellow mechanics in Boston. What they tried to do was to keep very close tabs on what General Gage was doing. When there were signs that General Gage was striking at the next major powder supply, which was in New Hampshire, Paul Revere made an earlier ride up to Portsmouth in very bad weather—in December—and he got the message there before General Gage's troops could seize that powder. . . . He made many rides before the midnight ride. . . .

The Boston Tea Party was . . . an act of violence and very carefully controlled. . . . They were throwing away the East India Company's tea, which carried a tax that they didn't wish to pay. This was an act of violence, [and] there were many moderates in America who were taken aback by it. Paul Revere was asked to ride to Philadelphia and New York to explain what had happened. After that he made at least five other rides to Philadelphia and New York and helped to organize an American resistance—this all in the period from December 1773 to April 1775.

The actual ride was on the eighteenth and nineteenth [of April 1775]. It [started] on the eighteenth. General Gage was again thinking about seizing more munitions and had been ordered by London to move with more force and speed. He decided to strike at Concord. There were about four thousand [British troops in Boston] on April eighteenth, and about nine hundred were sent to Concord. These were the cream of the army. They were special units that were called grenadiers and light infantry. . . . At about ten o'clock [at night] . . . they mustered, just on the back side of Boston Common, and then [they] were rowed across the Charles River by the Royal Navy. . . .

The phrase "One if by land, two if by sea" was a warning that was to be sent out of Boston by lantern signals in case Paul Revere himself was unable to get clear. . . . The signals were to be displayed in the highest building in Boston, which was the steeple of the Old North Church, as soon as Paul Revere and

Joseph Warren discovered that the British troops were moving by sea, that is to say, across the Charles River. . . .

So on that night at ten o'clock, nine hundred British soldiers took off to Concord across the water. The crossing point was chosen for secrecy, from the most remote part of Boston to an uninhabited part of Cambridge. When they got across they discovered that the reason it was uninhabited was that it was a swamp, and the British troops were [stuck] in that swamp until between 1:00 A.M. and 2:00 A.M.

[Meanwhile, Paul Revere was] on his horse, headed toward Lexington. . . . He got onto the Lexington road, which would have taken him directly there, and . . . saw two British officers in the shadow of a tree just ahead of him. They were part of a patrol that General Gage had sent to stop him. Paul Revere pulled his horse around, rode back at a gallop and then north to another town called Medford. This took him in a long, looping detour to the north and then to the west, but it took him safely around those patrols. . . .

Paul Revere, going from Medford, gets around to Lexington. He rode from Lexington Green to the parsonage where Samuel Adams and John Hancock were staying the night. The message he carried was addressed to them. They had been out attending meetings of the Provincial Congress in Concord. John Hancock was perhaps the richest man in Massachusetts; he was described as the milk cow of the revolutionary movement. . . . Paul Revere brought his message to the house, and there was a guard out front. The guard was a sergeant in the Lexington militia who did not know Paul Revere and was not impressed by this midnight apparition. He told Paul Revere not to make so much noise, people were trying to sleep. Paul Revere said, "Noise? You'll have noise enough before long. The regulars are out." It's interesting what he did not say. He did not say "The British are coming!" None of the riders said the British were coming . . . in 1775 these men still thought that they were British.

Paul Revere woke [Samuel Adams and John Hancock] and they talked. About a half an hour later [another rider, William] Dawes, arrived, and they all agreed that Concord should be warned quickly and that Revere and Dawes were the men to do it. So off they went again, riding on a second ride from Lexington toward Concord. It's about six miles between Lexington and Concord.

[While alerting citizens along the route, Revere was captured, but] the British let him go. They decided that they had to carry his news back to the British colony, the news that the countryside was alarmed. They went off at a high rate of speed to the east, and Paul Revere was allowed to go free. He went back to the parsonage, back to see if Sam Adams and John Hancock had gotten away. He discovered to his horror that they were still there. They were still debating over what they should do. This was now between 2:00 A.M. and 3:00 A.M. He persuaded them to get clear of Lexington as quickly as possible.

Then he met the clerk of John Hancock, who said there was yet another job that had to be done: John Hancock had left the secret papers of the Revolution in the tavern at Lexington Green. . . . So, back they went to the Buckman Tavern on Lexington Green. They went racing up the steps and found a huge trunk—it still survives today. It was very heavy. They had trouble picking it up. As they bent over the trunk Paul Revere looked out through the window. It was now nearly 5:00 A.M.—almost sunrise—and in that gray light before the dawn, he was one of the first to make out the sight of the British troops coming up toward Lexington Green. Out they went from Buckman Tavern with the trunk between then, staggering across Lexington Green. They went through the Lexington militia that were mustering there and carried their trunk beyond. As they went beyond, they could hear the [Lexington militia] commander, Captain Parker, telling his men, "Don't fire first. Stand your ground but don't fire first."

It was just about sunrise, just about five o'clock, and Paul Revere was behind the American militia, heading away from them. He heard a shot ring out, and he looked back and couldn't tell where it came from. He thought it sounded like a pistol shot, but he couldn't be sure. Many other people who were there thought they saw it come from several places. The Americans thought that a British officer had fired first, not the British infantry, but there were several officers mounted in front. They were, in fact, the patrol that had captured Paul Revere and they had gone back and joined the column. They were still in a state of panic almost, as they had been since they had met Paul Revere. They may have been the first to fire. The British eyewitnesses were quite sure that it was an American who fired first, perhaps a shot out of the Buckman Tavern. There were young men there who had been drinking, who were armed. . . . We don't know and will never know who fired that first shot.

There were seven people who were killed at Lexington. Everybody on the field agreed what happened after that first shot was fired. The British infantry fired a volley into the American militia, and then the militia were scattering, were dispersing, and a few of them fired back—not many. No British soldier was killed at Lexington. One was wounded and the horse of one of the officers was hit. Lexington was a very one-sided affair that way.

If Paul Revere hadn't been there that night, historians do not know if the people of Lexington would have been tipped off. . . . By midnight of his ride, Paul Revere had gotten to Lexington, and by 1:00 A.M. to 2:00 A.M. the word had been carried by other messengers as far as the New Hampshire border, which was nearly thirty miles north. These were eighteenth-century times and distances. That was normally a long day's journey. . . . My hunch is that Paul Revere really did make a difference. He made a difference mainly in the preparations before the ride in organizing the effort. This couldn't have been done spontaneously. The British commanders thought that the American troops must have mustered a day or two before their march, which they didn't do. Only by that kind of collective effort could this have happened the way that it did. Only by the organizing skills of people such as Paul Revere could that effort have been brought together.

AMERICANS CELEBRATE PAUL REVERE, particularly in moments of crisis—in the Civil War, as Longfellow did, and then again in World War II, when Esther Forbes wrote a very good popular biography that made Paul Revere into a "simple artisan," in her phrase, who became representative of an ordinary American capable of extraordinary things. . . . Then after that, Paul Revere became a cold warrior. He became a businessman on horseback and was a symbol of the union of capitalism and democracy. Then suddenly there was a reversal that coincided with Vietnam, and Paul Revere became the target for many American iconoclasts . . . the singing canary. . . . He became a truly villainous figure for the iconoclasts. It's reversing again today.

Paul Revere has a message for us as well. . . . We can see a kind of message, first of all, in what he was doing. For me it was mainly the collective effort in the cause of freedom. We forgot about both sides of it, sometimes. People on the left today, some of my colleagues in academia, tend to forget about American ideas of freedom. People on the right tend to forget about collective action. Paul Revere and his friends brought those two things together.

John Adams

---

by
JOSEPH ELLIS

*John Adams of Massachusetts (1735–1826) was a political philosopher, dele-
gate to two Continental Congresses, vice president, and our second president.
Historian Joseph Ellis, who appeared on* Booknotes *on September 5, 1993,
called his biography of Adams, published in 1993 by Norton,* Passionate Sage:
The Character and Legacy of John Adams.

JOHN ADAMS WAS A VERY WISE man and also a very fiery, emotional, vitu-
perative, sometimes angry, sometimes obscene fellow. [*Passionate Sage*] . . .
captured in a way . . . the kind of paradoxical character of this [man] otherwise
thought of as an icon—very human but also extraordinarily wise.

He was president for four years, from 1797 to 1801. . . . One of Adams's major
problems as president was that he followed Washington. . . . Whoever followed
Washington was in for trouble, because Washington's unbelievable reputation
and his sculpted serenity left him immune to criticism. . . . There were a lot of
problems that were festering, and whoever came in was going to take some heat,
and Adams felt that. He beat Jefferson in the election of 1796 by a narrow electoral margin, and then he lost by an almost equally narrow margin in 1800. There
is some speculation that the reason that he lost was a scurrilous pamphlet that was
not actually published by [Alexander] Hamilton but was put out by Hamilton
and published by others. The title was *Concerning the Public Conduct and Character of John Adams.* It was the kind of thing today you'd see in the *National En-
quirer*—an attack on Adams as a person who was unstable, who was unfit for
public office, who threw tantrums, who shouted obscenities at his cabinet. . . .

JOHN ADAMS WAS BORN October 30, 1735, in Braintree, Massachusetts; he died
on a marvelous date—July 4, 1826, about three miles from where he was born in
what then was called Quincy. . . . He lived to be ninety years of age. Despite the
fact that he was born and died in the same town, he traveled both geographically
and intellectually about as far as any American of his generation.

He was vice president for eight years [from 1789 to 1797]. He was the first
vice president. He was the originator of all of the interesting negative things

that you . . . say about the vice presidency, you know, "Not worth a bucketful of spit." . . . He became president right after that.

[As he left the presidency, he] appointed John Marshall as the chief justice of the Supreme Court, for which he was hated. Well, "hated" might be too strong a term. Jefferson didn't like [the appointment], and as the famous story of the midnight judges [goes] . . . Adams was sitting there in the Oval Office crafting the appointment letters, including the letter for John Marshall, thereby bequeathing to his successor a series of his own appointments. They were appointments for the Federalist party, which Jefferson would not really appreciate very much. Truth is, he had appointed Marshall many weeks beforehand. There wasn't some sort of final moment of unbridled, spasmodic hatred for Jefferson, not so at all. He did sign some letters for some minor officials on that last night, and . . . he didn't even go to bed. He took the stage out of Washington, D.C., at four in the morning on the next day and never attended the inauguration of Jefferson. He's the only sitting president in American history not to attend the inauguration of his successor.

HE HAD NO TEETH. . . . I don't know when he lost his teeth, but he didn't have them by the time he retired. He was the first president to occupy the presidential mansion in Washington, which was just being finished and was still unfurnished when he occupied it. He's sitting there . . . toothless and with very bad eyesight. . . . He claimed that he would have gone back to the law when he left the presidency in 1801 if he could talk, but he said he couldn't talk in public because his words were so slurred.

In response to requests [to] describe him[self] physically, he would always try to write back in a funny way. His standard reply would be, "I am a man with blue eyes, one head, two arms, two legs, and am five foot seven or five foot nine inches tall, I know not which."

HIS WIFE WAS ABIGAIL. She was certainly one of the great figures of American culture and history of this time, a woman who's not formally educated but generally regarded by her peers and by subsequent historians as one of the most learned ladies in the land. [She was] a real force politically and a partner for him in ways that would sell well in a contemporary notion of a partnership marriage.

He had four children. His eldest was Abigail, named Nabby, a daughter. Then John Quincy, the apple of his eye, who became president of the United States—John and John Quincy, the only father-son team ever to occupy the office of president. [Then he had] two other failed sons: Charles, who died an alcoholic in 1800 or 1801, and Tommy, who also had problems with alcohol and lived on until about 1832.

ADAMS READ A LOT. . . . Jefferson would say, "Heavens to Betsy, how do you do it? I don't see how you're reading all these things." Adams didn't only read books, he tended to battle with them. He was a contrarian, had a kind of dialectical temperament. . . .

ADAMS RETIRED TO HIS LITTLE HILL, his country estate, which a French visitor once described as the kind of place that a third-rate French lawyer would regard as appropriate. I think it's a nice place, the Adams homestead in Quincy. Adams started to make fun of the fact that everybody else who was of the Virginia dynasty had their own great estates. Washington had Mount Vernon; Jefferson had Monticello; Madison had Montpelier. Adams had to have something like that, so he created the term *Montezillo* as a kind of joke. *Monticello* means "big mountain," *Montezillo* means "small mountain," and it was a way of him sort of poking fun at himself.

ONE OF THE IRONIES is that they call Adams a conservative. He was not really a conservative; he was not really a radical; he was not really a liberal. Adams was a kind of person who thought in the style of Groucho Marx to reach the conclusions of Edmund Burke. He was a real weird combination, but he was a liberal in the modern sense of the term in that he believed that government had a constructive role to play in the shaping of national priorities. . . .

He was against slavery, and there's an interesting debate there. . . . As secretary of the Board of War and Ordnance during the American Revolution, he's a one-man secretary of defense throughout the early years of the American Revolution. He got these letters from a lot of people, including some black people, saying, "This is the opportunity to end slavery. The values of the Revolution, the values of the Declaration of Independence are clearly incompatible with the existence of chattel slavery." Adams said, "You're absolutely right. They are, but we can't afford to divide the Union now, North and South. South Carolina, Virginia will not be able, will not be willing to support our war efforts against Britain if we raise this issue now." Slavery was a doomed institution, he thought.

Slavery and that form of labor cannot compete with free labor. He presumed it was going to die a natural death; so did Jefferson. When it didn't die a natural death and, instead, spread by the latter years of both men in 1819, 1820, and they corresponded about this, Jefferson was prepared to endorse its expansion into the West. And he said, "By letting it spread, we'll diffuse it." Adams said, "How in heaven's name can a cancer become more malleable if it spreads? This is a cancer. We need to attack it now."

I REALLY DO THINK THAT ADAMS was a person who was speaking to us in ways that, to me at least, suggest . . . some important insights. In typical Adams fashion, they're not always the things we want to hear. They're not attractive, they're not pleasant, they're not sentimental or romantic. He's a real realist, and part of what Adams was saying, or should be saying to us, was that history, as does human life, moves in cycles. . . . The job of a great American statesman in the late twentieth century is to try and understand and figure out where the United States is in its own cycle. Nations, like people, have life spans. They have limited life spans. . . . The time when he and Jefferson were running the country back in the late eighteenth century and making decisions was the youth of America. We're past that now. We're the oldest republic in world history. We need to come to terms in a mature way with our own maturation. . . .

ON THE FIFTIETH ANNIVERSARY OF THE SIGNING of the Declaration, or the supposed anniversary, July 4, 1826, both Jefferson and Adams were nearing death. They were two of the last three of the original signers of the Declaration to still be alive, and certainly the most prominent. Jefferson had fallen into a coma the preceding evening and just before that had said his last words, which were, "Is it the Fourth?" One gets a sense that these men could will their own deaths and delay them a bit to make it a bit more symbolic.

Jefferson lingered on until 12:20 the next day in the early afternoon. Adams had risen the same day, ready to celebrate "the great jubilee of independence," as he called it, and fell ill in the morning. Just about the time that Jefferson died, he was carried downstairs and fell into unconsciousness, awoke briefly in the afternoon, and his last words were, "Thomas Jefferson survives," which turned out not to be true. . . .

They both, in effect, died on the same day, which was the fiftieth anniversary of the Declaration, and commentators throughout the country regarded this as a providential sign, as an act of God. There was a mathematician at Yale College . . . who estimated the probability or possibility of this occurring to be one in 125 million.

Thomas Paine

by
JON KATZ

Media critic Jon Katz calls Thomas Paine "the moral father of the Internet."
An essay on Paine's contributions to journalism appears in Katz's 1997 book,
Virtuous Reality, *which was published by Random House. Thomas Paine*
(1737–1809) fostered revolution with his pen. An English Quaker who emi-
grated to Philadelphia on the advice of Benjamin Franklin, Paine's pam-
phlets, including Common Sense, The Rights of Man, *and* The Age of
Reason, *influenced both the American and French revolutions. Mr. Katz told*
Booknotes *viewers more about Tom Paine on March 23, 1997.*

I WROTE ABOUT THOMAS PAINE on the Internet, in *Wired* . . . and I write
about him in this book. I basically said in the book that Thomas Paine, if he
were alive today, would be on the Internet. He couldn't get a job at any newspaper in America, because he certainly did not believe in objectivity. He was far
too outspoken and independent-minded to work in a newsroom. He would
not have liked corporate media in the least. So I think his spirit is very much
alive [on the Internet]. We are very free on the Internet. We can really say
things you can't say in traditional media. We can question the existence of God
if we wish. We can go beyond the sort of narrow confines of liberalism and
conservatism.

Freedom lives on the Web. . . . It sounds corny to say, and I would be embarrassed to say it in most newsrooms. But there's a passion for freedom, a
spirit of freedom, that is breathtaking on the Web.

I WROTE THIS PIECE for *Wired* magazine about Paine and what a great person
he was and how much I admired him. . . . His house is in New Rochelle, New
York. Today there is a little Thomas Paine museum, which is a funky little
place. . . . There's a hole in the ground where his grave was. This pamphleteer
who didn't like his work grabbed his bones and squirreled them off to England
on a boat, where they just vanished. No one really knows what happened to
them. . . . Every month or so, I get an e-mail from someone in England who
has a piece of him.

I don't know how these people get my column. I can't imagine that they're online. They're usually titled [aristocracy]. They'll e-mail that they liked my piece very much, and they know where Paine's femur is or his jawbone or his rib cage. I really think by the end of the year, I'm going to have him all reassembled, the little bits of him, in England.

[THOMAS PAINE WAS BORN in 1737 and died in 1809. He moved to the United States when he was thirty-seven years old and] wrote essays. . . . He wrote *Common Sense,* which was the country's first bestseller. He sold half a million copies of *Common Sense* in a country of three million people. He wouldn't take royalties for it because he was afraid people wouldn't be able to afford it. It's one of the reasons he died a pauper. When he was thrown in jail in France, he wrote *The Rights of Man;* he wrote *The Age of Reason.* He wrote three or four of the classic essays on individual liberty. He created political journalism with *Common Sense,* which was the first statement for individual liberty in North America. Some of his ideas were drawn from some of the British writers. . . . He did pamphlets. He did long, argumentative essays. I use him as an example of why I don't like objectivity very much, because if Thomas Paine were subscribing to the conventions of objectivity, *Common Sense* would have begun with "A spokesperson for the British says the colonies should remain attached, and a spokesperson for the colonists says it shouldn't." We'd still probably be part of the empire.

HE ENDED UP A WRETCHED and disliked figure. He was obnoxious. He was extremely opinionated and had a gift for alienating his friends. [He] was always whining about money, as writers still do today. But those three essays, *The Age of Reason, The Rights of Man,* and *Common Sense* really gave birth to the modern American media, to the idea of media as a force for change, to the idea of reasoned argument, and for the use of media as a guide to help us sort out some of the moral dilemmas that we have.

[Paine] wasn't in prison in France very long—less than a year. He was earmarked for the guillotine, but some friends of his marked the door in such a way that the guards were fooled, and they passed him by. He went over there to help the French Revolution, but he ended up being critical of them for being so brutal. He had a gift for provocation and for being in trouble wherever he went. But for me, he has always embodied the spirit of American media as it was meant to be. The loss of that spirit is crippling for journalism. Whether you're a liberal or a conservative, you're deprived of this sort of informed and passionate reason.

Thomas Paine said, "Here's my opinion. I'm up front about it. Here's how I reach my opinion. Here are statistics to support my opinion. Take it or leave it." That argument gave birth not only to media, but to the American Revolution.

In our time, it's somewhat shocking to people, who ask, "How can you say these things? How can you be so argumentative? Why aren't you being more reasoned, more balanced, more researched?"

The polemical essay, which is the one that American media was invented upon, is so shocking that I notice many of my reviewers don't even know what it is. . . . The idea of an argument is almost unknown in media, because you can only do it on these op-ed pages, and even then within a very militantly moderate context. The idea that drove me, in many ways to write the book . . . is the notion of a media that has lost this moral mooring, lost this connection with this man who worked very hard on his essays, researched them very carefully, filled them with facts . . . and then made very reasoned arguments.

Today you don't have journalists arguing a point of view. You have journalists who are paid to argue the same point of view every week and pretend to be passionate about it. It's the opposite of reason. It's like the cockfight every week where people get together and debate each other and score points on each other. It's one of the reasons Americans are so alienated from media, because these people aren't coming on sincerely with opinions. They aren't morally trying to persuade you to a point of view; they're taking money to appear to be passionate every week. It's particularly damaging for Washington journalists to be doing that because we probably need them to be clear more now than we've ever needed them. There's so much information coming out. It's from so many different quarters. . . . Thomas Paine would have said, "Here's what we should think about Bill Clinton, and here's why I think so. Here's what we should do about welfare, and here's why I think so." We could do it or not; we wouldn't have to take his point of view.

Thomas Jefferson

by
WILLARD STERNE RANDALL

Thomas Jefferson was born in Virginia in 1743. At age thirty-three, as a member of the Continental Congress, he was asked to draft the Declaration of Independence. After a two-term presidency, he returned to Monticello, his Virginia plantation, where he died on July 4, 1826. Willard Sterne Randall, a journalist turned historian, wrote Thomas Jefferson: A Life *in 1993 with Henry Holt. He appeared on* Booknotes *on December twenty-sixth of that year to discuss our third president.*

THOMAS JEFFERSON, as president, managed to keep himself open to a great number of constituencies. He also believed in equality among the officers of government. He abolished normal seating arrangements; every department had to have an oval table so no one sat at the head and no one at the foot. He received visitors of all kinds, people from the hustings, diplomats, with almost no fanfare. He was approachable. I know that's very difficult today, but any president today would [also] do well to try to keep himself open instead of just being surrounded by the old China hands, the palace guard. . . . Also, the inquisitive mind of Jefferson never stopped: he was always looking for new approaches and was not afraid to contradict himself frequently. He did rapid about-faces. He was a pacifist going into the presidency, yet he founded West Point and made war in Algeria.

He was against a strong central government and was a strict constructionist on the Constitution, and yet he used a congressional slush fund . . . when he needed to buy land, because he thought that was the wealth and the future of the country—the Louisiana Purchase. The flexibility of Jefferson is one of the most important things about him.

HE WAS BORN in Albemarle County, Virginia, the farthest settlement west, the last ridge, basically, before you got into the frontier. His father had settled Albemarle County, one of the two original settlers. He was a pioneer, a great giant of a man, Peter Jefferson, with legendary strength, the Paul Bunyan of the

Virginia frontier. He helped draw the boundaries of Virginia. He rode out on expeditions with chains and surveyors. Jefferson worshiped him and learned surveying and a love for books from his father, whose entire library was only forty volumes, but compared to the libraries of most people on the frontier at the time, that was quite a lot. Jefferson emulated his father, but he's very much like his mother, who was a Randolph, very refined, and he got his love of education from her.

There were so many [children] that he basically had to move out and go away to school. Our picture of a plantation of the time is something more out of *Gone With the Wind* than from reality. These were small farmhouses with eaves and dormers, and Jefferson was a tall boy. With five children at home, and then seven children at home by the time he was a teenage boy, there just wasn't room for him, and he went off to school. It was a big family. He was the older of two boys with a half-dozen sisters. When his father died, Thomas was only fourteen. He became the man of the family at fourteen.

His father had slaves. They had been introduced into the family gradually. As the indentured white labor supply dried up, the Jeffersons, like others, bought more land and bought more slaves. When Peter Jefferson died, he left his family thirty-four slaves. Most of Jefferson's slaves came by inheritance from his father; then when he married, his father-in-law died almost immediately, right after buying a whole shipload of slaves that nobody wanted and nobody could afford. So he instantly became the largest slave owner in Virginia.

When he was twenty-seven years old, he became a member of the Virginia House of Burgesses from the frontier county of Albemarle. He was also the youngest lawyer to practice before the General Court of Virginia, which was the supreme court of that colony. Jefferson, the lawyer, was much more important than he's been made out to be. Other biographers have touched on or summarized his [law] career, but in tracking him through his life, I quickly learned that his legal papers and his casebook and his record books still existed. They were out in a private collection in California. I was able to go out there and sit and hold them, and study them, and see that the man had almost one thousand law cases on the eve of the Revolution—many of them in areas that mattered a great deal to him. He would represent slaves without fee to try to win them freedom; he was one of the first to think about divorce reform. Divorce was illegal, as Henry VIII could have told him. Many of the areas that are considered quite modern, he had struggled with as a lawyer. He had been shouted down by the slave-owning oligarchy and the British officials in Virginia.

Out of the law courts, we get Jefferson the revolutionary, on his feet, writing brilliant opinions, very articulate, a better speaker than most biographers have let on. That, to me, explained for the first time why such a good lawyer as John Adams would defer to him to write the Declaration of Independence and the key documents of the Continental Congress. That never made sense to me before. What I knew about Jefferson basically was at age thirty-three he dropped out of the sky in Philadelphia and wrote the Declaration of Independence. What I found out in this research is that those early years were terribly important.

He was a marvelous writer, as he set out to be. He thought that the law should be in simple language so you didn't need lawyers like him. When he rewrote the laws of Virginia, he put them in laymen's language, got rid of the cobwebs. The Declaration of Independence is not only ringing rhetoric, but it's beautifully done, beautifully crafted. It follows an argument. He knew exactly how to craft an argument, and you can hear the beat get stronger and faster, the excitement of the writing as it goes on. I think he was a brilliant writer. I think others at the time thought so, too.

He was in the Second Continental Congress in 1776, one year only—filling an unexpired term. He became a member of the first House of Delegates, was the revolutionary governor of Virginia, and in three years literally rewrote the law of the largest state at the time, Virginia—126 new laws and a new criminal code. Then he went on to Congress again. He was the leading member of Congress for a few years, then became the American minister plenipotentiary, or ambassador, to France, replacing [Benjamin] Franklin, his mentor. Washington wanted him in his first cabinet, so he was the first secretary of state. Jefferson found it hard to say no to George Washington, as just about everybody else did. He became vice president to Adams by three electoral votes in the first contested presidential election. Then he defeated [John Adams,] the Federalist, and became the third president of the United States.

After the British burnt the first Library of Congress in the War of 1812, Jefferson offered to sell his entire library at Monticello—I think it was 6,500 volumes—at a bargain-basement price, so it's the nucleus of the modern Library of Congress. He was also vice president and then president of the American Philosophical Society. He sent off the first scientific expedition funded by the federal government, the Lewis and Clark expedition, personally wrote its instructions, personally had Lewis trained as its guide. He invented the first modern plow. He brought the dumbwaiter from Paris to the White House and then to Monticello. He redesigned the capital after L'Enfant did a first draft. He changed the relationship so the president's house was down in a gully and the president had to look up to Congress on Capitol Hill. That wasn't supposed to be that way originally, but he was always using his mind to rearrange and to adapt, if not invent, things.

He was very good at operating behind the scenes. He appeared not to be running, but as Adams and Hamilton and others found out, the appearance wasn't the whole story. He was very good at lining up support, bringing around state committees, very good at working in secret, something he learned as a diplomat in Paris. As a president, I have a very mixed view of him. He could be absolutely ruthless. While he founded the oldest political party, the Democrats, he trashed the Federalists and almost destroyed the two-party system for forty years and brought the spoil system into politics. When he believed in something, he believed in it so completely, he couldn't see the damage that he might do. I wouldn't like to see some of the things he did done again.

HE WAS MARRIED FOR TEN YEARS [to Martha Wayles Skelton]. She had conceived half a dozen times. She'd had a terrible time in childbirth as most women did then. She had lost their only son. He was very fond of her. She did not want, and he did not want, their children growing up with a stepmother. I think that was why she almost exacted a promise from him on her deathbed about raising those children [alone].

HE WENT TO PARIS when he was forty-one. His wife had died not long before that. He was desolate. He thought his life was over. He went mostly because Franklin had asked him three times to come, and as long as his wife was alive and sick, he couldn't see his way clear to leaving her behind. She wasn't up to the voyage. But when she died, he went, at Franklin's invitation, to help negotiate the peace with the British. That was all done by the time he got there, but he became the apostle of the new country, publishing *Notes on [the State of] Virginia* over there, along with Franklin, trying to show what this new country was about. He was there for five years, a vital five years. He was very close to [the marquis de] Lafayette. A lot of the early stages of the French Revolution took place at his dinner table in the American mission on the Champs Elysées. . . .

   He was in Paris from 1784 to 1789. He was there when the Bastille fell. The rioting was going on outside his windows. For months, he went out in his carriage to investigate. The crowds recognized him, and they would stop hitting the guards long enough to let him pass and then let fly again at the Swiss Guards. He stayed there about three months after the Revolution began and then came home.

[WHILE IN EUROPE,] Jefferson went over the Alps in a mule train in the wintertime to try to find products in Italy that he could bring back to adapt to the United States to help its infant economy. For months, he violated the laws of Italy and diplomatic immunity by stealing sacks full of unmilled rice. He thought the Carolinas needed not only a better grain of rice but one that didn't use slave labor, one that would grow in the hills, where so many slaves wouldn't be killed from malarial insects. He risked his life going into Italy and smuggling out this rice. He also brought back ice cream, pasta, and several other things. He was always looking for new things to bring back to the United States.

[MARIA COSWAY] WAS MARRIED to a British portrait painter, Richard Cosway, who came to Paris with a commission to paint a duke. Jefferson was introduced to Maria by John Trumbull, an American artist who was living with Jefferson. He was painting Jefferson's part of *The Declaration of Independence*— the famous portrait. . . . [Trumbull] took her around and took Jefferson around. . . . They hit it off. Many times they would all go off as a foursome, many times not. Jefferson saw her for the better part of six weeks before she went back to England. Then they corresponded for the rest of his life, less and less frequently, but until he was a very old man. . . . He was the patriarch, writing to her. She became a nun and the headmistress of a girl's school in Italy, but there was always this wonderful literary affair, if nothing more than that, between them.

They never did see each other [again]. He had several opportunities, but he decided to come back to America and go back into political life. Those years [in Paris] healed him from the terrible years in Virginia during the Revolution when he lost his home, his farms, and when his political career looked wrecked as well.

FOR UP TO SIX WEEKS [at a time, he had headaches and] he couldn't function in the daytime. . . . They usually followed some serious loss. When his mother died, he had a migraine that lasted for six weeks. When his father died, there's [another] hint of one in his correspondence. . . .

Mostly they called in someone who bled you and purged you, which I'm not sure helped a headache or anything else very much. He had one period in Paris for six weeks when he was absolutely flattened. He called in a doctor whom I don't think helped things. When he was secretary of state, he had another attack for almost two months. What cured it, usually, was shutting down and absolutely relaxing, so he took his first real vacation as a U.S. government employee on horseback, traveling up through New York and Vermont with [James] Madison. There, the headache went away, but he couldn't get away from politics: they were plotting the formation of the Democratic party. He hated office work . . . and [during] the periods of grief and intense study, or when there were controversies with other political figures, these bouts would come for six to eight weeks.

SIX TWO AND A HALF is the best estimate [of his height] I can come up with. He was thin, probably no more than 180 pounds. . . . A slave overseer who specialized in knowing the statistics about human beings said he was six two and a half, straight as a gun barrel with a wonderful bearing. He didn't walk with a cane until the last few months of his life. He exercised and rode a horse until the last few weeks of his life. He was virtually a vegetarian, although not slavishly so. For about forty years [of his life, each day] he had a glass of red wine, and it was always a good one. He preferred country ham and French cuisine equally, and he believed in being outdoors as much as possible. He took care of himself. He died with a full head of teeth, which was extremely rare in those days, and he had a shock of red hair.

He was not a foppish dresser. He usually wore the same things over and over again until they wore out. He liked a red doublet, and that became almost a uniform with him. When he went riding, he pulled coveralls on to keep his clothes clean. He could be fastidious. The one thing he wouldn't tolerate was somebody not taking care of his horses. He would come out with a white glove and run it along the side of the horse, and if the glove didn't come off white, he would yell at whoever was supposed to groom it.

SALLY HEMINGS [a slave with whom Jefferson was long reported to have had an affair] . . . did exist. This sort of thing happened all over the South. What fascinated me is how the story came about. Jefferson was attacked in his first presidential campaign by New Englanders as an atheist, "a man with a Turkish harem" was one phrase that was used from the pulpits of New England. He had a hired writer, a hack writer, James Thomson Callender, who worked for him attacking Alexander Hamilton and John Adams for years. When Jefferson didn't give Callender a high political office when he became president and basically refused to have anything more to do with him, Callender switched sides and attacked Jefferson in print in a Richmond newspaper. What I did was try to dig out the genesis of the story and how it was handled at the time. I actually found the first paragraph about Jefferson, and there's Sally. She's not given a last name, and there's the charge that they had a son and that she had gone to France with Jefferson when he became the ambassador there. . . . [The paper also charged that she] named her son Tom, and that she was the "African Venus" who presided as the hostess of [Jefferson's home,] Monticello. . . .

There were so many red flags on the field for me, I decided to dig into it as much as I could to try to find out, if possible, what the facts were. There was also a family story going back and forth in the private correspondence of biographers in the nineteenth century. The family's version of this, privately, was that there were mulatto children at Monticello but that they were not Thomas Jefferson's, that they were the children of Jefferson's nephews. The evidence seemed to lean to one of the two nephews that Jefferson had raised, [who were] sons of Jefferson's sister.

I came away from it wondering why it was still so important about Sally Hemings—why studies of Jefferson have been all but stopped by this one aspect. . . . [Because of the Hemings story, there is some current thought] that he was a hypocrite. Here was the man . . . talking about freedom and "all men are created equal," and he had a slave mistress at Monticello. Thomas Jefferson was reduced to that, as far as what we should know about him. [It's as] if we know one fact now, [and] it wasn't that he wrote the Declaration of Independence or founded the University of Virginia, but that he had a slave mistress.

JEFFERSON WROTE [much more than] the Declaration of Independence; [writing] is what he loved to do. The very last thing that he did when he lay dying was to sit up, in the middle of a coma. His hand moved in front of him as he tried to write one more letter. Writing was his favorite activity in life.

James Madison

by
LANCE BANNING

James Madison (1751–1836), a primary force behind the Constitutional Convention of 1787, was able to negotiate many of the framers' differences to build consensus for the final version of the Constitution. In 1808 he was elected president. Lance Banning appeared on Booknotes *on February 11, 1996, to discuss* The Sacred Fire of Liberty: James Madison and the Founding of the Federal Republic *(Cornell University Press, 1995).*

JAMES MADISON WAS SIMPLY the most important of the fifty-five men who had a hand in the actual writing of the Constitution. Essentially, he's the one who prepared the original ideas, the outline that the Constitutional Convention started with and then worked on throughout the summer to tailor it into the document that was finally approved. He played the leading role throughout that process.

It was an unimaginable effort that he was making. He had not only made elaborate preparations but . . . looked into the histories of the confederacies of ancient and modern days. He wished he could find out more about those than could be found out.

When this chance to create a new government came along, he thought we, his posterity, would be interested in having better records than he had himself. He not only took it on himself to play a vigorous role in the proceedings of the Constitutional Convention, but even while doing that, he took shorthand notes of the proceedings. Then when he went back to his rooming house at night, he spent a good part of his time writing those shorthand notes out into longhand. . . . They [are] our fullest record of what happened in the Constitutional Convention.

THE BILL OF RIGHTS: Madison has at least a strong a claim to being the author of it. He always denied that he was the author of the Constitution. He said this was the work of many heads and many hands. . . . [But] there would have been no federal Bill of Rights, at least in 1789, if James Madison hadn't undertook to draft the amendments, to sponsor them, and to push them through Congress over the opposition of a good many other congressmen.

The Bill of Rights comes out of an idea that goes way back in American and English history and, ultimately, even much further than that. It comes out of an idea that people as individuals enter into a political society for specific and limited reasons. When they do that, there are inalienable rights—that is, rights that cannot be alienated from a person—that they do not give up. There is an area into which government ought never to intrude. The idea was that one could at least partially define that area by spelling it out in a bill of rights. The Bill of Rights was framed in the Congress of the United States by Madison's sponsorship in 1789, the first year that our current federal government was in effect. Ten of the twelve amendments he sent out were ratified by the requisite number of states by 1791.

MADISON'S HOME was in the Virginia Piedmont in Orange County, near what now is Orange, Virginia, not too far from Charlottesville, at the foot of the Blue Ridge Mountains. His father was Orange County's leading planter, probably the largest landowner in the county. He was also a justice of the peace, a vestryman of the Anglican church, and the head of the county militia.

[James Madison attended the] College of New Jersey, which is now Princeton. . . . It was probably the best place on the continent to get an education at that particular moment in the 1760s. . . . It was considered that the moral, and maybe even the political, climate at Princeton was a better one than would have been the case in Virginia.

He held an enormous number of jobs. We're talking about forty years of very active public service that started when he was a member of the Virginia legislature. Then he became a member of the Continental, or Confederation, Congress, went back to the Virginia legislature for a while, became a member of the Constitutional Convention, a member of the Virginia ratifying convention, and then he went to Congress. He was a representative for a number of years. He went back to the Virginia legislature for a couple of years, then became secretary of state under Jefferson and ultimately president himself—[our] fourth president [in 1809].

[WHEN THOMAS] JEFFERSON [and Madison first] met [in 1777], there was an enormous distance between them. Jefferson was already a senior, very respected statesman and Madison was a young fellow, just starting out. They got involved closely with one another, basically, because they're both great advocates of religious liberty. Madison was a strong supporter of Jefferson's program to extend religious liberty in Virginia. . . . Their friendship would seal into the closest personal and political alliance in all of American history. . . .

They're very different in . . . size. Jefferson was a tall fellow, six foot two . . . maybe a little taller than that; maybe as much as six foot four. Madison was quite slight. Madison was about five foot six. Very often, comments are made on the difference in stature between him and many of the other great Virginia founders—Washington, Jefferson, Monroe. Those guys would have been very good sized men for our day and were nearly giants for theirs.

THE FEDERALIST PAPERS were the most important contemporary argument in favor of the Constitution at the time when the country was debating whether the people would ratify it. They appeared originally as a series of newspaper editorials . . . and then were republished as a pamphlet. There are eighty-five in total.

Hamilton wrote little more than half of them, probably 60 percent . . . of them. John Jay ended up writing only four. Madison wrote nearly all the rest.

They began [publishing *The Federalist Papers*] in the fall of 1787, and they extended into 1788, which were the months during which several states were holding conventions to ratify or to disapprove of the proposed Constitution. . . .

[Hamilton and Madison] seem so much in agreement in *The Federalist Papers* that there was one hundred years of argument about a few [pieces] whose authorship was in dispute. . . . Hamilton and Madison were both entirely convinced that this new Constitution, which the Constitutional Convention had written, was absolutely essential to deal with the problems of the country. They were both convinced that it would be safe for the country and that it would not fundamentally destroy its revolutionary principles. They were both entirely dedicated to it. They shared many agreements about it. But in the end, both of them wanted a stronger central government for not just different, but partially conflicting, reasons.

Once that central government went into effect and Alexander Hamilton began shaping its course in the direction that he thought it was necessary for the country to go, then Madison essentially originated an opposition to him, which Thomas Jefferson very quickly joined.

[Madison helped Jefferson shape the first American party—] the Jeffersonian Republican party, which is the ultimate ancestor of today's Democratic party. . . . One of the things that they did when they created the party was to encourage the circulation of information among the public by way of the newspapers. When they became intensely concerned about the direction that Washington's administration, under Alexander Hamilton's guidance, was going, they encouraged Philip Freneau to come to what was then the national capital and create a newspaper for the purpose of informing the people about what was going on in national politics. . . . They played a critical role in the course of American history by encouraging the development of a politically oriented media.

I suppose part of the reason [Madison and Jefferson] did that is that they came very quickly to realize that the country was so large that there was never going to be a way for a majority public opinion to form and express itself if you didn't have channels, like newspapers, . . . that could spread information.

[MADISON'S PRESIDENCY, from 1809–17] is usually considered . . . not his greatest moment. Madison certainly made his greatest contributions in the years surrounding the creation of the Constitution. A lot of people consider him very nearly a failure as a president—a very mediocre president at best. After all, we got into the War of 1812 under his watch. It's not a war that we [did very well in], although contemporaries at the end of that war had a very different feeling. They thought Madison had conducted himself very well.

MADISON WAS A BEAUTIFULLY CLEAR WRITER, but he was not a beautiful wordsmith. If you're looking for things that you can put up on the wall, if you're looking for the phrases like "We hold these truths to be self-evident" and those kinds of things, you don't find very much of that in Madison's writing. He was not the gifted penman that Jefferson was. Also, if Madison was a deeper figure, he was also a somewhat narrower one. His interests are primarily political and public, whereas Jefferson was this sort of renaissance man, this man of universal genius who had a hand in everything.

Through much of the early twentieth century probably, Madison was quite overshadowed [in public opinion] by Jefferson, with whom he worked so closely. Jefferson got all the attention; Madison tended to fade into the shadows. . . . This may still be true to a certain degree in the public mind, perhaps. But in the scholarly community and in books, Madison pretty well gets his just acclaim and recognition now. There's been probably as much scholarly interest in Madison over the last twenty years as there has been in Jefferson, and probably a general agreement among scholars, at least in the area of political thought: Madison was probably the better of the two thinkers and the more interesting, ultimately, the deeper [thinker].

Marquis de Lafayette

---

by
LLOYD KRAMER

The marquis de Lafayette (1757–1834) was a wealthy French aristocrat who resigned from the French army in 1776 to sign up with the American revolutionary forces. After the American Revolution, he returned to France, where he continued to represent the interests of the United States. In September of 1996, Lloyd Kramer talked to us about his book Lafayette in Two Worlds: Public Cultures and Personal Identities in an Age of Revolutions *(University of North Carolina Press, 1996).*

[MARIE-JOSEPH-PAUL-YVES-ROCH-GILBERT DU MOTIER, the marquis de] Lafayette was a unique figure in American history. He was a foreigner who had come to America during the Revolution and convinced the Americans that they were on the right track. He gave generously of his time and his money and become a hero for Americans. There were very few Europeans of his status or his visibility who embraced the American cause. . . .

He was about nineteen years old when he came [here in 1776]—it wasn't the United States until the American Revolution in 1777. He came on his own initiative. He bought a ship after receiving a commission from Silas Deane, the American representative in Paris. With his own money, he made his way to Charleston, South Carolina, and headed north to rendezvous with Washington's army.

He got a promise of a commission by Silas Deane. It had to be confirmed by the Continental Congress. When he got there, the Congress was uncertain about what to do. There was discussion. It was held up for a while. Washington finally told them that this man was important; they ought to give him the commission. He became an officer in the Continental Army, a general. . . .

It was quite unprecedented that someone would be given that rank, and so quickly. But he had established himself as someone who could help the Americans; he was from a very prominent family. . . . Washington and other people wrote to the Congress and said, "This man might be able to do us some good. We need all the help we can get." They were trying to develop an alliance with the French, and Lafayette was seen perhaps as a go-between, even though he was only nineteen years old when he arrived.

He immediately became a great admirer of George Washington. He thought George Washington was a brilliant leader. Lafayette's own father died when he was two years old, so he had never really had a father. When he came to the United States . . . Washington stepped into that role for him and became an adviser, a father figure, as well as a commanding general. When Lafayette had his own children, the first son was named George Washington Lafayette.

He was here for about two or three years. He went back in 1779 to try to see if he could encourage the French to send more troops and supplies. By then, the French had signed an alliance with the colonies, the revolutionaries. He went back to France and spent several months there, and then came back in 1780 with the announcement the French were sending an expeditionary force to join the American army. That's the force that then worked with Washington at the Battle of Yorktown.

That expeditionary force was a little over five thousand men. One of the frustrations that Lafayette and the Americans had was that the French would not send more troops; they had expected more.

[In the Revolution he was] a mediator, or go-between, sending information about what was going on here to his friends in France, urging them to take an interest in the American cause, representing the American cause to influential Europeans. Militarily, he became a commander of a light brigade . . . and tried to play a role in offensive strikes around New York that never came to very much. He was wounded in the Battle of Brandywine early in his career. That made him sort of a hero.

HE WENT BACK [to France] shortly after Yorktown in 1782. He came back for a short visit in 1784 to see how things were going. Then he didn't come back again until 1824.

In 1824, President James Monroe invited Lafayette to come and make a goodwill tour to visit the United States and receive the thanks of the American people for what he had done. He agreed to come. He arrived in August of 1824, and he was in the United States for thirteen months. He went to every state in the Union—all twenty-four states—and had a great, triumphal reception everywhere he went. It was a remarkable thing. It would be even more than a rock star might get at the end of the twentieth century.

They welcomed him in each city. They would often build an arch with various kinds of greenery. He would be escorted into the city. For example, in the city of Philadelphia, there was a tremendous parade. It was like Charles Lindbergh coming back from Paris in the 1920s. He was escorted in by carpenters and other workers and then by all the dignitaries. It was a great honor to be with Lafayette. Every politician wanted to get up next to Lafayette and be seen standing beside him.

He gave hundreds, thousands of speeches. . . . Whether he was speaking at a joint session of the U.S. Congress or to the local patriots of Biloxi, Mississippi . . . he always stressed that the American Revolution was a unique revolution. It had achieved something that no other revolution had achieved. . . . Americans had established better government institutions than other societies; they actually defended what he called the natural rights of man in their political institutions. . . .

He stressed that the evidence for all of this was the economic prosperity of America and the growth of the country from the 1780s to the 1820s. . . . [This was an] extremely popular [idea] with Americans because it confirmed their own image of themselves. One of the arguments I make in the book again and again is that Lafayette was important precisely because he helped Americans understand their own national identity by coming in as an outsider and saying, "These are the characteristics of your country." It was extremely important to the Americans to understand themselves in this way and to have it confirmed by someone from the outside.

LAFAYETTE WAS A PLEASANT PERSON. That is, he wasn't confrontational. He didn't like to alienate people. He would talk politely to people. Some people complained that as he got older, he had only the same ideas. He would tell the same stories; his ideas never evolved. This is a very familiar critique. People would say, "Well, what was it like to be with George Washington in 1777?" He was always telling the same stories, and as he got older, some people tired of that. But he was generous in his openness to people. He welcomed people to his home, and he was eager to be accommodating.

He was tall, close to six feet, which was pretty tall in that era. The sources talk about him getting heavier as the years go on, which I guess is a common enough problem. He was fairly stout in his later years.

He was married to [his wife Adrienne for] about thirty-four years. She died at a young age—she was only forty-eight. . . . They were married as teenagers. He was sixteen and she was fourteen. This was a fairly common pattern in the eighteenth century, among the aristocracy particularly, because these relationships were arranged to benefit the families. The Noailles family, which was Adrienne's family, was one of the most influential families in France. For Lafayette, this was a very prestigious marriage.

ONE OF THE INTERESTING THINGS ABOUT LAFAYETTE is that although he's been a hero in America for a couple of centuries, especially in the nineteenth century, he's very controversial in France. Many people in France don't like him very much, especially historians. He was a moderate during the French Revolution who alienated both the conservatives and the radicals. Therefore, the histories of Lafayette tend to repeat the political perspectives of the French

Revolution. He's dismissed as an insignificant, vacillating person who didn't really understand what was going on.

There were two main revolutions [in France]. There was the Revolution of 1789, to the late 1790s. He was very heavily involved in it the first three years. The other main revolution of his lifetime was in 1830, when the Bourbon monarchy was overthrown. Lafayette, in both of these revolutions, became the commander of the national guard, which gave him great influence within French society as the guardian of law and order in Paris.

He had troops, in fact, thousands and thousands of troops. After the revolution of 1830, he was the commander of the national guard for the whole nation, which probably had a million troops at that point. . . . These were not regular line troops; they would be like militia or national guard troops. He had major influence as a commander. . . .

When he was the commander of the national guard, he had a great interest in how to represent himself. He was a man on a white horse, not necessarily a great man on a white horse, but definitely a man on a white horse.

In the first revolution, 1789, the king was Louis XVI. Lafayette tried to make Louis XVI a strong supporter of constitutional monarchy. Lafayette was not a republican in the sense of wanting a republic without a king. He favored a regime in which the king would have certain authority as the executive of the government. He had a tense relationship with the king in 1789, 1790, 1791, because the nobles around the monarchy felt the king was giving up too much power, [and the monarchy was] losing its influence. And yet, for the people who were hostile to the king, Lafayette was seen as too sympathetic to the king. So he was attacked by the republicans on the left, and he was attacked by the monarchists on the right. . . .

When the king was overthrown in August of 1792, Lafayette saw that his position was doomed. He fled the country, whereupon he was captured and imprisoned. . . .

He was captured by the Austrian army and taken off to Austria and then to Prussia. He was put in a prison at a place called Olmütz, where he was in confinement for five years, solitary confinement most of the time. But at the end of that period, his wife Adrienne and their two daughters came to this prison and demanded permission to go [into his cell]. They spent a great deal of time with him at the very end. He got out in 1797, the year he turned forty.

[His imprisonment] had a major impact, because he had been a very active person, obviously. He had been involved in the military and revolutions and so forth, and here he was in isolation. It forced him to stop and think about what had gone wrong. He had to think about why the Revolution had failed, and in a sense it confirmed his point of view that the Revolution should not have become so radical. He was very alienated by the Terror. . . . The imprisonment altered his life; it made him more reflective and more of a reader and a writer.

WHEN I WAS IN PARIS doing my research, I met a historian, an American historian, who said, . . . "Oh, Lafayette, the dumbbell of the French Revolution." That just stuck in my mind. It's a sort of shorthand way of saying he was not very clever, not very aware of what was going on and naïve. . . . He was seen as someone who was [continually] telling [the same] stories about politics, about his career. In the end, the story was rejected by his contemporaries in 1792.

But I argue . . . that he was no dumbbell. The people he most admired from Washington to Jefferson to his own French colleagues, like the famous French political theorist and thinker Benjamin Constant, were all people who were involved in politics. For him, politics was the highest human good, like the Aristotelian idea of human beings as political animals.

John Quincy Adams

by
PAUL NAGEL

John Quincy Adams (1767–1848) was the son of the second president, John Adams, and Abigail Adams. In 1825, he became the sixth president of the United States. In 1830 he became the only former American president to serve in the U.S. House of Representatives. Adams family scholar Paul Nagel appeared on Booknotes *on January 4, 1998, to discuss* John Quincy Adams: A Public Life, a Private Life *(Knopf, 1997).*

JOHN QUINCY ADAMS WAS certainly one of the most complex personalities to sit in the presidency, where he had a miserable time. He was also one of the most intriguing figures in American public life and, perhaps, the most useful of all American public servants.

He was born in 1767 and died in his eighty-first year, in 1848. He spent twenty-one of those years living abroad, which shaped his outlook a great deal. Many of the other years he lived in Washington with retreats to Quincy, Massachusetts. He was born in Braintree, Massachusetts, near the south shore of Boston.

[His father was the] second president of the United States, John Adams. . . . John Adams claimed privately that he did more to write the Declaration of Independence than his sometime friend and sometime foe Thomas Jefferson. His mother was that remarkable woman Abigail Adams, whose critical apparatus when it came to sizing up public figures was really unrivaled and sharper than her husband's.

JOHN QUINCY ADAMS STARTED WRITING [his diary] when he went with his father to France at eleven years of age. He had an amazing fidelity to it, both in terms of writing it and in terms of making it useful introspectively and a brilliant treatment of what was going on—wherever he was at the time. He wrote until his first stroke [made it] very difficult for him to write . . . then his wife and his granddaughter would make his daily entries. He made entries almost to the day he died on the floor of Congress.

His father was one of the commissioners for peace . . . to bring about the end of the American Revolution. When that frustrated John Adams, he went to Holland, to the Low Countries, to negotiate financial support for the rebellious colonies. While they were in Holland, JQA—as a youngster—was a student at the University of Leyden. By then he was more facile in the French language than the English language.

Then the Congress wanted someone to go to St. Petersburg to see if Catherine the Great—a pivotal figure in European politics at the time—would come down on the side of the American cause, the revolutionary cause. They sent [former Continental Congress delegate] Francis Dana, who spoke no French, as a representative. . . . Somebody had to go with him to be an interpreter and to show him the ways of Europe. So whom do they send but a fourteen-year-old boy named John Quincy Adams. His first post was in Russia at St. Petersburg. . . . He accompanied Francis Dana. When that proved to be very frustrating—Catherine wouldn't even speak to them—he came back in the wintertime and spent a great deal of time in Scandinavia. He was having a great time. He was on his own.

It was about age twenty-eight, after he came back to the United States, that he spent a year and a half and graduated from Harvard. He struggled against depression to establish the only career he knew at the time, a lawyer, and was miserable at it. But he became an essayist. George Washington was proud of the support he was getting from this young fellow up in Boston and made him minister to Holland . . . and then to Portugal, where he didn't go. His father switched him to Berlin. He was a minister to Berlin—had a wonderful time until 1801, when his father, John Adams, lost the election to Jefferson and recalled him. [It was] a parental deed that John Quincy Adams did not appreciate. He wanted to stay in Europe, where he was surrounded by books and art and time to write—a good, comfortable life. He knew if he came back, he'd have to go into politics or law, both of which he dreaded.

He came back and then didn't go abroad again until 1809, when he was minister to St. Petersburg, Russia—our first minister to Russia—where he became a great friend of the czar. He was in Russia from 1809 until 1814. When the time came to try to end the second war with Britain, the War of 1812, he led the American peace delegation that wrote and signed the peace [treaty] that ended the war. Then he was sent to England as our postwar representative, where he stayed till 1817, [when he] came back to be secretary of state.

[He was our sixth president.] He was followed by, in his judgment, the unspeakable Andrew Jackson. He was preceded by James Monroe, whom he served for eight years as secretary of state.

How could a man as devoted to literature and science and a person who so disliked politics—I think he did; it wasn't just empty talk in his diary—how could he stay as long in politics, how could he run for president? He often said it was "a cup" he "hoped would pass." . . . He was secretary of state, and he had a lot of support in New England to be president. His final rationalization was that he could do as no one else probably could ever do: He would be a president of the whole people, he would be above party, and he would help build universal peace. . . .

But much of the last four years of his eight as secretary of state were devoted, whether he liked it or not, to demands upon him that were made upon every candidate. He tried to avoid them; his wife begged him that if he was going to try to be president, at least make a pleasant effort. He said, "If that's what it takes to be president, I don't want to be president," but he did, as it turned out.

When there was no majority vote in the Electoral College, the House of Representatives chose the president in February of 1825. On the first ballot, he was given a majority of the states. Each state has one vote. Jackson came in second, and all heck broke loose after that because it was claimed that Adams got the votes of Illinois, Kentucky, and Ohio—crucial for him—as a result of the support of Henry Clay.

THE POOR FELLOW REALLY WAS IMPOTENT as a president. . . . He won in the House of Representatives, it was claimed, because [of this] corrupt bargain with Henry Clay, who'd been one of the other [candidates] and who threw his support to Adams. He made the terrible mistake of naming Clay to be secretary of state, which in those days was the last step people took before they became president. He had not only a majority against him in Congress, but he was the victim of what was called a corrupt bargain.

The other reason he was powerless was because his ideas were so far away from what the public and particularly Congress could be interested in: support for education, federal support for science, federal support for a great national infrastructure of roads and canals. He made himself ludicrous. His cabinet begged him not to deliver in his first annual message a plea for the government of the United States to create an astronomical observatory.

His happiest times in the White House were when he was out in the garden on his knees next to the White House gardener. They raised their own vegetables in those days at the White House.

[ONCE WHILE HE WAS] PRESIDENT and was in high conference with the secretary of state, the door opened—as it happened people just walked in to [see] the president. The door opened, in walked this gentleman, who said he was just passing through Washington. . . . He just wanted to see a president of the United States—John Quincy Adams. The gentleman stood up, shook hands, [and JQA] found out he was a dentist. He told Henry Clay to take off, get lost, and had the dentist pull one tooth, clean his teeth, and had him come back the next day and finish the work. When he asked the dentist his fee, the dentist said, "No fee; I just want a letter of recommendation from you."

But a more interesting visitor was the doctor who'd been fired by the United States Army, a physician from the Medical Corps. . . . He wanted the job back. When the army wouldn't give it back to him and the president wouldn't over-rule the army, he said he'd come to Washington to kill the president of the United States. He walked the streets of Washington reporting that he was here to shoot the president. He entered the White House, went up the stairs to the president's office, and walked in. John Quincy Adams knew he was in town. He'd been warned by his friends not to take his usual morning walk. He always was up before dawn walking, oftentimes with Chief Justice Marshall. Adams stood his ground. The doctor, abashedly, told his story, and Adams said, "No, I won't overrule the army."

The man left. He came back several times. He quit talking about shooting the president. JQA said in his diary that the episode reminded him sometimes of the very narrow margin between life and death.

[WHILE HE WAS PRESIDENT] HE SWAM in the Potomac often. He competed against himself to see how long he could swim without touching bottom. He almost drowned once. The rumor went around the country that the president of the United States had drowned. He wanted to go [by boat] to the other side of the Potomac and swim back. His son John was with him, and John took one look at the boat and said, "I'll have nothing of that," and went back to the White House. Adams and his valet—a wonderful guy—went across, got halfway over, and the boat sank. Both of them had taken off their clothing. They managed to save a couple of pieces of clothing and swam to the other shore.

He sat sunning himself while [the valet] went back to the White House to get some clothes. Meanwhile, the rumor was picked up that the president . . . had drowned. When [JQA] got back to the White House, he was scolded unmercifully by the First Lady. He admitted that perhaps he'd been a little foolish—all of this is in the diary.

He met his wife in London. She was the daughter of America's consul in London, a man named Joshua Johnson, whose brother was the first revolutionary governor of Maryland. She came from a prominent Maryland family. . . . She was a very talented musician, linguist, writer. Her diaries, her poems, her letters, her commentaries on her husband are all in the Adams papers. She was torn over her husband's career—the way he was. She so wanted him to be remembered for what he wanted to be remembered for, as a scientist or a writer. She deplored his presence in politics because she knew he was un-suited for politics. But she was very loyal and she supported him eloquently.

JQA didn't truly appreciate her until late in life. He was something of a real macho, a male chauvinist type. . . . It was perhaps a reaction against the over-powering mother he had. He thought a woman's place was to stay home and be quiet. His wife Louisa often complained he wouldn't discuss politics with her, and she loved to hear about it. . . .

HE RAN FOR REELECTION and probably did a little better than one would expect. But he was roundly defeated by Andrew Jackson, who then began his eight years as president. He announced that he was going home to Quincy, to retire as completely as any nun would ever have retired. He was going to write a biography of his father and would perhaps do some writing in defense of his own views. He got back and found he was angry over his defeat; he felt much of his defeat was owed to the slaveholders and the southern block. . . . He was just a very angry man, so angry that he couldn't concentrate. His son begged him to sit down and work with his books, do what he always said he was going to do. But he was very upset. . . . It was . . . basically anger and a desire for revenge that sent him back to Washington [as a member of Congress]. Louisa first said, "Well, if you're going back to Washington, you're going without me." But she had sisters and relatives in Washington, and she came along with him. . . . He was in Congress from 1830 to 1848.

The Democratic party generally controlled Congress at the time. JQA certainly believed [the party] was pretty much the handmaiden of the southern bloc. . . . That bloc became disgusted in the mid-1830s with the arrival of petitions—cartloads of them, stagecoaches full of them—from all over New England . . . begging Congress to do one of many things about slavery. The southern delegation got Congress to adopt a resolution, a so-called gag rule, which said that any petition presented to Congress that touched in any way upon the institution of slavery would not even be received, much less read and discussed and referred to committee.

Adams considered this a gift from on high. He said, "I need a cause." The South just fell flat on its face with this because JQA, year after year, proclaimed that this was a violation of the Constitution, the right of petition, the right of free speech. Before many years had passed, he was the great defender of free speech. Gradually, northerners got up the courage to join him. Finally, before he died, the gag rule was repealed. It was a great moment in his life.

FOR ME, THE MOST INTERESTING DISCOVERY after working for over twenty years with the Adamses and thinking about JQA is to realize, and I hadn't recognized it, that he was frequently clinically depressed. He had an aunt who recognized it. In many ways, this helps explain much of his personality. Historians have said until very recently that there's been no more unpleasant, no more unlikable person in American public life who was so successful as John Quincy Adams. Much of it is due to his depression . . . a chemical problem when he was just becoming about age twenty, twenty-one.

He also suffered from hemorrhoids, and some people say it's quite possible that his grim feature was when that disorder—when he was sitting in the president's chair, elsewhere—bothered him. . . . He did a lot of his writing standing up because of that problem.

HE DIED WHEN HE WAS GOING ON eighty-one. He had a stroke while he was in Boston, which he just refused to retire with, and [through] sheer tenacity, he came back from it. . . . His final stroke is one of the most famous episodes on the floor of the House of Representatives. He was still fighting against the war over Mexico. It was a slavemongers' war, he said; it was a war to expand human bondage. He rose to object to a measure related to the war—the war was going on then—and he toppled over with a stroke. He was caught by the person standing next to him and taken to the Speaker's chamber, where he survived for a little while, long enough to ask to see his old friend and sometime enemy Henry Clay. . . . Clay came and wept at his side. It was all very touching. It became part of Washington folklore.

There was an outpouring of public grief for JQA after he died. Fifteen thousand people attended his funeral in the Capitol of the United States. The telegraph had just become useful at the time, so the word of his death went around the country. The train that bore his coffin to Boston traveled along amid universal grief. People just stood along the train tracks, took off their hats, and women wept. This was a champion of freedom of speech.

Andrew Jackson

by
JOHN MARSZALEK

Andrew Jackson (1767–1845), the seventh president of the United States, was born in Waxhaw, South Carolina/North Carolina. In 1796 Jackson became the first member of the House to represent the new state of Tennessee. In 1824 he narrowly lost the presidency to John Quincy Adams, but was successful in the election of 1828. In March 1998, author John Marszalek appeared on Booknotes *to discuss his book* The Petticoat Affair: Manners, Mutiny, and Sex in Andrew Jackson's White House, *published in 1998 by The Free Press.*

ANDREW JACKSON . . . COULD NEVER have been elected president during this [present] period in time. He couldn't have survived because of some of the things he did. . . . He was incredibly emotional, had incredible fits of anger. He was involved in all kinds of duels before being president. It just is inconceivable that anyone with his personality could survive the media coverage that modern-day presidents have.

When he ran for the presidency for the first time in 1824, he won the popular vote, but no one received a majority of the electoral vote. The result was that it went into the House. He thought, I'm the choice of the people, the people's president. They voted for me more than they voted for Henry Clay and John Quincy Adams. He simply sat back, expecting the presidency to be given to him. Clay was a very good politician, and he got together with John Quincy Adams. They worked a deal and Adams became president. Then a few weeks later, Clay became secretary of state, the stepping stone to the presidency. Jackson went crazy, went berserk. For the next four years of John Quincy Adams's presidency, the "corrupt bargain" was the cry that was used against John Quincy Adams.

The 1828 election came along. It was as dirty an election as there was in American history. And one of the dirty things that came out of this 1824 period was the attack on Rachel Jackson, that she was a bigamist, that she had, after all, married Andrew Jackson when she was not legally divorced from her first husband. She went through all of this; he went through all this. He was elected anyway in 1828 and was president until 1837, so he served two terms.

He was getting ready to go to Washington, and Rachel had a heart attack and died. He was convinced that what killed her were these attacks on her character and on her personality. He grieved. He literally grieved through his whole presidency. He gave his inaugural address wearing grieving clothes. He never got over this thing. Anything having to do with Rachel was just an indication of "these awful people out there trying to get me. Not only are they trying to get me, but they got my beloved wife."

I don't think [the scandal] had much impact, because Jackson was elected with a rather significant vote. But it brought the election down to a level of just absolute mud-throwing. The people supporting Adams were saying terrible things about Rachel Jackson, so the Jacksonians were making up stories about John Quincy Adams. For example, that when he was minister to Russia, he was actually a procurer of American women for the Russian czar. If you know anything about John Quincy Adams, that doesn't make any sense at all. But those were the kinds of things [that were said]. . . . Adams bought a billiard table for the White House and [people said] how awful and terrible that was, using government funds to do that. Adams said, "Well, no." He bought it with his own money, and it was really a used billiard table. Then they attacked him for bringing shabby furniture into the nation's White House. It was that kind of thing, just an awful sort of business.

JACKSON HAD SEVERAL DUELS defending the honor of his wife Rachel. In one incredible situation . . . the man, [Charles] Dickinson, that he was dueling against was supposed to be the best shot in Tennessee. The guy fired first and he hit [Jackson]. Jackson didn't move. Jackson [pulled the trigger of the gun; it] clicked and nothing happened. He [fired] again, shot Dickinson right in the stomach, killed him on the spot. Meanwhile, Jackson started walking away. Blood was dripping into his boot. The bullet was very close to his heart. It never [was removed].

Another bullet he got from Thomas Hart Benton and the Benton brothers in a big "debate," to put it mildly. He was shot in the arm. That bullet worked its way to the skin during the time he was president. Jackson said, "I don't want anything. I'm not going to take anything, not any whiskey or anything." He sat in a chair, holding his cane. The doctor took a knife out, opened the skin, and yanked the bullet out. Jackson got up and walked out [and went] on with his work.

ANDREW JACKSON IS ONE of the most intriguing people in American history because you can't pin him down. You can say, "He was a great nationalist. After all, he battled against nullification and he was going to 'hang John C. Calhoun from the highest tree.' " But he was really a states' righter, too. He was a great believer in states' rights. He was a great believer in limited government.

Nullification was the idea that a state, an individual state, could nullify the effects of a federal law within a state. For example, the tariff: South Carolina could pass a nullification ordinance, saying, "You can have the tariff, but it doesn't work in this state." Jackson said, "You can't have a union this way. You can't operate this way. I believe in states' rights, but not up to the point of destroying the union." He was a great lover of the union. One could argue the main reason why he was president of the United States was because of the Battle of New Orleans in 1815, this great victory over the British in the War of 1812. It was a strange situation because the war was really over when the Battle of New Orleans took place. But in this great victory, after all these difficulties in the war, we really put it to those British. Jackson came to symbolize this spurt of nationalism that grasped the country in the period after the War of 1812.

THE PETTICOAT AFFAIR . . . IS one of those events that every historian knows something about, but no one's really bothered to get into it in any great detail. It is a story of a woman who happened to be the daughter of a Washington innkeeper in the early nineteenth century. This was at a time when congressmen didn't bring their wives, their families, to Washington because Congress wasn't in session all the time, so they lived in boardinghouses. Margaret O'Neale was the daughter of one of these boardinghouse-keepers. She was a beautiful woman; she could talk politics; she could do a lot of things that women were not supposed to do during those days. As a result, stories developed about her that she was providing services to her clientele that she ought not to be providing. She developed a bad reputation in Washington society.

Margaret O'Neale . . . went from being a cute little girl who would sit on [congressmen's] laps when they would be talking—they'd left their children behind and she became their surrogate child—[to] by the time she got to be fifteen, sixteen . . . a beautiful woman. Then she had some romances—not with any of the congressmen, but with some army people.

She married a man named John B. Timberlake, who was a purser in the navy. Timberlake was not a good businessman. . . . He tried to work a shop out of the same boardinghouse area. He failed at all of these things and lost all kinds of money. He went back to sea again. Jackson came [to the boardinghouse] with John Henry Eaton [who] . . . had already been a senator for one term. He had already lived there. Eaton became very close friends with Timberlake and with Margaret. When Timberlake went off to sea, Eaton became her guardian. In fact, Timberlake gave him his power of attorney. The rumors really began then. This guy was off to sea, [and] his wife was fooling around with this senator, blatantly going out in public.

Washington society was abuzz about the fact that they saw John Henry Eaton and Mrs. Timberlake going off to parties together and sitting together at the boardinghouse and talking. All kinds of rumors developed. The whole thing exploded in April of 1828 when word came back that Timberlake was dead. He died during one of his cruises on a navy ship. He committed suicide. The story developed that he committed suicide because he'd heard about his wife fooling around with John Henry Eaton, couldn't stand the shame, and cut his own throat. Margaret insisted, and her family insisted, that . . . this was an accidental killing, that he suffered from terrible asthma, and in an asthma attack, he somehow cut his throat. We don't know. There's no way of knowing. People who were with him when he died later said that he kept talking about his wife and wished he were back with his wife and with his children. They had some children by that time. I don't think the idea that he cut his throat because he heard these terrible things about Margaret . . . holds water.

Eaton and Margaret married on January 1, 1829, which opened up another can of worms. She was violating one of the basic mores of a genteel woman. In those days, if a husband died, a wife was supposed to grieve for anywhere from one to two years—grieve to the point of wearing certain kinds of clothes and doing nothing. You weren't even supposed to sew because if you could concentrate enough to sew, that meant you weren't grieving for your husband enough. Interestingly enough, if a wife died, a husband grieved six months and went on and probably remarried. In any case, Margaret's husband died in April of 1828; January 1, 1829, they married, less than a year later. This was outrageous. . . . How could this woman flaunt herself this way? What happens next? Jackson appointed Eaton secretary of war and Margaret Eaton was now a cabinet wife.

All the cabinet officials, all the cabinet wives wouldn't have anything to do with her. Washington society snubbed her completely. Andrew Jackson— because of a number of things—spent the first two years of his presidency practically doing nothing else but trying to get Washington society to accept this woman as an equal. He failed. As a result, he fired his entire cabinet two years into his presidency.

[There] was a meeting of the cabinet. They were there for Jackson to prove that Margaret Eaton was as chaste as a virgin, and that's what they did. He brought in John Campbell, the preacher from his own church who was accusing her of a miscarriage. . . . The idea was that it was maybe more than a miscarriage. Whatever it was, it happened at a time when her husband was gone too long. So they sat there, and they didn't even debate this. Jackson provided the information and said, "This is it, people. She is as chaste as a virgin and I want you to meet with her, and that's that."

Jackson thought he'd won out. He thought he'd convinced everybody. He'd presented them all the facts, for heaven's sake. That should be the end of it. . . .

Nothing changed. The wives refused [to accept her]. The thing Jackson didn't understand, interestingly enough, is that in that period of history, it was not a man's decision. This was a woman's decision. Women had the duty to maintain virtue in society, so they made these decisions. It was the man's responsibility to follow along with his wife.

A BIG ISSUE GOING ON at the same time . . . was rotation in office, the idea of the new president bringing in his own people and firing, eliminating. That's what happens normally [today]. But in those days that wasn't supposed to happen. So this Eaton affair tied in with this rotation in office because they were saying, "Here's this barbarian from the West, this ruffian, this man who's hanged people in Florida, who's shot people in duels. He's coming in. He's the president. He's bringing in people like him. If you don't believe that he's bringing in really awful people, just look at the wife of his secretary of war."

[His cabinet resigned] . . . very cleverly. Some people say this was Martin Van Buren's finest hour. Van Buren said, "Andrew Jackson, things are not going well. People are saying that I'm responsible for this Eaton affair. I'm responsible for all this, and I want to run for president. So I will sacrifice myself, and I will resign from your cabinet." Then Eaton said, "Well, no, no, I'm really responsible, so I'll quit." His two friends resigned. Jackson then turned to his enemies, and he asked them for their resignations. They resigned, but it was a big to-do, and this was when the country found out about the Eaton affair.

[Everyone] couldn't believe it. They were shocked; they were titillated. But it really had no impact on Jackson's popularity or Van Buren's popularity. It didn't have any impact at all. Jackson brought in a whole new cabinet, just hired new people. This cabinet was, interestingly enough, a better cabinet than the first one.

THERE WERE SEVERAL REASONS [Jackson defended Margaret Eaton]. The major reason was all his life he has had this relationship with women where he felt he must defend them. His mother died at the hands of the British, he believed; she [actually] died from disease during the American Revolution. His wife died, he believed, as a result of these political scandals. He had a very strong feeling he must defend women.

In defending Margaret Eaton, he was again defending his wife; he was again defending his mother. He saw this as one big thing. And secondly, he saw this as a continuation of the assaults on him: "They're attacking Margaret Eaton, but they're really attacking me. They're really trying to get me because they [didn't] get me through Rachel, so they're trying to get me through Margaret." He believed in conspiracies. Everything was a conspiracy against him.

Henry Clay

---

by
ROBERT REMINI

Legendary orator Henry Clay of Kentucky (1777–1852) served as Speaker of the House, U.S. senator, and secretary of state. Despite several tries, he never reached the office he most desired—the presidency. Historian and biographer Robert Remini wrote Henry Clay: Statesman for the Union, *which was published by W. W. Norton in 1991. His interview aired on* Booknotes *on April 5, 1992.*

I HAD NEVER REALLY BEEN INTERESTED in Henry Clay, but in doing Andrew Jackson['s biography], I came upon Henry Clay. I found him funny, fascinating—a man I thought that really needed and deserved a modern, full-scale biography. He was Abraham Lincoln's ideal of a statesman. . . . Most of the ideas that Lincoln had early on about economics, about slavery, come right out of Henry Clay. Lincoln is like Henry Clay, to a very large extent. . . . Lincoln quotes Henry Clay in the Lincoln-Douglas debates, I believe, a total of thirty-seven or thirty-eight times. Clay told whimsical stories the way Abraham Lincoln did. Lincoln moved far beyond Clay in the late 1850s, and is a greater statesman, but this is the man who provided many of the ideas and programs that held the nation together when it seemed to be breaking apart over the Missouri question, over the tariff question, and over the acquisition of new lands in the Mexican War.

HENRY CLAY HAD AN EXTRAORDINARY CAREER. He was elected Speaker of the House in his first year, and on the first day of the first ballot. The Speaker had been intended by the Founding Fathers to be a kind of policeman, to control traffic. He made the office of Speaker of the House the most important position in the government, after the president, because he used it in order to direct national affairs and help formulate policy. They liked him; they elected him again and again. For ten years he was the speaker. No one in the nineteenth century served as long as he did.

He was born in 1777, during the Revolution, and he died in 1852. He was seventy-five years of age when he died of tuberculosis. . . . He was sent over by

President Madison to Europe to help negotiate the Treaty of Ghent that ended the War of 1812. He regarded himself as a very successful diplomat. He came back to the United States, was again elected to Congress, and when John Quincy Adams became president of the United States, he appointed Clay to be his secretary of state. He was secretary of state from 1825 to 1829.

When Adams was defeated by Andrew Jackson, Clay returned to his home [in Kentucky] but then was elected to the Senate of the United States. Clay became one of the most powerful men in the Senate. He, with Daniel Webster and John C. Calhoun, were known as the Great Triumvirate and were the powerhouses of the Senate in its golden years. Debate never equaled what was heard in the Senate from 1832 to 1852. They all died almost at once: first Calhoun, then Clay, and then Webster.

I've never added up those hours, those years, or the number of elections, but he was elected again and again without any trouble. The only position he couldn't win, and he desperately wanted, was president of the United States. He tried that three times, and failed.

HE WAS RAISED IN VIRGINIA. He was taught by George Wythe, who had taught Thomas Jefferson and a great many other luminaries of Virginia, so his whole background was what we call Jeffersonian Republicanism. But, it had a difference, you see. He inclined much more towards using the government to help advance the interests of this nation, and the interests of all sections, and the interests of all people in all classes. He was a man with real vision as to where the country ought to go and how it ought to get there. He had a system, an American system, he called it, of economic development, which would raise this country to a level of greatness which it has since achieved. And some people said, "That's Hamiltonianism, that's Federalism, it's not Republicanism." But he denied that, he always believed he was a true Republican.

CLAY WAS TALL—six feet and thin, very thin, cadaverous almost, with a large protruding nose and a slash across where his mouth should be. His mouth was so wide, they said that he couldn't whistle and he couldn't spit with tolerable accuracy. He had blue-gray eyes. Not particularly prepossessing-looking, but once he started to talk, he was another person altogether. George Bancroft said it was music itself to hear. I can imagine what that Senate must have been like, one that rang with the voices of a Henry Clay and a Daniel Webster, and a John C. Calhoun. It was indeed the golden age, and we don't have anyone like that in the Senate today, I assure you.

CLAY WAS IN WASHINGTON all alone. His wife was very domestic. She preferred the farm. She ran it. He would give her a check when he was leaving, to run the farm, and when he returned she would hand it to him and say, "I had no need for it." She did not like the social whirl. He loved it, and he went to all the parties. Usually he'd bring some woman with him, sometimes two women; one, they said, on each arm. You know Washington gossips, they always presume the worst. We don't know if he was carrying on any affairs, whether he was unfaithful. There was no documentary evidence whatsoever, but he enjoyed women, and they enjoyed him. It's amazing, when he was running in 1844, against James Knox Polk, the chairman of the Democratic National Committee was for Polk, but his wife was for Clay. She was making rosettes for Clay, who was running against Polk, and she said, "My husband is a Polk man, but I'm a Clay man." Women just liked him, and he, somehow, had exuded a kind of excitement and interest that attracted them.

The Clays were not a particularly attractive-looking couple. . . . But he always showed his wife a great deference and respect, regard and affection. She had eleven children by him. Most of the daughters died, six of them, and one son died in the Mexican War and another was committed to an insane asylum. . . . The two of them had a very unfortunate private life with their children.

CLAY WAS ALWAYS VERY CAREFUL when he said things that were provocative, to be sure that the individual knew that he wasn't trying to insult him. If the individual refused to retract what he said, then you challenged him to a duel, and your seconds would make the arrangements as to where and when. You would appear with your surgeon, take your position, and, according to the rules, you would come up to the mark. When the order to fire was given, you brought up your gun and you fired. Clay was once struck; he was injured in his first duel. That was his duel with Humphrey Marshall, when he got a bullet in the leg.

It was over a fight in the Kentucky legislature in which the Federalists were trying to prove that the Republicans were involved in all kinds of treasonous behavior. Clay got up and became very angry. He began to say things that became more and more heated. Then he finally rushed at the man to strike him. He had to challenge him to a duel, and they went across the river. They weren't going to pollute the sacred soil of Kentucky by killing one another, so they went over to Ohio. They took their positions. They had two rounds. Clay said he surely would have killed him on the third round, if it had been allowed, but the referee decided that it was enough—that his honor was taken care of. That was the end of it.

AARON BURR WAS THE VICE PRESIDENT of the United States, among other things. He wanted the presidency, but he was intended by the Republican party to be the vice president. He came out west and began to tell all kinds of stories to people as to what he planned. He bamboozled a great many individuals, including Henry Clay and Andrew Jackson. It is not known to this day just what he was up to. Finally President Jefferson said that there was a conspiracy afoot that would endanger the Union. The conspirators were to be apprehended, and the finger was pointed at Aaron Burr. Burr hired the best lawyer he could get in Lexington, Kentucky, to defend him, and that was Henry Clay.

Clay was a marvelous lawyer, especially before a jury. He was a great actor. He had the most mellifluous voice that you could imagine. It carried through a hall. People were mesmerized frequently by what he said. His manner was not oratorial in a traditional sense, with grand flourishes. It was very intimate. It was kind. He was more like a public speaker, with an actor's [touch]. He used his hands, his head, they said. He had props, such as his spectacles and his snuffbox, which he played with. It was almost impossible to beat him before a jury. Burr hired him to be his lawyer. He won the case for him, and Burr then continued on his way.

HENRY CLAY BELIEVED THAT SLAVES had to be freed. They all had to be sent back to Africa—[he believed that] the two races could not live together. He feared . . . the blacks would assume political power and would do to the whites what the whites had done to them. Socially and economically, there would be conflict, so it was something that could not be bridged. The only solution, he felt, was a gradual emancipation in which, as they were emancipated, they were returned to Africa. These are thoughts, I believe, that Abraham Lincoln had until the end of the decade of the 1850s. Then Lincoln was radicalized and his views did change. But they had this racist notion about the inferiority of other races, and that was not the black race alone—that included Indians, who were treated as though they were of a lower order.

Henry Clay knew that slavery couldn't last. . . . I believe Henry Clay believed that all men are created equal—in principle. He said that several times. In actual practice, you know, no two people are equal. One has more talents than the other. It was his plan to pick a date—he didn't care which date, but some date—say 1850 wherein . . . those blacks born after that date would become free at the age of twenty-eight if they were male and twenty-five if they were female.

He later backed that up a little to males [being freed at] twenty-five and females twenty-one. Those born before that date, 1850, would remain slaves for the rest of their lives, and they would die out. Those slaves born after, becoming free at the age I've indicated, would be apprenticed, would learn to read, write, and cipher, and in the last three years of their enslavement, they would earn wages, which they could use to set themselves up in Africa. Once they became freed, then they would be transported back to Africa. That was his plan. He believed that the principles of population and economics would destroy slavery. He thought there would be more and more whites, as the Irish were coming in, and Germans were coming in, lowering the labor costs, so that it would be unprofitable to have slaves. [He hoped] that the South would voluntarily give up slavery and hire free white labor, and that would help to solve the problem too. Maybe by the end of the century we wouldn't have any slavery. There wouldn't be any war. There wouldn't be bloodshed. It didn't work, of course.

Frequently Clay was asked, "Why don't you be the example to everybody else and free your slaves, since you say you hate slavery?" He told this man to mind his own business, but he went on to say, "What are you going to do about the slave that I free who is sick, who is old, who is imbecilic, who is a child? They have to be taken care of—who's going to take care of them? The state? Obviously not. By just simply freeing them, you are not helping them at all. What you are doing is reducing them to abject poverty and death." He said that that was no answer at all. It had to be gradual, it had to be systematic, and there had to be a plan behind it.

As soon as I got into Henry Clay, I realized what an extraordinary figure he was. How important he was, not only for the growth of this country, but its preservation as well, in holding it together. Some historians feel, and I'm one of them, that had the South seceded in 1850, as it threatened . . . that they might have made good their secession. If there had been a war, they would have won it in 1850, but this was prevented by Clay with his ideas that constitute the Compromise of 1850. [It gave] the North ten more years to gird its industrial strength, find Abraham Lincoln, and even then they had a really hard job of beating the Confederates and forcing them back into the Union. He was a very significant man for the development of this country as well as its preservation.

To be a good public servant, you have to divest yourself of any personal motives, any private needs. You're not there because you want money or to acquire power; you are there to serve. And these men—Henry Clay and Andrew Jackson—believed they were serving the American people and that they both had goals, ideas, and programs that would do that.

John C. Calhoun

by
IRVING H. BARTLETT

On September 18, 1994, Irving H. Bartlett appeared on Booknotes *to talk about* John C. Calhoun: A Biography *(W. W. Norton & Company, 1993). John Calhoun (1782–1850) served as vice president under both John Quincy Adams and Andrew Jackson. In 1832, he resigned because of his support of states' rights to nullify federal laws. He was later elected to the Senate, representing his home state of South Carolina.*

He WAS BORN IN ABBEVILLE, South Carolina, in 1782. Abbeville is in the back country near the mountains in western South Carolina. Clemson University is the site of Calhoun's [former] plantation. . . . All that remains of John C. Calhoun's presence is the house, which was called Fort Hill.

He had bushy hair that went straight up on his head. Later in life, it fell down to his shoulders. He was tall. He was thin. He was very intense. He was probably unsurpassed in his own time as a parliamentary speaker. But he was not a ceremonial speaker like Daniel Webster. He showed to best advantage in the give and take of debate in the Senate. He was a fierce partisan for his particular points of view. He was accused of being too cerebral, too abstract. . . .

Calhoun was unflinching in his defense of the South, his defense of South Carolina, and his defense of slavery. He didn't give an inch. It was as if he was a locomotive that was frequently off course in the minds of his detractors and his opponents but couldn't be stopped. It was this aspect of Calhoun that encouraged the image of the cast-iron man. In my book, I was interested in exploring this. I found, like most stereotypes, it had some basis in fact. Clearly there aren't any cast-iron people; there are human beings. There was a story that . . . Calhoun once tried to write a poem to his sweetheart before he married her but couldn't get by the first word, which was "whereas." I was able to find in the Calhoun papers a love letter in which Calhoun is clearly smitten. Although I don't know that he ever tried to write any poetry, he had the feelings that other people have. But his public persona was of this fierce, unrelenting, determined defender of the South and slavery.

JOHN C. CALHOUN was in the House of Representatives from 1811 until he became secretary of war in Monroe's administration in 1817. He was secretary of war until 1824. [After serving as vice president,] he went to the Senate, where he remained until 1844. He resigned to run for president in the election of 1844. That campaign didn't work out; but it was as close as he ever came [to the presidency]. . . .

He was, in a sense, licking his wounds . . . [when] a vacancy in the secretary of state's place in [President Tyler's] cabinet came up, and he moved into that position. [In 1845, when James K. Polk became president,] he was asked not to stay on as secretary of state. He talked about retiring, but the people in South Carolina, his friends, wouldn't let him stay retired. They sent him back to the Senate, and he died as senator.

HE WAS A REPUBLICAN; that is to say he believed that government should be kept lean, that government should be led by people of ability and integrity. He believed that people like himself, with education and a sense of morality and civic virtue, should play an important role in politics. He believed that politicians should always have the long-range interests of the country at heart and not settle for short-range gains. He was a lifelong politician who was constantly knocking politics.

CALHOUN WAS CERTAINLY THE ONLY MAN, the only vice president, who got into an open fight with a president, a very severe fight at that, and then resigned.

South Carolina and the South generally were opposed to the tariff policy of the federal government. The South was heavily involved in staple agriculture, which meant exporting, and the tariff was alleged to hurt the South. The way they put it in common language was that a protective tariff forced southerners to buy high and sell low.

In the 1820s, the price of cotton plummeted. It was twenty-seven cents a pound in 1815, nine cents a pound in the mid-1820s. The tariff was perceived as being the culprit. It was not. It was more complicated than that. Cotton was cheaper in large part because too much of it was being produced as new cotton lands were opening in the Southwest, but it became a symbol of southern oppression. Calhoun was called upon to defend the South. He did this by developing a theory of constitutional government in America which held that . . . when the [states] entered into the federal union, they retained their sovereignty, delegating to the federal government specific powers—powers over foreign policy, some powers over commerce—but the federal government was not given the specific power to pass a protective tariff. It was only given power to put duties on imports in order to raise revenue. Calhoun held that in the final analysis, each state retained the right to negate a federal law if it found this law threatening its own welfare. This was the power of nullification.

He wrote a statement about this when he was still vice president. There's a lot of irony here. He was elected vice president in Andrew Jackson's first administration [in 1829]. This was the election in which "the people" presumably took over. A great majority of the people swept Jackson into office. The theory of nullification that Calhoun was articulating was essentially an attack on majority power, and he was writing it as vice president–elect. At the same time he was swept into office by a large majority vote, he was writing a theoretical statement denouncing the unlimited power of the majority. Ultimately, South Carolina attempted to nullify the tariff of 1832, which kept duties high. . . . A great confrontation between the federal government and the president, Andrew Jackson, and South Carolina and the vice president, John C. Calhoun, ensued.

Calhoun quit. But he was almost finished with his term of office. At that time, it was clear that Van Buren would be the vice president in Jackson's second term.

EDMUND MORGAN, WHO WAS PROFESSOR of American studies at Brown when I went to graduate school there, . . . wrote a wonderful book about Virginia in which he showed that ideas of liberty and ideas of slavery grew hand in hand in the colonies. He even hypothesized that . . . slavery somehow made it easier for them to experiment with new forms of government. . . . I found the same thing to be true in South Carolina: that is, as Calhoun was growing up, the [population of the] back country in South Carolina was getting blacker and blacker. Slavery was expanding to the frontier, to the back country. As it expanded, life became more and more civil for white people. It wasn't ever good for the slaves, obviously. But Calhoun in his experience always saw slavery as a civil institution, as an institution that encouraged civility and law and order and all the rest of it. Trying to understand that is very important for all of us. I mean, we have to understand that slavery was there at the beginning along with liberty—a very flawed situation, obviously, but that's the way it happened.

Calhoun, at one time, owned . . . about one hundred [slaves]. . . . He doesn't say much about his slaves in his letters. My conclusion is that he was a just master. . . . A just master was a person who believed in slavery, who assumed that slaves were inferior to white people, that being owned by white people was perfectly proper. But it meant that slaves had to be treated well. It also meant that slave owners were supposed to live up to a high standard of conduct.

Slavery created a distinctive culture in which honor became very important. We tend to think of that in terms of the prickliness of Southern slaveholders—

their willingness to resort to duels. But there's a good deal of scholarly literature which indicates that honor was a key value in the South. . . . [Also,] think of Benjamin Franklin and his advice. What are the values that he was encouraging his countrymen to emulate? Shrewdness, competitiveness, and acquisitiveness. It was this culture that formed Calhoun and this culture in which he, for many southerners, symbolized the ideal. He was willing to discipline slaves. He had them whipped when they ran away. He talked about the importance of having moral slaves. He would get very upset if he thought his overseer was giving a slave who was hired out too much of the money he was earning. . . .

Calhoun was never aware that he was living in a particularly privileged situation. He never felt any guilt about slavery. He assumed incorrectly, I assume, that the slaves were content with their lot. . . . Calhoun . . . never used the word "nigger." Never did I find a single thing in the papers which was derogatory to slaves as individuals. He never treated them derisively but would have insisted to the death in their inferiority. That was the basic assumption on which slavery rested. He had to believe in that. This led to one of the sorriest episodes in his life when he accepted at face value a ridiculous account in the census of 1840 about the plight of free black people in the North. The census was essentially a racist census and purported to show that free black people were mentally ill in ridiculously high numbers. Sometimes the number of insane blacks was greater than the total number of blacks in a given community. Calhoun actually drew on this census in an important diplomatic paper that he wrote as secretary of state while he was attacking British philanthropists and abolitionists and trying to show that the American system of slavery was the way to go.

[IN THE LAST YEAR OF HIS LIFE,] . . . CONGRESS was trying to decide what to do with the territory acquired . . . in the [Mexican] War. There was a big argument over whether slavery should be allowed into this territory. . . . A famous piece of legislation had been introduced, the Wilmot Proviso, which would have prevented slavery from being practiced in the new states that would come out of this territory—New Mexico, California. Calhoun was adamantly [opposed to] this. A lot of people said, "What difference does it make? Slaves aren't going to be taken out there anyway. They're not going to be on the desert; they're not going to be in California."

But Calhoun saw that the principle was vitally important. It was natural for southerners to feel terribly offended. South Carolina had contributed, given its small size, more soldiers to the war in Mexico than almost any other state. What sense could it make to a South Carolinian to be told now that he couldn't take his slaves to territory [won in] . . . the war? Calhoun was very strong in refusing to compromise on this issue. He was insisting on the rights of nullification that he had enunciated twenty years earlier. At the same time that this was going on, Calhoun was writing his great political and theoretical works, *Disquisition on Government* and *The Discourse on the Constitution [and Government] of the United States*. Eventually, there was a compromise, one of the most famous in American history, the Compromise of 1850, engineered in part by Henry Clay and Daniel Webster and other people.

Calhoun made his last speech as a statement against the compromise. His diseases, essentially heart failure and consumption, were so far advanced that although he had been able to write the speech, he could not deliver it. A friend, a senator from Virginia, actually read the speech to the Senate while he sat enveloped in a large coat that hid his emaciated form. It was one of the dramatic moments in the history of the Senate.

He died in 1850. [They brought his body into the Senate to lie in state.] It was customary for famous senators. Then they took him to South Carolina. He was buried in Charleston. His tomb is there. He wouldn't have liked that. He didn't like Charleston particularly. Charleston represented super sophistication and expensive ways of life and luxury. Calhoun was pretty much of a puritan, a southern kind of puritan. His wife had planned for him to be entombed on the plantation. That's what he would have liked. But it was handled as an affair of state, and the governors and the powers that were in effect in South Carolina at that time decreed otherwise.

Winfield Scott

---

by
JOHN S. D. EISENHOWER

Winfield Scott (1786–1866), a soldier in the War of 1812, was appointed general in chief of the army in 1841. He commanded the U.S. forces (1846–1847) in the war against Mexico. In 1852, he made an unsuccessful run for the presidency. Toward the end of his career, he helped defeat the Confederacy before retiring in October 1861. John S. D. Eisenhower's biography of Scott, Agent of Destiny: The Life and Times of General Winfield Scott, *was published by The Free Press in 1997. He told us General Scott's story on April 19, 1998.*

GENERAL WINFIELD SCOTT was our most prominent general of the nineteenth century, up to the Civil War and including the first few months of the Civil War. He was an astonishing man. He served under fourteen presidents. He was our number-one hero in the War of 1812 until the Battle of New Orleans, when he was supplanted by Andrew Jackson. He led the expedition that landed at Veracruz and took Mexico City in 1847. He was instrumental in moving Indians to the western parts of the United States. He was Lincoln's general in chief at the beginning of the Civil War. . . . He did have a tendency to get political every now and then, which was one of the unfortunate things about his career.

HE WAS BORN NEAR PETERSBURG, Virginia. . . . He went to school at William and Mary for a couple of years. He was always very impetuous and full of his own opinions, even when he was very young. I sometimes thought that he got his pomposity from being a general too long, but that's not true; he had it when he was born, for some reason or another. He left school. In those days, you could work under a lawyer and get your law degree on that basis; that's what he did . . . until 1808.

A friend took him in to see President Jefferson in . . . 1808. His friend said, "Mr. Scott here, he wants to be commissioned straight as a captain." Jefferson was preoccupied by other things, but he tolerated all this and talked to some other congressmen. Finally he says, "All right. If I get the augmentation of the army that I've asked for, I'll commission you as captain." He served from 1808 to late 1861—that's fifty-three years—and was a retired officer for the last five years of his life. Within just a few years, in 1814, he was made a brigadier general; 1814 to 1861 and an active-duty general officer. Wow.

SCOTT WAS PUT BEFORE a [military] court three times in his career. This was quite legitimate. . . . He was brash. There was a General James Wilkinson, who was really a bum. He was on the payroll of the Spanish when he was wearing an American uniform. He was down in New Orleans with the bulk of the army because we were expecting possible war with Spain. Wilkinson put the army in an awful sump hole where [there were] diseases. . . .

Scott couldn't keep his mouth shut. He kept declaiming his criticisms of Wilkinson. Scott claimed Wilkinson was just as great a traitor as Aaron Burr was. That didn't sit very well. Wilkinson had some friends around who reported what Scott said. They court-martialed him [in 1809]. The only thing that saved him was that everybody else felt the same way, so they worded [the verdict] very carefully—"unofficer-like conduct." Now by the Articles of War, if you say "conduct unbecoming an officer and a gentleman," that's curtains. You're dismissed. But they weaseled it around, "unofficer-like conduct," and they just suspended him for a year. It was a wonderful thing that happened to him, actually.

Scott took off for a year. He was going to go back into law, but his friends discouraged him. Instead, he studied the military profession for one solid year and came out the most professionally knowledgeable officer in the army, as a youngster. It put him on this road toward military professionalism, which is really what he was: our foremost military professional.

HE FOUGHT THE BRITISH to a standstill—the first time in the war [of 1812] that Americans had fought the British regulars to a standstill. My God, he was popular. Three weeks later, with all of this rise and furor of popularity, he was wounded very badly at Lundy's Lane. He's made a major general. Well, here's this guy—this is 1814—he was twenty-eight years old and a major general, outranking almost everybody in the army . . . and he's still a kid. He had a lot to learn by way of administration, particularly about finesse, and he had a lot to learn about humility, which he never did learn.

Scott really loved panoply. . . . When he would go inspect troops, he'd have his whole staff line up. He'd go in full dress. When he first bought his full-dress uniform, he admitted that he locked a door, put up two mirrors, and paraded for two hours, admiring himself in that uniform. He loved any picture of himself. I've never seen Scott in a picture in which he's not decked out with epaulets and full regalia. He was pompous. While he was very good with his troops . . . [he became known as] "Old Fuss and Feathers." That was one of his downers.

HE MARRIED MARIA MAYO in 1816, a very prominent debutante of Richmond, Virginia. Her father was a Virginia aristocrat, more so than Scott. Her father was not terribly enthusiastic about the marriage because he was unimpressed by Scott's fame and military prowess. He thought more about the status of where he stood in Virginia. But he gave his assent. The two produced seven children, of whom three survived to adulthood. Maria and Winfield were very fond of each other, proud of each other, but they were both prima donnas used to having their own little coterie of admirers around them. So they were sometimes in a little competition. She developed respiratory problems later on and spent an awful lot of time in Europe. . . . She died there.

He was absolutely terrific in the Mexican War. . . . The Mexican War was the manifestation of the doctrine of Manifest Destiny. It was brought about by a great urge, a movement in the United States, to move from where we were with the Louisiana Purchase and take the southwestern part of the country and reach out to the Pacific. As a result of the Mexican War, which was engineered by President James K. Polk, the borders of the forty-eight contiguous states became almost what they are today, except for a little sliver of land that was purchased later.

It was a war that was very interesting from a military point of view. Nobody wanted to conquer Mexico, they just wanted those territories. The president tried at first to send Zachary Taylor into the northern part of Mexico, within occupied California. . . . But the Mexicans absolutely would not cede any territory. . . .

Scott was President Polk's last choice . . . because he was a political rival. He was sent with twelve thousand men to land at Veracruz, way down on the Gulf of Mexico, and march inland over the same route that Cortés had used three hundred years earlier to take Mexico City.

Once Scott had Veracruz, Tampico, and Mexico City, the Mexicans finally said, "Get your people out of here; we'll sign this treaty." They have always resented it. It took over half the territory they claimed but did not control. It was a grimy episode in American history but one that's been beneficial in the long run.

[In 1817] Andrew Jackson, who commanded the West, had a run-in with the War Department. The War Department tried to send an order for an engineer officer [under Jackson's command] to report to Washington. Jackson protested, putting out his own order saying, "Any orders that come to you from the War Department, ignore them until you hear from me." Now that is pretty bad insubordination because the War Department established his command to start with.

Scott was at dinner with New York governor-elect DeWitt Clinton and . . . somebody asked Scott his opinion of [Jackson's order]. Somehow, the word "mutinous" got out. "Mutinous" got back to Jackson, who wrote Scott a fairly icy, but correct, letter. Scott, who never got over being a lawyer, wrote him a great tome about the legalities of Jackson's errors. That was enough. Jackson called him "pimp of the War Department"; he called him all sorts of names in this letter and said, "If you wish satisfaction, I can be reached at this address."

Scott, for once, used a little sense. He thought it over a long time and said, "I've got a no-win situation here. Either I get killed, which is undesirable, or I kill the great hero of the country, putting me in a class with Aaron Burr," who killed Alexander Hamilton. He cited all sorts of spurious [reasons]—religion, among other things—why he could not issue a challenge. Jackson consoled himself by telling people he would cut Scott's ears off. It blew over and four years later, they made up.

Meantime, Scott thought Governor Clinton was responsible for the word getting to Jackson about what he said. He issued a challenge to Clinton, who likewise and wisely passed it up. The political foes who knew everything about Scott said, "Well, look, you passed up a duel with a fellow who'd probably kill you, and you challenge somebody else that you would probably kill. Now what kind of a brave soldier is that?"

[SCOTT WAS NOMINATED FOR PRESIDENT by the Whig party in 1852.] The Whig party was organized in 1832. . . . It encompassed people of all persuasions who were against Andrew Jackson. That meant an awful lot of the southerners and also, much more heavily, northerners. . . . The Whigs collapsed because they had no . . . unifying philosophy. They were split badly over the Fugitive Slave Act—it was an unpopular act that the abolitionists in the North could barely stomach.

Scott's pomposity made him probably the worst candidate we've ever had nominated for president. He was a wonderful soldier, certainly our greatest soldier in at least the first half of the nineteenth century, but a hopeless politician. His big Achilles' heel was his pomposity and his ego, and that showed through.

Scott's [political] handlers—[New York Whig leader] Thurlow Weed and William Seward, who bought Alaska—said, "Keep your mouth shut. Don't open your mouth about anything." With Scott, that was impossible. When the reporters came around and he learned about his nomination, he said, "I shall support the platform." Oh, boy, there went the election right there. [He lost the election. The electoral vote was 254–42.]

Franklin Pierce [won]. He was a rather admirable fellow, a New Hampshire Democrat. . . . Pierce served as a brigadier general—after having signed up as a common soldier—under Scott. That made it a little painful for Scott, to be so roundly beaten in a presidential election by one of his previous subordinates. But Pierce was a congenial fellow, and they got along all right.

[AT THE END OF SCOTT'S LIFE,] I would say he was quite serene. He knew that he'd done great things in guarding Lincoln's inauguration and in forming the army that [General Irvin] McDowell commanded at the First [Battle of]

Bull Run. The fact that we had an army at all in the Civil War was due to him. But he was, by this time, seventy-five years old. He had diseases from the Mexican War, he was overweight, and he picked up a subordinate who was not very loyal, George B. McClellan. Even though George McClellan said all sorts of nice things about Scott, he undercut him. He absolutely ignored his orders. Scott tried to resign a couple of times. Then he went to New York City in the wintertime and West Point in the summers. He lived to attend the Lincoln funeral in New York. He died at the age of eighty [in 1866] rather quietly—and I don't think unhappily—right after writing his memoirs.

Sam Houston

by
MARSHALL DEBRUHL

Sword of San Jacinto: A Life of Sam Houston *was published by Random House in 1993 as a bicentennial birthday tribute to Sam Houston. Houston (1793–1863) died a hero of the Texas Revolution, having served as congressman, senator, president of the Texas Republic, and governor of the states of Tennessee and Texas. Author Marshall DeBruhl detailed Houston's life in a* Booknotes *program that aired on May 2, 1993.*

SAM HOUSTON WAS THIS GREAT NATIONAL FIGURE. That's what one has to keep in mind, that he was this extraordinary Virginian who was born in the eighteenth century . . . but who did his great work and achieved his great fame much farther afield than those who went to Philadelphia or Washington. He had two great political careers: one in Tennessee, where he was an attorney general, major general of the militia, a two-term congressman, and then governor—all before he was thirty-four years old, and then he had another career in Texas and in the United States Senate.

HOUSTON LOVED TO DRINK and run around with older men, but he always married young women. All of his male friends were much older than he and were mentors, really. But he always was attracted to young, very, very young women.

His first wife was a young woman from Gallatin, Tennessee, named Eliza Allen. She was the daughter of a prominent Tennessee family. Houston was thirty-six years old; she was twenty. It was an arranged marriage. The family was very ambitious for their daughter. Remember, he was pretty much on the road to being president of the United States at that point. He was a young governor of Tennessee, had already served in the Congress of the United States. He was Andrew Jackson's protégé. There was a very good chance, if this marriage hadn't derailed his political career in Tennessee, that he could have gone on . . . to be president of the United States. . . .

He married her on January 22, 1829. They were married for eleven weeks. Jackson had just been [elected] president and was on his way to Washington to be inaugurated. Houston stayed behind to marry in Gallatin, but the marriage collapsed almost immediately, and she left him in April of that year.

He resigned the governorship. He spent a week or so drinking in the Nashville Inn, where he was living, and then wrote an eloquent and brilliant letter to the people of Tennessee resigning the office. [Then he moved] to the West to rejoin his Indian friends in the Arkansas territory, which is now Oklahoma. He spent the next three years alternately in and out of Arkansas and Washington, drinking; he married the niece of the Cherokee chief Ooleteka. That was his second wife, Tiana Rogers.

He had met her earlier when they lived in east Tennessee, before the Indian removal to the West, . . . and he knew her father and her brothers. They were great friends of Houston's. . . . As a teenager, he had run away from home and lived with the Cherokees. So he just simply picked up with them again when he moved to the West. They lived together as man and wife near Fort Gibson in what is now Oklahoma . . . for almost three years, from 1829 to 1832.

His third wife, Margaret Moffette Lea, was an Alabama belle from Marion, Alabama. When Houston was wounded at the Battle of San Jacinto and was taken to New Orleans for medical treatment, he arrived with this very dramatic entrance. . . . This young girl—she was seventeen then—was on the pier in New Orleans. She was visiting family in New Orleans. She saw him and was taken with him. Then three years later, she met him and married him in Alabama when he was visiting there. He was forty-six and she was twenty. . . .

It was obviously a great love match. You read their letters—there are hundreds of letters. They had eight children, the youngest of whom, Temple Lea Houston, was only two when Houston died at age seventy. She was clearly in love with her husband. She was a very beautiful young woman and very religious—extremely religious Baptist and certainly a teetotaler.

He was a heavy drinker. It was a serious problem. Presumably his third wife sobered him up, but I'm not convinced of that. He drank bitters and it's eighty proof. It's the equivalent of bourbon, really. . . . [He drank] up until maybe his last ten years, when he became sort of the darling of the temperance movement. That was one of those things that swept the country for a while. He made speeches on behalf of temperance later, but that was when he was sixty years old.

THERE WAS A . . . GREAT SCANDAL when he beat up a congressman, Stanbery, from Ohio, who had libeled him on the floor of the House of Representatives. Houston beat him up on Pennsylvania Avenue and crippled him, really. They brought charges against him and Houston was arrested and tried before the House of Representatives. . . . Jackson's famous comment when he'd heard what Houston had done [was that] he wished he had more Houstons to cudgel the brains of Congress. . . .

The great trial in the House of Representatives became almost like the Oliver North hearings; it just transfixed the country. Dispatches went out everywhere, and all the papers were covering it. . . . Houston was [found] guilty. The night before he had been drinking with the Speaker of the House, who was a friend of his, and James K. Polk, and Daniel Webster, and various other people who were all his pals. . . . [He received] just a minor reprimand. But then he was taken before a judge in Washington and fined five hundred dollars. Later Jackson remitted the fine and pardoned Houston. . . . He had friends in high places.

THERE ARE SEVERAL THEORIES [as to why Houston went to Texas]. Americans love conspiracy theories. One theory is that he was dispatched by Andrew Jackson to separate Texas from Mexico. Jackson always assumed that Texas had been part of the Louisiana Purchase and that it belonged to the United States. He thought [the border] extended all the way to the Rio Grande or the Nueces, really. . . .

Llerena Friend, who wrote another biography of Houston years ago [had another theory]: Why was Houston in Texas? To make a living. . . . He had his whole political career collapse in America with the dissolution of his first marriage and the great scandal. He had no future left in Tennessee—or even in Arkansas, for that matter, where he had moved. His future lay somewhere else, and Texas was the place to go.

THE BEGINNING OF THE TEXAS REVOLUTION was when . . . Mexico gained its independence from Spain; the trouble began right there. This area called Texas or Tejas was not inhabited. There weren't very many people there, so the Mexican government had a policy of encouraging immigration from the United States. Stephen Austin or his father, Moses Austin, began this enormous land grant in Texas of hundreds of thousands of acres—millions of acres, really—and then recruited colonists to come down there. The seeds were sown then for revolution because you ran head-on into an autocratic government of Mexico and these people who were basically libertarians from the north.

The trouble began in the 1820s when the first colonists arrived. . . . Mexico became more and more despotic under a succession of people, but chiefly under Antonio López de Santa Anna. . . . He decided that this colonization should stop from the north; he was going to tighten the screws on these colonists who were causing him some trouble. But these people were from America and weren't going to put up with it. One thing led to another, and the whole situation rapidly unraveled.

Houston arrived there in 1832 . . . from the Arkansas Territory, where he was living. . . . He crossed the Red River into Texas, went on to Nacogdoches, and then joined up with Stephen Austin's colony in a place called San Felipe de Austin, where Austin's headquarters were. He was given his land grant and set up a law practice in Texas.

Later, when the revolution was heating up, Austin went to Mexico to negotiate with Santa Anna for more civil rights and liberties for the Anglo settlers of
Texas. Austin was thrown into prison. He spent over two years in the Mexican
jail. When he came back . . . the course had been set for a full-scale war against
Mexico. Sam Houston was there and since he'd had all this military experience,
he was made commander in chief of the Texas army . . . in late 1835. The revolution was very short; it lasted only a few months. The Battle of San Jacinto was
only eighteen minutes.

THE BATTLE OF THE ALAMO happened in March of 1836. Houston had sent
James Bowie and James Bonham there to tell them to blow up the place and
abandon the Alamo. It was in San Antonio, Texas. There are five missions, and
the Alamo was one of them. The Mexican church had established the missions
for pacification of the Indians and to assimilate the Indian tribes. . . . It had
been closed down. It was in ruins, really. There was a small fort built around it.
The Texans had decided to fortify this place and hold it against the advancing
Mexican troops.

But Houston had told them to get out of there, then to blow it up and
bring the available ammunition and horses to join his army in the east. He was
trying to organize a full-scale army, you see. Well, Bowie and Bonham got to
the Alamo and [Commander William B.] Travis and they decided that they
would hold it; that they would defend it against the Mexicans, which was folly.
It led to this terrible disaster . . . 180 men were killed at the Alamo and . . . 340
men killed at Goliad. That's quite a number of able-bodied men shot down.
Houston would have had that force, plus their ammunition and their arma-
ments for his army. But it was lost to him because of this folly.

HIS ENEMY SANTA ANNA called himself the "Napoleon of the West." He
had, indeed, had great successes as a soldier in Mexico against the Spanish
forces for the revolution against Spain. Then his march across Texas was one
victory after another. He won the battles and then he shot everybody afterward. . . . At the Alamo, after they had surrendered, he executed people—
there were a few survivors, including Davy Crockett. Then a few weeks later,
at this place called Goliad, Texas, they overran James Fannin and his men.
They marched 342 men out and executed them there—just shot them down
in cold blood.

Houston had retreated across Texas before the Mexican army, and that's another subject of great dispute: Was he really running or was it a strategic retreat? My feeling is it was a strategic retreat. He was drawing Santa Anna
farther and farther into what was Anglo Texas. That's where all the people were,
in east Texas. He ended up on this place called Buffalo Bayou, just outside of
present-day Houston. There, with his back to the water, he decided to attack
the Mexican army, which outnumbered him two to one. On the afternoon of

April twenty-first of 1836, they stormed across that field there and in just eighteen minutes conquered the Mexican army. . . . What it did was eventually give Texas to the United States; annexation came later. And it led directly to expansion all the way to the West Coast. All or part of six states resulted from this great battle. It was one of the great battles in history.

Austin, Texas was named after Stephen Austin, who is rightly called the Father of Texas. People say Houston was the Father of Texas—[but] he was actually the father of Texas independence. Austin is the man who [first] got the colonists there. . . . Houston was named after Sam. It was a place called Harrisburg, but it was burned during the revolution, and when they rebuilt this new town and laid it out, they named it after the victorious general, Sam Houston.

He's one of these great American figures who deserves to be known more than he is. People know who he is, but Americans don't realize what a great national figure he was. For example, he was in Washington for thirteen years in the United States Senate [representing Texas]. The two great issues of the time were . . . secession and the slavery issue.

He absolutely was adamant in his defense of the Union, that we could not allow this great calamity of secession to happen. He warned the people of Texas what would happen to their young men and to their farms and plantations and to the whole South, for that matter, if they pursued this folly of secession. Lincoln offered to send fifty thousand troops into Texas to keep it in the Union. Houston refused to do that because there would be even more bloodshed; that puts him right up there with the American heroes. . . .

Anything that threatened to break up the Union, Houston was absolutely opposed to. . . . Earlier, he had gone through the great battles against the Nullifiers with Jackson in Washington in the 1830s. . . . [It was clear even then] that this issue was not going to go away. Houston [opposed] the whole idea of the extension of slavery into the territories. He had voted against the Kansas-Nebraska Bill and the repeal of the Missouri Compromise, which made him anathema to the slaveholders in Texas.

He was [a slaveholder himself], but he was opposed to extension of slavery and the reopening of the slave trade. He was convinced that it was a dying institution and . . . felt it should be allowed to die out gradually. Because there were almost four million slaves in the South, it was an issue that certainly was not going to go away. He went back to Texas and was elected governor because the common people adored him. . . . But he still would not go along with the rest of the South in the secession movement, even refusing to call a secessionist convention till he was forced to do so. Then in March of 1861, just after the Lincoln inaugural when everybody was seceding, he wrote this famous letter to the people of Texas that he could not and would not go along with [secession]. The next day—this was March 15—he was called in front of the Texas legislature to swear an oath of allegiance to the Confederacy. But he refused to leave his office and go up to swear the oath. He was deposed from the governorship then and went home to Huntsville.

He died in Huntsville, Texas, [when he was seventy] in this rather eccentric house that he and Margaret had rented. They had no money. They had land, like most southerners. They were land poor. They'd gone back there after he was deposed from the governorship of Texas; [it was] a place that he had liked and where they had lots of property. It was called the Steamboat House, this rather strange-looking building that looked like a Mississippi riverboat. This eccentric man had built it in Houston. It appealed to Sam, and so he rented it. He and Margaret and their children were living in the house when he died.

He had been asked, or people were forever talking about, doing biographies of Houston. In a letter to a prospective biographer, he said, "Your idea of writing a book about me interests me. I have not sought to live in vain." . . . I thought that that was a wonderful epigram for him. . . . He certainly did not live in vain.

Sojourner Truth

by
NELL IRVIN PAINTER

Sojourner Truth (1797?–1883) was an abolitionist, women's rights activist, and former slave. She successfully sued and won the right to bring her son out of a life of slavery. On December 8, 1996, Nell Irvin Painter appeared on Booknotes *to talk about her biography* Sojourner Truth: A Life, a Symbol, *published in 1996 by W. W. Norton & Company.*

SOJOURNER TRUTH means "itinerant preacher." . . . She was not born a slave in the South, as many people assume. She was born a slave in Ulster County, New York, along the Hudson River, in about 1797. We don't know exactly when because nobody was keeping track at that point. She died in Battle Creek, Michigan, which was kind of the Berkeley of its day, in 1883.

She spent the first part of her [freed] life—the late 1820s until 1843—working as a live-in household worker. That's how she supported herself. But she also belonged to a group of enthusiastic religious folk. Then in 1843 the Holy Spirit told her to change her name [from Isabella to] . . . Sojourner Truth. She started wandering off to Brooklyn, then along Long Island, then up the Connecticut River valley and stopped in Northampton [Massachusetts]. Over a period of time she became a feminist and an abolitionist. We know her as a feminist abolitionist.

[SOJOURNER TRUTH USED SMALL CARDS as a fund-raising tool.] They were called *cartes de visite.* They were about baseball-card size [and featured a photograph of Sojourner Truth]. . . . They were inexpensive because you could do four or eight or ten at one time, then develop them and then just cut them up. All sorts of people had them. . . . She used one caption over and over again [on the cards]: "I sell the shadow to support the substance—Sojourner Truth." What she meant by that was "I sell the shadow," which was the photograph, "to support the substance," which was her bodily substance.

SHE WAS INJURED in her last year of slavery. But interestingly enough, even though other people harped on her experience of having been a slave, in none of her pictures does she display her slave wound. She never shows that hand prominently. She never shows the scars on her back or anything like that. . . .

Remember that in the North, we're not talking about a land of plantations: 99.5 percent, 99.9 percent of the enslaved people in the North were on farms. There were one or two enslaved people working with handymen or hired girls or men. . . . They would have been pretty much by themselves as black people. It meant that they were much more like all the country people around them.

Her first language was Dutch because that was the language of the working people around her. When she was living with [one family,] the Dumonts, for instance, she would get up in the morning, start the fire in the kitchen, peel the potatoes, put them on to boil, go out, milk the cows, bring back the milk, fix the breakfast, and then, after the family ate, she'd clean up. Then she'd go out in the field. She did everything.

Her parents were perpetually depressed. They were also enslaved. They were relatively privileged because they had their own house and their own garden. . . . But they had lost ten to eleven to twelve children to the slave trade. Losing a child like that is like having your child die; we know how traumatic that is. In the first few pages of Sojourner Truth's narrative, she [explains] that her parents would sit around the fire and tell her about her siblings who had been sold away. Her mother would take her out, look up at the stars, and say, "See those stars? Those stars are shining on your brothers and sisters. We don't know where they are, but we're all under the same heaven. . . ."

I began to really focus on what it must have been like to live in a family where your parents were lamenting the loss of their children. I began to understand the psychological weight of having been enslaved, of having been beaten, of having been fondled by your mistress. We now know what is likely to happen to people after those experiences. People who suffer that kind of brutality are greatly at risk of depression themselves, of low self-esteem, of difficulties with sexuality and with anger at themselves and at others, and more importantly, of passing this on to the next generation and the next generation. It's transgenerational.

SHE MARRIED ONCE IN SLAVERY to a man named Thomas and so far as I know, Thomas was the father of all her children. From what I can tell, they had a reasonably happy but not romantic life. They had planned to have their little cottage and their little garden by themselves. That didn't work out. When they were emancipated, Thomas decided to stay in Ulster County. He was much older than she. She decided to seek her fortune in the city, which many country people were doing at the time. He died in the poorhouse, probably not too long afterwards.

The first commune [she joined] was the Kingdom of Matthias—this was the early 1830s—first in New York City then in Westchester County. Matthias was a Scots-American born Robert Matthews, who, like many others in New

York . . . was inspired by Charles Grandison Finney, the great evangelist of the 1820s, 1830s, and 1840s. [Matthias] was a man prone to religious enthusiasms. One day in Albany, he was shaving and the Holy Spirit spoke to him and said, "You can't shave anymore. You are a Jew, and true Jews do not shave." He stopped shaving, and then God told him to go to the West and preach his truth. He left and went to the West and came back and then ended up in New York City.

At this point, Isabella—Sojourner Truth—was living with people who shared her religious enthusiasms. One day Matthias came knocking and Isabella opened the door. Here he was, looking like . . . Jesus with his beard and such. She said, "Art thou the Christ?" He said, "Yes, I am." And all of them fell together washing each other's feet, understanding each other, taking each other in and becoming a family. That family grew, moved, and occupied the home of a wealthy couple up in Mt. Pleasant, now Ossining, New York.

Matthias felt that there was Gentile law and there was his law. People who got married under Gentile law didn't have to stay married. So he plucked out the wife of the man who owned the big house in Westchester County and said she was his "match spirit." This set all sorts of family matters roiling. . . . It was free love. . . .

The second commune was an industrial commune. This was in Northampton, Massachusetts—the Northampton Association of Education and Industry. Here, the people were not particularly religious. They were ecumenical as far as religion goes. But they were anti-slavery; they were for women's rights. It was there that Sojourner Truth discovered abolition and women's rights. She got there in 1843, in the fall or early winter. . . . She only meant to stay there for the winter and then continue on her way. But she liked it and she stayed. She outlived the commune, which fell apart in 1846. . . .

This was a Utopian community. *Utopia* means both "no place" and "good place." It was a place that would be set off [from society] where people would try to perfect human life. . . . In our generation, we can think back to the 1960s with the hippie communes. It was very much that kind of an impulse—to pull away from the corrupted world, to make a better place that would hopefully grow and spread its beneficent influence to the rest of the world.

Everybody in the commune put everything together. They were paid a few cents an hour, so they had everything they needed. They lived in a large building . . . and bathed in the creek. I hate to think of what it was like in January.

At that point she felt that she was with very good-hearted people who were not white supremacists. As I worked on this book, I was . . . floored by the level of white supremacy in this country in the nineteenth century. You almost could not find anybody who didn't believe that white people were better than black people [and felt that] black people should just be out of sight and just do work. These were some of the few white people who were not shackled with this white supremacy. She found that it was a comfortable place psychologically. She was able to have her daughters there with her. She did work like everybody else. . . . [The abolitionist] Frederick Douglass was not a member, but he and William Lloyd Garrison . . . the most prominent anti-slavery person in the United States . . . and others would come to western Massachusetts, kind of like a progressive summer camp. . . . George Thompson, who was visiting, was the person who began to take Sojourner Truth out as an anti-slavery lecturer.

THE *NARRATIVE OF SOJOURNER TRUTH,* first printed in 1850, with another big edition in the 1870s and a final edition in the 1880s, was an ex-slave narrative. It was Sojourner Truth, who did not read or write, talking to another woman named Olive Gilbert, who was writing down Sojourner Truth's experiences as a child and a young woman. Since this first came out in 1850, it does not include the kind of high moments that we now know of Sojourner Truth's life, because it was published before she became an itinerant abolitionist.

[As for] being known, her break comes in 1863, when Harriet Beecher Stowe wrote and published an article called "Sojourner Truth, the Libyan Sibyl." People who had been rubbing shoulders with her for years could see her for the first time; all of a sudden she was a VIP, she was somebody.

SHE WORKED IN WASHINGTON, D.C., with the freed people, the refugees who were pouring into the District from Maryland and Virginia. After the war ended, there was not a lot of work, and they were a displaced people. She and another woman worked for a while trying to have [the freed slaves] put in jobs in Battle Creek, Michigan, and Rochester and other places in New York. But that was extremely expensive and difficult. Then she thought, Well, if some of the western land could be set aside for these people, they could settle in the West and have their own institutions, farms, and be self-supporting. That was her ideal. Nothing came of it, but she was delighted with the exodus to Kansas of 1879.

[She met with three different presidents.] The best known meeting was with Abraham Lincoln. [There is a picture of the meeting] painted ten years after Sojourner Truth's death and, of course, many years after Abraham Lincoln's death. It's very famous, because people liked the idea of these two giants meeting and respecting each other—the proof of that is that Sojourner Truth is sitting down and the president is standing up. On second thought, I think everybody would realize [that Lincoln deferring to her] is highly unlikely.

SHE WAS ILL for the last three years or so with ulcers on her legs. It might have been diabetes; we don't know. She died in Battle Creek [in 1883, which] had been her base since the 1850s. She's buried in Oak Hill Cemetery, which is a fancy cemetery. . . .

[TODAY,] THERE ARE ALL SORTS of Sojourner Truth symbolic . . . things that you can buy to wear or display to show that you are for strong black women, for strong American women, or for multicultural feminists.

I do know that for the rest of our country and perhaps for the rest of the world, Sojourner Truth and I are grouped together as black women. I don't mind that. In that sense, I am connected to her, just as I am connected to all other black women in this country over time. We do have extremely different experiences. One of the things I was trying to do was to humanize Sojourner Truth, to show her as an individual with her own life and her own experiences—in addition to being a symbolic black woman.

1800s

Most of us are not going to be Freud and most of us are not going to be Martha Graham. But are there some lessons which we can learn from extraordinary people which might make us more effective as just ordinary people trying to have a decent life?

—Howard Gardner

Ralph Waldo Emerson

by

ROBERT D. RICHARDSON, JR.

For much of the nineteenth century, Ralph Waldo Emerson's (1803–82) unique voice spoke to America through lectures, poetry, and essays. His ideas inspired other writers and activists of his age like Henry David Thoreau and Margaret Fuller. On August 13, 1995, Robert D. Richardson, Jr., talked to us about Emerson—The Mind on Fire *(University of California Press, 1995).*

THE PICTURE THAT I USED TO HAVE of Ralph Waldo Emerson was of a cold, plaster saint. His bust was up in schoolrooms everywhere; a lot of other people picked up the notion that Emerson was this cool, distant saint. One day, I was in his house in Concord, looking on the walls, and there was a picture of a volcano in eruption—right where you come in the front door. It's very striking because it's not a very good painting, but it's very vivid and very colorful. I kept wondering and wondering about this painting. Finally, I began to notice that the image of fire and volcanoes—the notion that humanity is all connected the way volcanoes are connected by a fire under the earth—was Emerson's leading idea. He came to think that just as each volcano was an outlet for the fire under the earth, so each person is an outlet for the humanity that unites us all.

HE WAS BORN IN 1803 and he died in 1882, so his life covered two-thirds of the nineteenth century. He lived to see the Civil War and its aftermath. . . . He lived in Concord, Massachusetts, although he wasn't born there. He was born in Boston. He moved to Concord eventually and became very much a citizen of Concord. And while it's sometimes been said that there's no great sense of place in American literature—D. H. Lawrence once famously complained about that—that certainly isn't true of these Concord writers—Henry David Thoreau, Emerson, Nathaniel Hawthorne, Louisa May Alcott. They have a very strong sense of place.

Henry Thoreau was just fifteen years younger than Emerson. He died in 1862, just as the Civil War was under way. He died young, and Emerson lived on, but they were both in Concord at the same time. They were very close friends. They had a lot of intellectual horsepower, and they didn't always get along perfectly. There were some spats and some falling-outs, but Emerson, even when his memory was gone as a very old man, remembered Thoreau as his best friend. Without Emerson, I don't think there would have been a Thoreau.

They were writers, but they found their way to writing. It wasn't really a profession the way it might be thought to be now. Emerson started out to be a preacher, and he had some difficulties with that. He went to college. He eventually went to divinity school. . . . But he couldn't live with the institutional church. He was a deeply religious person all his life . . . but had trouble with anything that was institutionalized.

His first wife died early and tragically. About the same time that she died, he had his crisis of conscience and his break with the church. . . . She died of tuberculosis after they had only been married a short time, less than two years, and it absolutely tore him up. Somehow in that loss of her, he also lost his willingness to go on being a minister in an institutional setting.

I started the book with the moment when the young Emerson, who is a minister, is walking out to Roxbury to visit the grave of his wife, and he opens the coffin of his wife, who has now been dead a year and two months. . . .

He said in his journal that he walked out and opened the coffin. Not the tomb—he opened the actual coffin. The reason for it has been speculated on a great deal. For some biographers and some readers, it seems so macabre, and [they act as if] they've thought that perhaps he imagined it or hallucinated it, but it's right there in the journal. There were other people in the nineteenth century who did similar [things]—who opened the coffins of recently dead loved ones. I think the reason—and one has to say that it's a guess—but I think it was because he couldn't really believe she was dead.

He was writing in his journal to her as though she were alive. She was very beautiful, very young. He couldn't accept the idea that she was dead. I think this was his way of letting her go. It also is the essential Emerson. He had to see for himself. He had to, with his own eyes, see. His hunger for personal, direct, immediate experience is really the basis of his whole life.

HE WENT TO EUROPE [after his first wife's death]. He traveled through Europe to think things over. He became more and more convinced that the modern world was going to revolve around science. He came back and began a whole new career as a public lecturer on science. . . . He then rapidly branched out into other things. He founded the new lyceum movement, which was a sort of working people's lecture series movement. . . . He began to travel around—first around eastern Massachusetts and then more widely around New England—and eventually wherever the railroads ran throughout the country, giving lectures. He would give as many as eighty public lectures a year, and there'd be a train trip and a stay in a cold hotel. . . . He was on the lecture tour for four or five months every year for twenty-five years. What Emerson really was, was a public lecturer, and then when he came home, he would recharge the batteries, read, try to write, get back to his family.

He would often give the same series of lectures in different places, and he had to beg the newspapers not to print what he had lectured about in each city because if they printed it too carefully or made verbatim transcripts, it would make the same lectures difficult to use. But he wrote a new set each year and often, in a given year, would use sets from various years. He kept very careful track of where he had given what talk. The general setting would now be considered adult education. He did not go to universities. He was not the equivalent of what one now calls an airport intellectual, who goes from university to university and talks only to people in those places. The lyceums were really organized for working people, for people who were self-made or trying to be self-made, what we would now call a general audience.

HE WAS A FAIRLY TALL MAN. He stood six feet tall, which was tall in those days. He dressed, various people said, like a prosperous farmer. He wore black suits, but so did farmers in those days, and he had a coat and tie, but so did his farming friends. People were much more, to our eye, formally dressed, but his clothes were sort of shabby, and they didn't fit terribly well. When he took out his money to pay for his transatlantic passage, the captain noticed that he had twine wrapped around his wallet many times; he had to unwrap it all, take out the money, pay for the passage, wrap the wallet back up, put it back away. When he stood up to lecture, he had a very plain style, and he read his lectures, though he practiced them and he knew where the emphasis would come in any given word. It wasn't "Hitch your wagon to a star," it was "Hitch YOUR wagon to a star."

HE WAS A VERY WELL KNOWN figure, and he was invited . . . back again and again as a leader of the billing. He went back to Ohio for twenty-five years. He was invited back each time, and gradually, more and more people heard him. It's how he got his fame. He was a good speaker.

He became very famous rather early. In a piece called "The Divinity School Address," he attacked what he called historical Christianity, meaning a view of Christianity that depended upon miracles and the Bible and a historical figure . . . rather than being based in human nature. The piece drew immense attention. That was 1838, and from then on, he was really well known. He was infamous as well as famous. Mothers would take their children and cross the street with them so that they wouldn't have to meet "Mad Dog" Emerson, who was considered by the religious establishment a completely wild man.

HE WAS A PACIFIST for a while in an era when it was a very complicated matter—because the whole of Emerson's early career was under the shadow of the coming Civil War. One has to remember that in 1860 the war broke out and engulfed the nation. Everybody had to take sides or felt forced to take sides. The movements that he was interested in—anti-slavery and, to some extent, women's rights—inclined him toward other new movements. He was very sympathetic with the idea of peace, and he gave a lecture at a peace conference. The lecture was called "War," but it's actually about peace. But one has to say that as it became clear that there was going to be a fight between the North and the South, he came to think that perhaps it was necessary and inevitable. He was not willing to let slavery stand. He was not willing to sit by, and when the war came, he accepted it.

A TRANSCENDENTALIST, IN THOSE DAYS, was a person who belonged to a loose little collection of outsider intellectuals. They had a hard time with the reigning philosophy in the colleges, which was that everything in our heads has come there through experience; there's nothing in the human being but the famous Lockean *tabula rasa,* that the mind is a blank slate on which experience writes itself. . . . The transcendentalists believe that there was already something in the mind that took in experience and shaped it. . . .

Transcendentalism came to mean something different for each of these people. It began with an affirmation of the autonomy of the individual, because it celebrates the freedom of the individual. Politically it meant that they had to fight for freedom for everybody else, and so it pulled some of them into the anti-slavery movement. It pulled others into the women's movement. It pulled others into education. One of them, Elizabeth Peabody, founded the kindergarten movement in this country. Others became interested in American Indian rights. . . . Margaret Fuller became the first full-time reviewer for an American paper. Thoreau became interested in the anti-slavery [effort]. Emerson spent years on anti-slavery. Transcendentalism began as a personal philosophy and ended up pushing all its members into reform. They became a group of reformers.

He met Abraham Lincoln in Washington during the course of the war, early on when the issue was whether or not and how soon to proclaim emancipation. Emerson was . . . invited to Washington by the Smithsonian to give lectures. . . .

Emerson's hope was . . . that they could get Lincoln to announce the Emancipation Proclamation, and they could then publicize it. Then he wouldn't be able to back down from it. It was really the politics of how to get the Emancipation Proclamation issued. Once it was issued, there were big public meetings in the North. Emerson went to one in Boston and wrote a hymn for it and brought people roaring to their feet singing "The Boston Hymn."

HIS FIRST BOY WAS NAMED WALDO, and he died at the age of five of scarlatina, which came on very suddenly and very tragically. . . . He was a sunny, cheerful boy, and he died very suddenly, and that was another tragedy. Emerson's life was marred by tragedy.

After his wife died, his two younger brothers died, both of whom were considered more likely prospects for success in the world than he was. And then his first child, first son died, and he opened his coffin fifteen years later, too, on the occasion of moving it to Sleepy Hollow . . . Cemetery. He wrote in his journal and he told his family when he came home that he'd opened the coffin and looked in, but he said, "No more."

We never know what he saw in there, but one of the things that I noticed as I was putting the book together and assembling the chronology was that Emerson's real creative life, that volcanic outpouring, falls entirely between these two glimpses into the grave, these glimpses not simply of the dead but of his dead. From that, I came to see better than I ever had before that Emerson's achievement really was based on facing the abyss, on facing tragedy, on facing loss; that the idea of him as an easy optimist, the idea of him as someone who somehow hadn't earned his right to be self-reliant, was nonsense. In fact, this man's entire life was based on loss and on a kind of powerful facing up to loss that's not common. It's hard to imagine, hard to do.

Robert E. Lee

by
EMORY THOMAS

Emory Thomas discussed Robert E. Lee: A Biography *(W. W. Norton, 1995)*
with Booknotes *viewers on September 10, 1995. Robert E. Lee (1807–1870) was*
offered field command of the U.S. Army on April 18, 1861. He declined the offer,
instead resigning from the U.S. Army to fight with his home state of Virginia.
General Lee commanded Virginia's forces throughout the Civil War until he
surrendered to General Ulysses S. Grant at Appomattox on April 9, 1865.

ROBERT E. LEE WAS A GREAT GENERAL who was a great man. He was a
greater man than he was a general. That's why he excites so many people. They
know he's great. Not all that many people know exactly why, but they perceive
his greatness, which probably has something to do with the tragic events in his
life more than the victories and the successes.

He had a birth defect. The birth defect was his father, who was a hero in the
revolutionary war, a prominent public figure who had some problems with integrity and rascality and insolvency that drove him out of the House [of Rep-
resentatives], out of the country, one step ahead of his creditors when Robert
was a young man. He died trying to come back to the country . . . when
Robert was on the brink of being a teenager. Lee spent most of his life trying
to forget who his father was and also trying to live down his father's infamy.

[Lee's father,] Light-Horse Harry Lee, spent time in two debtors' prisons,
one in Westmoreland County at Montross, Virginia, ironically where he once
served as a "Gentleman Justice." . . . He fell on evil times. He spent a lot of
money; he borrowed a lot of money. He was a pretty reckless speculator in land
and other schemes. He got to the point of not being able to satisfy his creditors. He was holed up inside Stratford Hall, the old Lee mansion, with a chain
across the door trying to keep the creditors away, but he couldn't. They finally
arrested him and put him in jail for debt.

He was also in jail in the Spotsylvania Courthouse. He once wrote a letter to
then-president Madison recommending one of his relatives as a federal judge. I
don't know what the Anglo-Saxon equivalent of "chutzpah" is, but whatever it

is, Light-Horse Harry possessed it in great abundance because it takes a great man of gall to write a letter from jail recommending someone to be a federal judge. . . .

THE FIRST THING ROBERT E. LEE did that attracted anybody's attention was attend West Point. There he was second in his class, accumulating no demerits. This was not unheard of, but [it was] rare. For the next seventeen years, he enjoyed some significant success as an engineer. . . . He diverted the course of the Mississippi River, making St. Louis continue on as a thriving river port instead of throwing the river over to the Illinois shore, which would have made Brooklyn, Illinois, [an important] port.

For the next seventeen years of his life, he was a warrior, beginning in the Mexican War. He served on the staff of General Winfield Scott and was very important in several of Scott's victories in the campaign from Veracruz to Mexico City. He then was superintendent of West Point for a time. He worked on some other engineering projects briefly but then went off to Texas, changing his branch to the cavalry.

[ROBERT E. LEE MARRIED MARY CUSTIS] in 1831. In a way, they'd always known each other. They were distantly related. Robert E. Lee's mother, who was really the heroine, the one who kept that family together, insisted that her children enjoy the genteel upbringing that she believed they deserved. She went on protracted visits—primarily, to keep from having to make ends meet at home—to various relatives and close family friends. One of these friends was Mary Fitzhugh, who'd married [George Washington's stepson,] George Washington Parke Custis. They visited Custis's home, Arlington House [situated on a hill above the Potomac River on the grounds of what is now Arlington National Cemetery]. The two children knew each other at that time and continued to know each other in a circle of friends in northern Virginia.

[Mary Lee] was rather sickly. . . . Some of it had to do with having seven children in roughly fourteen years. After one childbirth, she had a terrible infection that really wracked her and, as Robert pointed out, affected her brain. She became very apprehensive and very concerned. . . . She didn't want to go anywhere or see anybody. . . . On another occasion, she had been ill so long and her hair became so tangled that she became frustrated and cut it all off. [Robert E.] Lee wondered what in the world he was going to do with this wife with a crewcut, but I guess it grew back.

HE [RETURNED FROM TEXAS] to northern Virginia, near the Washington, D.C., area, at the death of his father-in-law to settle his estate. He spent the next two or three years doing that. In the course of that experience, he happened to be on hand during the [abolitionist] John Brown's raid on Harpers

Ferry in October of 1859. Lee had a great role in putting down that raid and capturing John Brown. Lee doesn't get credit for this, but he endured a hostage crisis such as we're all too familiar with in these times because John Brown had thirteen hostages inside that famous fire engine house. . . . Lee was able to get those hostages out, none of them harmed, and capture John Brown at the same time.

HE WENT BACK TO TEXAS rather briefly, but significantly, because at this point he had a chance to be a landed planter in the course of dealing with his father-in-law's significant wealth, but he chose to stay in the army. He went back to Texas, rejoined his regiment, and there he was when the secession crisis boiled over. At that point he came back to northern Virginia, turned down field command of the United States Army offered to him by [General Winfield] Scott, resigned from the [U.S.] Army, and shortly thereafter accepted command of the army and navy of the state of Virginia. Thus he began his Confederate career. He . . . came to command ninety-two thousand troops in the Seven Days' campaign . . . in the spring of 1862. Before that Lee had never really commanded anybody but those marines at Harpers Ferry.

In addition, in this first year of the Civil War—1861 and the spring of 1862—Lee had traveled around enough and experienced enough of the war to know that it was going badly, that the Confederacy was not really prepared to fight this war.

He was made a full general, one of the first eight full generals, by President Jefferson Davis, more so for political reasons, and also because Lee enjoyed a significant reputation. . . . A lot of people believed that Lee was a great warrior. . . . He looked like a general. He was the handsomest man in the United States Army and his pictures reveal that. . . . He was five eleven, but [he wore size four and a half C shoes]. He had tiny, tiny feet. . . . I get these numbers from Edward Valentine, who did a sculpture of Lee. He was supposed to do it from life. He did take the measurements while Lee was still alive, and one of the things he measured were those feet.

HE KNEW [GENERAL ULYSSES S.] GRANT and even visited Grant in the White House when Grant was president. But that relationship was kind of testy. . . . No one really knows what went on when the two former enemies went into the White House, closed the door, and spoke privately, but I'm not sure that it was a very jolly meeting.

Lee met Grant in Mexico when they both served there. Grant was a young lieutenant; Lee was a captain. That meeting couldn't have been very consequential, and only Lee remembered it. I'm not even sure Grant did. Certainly the two knew each other from 1864 in northern Virginia and all the way to [Lee's surrender at] Appomattox.

The Second [Battle] of Cold Harbor, [Virginia,] on June 3, 1864, was a terrible mistake on Grant's part. It was essentially a series of frontal attacks against the entrenched Army of Northern Virginia; it was slaughter. It was really over in one morning and an awful lot of people were dead, wounded, and dying out there on the battlefield. In the wake of other battles, generally the general who had lost . . . would ask for a truce to retrieve the wounded and bury the dead. In this case, Grant didn't want to admit that he'd lost. He sent Lee a message through a white flag. . . . Lee was just as stubborn and made Grant ask in the regular manner.

The sparring went on for five days, during which time the poor guys out there, the ones who were wounded, were screaming, crying, calling for water, calling for help, and asking to die. We're talking about the pride of a couple of generals here. Well, maybe the corporate pride of their armies was at stake, too. But I don't think either one of them covered themselves with a great deal of glory in this instance. By the time they went out there to retrieve the wounded, a lot of wounded had slipped back to their own lines at night or been hauled away during the dark. By the time Grant finally said, "Okay, okay," and asked for the truce in the accepted way, there were only two people alive. Everybody else was dead.

On April 9, [1865,] to be precise, [Lee] surrendered. He didn't surrender all of the armies. He didn't think that was within his authority. He only surrendered one army, the Army of Northern Virginia, that he had actively commanded ever since June first of 1862.

[AFTER THE WAR] HE ACCEPTED, somewhat haltingly, the presidency of a tiny liberal arts college in Virginia, Washington College, named for George Washington and endowed by Washington initially. Washington College was the only college around anywhere nearby that had any money at all, because they still had that endowment. They had to convince the state of Virginia to turn loose the money, but they had it. Lee took the reins of this school and led it for the last five years of his life. It is now Washington and Lee University, named for both Washington and Lee. He was a very creative, imaginative educator. Some of the most exciting ideas that he had in his life came very near the end of his life.

But in many ways these were frustrating years. Clearly, he had lost a very large war. He wrote to a friend, "I am perceived—I'm seen as such a monster now"—that is, he was a rebel. He was the enemy. But he . . . took this struggling little liberal arts college, he transformed the curriculum, introduced elective courses, brought in the sciences, brought in applied science—what we would call engineering—and abolished compulsory chapel for the students. He went every day himself, setting an example that way and attracting students to chapel.

Lee's religious life is probably best summed up in a line that he wrote in a letter and also in an essay that he wrote in the back of a diary that he was keeping in the 1850s. He [wrote] about the moral development of children that "the great duty of life"—and when somebody says the great duty of life, you perk up and pay attention—"the great duty of life is to see to the happiness and welfare of our fellow man." He believed that selflessness was the greatest good. And, conversely, the greatest evil, the source of any sin in the world, was selfishness. He lived that out, and that's a big part of his moral and religious thinking.

I try to point out that Lee was what we would call a very liberal Christian. He's often seen as this pious, hidebound, rigid, authoritarian moralist. But I don't think so. Many of the things that he did in his life as well as those lines [he wrote] about the happiness and welfare of our fellow man reveal him as this very open, warm, humanist Christian.

HE DIED IN 1870 . . . AT Washington and Lee University, of a stroke. His last real act on the public stage was in a vestry meeting in which they were trying to balance the budget. The thing had gone on for three hours. Finally, in order to end it, in order to resolve the controversy, Lee said, "I will make up that sum." He would give the fifty dollars or so necessary to balance the budget and to pay the rector. . . . He came home. His wife chided him for being late, which was moderately funny because it was she that was always late. He went to the head of the table and attempted to say the blessing over the supper and couldn't do it. His mouth opened but no words would come. He sat down. He was flushed, and he had a stroke, a rare stroke that did not provoke paralysis. He lingered for a couple of weeks and died on October 12, 1870, having been silent all those days. The people who watched by his bed couldn't get over that silence, but really, what was more appropriate than for Lee to die silently. He wasn't a man of words; he was a man of deeds.

Salmon P. Chase

by
JOHN NIVEN

Salmon P. Chase (1808–73) was Abraham Lincoln's secretary of the treasury during the Civil War. He later resigned that post and was appointed by Lincoln to the Supreme Court. Chase had previously served as the governor of Ohio from 1855–60 and was twice elected to the U.S. Senate. John Niven appeared on Booknotes *on May 28, 1995, to discuss* Salmon P. Chase: A Biography, *which was published that year by Oxford University Press.*

SALMON P. CHASE WAS A VERY IMPORTANT statesman in the nineteenth century. When he became Abraham Lincoln's secretary of the treasury, Chase and [secretary of state] William Seward were better known to the public than Lincoln was. Chase had been around for a long time. He had a big reputation as a defender of fugitive slaves. He had been the first Republican governor of Ohio. He had been the U.S. senator before that on the Free Soil ticket. He was actually the founder of the Free Soil party and coined the famous slogan "Free soil, free labor, free men," which energized the Free Soil movement, a third-party movement that didn't get anywhere but certainly advertised Chase.

He lived from 1808 to 1873. He was sixty-five when he died, a man who was supremely industrious and supremely ambitious. . . . Lincoln referred to him as having ambition [like] a maggot in his brain . . . . He tried to ease Lincoln out of the nomination in 1860. Then, while he was an important member of the cabinet—secretary of the treasury—he constantly [engaged in] intrigue, trying to get the nomination away from Lincoln in 1864. He was not successful.

CORNISH, NEW HAMPSHIRE, [his hometown, was] a town that was dominated by the Chase family. His father was named Ithamar Chase, and he was a very prosperous farmer, a state legislator, a senator in New Hampshire, and a selectman: in other words, a leading figure in the town. . . .

His father died when Chase was eight years old. By that time the family had lost a good bit of their money. They had moved to Keene, New Hampshire, where father Chase, Ithamar Chase, had invested in the glass business at the wrong time, sold his farm, and lost all of his money. They went from relative affluence to near poverty. This had a tremendous effect on Chase. He had numerous uncles, all of whom had gone to Dartmouth College, but not his father; he's the only one who did not. One uncle became the bishop of Ohio— the Episcopal bishop. They were all the way up in the social hierarchy of New England in the early nineteenth century. His mother shipped him off to Ohio under Uncle Philander's tutelage when he was just a kid, nine, ten, eleven, something like that. He spent two years in Ohio with his uncle, which he hated; he hated the whole interlude. The bishop was a really tough, tyrannical person and beat Chase quite a bit, extracted a lot of labor from him, cheap labor. . . .

Then Uncle Philander decided he would leave. He became president of Cincinnati College. They were there for about a year, the Philander Chase family, including Salmon. Then the bishop decided to go east and go to England to see if he could raise money to found a college. The family went east. Then Chase, who had about a year at Cincinnati College, went to Dartmouth. The uncle went off to England, raised money, and founded Kenyon College in Ohio.

Chase went to Washington after he got out of Dartmouth with vague thoughts of a teaching career. And he went to Washington, where another uncle was a senator from Vermont. Chase came from a distinguished family, and he managed to luck out. He ran a school, a boy's school in Washington. While he was there, he came in touch with William Wirt, who was attorney general in the Adams administration . . . a friend of Jefferson, Washington, an old republican from way back and an essayist and lawyer. He was a foment of influence, in my opinion, in Chase's life. Whereas the bishop was a harsh, unrelenting individual emphasizing work, Wirt was a genial eighteenth-century man and a distinguished essayist and literary figure. He had a lot of beautiful daughters, and they took Chase in. His Washington career was pleasant while the Wirts were there. He studied with William Wirt and took his law education from Wirt and passed the bar. When the [Andrew] Jackson administration came in, the Wirt family moved to Baltimore. Chase then took the bar examination in the District [of Columbia] and then went out to Cincinnati in 1829.

[While there,] he wrote a petition for a Quaker group, which was introduced in Congress, but he didn't take any particular side in this early period until there was a riot in Cincinnati against abolitionists involving James Birney, a prominent abolitionist who had come from Kentucky and was running a newspaper called the *Philanthropist*. Chase took the side of Birney because he promoted law and order. Anarchy in the streets occurred when Birney's press was broken up. That energized Chase to become more involved in the antislavery movement.

He was elected to the first Cincinnati city council, then the legislature. He was elected senator in 1849 on the Free Soil ticket; he served a six-year term.

Then he ran for governor. . . . He campaigned and won the election. He was governor for two terms, four years. And then he was reelected as U.S. senator in 1860.

HE WAS A FREE SOIL SENATOR in 1850. A Free Soil outlook . . . meant wherever Congress had power, territories, high seas, District of Columbia, they should vote against slavery. Not in the States, where [slavery] was established and protected by municipal law, local law, but everywhere else where Congress had power. . . . Then in 1854, Stephen A. Douglas, in an effort to solve, as he thought, the agitation against slavery . . . borrowed the "popular sovereignty" idea, where the inhabitants of a given territory would decide for themselves whether that territory went free or slave. Douglas was a nationalist and a moderate, but, in this case, he followed the pressure from the southern senators, the slave-state senators. . . .

Chase and some of his colleagues wrote what they call the *Appeal of the Independent Democrats in Congress,* a fiery document accusing Douglas of all sorts of chicanery and slave-state conspiracy. . . . [Chase made this] appeal to the independent Democrats, which really energized the anti-slavery feeling in the North and was a body blow to Stephen A. Douglas.

[HE WAS SECRETARY OF THE TREASURY FROM] 1861 to the end of June 1864. [Two days after being sworn in as senator for the second time, he had resigned to take the post.] Lincoln took all of his competitors, both former Democrats and former Whigs, to form his coalition government. He offered the State Department to Seward, and he offered the Treasury Department to Chase. Lincoln tried to make a balance between geography, geographical areas, and prior political involvement. . . .

After a while, [Chase's] insidious ambition and his efforts to undercut Lincoln caused an estrangement. Lincoln put up with him until 1864; then, over a patronage dispute, he finally gave in at the wrong time and accepted Chase's resignation.

When Lincoln accepted his resignation, which upset Chase—he didn't think it was going to be accepted—Chase yearned for more public duty and more public composure. He'd always thought about the Supreme Court as a possible place anyway, and so he lobbied for himself. . . .

Lincoln, who was under great pressure at the time, decided he had to have a progressive, or radical, person. He had high respect for Chase's abilities, rather lower respect for his deviousness and his intriguing qualities. So finally, he decided to . . . respond to the pressure, and he appointed Chase. He [became chief justice] from December of 1864 until his death in May 1873.

SALMON P. CHASE WAS THE PRESIDING OFFICER, as the Constitution provides, [during Andrew Johnson's impeachment trial]. [Johnson was impeached by the House] . . . predominantly because Johnson was considered to be a stumbling block for Reconstruction. He had been a Democrat—he was a war Democrat—but he was very conservative. He had a Jacksonian approach to politics. This didn't set well in the period after the war, when they were trying to determine . . . peace terms for the South. Johnson wanted lenient ones and the Congress, spurred on by the radicals and the progressives, wanted much more stringent ones. They passed [the] Reconstruction Acts. All of these acts—[the] Freedman's Bureau Act, Civil Rights Act, Fourteenth Amendment—all these were bitterly opposed by Johnson. . . .

The Constitution says the chief justice shall preside at any trial of the president. Chase, being Chase, decided to expand his role. Chase raised the point with the Senate Committee on Rules. As chief justice, he wanted not only to be presiding officer, but to be like the vice president—have a [tie-breaking] vote and also to rule on the competency of witnesses. In other words, as Chase said, he wanted to make it as judicial a trial as possible, and not a legislative or political trial.

He managed to get his way. On roll calls and things like that, there were efforts to deprive him of this [power], but they didn't succeed. So as chief justice and presiding officer, we owe a lot to Chase for making sure that Johnson was not found guilty; it would have wrecked our system of government. Johnson was acquitted by one vote. They brought it up again a couple of weeks later and the same thing happened. Finally the Senate gave in, and Johnson completed his term. He only had about seven or eight months to go anyway.

CHASE BEGAN TO GET SICK in 1868 or 1869. He had a heart attack and recovered from that. In 1869 or maybe 1870, he then had a bad stroke. He recovered but was put on a diet. . . . He tried to resume his regimen in the Supreme Court, but even he began to realize that his health was shattered. [He died in 1873.]

[HE] CERTAINLY WAS A GREAT MAN as far as American history in the nineteenth century. He is important to historians, much more than to, perhaps, the casual reader. He actually had a lot to do with bringing on the Civil War. . . . But he was a man of all sorts of paradoxes; it is very difficult to get a handle on him. As far as the anti-slavery impulse that he cultivated, he was genuine about this, even though it also, incidentally, helped his political career.

Abraham Lincoln

---

by
DAVID HERBERT DONALD
HAROLD HOLZER
MARK NEELY, JR.
MERRILL PETERSON

Abraham Lincoln (1809–65) was the sixteenth president of the United States. Many Lincoln scholars have visited Booknotes, *including Mark Neely, Jr., for* The Last Best Hope of Earth *(Harvard University Press, 1993); David Herbert Donald for his award-winning* Lincoln *(Simon and Schuster, 1995); Merrill Peterson for* Lincoln in American Memory *(Oxford University Press, 1994); and Harold Holzer for* The Lincoln-Douglas Debates *(Harper-Collins, 1993). Here's a sampling of what they discovered.*

Mark Neely, Jr.

The Last Best Hope of Earth:
Abraham Lincoln and the Promise of America

LINCOLN WAS BORN IN 1809, near Hodgenville, Kentucky. His father was named Thomas and his mother was named Nancy Hanks Lincoln. His mother was illiterate; his father could, as Abraham said later in his life, "bunglingly sign his own name but was otherwise illiterate." Thomas Lincoln, his father, hadn't had many opportunities in life. Abraham Lincoln's grandfather, after whom he was named—Thomas Lincoln's father, Abraham—had been killed by Indians while settling a farm in Kentucky, and that left Thomas without many opportunities in life. Even so, he managed to buy, with cash, three different farms in Kentucky and was attempting to better himself. But he became the victim of the system, and the system was a very bad land-title system. They didn't have title insurance in those days, so when you bought a piece of land in Kentucky, as Abraham Lincoln's father did, essentially you didn't know what you were getting.

Kentucky [in the early 1800s] was a crazy quilt of overlapping land claims. You were responsible for the survey yourself. The survey was conducted by the system of metes and bounds, so that the boundaries of these farms would be described in the documentary record as "trees and rocks and streams," all features of the landscape that moved, and so most of the pieces of land in Kentucky had disputed title. Thomas fell victim to this and in disgust left with his seven-year-old son Abraham for Indiana, where the land was surveyed by the federal government and came under the land ordinance of 1785, laid off in neat mile-wide squares, and title was much more secure.

His MOTHER DIED when Abraham was nine years old. Within a year his father remarried a widow named Sarah Bush Johnston Lincoln. She proved to be a wonderful mother. No one that I know of in the many books written on Lincoln ever says an unkind word about Sarah Bush Johnston. He had a younger brother, who died at a very early age, and an older sister, who died in childbirth. Lincoln . . . grew up in what we could consider pretty rough circumstances in rural Indiana. He [learned about] death at an early age. It left him with a tragic view of life and mixed feelings about his hardscrabble past.

No one knew Abraham Lincoln was going to grow up to be president of the United States, so there was no one around taking notes on his childhood development. We wouldn't know anything about it at all because Lincoln was a modest man—he didn't write an autobiography; he didn't keep a diary. He was a genuinely modest man—a little secretive, in fact, about his past. But we do know something about those early years because once he became famous— actually, after his assassination—his former law partner, William Herndon, conducted what we would call an oral history. He went and interviewed, either in person or by letter, old settlers in Indiana and Illinois who knew Lincoln when he was a youth. Those reminiscences tell us what we know about the early years of Lincoln's life, substantially.

The interviews are fraught with great difficulties in use. As you can imagine, if someone came to interview you and you'd grown up with Abraham Lincoln and someone asked you, "Did you know Abraham Lincoln?" you'd say, "Sure, I taught him everything he knew." They tended to exaggerate the person's role in Lincoln's life, and they're not altogether trustworthy, but they tell us something.

He LIVED IN INDIANA for fourteen years. He left the state when he was twenty-one. Lincoln and his family moved to Illinois in 1830. They moved first to Coles County, and Lincoln helped his father build a cabin there, but he left his father's roof at that point. Lincoln did not get along very well with his father. We don't know why. People can speculate. My own speculation is that Abraham Lincoln was a very ambitious boy and a very ambitious man. His father, by the time his son knew him well, was beginning to lose his ambition. Those farms he'd bought in Kentucky and the sour experience there of having the title spoiled and then moving to Indiana . . . and to some degree maybe the people he associated with, sapped Thomas's ambition. So by the time Lincoln had a conscious view of his father, he may have seen him as somewhat ambitionless. I don't know. That's purely speculation. But at any rate, he did not get along very well with his father and left his roof for good and went to live in New Salem, Illinois. New Salem is . . . a ghost town now maintained as a park site. But [at the time] it was a small log-cabin community near Springfield, Illinois.

IT'S INTERESTING THAT LINCOLN became a politician before he became anything else. . . . He ran for public office when he was twenty-three years old in a new state. He lost the first time, but the second time he won. . . . When he went to the state legislature, he met people with bigger horizons than New Salem. Among them was John Todd Stuart, who was a prominent Whig, and he encouraged Lincoln to study law. Lincoln's prospects were not very great, and at one point he thought maybe he'd become a blacksmith. He needed some outside encouragement. He just had such meager education—only a year's formal school. He didn't learn polished grammar until after he was twenty-one years old. He didn't learn plane geometry until he was forty. He thought his educational background was too limited to become a lawyer, so it took some encouragement from somebody else. But Stuart encouraged him and Lincoln started reading on his own, and by 1836 he would become a lawyer.

TYPICALLY, IN NINETEENTH-CENTURY AMERICA people got so excited about politics that by the time elections rolled around there were often scuffles in the streets, [beatings with canes] of newspaper editors who had printed some calumny about a politician, and . . . sometimes a little violence at the polls. When political campaigns got very heated and bad words were spoken, sometimes a politician would challenge another politician to a duel. Lincoln was challenged to a duel by a Democratic politician named James Shields. It was a very interesting event in Lincoln's life.

Lincoln avoided fighting the duel. That tells you something about him that's important, that is that he was to some degree a little exempt from the rougher standards of masculine behavior in nineteenth-century America. He didn't like to hunt. He was not a violent man. Although a good wrestler, he didn't have a vengeful nature, and he wasn't about to fight a duel. So being the challenged party, it was his privilege to stipulate the weapons. Lincoln stipulated that they fight with large cavalry broadswords. A plank was to be placed on the ground over which neither party could cross, and they were to duel with these swords on either side of this plank. The trick here is that Abraham Lincoln was six feet four inches tall and had a very long reach, and Shields was rather shorter. So it was a completely unfair contest and ridiculous. By setting these terms, he, in a sense, was making fun of the institution of dueling, and yet he went along far enough to set the terms. Later he was ashamed of this and didn't want to talk about it.

HE MARRIED MARY TODD LINCOLN [in November, 1842], also a Kentuckian, but who came from a much more privileged background, well educated. Women did not have many educational opportunities, especially west of the Appalachians. She had been to finishing school. She spoke French fluently. She had an extraordinary interest in politics for a woman in the era, and she was, for Abraham Lincoln, quite a catch.

She moved in the most exalted social circles in Springfield. She had gone there to live with her sister who was married and living in Springfield. They met in the political society of Springfield, probably at a social occasion.

HE SERVED FOUR TERMS in the Illinois legislature. Then there was a brief period in which he didn't hold public office, but he was basically angling to get to be congressman from his district. In 1846 he was elected to the United States Congress. He served one term in that Congress from 1847 to 1849, the only national office he held before becoming president [in 1861].

Harold Holzer

The Lincoln-Douglas Debates

LINCOLN WAS THE PHYSICAL OPPOSITE of [his political opponent] Stephen A. Douglas. . . . Douglas was called "the Little Giant," and Lincoln, at that point, was known by the nickname "Long Abe." He had served in the 1840s in the Congress as a Whig, and he was a co-founder of the new Republican party, a leader of the Illinois Republicans, and a well-known, successful attorney. He was mostly known as a party leader and a public speaker on behalf of other candidates. He had tried for the Senate a few years earlier in a campaign that was not really a campaign. It was just decided in the legislature with no pre-campaign, no debates, and he had nearly made it, but his party forsook him during the balloting and elected a different fellow. He was making his second real effort for the Senate, and this time he said he would only do it if he was nominated for the Senate in advance, which was not the practice in those days.

The Republicans met in convention, and they nominated Lincoln as their first and only choice for the United States Senate. Lincoln responded with his famous "House Divided" speech—that was his acceptance speech—and thereupon a campaign began.

The process began in an interesting way. Douglas was much better financed than Lincoln and much better known, even in Illinois. Lincoln was having trouble getting attention for his nascent campaign. He devised this idea that he would follow Douglas around to wherever Douglas was campaigning, and after Douglas gave his speech, Lincoln would give a speech in the same place and thus, he said, "I'd have the last word on him."

In Chicago, Douglas spoke in the afternoon; Lincoln spoke in the evening. In Springfield, their hometown and the state capital, Douglas spoke one day and Lincoln followed him the next day. Well, the Democratic press started to make fun of Lincoln. They said that it was as if he was a circus performer picking up with the menagerie and moving from town to town. The Republican paper, the *Chicago Press and Tribune,* now called the *Chicago Tribune,* proposed this idea of joint debates. Lincoln picked up the case immediately and challenged Douglas to debates. Douglas knew from the beginning that this process could be of no benefit to him. He was coasting at that point. He had a stacked legislature there that was almost certainly going to reelect him to the Senate to begin with. The last thing he needed was to waste his time facing Lincoln face to face—of course, as close to face to face as they could get, one fellow being five foot two and the other being six foot four—but the code of honor of the West dictated that you couldn't very well refuse.

Douglas had to accept the debate challenge, but he drew the line when Lincoln said, "Let's meet one hundred times all over the state." Douglas said no. Lincoln said, "How about fifty times?" Douglas said, "Forget it." Douglas said, "We'll meet in the county seats of each of the counties, and we'll leave out Cook County, because you already followed me in Chicago, and we'll leave out Sangamon County, because you followed me in Springfield. So that leaves seven counties, we'll meet in seven county seats. Take it or leave it." Lincoln took it.

Each debate was three hours, incredibly enough, and the format was nothing like the debates we have today. The first speaker, the opening speaker, spoke for sixty minutes without stop, and then the rebuttal speaker spoke for one and a half hours—ninety minutes, again uninterrupted. Finally, the first speaker had thirty minutes to answer the rebuttal—three hours altogether each time. Audiences not only endured it in both the blazing heat in August in Freeport, for example, and Ottawa but in the freezing rains that suddenly whipped up in the fall. They loved it. It was spectacle; it was theater; it was religion; it was Fourth of July. These were the biggest events to hit the prairie in these people's lifetimes, and they knew it.

How would he do today in politics? It's very hard to transpose the Lincoln who could [only] afford to wear ill-fitting clothes and travel by coach during these debates. He generally looked like he had just slept for twenty-five or thirty hours in his suit when he arrived, didn't shave often enough, and didn't tend to his hair the way our candidates and leaders do today. But obviously he was smart enough to have adapted, and he probably would have been extremely persuasive.

Presumably he would change some of his politics to update himself to the twentieth century. I think he was endlessly fascinating. He was mysterious, though. He managed, even with the best of his friends and the closest of his acquaintances, to leave a veil of mystery, something untouchable. You read the reminiscences of the people who claimed to have been closest to him, and they were probably the closest, because there were no others, and there was something they couldn't touch. There was something they didn't know. There was a line that he drew. They didn't know about his childhood. They didn't know much about his family life. He didn't invite many of them home. They didn't know much about what he was thinking. He was a very, very private, close-mouthed person. At the same time, he was a gregarious politician, an enthralling speaker and a great storyteller.

David Herbert Donald

Lincoln

IT'S IMPORTANT TO REALIZE that Lincoln, contrary to myth, did not emerge as the opponent of slavery and the advocate of equal rights for blacks; he came to this very slowly. By the end of his life, he was almost there. But well into the war years, he was still saying pretty much the same thing.

He called a group of African-American leaders to the White House—the first time an American president had ever met with black leaders—to urge them to colonize in Central America. "Get out of this country; show that you can set up an independent, free society under American protection in Panama. This would do much to end the institution of slavery, to remove racial prejudice." He went on to say, "You and I are not equal. Whether this is right or not is not for us to discuss." By this time he had shifted. Earlier—there was no question in the Lincoln-Douglas debates—he was saying it was quite all right for us to have superior and inferior races. By the presidency he was saying, "Whether this is right or not, there's no point in our discussing it." He meant "I don't think it's necessarily right, but public opinion says we have got to deal with this and the way to deal with it is through colonization."

The black leaders turned down his offer, quite reasonably, pointing out that they had been in this country as long as his ancestors had been in this country. Gradually, Lincoln, watching the accomplishments of black soldiers in the Union armies, watching the progress made by blacks in states like Louisiana as they were reconstructing, came to see that blacks were capable of citizenship. He favored allowing at least the intelligent and the educated and those who served in the army to vote. He was perhaps moving further than that by the end of his life. So it's a mistake to have a kind of candid shot of Lincoln at any one point and say, "These were Abraham Lincoln's racial views." They were constantly changing and moving in a progressive fashion.

HIS FIRST ABSOLUTE PRINCIPLE was devotion to the Union. This was, [Whig representative] Alexander Stephens said, "a kind of a mystical belief for Abraham Lincoln." He simply would not tolerate its ever being challenged or questioned. He was never prepared to say "There might be some good to be had from dividing the country or allowing the South to go in peace." Or one could do a calculus on this and say, "Six hundred thousand men were killed and wounded in this war. Was the Union worth that?" For Abraham Lincoln it was. There was never any question; the Union was absolute.

His second principle added to this as the war went on was freedom. He'd always been in favor of freedom, opposed to slavery, but not sure he could do anything about it until the necessities of war pushed him in that direction. With the Emancipation Proclamation came the second war aim. Toward the very end, he was beginning to add the third: equality. These were his guiding principles.

[His] OLDEST BOY WAS ROBERT TODD LINCOLN, who grew up to be a Harvard graduate, secretary of war, minister to Great Britain, and so on. Then the next little boys were Edward, who died young; Willie, the little boy that died in the White House; and Tad, who survived the assassination year only by a few years. He died in his early teens. He had a lisp and probably a cleft palate, so he was never very clear in his articulation. But there were four boys. Lincoln was devoted especially to the young ones, whom he just doted on. The little boy, Tad, would come in and interrupt cabinet meetings with his bad speech. He would say, "Papady, Papady, Papady," and only Lincoln would understand he meant "Papa dear." Something had to be done instantly. Lincoln would break off discussion of a national banking act to go take care of whatever Tad's needs were. The little boy would fall asleep on his couch in the cabinet room. Lincoln would take him up to bed with him at night. He loved that little boy. But his heart really belonged to Willie, the little boy that died in the White House. That was the great tragedy of the Lincolns, because he was the brightest of all the Lincoln children.

HE WAS NOT A MODEST MAN. His secretaries were the best judge of this. . . . [People] would come to the White House and they would think, I'm a graduate of Harvard University. I have degrees from so-and-so. I'm a principal leader of this business. . . . They would look at this fellow in the White House who had no experience, really, who had to learn on the job, who was uncouth in appearance, who seemed to have folksy, down-to-earth manners and no polish at all, and they all thought they were better than he was. Lincoln was never taken in by any one of them. He was never embarrassed by any one of them. He knew perfectly well that he was their intellectual superior. He was smart enough not to let them know it—or try not to let them know it. But he knew it very well.

[HE WAS RE-ELECTED IN] 1864—overwhelmingly, providing you remember that the Confederate states were out of the Union and therefore not voting. If they'd been back, it would have been a very close call. Lincoln himself thought he was going to lose that election until the very end. In August, he wrote a memorandum saying, "As of this moment it appears this administration is going to lose," and he developed a strategy of what he would do in those circumstances. So the victory—while on paper it seems very impressive—was not perhaps such a wide victory. It was about 54 percent, but 54 percent with your enemies not voting is not such an overwhelming vote.

Inauguration Day was in March. It was cold, but nevertheless the sun came out just as he gave his inaugural address. . . . I think it is the shortest inaugural address, and it was not what his listeners expected to hear. Aside from the first sentence or two where he said it was his duty to make such a speech, he did not refer to himself at all. He did not review the events of the past four years or say "We've claimed these victories" and so forth. . . . He reviewed very carefully and thoughtfully the causes of this war and what he thought the future was going to be. He made no pledge, no promise. "Earnestly do we hope, fervently do we pray that the scourge of war will pass from us," but he didn't say it was going to end tomorrow or in a hundred days or three years.

WHEN LEE SURRENDERED at Appomattox [on April 9, 1865], that really was the end. The night of April 14, Lincoln was ready for the celebration that everybody [else] was rejoicing in. Lee had surrendered. The soldiers were coming back into Washington. [Union commander General Ulysses S.] Grant was in town. It was supposed that Lincoln and Grant and Mrs. Lincoln and Mrs. Grant would be at Ford's Theater that night as kind of a spectacle, for soldiers to see them, to see that victory was really there. The theater party broke up for a variety of reasons; different people were otherwise engaged. Mrs. Grant did not like Mrs. Lincoln and would not go to the theater with her. So she invented an excuse to take Grant off and out of the picture. Finally, with [their friends Major Henry] Rathbone and his fiancée, Lincoln went to the theater to see *Our American Cousin.* John Wilkes Booth went, too.

The initial plan was not so much to kill as it was to kidnap. They would kidnap Abraham Lincoln and hold him hostage [in exchange] for Confederate prisoners in the North. If this could be done—there were some two hundred thousand Confederate prisoners held in the North—if they could be freed, Confederate armies could regroup, and the Confederacy could live again. When this failed, and they realized it was not possible—how do you kidnap a six-foot-four-inch man in a public place without any disturbance?—then the Confederacy was falling. John Wilkes Booth thought the only solution was not kidnapping but assassination: He would assassinate Lincoln. He would assassinate Secretary of State William Seward. He would assassinate Vice President Andrew Johnson and then maybe others as well. It would be a sweeping out of the top echelon of the Union government.

[Abraham Lincoln was shot around ten-thirty that night. He was] . . . taken across the street to the Petersen house . . . on 10th Street in Washington. . . . He died the next morning at 7:22.

Merrill Peterson

Lincoln in American Memory

[IT TOOK TWENTY DAYS TO BURY LINCOLN,] because he was transported across the country on a funeral train, all the way up through New York. Basically the funeral train on his trip home to Springfield followed the route that he had taken from Springfield to Washington in 1861 to be inaugurated president, with some minor variations. It was an incredibly moving event, with tremendous impact on the minds and emotions of the American people. There were other events after that. There was a national fast day proclaimed for Lincoln, a national day of mourning for Lincoln after the funeral proclaimed by President Johnson. There were a lot of things that had to do with the closure of the Civil War.

LINCOLN WAS . . . A HUMANIST; an American humanist. But he's not a humanist in the sense that [Thomas] Jefferson was—an educated humanist, a learned humanist, a man of books and learning and so on. Lincoln, later in his life, saw the tremendous excitement of that, but he didn't have the opportunity to do anything about it. . . . Lincoln was a man who appealed to the heart. I think Lincoln was very much a man who had an affectional relationship to the American people, or the American people developed an affectional relationship with him. That's partly because of the tragedy, the pathos of the assassination. It's also because of the qualities of his personality that were so endearing to many people and so mysterious in many ways.

"APOTHEOSIS" MEANS "MAKING INTO A GOD, making immortal." . . . One of the interesting questions that one has to ask right at the outset is: Would Lincoln have been as famous if he had died a natural death or if he had lived longer? To what extent did the assassination—in the circumstances of that time, right at the very end of the Civil War, one day after the American flag was raised again in Charleston, South Carolina, on Good Friday, which immediately evokes the whole symbolism of Christ—to what extent would he have become such a saint and hero if that had not happened?

There was plenty of evidence that Lincoln was being recognized as a very great man both in America and abroad for a year or more before his death, certainly after his reelection as president and his second inaugural address, which was actually only about six weeks before his death. He was being recognized by learned, educated people, not only in this country but around the world, as a very great man.

Walt Whitman

by
DAVID REYNOLDS

Walt Whitman (1819–92) is one of America's foremost poets, whose talent was not recognized until decades after his death. On April 28, 1996, David Reynolds talked about "the Good Gray Poet" and his book Walt Whitman's America: A Cultural Biography *(Knopf, 1995), where he takes a look at the poet himself and at the times in which Whitman lived.*

WALT WHITMAN HAS BEEN SUCH A CRUCIAL figure in the formation of American culture and the American spirit. . . . He was a man who, above all, saw himself as absorbing America. He said the proof of the poet is that his country absorbs him as affectionately as he has absorbed his country.

He was born in 1819 on Long Island. His father was a struggling carpenter who just barely made it above the poverty line. His father struggled [also with] farming on Long Island. Then just before Walt turned four, his father took the young family to live in Brooklyn. . . . When they moved there, it was a little town numbering about seven thousand in population. His mother was of Quaker stock. Walt was always very devoted to his mother, even though she was only barely literate; when she wrote him letters, she never capitalized words, rarely used punctuation. . . . Nevertheless, he said, "I have a kind of tribal feeling about my parents and about my siblings."

There were eight children, one of whom died in infancy. It was in many ways a troubled family. Walt's youngest brother Eddie was retarded from birth and possibly epileptic. His older brother Jesse went insane, and Walt had to commit him to the Kings County lunatic asylum [in New York]. His sister, Hannah, ended up going psychotic and was married to a neurotic artist who also ended up in an asylum. He had another brother, Andrew, who became an alcoholic and who died early of throat cancer. I mention all of these things because Walt Whitman was above all the poet of joy, of optimism, of faith and hope. Too many people nowadays look upon Whitman and say, "He lived in a simpler age. He lived in an age when, people could speak about the miracle of the commonplace in such an easy way." That wasn't at all true. I mentioned his father's near poverty. His father also apparently struggled with alcoholism. I mentioned several of his siblings having problems. And yet Walt stands for us as an example of somebody who managed to overcome incredibly severe private misfortune to forge a new kind of affirmation in his poetry.

He didn't have much formal schooling. He left school when he was age eleven; he just barely got beyond elementary school. . . . He had to become a law clerk and then work for newspaper offices in Brooklyn just to help the family keep going. What's really remarkable about people like Whitman, about Herman Melville, about a lot of writers back then, was that there was a certain faith in self-education. Melville once said, "A whaling ship was my Yale College and my Harvard." [It is the same] for Whitman, too. Even though he had very little formal schooling, he had this voracious interest not just in reading, but in experiencing life in general. He can set an example for a lot of people nowadays—that there is such a thing as learning by yourself. Going to school is so important, but it's what school does to you, how it inspires creativity in you and the thirst for new knowledge [that matters]. This is what he really embodied.

He respected the marriage institution. He actually advised many of his friends to get married, but the presumption is that he was homosexual. He had many romantic relationships with younger men. Late in life on the other hand, when he was approached by John Addington Symonds, who was a European homosexual, and asked, "Don't your homoerotic poems"—the *Calamus* poems—"imply this sexual relationship between men?" At that time Whitman said, "These are damnable, morbid inferences, and I completely disavow them." A lot of people have said, "He was just covering up." I think that the truth lies in the middle. He didn't perceive that word *homosexuality* [as we do]—it wasn't used until the 1890s. He really didn't perceive himself in quite the terms that Symonds, who was this European intellectual, saw him. He saw himself as a working-class comrade. He "sold himself," quote, unquote, in much of his poetry as that. . . .

He did apparently have certain one-night affairs with women. There was a reference in one letter to "that lady who called you such a good bedfellow, Walt." One of his friends wrote that. Supposedly he had what he called a "sweetheart," a woman in the late 1850s or early 1860s. But in terms of becoming close to marriage, he never did that. . . .

When he was teaching on Long Island in a little one-room schoolhouse . . . in the town of Southold, Whitman was allegedly denounced from the Presbyterian pulpit by . . . Ralph Smith for allegedly having had affairs with some of his male students. . . .

This group of citizens supposedly tracked Whitman down in his house, dragged him out, and tarred and feathered him and supposedly rode him out of town on a rail. Mainly this was a story that was passed down orally through generations. . . . I got in touch with the only living descendant of the Whitmans, a descendant of Mary, his sister, who was living in Greenport, right near Southold. . . . Her husband actually is the one who said, "Yes, I have heard this from the word go in my family, that this Southold thing happened, and that Walt Whitman has therefore been considered the black sheep of his family because of this." . . .

The story was that he was tracked down, beaten, and driven out of town and that a kindly nurse named Selina Danes nursed him back to health. I think that those moments of anguish [made their way] into some of his poems. . . . There's one called "Trickle Drops" in which he describes being beaten and the drops of blood oozing out of him. I pose the theory that maybe there was some real trauma here, either in Southold, maybe even somewhere else. Who really knows? Sometimes the moments of anguish in his poetry have a real vividness that might possibly be tied to moments in which he suffered some kind of persecution. . . .

He had formerly been a very boring conventional poet. Suddenly he erupts in this kind of violent, subversive language in the early 1850s in which he rails against things like the fugitive slave law. The country was on the verge of civil war. He was totally disgusted by the betrayal of American ideals on the part of party leaders whom he had once revered. Suddenly this new voice comes in, this brash, defiant, anti-authoritarian voice comes in, and this leads directly to the 1855 edition of *Leaves of Grass*. In the preface, he denounces what he calls "the swarms of cringers, doughfaces, lice of politics that infest the whole American government." Suddenly we have this new, fresh voice who is, on the one hand, denouncing these corrupt public figures but at the same time affirming so many other things: affirming the common man, the common individual; affirming people of all races and all creeds.

When *Leaves of Grass* first appeared in 1855, the poems were very free-flowing. Instead of commas, there were ellipses, periods, a very unconventional use of punctuation. A lot of times he didn't use any punctuation at all. It was a radical, fresh kind of poetry. It was a wonderfully brash, defiant, individualistic, also a very loving, open kind of poetry. Then slowly, as he found himself in different cultural conditions and responding in different ways, he changed his poetry. He did retain most of the early poems, but at the same time he added more conventional commas where there used to be these very unconventional ellipses. He somewhat tailored his poetry, his later poetic voice, to more conventional, middle-class tastes.

HE WORKED FOR THE GOVERNMENT [from 1863 to 1873]; he went to Washington to seek out his . . . brother George, who was wounded at Fredricksburg. He said, "Well, I'm just going to stay here for a couple of weeks." Turns out that he actually stayed there for ten years working as a government clerk. He ended up in the attorney general's office. He had worked previously at the Bureau of

Indian Affairs, mainly as a government clerk. Today he might even be considered a kind of government drudge, sort of a glorified secretary and so forth.

He saw [Abraham] Lincoln often in the streets, and he said that once or twice Lincoln would nod to him. In Washington in those days it wasn't like today, where the president is usually, for most people, just an image on the TV screen. In those days, you could actually even make an appointment with Lincoln and see him in the White House. Whitman himself never did that, but he did see him on the street often, and he gained an incredible admiration for, almost a fixation on, Abraham Lincoln.

His most popular poem was "O Captain! My Captain!" Whitman was asked many times to give this lecture he had written called "The Death of Abraham Lincoln," in which he relived the assassination. He thought that, in this moment of assassination, America came together in grief over the death of its martyred chief. In a way, Lincoln accomplished the kind of social unification that Whitman had hoped his own poetry might accomplish. He thought that because Lincoln became such an important cultural icon, that he himself would be the perpetuator of Lincoln's memory.

LATE IN LIFE, WHITMAN BECAME swept up in some of the racist attitudes of his day. And he got swept up in what was called ethnological science, which predicted the extinction of certain allegedly inferior races and so forth. On the other hand, there are many incongruities in people that I think ultimately have had a very positive force in American society, and Walt Whitman was one of those. Abraham Lincoln, for example, thought until about 1862 that African-Americans, when they were released from slavery, should be colonized in Liberia, should be sent abroad. Harriet Beecher Stowe, who wrote *Uncle Tom's Cabin,* at the end of *Uncle Tom's Cabin* says, "Well, I believe that blacks should be educated and then shipped abroad." Thomas Jefferson was a slaveowner, and yet Jefferson, Stowe, and Lincoln in their own ways were forces for freedom. They opened the door. Maybe they didn't walk through that door themselves, but they opened the door. They reflected the inconsistencies of the culture, as did Walt Whitman, ultimately—later on in life, in particular.

[HE DIED OF] JUST ABOUT EVERYTHING. He had been pretty badly diagnosed by doctors who generally had no understanding of strokes. He had suffered several strokes—which left him partly paralyzed for the last nineteen years of his life. He also was riddled with tuberculosis. It's absolutely shocking that he survived the last four months of his life with only one sixteenth of his normal breathing capacity. He was lying in bed and his doctor thought he would last maybe about three or four days. But he, through almost sheer willpower, [lasted longer]. I am also convinced it was his kind of optimism [that kept him alive]. He always said, "Cheer: what better religion is there than simple cheer?"

Susan B. Anthony

by
LYNN SHERR

Susan B. Anthony (1820–1906) devoted the majority of her eighty-six years to crusading for women's equality. Although she died before seeing women get the vote, she was a path breaker in the women's suffrage movement and was one of the co-founders of the National American Woman Suffrage Association. ABC correspondent Lynn Sherr appeared on Booknotes *on March 5, 1995, to discuss* Failure Is Impossible—Susan B. Anthony in Her Own Words *(Times Books, 1995).*

IN 1906 [WHEN] SHE WAS EIGHTY-SIX YEARS OLD, women did not yet have the right to vote. She was attending a suffrage meeting here in Washington, D.C. It was her birthday celebration. February 15, her birthday, was always celebrated by the suffrage groups. President Theodore Roosevelt sent greetings to that particular meeting. She was quite frail at the time. She stood up and she looked around the room. She acknowledged that there was not yet the right to vote for women, and she said, "But with all the help, with people like we have in this room, failure is impossible." That was her last public statement. One month later she was dead. The women in the suffrage movement and the men took that phrase "failure is impossible" and made it their motto. It took another fourteen years, but we finally got the Nineteenth Amendment, and that became the symbol of Susan B. Anthony.

SHE WAS BORN IN ADAMS, Massachusetts, the upper-left-hand corner of Massachusetts in the Berkshires. Her house is still standing. It's a private house now, so you can't go in and visit. What you can visit . . . is the Quaker meetinghouse where she and her family worshiped. It's not open for worship anymore, but you can take a little tour. It's this beautiful, very honest, very direct building. You walk in there and you understand immediately where it came from, because there's a real sense of holiness; there's a real sense of equality. It was in that meetinghouse that she learned that women were equal to men, because the Quakers always said women and men are equal. She had an aunt who preached there. There were no other religions where women could preach. . . .

The Quakers not only believed in the equality of men and women, they absolutely did not tolerate the evil practice of slavery. These were two things that were just part of her nature, and she got them from the time she was a child. . . . She attended church most of her life. She wound up going to the Unitarian church in Rochester. When their family moved to Rochester in 1845, her father, who was a very liberal Quaker, split with some of the Rochester Quakers because they were not liberal enough for him and because they did not believe in abolishing slavery. . . . She attended the Unitarian church there for the rest of her life. . . . She liked to hear the sermons. She was not an orthodox religious person. At the big suffrage meetings they had in Washington every January, [with] hundreds of women, she always had to be reminded to call for the opening prayer. She would say, "That's because as a Quaker, I'm used to praying in silence." She didn't believe in reading prayers. She didn't talk about God a lot. What she talked about was humanity.

WHEN THE ANTHONY FAMILY MOVED to Rochester in 1845, Frederick Douglass had just moved there himself. Douglass published his antislavery newspaper, the *North Star,* from Rochester. He was a very close friend of Susan's father, Daniel Anthony. Every Sunday at the Anthony family farm, all the famous abolitionists in the country would gather—including Frederick Douglass—to talk about ways to abolish slavery. Susan B. Anthony had the equivalent of a Sunday-morning TV talk show in her backyard every single week. These were the most important people in the country talking about the hottest issues in the country. . . . Frederick Douglass remained a lifelong friend. . . . The very last thing he did the day that he died was to attend a suffrage meeting in Washington, D.C. Susan B. Anthony delivered a eulogy at his funeral.

SHE STARTED OUT DOING ABOLITION WORK . . . and she was a temperance worker. She was against alcohol, and that was a very big movement at the time. It sounds silly today, but alcohol was just not regulated; every other shop on a block was a liquor store. Many, many men would get drunk all the time, abuse their wives, abuse their children, abandon them. Susan B. Anthony was a reformer by nature, and so she took out after alcohol. It was while she was lecturing about alcohol [that] she discovered the real problem: Women needed [money] of their own in order to deal with the problems that were affecting them. That's what turned her to women's rights.

[1850] was a miserable time to be a woman in America. Married women had it worse than single women, believe it or not. There were no rights for married women because everybody was governed by a law called Blackstone's old

English common law, which said, "The husband and the wife are one, and that one is the husband." Wives were property. You could not own property; you could not sue or be sued; you could not keep money that you earned yourself; you could not get custody of your children; you could not ask for a divorce; and if you ran away—because frequently men were so abusive that women would run away—the husband was entitled to grab you back and beat you. That was legal.

She was known as "the General," and in one of my chapters I refer to her as "General Anthony" because she was able to take all these things that happened and focus them. She understood that for all the things that women were trying to get, none of them was as critical as the vote. No matter what we got in the legislatures, no matter what happened, it could all be voted out by the very same men who had voted it in the first time. She understood that women needed the vote in order to get and keep all the rights they ever wanted to have.

She was a wonderful speaker. She was very persuasive. A lot of people didn't agree with her—in fact, the majority. Does it surprise you to learn that not only the majority of men, but the majority of women did not want the right to vote? Yet they found her so charming that they would listen to her. Obviously some people figured out that women are equal and women should have the right to vote. What she was saying was common sense. . . . After a decade or so of utter ridicule, of being caricatured in cartoons, of being burned in effigy once, of having eggs thrown at her, it turned out that people thought she was quite wonderful. Even if they didn't agree with her they had great respect for her.

Men were saying things like "Women are too emotional to vote. It will disrupt the family. Why can't women just tell their husbands or brothers or fathers or sons how to vote? The men should vote for the women." In the Senate they were extraordinary. . . . They were very polite, but one stood up and said, "The trouble with women having the vote is they'll get involved in politics. That means sometimes going to caucuses, some of which are held at night. Women are not suited for nighttime caucuses." Women said the same things: "We don't want to be taken off our pedestal. We like being protected. We do not want to have to bother with this." Everybody said, "It's going to lead to divorce. It's going to lead to too many independent women."

In 1905, Grover Cleveland, after he was president, wrote an article in the *Ladies' Home Journal* about how terrible this new movement was, what an awful thing it was doing to women and to the marriages of the country. He pointed out that it had a dangerous undermining effect on the characters of wives and mothers. He felt that a good wife was "a woman who loves her husband and her country with no desire to run either." He also said, "The hand that rocks the cradle rules the world," meaning women should be content to be wives and mothers. . . . Susan B. Anthony was livid. She was interviewed by a reporter in Rochester who came knocking on her door. . . . She said, "This is nonsense. What does he know about what women want?"

SHE HAD A BAD RIGHT EYE. . . . We might refer to it as a wandering eye today. . . . She had some surgery, which made it even worse. She had a touch of vanity to her. . . . She just wasn't this prim, proper, uptight lady we think of, or this very dour profile on the one-dollar coin. She had great personality, and she was quite vain about that wandering eye. You will almost never see a front-on photograph of her. She always would turn her head, and that's why we have all those profile pictures of her.

THERE'S QUITE A LOT OF EVIDENCE from her diaries, from her letters that she was courted a lot as a young woman. You can practically see her fluttering her eyelashes and braiding up her hair. . . . She talks about suitors, but nobody ever quite made the grade. As she grew older and grew greatly respected and very famous for all of her work in women's rights and suffrage, reporters would always ask her, "Why did you never marry, Miss Anthony?" She'd change the answer all the time. It was generally things like "Well, nobody wanted to marry somebody with views, and I always had views." Another time she said, "The ones I liked never liked me, and the ones who liked me I didn't like." Very contemporary feelings, right? My favorite answer she gave was to Nellie Bly, the great journalist. . . . She said, "Well, when I was a young woman, if you married wealthy, then you became a doll. If you married poor, you were a drudge." She said, "Think of it. I would have been either a doll or a drudge all my life." . . .

Just for the record, I found no evidence of any romantic relationship with a man or with a woman [although] she had many, many close female friends. She really was devoted to her work.

[S]HE WAS SINGLE all of her life, yet she was one of the first to lobby for property rights, legal rights for married women. She went in the dead of winter through fifty-four of the sixty counties in New York State with a petition . . . for a married women's property rights law that would be presented to the New York State legislature. It was just incredible. You know how cold it is in upstate New York, yet she did the whole thing. She went around, she would speak, she would cajole, she would beg, she would lecture. She and [Elizabeth Cady] Stanton got that law passed in New York. Having finished that, they went on to other things. A few years later, the law was rescinded by the same men that had voted it in, which was proof of the fact that women needed the vote in order to get anything to stay.

SHE . . . MET WITH EVERY SINGLE president after Lincoln, met with them in the White House. She addressed every Congress after 1869. If you go to the Library of Congress, you can open up these wonderful scrapbooks that she kept. You will find in them a folded-up seating chart of all the members of Congress. . . . She liked Mrs. [Rutherford B.] Hayes because of her temperance work. She would correspond with her regularly. She wrote everybody. Anybody that she thought could help the cause she would write.

SHE WAS PERFECTLY AWARE of how famous and important she was, but she was very humble. It was suggested that there be a statue of her. She said, "No . . . I never liked the idea of a woman's statue being out of doors, particularly in the rain. She must get all wet and cold." Unfortunately, everybody listened. There's no public outdoor statue of Susan B. today. . . .

Back in the 1970s we used to use this phrase: "Women's liberation is men's liberation too." We thought we were terribly clever. I thought whoever said it had invented it. It turns out Susan B. Anthony understood that as well. She was the one who was saying back in the 1800s "Once we get women to their full equality and independence, then men will be freer also. Families will be better off when men can stay home and do more of the child-rearing." . . .

This woman has a lot to teach us. This woman was more than just a crazy old spinster who ran around in bloomers campaigning for the right to vote. This woman was a feeling, caring, vibrant, funny, creative individual who still speaks to us today—not only about women's issues. She has wonderful things to say about tabloid journalism; she hated tabloid journalism. Back in 1893, she said, "Get the murders off the front page." She was just so wise. I hope that a new generation will discover her, because I'd like to see her brought back into our lives.

Ulysses S. Grant

by
GEOFFREY PERRET

Born in Point Pleasant, Ohio, Ulysses S. Grant (1822–85) was appointed commander of the Union troops in 1864. A popular war hero, Ulysses Grant went on to become president of the United States, serving two terms (1869–77). Geoffrey Perret, author of Ulysses S. Grant: Soldier and President *(Random House, 1997), came to* Booknotes *on October 12, 1997, to discuss the life of our eighteenth president.*

Ulysses S. Grant is fundamental. No Grant and there would have been no victory in the Civil War for the Union. The Civil War would have probably ended in a stalemate with a negotiated peace rather than a surrender. Now what kind of peace that would be, I don't know. But I believe that Grant was the only general who could coordinate the Union's strengths and bring them to bear on the Confederacy in time to ensure Lincoln's reelection in 1864.

He was born in 1822 in a hamlet in Ohio. He didn't live long enough; he died at the age of sixty-three, a victim of those cigars that he smoked. He was a very heavy cigar smoker during the Civil War for fairly obvious reasons. He got cancer of the esophagus and died in 1885.

He was baptized Hiram Ulysses Grant. When he went to West Point, he foresaw the future: His luggage was going to have the initials H.U.G. He was going to be known as "Hug" because everybody at West Point had a nickname. He didn't want to be called "Hug." When he got to West Point, he reported to the adjutant and said, "My names is Ulysses Hiram Grant."

The adjutant said, "No, it's not. Your name is Ulysses S. Grant." The congressman who appointed [Grant to West Point] had made this appointment on the very last day of his term in Washington. The congressman was probably surrounded by packing cases and preparing to get out of town; he had a lot of things to sign. He thought, What is that Grant boy's name? Something Ulysses? Ulysses something? He wrote down Ulysses S. Grant. . . .

[The Congressman thought Grant] had to have a middle initial of some kind and guessed that it was S for Simpson [Grant's grandmother's maiden name]. The adjutant then explained to Ulysses Grant that because the appointment was made out in the name of Ulysses S. Grant, that was who he was and as long as he was in the army, that was who he would be.

GRANT'S TIME IN MEXICO [from 1846 to 1847] was absolutely essential to his education as a soldier. Grant was a fundamentally modest man, but he was immensely proud that he had participated in ten battles in Mexico.

It was then that Grant discovered that although he deplored the human cost of war, he was susceptible to the drama. Once he found a way to participate in a battle, feeling that he was doing his duty, that this death and destruction could be justified on moral grounds, he discovered that he had a soldier's vocation. That came as a surprise to him.

WHEN HE CAME BACK from Mexico in 1847, he was finally able to marry his fiancée, Julia Dent. They'd been engaged for four years at that time. The [Mexican] War had kept them apart. . . . When he came back, the first thing he did was marry her. They were married for the next thirty-six years.

It's ironic, but the most famous drunk in American history was not a heavy drinker. The trouble with Grant was that he could get drunk on two drinks. Not only that, he would start walking into the furniture and need the wall for support. It was obvious when Grant had been drinking. . . . There was only one reason why Grant drank and that was he was deeply and passionately in love with his wife.

Grant's marriage was not a limited partnership. It was a romance from beginning to end. When he was away from Julia for very long, he felt desperately lonely. He missed her tremendously. He would start drinking. It's also true that during the Civil War, after some big battle, Grant would have a couple of drinks. That was more or less a release of tension. But while he was preparing for battle, while battle was in progress, he never touched the stuff.

The presence of a bottle in Grant's tent invariably indicated the absence of Julia. When the war ended and he was able to spend all of his time with his wife, he hardly ever touched anything except maybe to sip a glass of champagne at a state banquet in the White House.

[HE WAS PRESIDENT FROM] 1869 to 1877. The white vote was split more or less fifty-fifty between the Democrats and the Republicans. It was the blacks, allowed to vote for the first time, who really put Grant into the White House. This is the election of 1868. He won by something like 51 percent to 49 percent.

[The Grant White House] was pretty informal. When Lincoln and Johnson were there, presidents . . . didn't treat it like a home. Julia was the one who changed that. She had three children to raise. She was determined to create a home for them in the White House. She had the gates locked so the children could play on the White House lawns; they couldn't have people staggering in there half drunk and passing out under the trees on the South Lawn.

She made the staff improve their [personal] appearance. She had the whole interior redone. . . . Julia got rid of the chipped paint, the broken furniture, and turned it into a comfortable, pleasant home for herself and her husband and the three children. That was the first time anybody had done that with the White House.

Grant the president turned out to be a surprise. When I was in college, I did the one-year survey course of American history. I had an excellent teacher, and I remember the afternoon he said, "Now we will consider the rating of the presidents. . . . At the top, we see the faces of George Washington, Abraham Lincoln, Thomas Jefferson. We move down to the middle and we have people like Grover Cleveland. . . . We keep on moving down. As we look down towards the earth, what do we see staring up at us? The bearded visage of Ulysses S. Grant. The only thing below Grant is the eyebrows of Warren Gamaliel Harding."

So it came as a surprise to me to discover that Grant was not a failed president. He was not a great president, but he was a competent, middle-of-the-road president. There were a lot of scandals associated with his administration, but that was comparatively new. Financial scandals were not a part of the presidency until the Civil War because, until then, America was a country where people and the government didn't have a lot of money. The Civil War created a huge national debt. More than $400 billion in greenbacks was put in circulation. There was a lot of money around, and money changes people. It changed America.

Reconstruction, which should have been the big moral crusade following the Civil War, had been killed stone dead by Andrew Johnson. Grant couldn't revive it; Lincoln could not have revived it in that condition. The biggest problem the government faced was the national debt. . . . Meantime, you have the rise of industrial America, and there's a lot of money around. Railroad companies were happy to bribe any congressman they could shove money onto.

The two biggest [scandals] were the Crédit Mobilier scandal, which involved a railroad company, and that wasn't really Grant's scandal. During the Andrew Johnson administration, Crédit Mobilier had paid off at least fifty congressmen. It gave them stock in the company, and the stock rose in value. But they hadn't had to pay for the stock.

Democrats took the stock; Republicans took the stock. The finance company for the railroad needed a grant from the government, a huge amount of land. With the land as collateral, the finance company could then raise money. They'd get a mortgage on the land.

The important thing was to get Congress to approve giving huge amounts of federal land. Crédit Mobilier handed out the stock and was able to finance the railroad. The stock rose in value. These congressmen, in effect, had a financial interest in this. The scandal broke, but it broke during the Grant administration. Somehow Grant was blamed or tarnished by what was really an Andrew Johnson scandal simply because it came to light during Grant's presidency.

The other big scandal was the whiskey fraud scandal. For some time in border states, the way Democrats financed their political campaigns was to siphon off some of the whiskey tax that was imposed during the Civil War as a way of helping to finance the war. The tax collectors would hand some of the money over to the federal government, but they would keep some of it to finance political campaigns.

After the 1872 election, the Republican party needed a new moneybag, and it could not find one. The Republicans in some states started engaging in their own whiskey tax fraud in order to finance Republican campaigns. . . . Grant had no idea that this was going on. It was the same problem we're dealing with now: How do we finance campaigns? The problem is still here. But the solution for some people then was to take some of the whiskey tax money.

With all these scandals swirling around him, Grant was in a unique position. He was the first president who had to cope with a lot of financial scandals, and people were horrified. "What has happened to our government? We have all these financial scandals." But it was the era that had changed; it was not [caused by] one man. No man could have stopped that. Ever since the Gilded Age, most American administrations have had financial scandals. But Grant was personally blamed because his scandal was the first.

HE LEFT THE WHITE HOUSE in March of 1877. Two months later he set off on a voyage, and he was gone for two and a half years. He went to nearly every country in western Europe. He went to Russia. He went to Egypt—which he probably liked better than almost any other place that he'd visited up to that point—went to Jerusalem, sailed on to India, went to China, went to Hong Kong.

He was received almost as if he were [still] president. Nobody had done this kind of thing before Grant. Wherever he was received, he was received as a great soldier, and he astounded his hosts by refusing to go to military reviews. He hated parades. He wouldn't even look at pictures of military art if he could avoid it. He traveled on to Japan, which, strangely, was the one place where he wasn't able to avoid a military review.

From there, he wanted to go to Australia, but there was no way of going to Australia without stopping at a lot of other places along the way and Julia did not like traveling. Julia said, "Ulysses, I've had enough of this. I want to go home."

[HE DIED IN] 1885 . . . OF THROAT CANCER. It was an agonizing way to die. The doctor would paint cocaine on this cancerous growth during the day in an attempt to ease the pain. Then he had morphine at night to help him sleep. But even the morphine didn't make much difference, the pain was so agonizing.

He's buried in New York, but that was not his choice; that was his wife's choice. Grant wanted to be buried at West Point, and he wanted his wife to be buried alongside him. At that time, you could not be buried at West Point unless you were a West Point graduate. Your wife certainly couldn't be buried with you. Had Grant ever expressed any desire to have his wife buried with him at West Point, I have no doubt that Congress would have passed whatever bill was necessary. But . . . Grant was the last man in the world ever to ask for a favor.

He died virtually a pauper. . . . He had nothing. Somehow, that too is all of a piece with Grant's life, the fact that he never really had a home of his own, that he was not interested in possessions, fame, power. He left the world about as poor as when he'd arrived.

Rutherford B. Hayes

by
ARI HOOGENBOOM

Rutherford B. Hayes (1822–93), nineteenth president of the United States, was a lawyer and Union officer before entering public life. He resigned his position as governor of Ohio to run for president in 1876. After winning the contested election, Rutherford Hayes embarked on a presidential term noted for its civil service reform. Ari Hoogenboom argues in his book Rutherford B. Hayes: Warrior and President *(University Press of Kansas, 1995) that Rutherford Hayes's progressive agenda is deserving of greater recognition. He appeared on* Booknotes *on July 2, 1995.*

MOST AMERICANS DON'T KNOW RUTHERFORD HAYES from James Garfield or from Chester Arthur. The questions frequently are "Well, did he have the long beard?" The answer is "Yes, he did." He had a very full beard. Other than that, most people don't have a crisp, clear idea of Hayes unless it's in connection with the end of Reconstruction and in connection with the disputed election [of 1876].

The election of 1876 dragged on into 1877. . . . Hayes was not officially declared the winner until a couple of days before his inauguration in March of 1877. . . . He did not have a majority of the votes that were cast. He was elected by one electoral vote and that only after a long dispute in Congress over whether the electoral votes of South Carolina, Florida, Louisiana should be counted for either Hayes or his rival, Samuel J. Tilden of New York.

HAYES GRADUATED from Kenyon College in Ohio. He read law briefly at Columbus, Ohio, and then he went to Harvard Law School. Hayes, after graduating from Harvard Law, had a choice of going to Columbus, where his mother and sister were, who would try to tell him how to live his life, or going to Fremont, Ohio, where his uncle was, who would be a little more easygoing and could steer some business to him. Hayes went to Fremont and began practicing law.

Ultimately, he went to Cincinnati. He found Fremont was simply too small a town for him to really make a name for himself in the law. Lucy Webb was in college there. They got married fairly soon after he arrived in Cincinnati. She was the first First Lady to have a college degree.

HAYES VOLUNTEERED AND SERVED exactly four years in the Civil War. He was a colonel; he regarded himself as one of the good colonels. He did become a general ultimately, but as he said, "I never fought a battle as a general." His promotion to general came after he fought his last battle and was wounded for the fifth time. . . . No president of the United States has seen as much front-line action as Hayes did. No president was wounded as many times. . . . One [wound] was very serious. He was shot in his left arm, and the bone was broken but fortunately not shattered. If it was shattered, they would have hacked it off because they didn't try to set any bones that were shattered.

In the army, as a colonel, he typified in many ways the value of the civilian officers, because Hayes was able to mediate between the West Point–trained higher officers and the volunteer soldiers and officers in the army. Hayes understood both sides. When the Twenty-third didn't get rifled muskets—they started out with smooth-bore muskets, very inaccurate weapons, and they didn't get them when they were promised—the men were virtually mutinying. Their West Point commander over Hayes didn't quite understand the men, but Hayes spoke to the men, calmed them down, told them guns would be coming, to be patient, to remember the goal that they had: to preserve the Union. He also got back to the immediate commander and calmed him down. . . .

He was still in the army when he was elected [to Congress]. But Congress didn't meet until December of 1865, so he didn't miss any sessions in Congress. [He was elected] governor [of Ohio] three times. . . . The third term was interrupted by the presidency. As governor, he was instrumental in the passage of the Fifteenth Amendment—that's the Voting Rights [Amendment]. He pushed that through the legislature of Ohio. . . . He was also instrumental in establishing Ohio State University.

HAYES BECAME INVOLVED in social causes after he was president of the United States. He was very much involved in education and movements to educate poor southerners, mostly black children. . . . He was head of the Slater Fund, and money was used from the Slater Fund to help educate blacks in the South. He was also ardently in favor of a piece of legislation that never passed called the Blair Bill, which would have given federal funds to poor school districts throughout the nation, primarily in the South and in the West. He wanted that bill passed very badly in order to provide educational equality, which would provide, he thought, equality of economic opportunity.

One of the social causes that he was interested in was prison reform, a very unpopular sort of thing to do. He also opposed the death penalty. He always

felt people could be, somehow or other, rehabilitated—again, through education. Everybody could be aided by some kind of training.

He was very much opposed to slavery and defended runaway slaves. Early in
the Civil War, he was convinced that the war was a crusade to end slavery. He
felt that a good half of his life was spent in a crusade against slavery. Lucy [also
influenced him] to a large extent. Lucy had abolitionist sentiments in her family, and Hayes had always been antislavery but never strong enough to do much
about it. But after he married Lucy, he began defending runaway slaves.

THERE WAS SOME ALCOHOL served at their first state dinner for some visiting
royalty from Russia, but Hayes decided not to have any in the White House. It
pleased his wife, whom people now refer to as Lemonade Lucy, which is quite
unfair. Nobody referred to her as Lemonade Lucy at the time. Hayes made the
[no alcohol] decision. He didn't like to see congressmen in their cups, primarily. He also made that decision for sound political reasons: Hayes was opposed
to prohibition. He was in favor of temperance. He himself was a temperate
drinker, until he went into the White House, but then he became a total ab-
stainer in the White House. . . . He thought a good example would be set by
him and Lucy not serving wine in the White House. . . .

It basically was a shrewd political move, because those who drank didn't care
whether Hayes had liquor in the White House or not and those who didn't
drink were very happy about it.

[HE WAS THE FIRST PRESIDENT to have a phone in the White House.] . . . It
wasn't of much use, because hardly anybody else had a telephone. They had a
telephone connection with the Treasury Department. Most of the White
House communication was actually by telegraph.

Hayes traveled more than any [other president] up to that date. They called
him Rutherford the Rover. [He traveled by train], mostly. He went on long
trips late in the summer, after business was pretty much wrapped up in Washington—late summer, early fall. He didn't campaign. He wouldn't campaign
for individual candidates, but he would preach the particular policies that he
was very much in favor of. He would give these rather short speeches—sound
bites—that would elaborate on one issue and wouldn't tire the audience but
would hammer home his point of view. . . .

He was the first president to travel to California to put across policies that he
favored. In other words, he anticipated presidential politics of the twentieth
century. In many ways, he—and a lot of people say this about a lot of presidents—was the first modern president. He fought battles with Congress over
the power of appointment, and he won. At the end of his presidency, he was
making the appointments he wanted to make. He defeated the notion of sena-
torial courtesy. He had a tremendous battle with the Democrats over vetoes. . . .

The Democrats were attaching riders to appropriations bills, but Hayes vetoed them. . . . Their legislation was [intended] to repeal enforcement acts to the Fourteenth and Fifteenth amendments—the civil rights amendment and the voting rights amendment. The veto, which he used very freely, enabled him to prevent the Democrats from pushing through legislation that Hayes did not want.

[RECONSTRUCTION] BEGAN IMMEDIATELY after the war—well, toward the end of the war, actually—and lasted, technically, until 1877. Hayes is renowned, or castigated, for ending it, but that's kind of an exaggeration.

The end of Reconstruction in 1877 meant the removal of the federal troops that were supporting Republican governments in the capitals of New Orleans in Louisiana, and Columbia in South Carolina. . . . These Republican governments, supported by federal troops, had control of only a few square blocks around those capitals. The rest of those states had already been taken over by rival Democratic white supremacy governments.

The big problem for Hayes when he came into the White House was that Reconstruction had ended, except in those two places. Hayes was faced with the problem of what to do about these Republican regimes that were still existing by a thin thread in both of those states. What it boiled down to was that Hayes did not [need to make] a decision on whether to withdraw those troops. His decision was when would he withdraw those troops and what could he possibly extract from the southerners in exchange for withdrawing them? . . . He was elected with the poorest of mandates. The whole country was suffering from a great depression, and people were really more concerned about getting a job rather than politics in the South. Northerners were no longer interested in maintaining a military presence in the South—what its enemies called a bayonet rule. The Democrats had control of the House of Representatives, and the Democrats had already refused to appropriate money to the U.S. Army. The U.S. Army was small and very weak—about twenty-five thousand men, most of them out in the West, along the Mexican border as well.

It was an impossible situation for Hayes. Without any support from public opinion and with his poor mandate, it was impossible for him to sustain Reconstruction. Ulysses S. Grant had already ordered the withdrawal of troops from Louisiana at the end of the controversy over the disputed election. Hayes, in all probability, countermanded that order, because it never really was carried out. . . .

What Hayes did was extract from South Carolina and Louisiana Democrats solemn promises that the civil rights of black and white Republicans would be carefully preserved, and also that equal educational opportunities [would be offered], which Hayes felt were terribly important. This was pledged by the Hampton government in South Carolina and the Nicholls government in

Louisiana, Democratic governments . . . but they reneged on their promises within six months, certainly within a year.

HAYES WAS PRESIDENT for one term, [then went] back to Spiegel Grove in Fremont, Ohio. [He] died in January of 1893, twelve years [after his presidency, at age seventy-one]. He hadn't been in bed since his very serious wound in the Civil War . . . until he had this heart attack.

[His wife] . . . died in 1889. He missed her dreadfully. He was very much devoted to her, and, as he said, "The life has just gone out of the house," and pretty much out of his life. But on the other hand, he would get interested in these educational projects. He was always interested in young people and found himself refreshed by them.

At the end, he was really a precursor of the Progressive movement. He was opposed to what he called plutocracy, a maldistribution of wealth. He was very much in favor of traditional republicanism—that's with a small *r*—values of political equality, of equality of economic opportunities for everybody. That's why he stressed education so much.

George Pickett

by
CAROL REARDON

George E. Pickett (1825–75) was the Confederate major general who led the charge now named for him in the Battle of Gettysburg. Carol Reardon, the author of Pickett's Charge in History and Memory *(The University of North Carolina Press, 1997), came to* Booknotes *on February 8, 1998, to discuss the general's life.*

PICKETT'S CHARGE WAS THE LAST great Confederate attack on the third day of the three-day battle at Gettysburg, [Pennsylvania]. Gettysburg took place in the middle of the Civil War, July of 1863. A lot of people call it the turning point of the Civil War. The one single action that seemed to sum it all up, the one that brought the battle to a decisive end and made it a Union victory, was Pickett's Charge.

One of the reasons why I wrote this book was because I was very taken with [journalist and author] . . . George Stewart's comments. He said—and I'm paraphrasing a little bit here—"If we grant, as most Americans would, that the Civil War is the most dramatic moment in our history and that Gettysburg is the turning point of that war, then it would seem to me that Pickett's Charge, on the third day of Gettysburg, was the turning point of the most dramatic moment of the Civil War." In other words, the most dramatic moment of American history comes down to Pickett's Charge; it's the pivotal moment in American history. That struck me as just an absolutely stunning comment, and it's one of those little sound bites that sticks in your memory. . . .

There [is] this image of . . . Pickett's Charge that is much larger than life. But if you looked at the thoughts of the men who actually fought in it, they didn't see it as something incredibly exceptional. . . .

As I got to know the soldiers who actually fought the battle, as I got more intimately familiar with the battlefield itself, I began to realize something slightly different: that our first stop has to be with the soldiers who fought there themselves. They didn't see a turning point, they didn't see the climax of American history; they saw just another battle. If you read their diaries or their letters right after the battle they say, "I've been in the hardest fight I've ever been in. Glad I'm alive to tell you about it," end of story.

THE . . . FOCUS OF ATTENTION during the summer of 1863 was in south-central Pennsylvania. Robert E. Lee's army—the Army of Northern Virginia—had been victorious at a battle called Chancellorsville in May of 1863. They were taking advantage of their victory by marching north into Pennsylvania. We're not sure entirely why Lee decided to move north at this time. He would say in his report afterwards that he wanted to give Virginia farmers a breather and allow them to have one harvest season not disrupted by the marching of armies across their farms and to perhaps relieve pressure on Richmond from some Union forces in that area. He was marching north and the Union army was marching after them in pursuit.

It was a hard thing for the North to deal with a major Confederate army on northern soil . . . especially so close to Washington, the capital. . . . Gettysburg attracted a lot of attention, because if you look at it on a map, it looks like the hub of a wheel. Eleven roads came into Gettysburg from all directions. It's almost a natural concentration point for any armies marching anywhere in that area. Nobody planned to fight at Gettysburg. Gettysburg was almost a magnet that drew the two armies together.

UP UNTIL JULY OF 1863, almost every time Robert E. Lee had taken his army into battle, he had won, and sometimes won very decisively—Fredericksburg, Chancellorsville. He didn't really win at Antietam, but he was still on the battlefield when the battle was over. At the Second Battle of Manassas, he cleared the Union army right off the field. At the Seven Days battles outside of Richmond, he forced back an army bigger than his own. The Union army had gotten within five miles of Richmond, and Lee pushed them back. He'd been remarkably successful in a little over a year in command of the Army of Northern Virginia. His soldiers were accustomed to winning. But after July 3, 1863, they had to deal with a very unaccustomed feeling, one of defeat.

IF YOU TAKE A LOOK at the attack that becomes known as Pickett's Charge, strictly as an exercise in military tactics, it was very ordinary in Civil War terms. That same ground that Pickett charged across on July third was also charged across on July second, but that attack has no special name. . . .

Whenever we talk about Pickett's Charge, what most people think about is the charge of General George Pickett's division, his three brigades of Virginians. . . . They advanced from the main Confederate battle line on Seminary Ridge across a rolling valley. It's not a wide-open plain, nice and flat, like a lot of people think. It's very rolling. It provides a great deal of cover and concealment, a lot more than might be readily apparent unless you walk across it yourself.

From over on Seminary Ridge, Robert E. Lee was able to look out and see that clump of trees and see the basic outline of the Union center and say, "That's your target." General Pickett's men get . . . an awful lot of the attention here, but they were not the only troops who made this charge that day. . . . There were more troops involved under the command of General James Johnston Pettigrew of North Carolina and General Isaac Trimble, a Marylander who was commanding two North Carolina brigades that day.

Lee's total army in Pennsylvania would have been about seventy-five thousand strong. . . . There were about ninety-five thousand Union troops. By tradition, the charge began at one o'clock in the afternoon with an artillery bombardment. We say "by tradition" because one of the few people who wrote down a note about when the bombardment began looked at his watch and it said 1:00. But we have a few other people who apparently looked at their watches and said 2:00, 3:00, 2:30, 2:45. Watches were not mass-produced at that time. What you have is history given to us by a whole lot of individual watchmakers and their individual skills.

This artillery bombardment lasted anywhere from—depending on who you read—twenty minutes to four hours. I guess it depended on where you were standing at the time—if you were enduring it, [it felt like] four hours. After the artillery bombardment ended, the [Confederate] infantry moved forward. From the time they left the shelter of Seminary Ridge, fought their battle on Cemetery Ridge, were defeated, and returned, the whole attack, fight and repulse, took about one hour. That one hour certainly has made a lot of history.

The wall was a boundary marker; it extends several hundred yards north-south, where most of the fighting in Pickett's Charge took place. It's a wall that angles back to the east, deeper into the Union position for about seventy-five or eighty yards, and then angles back north again. It was used by the Union soldiers as a defensive position. It was strengthened by using fence rails and other loose rocks that were around. The rock wall had great significance then and it would for generations to come.

We don't know how many went in. It's really very difficult to figure out how many died, but usual estimates will say [there was] somewhere around 60-percent casualties.

We've been sensitized to believe that this battle was the turning point of the war, that [Lee's surrender at] Appomattox was a given after Gettysburg. But Appomattox was almost two years in the future. . . . We're beginning to realize that, at least in the minds of the Confederate soldiers who marched away, they were befuddled by this defeat. They certainly felt deeply the personal loss of so many friends in Pickett's division and in other Confederate units. There was an awful lot of finger pointing going on trying to figure out why the Confederates lost. This [loss] was unusual; they didn't know how to deal with it. It's almost a natural reaction to look for scapegoats, to blame somebody for it. Part of that helped shape the history of Pickett's Charge, because when the Richmond newspapers talked about this great charge, they wrote about how well General Pickett's Virginians did, but asked why they didn't completely succeed.

They didn't completely succeed because the other troops in the charge, those from North Carolina, Tennessee, Alabama, Mississippi, failed in their duty. That's perhaps one of the reasons why we don't read about them, because the Richmond press refused to write about them or blame them. . . . Later on, when we try to find historical sources, we can find a lot about Virginians, but all we can find about the other people in the charge is somehow they made mistakes, they failed, that the whole defeat belongs to them.

GEORGE PICKETT WAS A VIRGINIAN, a graduate of West Point who graduated last in his class—not a mental giant by any stretch of the imagination but, generally speaking, a good soldier. His men adored him. He had a background in the Mexican War—fought Indians out West. In 1863, he commanded a division of three brigades of Virginia infantry in Robert E. Lee's Confederate army.

I can't say with any authority whether or not Pickett had a drinking problem. It was a rumor. In this case, it was one that was used against him, but it's an interesting story. George Pickett was held up as a hero by his men and by much of the South for quite some time, until the early 1890s, when a little article appeared in the Richmond newspaper that said, "Almost anybody who was at Gettysburg has heard this story . . . George Pickett was not in the front lines with his men at Gettysburg and he wasn't even on the field."

The story went on about how several of Pickett's staff officers were behind the lines drinking whiskey at the so-called whiskey wagon. The officer who basically made this public was one of Pickett's own men, Kirkwood Otey, a major in 1863 who would rise to the rank of colonel, who was wounded early in the charge. He went back to have his wound dressed. What he ended up finding out was that they didn't have any chloroform to take care of the pain. He was told to go over and get a cup of whiskey. When he did, he found Pickett's officers there, or so he said. . . .

There would be other officers who would say that Pickett liked to carry himself like a gentleman, and that meant eating and drinking like a gentleman. But what does that mean? We're not quite sure. One of the most intriguing things is that right after the Battle of Gettysburg, Kirkwood Otey found himself being court-martialed. One of the charges on which he was court-martialed was drunkenness on duty. Was his story retaliation, thirty years later? Was that perhaps part of the issue? We don't know.

I SUSPECT PICKETT'S CHARGE remains in memory because Pickett's men were among the first, as a group of former Confederate soldiers, to embrace the cause of national reunion. In 1887, the twenty-fourth anniversary, Pickett's men and the Philadelphia Brigade, the Pennsylvanians who actually held the stone wall at the angle where the Confederates broke though, had a reunion at Gettysburg. . . . This was hailed by some to be a remarkable display of the end of sectional ill will and the beginnings of working together for a common future. . . . Several hundred Pennsylvanians, several hundred Virginians all got together and talked about "The war is over. Let's look to the future. Let's bury our hostilities and work together for the common good of the entire country."

George Armstrong Custer

LOUISE BARNETT

Although George Armstrong Custer (1839–76) graduated last in his West Point class, he went on to forge a brilliant career as a soldier during the Civil War. Louise Barnett visited Booknotes *on October 13, 1996, to talk about her biography* Touched by Fire: The Life, Death, and Mythic Afterlife of George Armstrong Custer *(Henry Holt, 1996) and the general's famous last stand at Little Bighorn.*

GENERAL GEORGE ARMSTRONG CUSTER was part of that generation that was touched by the fire of the Civil War. He had a splendid, heroic career as a general in the Civil War. Afterwards, the time when he becomes very interesting to me, at the age of twenty-five, he was one of 135 unemployed major generals. He had to redirect his life. For the first few years, it wasn't easy. Then he found a new career on the frontier.

He had tremendous achievement during the Civil War, and in a way that seems breathtaking to me. For example, he captured the first enemy battle flag of the Army of the Potomac. By the same token, at the end of the war, he received the flag of truce of General Lee. He was involved in these two moments of great symbolic, as well as historical, significance. Everything in between was a series of compelling victories for Custer. He really did live the role of the romantic knight on a charger.

There are many instances of his courageous behavior. He saw a private shot and killed on the fighting line. He risked his own life to rescue this man's body, because he said he couldn't stand to think of it being riddled with bullets if it remained there. On another occasion, a sergeant was badly wounded. Custer leapt from his horse, put the wounded man on the horse, and sent it back to the rear, and then waited to be rescued himself. This is in the heat of battle. Actions like that seemed to be second nature to Custer.

"Custer's luck" was an expression that people made up during the Civil War to explain his incredibly fast rise to prominence. He was always in the right place at the right time. It seems to me that you have to give Custer credit for more than this. He was in the right place at the right time, but he knew how to make the most of those opportunities, which many people would not. I think, for example, of what happened to another man, Elon Farnsworth, who was appointed brigadier general at the same time that Custer was.

Both of them became generals right before the Battle of Gettysburg. Both were under the command of General Judson Kilpatrick, whose nickname was "Kill-cavalry" because he was so reckless with the men under his command. Custer managed to somehow get his orders from Kilpatrick countermanded by another general. As a result, he played a significant part in the Battle of Gettysburg.

When Pickett was charging against the Union front, [Confederate general Jeb] Stuart was coming around the rear with the idea that they would cut the Union forces in half. Custer actually prevented Stuart from carrying out his part of that strategy, because he got himself out from under Kilpatrick's orders. Farnsworth, on the other hand, was ordered to make a suicidal charge by Kilpatrick. Farnsworth even questioned Kilpatrick and said, "Are you certain you want me to do this?" Kilpatrick insisted, and Farnsworth, only a few days after his appointment to the rank of general, was killed, along with many of his men. Custer somehow was able, even under a leader like Kilpatrick, to not only keep himself alive but to play a distinguished role.

[HE WAS COURT-MARTIALED] TWICE, actually. The first was not terribly significant. It happened at West Point right after his graduation. It was a very minor thing and did not set him back. The serious court-martial happened in 1867 on the Kansas frontier. Custer [was] making a very difficult transition from his success and achievement in the Civil War to the vast plains of the frontier, which was a very marginal and unrewarding kind of duty—chasing Indians who could never be caught. He had no opportunity to show his skills in battle. He experienced a crisis that caused him to lose his head as a commander, to go AWOL, essentially, in order to get back to his wife. That was the pressing motive of his leaving his men, taking a long forced march to get to her . . . no matter what.

He was out in the field, and he headed back for the fort where he thought he would find her. She wasn't there, so he woke up this commanding officer in the middle of the night and said, "I'm taking a train that leaves in fifteen minutes to go to the next fort to see my wife." The next morning, when his commanding officer, Colonel A. J. Smith, got up, he realized that this was highly extraordinary. Custer was placed under arrest and court-martialed for this.

Custer became very involved in his own defense and presented what he thought was a strong defense. . . . He got a rather lenient sentence. Someone else might have been simply dismissed from the army permanently. He was suspended for a year.

[HIS WIFE], LIBBY, WAS A CHEERFUL, kind person of the sort that people instantly like. She was unassuming, attractive. People were drawn to her. I have great admiration for the way that she recreated her life after the tragedy of losing her husband to whom she had been tremendously attached. They had a very intense love marriage. When he was away, he would write letters that were sometimes as long as one hundred pages.

I read through them. One of them ends with the comment "Do you think this letter is too long . . . ?" He would often end by saying that "I've got to stop now, because it's late at night, and reveille is only in another couple of hours." He had tremendous energy and enthusiasm for his wife. He could go without sleep. After a hard day's riding on the march in the field, he could write letters late at night to his wife.

They were married for twelve years. Then Libby Bacon Custer was a widow for fifty-seven years. I find her life almost as interesting as his because she devotes her widowhood single-mindedly to projecting the image of her husband as a great hero. . . . Being his widow did become a profession for her. She wrote three books of memoirs, which were all bestsellers. She became wealthy giving lectures about their life on the frontier.

WHEN [CUSTER] WENT BACK to the frontier [after his suspension], it was in response to a telegram that Phil Sheridan had sent him saying, "Almost all of the officers here are calling for you to come back. You're the only man who can lick the Indians. I'm counting on you." Custer got up from the dinner table, packed his bag, and left, even before the return to command had become official. He came back with a new spirit and won a victory over an Indian village, the Battle of the Washita, in late November of 1868. . . .

Many people at the time, and many historians afterwards, have felt that the frontier army represented the dregs of society. It was very poorly paid. Conditions were harsh. Supplies were often awful. On the frontier, Custer found some bread that was stamped 1861 that was really moldy and couldn't be eaten. Yet they had nothing else. The frontier army, in a way, served as a kind of French Foreign Legion for us. Often men who were wanted by the law, or who were escaping wives, getting away from entanglements of various sorts, would end up in the frontier army, as did newly arrived immigrants who didn't speak enough English to get another job. Custer went from commanding volunteers, middle-class men, very often like himself, who were fighting because of love of their country, to commanding men who seemed just impossible as soldiers. You can see that this affected his attitude, that he isn't as caring about his men on the frontier as he was known to be during the Civil War.

THE LITTLE BIGHORN is located in southeastern Montana in an area that was not yet part of the United States at the time that the battle was fought on June twenty-fifth, 1876. It was a territory that was occupied by various Indian tribes, not really settled at the time, in fact, not even accurately mapped, which was one of the problems that Custer encountered in fighting a battle there.

It's been very difficult for our nation to understand how this famous fighting force, the Seventh Cavalry, led by this distinguished ex–Civil War general . . . and all of the men with him—five companies of cavalry—had been wiped out by people that they regarded as primitive savages. At the time, people were no longer thinking about Indians as important enemies of the United States. They felt, and they were historically right, that the struggle for possession of the continent had long been settled. This was just a kind of mopping-up operation. No one had the slightest expectation that Custer and his force would be wiped out or defeated.

The total [number of soldiers] killed was 265. A very small number when you think of Civil War battles. One of the points that I make in the book [is] how astounding it is that this battle has lived on in our national consciousness when relatively few people were involved in it.

Very early in the morning of that day, Custer believed that the Indians who were gathered in that valley . . . had discovered the presence of his force and that they would probably melt away, the way Indians usually did, if he didn't attack immediately. His plan had been to attack on the following day. He simply went into a kind of crisis mode, led his troops down into the valley, divided them into different commands. This is what is controversial about his strategy, the fact that he divided his small group—small in relation to the enemy. But you have to keep in mind that he had no idea of the size of the enemy at that time. This was the greatest gathering of Indians on the North American continent. No intelligence of any sort indicated that there would be that many Indians amassed at the Little Bighorn. Custer's actions were reasonable given the fact that he had no idea of the size of the enemy that he was confronting.

It was expected that even a small group of well-trained cavalry would be able to hold its own and even defeat much larger numbers of Indians, because the fighting style was so different. It was usually felt that the soldiers had an advantage over the Indians. That wasn't true in this particular case. For one thing, the Indians were fighting on their home territory. They had their village with women and children on the site, and this motivated them to fight fiercely to protect them. Most likely, they even had better weapons than the troopers they faced. There were many reasons why they had the advantage. They attacked from a concealed position, whereas the troopers were out in the open. When Custer did divide his command, it's pretty clear that he was doing it as a reconnaissance rather than formulating a battle strategy. He would have done that later had it been possible. But by the time he discovered the extent of the village—how large it was—it was too late.

There were three thousand warriors [in the battle]. . . . The Indians always maintained that they had very light casualties. The reason we don't know is because they always removed the bodies of the dead and wounded from the field of battle. They left no trace of how many casualties they took. But we do know that people who survived that fight on the Indian side continued to die for months after that, so that probably there were more casualties than the Indians first admitted, possibly even as many as the whites sustained.

The shock that people experienced when Custer and his famous Seventh Cavalry were wiped out by the Indians somehow led people to keep refighting that battle ever since to try and find some explanation as to why Custer and his troopers were wiped out. To me, it's obvious: The Indians were the better fighters, for many reasons, on that particular day. I think it's been very hard for our culture to face that because of the inherent feeling that we—meaning at that time, white America—should always be able to defeat an enemy coming from a radically different culture, like the Indians.

John D. Rockefeller, Sr.

by
RON CHERNOW

John D. Rockefeller, Sr., (1839–1937) was the richest man of the nineteenth century. Rockefeller founded Standard Oil and dominated the American oil business until a 1911 Supreme Court antitrust decision forced the breakup of his empire. Ron Chernow, author of several award-winning books on the banking industry, appeared on Booknotes *on June 21, 1998, to discuss* Titan: The Life of John D. Rockefeller, Sr., *(Random House, 1998).*

JOHN D. ROCKEFELLER, SR., WAS DESCRIBED by William James [an American philosopher] as the most strongly bad, and strongly good, human being he had ever met. That expresses it as well as anyone has ever expressed it. He was a man of such profound and baffling contradictions, a man who is simultaneously the most ferocious of the robber barons and the most farsighted of the philanthropists. These two seemingly disparate human beings were rolled up inside one body and one mind. That was really my task, as the biographer, to try to make sense of the two halves of this whole.

The significant thing about the Rockefellers is that they were great institution-builders. John D. Rockefeller not only created Standard Oil, which was the largest business empire on earth, but he created the most extensive philanthropic empire, which includes what is today the University of Chicago, Spelman College, Rockefeller University, and the Rockefeller Foundation. He has cast such a long shadow because he created these permanent corporate forms, both in the business world and the philanthropic world.

In terms of the business empire, although the Standard Oil trust was broken up by the Supreme Court in 1911, it gives you some idea of the size of that trust . . . to know that the heirs include what are today Exxon, Mobil, Amoco, Chevron, Conoco, ARCO, BP America, Chesebrough-Pond's, and two dozen other companies. I don't know that the business world has ever seen an agglomeration of wealth and power on the scale of Standard Oil.

What I quickly discovered is that when you're writing about John D. Rockefeller, you don't feel like you're writing about a human being; you feel like

you're writing about a sovereign state. I had millions of documents to use. . . .
I did [interview some living Rockefellers]. The family was guarded but cordial.
I had a couple of very nice conversations with grandson David Rockefeller. . . .
Because John D. senior lived so long, grandsons David, Nelson, Laurance, and
all the rest [got to know him as adults. By his death,] they had graduated from
college; they had married; they had started in their business careers. David
Rockefeller said to me, "Gee, there are so many things I wish that I had asked
Grandpa." What he didn't realize is that Grandpa studiously avoided certain
topics. In fact, when Nelson was a senior at Dartmouth, Nelson wanted to do
his senior thesis on Standard Oil and vindicate Grandpa against his critics. He
wrote to his father, John D. Rockefeller, Jr., saying, "I so admire Grandfather.
Do you think you could arrange for me to speak to him?"

Most grandfathers would leap at the opportunity to tell war stories about
their business career. A few weeks later a letter came back from his father saying that "Grandfather has no desire to talk about Standard Oil." I make much
of this in the book because in most families there's a very rich oral history,
whereas the Rockefeller family is a family that's riddled by strange silences and
taboos.

RANDOM HOUSE ASKED ME to write about John D. Rockefeller after I finished my book *The Warburgs* [Random House, 1993]. I must confess to my
embarrassment, I thought it was an absolutely ghastly idea. I had done these
family sagas and I was very eager to do a pure biography, which I thought
would be more compact and cohesive. I told my editor at Random House, Ann
Godoff, that I thought Rockefeller was the worst subject imaginable—that he
just seemed to me cold, wooden, mechanical, ruthless, a man without any interior life that I could see. She suggested that I visit a place called the Rockefeller Archive Center that was set up by the family and is run by a team of
independent archivists.

It was a strange day that I spent there because I was almost trying to wriggle
out of the project. I told the archive director that I was not interested in Rockefeller because he had no voice. He didn't seem to have an inner life. I said to
him, "I don't hear the music of his mind, so how can I write a biography about
him?" With that, he produced an interview that had been privately conducted
[by a family acquaintance, William Inglis,] with Rockefeller between 1917 and
1920. It was part of what was supposed to be an official biography that was
never published.

Suddenly, here was this man who had no voice, who was so reclusive and secretive, and I have a seventeen-hundred-page transcript where he gives a blow-
by-blow account of every major twist and turn of his career. At that point, I
encountered a personality that I hadn't encountered in any of the previous
Rockefeller biographies. Rather than this cold, mute, reserved figure, here was

someone who was fiery; he was often funny, and he was amazingly analytical. In fact, he was quite brilliant.

I hasten to say he was often sanctimonious. I can see that there was a lot of self-delusion and rationalization. He evaded a lot of questions about the most controversial aspects of his life. But I saw just how much time he had privately invested into analyzing what he had done. Having written, for instance, about J. P. Morgan, who, at most, could concentrate on something for five minutes, here was somebody who had spent decades analyzing what he was doing, who had a brilliant strategic sense of the oil industry. . . .

Rockefeller was someone who did the exact same things at the exact same times every day. Right before they went out on the golf course every day, [William] Inglis would interview Rockefeller for half an hour to an hour. Rockefeller would recline on a couch with his eyes closed. Often, as Inglis was reading the question to him, Rockefeller appeared to be dozing, and then Rockefeller would suddenly snap his eyes open and give a very precise answer. The structure to that interview must be unique in American economic history, if not history in general. Inglis took the writings of Rockefeller's two most famous muckraking critics, Henry Demarest Lloyd and, most notably, Ida Tarbell, and read paragraph by paragraph to Rockefeller the most scathing charges against him. This was a fascinating document, having him confront his most severe critics. . . . As soon as I saw it, I knew that I wanted to write the book. I knew that this was a rare historical opportunity of taking someone who was seemingly so familiar to the public and saying to them, "He's completely unfamiliar. You don't know what he was like at all, because he didn't want to share it with anybody."

NELSON [ROCKEFELLER] VERY MUCH IDENTIFIED with his grandfather. He revered him. Nelson felt that he was very much the standard bearer in that generation of the family, even though he was the second son. He had a way of nudging his older brother out of the limelight. Incidentally, Nelson and JDR senior were born on the same day, which Nelson took as a very important sign that he was destined to carry on the family tradition.

JOHN D. ROCKEFELLER, SR., WAS NEARLY ninety-eight when he died. In the early 1900s, he announced that he planned to live to the age of one hundred. One thing about John D. Rockefeller, when he set his mind to doing something, he had an extraordinary ability to focus his mind and he almost always achieved goals. . . . He became something of a New Age health fanatic. He had all sorts of theories in terms of how he could prolong his life. This was the bane of his luncheon companions, but he used to chew food ten times before swallowing. Guests who observed him closely said that even when he had liquid in his mouth he would swirl it ten times before swallowing. This meant that people who were absolutely thrilled to be invited to the luncheon table of the world's richest man found themselves, after twenty minutes, finished with their own food and for the next hour watching John D. finish his.

THE IDA TARBELL ARTICLES in *McClure's Magazine* ran from 1902 to 1905. They had a powerful impact. The articles came out in serial form, which meant that each issue of *McClure's* had a larger circulation. . . . With each new installment, more Rockefeller critics would come out of the woodwork, so that the circle of sources kept growing with each issue.

By an extraordinary historical coincidence, Ida Tarbell was publishing this series just as the man in the White House, Teddy Roosevelt, was looking to single out one notorious trust for an antitrust case in order to make an example of it. It was really Ida Tarbell who turned John D. Rockefeller into the most hated man in the country. She brought all of the evils of the Standard Oil trust to public attention, just at the moment when Teddy Roosevelt was not only looking for a big, brutal, rich, unrepentant trust, but for one that the public felt strongly about.

It took tremendous courage to take on Standard Oil. Tarbell's father, who had been an independent oilman crushed by Standard Oil, warned her that her life would be in danger if she took on Standard Oil. The strange thing was that far from being crushed by Standard Oil as she was researching it, this lady kept taking shots at Standard Oil over a three-year period—and didn't take any fire in return. Rockefeller missed two major things that were going on in American life: one was the power of the press. Ida Tarbell was able to take on a complicated subject—to slice open Standard Oil, dissect it, give an accurate chronology of it. No previous generation of reporters had been able to tackle such complicated issues.

Rockefeller also did not realize that with Teddy Roosevelt, power was migrating from the legislative to the executive branch. For the first time, the federal government felt that it had both the right and the power to take on the largest corporations in the country. So there was a very powerful dialectic at work between Teddy Roosevelt and muckraking journalists like Ida Tarbell. The combination overwhelmed Rockefeller, who felt that he didn't need to dignify the series with any response. It was a fatal mistake. Standard Oil did not hire its first publicist until 1906, the year after the Ida Tarbell series ended. Today a corporate executive in a similar situation would probably have a team of thirty or forty public-relations people working around the clock.

ROCKEFELLER WAS NOTORIOUS from the time that he was a young man. The oil industry, like the computer industry today, was created by young men, which is often the case with new industries. After Colonel Edwin Drake struck oil in Titusville, Pennsylvania, in 1859, there was a wild, rip-roaring, gold rush atmosphere. It wasn't the kind of thing where old, settled people rushed off to western Pennsylvania. It was all of these young guys who had just been demobilized after the Civil War.

Rockefeller created Standard Oil in Cleveland in 1870. He quickly realized that the most significant factor in the competitive rush to dominate oil was transportation because, basically, one company's oil product didn't differ that much from another. Rockefeller created a conspiracy with the railroads called the South Improvement Company that gave preferential rates to Standard Oil, and at the same time gave punitive rates to Rockefeller's rivals.

When news of this leaked out in western Pennsylvania, Rockefeller was burned in effigy. There were huge torchlight parades in towns like Titusville and Oil City and Franklin and the other centers of the oil region. There was so much protest that this conspiracy was disbanded. But during that time when the conspiracy was alive, Rockefeller took over twenty-two of the twenty-six other refineries in Cleveland. His competitors felt that they could not possibly compete with Standard Oil, which was in cahoots with the railroad. This was a very significant moment. It was the first time that his name appeared in the newspaper. Even though he was controversial in the oil industry, it was many years before the general public realized that one of the ten richest and most powerful men in the United States was this John D. Rockefeller who controlled the oil-refining industry. By the late 1870s, even before he had reached age forty, he controlled about 90 percent of all the oil refining in the United States.

PEOPLE WHO DEALT WITH HIM in a business situation talked about his eyes, these piercing eyes that would just drill holes through you. William James said that he was the most suggestive and formidable personality he had ever met. Later on, Rockefeller became this sort of laughing geezer handing out dimes. I wrote about that. He became a rather colorful, eccentric old man, and that's fun.

Later on, he also wore a wig. He had lost all of his hair. He suffered from something called alopecia. In 1901, he lost not only all the hair on his head; he lost all body hair. This was a great tragedy in his life because Ida Tarbell came along a year later and did this series portraying him as a monster. Since he was hairless and suddenly looked old and ghoulish, his appearance seemed to ratify what she was saying in the series. The timing was particularly unfortunate for Rockefeller.

HE MARRIED INTO A FAMILY called the Spelmans, a wonderful family. They were not only ardent temperance activists, but they were ardent abolitionists who had been conductors on the Underground Railroad. They'd had Sojourner Truth in the house. Then Rockefeller went on to found Spelman College to educate freed female slaves. There's no question that he felt deeply about abolitionism.

Laura Celestia Spelman was about twenty-five years old when she married John D. Rockefeller. Her nickname was Cettie. They got married in 1864. She was a very bright, lively, intelligent young woman, a kind of bluestocking. She was a schoolteacher. She went to college at a time when that was extremely rare. She believed strongly in abolitionism and temperance. Later on, as the years went by, she became an almost suffocatingly pious young lady. She lost a lot of this intellectual vitality that you saw early on. One thing that many people have speculated . . . is that, as the drumbeat of criticism against Standard Oil grew louder, she took refuge in the church. She became a kind of unreal and otherworldly person who talked in a very high-flown religious rhetoric. It's strange that John D., who was accused of being the greatest corporate criminal of the age, went home to this household that was drenched in Baptist piety and felt no discontinuity whatsoever.

WHEN HE WAS IN HIS TWENTIES, his father, who was a bigamist and had abandoned the family, [left] John D. to single-handedly support his brothers and sisters and his mother. His father, William Avery Rockefeller, was a colorful, raffish mountebank who even in John's childhood would disappear for weeks or months at a time. John D.'s cunning side, the rascality, clearly comes from his father. His mother, Eliza, was very strict, very pious. All the thrift, discipline, industry, religiosity come from the mother. Here you have the product of these crazily mismatched parents, who then produce, quite logically, a crazily contradictory son.

HE DID [SOME THINGS THAT WERE ILLEGAL]. A lot of the things that he did were certainly unfair. I uncovered a lot of correspondence where he was directly paying off different politicians, and at the time to directly pay off a politician to kill a piece of legislation was illegal. Sometimes they used different subterfuges and would hire somebody as legal counsel.

Rockefeller often pointed out that most of his business career was played out before the Interstate Commerce Commission was created in 1887, which outlawed railroad rebates, and before the Sherman Act was passed in 1890, which outlawed combinations in restraint of trade. But what you saw with Standard Oil was that even when those two landmark pieces of legislation were enacted, the behavior of the trust didn't change at all. You can see in the [company] papers, they just tried to figure out different ways to circumvent the law. Basically, John D. and his colleagues regarded government regulators as nuisances to be bypassed wherever possible.

[In 1896, he gave $250,000 to the William McKinley campaign for president.] That would be several million dollars today. He didn't like politicians. He felt that politicians were basically parasites who shake down businessmen. All of this bribery he saw as extortion—politicians shaking *him* down, rather than *his* paying off the politicians. He regarded these payments as a business expense. He had very little interest in conventional politics. He was never somebody, aside from writing a check, who would get involved in a political campaign.

If you look at the late nineteenth century, the people who were really building the country were the businessmen, not the politicians. [Today] if someone were to ask you whether you would rather read a biography of John D. Rockefeller or Andrew Carnegie, let's say, than Rutherford B. Hayes or Benjamin Harrison, or if they asked you which two were more important, we would all say Rockefeller and Carnegie. This was a period of tremendous political squalor [however it was] partly caused by the business interests themselves.

THE IMAGE OF JOHN D. is that he made a pile during his career and then gave away a pile afterwards. . . . That's a cliché: The businessman makes a bundle and then sanitizes the fortune by giving it to good works. What makes John D. so much more fascinating and enigmatic and compelling a character is that he was making money as fast as he could from the time he was a teenager and giving it away as fast as he could. He was a Baptist. He was tithing as a teenager. By the time he was in his early forties, he was creating Spelman College in Atlanta, then Spelman Seminary to educate emancipated female slaves. By the time he was in his early fifties, he was single-handedly creating the University of Chicago. By the time he was in his early sixties, he was single-handedly creating the Rockefeller Institute for Medical Research, today Rockefeller University, the first major medical research institute in the United States. He was creating General Education, the world's largest educational foundation. He was creating huge philanthropic institutions throughout his career and not publicizing them. It's clear from his papers that, if anything, he found the idea of publicizing what he was doing very distasteful.

Frankly, it was for selfish reasons that he didn't want publicity. When there was an article in the newspaper about one of his large bequests, he would receive, on average, fifty thousand letters soliciting money within the thirty-day period after the appearance of such articles. His philanthropic adviser, Frederick T. Gates, said, "Mr. Rockefeller was stalked and hounded like a wild animal." Everywhere he went, everybody, from the most noble to the most ignoble, was soliciting him for money.

His net worth peaked in 1913 at $900 million, which translated into contemporary dollars is $13 billion. It does not sound like very much, but it doesn't begin to tell the whole story. He had $900 million in 1913. The entire federal budget in 1913 was $715 million, so he could have personally paid for every federal employee and expense and had money left to spare. The total accumulated national debt that year was $1.2 billion, so he could have retired three-quarters of the total national debt.

Bill Gates's wealth only represents one half of 1 percent of today's gross national product. Rockefeller's wealth represented 2.5 percent of today's gross national product then, which is why people claim with some justice that John D. Rockefeller was the richest man in American history.

HE WAS GREAT FRIENDS with Will Rogers, and Will Rogers came up with a lot of funny lines. They used to golf together, and one day after Rockefeller beat him at golf, Will Rogers said to him, "Gee, John, I'm glad I lost to you in golf. The last time I beat you the price of gasoline went up a dime."

ROCKEFELLER'S WIFE had been a sort of professional invalid for the last ten or twenty years of her life. . . . She was confined to a wheelchair during the last few years of her life. . . . After she died in 1915, John D. lived another twenty-two years. There's no evidence, during all the years that his wife was an invalid, that he ever cheated on her. He seems to have been a model husband—one of his many contradictions. . . .

As soon as she died, he developed a real roving eye. He [had] this afternoon ritual where he went out with a party of people in a large touring car. He always sat tightly wedged between two buxom women on either side. He had a blanket that he drew over their laps and up to their necks, and his hot, itchy fingers would stray under the blanket. Rockefeller lived his adolescence in his last years, whereas when he was a young man he looked very old and serious, and when he was an old man he looked rather jaunty and young. He seemed to keep getting younger and even slightly silly as he got older.

PREVIOUS PAGE: Edmund Morris stands in front of a painted profile of Ronald Reagan which hangs on the wall of his Capitol Hill townhouse. The painting is by Tom Bostelle. (*All photos courtesy Brian Lamb*)

ABOVE: Sylvia Jukes Morris, wife of Edmund Morris, also did her writing and research for *Rage for Fame: The Ascent of Clare Boothe Luce* in their home on Capitol Hill. Here she is shown in her third-floor study.

OPPOSITE: Robert Bartley, author of *Seven Fat Years: And How to Do It Again*, in his *Wall Street Journal* office on Liberty Street in New York's financial district. He has been the editor of the paper since 1972.

OPPOSITE: Juan Williams in the Supreme Court of the United States. A portrait of Thurgood Marshall hangs behind him.

ABOVE: Feminist activist Betty Friedan in the Rotunda of the U.S. Capitol. Behind her is a 26,000-pound sculpture of Susan B. Anthony, Lucretia Mott, and Elizabeth Cady Stanton, all three leaders in the woman's movement. Following an act of Congress, the statue was moved from the Capitol's Crypt to the Rotunda in May 1997.

ABOVE: David Reynolds stands in front of the brown-shingled house in Old Westbury, New York, where Walt Whitman was born.

OPPOSITE: Robert Richardson at Ralph Waldo Emerson's home in Concord, Massachusetts.

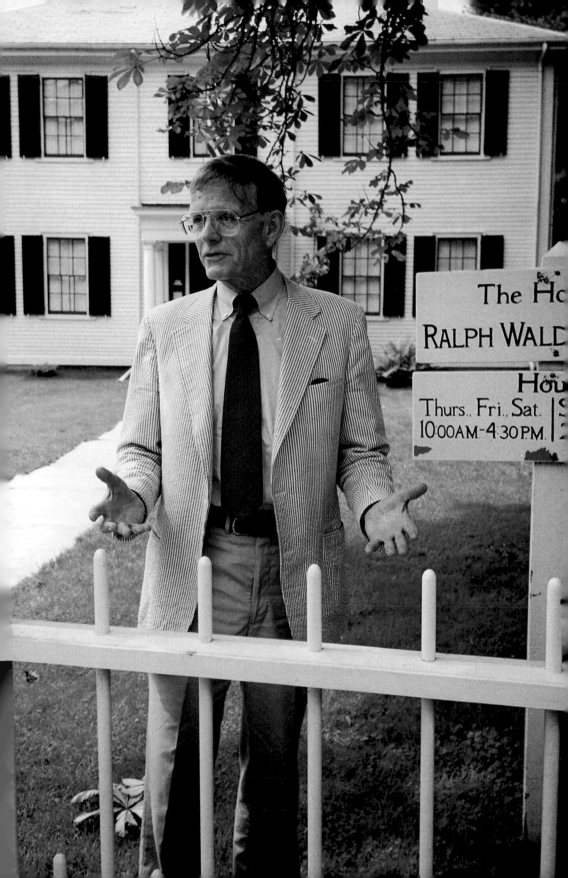

PREVIOUS PAGES: (*Left*) Edward Epstein in his Upper West Side apartment in
Manhattan. Behind him is a portrait of Mr. Epstein painted in 1977 by Byron
Dobell. Mr. Epstein is holding tapes of Armand Hammer's phone conversations.
(*Right*) Neil Baldwin in Thomas Edison's laboratory. The national historic site is
located in West Orange, New Jersey, and is open to visitors.

ABOVE: Monica Crowley at the former Nixon home in Upper Saddle River,
New Jersey. President Nixon lived here for ten years. Ms. Crowley's second book
on Nixon was published in 1998.

Sam Tanenhaus is pictured in front of Whittaker Chambers's childhood home in Lynbrook, Long Island.

ABOVE: Anita Hill signs an autograph in Kansas City, Kansas, as her nephew
Eric Fennell looks on.

OPPOSITE: Lloyd Kramer, with the White House behind him, sits in the park
named for the Marquis de Lafayette.

CALVIN COOLIDGE
1872
BORN PLYMOUTH, VT.
1895
GRADUATE, AMHERST COLLEGE
1897
ADMITTED MASS. BAR ASSOC.
1898
CITY COUNCILOR, N'TON
1901
CITY SOLICITOR, N'TON
1906, 1907
STATE REP., MASS.
1909, 1910
MAYOR, CITY OF N'TON
1911--1914
STATE SENATOR, MASS.
1913, 1914
PRESIDENT, MASS. SENATE
1915--1917
LT. GOVERNOR, MASS.
1918, 1919
GOVERNOR, MASS.
1921--1923
VICE PRESIDENT, U.S.A.
1923--1929
30TH PRESIDENT, U.S.A.
1933
DIED NORTHAMPTON, MASS.

PREVIOUS PAGES: (*Left*) Former Secretary of Defense Robert McNamara in his I Street office in downtown Washington, D.C. (*Right*) Katharine Graham in her Georgetown home where she wrote her Pulitzer Prize–winning autobiography.

ABOVE: This monument to Calvin Coolidge, detailing his public offices, stands on the lawn of the county courthouse in Northampton, Massachusetts.

Oliver Wendell Holmes

by
LIVA BAKER

Oliver Wendell Holmes, Jr., (1841–1935) fought in the Civil War, then re-
turned home to Massachusetts to attend Harvard Law School. Theodore Roo-
sevelt appointed him to the Supreme Court in 1902, where he served for over
thirty years. Liva Baker recounted Holmes's life and legal career in The Justice from Beacon Hill: The Life and Times of Oliver Wendell Holmes
(HarperCollins, 1991) and for Booknotes *on September 8, 1991.*

OLIVER WENDELL HOLMES was the son of Dr. Oliver Wendell Holmes of
Boston. He was a federal Supreme Court justice from 1902 to 1932. He was on
the Massachusetts Supreme Court for twenty years before that. He wrote a
book, *The Common Law,* which was a seminal book in legal history. . . .

[He was known as] the Yankee from Olympus, the magnificent Yankee. He
was a legend for so long. His father began it, but he made his own legend. He
was the darling of the Progressives. His dissents from some of the court majority opinions were forceful, and he was very articulate. He made [himself into]
a legend, but other people helped him along. His father helped him by publishing—I guess it was in 1862—*My Hunt After the Captain,* about his search
for [his son] after he was wounded at the Battle of Antietam.

JUSTICE HOLMES HAD A LOT of courage. He was willing to go on his own.
That's sadly lacking in all of our society today. I don't know about the people
on the court now. I don't know whether they have any courage or not. It's certainly lacking in our society. People are not loners; they're lemmings now.
Holmes had a lot of courage, and he spent all those nights reading by himself
in a city that really didn't appreciate his work, his scholarship. He was willing
to go it alone. He had a lot of courage in the Civil War, too. . . . [And,] he had
the courage to buck Theodore Roosevelt, who had appointed him.

His father was a physician, an essayist, a biographer and a poet of sorts. It
wasn't great poetry, but it was certainly well known. His father also had a great
deal of courage. He wrote, when it was certainly not popular to write, a paper

on childbed fever and how it was transmitted from bed to bed by the doctors and nurses and the midwives. That sure set the medical establishment on its ear, but he had the courage to stick by his guns.

THE CIVIL WAR WAS THE SINGLE most important thing in Justice Holmes's life. He was never really mustered out psychologically; he fought that war for the rest of his life. The metaphor of the military was in his writings. It gave him a certain detachment. If you see your friends being killed . . . all the time and you don't have time to stop and do anything about it, you can become somewhat detached. It also distanced him from other human beings somewhat— the thought that perhaps he would lose them in some way, so he didn't ever want to get too close to people and really be dependent on them.

He fought in the eastern peninsula [of Virginia,] in the Peninsular campaign. He was in a place called Ball's Bluff, which was probably the biggest mismanagement of that part of the war. They sent the Union soldiers up a 150-foot-high bluff as the Confederates just sat there and peppered them. . . . That was where he was wounded the first time. He was at Antietam, and then he was on the road to Chancellorsville—he was between Fredericksburg and Chancellorsville—and he got hit again.

He sometimes thought of himself as an accidental survivor. He felt that he had to atone for that in some way and make it worthwhile that he survived. Several times during that war, other people were in places where he might have been, and so he survived. One of his favorite books was [Herman] Melville's *Moby-Dick*. On the last page, the hero is floating in a sea supported by a coffin. I have a feeling that [image] went right to Holmes's heart. . . . If he had moved two inches, two of the times he was hit, he would have been dead, too.

HIS SENIOR YEAR AT HARVARD, he enlisted [to fight in the Civil War]. He was in until the summer of 1864—1861 to 1864. He came back from the war and went right into Harvard Law School. Then he went into private practice for a while. For the next decade and a half, he went in and out of private practice. He also did a lot of scholarly things. Then at the end, he wrote his book *The Common Law.* The point [of the book] is that law is not static; it's evolutionary, Darwinian. Natural selection plays a part in the law as it does in the structure of the horse, or the elephant. Law responds to the needs of society and is constantly developing. It was a seminal work at the time.

He was in his early forties when he told a friend that he wanted to be chief justice of Massachusetts and then he wanted to go on to the United States Supreme Court. Whether he thought he'd actually make it, I have no idea, but he told somebody that that was his ambition.

I often thought I should have written a little something about the role of accident in his life. [His appointment to the U.S. Supreme Court] was an accident, too. McKinley was assassinated and Theodore Roosevelt was then president. Theodore Roosevelt and [Senator] Henry Cabot Lodge were close friends. There was a point in Lodge's life when he was an outcast in Boston. Holmes walked across the street and stuck out his hand and shook hands with him publicly on the street so that everybody could see it. That was courageous for Holmes. . . . It wasn't a great deal, but Lodge never forgot that Holmes was kind to him when he was an outcast. Lodge went to his friend Theodore as soon as there was a vacancy on the Supreme Court and pushed his friend Wendell Holmes.

Henry Lodge was the junior senator from Massachusetts. He had been a history instructor at Harvard whose courses Theodore Roosevelt avoided because he was too hard a taskmaster, but they became great friends. Lodge moonlighted with the Massachusetts Republicans and worked his way up, left Harvard, and went into politics full-time. He was eventually elected representative and then senator.

[Roosevelt] asked a lot of questions of Lodge. He wanted to make sure that they got somebody who was politically with them. They didn't want any mavericks on that court. Roosevelt was in his trust-busting phase . . . and they wanted to be sure they were going to get somebody who would go along with him.

Holmes went down to [Roosevelt's home in] Oyster Bay, [Long Island], one summer afternoon and talked to Roosevelt. Roosevelt then said to him, "The appointment's yours, but don't announce it for a few days. Let me talk to Cabot Lodge and the other senator from Massachusetts . . . and get things straightened out before I announce it." It was a week or two before it was actually announced.

[POLITICALLY, HOLMES WAS] A EUNUCH. He didn't like politics. He was talked [to] about running for office at one time. He wouldn't have anything to do with it. . . . He seemed to understand politics, but he just didn't want any part of it. He was a Republican as far as the party goes. He voted, but politics wasn't his thing at all. . . .

Roosevelt and Holmes were [friends] for a while and then Holmes disagreed with Roosevelt about two years after he got on the court. . . . [What put a wedge in their friendship was] a case called *Northern Securities.* Roosevelt was in his trust-busting phase, and Holmes didn't think that in this case the trust ought to be busted, and he dissented. It was one of the first big decisions after he was on the court. Roosevelt said, "I'm not going to invite him to the White House again." He did invite him again, but as Holmes said, "Things were never the same after that."

I THOUGHT HE WAS A GREAT CIVIL LIBERTARIAN when I began. He had done some very nice libertarian things, but not for the reasons I thought. I thought he was shouting all the time about civil liberties, but he wasn't. There were only a few [truly libertarian decisions], like the famous one that the Constitution allows freedom of thought, not only for the thought that we agree with, but for the thought that we hate. For me, that's a rallying cry. I think that's wonderful. But he didn't say many things like that. [At least] not as many as he was thought to have. . . .

He was not a great dissenter . . . [but] it was the quality of . . . the dissent, the pungency of his writing. Also, he was known. There was even an Oliver Wendell Holmes PTA in Cleveland or someplace like that, so I guess people did know about him.

FANNY HOLMES WAS HIS WIFE. She was very reclusive. She covered her tracks. She remains to me somewhat of an enigma. I think she did it deliberately. Somebody once pestered her about giving them a picture and she finally gave in and said, "All right. I'll get you one." She gave them a picture of a Buddha. She kept the shades drawn in her house. Literally and figuratively, the shades were always drawn with Fanny Holmes.

She died . . . in 1929, . . . before he did. For a long time afterward, he had a terrible time, but he'd lived through the Civil War and seen a lot of his friends killed. Grief distracts from the business at hand. On the other hand, the business at hand distracts from grief, and that was pretty much the way he operated. He was back on the court within a couple of weeks. The details of getting her affairs cleaned up helped him a lot. She died in . . . the end of April and then he went to Massachusetts for the summer to their summer home where they had gone for a lot of years. He was very lonely, but people there tried to take up the slack and kept him very busy to the point where he got tired of being kept busy. But she had left a great hole in his life.

ALGER HISS WAS ONE OF HIS SECRETARIES . . . what today's law clerk is. He [hired] young men after their last year at Harvard Law School. . . . Secretaries, as they called them then, did things like balance his checkbook and run errands for him. The most important thing they did was be available for what he called a "good jaw." He liked to talk to them. He liked their bright, young, inquisitive, adventuresome minds. He loved to talk to them about what was going on at Harvard Law School and what was going on in the law. He found that very stimulating. That was their main purpose. They didn't write the opinions. They looked up some legal citations, but nothing more.

[HE WAS ON THE SUPREME COURT until he was] ninety-one. . . . It was said in his later years that he became more and more dependent on [Supreme Court justice Louis] Brandeis to give him a hand with some of the legal citations and perhaps some of the reasoning. He wasn't quite up to it in his last few years, but into his eighties he was pretty good. Then maybe after eighty-five or so, he began to slow down some. . . . He worried about it a lot, too, whether he should keep on. His friends, of course, as friends often do, said, "Oh, yes, sure. We can't live without you. You've got to keep going." They finally did have to ask him to leave, though.

Oliver Holmes . . . along with Brandeis . . . helped bring the court into the twentieth century. Both Holmes and Brandeis, although they came at it from very different places, were believers in the Constitution as a living document, responsive to the needs of society. That's what brought the court into the twentieth century. Before that, the court was static, and the Constitution was treated as a static document. It was natural law. It was law and nature transmitted by divine will—immutable, eternal, and there was no changing it. The justices would say, "Well, that's not constitutional because the Constitution doesn't allow that specifically." Holmes would say, "It doesn't say it's not unconstitutional, so it's all right."

Thomas Edison

by
NEIL BALDWIN

Thomas Edison (1847–1931) was the inventor of the light bulb and the phonograph. His experiments with motion pictures and the founding of the General Electric Company helped usher in the twentieth century. On March 19, 1995, Neil Baldwin talked to our audience about his book Edison: Inventing the Century, *published in 1996 by Hyperion.*

Edison's known for over one thousand patents: the phonograph, the varying permutations of the telegraph, the electric pen, the concrete house, the storage battery, the phonograph cylinder, the disc record, all sorts of dynamos, every component of an electrical system. One of the points I try to get into in the book is that it isn't just these free-standing inventions we should think of when we think of Edison; we should think of systems of inventions.

The light bulb, which is the most familiar to all of us, the one that we grow up learning about, really is one component of an entire system of delivering electric power to domestic and corporate settings. You have to think of the dynamo that generates the electricity, the wire that goes under the streets, the wire that goes from the streets to the actual apartment or factory, the fuses, the measuring system for the meters, the filaments of the bulb—in addition to the bulb itself at the very end. Edison actually spoke about his pride in the entire system that he created. That was, in his mind, the real invention, rather than just the bulb, or the lamp as it was known in those days.

He was born in Milan, Ohio, which is a little town—it's still very much the same way it was in the 1840s. It's about sixty miles west of Cleveland. His forebears were Canadian. His father came over from the north country and set up a shingle shop. Edison was one of seven children. . . . His mother's forebears fought in the revolutionary war, so there was kind of a strong patriotic strain to his background.

As a little boy Edison was chastised by his teachers for not listening in class, daydreaming. It wasn't that he wasn't listening. It was that he couldn't hear. The teachers chastised him in front of the class, and when he was seven years old, after only three months of schooling, his mother came in and yanked him out of there; he never went back to school again. He was home schooled for quite a long time. As a consequence of his progressively degenerating hearing, he became a very introspective child. He became a voracious reader, literally an autodidact who, as an adult, had a standing order at Brentano's Bookstore for every single new book that came in to be shipped directly to his home.

He lived in Milan, Ohio, till he was eight years old, and then his family moved to Port Huron, Michigan. He worked for the Grand Trunk Railroad, which was a line that ran down to Detroit from Port Huron. That was when he began publishing his own newspaper on the train, typesetting it by hand, publishing it, and selling it to all the people on the train. He also worked on his father's truck farm growing vegetables and sold those on the train. He was extremely adept for a teenager.

He learned telegraphy at the train station nearby in Mount Clemens, Michigan. Gradually it expanded his universe. During the Civil War, he was an itinerant telegrapher throughout the Midwest, living in various towns and working part-time, learning the craft of telegraphy, which was a very common profession for young men of that period. He moved to Boston when he was about twenty years old, then New York, then Newark and Menlo Park. [He spent] the rest of his life in New Jersey. Most people think of him as being a New Jerseyite, but he had his formative years in the Midwest.

Telegraphy was a very nascent industry that grew up in tandem with the railroad. You have to see them as brothers in technology. Telegraphy progressed in complexity in the 1850s, 1860s. I always like to say that Edison grew up with the railroad. He was born at a time when canals were the major infrastructure system used for commerce. . . .

The rise of the railroads, the change in the way in which goods and information were transported, necessitated an upgrade in the accompanying technology. He defined his era and was defined by his era. He had his ear to the ground in the sense of what was required by this growing nation. He understood the first telegraphy that he got into was between businesses—very rudimentary—I guess now you would call it a local area network. . . . Edison saw that the best way to grow an industry was in concentric circles. He started by marketing these telegraphic services to related businesses in a community. I think he really had a sense of the pulse of corporate America because, you have to remember, this is the late 1860s, early 1870s we're talking about. He always had one eye on the future when he was developing his inventions.

He opened his own shop right outside of Newark, New Jersey. This would be about 1870 or thereabouts. He was twenty-three, twenty-four years old. That was where he met his first wife. Her name was Mary Stilwell, and her family was from Newark. She was working for him in a clerical capacity. She was a very attractive, very young, blond, gray-eyed woman.

She bore him three children over thirteen years. This was the period when Edison was building his empire. He was proud of the fact that certain times of the year he was away from the home for one hundred nights in a row working in the lab.

I can definitely say that Mary Stilwell was a very lonely woman. She was depressed. The few letters of hers that survive talk about her being alone, that Edison wasn't here. "My husband is not here. I have terrible headaches," she would say. "My head is splitting." She became a drinker. We know this from the bills that she saved for her accounts with a liquor store. She was a big sherry drinker, and she gained a tremendous amount of weight toward the end. She became a compulsive eater also. When you compare some of the pictures of her toward the end—and again, we're talking about a woman in her twenties—to her wedding picture, you almost can't recognize her. She was a neglected woman with three little kids and a husband who wasn't around. I don't really know the actual physical cause for her death, but she died very young, very sadly, and alone.

With the second wife, our story changes 180 degrees. You have to put this relationship in the context of a man who has achieved a certain level and a certain lifestyle, is quite young and still has three children to take care of. Edison was one of those people who had to be taken care of by a woman. I don't think he would have admitted that, in so many words, but there's no question in my mind. He met Mina Miller through family friends in Boston when he was recently widowed. He was associating with some of his bachelor friends and they were trying to connect him with eligible young women. . . . Mina was a self-possessed, talented, beautiful young woman. She was only nineteen when he met her, but she was much more educated and, I believe, much more self-possessed than his first wife.

WHEN YOU START TO LOOK at the structure of Edison's work, you find out that the other root of his genius was his ability to hire the best people, people who stayed with him for decades: Charles Batchelor, John Kruesi, William Kennedy Dickson, Jonas Aylsworth, Francis Upton. . . . These were the people who were behind the scenes, making the tremendous research and development contributions to Edison's corpus of work. When the time came to file the patent, their names were put subsidiary to Edison's; the patent was filed under Edison's auspices. They were taken off salary and given a percentage of the gross revenues for these inventions in perpetuity.

The trade-off for these people was anonymity in the history books until recently . . . but college education for their children, a house, and a secure income.

When you ask about his friendships—these were very tight colleague relationships that were predicated upon involvement in these great inventions.

In 1896, Edison met Henry Ford and that's a different genre of friendship. . . . By that time Edison was a revered icon in the mind of Henry Ford, who was working for the Detroit Edison Company. He was actually an employee of Edison's, by extension. . . .

Ford went to a convention of Edison managers in Long Island, at which Edison gave a speech. Someone brought Ford over to Edison's table and said, "Here's a young man who's beginning to work on the internal combustion engine." He sat down next to Edison and sketched on a napkin his design for the stroke engine he was working on. Edison pounded his hand on the table and said, "You've got a good idea. Keep at it and one day, you'll become a success."

There's a certain apocryphal strain to that. But the fact is, Henry Ford was Thomas Edison's greatest admirer. At times, when Edison was having problems financially with his cash flow, Ford would commission him to design a battery for the Model T. He gave him a loan of $200,000 or $300,000 to get him through and helped support Edison at the end of his life when he was doing research on the rubber plant.

IF YOU LOOK AT THE STATEMENTS EDISON MADE about the rationale behind some of his inventions, you will find statements akin to Henry Ford's "I will build a car for the great multitudes." . . . I don't know how familiar people are with Edison's work with prefabricated housing for working people. Edison was convinced that he could design a concrete house that would be poured into a mold in one day. . . . He had a concept that he would build huge housing developments very cheaply for the working man to allow him to provide the American dream of the home . . . for his family.

When he was producing phonograph records, his main goal was to promote music that was palatable to the masses and that conformed to his taste. His taste in literature ran to poets such as Longfellow, who was his all-time favorite. He had a very mainstream sensibility and he believed that he was in a position to disseminate this through Thomas Edison Industries. That's why I say [he was] a populist.

A VARIETY OF EAR PROBLEMS afflicted Thomas Edison, yet I would say he only became totally deaf toward the very end, which, ironically or paradoxically, is when he entered the record business and started auditioning opera singers and instrumentalists. In those instances, he would put his entire head inside the megaphone of the phonograph—stick it all the way in there—and turn the volume all the way up. In one or two instances, when a pianist was auditioning, he would literally clench his teeth around the frame of the piano. The vibrations would come through his jawbone, and he would sense the music in that way. I've seen the teeth marks on the sides of the piano in Thomas Edison's home. He signed off on every single recording that was made for his record company, even as his hearing was practically nil.

NAPS WERE IMPORTANT to Edison. Some of the stories that we've all grown up with about Edison not needing any sleep really bear looking at. A more accurate way of describing it would be that he could survive on four or five hours of sleep a night. His pattern was such that he liked to stay up late after everyone else went to sleep, be upstairs in his study. At that time he had what was called a thought bench up there, which was a place where he would sit when he was totally quiet and totally isolated. He could reflect and really distill his thinking and sort out what he was going to do the next day while the whole rest of the family was asleep.

During the day, as an older man, he would get tired and he would have to take these catnaps. He was known for being able to fall asleep in the most inhospitable circumstances. He could literally sleep anywhere. Then he would wake up refreshed after five or six minutes.

HE ENDED UP DYING of pretty much a system breakdown, you might say. He had congestion of the lungs. He had very serious digestive problems as an older person. . . . He'd lost a lot of weight and became very weak. It wasn't a question of his heart giving out or his brain giving out. It was pretty much his respiratory system and his digestive system combined.

He lived from 1847 to 1931, so that's eighty-four years. That's why actually "Inventing the Century" was a concept that I thought very carefully about. I feel he represents the era and is a representation of the era at the same time. He exemplifies the century, the waning of one era and the beginning of another, as well as being a major prototype of the time. He defined the time and the times defined him.

Woodrow Wilson

by
AUGUST HECKSCHER

Woodrow Wilson (1856–1924) was a university professor and then president of Princeton University. In 1912, he was elected president of the United States. After his dream of a League of Nations was turned down by Congress shortly after World War I, his health deteriorated. August Heckscher, author of Woodrow Wilson: A Biography *(Scribner, 1991), appeared on* Booknotes *on January 12, 1992, to discuss our twenty-eighth president.*

Woodrow WILSON WAS A PRODIGIOUS worker and very fascinating in his youth: lively, spirited, witty. He was voted year after year as the most popular member of the faculty at Princeton University. . . . But the most fascinating period in some ways is when he left the university and stepped out into the world of politics in 1910. For two years he was governor of New Jersey, and in 1912 he was elected president of the United States, so it was a meteoric career. He emerged on the political scene with enormous vitality, with great eloquence, striking a new note with humor and modesty where otherwise there had been bombast and exaggeration.

He was born in Staunton, Virginia, in 1856, just thirty years after John Adams and Thomas Jefferson died. How short our history is when you think of it. He was born a southerner in Virginia. He lived all his youth in the South. His father was a very distinguished clergyman and himself a great preacher who inspired the son to the concept of oratory, which he did pursue. He lived in Augusta, Georgia, during the Civil War, where his father had a big Presbyterian church. He lived in Columbia, South Carolina, during his teenage years; he lived in Wilmington, North Carolina, at least the family did, while he was mostly at Princeton. Then he married a girl from Rome, Georgia. He was about as southern in his upbringing as you [could imagine].

Wilson was, in all his early writings and all his thinking, a nationalist. He believed the Civil War was over, which a great many people at that time doubted. In one famous debate when he was a law student at the University of Virginia, he said, in effect, "Now I will tell you something that will shock you: I am glad that the South lost the Civil War." He then went on to picture very eloquently the stricken Union, the broken nation, the disadvantage the South would have been at in terms of manufacturers, and so on.

From the beginning he rose above the South. He never had a southern accent, for example. It's often asked whether his problems with civil rights, when he became president in 1913, did not have their source and their roots in the fact that he was a southerner with a southerner's prejudice. . . . I think there were other reasons. Wilson himself was very liberal in the deepest sense. He was absolutely nonsectarian in his views. He appointed the first Jew to the Supreme Court of New Jersey. He appointed the first Jew to the United States Supreme Court. He made a Catholic his private secretary and so on. He recognized blacks as a race that needed help and education if they were going to play their part in the national life.

DEMOCRATS HAD TAKEN OVER the House in 1910 and they also controlled the Senate, so he came in as president with his own party, which was what he wanted. . . . But in 1918, the congressional elections went against Wilson and he had a hostile Senate. . . . He could never really work closely with it. . . .

Wilson re-established a principle dead since almost the founding of the Republic, where the president goes down to Congress and delivers the [State of the Union] message himself. [Past presidents had] sent messages that were read by the clerk that were long and dull. But Wilson appeared [in person]. It was an absolutely unbelievably dramatic thing. He had an office in the Capitol that hadn't been used since Lincoln's days, and he would go down there and consult with the members of his own party and members of the opposition party, too, when he was promoting legislation. It was a very dramatic moment in American government. He himself had written that "the president has the great power of standing alone for all the people." The Senate and the House were elected by particular constituencies. The president was elected by all the people and he had to speak for the whole people so far as he could. Insofar as he did speak for them, Wilson wrote, he was invincible.

WILSON SUFFERED IN THE FIRST TWO YEARS of his presidency the great disaster of his wife's death. She died in August 1914, almost the same day as World War I broke out. Wilson was caught in that vortex of [world] events and at the same time caught in a private sorrow that caused him a deep depression for several months. Then to go on, he met, about eight or nine months later, Edith Bolling Galt, [a widow] with whom he immediately fell in love. He carried on a passionate courtship with Mrs. Galt and married her about sixteen months after his first wife's death. . . .

[When he first met her,] Wilson was just beginning to emerge from this deep depression. He loved to motor around Washington way out into the country, and one day as he was passing Dupont Circle, he said to his private physician, who usually was with him and was a good companion as well as a good doctor, "Who is that beautiful woman that I see walking down the street?" By an extraordinary coincidence, it was [Edith Galt], whom the doctor, Cary Grayson, knew well, and that in a strange way was the beginning. But it was only afterward that she came, by chance, to the White House as a friend of the president's niece. . . .

[The pair] came in from walking in the rain. They were in the little White House elevator and the door opened: there was the president of the United States. Wilson had his first real glimpse of his future wife wearing muddy shoes, as she said.

Mrs. Galt was a southerner and she had great pride. She had . . . an unhappy first marriage[, but] her first husband had died. She was living in Washington, a jaunty figure—the head of the Galt Jewelry and Silver Company. The first woman in Washington, she prided herself on saying, to drive an electric car, and a woman who paid great attention to her looks and her style. She was indeed the first First Lady whom the crowds noticed because of what she wore, because of her Paris gowns and things of that sort. . . .

After that first meeting when she emerged from the elevator in her muddy shoes, he invited her to dinner at the White House several times. She'd come with members of the family. Then one night in May, they went out on the porch of the White House and the other families tactfully withdrew. There, Wilson proposed to her and she turned him down. [He wrote her this letter the following day:]

Here stands your friend, a longing man in the midst of world affairs, a world that knows nothing of the heart he has shown you and which would as lief break it as not. . . . Will you come to him sometime without reserve and make his strength complete?

. . . These letters between Woodrow Wilson and Mrs. Galt in their courtship phase are great literary love letters. But the letters to Wilson's first wife, whom he had married in the 1890s, are also extraordinarily frank and romantic in every sense.

WILSON'S GREATEST CONTRIBUTION was the vision that, tragically, was not realized. It is a vision that we are still trying to fulfill: a world made up of democratic states, free states as we tend to call them today, self-governing, brought together under an overarching international organization that would preserve peace, engaging in free trade, maintaining human rights, disarmed because they didn't need arms. . . . Today that vision still is very much with us.

The League of Nations became essential to Wilson as the horrible slaughters of World War I drew to an end. He saw it as the only means that would justify the great sacrifices that had been made by England and France and other countries, and indeed, at the end, by our own country. It would mean peace for the world in the future. It would redeem the horrors of the war. . . . So in Paris, where the Treaty of Versailles was framed, he got the League of Nations at the top of the agenda. He got the assembled nations to approve it and to commit themselves to it. It was a great act of statesmanship on his part. As the peace conference went on, he more and more saw the League of Nations not only as a peacekeeping institution, but also as a kind of supreme parliament. It was going to straighten out many of the mistakes that the statesmen of that time were being forced to engage in. Wilson believed that a better period in world opinion—a more sane and just opinion—would develop and would reflect itself in the League of Nations, that the flaws and the errors of the peace were going to be corrected by the League. All that happened and then the League was defeated in the Senate, and we never joined it. It went on in Europe and then lived between the two wars. I don't think one ought to take away from Wilson the fact that he created the League. One has to look at that terrible political defeat that left the United States on the outside.

He had a very severe stroke . . . in October of 1919. It was seventeen months before the end of [his second] term. He'd come back from the western tour, which had been shortened because there were very alarming symptoms. He was a very ill man. He came back to Washington, walked from his railroad car to a waiting car, rode to the White House, and two nights later he suffered this very severe stroke. . . .

The country as a whole didn't know that Wilson had suffered a severe stroke. The bulletins that were issued emphasized the fact that he was exhausted, that it was a sort of nervous breakdown, and that he would be able to carry on. . . . The [White House inner circle] believed that his life hung by a thread.

Three people who were close to the president carried on the affairs of government: Mrs. Wilson, his secretary Joseph Patrick Tumulty, and his doctor, Cary Grayson. Now the question is: Did they run the country or, more particularly, did Mrs. Wilson run the country? The president was totally disabled by this stroke for a period of about two months. Then he was in a wheelchair, and he learned very slowly that following spring to walk painfully and to mount one step at a time. But he really remained a cripple through the rest of his life. . . . Wilson . . . was a stricken man [when he] returned, never to make a speech again except for brief speeches after he'd retired. . . .

Did Mrs. Wilson run the government? Well, my answer to that usually is the government didn't run during these seventeen months. The departments carried on their work, the annual message was pieced together largely by Tumulty from reports that were made by the cabinet members to the White House; it was a period when nothing was initiated, nothing new was undertaken. The country was turning away from the war back to private business and was much more concerned with making money than with political innovation or political leadership. The country really drifted during that period.

In Congress they would joke, "Another bill has come down from Tumulty." They would examine the signatures on bills and proclamations to see whether they were Wilson's. Sometimes they were not; they were a rubber stamp. In the country as a whole, the word got out that the president was seriously ill. After several months, diplomats went to see him to present their credentials and would write home to their own governments about the pathetic spectacle that occurred: where once an intensely vibrant man—a giant, if you will—had been, there was just this bent, stricken figure. He was often wearing a kind of baseball cap that came down over his eyes, often with a shawl over his shoulders, often unshaven and so on. It was a tragic thing.

He was terribly, terribly bitter in the end. . . . The Republicans in the Senate had proved absolutely unyielding, and Wilson, when the final [League of Nations] struggle in the Senate came up, was a fallen man. He was a man not capable of making a public speech, not capable of negotiating. All he could do was lie in his bed or sit in his wheelchair and say no. He rejected the compromises that were proposed to him by the Senate, one after the other. . . . Finally, the whole thing was withdrawn and there was a complete wreckage. We never signed the Treaty of Versailles and we never joined the League.

He retired with Mrs. Wilson to a very handsome house on S Street, [in Washington, D.C.] and there he lived out four years [until] he died in 1924. . . .

[TODAY] WE ARE IN A PERIOD where Wilson's ideas are again coming to the fore. Emerson said of John Brown, "We meet him wherever we turn." We begin to meet Wilson again, wherever we turn. . . . Whether we'll be able to achieve everything that Wilson strove for is still doubtful. It may need another half a century and it may even need more wars before we're able to get there. Many of his problems still live with us, and he'll be there when we try to solve them.

Theodore Roosevelt

---

by
NATHAN MILLER

Theodore Roosevelt (1858–1919) was born in New York City and graduated from Harvard in 1880. In 1898, during the Spanish-American War, he led the Rough Riders up San Juan Hill in Cuba. He was elected in 1898 and served until 1901 as governor of New York and then became vice president under William McKinley. When President McKinley was assassinated in 1901, Teddy Roosevelt succeeded him as president. Nathan Miller, author of Theodore Roosevelt: A Life *(Morrow, 1992), appeared on* Booknotes *on February 14, 1993.*

TEDDY ROOSEVELT BELIEVED that life was a great adventure and the great sin was not living life as a great adventure. He also did a number of things for the country. The greatest thing he did was that he understood that the presidency is, as he said, "a bully pulpit." Everybody copies those words today. He believed the job of the president should be to lead and to educate, and he tried to educate the American people to the needs of the day.

Roosevelt was not liberal or conservative in the sense that we use the terms today. He believed that the government should be used as a buffer to meliorate the conditions of the time. It should stand to prevent the conservatives of the day from taking over the country and also prevent radicalism from getting a stranglehold on the country.

He started the conservation movement insofar as the federal government is concerned. He took millions of acres out of the grasp of speculators and put them aside for the nation. He was the first conservationist president. He probably knew more about conservation than any "green" today. But at the same time, he was not a tree-hugger in the sense that he believed these things should be just put away and not used. He believed that if resources could be used in a fashion that did not destroy them, they could be used for the benefit of the public. He also brought in the Pure Food and Drug Act, the meat inspection acts, a lot of other things that we take for granted today.

HE WAS BORN IN NEW YORK CITY—in fact, he was the only president born in New York City—in 1858. His parents were quite distinguished people. His father, Theodore Roosevelt, Sr., was a philanthropist. He had inherited $1 million from his father, C. V. S. Roosevelt, and he spent his lifetime doing good.

In the beginning, Theodore did not go to school. He was taught by his aunt, Gracie. He was considered too delicate. His health was bad. He had asthma. . . . He did not see any organized school until he went to Harvard at the age of eighteen. At Harvard, he studied natural history—in those days natural history was more than it is today. It covered a lot of fields that we wouldn't consider natural history today. He intended to be a natural scientist. But he met [his first wife], Alice. He realized that [to be a scientist] he would have to go to Germany to study for several years and he did not want to leave her. So he switched from the study of natural history to the study of law. . . . He was too bored with law to stay with it. He left law school after two years. He wrote a book at the age of twenty-four that became a great success, *The Naval War of 1812.* More than a century later it's still the standard work on the subject. He got into politics, was elected to the state legislature of New York, and was in Albany at the age of twenty-five.

He met Alice Lee at Chestnut Hill, outside of Boston. His close friend at Harvard was Richard Saltonsall. Saltonsall, who lived in Chestnut Hill, invited Roosevelt home for the weekend. The Lees lived next door. He met Alice one day on the garden path between the two houses. As he said, it was love at first sight.

I am the first to use the correspondence between Theodore Roosevelt and his first wife, Alice Hathaway Lee. After she died in childbirth in 1884, it was thought that T.R., in his anguish, had destroyed all the letters that they had written during their courtship and marriage. But as it turned out, he had not. They'd been put away, and they'd come into the possession of Alice and T.R.'s daughter, who became Alice Longworth. After her death in 1980, it was found that she had all these letters, had been sitting on them. She thought they were too sentimental to be shown to the public and had not reported their existence. After her death, the letters went to Harvard and were sitting in a box. I opened it, and there they were. There's some lovely material in them and some tragic material, too. There's a note in there in which Alice announces that she is pregnant for the first time. She had some difficulty becoming pregnant . . . and she was so enthusiastic. You read it, and you know that she's going to die in childbirth, and it's just so sad to read this. Also I found a little bundle of tissue paper in the box. I unwrapped it and there was a lock of Alice's hair carefully wrapped up and preserved for so many years.

T.R. married Edith Kermit Carow about three or four years after the death of Alice. He had been friendly with Edith throughout his childhood. He had first known Edith when they were both about five years old. . . .

HE WAS A STATE ASSEMBLYMAN [in New York] and it was extremely important in his career; this was the beginning of his career in politics. In his second term in the state assembly, he advanced to . . . minority leader. From there he went on to other jobs, but the job as state assemblyman made him a prominent public figure, because he led reforms against [corruption] in New York City. This gave him tremendous publicity and made him . . . the most famous politician in New York State.

He volunteered for the army at the beginning of the Spanish-American War [in 1898]. He always had this idea of having a regiment of mounted rifle-men. When the war broke out, he put this idea forward to the government. It was accepted. There were three regiments of mounted riflemen organized—the First Volunteer Cavalry. The Rough Riders were the only ones that got into ac-tion, and when they went into action, they did not go into action on horse-back. Their horses were left back in Florida, where they debarked from, and they went up San Juan Hill on foot, except for T.R., who partially went up on horseback and was a target for every Spanish rifleman in the area. Finally they reached barbed wire, and he got off the horse to hack at the barbed wire and went up the rest of the way on foot, too.

They were trying to take Santiago, which is on the south shore of Cuba and where the Spanish fleet was holed up. . . . The navy was blockading Santiago but couldn't go into Santiago after the Spanish fleet because of the mine fields. They thought if they could capture the city, the fleet would be forced out and destroyed by the navy, which actually did happen.

He got out of the army in September and was elected governor of New York in November. He began his administration on the first of January, 1899. The terms of governors at that time were only two years. At the end of his first term, the political boss of New York State, Tom Platt, wanted Roosevelt out of Al-bany. He was just causing too much trouble; he was too much of a reformer. Platt decided to elevate him, to kick him upstairs to the vice presidency—[as] he put it, to have T.R. "take the veil."

[On September 6, 1901,] McKinley was visiting the Pan-American Exhibi-tion at Buffalo. The place had been thrown open, anyone who wanted to could greet the president in person. There was a line of people . . . and a man came up to the president with a bandage over his hand. The president stuck out his right hand to shake hands with this fellow. The fellow raised the hand with the bandage. There was a gun in the hand . . . and he fired into McKinley's stom-ach two or three times. McKinley fell back, seriously wounded, and died about ten days later.

T.R. was giving a speech on an island in Lake Champlain, New York, when the word was received. . . . He hastened off to Buffalo and remained there for several days. It appeared that the president was recovering, so they thought it was a good idea if the vice president left. It would show the country that the president was doing better and confidence would be restored. T.R. went off into a hunting expedition in upstate New York. While there, he received word that the president was dying and he should come back to Buffalo. There was a wild ride—a buckboard to get him to the nearest train station, which was fifty miles away. They covered fifty miles in a night, this tremendous ride through the mud, around the mountainsides. Roosevelt's account of it is quite vivid. They reached the train and, while waiting for the train to leave for Buffalo, he received a telegram that expressed everything in one sentence: The president died at such-and-such an hour this morning. He was now president.

He was the youngest man ever to become president of the United States. . . . He had presided over the Senate for three days. That was his only service as vice president.

He became president again in 1905—on his own right, as he said. In the beginning [of his presidency] he tried to cultivate the Republican party and the Republican bosses, led by Mark Hanna. Then he began to move out more on his own. He tried to build his own political strength in the country, particularly in the South, where Hanna had control of the delegates. He made his first really independent move in the coal strike. . . . He settled the strike almost single-handedly. Until then, a president had never intervened in a labor dispute except to send troops to shoot down the strikers. T.R. believed that the strikers had a good argument: they were underpaid and overworked. He took a hand in . . . seeing that the strike was arbitrated and that the coal miners got a fair shake—as he put it, a "square deal." The Square Deal became the symbol of his administration, just as the New Deal became the name for Franklin Roosevelt's administration and the New Frontier John F. Kennedy's.

T.R. SAID THAT HE'D GOTTEN the phrase "Walk softly and carry a big stick" from the McGuffey readers [standard texts given to schoolchildren of the day]. It meant, in foreign policy, that the United States should negotiate, should arbitrate, but always have a big stick at hand in case reasonableness would not be met. In his case, the big stick was the navy. He built up the navy to a large and important force that became the third- or the fourth-largest navy in the world.

ROOSEVELT WROTE 150,000 LETTERS in his sixty years of life, plus forty books, plus tons of magazine articles. He was constantly at work. T.R. also read a book a day. He would pick up a book in the morning and finish it by evening. . . . He speed-read. You didn't have speed-reading in those days, but he read very quickly. He had a photographic memory, and he could just whip through a book. He kept a book at the door of the White House. While waiting for guests to arrive, he'd pick up the book, read a page or two. When the guests arrived, he'd put the book away on the stand. The next time he was in that area, he'd pick it up and start reading again until he'd finished it.

Roosevelt would bubble over—his energy was so tremendous that he never seemed to sit down. He bounded—he did not walk. He would leap out of his chair to talk to people. A perfect example would be the way he gave news conferences. There were no formal news conferences when T.R. was president. News conferences did not come in until later. But every day he would meet the White House press corps, the six or seven reporters covering the White House, informally. He would be shaved at noon, and he would walk into the room, he would sit down in the chair, the barber would put a sheet over him to cover him, lather up his face, and the president would answer questions. But periodically, he'd get so excited while answering a question he'd jump out of a chair while the barber was all set to shave him. Then he'd sit down and smile at the barber. And the barber would try again to shave him. As one correspondent said, it was like a three-ring circus, watching the president be shaved.

IN 1908, T.R. DECIDED not to run for president . . . He thought that too many people were claiming that he was a dictator and it was best to step down. He turned the presidency over to his hand-selected choice, William Howard Taft, who had been secretary of war and his very close friend.

After he left office, he went off on an African tour, and while he was on the African tour, rumors began to reach him of the difficulties that Taft was having. He felt that Taft was betraying his positions, particularly in the case of conservation. Taft was no conservationist. He turned some of the reserves that Roosevelt had established over to exploiters. Taft was more conservative than Roosevelt. Roosevelt had not really realized how conservative Taft was. . . .

He had become so frustrated with Taft that he decided to run [in 1912] for the Republican nomination. There was no rule then against a president running for a third term, just the unwritten Washington rule. . . . T.R. ran in every primary; he won every primary. He tried to influence every delegate that he could influence that was not elected by the primaries. But the old guard controlled a majority of the Republican convention. When they got to Chicago, T.R. was counted out by the old guard. He stormed out of the convention, threatening revenge.

In the meantime, some of the more progressive Republicans and Democrats had gotten together and sponsored T.R. as a Progressive party candidate, a third-party candidate. He resisted at first. . . . Woodrow Wilson had been nominated by the Democrats and Roosevelt knew that if he split his party, Wilson would win. He resisted up to a certain point and then he was convinced, told by Progressives that they had put all their hopes in him. They had abandoned the party and he owed it to them, out of loyalty, to run in 1912 as a third-party candidate, which he did. Some people attribute T.R.'s running in 1912 to pique or to jealousy of Taft. Some even say he was insane—a lot of people used to say that T.R. was insane because of his violent motions and fast talking. This was the only way they could explain it.

But he did not do this out of pique, he did not do it out of jealousy of Taft. He did it out of loyalty to his fellow Progressives. At least that's my interpretation.

ROOSEVELT WAS SHOT in 1912, campaigning for a third term as . . . the Bull Moose candidate. He was in Milwaukee towards the end of the campaign, and he was climbing into his car in front of a hotel on his way to give a speech. As he got into the car, he turned. Suddenly, a man in the crowd pulled out a gun and shot him in the chest. As Roosevelt later said, he felt like he'd been kicked by a horse. He fell back into the car. Then he remembered what he'd once been told when he was in the army—to [try to] cough up blood to see if he'd been wounded internally. He did not cough up blood, so he knew that it was not a very serious wound.

He immediately demanded to be taken to the hall where he was to give the speech and stood up for ninety minutes giving the speech while he had a bullet in his chest. Blood was pouring over the front of his shirt. Then he allowed himself to be taken off to the hospital. He said it took more than that to kill a bull moose.

He had always talked about bull moose. "I feel like a bull moose," he had often said. . . . He was a big-game hunter and the bull moose was a symbol of large and royal animals. That's what gave the name to the third party, to the Progressive party, which was known as the Bull Moose party.

The bullet had been deflected by a copy of his speech. The speech was quite long. It was fifty pages, folded over his chest. There was a bullet right through the speech. Also his eyeglass case, which was metal, had deflected the bullet. When the doctors examined him, they were quite surprised that he'd not been seriously hurt. It was an immense muscular development of his chest that had stopped the bullet from really entering and doing serious damage. The man who shot him was John Schrank. He was somewhat deranged and an anti–third-term fanatic. . . . He was not executed because he had not killed the ex-president.

ROOSEVELT RAN SECOND to Wilson [in 1912]; Taft ran third. Taft is the only incumbent president to run third in an election.

T.R. LIVED TO BE SIXTY YEARS OLD. He died of an embolism. He was worn out from the various things that he had done throughout his life. At the instructions of his father, he built himself up physically, and in doing so, he strained himself. One of the doctors who had examined him before his first marriage, at the age of twenty-two, advised him to be very careful how he lived the rest of his life—in fact, advised him against running up and down stairs. T.R. said, "If I have to live a life like that, I'd rather not live it," and proceeded to live a very vigorous and active life.

W. E. B. Du Bois

by

DAVID LEVERING LEWIS

David Levering Lewis's Pulitzer Prize–winning biography of W. E. B. Du Bois delves into the life and times of the civil rights leader, who lived from 1868 to 1963. Dr. Lewis joined us on January 2, 1994, to discuss volume one of his two-volume series, W. E. B. Du Bois (1868–1919): Biography of a Race *(Henry Holt, 1993).*

WILLIAM EDWARD BURGHARDT DU BOIS was a man who lived about ninety-five years. His life spans the twentieth century, its issues and its major personalities. He was born in the North, in Great Barrington, Massachusetts, a small town in the Berkshires, and educated at elementary and high schools there. Then he attended college at Fisk University in Tennessee, took a second bachelor's at Harvard and went on to obtain a Ph.D. in history from Harvard. [He] was the first African-American to be awarded the doctorate.

Before he did that, he spent about two years at the University of Berlin pursuing economic studies. . . . When he came back, he taught . . . at the University of Pennsylvania; he wrote a book called *The Philadelphia Negro,* which is one of the first books of urban sociology in America. He then went on to Atlanta University, and for ten years he superintended the pioneering Atlanta University Studies, which simply [studied] the whole gamut of African-American and southern life.

He retired from teaching to be the editor of the NAACP's magazine, *The Crisis,* from 1910 to 1934; he was also a co-founder of the National Association for the Advancement of Colored People. It was he who insisted that it be "colored" not "Negro," not "African," not "black," but "colored" because he wanted the association to have a mission and mandate that would address itself to the larger issue of darker peoples everywhere. He was always thinking a bit ahead of the administrators, bureaucrats, and colleagues for whom the immediate and pragmatic were more compelling.

He was controversial. Every position he struck up was the only position, from his point of view. With great articulation, both verbally and in prose, he would espouse his position. Then a few years later, he might well strike up another position, which, while not in direct contradiction to the previous position, was more than a shade different. Many of his allies found themselves puzzled as, in his long life, he took a variety of positions that were somewhat paradoxical.

Underneath them all, though, was a principal consistency that racism must be combated, that human rights must be affirmed, that economic justice was the key to the eventual accomplishment of parity and the enhancement of the great majority of the life chances of peoples.

DU BOIS IS ONE OF THOSE PERSONS who brought a lot of internal fire. If you were measuring the force field of that personality, the needle would have gone up high. He just came into the world with quite a bang, quite a bit of pizzazz. But then there was [also] a great deal of self-conscious cultivation of the mind.

I began coming across little graphs of his workday: so much to do in the morning, so much in the afternoon, so much in the evening. They grew longer and longer until, finally, there were these scrolls that outlined every single thing he would be doing for a week and then two weeks, then a month. In the morning, after a cup of coffee, there would be reading, then writing a book, then there would be reading a novel, then there would be correspondence. This was unvarying. It's simply a formidable schematic for productivity.

Think of [German philosopher] Immanuel Kant. People in the university town used to set their watches by Kant as he walked by. Du Bois had that same kind of precise regularity. I suppose that was why at times he appeared brusque, arrogant, and aloof, because he knew that he didn't have time for the sociability that would take time away from that schedule.

HE ARTICULATED THE IDEAS of Pan-Africanism, though there were others who had these ideas. Pan-Africanism was the philosophy of the common destiny and purpose of people of African descent, who must work across boundaries, across lines, in concert in order to throw off the shackles of imperialism, whether it was the naked variety of actual occupation on land or whether it was the market manipulation of countries by more powerful northern and European palatines and governments.

The reason was probably best summed up in his turning-point book, *Black Reconstruction,* which was published in 1935. People in slavery, obviously, would have a performance level that would leave a great deal to be desired—that was the nature of the . . . institution. After emancipation, however, the consensus of American historians was that African-Americans hadn't come up to snuff, that there had been an experiment called Reconstruction. It had been a great mistake and extravagance in terms of the corruption and stupidity it obtained.

It was Du Bois who was to go back to the sources and show that Reconstruction had been quite a different experiment. Its failings had to do with the refusal of the federal power to follow through, on the one hand, and on the other, the decision to allow the white South to erect a system of racial supremacy. In that situation, where the civil rights of the African-American and his economic rights were repressed and controlled by white southerners, it was simply not in the cards for African-Americans to achieve their full potential.

[HIS RELATIONSHIP WITH BOOKER T. WASHINGTON] was such a titanic misunderstanding and contretemps that it divided the African-American community. There are still echoes of that detonation even today. Washington was the principal of Tuskegee University, the leading institution in the Deep South that offered vocational and industrial education to its student body. But more than that, he was the man who had famously spoken in Atlanta, Georgia, in 1895 at the Cotton States International Exposition when the South was putting its best foot forward, claiming that it was rising from its ashes, was the place to invest, and was a place where racial problems, indeed, were well in hand.

Washington spoke at that international show. There he proclaimed that the African-American should, in effect, renounce his civil rights and in return enter into a bargain with the white South, in which for the renunciation of the vote, the white South would encourage the African-American in humble pursuits—industrial, vocational. The trade-off would be that in time, with frugality and patience, there would be, perhaps, a restoration of those rights—but that would be far down the road.

But by 1903, it was clear to Du Bois that a bargain in which you give up the one thing that gives you leverage is no bargain at all but an institutionalized exploitation. . . . Du Bois realized that he had to increasingly assume the role of adversary. He did so reluctantly; it took him away from his scholarship. He was not a leader of numbers of people. Camaraderie didn't come easily to him. But, increasingly, he found himself in the crosshairs, as I put it, of Booker Washington. Finally, he threw down the gauntlet in that essay included in *The Souls of Black Folk* . . . which announces that Washington does not speak for, as he called them, the members of a "talented tenth." These were the African-Americans for whom . . . their renunciation of civil and social equality was simply appalling. They were mostly northern, and they were all college educated. That small group rallied to Du Bois, and over time it grew as a critical mass. Finally, Booker Washington was no longer the spokesperson for the majority of his people: Du Bois was.

[THE NATIONAL ASSOCIATION for the Advancement of Colored People was founded] in 1910 at Cooper Union, the historic forum for founding movements in New York City. Du Bois was present with those Progressives who used to be household names: [reformer] Jane Addams; Oswald Garrison Villard, the owner of the *New York [Evening] Post* and *The Nation* and the grandson of William Lloyd Garrison, the great abolitionist; William English Walling, one of those well-bred socialists of the period; Mary White Ovington, another powerful socialist. . . . They were people who believed that America was in the grasp of mammon; that the cities were polluted; that politics was corrupt; that government was at the beck of the highest bidder. They wanted to reform and save America, to make it once again a city on the hill.

In the area of race relations, they saw the movement of racial tensions out of the South into the industrial North as a great threat to the civility of society and to its order. There had been a quite terrible riot in 1908—the real trigger for the founding of the NAACP—in Abraham Lincoln's burial place in Springfield, Illinois. It was a pogrom where hundreds of people were maimed and murdered. Out of that atrocity came "the call," as they would say, which brought the Progressives, black and white, to Cooper Union to found what became the NAACP.

It had an important component in the movement that Du Bois himself had started earlier in 1905—the Niagara movement, exclusively made up of African-American men, and later women, "talented tenth" types. Booker Washington was still vigorous and able to restrict the success of that movement. It was only when there was a confluence of white progressivism and African-American civil rights that a movement that could effectively combat white supremacy and Booker Washington came on line: the NAACP.

DU BOIS JOINED the [Communist] party when almost everybody else was leaving it, when it was, if not on its last legs, institutionally battered to the point that its membership was reduced to a rump. He joined in October 1960, just as the Russian Revolution's anniversary was being celebrated. He did so in order to Homerically thumb his nose at what he saw as the increasing rigidification of politics in America, the triumph of the Cold War, as he saw it, the division of the world into two armed camps. He was even skeptical about the long-term significance of the civil rights victories of the 1950s because, once again, he looked beyond the desegregation of facilities and the integration of schools and those firsts that were so impressive.

He looked beyond that to the economic reality that not much had changed, and there was no good reason to anticipate that a great deal would. To the extent that things did change, they went down to the credit or the benefit of a small African-American middle class. You would then have a class divide within the group, which would further impede the struggle for civil rights.

He was tried in 1951 in Washington, D.C., as a foreign agent, which was ludicrous. The Justice Department spent about a half million dollars, which was [big] money in those days, trying to find evidence abroad that Du Bois was the conduit of funds and subversive ideas at the beckoning of the Comintern. Not so. The transparency of the charges was so much so that the judge threw out the case in three days. But Du Bois, looking around for support, didn't find any within the African-American community.

There were some exceptions: the poet Langston Hughes; [singer] Paul Robeson; E. Franklin Frazier, the distinguished sociologist; and a few others. But that "talented tenth" absented itself from his defense. That had a great deal to do with Du Bois's decision . . . about the role of this bunch of people. The . . . disenchantment then pushed him even farther left. But I don't think it was bitterness that did it as much as it was a genuine alarm on his part: If he didn't begin to say something about the quiescence of this leadership class, its sponginess, its smudginess as some things began to happen that should have been applauded in the area of the breakdown of racial segregation, [then] no one else would. He then would deserve his mission in life, which was always to be the great scold, the exemplar, the model, the seer, the prophet.

He went to the Soviet Union and was treated like a head of state. He then went on to China with the same sort of treatment. If the Soviet Union hoped to encourage people within the United States and elsewhere to look upon Marxism, communism, scientific socialism with increasing favor, then Du Bois was useful in that regard. . . . Here was the most impressive African-American intellectual, a man who was deemed widely to be the father of Pan-Africanism, the founder of the civil rights movement, and now in the 1950s, his politics were such that the Soviet Union thought it appropriate to bestow upon him the Lenin Peace Prize.

HE DIED IN GHANA just on the eve of the civil rights march on Washington, that historic assemblage here around the Reflecting Pool in 1963 on August 28. I say that he timed his death, his departure with cinematic poignancy because just before Martin Luther King stepped up to the microphone to deliver his memorable "I Have a Dream" speech, Roy Wilkins, the head of the [NAACP], stepped up to the mike to say that Du Bois had died.

Many people weren't quite sure who he was, but almost everyone realized that this was a significant passage. . . . In a sense, the baton passed from this great figure, who had been the source of so many ideas and strategies combating civil rights, to a younger man with a somewhat different approach, but nonetheless certainly an heir to Du Bois.

DU BOIS WAS EXCEPTIONAL, above all, in this way: At ninety-five, he was more radical than he was when he was twenty-five, and he was more radical in most Americans' eyes. That is quite extraordinary, that a man who has the option to accept any number of honors chooses this lonely vigil of reproach and imprecation and exhortation. . . . Du Bois, in the service of human rights, gave up the comfort and the laureates that he might have had. He put it well himself. He said, late in life, "At fifty, had I died, I would have been championed. At seventy-five, my death was practically requested."

That, for him, was an achievement in its own perverse way. He continued to raise issues, he continued to examine and to probe and to deplore until finally his last decision was so egregious from the point of view of orthodoxy that people simply ran the other way and pretended to forget about him.

Marcel Proust

by
SHELBY FOOTE

In 1909, Marcel Proust (1871–1922) began work on Remembrance of Things Past, *a seven-volume novel that consumed his life. When author Shelby Foote appeared on C-SPAN's* About Books *on December 8, 1996, to discuss* The Correspondence of Shelby Foote and Walker Percy *(W. W. Norton, 1996), he told us about the important role Proust's work has played in his life.*

ONE OF THE RECURRENT THEMES in [*The Correspondence of Shelby Foote and Walker Percy*] is my trying to get Walker to read [the volumes of] Marcel Proust—from start to finish. I am preaching the doctrine of Proust. I never did get him to read any farther than *Swann's Way* and barely into [*Within*] *a Budding Grove.*

Marcel Proust was a French writer, the greatest writer of this century. I'd put him right up there under Shakespeare. He wrote this very long novel translated as *Remembrance of Things Past* or *In Search of Lost Time.* He combines all the talent in a novelist that I know of—psychological insights as great as Dostoyevsky, writing skill as great as Tolstoy. His ability to tell a story is as great as any writer, his creation of characters is right up there with Dickens. Proust seemed to me to have all this talent, plus this enormous talent for organization. You don't see that until you have read *Remembrance of Things Past* several times. You begin to see how he is driving that story the whole time.

The point of his novel is a very gloomy one. It's that society as we admire it from a distance is not at all what we think it's going to be. There are a bunch of idiots up there. There are many points to it. The main point is that salvation lies in art. Art can save us from all these disasters that accompany our living and dying. [But] that's an oversimplification. If you ask most people, they would say that he believed in involuntary memory. That is, he believed that a sudden dank odor or a waft of cold air could call back a memory far better than you ever could in your conscious memory.

He believed that your intellect would distort the image but your physical sensations, which we call involuntary memory, were the ones that could be most trusted. The most famous one [for Proust] being [the taste of] a madeleine dipped in tea, which brought back his childhood to him.

MARCEL PROUST WAS THE SON of a very well known French doctor. His mother was Jewish. He was raised in luxury. During his father's lifetime—his father died when Proust was under thirty—he must have been the despair of this man, this great doctor, because this boy appeared to care for nothing but society and frivolous literature. I often think of Dr. Proust going through that, knowing that his son was going to be a total loss. But he turned out to be one of the greatest writers who ever lived.

He lived in Paris, always in Paris. He had a cork-lined room. He had the room lined with cork as an insulation against noise. He didn't want to be distracted by noise. I lately found out that, after Proust died, the cork was taken off the walls and made into bottle caps. Which is a sad end for the lining of Proust's writing room.

Marcel Proust was homosexual, exclusively. No, he never even considered marriage—although he talks about it every now and then. He died when he was 51, about the same age as Shakespeare.

You can go to this place called Illiers [near Chartres, France]. There is a Proust shrine there—[the Musée Marcel Proust]. Proust is generally recognized as being one of the three great writers of this century. You could stretch it to half a dozen and he would be there in any case, but if you narrowed it down to three, there's Proust, James Joyce, William Faulkner.

TWO THINGS [MAKE A GREAT WRITER]—dedication and combination of talent and character. If you are lacking either one of those, you can never be a great writer. Talent is an ability to learn how to put words together. Character keeps you at the desk working away when it's hard. You have to have that combination if you want to be a real writer.

Proust wrote *Remembrance of Things Past* over a period of approximately fifteen years. It came out in seven different novels. The first one was published before the First World War. The second one was delayed because of the war and was originally going to be in two volumes. He began to expand that second volume until it stretched to six novels.

Today there are many, many Proust enthusiasts. Proust, however "precious" people may want to call him, is not that at all. He's like Dickens. He's in The Modern Library [collection]. He sells to this day. He is a delight to read, but you have to like language. You have to appreciate a stylist or you might find it almost impossible to read.

YOU CAN COUNT OUT what I believe [I have] accomplished in my life by how many times I have read Proust. When I finish anything and I think I have earned the right, I take off two months or however long it takes to reread *Remembrance of Things Past.* I have reread it nine times now from start to finish. It's seven novels long, about one million, two hundred thousand words. I read about seven or eight hours a day. I read slowly and with a good light because all through my childhood I had been told, "Shelby junior, you are going to put your eyes out if you don't put a good light on your face."

For my seventeenth birthday, my mother gave me the new Random House four-volume edition of *Remembrance of Things Past.* The date she gave it to me is written on the front page. On the first page of the last volume—the overleaf or the flyleaf—I [wrote down the date of each time I finished rereading the book]. There's a huge gap of twenty years while I was writing *The Civil War* that I didn't read it.

If I met him, I'd say, "Monsieur Proust, I admire your work enormously. It's meant everything to me in my lifetime."

Calvin Coolidge

by
ROBERT SOBEL

Calvin Coolidge (1872–1933), the thirtieth U.S. president, began his career in local Massachusetts politics and worked his way up the political ladder one rung at a time. He was a city solicitor, state representative, mayor, state senator, lieutenant governor, and governor. He was elected vice president in 1920 and succeeded to the presidency on Warren Harding's death in 1923. He was elected the next year in his own right. On August 30, 1998, Robert Sobel talked to Booknotes *viewers about* Coolidge: An American Enigma *(Regnery Publishing, 1998).*

CALVIN COOLIDGE WAS AN ENIGMA because the people in his time didn't really understand him, and I don't think we understand him today. He was a very complicated individual.

The complication was that he was what he seemed; there was no artifice. [Historian] Robert Ferrell once said that there are three presidents in the twentieth century who could have lived without becoming president, and one of them was Coolidge, the other one's Harding, and the third was Harry Truman. . . . Coolidge was a straightforward, honest man. His enemies said of him that "You may not like what he stands for, but you know he believes it, and you know he'll deliver. He will work very hard, and he will always be honest to what his beliefs happen to be." That's the way he was.

He was born in Plymouth Notch, Vermont. . . . There's a house, a church, a store, a cheese factory, and a visitors center, which, of course, came later. He lived there until he was in his early teens, then he went away to school, Black River Academy.

His father was the typical big fish in a little pond. He owned a store for a while before he sold it to his brother-in-law. He was an official in town, a justice of the peace, sheriff. He went to the state legislature for a while. He speculated in land. Calvin Coolidge always said that he was never half the man his father was. He admired his father greatly.

Coolidge was penurious, but often he still did not have enough money. His father provided his money. He told his father his hopes and his fears. . . . At one point, his father said—after Coolidge became a lawyer and didn't know what to do with himself—"Maybe you can get a job as a clerk someplace." Coolidge said, "I didn't become a lawyer to become a clerk." But it was always, "My dearest father." Whenever they met, they'd kiss. You had the president of the United States meeting his father, Secret Service around, the press, and he would kiss his father. It's just the way he was. He was not going to change just because he became president of the United States.

He went to college at Amherst in 1891, and he was chosen by the senior class to deliver the Grove Oration, which is supposed to be a humorous speech. He was the funniest person in the class . . . Will Rogers said Coolidge was the funniest person he knew. So, he delivered the Grove Oration, and in the audience was a man called Field, a lawyer from Northampton, Massachusetts. Field heard the speech and said, "I wanted to meet this man because I like to laugh." Coolidge wanted to go to law school or read for the law. He decided to read for the law, and he went into Field's office, which was in Northampton, Massachusetts, and he read for the law for two years. Then Field put him up for the bar and he became a member. . . . Then the question was: Where would he practice? He considered many places. He considered going back to Vermont. But he decided to open up an office in Northampton, and there he stayed.

[He started in local politics, winning offices on] the school board and things like that. . . . He would go up the rung, one step at a time, up the ladder. . . . In all, he ran for office nineteen times. He was elected seventeen of those times. No person who became president ever ran for office more than he did. He was once asked when he was vice president if he had any hobbies. He said, "Yes, running for office."

There was something about him. . . . He knew his constituents and the constituents knew him. Long before there were Reagan Democrats, there were Coolidge Democrats. Coolidge used to go out after the Democratic vote, and he said that "If a Democrat votes for me, that's two votes—one less for my opponent and one more for me." He rang doorbells. He stopped people in the street. He was not a backslapper, don't get me wrong, but he was a very effective campaigner, and he had this reputation for honesty and courage. People liked that. And he cracked a lot of jokes.

[He was nominated as the vice presidential candidate during the 1920 Republican convention.] The political bosses wanted someone else. . . . [Warren] Harding became a reluctant presidential candidate. They picked the vice presidential running mate, Irvine Lenroot, a senator from Wisconsin. And Lenroot was nominated. The seconding speeches came in and the president—the presiding officer—recognized Wallace McCamant, a delegate from Oregon, who didn't like the way the bosses were controlling things. McCamant had read a book by Coolidge—his speeches called, *Have Faith in Massachusetts,* and he liked what he read. So he nominated Coolidge. The convention rose up in a roar and selected Coolidge. Coolidge got the nomination. A senator from New York who had been to every convention since the Republican party was founded wrote a letter to Coolidge saying, "I have never seen anything like it. These things are not supposed to happen."

This guaranteed several things. In the first place, it guaranteed that Coolidge would not be part of the establishment in Washington. He was an outsider. They didn't want him. Of all the vice presidents who succeeded to the White House after the death of a president, only one before him had gotten the nomination, and that was Teddy Roosevelt. . . . The idea was in 1923 that if Harding ran for a second term—and everyone thought he would—Coolidge would be dropped from the ticket and he'd go back to Massachusetts. . . . But Harding died. . . .

Coolidge became president in August of 1923. . . . Washington is awfully hot in August. There was no air conditioning, so the city emptied out, and Coolidge went back to his father's house in Plymouth Notch. His father wanted him there because there were some repairs to be done: chopping down a tree, getting some shingles on the roof. . . . He went to sleep that night [of August 2] . . . [when] Harding died on the West Coast, San Francisco.

They called the general store, which was across from the house, and the proprietor was asleep. . . . There was no telephone at the Coolidge house, no electric lighting, no indoor plumbing. It was a very primitive house.

They called . . . and got some newspaper people . . . and the Secret Service, and they came to the house at 1:00 in the morning. They knocked on the door, and Coolidge's father answered with a lantern in his hand [and said], "What is it?" "President Harding has died. We have to speak to Calvin Coolidge immediately." He called upstairs, and Coolidge later said, "I knew something was wrong from the tone of his voice." He came downstairs. He learned about Harding. He went upstairs, got dressed, prayed, went across the street to the general store, which by now was open, and called Washington to find out what he had to do.

They said, "You have to be sworn in immediately." "Well, who can do it?" "A judge." "There's no judge here. My father's a notary public. Could he do it?" The answer was, "Yes, he can." So he went back into the house, and by the lantern, with his father holding the family Bible, Coolidge was sworn into the presidency at a little after 1:00 in the morning.

He went back to bed, got up the next morning, washed up, dressed, walked out, got into the car. As he walked out, he noticed a stone was missing from the step. He said to his father, "You better get that fixed." He got into the car, started driving off, and he told them, "Stop." The car stopped. He went to the family cemetery and visited his mother's grave. He prayed, got back into the car, and he was off to the train.

Calvin Coolidge did not want to change things. He wanted to carry out the pledges that Harding made, then he made a few of his own in the next election.

He wanted to cut the taxes, which he did. [When he left office] the national debt was two-thirds of what it was when . . . he came in. You had peace, prosperity, low inflation, low unemployment. He never took credit for this, by the way. [He let] the economy do that.

[He had a smaller staff in the White House than he did as governor of Massachusetts] . . . just one secretary. And no telephone on his desk. He thought it was unseemly. He thought it was undignified. Presidents should not make telephone calls from their desks. Besides, people might eavesdrop.

Grace Coolidge was a teacher of the deaf and dumb. She's considered by some the first modern First Lady. She was a charming woman, very talkative. She was once asked why, and she said, "I have to talk for two," because "Silent Cal" had the reputation of not talking very much, which was not a deserved reputation, by the way. . . . He met his wife when he was a lawyer. The story was that he was standing in the window of the house where he boarded, shaving himself, with a hat on his head. She looked up at the window, saw this strange apparition, and she laughed. He looked at her and he said later on, "I decided on first sight that I was going to marry this woman." She asked him after a while, "Why did you wear the hat?" He said, "To keep my hair out of my eyes. It kept on falling over, so when I shave, I put on this hat."

He courted her for a while. Her parents didn't particularly care for him, but they married and had a very happy marriage. She was considered to be an activist First Lady, but compared to Eleanor Roosevelt, she was not. The Girl Scouts were an important thing for her. She had a wonderful sense of humor. She was a charming, attractive person. Coolidge, who was not very demonstrative in public, except with his father, loved to go shopping for clothing for her. He bought her hats, things like that.

[Grace Coolidge secretly smoked.] Coolidge also smoked—cigars, but he did not want to smoke cigars in public. It sets a bad example, he said. Prohibition began after World War I and lasted through the twenties. All three Republican presidents didn't like it. Harding drank. Coolidge did not. Harding served liquor in the White House, but Coolidge would never do this [even though] he disapproved of Prohibition. Coolidge, if he were around today— and it's hard to say what he would be like—would probably be a member of the Libertarian wing of the Republican party: Don't interfere with people's private lives. Leave them alone. Let them have privacy. He said, "It's the law and the law says we have to have Prohibition. I'm here to enforce the law so I'll enforce the law," which is what he did.

One of the important developments during Coolidge's administration was the war [the United States] did not get into. Mexico had a revolution. They were nationalizing properties, including American properties. There was a conflict with the Church, and there were some Americans who felt we should intervene. Remember, we had intervened under Wilson, and we had the Mexican

War. . . . When Cuba became communist ninety miles off our border, there's Mexico, looking as though it's becoming communist [too]. This is the period right after the great Red Scare of the 1920 period.

Secretary of State Kellogg was talking war, and Coolidge did not want this. . . . Coolidge called an old college chum of his, Dwight Morrow, and said, "I want you to go to Mexico and become our ambassador." Morrow said, "Well, what are my instructions?" Coolidge said, "To keep us out of war with Mexico." That's exactly what happened.

Coolidge was one of the most graceful writers of the English language that we've had in the White House. His autobiography is 254 pages long. He wrote it in about six months. It is beautifully written. I read his book when I was in my twenties. I wasn't thinking about writing a Coolidge biography; I just picked it up. I was struck by how this man was a master of the language. Many of his speeches are this way. Teddy Roosevelt used the White House as a bully pulpit, everyone knows this. Coolidge did, also. He gave many speeches on morality, on ethics, on how we're responsible for each other. He was very much affected by a college teacher called Charles Garman, who was a transcendentalist. Coolidge was a religious person; not a churchgoer; he didn't belong to a church until he became president. He was a Congregationalist. But he would lecture the American people on how we have to be decent to each other. Those speeches on race relations, for example, are something. He went to [historically black] Howard University and delivered a commencement address, the first American president to do this. It was a speech on race relations.

He was [once] asked to get a black candidate in New York off the ballot, a Republican. He wrote back saying, "The black soldiers fought in the war for us, for all of us. There were no cases of desertion or anything like that. [They] have every right to be as much Americans as the rest of us."

He was called "Silent Cal" by reporters at the time. It wasn't because he didn't speak very much. He had two press conferences a week. He delivered more speeches per week, on average, than any president in American history. . . . The press loved him. He would ask for questions in advance, he'd read them off, he'd answer whatever questions he wanted to answer. . . . We have the transcripts. He was amazingly up on the issues. He knew quite a bit.

He wrote all his speeches himself. . . . Coolidge used the radio quite often to deliver speeches. He was voted in 1925 the fourth most popular radio personality. The first three were singers. Will Rogers came in seventh.

In one speech, he said, "Do the day's work." "If it be to protect the rights of the weak, whoever objects, do it. If it is to help a powerful corporation, do that. Expect to be called a 'stand patter,' but don't be a stand patter. Expect to be called a demagogue, but don't be a demagogue. Don't hesitate to be as revolutionary as science. Don't hesitate to be as reactionary as the multiplication table. Don't expect to build up the weak by pulling down the strong. Don't hurry to legislate. Give administration a chance to catch up with the legislation. We need a broader, firmer, deeper faith in the people, a faith that men desire to do right, that the commonwealth is founded upon a righteousness which will endure, a reconstructive faith that the final approval of the people is given not to demagogues slavishly pandering to their selfishness, merchandizing with the clamor of the hour, but to the statesmen ministering to their welfare, representing their deep silent, abiding conviction."

Coolidge made many speeches like this. The most famous speech [was in] 1925 before the newspaper editors, where he supposedly said, "The business of America is business." Well, the actual quote is, "The chief business of the American people is business." The headlines the next day said, "Coolidge calls for more spirituality in American life." They didn't mention, "The business of America is business" because he went on to say, "The chief ideal of the American people is idealism. And any newspaper which forgets this will not get very far. The American people are idealistic people." He gave many speeches in which he said that—"Riches didn't make the Declaration of Independence. The Declaration of Independence gave us the freedom to become wealthy."

One of Coolidge's neighbors in 1920, when they were talking about him running for the presidency, said, "Calvin Coolidge would probably make a very good president, but he won't be a very demanding president. He won't be a very exciting president." The reason is that Calvin Coolidge didn't take chances. If Calvin Coolidge had been a baseball player, he would have hit a lot of singles and he wouldn't have struck out very often. But he wouldn't have swung for the bleachers. He wouldn't have hit many home runs, because if you want to hit a home run, you have to take a chance on striking out. Mark Sullivan, the great journalist of the time, said, "Coolidge is the kind of person who climbs a ladder rung after rung. He won't take the next rung until his foot is secure on the bottom rung." This is the way he was.

Coolidge ran in 1924 . . . without making a single political speech, not one. Amazing. He dedicated dams; he would talk about Boy Scout things and Mother's Day and little things like that, but he didn't make political speeches— Coolidge would never mention his opponent's name in a speech, on any level, [even] when he was running for governor.

The [death] of his son, Calvin Jr. . . . was a very sad story. This was during the Democratic Convention in New York, in '24. Calvin [Jr.] was playing tennis, and he stubbed his toe, and it became infected. He was [sixteen] years old. He died, and Coolidge wrote in his autobiography that when he died, all the glory of the presidency went with him. Coolidge was dogged by death throughout his entire life. His mother died when he was a very young boy. He loved his mother. Then his sister died, his only sibling. People were always dying at critical points in Calvin Coolidge's life. When his father died, he was crushed.

I think [his son's death] had to have a large impact, especially [with his son being] so young and [dying] in such a strange way. . . . But he kept on working. . . . The Ku Klux Klan had a march in Washington that year, over 20,000 attendees. Coolidge was not in the White House, but a few weeks later he gave a talk on the subject, and he said, "We all came to America on different boats, but we're in the same boat now, and we have to learn to get along with each other." He was a very strong person on civil rights. So, he kept on working, despite the death of his son.

[He didn't run for a second term for] several reasons. One reason was the death of his son. The second was that if he ran and won—and he probably would have won—he would have been in the White House longer than any person in American history. He didn't think that was right. He had done everything he had set out to do. The country was in fine shape; there were no crises. So he decided to step down.

It was the anniversary of his having become president, and he had his press conference. He said, "Come back in the afternoon. I'll have more for you." When the reporters came back, he gave each one a slip saying, "I do not choose to run for the presidency in 1928." There was a stampede to the telephones, and later on, his host told Grace Coolidge, "Boy, he sure gave us a surprise, didn't he?" And she said, "What are you talking about?" He said, "Well, he decided he's not going to run for the presidency." Grace said, "Oh, my God, he never told me." It created a furor.

[After] he left the White House, he did a lot of writing and made a lot of money. . . . He wrote his memoirs. He wrote magazine articles. He wrote a newspaper column for about a year. It wasn't very good. He was asked to write a dedication—a five-hundred-word dedication, the history of the United States for the Mount Rushmore memorial. There's a *Liberty* magazine cartoon showing Coolidge sitting there thinking, and saying, "Calvin Coolidge is asked to write a 500-word history of the United States, and he's trying to think up 200 words of padding."

[Journalist] H. L. Mencken didn't like many people in politics. He had nothing good to say about anyone. He had some bad things to say about Calvin Coolidge, except for one thing when Coolidge was alive. He said, "He writes English beautifully." For Mencken, that was quite a statement. Then when Coolidge died [in January of 1933], he said that Coolidge came between two presidents whom Mencken didn't particularly care for, but he was a man of solid credentials and Jeffersonian principles. If ever we get to the point where once again we want Jeffersonian principles alive in our republic, perhaps we will give Calvin Coolidge his due.

Will Rogers

BEN YAGODA

Will Rogers was a plain-speaking humorist who became so popular that many people wanted him to run for president. By the end of his life (1879–1935), Will Rogers was an American folk hero. Author Ben Yagoda published Will Rogers: A Biography *in 1993 (Knopf) and appeared on* Booknotes *on September 25, 1994, to discuss his book.*

WHEN HE DIED IN 1935, Will Rogers was described by Joe Robinson, the majority leader of the Senate, as "America's most famous private citizen and probably its most beloved private citizen." This was one of the things that struck me when I started doing research for this book—how incredibly famous and popular he was at the time, and how today, especially before the Broadway musical *Will Rogers Follies* was such a success, he was more or less forgotten. . . .

I didn't know much about him at all. Until I started the book it was sort of a name, an image of somebody throwing a rope or a lariat and his two famous quotations: "I never met a man I didn't like" and "All I know is what I read in the papers." That was it. . . .

Will Rogers did many things—the movies, the column, the radio. There were no ratings then, but he had a weekly show in the early 1930s that was probably the second-highest rated show after *Amos 'n' Andy* in the country. It was on Sundays, and churches reported downturns in attendance when he was on. The other thing he did, and sort of pioneered, in the late 1920s, was the lecture circuit. He went on a one-man show around the country. It's more common today. . . . He would go to six or seven cities a week and do a show. He'd just sit on the stage. Well, he'd start off standing. The show would be two and a half, three hours long, and at the end, he'd just be sitting on the edge of the stage dangling his legs and say, "Go on home, I'm sick of looking at you," to the audience.

He was funny. He was humane. He was never mean-spirited, never bitter. He could be pointed and sharp, but the reason why he was so beloved was that his basic humaneness came through everything he wrote.

WILL ROGERS, IN HIS COLUMN, had become an extremely important political voice in the country. There was an article written at the time wherein a Washington politician was quoted as saying, "We could never have another war in this country unless Will Rogers is for it." He was humorous, but he was also serious. He was both.

There's no real parallel today I can think of. People like Molly Ivins are somewhat close. He said things in a humorous way, but he had a very strong point of view. He was read by 40 million people every day. They would pick up the newspaper at the breakfast table and read what Will Rogers had to say. A lot of people didn't know what they thought about an issue until they read Will Rogers.

In 1928, the old humor magazine *Life*—not the picture magazine, this was a humor magazine—had run "Will Rogers for President." It was a joke. . . . The funny thing was that many people didn't take it as a joke. [Industrialist] Henry Ford for one, who was a friend of Rogers, wrote in to say, "Hey, let's take this seriously. Rogers would be much better than who we have in the White House now." . . .

People started saying, "Why not Will Rogers?" He was a humanitarian. He'd gone on relief tours to help people suffering from drought. Several newspapers put him up as a candidate. The governor of Texas endorsed him. Some Democratic groups in various states said, "He's our candidate, too." There was a real groundswell of support, so much so that Franklin D. Roosevelt, who was the front-runner for the Democratic nomination [and] . . . a longtime friend of Will Rogers, wrote him a letter, in essence saying, "Don't run. You're a lifelong Democrat." "Don't do anything to make the donkey chase his own tail" was the way he put it. He didn't say in so many words "Don't run," but the meaning was clear.

He really didn't have to worry. Rogers never gave any serious thought to [running for president]. He valued his freedom. He was making close to a half million dollars a year from his column and from his movies. He was also the biggest movie star in Hollywood in 1933. He was voted the number-one box office attraction in the country by the nation's theater owners. The president at that time made much, much less than that. . . . And he just knew, he was wise enough and smart enough to know, that he wasn't cut out to be a politician. . . .

WHEN HE TOURED EUROPE in 1926, he had a meeting with Italian dictator Benito Mussolini. Even then Mussolini was a controversial character [although] it wasn't as clear that he was a force for evil in the world as it later became. He had usurped powers and was on his way to becoming a dictator.

[There] is a photograph that Mussolini inscribed to Will Rogers. It's of Mussolini horseback riding, jumping over a bar. It says "*Al Senor Rogers*," to Senor Rogers, "*complimente*," compliments of Mussolini, "28th Maggio," of May 1926. To my mind, one of Rogers's weak spots was that he had a liking for dictators. He had one quote to the effect that as long as the dictator makes the right decision, there's nothing wrong with him. To our ears today, that sounds really off the mark. I think that was a legitimate criticism of Rogers. One of the reasons he liked FDR so much was his strong presidency. He tried to take powers away from Congress. Rogers liked that. He just didn't like Congress. He didn't like the endless posturing debates back and forth.

A lot of his criticisms were well taken. But as a commentator, he often went back and forth between wanting to be taken seriously [and being taken lightly]. [He'd] take positions on issues of the day and [then] almost retreating into comedy, make statements tantamount to "Well, just kidding." He never wanted to go out on a limb—except in rare instances. One of them was when the Depression happened. He was so outraged by [the Depression] that he felt government should take action. For the most part, he would often retreat to comedy. His comments about dictators, about Mussolini, are an example of where he didn't really want to follow through. He wanted that safety net of being a comedian and a humorist.

HE SENT THIS [telegram] several weeks after [Franklin] Roosevelt won in a landslide and Roosevelt was at Warm Springs, Georgia, where he went for the healing waters for his polio . . .

> I diden't wire you on your election because I knew you wasen't reading any of em anyhow. Now that all the folks that want something are about through congratulating you, I thought maby a wire just wishing you could do something for the country when you get in, and not wishing anything for me, well, I thought the novelty of a wire like that when it was backed up by the facts might not be unwelcome. Your health is the main thing. Don't worry too much. A smile in the White House again—by the way, when was the last one—why it will look like a meal to us. It's the biggest job in the world but you got the most help in the world to assist you.
>
> Pick you some good men. Make em responsible for their end. If Europe don't pay up [and that was about the debts from World War I that were still owed to us by European nations] well, fire your sectry of the treasurer and get one that will make em pay. If people are starving and your granaries are full, thats your secretary of Agriculture's business is to feed them, too. If Nicaragua [even then a hot spot]—Nicaragua wants to hold an election, send em your best wishes but no Marines.
>
> Disarm with the rest of the world but not without it. And kid Congress and the Senate; don't scold them. They're just children thats never grown

up. They don't like to be corrected in company. Don't send messages to em, send candy. Let your secretary of State burn up the notes that come from Europe. Dont you have to attend to a little thing like that. Europe's not going to do what they've threatened to do. All those things are just something to give diplomates an excuse for existing. Keep off the radio until you've got something to say, even if it's a year.

Be good to the press boys in Washington, for they're getting those merry-go-rounds every few weeks now. Stay off of that back lawn with your photographers unless you got a Helen Wills [the tennis star] or your fifth cousin, Alice Roosevelt Longworth. Nothing will kill off interest in a president quicker than weeklies with chambers of commerces and women's political organizations.

Now, if some guy comes running into your office telling you what Wall Street was doing that day, tell him, "Wall Street? Why there's 115 million of my subjects that dont know if Wall Street is a thoroughfare or a new mouthwash. Its happenings don't interest me." Why, Governor, you can go in there and have a good time. We want our President to have some fun. Too many of our presidents mistake the appointment as being to the Vatican and not to just another American home.

THERE WERE RUMORS that spread when Rogers was around that he really had an Oxford education and was just putting on that cowboy pose. Not true. He never graduated from high school. His father, who, as I said, was a wealthy rancher, sent him to very good schools, but Will never got along with school. He left before graduation in high school to become a cowboy in Texas. He didn't have a lot of learning, never mastered punctuation, capitalization, spelling, anything. Early in his writing career, copy editors would clean up that stuff, put in the correct spelling and correct punctuation, until wisely his editor said, "No, don't do that. That's part of what makes Will, Will." So it was not a put-on. Later in his life he got so fed up with capitalization that he got a typewriter that had only capital letters on it, so the question of a capital or a lowercase letter would never come up. But it wasn't an act. That was him.

ONE OF THE THINGS that drove his life at the time was he wrote a daily column that [appeared] in four hundred newspapers around the country, including the front page of the second section of *The New York Times*. He was the first signed columnist *The Times* had, and its only columnist for a long time. He wrote a daily column of a few paragraphs and then a weekly column, a much longer piece. He had a need to fill that with material. There was only so much that he could generate out of his head, so he would go on trips. He loved to travel, but part of the reason to go on trips was just to gain material for his column.

Wiley Post was trying to explore possible air links between the U.S., Alaska, and Siberia for air-mail routes. He needing funding for his trip. Will Rogers was very rich, had plenty of money, loved aviation. It seemed like a perfect match. He'd always wanted to see Alaska. So they went up there, and they toured the future state, for some weeks. Then finally they were going, only to gather material for Will's column, to Point Barrow, which is the northernmost point in the Western Hemisphere. There was a man there, an old trader and trapper who Will thought would be great material.

They took off from Fairbanks. Then Wiley got lost. It was a cloudy day. He couldn't spot the coast where they were. They landed beside a lagoon that was only a few miles away from Point Barrow. They found an Eskimo there [who] . . . gave them directions to Point Barrow. They took off, and after the plane took off, it immediately turned around and crashed, killing both men instantly.

HE WAS SUCH A REMARKABLE person . . . he did so many things. . . . Times have changed so much. The 1920s and 1930s were the last time when someone could adopt that many roles. Occasionally [today] you might [have a star who can] cross over to another medium, but society is fragmented today. . . . [For example,] Michael Jackson is the king of pop, but Rogers was the king of movies, the king of newspapers, the king of radio, the king of the lecture tour, the king of politics.

Albert Einstein

---

by
DENIS BRIAN

*Albert Einstein (1879–1955), who was born in Ulm, Germany, became rec-
ognized as one of the world's great thinkers when he developed the Special
Theory of Relativity in 1905. For twenty years, author Denis Brian researched the Einstein archives; the result was* Einstein: A Life, *published by
John Wiley and Sons in 1996. Denis Brian appeared on* Booknotes *on August 4, 1996.*

I DEVOTED A CHAPTER to Einstein's brain. It was such shocking news when
I found out that somebody got his brain. It was exactly what he didn't want to
happen. He told everyone that he didn't want any physical part of him to remain. He didn't want any memorials made to him. He didn't want his home
made into a memorial. When I heard somebody had his brain and they were
slicing it up to find out clues to his genius, I thought that this is perhaps the
worst thing that could have ever happened to this man.

Several scientists have it. The man who took the brain has most of it. A Japanese scientist has some, and there's a doctor in Philadelphia who has other
parts of it. The conclusion is that it's absolutely ridiculous to search for genius
in the brain. All they can say about it is it was remarkably healthy for a man
his age.

The man who did the autopsy took it. . . . He purportedly asked Hans Albert, Einstein's son, if he could have the brain for medical reasons, for research.
He was given permission as long as there was no publicity about it. Immediately there was publicity in *The New York Times,* saying the brain was available.
The man was at Princeton at the time, and he stored it in his basement. When
he divorced his wife, he left the brain with her for a time. She was very angry
about it, saying things like, "I wish they'd get this damn thing out of here."
Thomas Harvey was his name, from Wichita, Kansas. . . . He says that he may
give this brain to the Hebrew University if they ask for it.

The man who had been his eye doctor in Princeton somehow appeared at
the autopsy, asked if he could take the eyes, and was given permission. He has

stored them in a bank vault ever since, and he says he's done it for his venera-
tion for Einstein, not for any scientific purposes.

ALBERT EINSTEIN WAS AN EXTRAORDINARY MAN who had a tremendously
hard life as a young man. When he finished college, he almost starved because
he couldn't get a job. He had antagonized his professors at the Zurich Polytechnic, and he was the only one of his colleagues who didn't get a job at that
college. The problem was he didn't know how to handle authority. He treated
the professors in the same pleasant, easygoing way that he treated the cleaning
women, and the professors in those days in Germany expected to be treated
like minor royalty. They said he knew it all, he wouldn't listen to them. He
missed all the lectures that didn't interest him, such as math. The math professor said he was "a lazy dog"—his summing up of Einstein. But to his friends,
he was intriguing, dynamic, spontaneous. One, a man called Marcel Grossmann, who knew him at college only in these early days, went home to his parents and said, "I've met a man who one day is going to be a very great man." It
was an incredible prophecy when everybody else was saying, "He's a lazy dog.
He's not going to make it."

HE WAS ABSOLUTELY BRILLIANT. [Before I did this book] my knowledge of
physics was practically nonexistent. I read up on physics, and I interviewed
Nobel Prize–winning physicists. All of the people I spoke with before I did this
book—every one of them said there was nobody that could match Einstein for
brain power.

I got interested in doing a biography of Einstein in 1972. I telephoned his
secretary, Helen Dukas, about something entirely different, and she began to
talk about a séance that Einstein had attended in California in 1931 with his
friend [writer] Upton Sinclair, who was very interested in psychic phenomena.
At this séance, she was scared out of her wits. She was sitting in an adjoining
room where the séance was taking place, and there was suddenly a ring at the
door; she thought it was a spirit appearing. It was actually somebody with a letter. Nothing happened at the séance and the people organizing it, including
Upton Sinclair, gave the usual answer, "There are unfriendly spirits in the circle." One of the unfriendliest would have been Einstein, who was a complete
rationalist, who said, "Even if I saw a ghost, I wouldn't believe it." But strangely
enough, he believed that telepathy might be possible.

Helen Dukas became his secretary in 1928. She was scared out of her wits
when it was suggested she should be his secretary, because, like me, she knew
nothing about physics. But she was persuaded to go and see him. He was very
ill at the time. He was in bed. He had a very badly strained heart. She was taken
upstairs by his wife—his second wife, Elsa, who was also his cousin. Einstein
immediately put her completely at ease with a few soft jokes.

Miss Dukas became absolutely tough in defending him, a real watchdog. She scared people off—strangers who tried to see him and badger him. She devoted her life absolutely to him. After his wife Elsa died in 1936, she was his housekeeper.

HE WAS NOMINATED for a Nobel Prize on eight occasions over eleven years. It took so long for him to get one because the judges didn't understand relativity. It had not been experimentally proved until after World War I, when [British astronomer Arthur] Eddington did an experiment proving it to be accurate. Also there was a definite anti-Semitic tinge in the people who voted. One man was a very close friend of Hermann Göring's and [Einstein was] Jewish and very pro-Jewish. . . . In fact, when they gave him the prize in 1922, it was for the photoelectric effect, another of his discoveries, which today we make use of in automatic opening doors—the electric eye, we call it.

THE THEORY OF RELATIVITY has many aspects to it. . . . E = mc^2 [is] the most dramatic part of it, which means that in everything physical in the world, there is tremendous energy that can be released. Everything can be transformed into energy. Energy equals mass times the speed of light squared. The result of that is the atomic bomb when the atom was split and the chain reaction took place. Einstein didn't know it could be done at the time. But the equation proved what was there.

It also has a lot to do with the movement of planets and speed of planets in space. Up until then Newton and everyone else believed there was an invisible ether that pervaded the entire universe, and that everything in it, all planets, the speed of them, should be judged against that ether. It's as if you imagine the ocean. Under the ocean there are submarines and swimmers and everything, and their movements and speed is judged against the ocean. Einstein said, "Let's forget about the ether." It doesn't exist, in fact. "Everything should be judged relatively to each other, one planet against another. It's all relative."

One other thing about the Special Theory of Relativity that's very important is that no two events can be described as simultaneous or happening at the same time except in your own environment. The extension of that is that events happening—stars moving, for example—they're millions of miles away from us, millions of light years away from us. If you want to calculate what's happening there, you've got to take into account the space that's traveled and the time it takes.

When this theory was propounded by Albert Einstein he was twenty-six. Four or five of his tremendous theories came out all in the same year, all almost in the same month, when he was twenty-six years old.

His formula showed that the atomic bomb was possible. But it would only have been possible if the atom could be split; it wasn't for another twenty-five years.

HE WAS BORN IN A LITTLE CITY called Ulm, in southern Germany. Then he moved with his family to Munich. His father was an electrical engineer, and he didn't do very well in Ulm, so he moved to Munich, which was an up-and-coming city. He lived there till he was fifteen, when his family all moved to a place near Milan where there was more opportunity for electrical engineering. Einstein was left in school [in Munich] at fifteen. He hated it—hated being left by his family—and wasn't doing well at school, wasn't getting on well with the teachers or the students. He persuaded a doctor to say that he would have a nervous breakdown if he wasn't allowed to leave and join his family.

He was also in Switzerland for quite a long time. He took an exam for Zurich Polytechnic and failed it, to his relatives' amazement, because by that time he was considered a potential genius. He was brilliant at mathematics but he'd taken it a year or so younger than the average age. He had done so well at mathematics, they said, "If you graduate from high school . . . you can come straight in without retaking the exam."

He went to a high school in Switzerland where he absolutely had a marvelous time. He fell in love for the first time with his teacher's daughter. He lived in the house with a teacher and the teacher's children. He did very well. He became a terribly enthusiastic violin player. Then he went from there to Zurich—went to the polytechnic for four years, graduated, fell in love again, [this time] with the woman he married, Mileva Maric, and then they moved to Bern. He lived in Bern for a while.

Mileva Maric was pregnant before they got married with a little girl who was born in Serbia. She went home to have the baby. . . . It's assumed that friends of the Einsteins had her adopted, but the fate of this girl is a complete mystery. Various people have tried to find out. I don't know if they call them illegitimate today, but she was born before [the marriage]. The extraordinary thing is Einstein was looking forward to the birth of this child very much, talking about seeing it when it came back. But there are all sorts of reasons why it would have been terribly difficult for them to have had the child with them then.

When they moved to Bern, after he couldn't get a job and almost starved, he started a little academy of his own, teaching two friends. He made lifelong friends tutoring. Mileva also did a little tutoring. . . . Then, through this friend, Marcel Grossmann, he got a job in the patent office in Bern. What he had to do was look at the patents that people sent in and their descriptions of the patents and clarify them, simplify them, see if they worked, and recommend whether they should be considered. It was a great help to him, because it focused him very much on being succinct about describing things and looking immediately for flaws.

After about seven years in the patent office in which he was doing fairly well, he was promoted. They thought very highly of him. He got a chance to be a lecturer in a Bern university; a professor [there] had taken a great interest in him. He was a very poor lecturer to start with. Then he got his Ph.D. at the University of Zurich. And from the University of Zurich, where he taught, too, he went to Prague University.

He first came to the United States in 1921. He came with Chaim Weizmann to raise funds for a Hebrew university, and they did a lightning tour of all the major cities. His next visit to America was in 1931, when he went to California. He went to the University of California, to Caltech. It was from Caltech, where he went a few years running in the 1930s, that somebody wanted him for what was to be the Institute for Advanced Study in Princeton, a new organization. He went to Princeton in 1933, when Hitler and the Nazis had declared him public enemy number one, and there was a price on his head.

He was hated by the Nazis because he was almost regarded as the representative of Jews in Germany, the representative of Jewish intellectuals. And he spoke out against the Nazis. When they put a price on his head and people threatened to kill him . . . his wife begged him to stop talking out against the Nazis, to keep quiet, his life was in danger. He refused to keep quiet. He said, "I wouldn't be Einstein if I kept quiet." He was a very courageous man.

When Einstein heard through secret information through Switzerland that the Germans were probably working to create an atom bomb, he realized they could win the war and destroy civilization. He was persuaded by Leo Szilard, a former student of his, also a brilliant physicist, and Eugene Wigner, another physicist, to write a letter to President Roosevelt, warning him that the Germans were not allowing uranium to be sent out of Czechoslovakia; that there was very good information an atom bomb was in the works; and that he should get onto it for the Americans.

He renounced his German citizenship and for a time was a citizen of no nationality. Then he got Swiss nationality. And eventually, in 1940, he became an American citizen.

His interest in [his appearance] was absolutely nil, including his long hair. He tried to simplify everything. . . . Einstein used to shave only with water, and it was very painful. [A doctor friend, Thomas] Bucky gave him some shaving soap one time—introduced him to it. Einstein used it, said it was marvelous, and then went back to water again because it was just simpler.

I've heard his voice on radio and also in documentary films of him. It's a very quiet, gentle, slow, musical voice, which is an incredible contrast from this dynamic young man. . . . A German accent always, with things like "I tink I will a little study" and "She is a very good theory."

Einstein was a great laugher. He laughed at almost any joke anyone told him, even if he'd heard it several times, people said, because he was so kind and didn't want to hurt people.

He was about five foot six. In later years he was a bit heavy, but he had quite a good physique . . . in good shape, quite muscular. He loved rowing.

Never drove a car, but loved [piloting] his simple little boat. I don't think he had any protection, any floating device, and would drive it daringly at other boats and just swerve aside at the last moment. He loved sailing. He loved playing his violin. There was this spontaneity in him as a young man. Once, he was told somebody in an attic was playing Mozart on a piano. He didn't know who it was, but he broke into the house, ran up, said "Keep playing." He had his violin with him, and he finished this piece with this old woman.

HE WAS MARRIED TO MILEVA from about 1900 to 1918, about seventeen years. [They had] two boys. In their young days, he was an adoring father. They adored him. He was very playful with them, and they found him fascinating. He was very interested in their upbringing. But when the divorce happened, he remained in Berlin, and she went back to Switzerland . . . and they remained with her pretty well for the rest of their lives until they grew up. The youngest boy went into a mental asylum as a schizophrenic. The eldest boy came over to America and became quite a prominent engineer.

Einstein began to have an affair with his second wife during World War I. He was very unhappy with Mileva. Whatever happened to the first baby girl caused his first wife to be terribly miserable and depressed. . . . And then he became interested in his cousin, Elsa. . . . He was very ill in World War I because of the diet they had in Germany, and she helped save his life. They became very close and friendly, and then they married. . . . That marriage lasted until she died in 1936. She came to Princeton with him.

He never remarried. He had many offers of marriage . . . mostly in the mail. He was very fond of women. He had the almost typical view of men in those days that women were not as bright as men. In one rather embarrassing interview, he said that "in women, God may have created a sex without brains." . . . But, he must have found out quite differently when he met his first wife, Mileva, who was studying physics at Zurich Polytechnic with him. So over the years, he [developed] a greater, higher view of women.

HE WAS A TREMENDOUS PACIFIST until the Nazis came to power, and also during the Spanish Civil War, when he realized that the democracy was completely at stake. Then he was a realist, and he disappointed pacifists by saying, "The democracies have to rearm to survive," and when Israel was threatened, saying, "Obviously, a small country has a right to defend itself."

He was a tremendous liberal. He belonged to the Social Democratic party.

In Germany, the strongest platform they had was social justice for all and that the major industries should be either owned by the government or controlled by the government. Because he was a liberal during the McCarthy era and the cold war, and because he saw the Soviet side of things against the American side of things, people thought he was a Communist. But he was the farthest thing from a Communist. He hated tyrannies of any kind. He hated the Stalin regime. But he would argue that the Americans were making mistakes, too.

The FBI had a 1,600-page file on Albert Einstein. Almost all garbage. They would take anything that came, often from lunatics or anonymous people writing from anywhere, accusing him of working on a death ray, of a plan to take over Hollywood and make it the movie capital for Communists. . . . Hoover himself seemed scared all his life to interview Einstein, because of influential friends. And when they couldn't get to Einstein or find anything about him . . . they started investigating Helen Dukas and looking at all her outgoing mail and incoming mail and doing tests on all the letters. It was absolute nonsense because they were the most innocent people in the world, the most democratic people in the world.

HE WAS OFFERED THE PRESIDENCY of Israel in 1948, when Israel became [a nation, but] he was very ill. He said that it was not a job he could do, really dealing with people. Yet despite the fact that he claimed to be a man who loved to be alone, he had more close friends than anyone I know about and communicated with more people.

He died in 1955 at seventy-six. I think I would have loved him. This is a motive for writing biographies—[to get to know] people you would like to have known very much.

H. L. Mencken

by
CHARLES A. FECHER

H. L. Mencken (1880–1956) was a Baltimore-born journalist who co-founded The American Mercury *magazine. Charles A. Fecher came to our studios on January 28, 1990, to discuss the never-before-published entries he collected in* The Diary of H. L. Mencken, *published in 1989 by Knopf.*

H. L. MENCKEN WAS A NEWSPAPERMAN, magazine editor, author, philologist, and critic of the national mores from about the turn of the century, 1900, up until the time of his death in 1956. He reached the peak of his reputation in the 1920s and 1930s, when Walter Lippmann called him the most powerful person of influence on this whole generation of educated people. *The New York Times* called him the most powerful private citizen in America.

Mencken wrote a series of articles for the Baltimore *Evening Sun* that were known as the Monday Articles. They appeared on the editorial page of the *Evening Sun* every Monday from 1920 until 1938.

No other man in American literature has ever written like him. The style is utterly unique. He's one of the great humorists in American literature. There are passages by him that you can't read without bursting into guffaws. Style is only one aspect of a writer's equipment. He must also have ideas to express. And Mencken did. The range of his interests and activities was enormous. He wrote about politics, literature, civic affairs, politicians—mostly, I would say, politicians. He didn't like any of them. He said that a good politician is as unthinkable as an honest burglar.

He commented from a conservative point of view. If you could reduce his political philosophy to a sentence or two, he was in total agreement with Thomas Jefferson that the best form of government is that which governs the least. Mencken thought that government had no business whatever intruding into the lives of its people. The government existed for two things: to repel foreign invaders and to maintain domestic order and tranquility. This was the source of his hatred of Franklin D. Roosevelt, who came along and created the CCC, the NRA, the NLRB and all these other government agencies, the Social

Security Act, welfare, and so on. All of this, to Mencken, was anathema because he didn't believe that government had any business in such areas.

WHEN MENCKEN DIED, he left his diary, along with a mass of other papers, to the Enoch Pratt Free Library in Baltimore. . . . The diary and some other papers were given to them with the stipulation that they could not be opened until twenty-five years after his death. The twenty-fifth anniversary of his death was in January of 1981. It wasn't until a number of years after that that the library decided to publish the diary.

The diaries are much rougher [than his published works]. They don't have the finished, polished style of the published books. They don't have the high humor of the published books. This is not to say that they're serious or somber in tone; they're not. It was impossible for him to write anything somber. But he was complaining about his health, which he did constantly. . . . [He was a hypochondriac,] one of the worst in the world.

There's no doubt that in later years, [his health] declined. He was a candidate for high blood pressure and a stroke. It was a stroke that eventually finished his career. I don't know how much of the complaining about his health in the diary was genuine and how much was just hypochondria.

His diary reveals a strain of anti-Semitism, of racism, of what the media has called bigotry. It reveals a pro-German sympathy. None of this was entirely new. Anyone who was familiar with Mencken's work would have known that those things were in there. It's simply that in the diary, they are stated more strongly and starkly than they ever were in what he published during his own lifetime.

I can't pretend to explain it. There was unquestionably an overt, or I should say a covert, anti-Semitism in the air and culture of that time. It wasn't the kind of psychotic and murderous anti-Semitism that occurred in Germany with the rise of the Nazis. It was a more quiet thing.

Mencken's whole background and culture was German. Three of his four grandparents were German. His father and mother were German. In those days, a great deal of the Baltimore population was German. He grew up absorbing German ideas and German culture. The Germany that he loved—and an important distinction has to be made here—was the Germany of Bach, Beethoven, Schubert, Brahms, German beer. It was hard for him to feel—both in World War I and again in World War II—any strong anti-German sentiments.

At the same time, I think it would be wrong to say he was pro-Nazi. Nothing in his writings gives the slightest indication that he approved of what Hitler was doing in Germany. It has to be admitted he never wrote anything against it. He should have, of course. Why he didn't is a mystery. . . . No one who knew him has ever been able to explain [why].

Mencken was, above all else, a newspaperman. He was probably the greatest journalist this country has ever seen. . . . The fact is not changed because the diary reveals some disagreeable aspects of his personality. It reveals his weaknesses as well as his strengths.

HE WROTE WITH A BLUDGEON. He hurled thunderbolts at everybody. But according to everybody who ever knew him, he was one of the kindest, most courteous, most gentle, and most considerate persons you could imagine.

He was only married once, at the age of fifty in 1930. [He was married for] five years. He had met her seven years before they got married, and there's no doubt that he was deeply and romantically smitten by her from the very beginning. There was an eighteen-year age difference between them. When they married, he was fifty and she was thirty-two. His wife was in poor health; she had a number of serious operations over the time that he knew her. When he married her, the doctors told him that she did not have more than three years to live. Actually, she lived five. He said in the diary that they were the five happiest and most fulfilling years of his life. There's no doubt that her death left a tremendous void in his life. Not all of his activities ever sufficed to fill that up. His wife was a beautiful, charming, intelligent woman. He wrote so often of how much he missed her, that hardly a day went by that he didn't think of her. Every day, he thought of something he wanted to tell her or saw something he wanted to buy for her.

HE WAS AN INCURABLE CONSERVATIVE and Tory. I suppose a number of reasons would have contributed to it—his solid Germanic background, the flavor and atmosphere and culture of Baltimore in that period, the fact that his father owned a business, which he wanted Henry to succeed him in. His father was, in at least a modest sense of the word, a capitalist. Mencken believed in the virtues of capitalism and bourgeois values very much.

He was one of those very rare creatures, a financially successful author. He did not get the kind of advances on his books that you get on some books today. He didn't believe in advances; he never took one. He took his royalties when the book had been published and was selling, but he never took an advance in his life.

[HE EDITED *THE AMERICAN MERCURY* MAGAZINE.] It was primarily devoted to political and social commentary, some literary criticism and some fiction and poetry. . . . It dealt with the social, political, economic problems of that era, and many people, many writers contributed to it. It has been said that it was a one-man magazine, which it was really. It reflected Mencken's personality. Anybody whose ideas differed from Mencken's wouldn't have much chance of getting published in it. It was even said that Mencken rewrote the articles that were contributed to it so that they would reflect his views. He himself denied this, and I believe that his denial was sincere.

Mencken published black writers in *The American Mercury* at a time when there were very few markets for the work of black writers. He encouraged his publisher, Alfred Knopf, to bring out their books. He played a very important part—an inspirational part—in the Harlem Renaissance of the 1920s. He knew and was on friendly terms with and corresponded with many important black people of that period. He and his brother had two black women who cooked and cleaned for them. He was very fond of them, took the most complete care of them. He paid their medical bills if they got sick. Here you have what I call egalitarianism. But at the same time, there's no question that he thought that black people were inferior to white. In speaking of these two black women who worked for him, he speaks of their belonging to the Afro-American race and bearing many of its psychological stigmata.

"It is impossible," he held, "to talk about anything resembling discretion or judgment in a colored woman. They are all essentially childlike, and even hard experience does not teach them anything." Now are you going to ask me to explain the paradox here? I can't. . . . He was a complex and contradictory person.

There are indications of anti-Semitism and of his feelings about black people scattered here and there in his published writings. I think that most of us—I was one of them—just skimmed over this and ignored it and did not let it get in the way of our admiration for him.

THERE'S NO QUESTION that he became very crotchety and stubborn and set in his ways [as he grew older]. He must not have been an easy person to get along with. He was one of the great humorists of the time, in person as well as in print. For the most part, I don't think he ever lost his good humor or his ability to relate to people and his generosity and politeness to them. But he did become set in his ways. There were certain things that he believed, and the rest of the world believed otherwise, which meant that the rest of the world was wrong and he was right.

My own fear, when the book hit the stands and all the hullabaloo started, was that it might permanently damage his reputation. Now I'm not so sure. I believe that he will survive in spite of the new material that's coming out about him. I say that because *The American Language* [his book on American English], for example, is still one of the greatest works of scholarship of our time. His three-volume autobiography, the *Days* books, still makes the most delightful reading you can imagine. He remains one of the most important and influential critics in the first half of this century.

Franklin Delano Roosevelt

---

by
DORIS KEARNS GOODWIN

In 1994, Simon and Schuster published historian Doris Kearns Goodwin's book on the Roosevelts, No Ordinary Time: Franklin and Eleanor Roosevelt: The Home Front in World War II, *which examines the life of Franklin Delano Roosevelt (1882–1945), our thirty-second and longest-serving president. She discussed her work on* Booknotes *on January 1, 1995.*

I CAME TO AN UNDERSTANDING that these two characters [Eleanor and Franklin Roosevelt] both needed other people to meet the untended needs that were left over as a result of their troubled marriage. What I came upon was a sense that the second family quarters of the White House were really like a residential hotel during these years. There were about seven people living there, all of whom were intimate friends of either Franklin or Eleanor's.

Harry Hopkins had been Roosevelt's chief New Deal man, in a certain sense. During the 1930s he was the head of the Works Progress Administration. He had been a social worker originally. When the war broke out in Europe, in May of 1940, Hopkins was staying overnight that night at the White House, and Roosevelt decided that he wanted him nearby. He didn't want him to go home; he needed somebody that he could talk to first thing in the morning, talk to late at night. He made Hopkins his chief adviser on foreign policy. Hopkins went to see Churchill before Roosevelt met him, went to see Stalin before Roosevelt met him. It was unprecedented. He makes Henry Kissinger look like a mild-mannered guy in terms of the kind of power that Hopkins had. And he was incredibly loyal to Roosevelt.

WINSTON CHURCHILL WAS AN INCREDIBLE CHARACTER during this period. He would come and stay for three or four weeks at a time. His habits were so exhausting that nobody else could sleep during the period of time he was there. He would awaken in the morning and have wine for breakfast. He would have scotch and soda for lunch; he would have brandy at night, smoking his cigars until 2:00 A.M. When he would finally leave, after being in the suite for three or four weeks, the entire White House staff would have to sleep for seventy-two hours to recuperate from Churchill's visits.

THE PERSON THAT I'M INTERESTED IN with Franklin is not simply Lucy Mercer. Everybody assumes she was the central romantic figure in his life because she had an affair with him back in 1918, [which] almost broke up his marriage. There was another woman that had an even more central role to play in his life, and that was his secretary, Missy LeHand. She had started working for him when she was only twenty years old, in 1920. She loved him all the rest of her life. She never married, and everybody in Washington knew that she was really his other wife. When Eleanor traveled, which she did 200 or 250 days a year, she was the one who took care of Roosevelt. If he had a cold, she'd bring the cough medicine to the White House. If he were grumpy during the day, she'd arrange a poker game at night. He had this cocktail hour every night, and somehow she'd be the one to be his hostess. She really was, on a daily basis, the closest person in the world to him. That's the relationship I'd like to know more about.

In the middle of the war, after Eleanor rejected Franklin's request to stay home and be his wife again, he got so lonely that he asked their daughter Anna to come and take Missy LeHand's place. Missy, by that point, even though she was only in her early forties, had had a stroke, and she could never speak again. It was one of those devastating things for Roosevelt during the war years. What happened is, in some way [Anna] became her father's daughter. She had long legs, she was tall, she loved cocktails, she could gossip at night with him—all the things that Eleanor never found it easy to do, Anna did. After a while, Eleanor began to feel displaced by her own daughter, so it was a very complicated set of relationships that developed during this time.

HENRY MORGENTHAU WAS FDR'S SECRETARY OF THE TREASURY. He's the subject of one of my favorite stories in the book. Roosevelt had an annual poker game: every year, it would always be held on the day that the Congress was going to adjourn. The rule was that whoever was ahead at the moment the Speaker of the House called to adjourn would win.

On one particular night, Morgenthau was way ahead when the Speaker called to tell Roosevelt he was adjourning at nine-thirty. Roosevelt pretended that it was somebody else calling—"I'm sorry, I can't talk to you. I'm in the middle of a poker game." They continued playing, until finally at midnight, Roosevelt started winning. He whispered to an aide, "Bring the phone to me." The aide brought the phone. He said, "Oh, Mr. Speaker, you're adjourning now. That's fine." Roosevelt won the game. Total manipulation. Everything was great, until the next morning. Henry Morgenthau read in the newspapers that the Congress actually adjourned at nine-thirty. He was so angry that he resigned as secretary of the treasury, until Roosevelt charmed him back into it. There was a real camaraderie among the cabinet members, at the time. They could play poker together as well as work together.

[Secretary of the Interior Harold] Ickes resigned several times. He'd get upset about policy issues, and he would resign. Roosevelt wrote him a very gracious letter saying, "You can't resign. I need you. You're so important to me, and you're absolutely right." Ickes then wrote back saying, "When I read your letter, I got fluttery all over. I couldn't believe it." It showed the kind of awe, in some ways, that they felt for this man who was their president.

FDR WAS NOT ONLY AN ONLY CHILD, but his father was a sickly man from the time he was young. His mother was a very young mother who was told she could never have other children after Franklin was born, because it had been a tough birth. All of her love, which was large, got focused on this child. She gave him probably the greatest asset a mother can give a child—that sense of unconditional love. But because he was so important to her, she never allowed him the freedom to feel like he could stand apart from her. You have the feeling that she hovered over him all of his life, even though maybe that's the source of his confidence. One of my favorite quotes by Churchill says that when you met Roosevelt—and I think Sara Roosevelt created this in her son—he had such inner élan, such confidence, such sparkle that to be around him was like opening your first bottle of champagne. But if only his mother had known when to separate, I think he would have had an easier time with intimacy.

CAMPOBELLO WAS THE PLACE that had been his mother's estate when he was a young boy. It's up off the border of Maine and Canada. It was a beautiful summer home that had been very much a part of Eleanor and Franklin's early romantic days. But it was also the place where he got polio.

In 1921, when he was only thirty-nine years old, he contracted [the disease]. One of the things I understood more by doing this book than I ever had before was how much that paralysis was a part of his everyday life. I, like so many people in the country, had assumed that he had conquered the polio somehow and was simply left a bit lame. But, in fact, he was a full paraplegic. He couldn't even get out of bed in the morning without turning his body to the side of the bed and being helped into his wheelchair by the valet. He couldn't really walk. He had thick braces on, and if he leaned on the arms of two strong people, he could appear to be maneuvering himself forward.

He had an annual dinner for the patients at Warm Springs[, Georgia]. He had originally created the whole Warm Springs rehabilitation center in the 1920s. He went down there initially because the hot springs that came out of the ground naturally in that area were thought to help people with polio. Lots of patients would be down there. I think somehow his contagious confidence helped them to get through their own polio. He liked to spend every Thanksgiving with them. That was a pledge he had made.

I interviewed Betsey Whitney, who had been married to Jimmy Roosevelt—the Roosevelts' oldest son. She said she asked FDR once, in the middle of the war, How do you fall asleep at night with all the burdens that you have to face? As soon as he told her the answer, I knew that that polio was still a huge part of his imagination, because he described that he had his own method of counting sheep: He would imagine that he was a young boy again, at Hyde Park, and there was a favorite sledding hill behind his house . . . that led to the Hudson River, far below. During the presidency, as he's falling asleep at night, he would imagine that he was a young boy again, getting on that sled. He said he knew every curve of the hill. When he would get the sled to the bottom of the hill, at the river, he would pick it up, run to the top, and do it over and over again, until he fell asleep. As soon as I heard that, I thought, My God! This man is the most powerful man in the world, and yet he's imagining, when he falls asleep at night—and getting solace from—the idea that he can run, sled, walk again, the very things that were denied him at the height of his powers at thirty-nine years old.

HYDE PARK WAS THE MOST IMPORTANT PLACE for both Eleanor and Franklin. During the whole presidency, he went something like two hundred times to Hyde Park. He would get there by train. He would often get on the train in Washington, maybe at ten or eleven at night, and it would reach Hyde Park by the morning. He'd sleep on the train. He loved traveling by train. He had his own compartment. Because of his polio and his paralysis, he didn't like fast-moving transportation. He hated airplanes, but he could feel grounded on the train. Eleanor was just the opposite. She liked to get places fast, so she only liked to travel by plane, but she would go with him by train, as well.

LUCY MERCER HAD AN ESTATE in Allamuchy, New Jersey. He loved to figure out maps . . . so he figured out the railroad lines and knew that if he went along a different pattern—and he had to convince the Secret Service it was safe for him to do this—he could spend an afternoon with Lucy. Now, this was not until the last year of his life. Some people had assumed, myself included, that he probably had known Lucy all of his life. I had heard about this affair that began back in 1918. I knew he had seen her and was with her when he died, so I thought maybe it had happened all the way through that period of time. But the truth was that he had kept his pledge to Eleanor not to see her again until the last year of his life, after Eleanor had refused to be with him and be his wife again, after Anna had come back into the White House, and after he was diagnosed with congestive heart failure. . . . I believe [Franklin] knew in that last year that he was dying. He went to Bernard Baruch's plantation in April of 1944 to recover, and it was there that he saw Lucy Mercer, essentially for the first time since 1918. She had just lost her husband, Winthrop Rutherfurd, who had been a very wealthy businessman . . . so she was widowed. I believe, when he saw her then, that what it did more than anything was to awaken in him a memory of what it was like when he was young, before the polio. He had known Lucy three years before his polio attack. Now, before his heart was giving way, he decided that he wanted to see her regularly.

She had been a social secretary, working for Eleanor. When he was assistant secretary of the navy, Eleanor and Franklin moved to Washington, in 1914. Eleanor felt worried about the whole social circle of invitations, because you had to know which A list, B list you belonged to. She hired this young woman, Lucy Mercer, who came from a blue-blood family in Washington and yet needed money because her father had been an alcoholic. Lucy came three or four days a week and worked for the Roosevelts. Somewhere in that period of time, between 1914 and 1918, a relationship developed between Lucy and Franklin.

It came to an abrupt end when Eleanor happened to come upon a packet of love letters that Lucy had written to Franklin. She later said, when she opened these letters, that the bottom fell out of her world. She actually offered Franklin a divorce immediately. I'm convinced it was the last thing he wanted. I think he had never meant for the marriage to be over by his relationship with Lucy. In some ways, I think Lucy's attraction for him was that she was confident, she was gay, she was easy, whereas Eleanor, during that period of her life, was still haunted by the insecurities of her own childhood. . . . But when confronted with the thought of losing Eleanor, it was the last thing he wanted.

Certain members of the press knew about Lucy Mercer. They knew that Missy LeHand lived in the White House. They knew there was an unconventional set of relationships in the White House. They certainly knew that Roosevelt was a paraplegic. Yet there was, then, a certain sense that a president's private life is his private life, unless whatever he was doing had an impact on his public activities. I talked to one old reporter who said, "Who are we to judge? We're not angels ourselves, so it wouldn't be sporting somehow to report on these unconventional relationships in the White House."

It's scary to think about [today's standards being applied to them], because if Eleanor and Franklin had not been allowed that network of friendships in the White House that allowed them to sustain themselves while they were going through the difficult days of depression and the war, they wouldn't have been as strong as leaders as they were. . . . In some ways, if we hadn't had, at that time, that kind of space for their private lives, they wouldn't have been replenished as political leaders.

AFTER HE CAME BACK from the Yalta Conference, and after he gave this major speech to the Congress in March of 1945, everybody could see that his health was failing. Somehow when he went to Warm Springs, Georgia, there had always been this sense that he would recuperate. . . . They decided that he'd make an extended trip to Warm Springs. He brought with him his two spinster cousins, Laura Delano . . . and Margaret Suckley, and they kept him company. . . . For the first week or so, it seemed like he might be getting a little bit of his bounce back, getting some weight back. He had been losing weight tremendously in that last year.

And then at a certain point, he invited Lucy Mercer to come and stay with him. She arrived about four or five days before he died, stayed in a little guest house right across the way from his Little White House, and brought with her a painter friend, Madame Shoumatoff, who wanted to do a portrait of Roosevelt. He seemed to be getting better. He took these little driving trips with Lucy. There was this favorite place he had, Dowdell's Knob, where you could see the whole valley in Georgia. Lucy later wrote that she'd never forget that day when he talked to her about all the plans he had, after the presidency, and what he hoped to do with the world, and how he still had idealism left about what the world would be like after the war.

Then on a certain morning, he woke up, and people surprisingly thought that he looked better than he had for weeks. His color was radiant almost. Probably it was, as doctors later said, that the embolism that later killed him was already beginning to be felt in his skin and in his coloring. But he nevertheless kept everybody company. . . . All that morning, he was talking to Lucy and her friend, Madame Shoumatoff. The two spinster cousins were there, and then, suddenly, in the middle of talking to them, at about noon or so, on April 12, he suddenly said, "I have a terrific headache," and he slumped forward. One of the cousins went over to him, thinking he had dropped his cigarette or something, and then she realized that he had become unconscious. So immediately they called for doctors, they called for help, and they carried him into his bedroom. Lucy knew enough to leave at that moment. . . . He died about an hour and a half later. He never regained consciousness. They finally called Eleanor and told her. She was in the middle of giving a speech in Washington when she found out. She knew, she said, the minute the phone rang, that something had happened. She could just feel it.

As ELEANOR TRAVELED THE COUNTRY AGAIN that summer, everywhere she went, people kept telling her how much they loved her husband. People that she had thought were her people—the poor people, taxi drivers, porters—felt that their lives were so much better off, at the end of the war, than at the start. She'd been fighting him all through the war. She wanted the war to be a vehicle for social reform on civil rights, on day care in the factory. She kept wanting more than he could provide. But now she saw, she later said, in the summer of 1945, that the country was indeed a better place; that blacks had worked in factories they never had before, [and] they'd done well in the military; that women had this great sense of mastery from having been 60 percent of the workforce during the war; veterans were going to college on the G.I. Bill; unions were stronger than ever before. She said that as she heard all these tales, she began to feel a sense of how much the country owed to Franklin Roosevelt. And, as she felt that, she was somehow, amazingly, able to forgive him for what had happened. . . . It was so wonderful for her that she did, because it meant that the rest of her life, those next seventeen years, instead of harboring bitterness toward her husband, she loved him even more, in some ways, than in life. She was able to incorporate all of his strengths into herself. . . . She became partly more like him. She was a much better politician after his death than before, because now she had to be both of them, not just herself.

It was an amazing end to this story. It makes you realize, if you looked at this story from the outside in, as the media would probably do today, they'd accuse him of infidelity; they might accuse him of harassment for his relationship with his secretary, Missy LeHand; maybe accuse Anna of betrayal of her mother; and yet none of those labels would be right. I'm absolutely convinced these people never meant to hurt one another. They were simply trying to get through their lives with the best possible mixture of love and respect, through work and affection. It seems to me that the challenge is not to do what's so prevalent today in biography—to expose, and to label, and to stereotype. What I really wanted to try and do was to extend empathy, to understand why they needed all these relationships, and not to judge them harshly because of their own human needs.

Thank God for the country, and for themselves, these opposite temperaments attracted when they were young and had enough to keep them going through this long marriage.

Eleanor Roosevelt

---

by
BLANCHE WIESEN COOK

Blanche Wiesen Cook is working on a multi-volume biography of former First Lady Eleanor Roosevelt (1884–1962). She joined us on April 11, 1993, to talk about her first volume, which details Eleanor Roosevelt's birth through the first Roosevelt inaugural. Eleanor Roosevelt: Volume 1: 1884–1933 *was published by Viking in 1992.*

PEOPLE REALLY MADE FUN OF HER and called her ugly and buck-toothed and scraggy. People really said the most awful things about her physical appearance. The fact is that as a young woman, she was really rather attractive. She was six feet tall, and her eyes were incredibly blue—a real cobalt blue that was just astounding—so that you really didn't notice her overbite as the first thing. But the press and the photographers were very mean to her. She was rather consistently attacked in the press.

When I think of Eleanor Roosevelt I think of power—women, politics, and power. I think of decency and dignity, which was her lifelong ambition for all people. She thought everybody should live in a situation that guaranteed decency and dignity. . . . During that awful waiting period between the election and the inauguration, Eleanor Roosevelt attended the intermission between the second and third acts of *Simon Boccanegra* at the New York Metropolitan Opera House. She stood up and made a political speech and said that she had been disturbed by how much homelessness and how much poverty there was right here in New York City. She spoke to the Metropolitan Opera audience and said, "When you see these terrible images, you have to do something. All of us have to do something. We can't just go on and look at all of this poverty and all of this homelessness and not reach down into our own pockets and our own hearts and not do something in this most wonderful country. This situation should not exist." That sort of startled me when I first read that. Imagine the First Lady doing that today. . . . It really is a ghost out of Christmas past.

VOLUME 1 OF MY BIOGRAPHY goes from 1884, when Eleanor Roosevelt was born, up to 1933 and ends when the Roosevelts enter the White House. Volume

2 picks up in that period . . . then it goes to the end of her life. She died on the seventh of November, 1962.

When I went to look at her papers, I discovered that we just didn't know very much about her. In fact, nobody had ever looked at her wonderful feminist writings in the 1920s. She was a hero. She was a terrific organizer. In 1924, just to give you one example, she was head of the Women's Democratic Platform Committee . . . [with whom] she called for full employment, national health care for all Americans, America's entrance into the League of Nations and the World Court, which the U.S. did not join. By the way, that campaign resulted in her vast FBI file. . . . The biggest single individual file is Eleanor Roosevelt's file. It's an FBI file that goes on for three thousand pages.

I think everything in her FBI file would make her very proud. J. Edgar Hoover was a maniac when it came to race. He was a terrible bigot. I divided her file up into subjects; the largest subject file is everything Eleanor Roosevelt ever said against lynching, everything she said against segregation, everything she said on behalf of racial justice. Hoover wrote really insulting remarks about "this old hen" and "here's the old cow doing it again" along the margins. In her file, there are some sleuthing activities. He kept a daily watch on her. . . . His goal was to vilify someone as important as Eleanor Roosevelt. It's quite an amazing file.

SHE WAS BORN IN NEW YORK. Her mother was from a little town, Tivoli, north of Hyde Park, and that's where she grew up. She lived there until she went to school in England—Tivoli and New York City. She didn't go to college. She went to this school for three years run by a woman named Marie Souvestre, which was like a finishing school, a pre-collegiate academy for the royalty and ruling class of the fin de siècle. . . .

People didn't know how much tension there was within the [Roosevelt] families, although it was in the press in 1891 when Eleanor Roosevelt's father was declared insane by his brother Theodore Roosevelt. It was four-inch headlines in the *International Tribune* and in the *Herald Tribune* in New York. It was all over the newspapers. That class, that ruling Knickerbocker class, knew about it.

It's very important to know that Eleanor Roosevelt was the daughter of a great alcoholic. Her father, who was Elliott Roosevelt, Theodore Roosevelt's brother, died at the age of thirty-four of alcoholism. Eleanor Roosevelt was ten when he died. Her mother died when Eleanor was eight and was a very abused and unhappy woman. So Eleanor Roosevelt always had a tremendous empathy with people in want and people in need and people on the margin. That's an important part of her life to understand.

She was brought up by her grandmother and her uncles and aunts, many of whom were also alcoholic. She said the favorite years, the best years of her life were when she went off to England to school at Allenswood, where she met a liberal spirit who encouraged Eleanor Roosevelt to grow and develop and be herself. That was her liberation. In fact, she said the happiest day of her life was the day she made the first team in field hockey. That's interesting because one of the other myths about Eleanor Roosevelt is she was not athletic, she was not competitive. . . . I thought it was interesting, too, that when she was in the White House she wrote to a friend, "I intend to earn as much money this year as Franklin earns as president." She was going to earn that money as a broadcaster, as a journalist—and she did. Seventy-five thousand in 1933 dollars, which in terms of today's inflation is the salary of a CEO—about $350,000. We would consider that a great conflict of interest today, wouldn't we?

FRANKLIN WAS HER FIFTH COUSIN, once removed, and she met him first when they were children when she was about two. There is a story that he carried her on his back and played around Hyde Park when her parents brought the children together. Ironically, her father Elliott was FDR's godfather.

[Her uncle, Theodore, offered them the White House for their wedding.] She didn't want to get married in the White House. She wanted to get married among her mother's people. Her godmother hosted her wedding party, and that's what she wanted. She was very committed to getting married among her mother's people.

When Eleanor Roosevelt got married, Theodore Roosevelt was very garrulous and took over the show. It became Theodore Roosevelt's show. It was St. Patrick's Day and it was quite a circus. He arrived, he had a few minutes, he dashed in. He walked her down the aisle. All of the guests left Eleanor Roosevelt and Franklin Roosevelt and went off and listened to T.R., the president, take off and carry on. Eleanor Roosevelt was really in the background of her own wedding

[Franklin and Eleanor] met in 1902 and they had a sort of secret romance. One of the really wonderful parts of this book is the love story between Eleanor Roosevelt and Franklin Delano Roosevelt. Their courtship letters are as ardent as anything that Eleanor ever wrote. The sad thing is that Eleanor Roosevelt destroyed all of FDR's courtship letters when she discovered his affair with Lucy Mercer in 1918. That's a very sad loss to history.

I thought that his affair with Lucy Mercer was his adolescent rebellion. FDR was a mother's boy who was very good. He plunged into an early marriage at the age of twenty-one, and he was a very devoted son and husband. Then he had this affair, while Eleanor Roosevelt was off doing good works and taking the children to Campobello, with her friend and social secretary, Lucy Mercer.

Their children ranged in age from three to ten while this affair was going on. She knew nothing about it. She was devastated. She was devastated in part because she thought that her marriage would be unlike her parents' marriage and that it would be perfect. She was very romantic about her marriage.

He was assistant secretary of the navy. After reviewing the naval stores during that great flu epidemic of 1918, they got a wire. She and Sara Delano Roosevelt, his mother, got a wire to meet the ship with an ambulance because FDR had double pneumonia and was reeling from this flu epidemic. That night, she unpacked his bags and there, presumably tied in that proverbial red ribbon, were all of these love letters from Lucy Mercer. She offered him a divorce. He said he would not see [Lucy] again, that he would break it off. They didn't get divorced, and their lifelong friendship and partnership is one of the wonders of the twentieth century.

They really did forge a healing partnership and friendship. But then, very much, he went his way and she went her way—not unlike the Edwardian courts of their contemporaries. . . . In 1923—and this is an important key to understanding what happens later when Eleanor Roosevelt decided she could have a life of her own—FDR picked up with a woman named Missy LeHand, who was his secretary during the campaign of 1920. . . . From that point on— and he had polio at this time—she was his primary companion, his primary friend when they went off to warm waters off the Florida coast where Eleanor Roosevelt couldn't stand the life. . . . LeHand lived in the executive mansion; during the White House years she lived in the White House.

In 1923, after LeHand arrived—Eleanor Roosevelt always treated her as a junior wife—Eleanor Roosevelt wrote an extraordinary article called "The Women of Tibet" in which she said, "It has been brought to my attention that the women of Tibet have many husbands, which seems to me a very good thing since so many husbands have so many wives." That is the context for [her relationship with] Earl Miller and for Eleanor Roosevelt's later liberation, which does include other people and other emotional enthusiasms.

Eleanor Roosevelt had two friendships where the people were there for her alone. Eleanor Roosevelt always said what a woman wants most in life is somebody who is there for you alone, who puts you first, who puts your needs, your feelings, and so on first. The first of those friendships was Earl Miller, who was her bodyguard. The relationship between Eleanor Roosevelt and Earl Miller was just completely ignored and dismissed as a mother-son thing.

There were two moments when I began to rethink that friendship. For a long time I too accepted—"Oh, well. It's just a mother and son thing." He was a very handsome state trooper. He built her a tennis court. He taught her to dive. He taught her to shoot from the hip and to be a good shot. He was a hunk. At one point I decided we had to look closer—it was not just his gorgeous legs—when I thought, Well, why not? We need a new historical category: Why Not? The two things that made me really think that is, one, I discovered he was political . . . and [two,] he cared about the same issues that she cared about. . . . I realized this was not just a gorgeous hunk and the lady; this was a substantial friendship. Then I did some simple arithmetic. This mother-son thing sort of falls apart when you discover that Eleanor Roosevelt was forty-four and Earl Miller was thirty-two when they first became very great friends.

LORENA HICKOK WAS ASSIGNED to interview Eleanor Roosevelt. That first interview, Lorena wasn't interested in women's stuff. She was a hard-nosed "I do news" reporter. She did the Lindbergh case and she was previously assigned to the governor, and so to interview the First Lady was like "Why do I want to interview the First Lady?" But she was very taken with Eleanor Roosevelt. She wrote that she always wanted to get closer to Eleanor Roosevelt, but Eleanor Roosevelt always kept her at arm's length, and her arms were very long. Finally she was assigned to write some good essays, keep her eye on the First Lady–elect, and Lorena Hickok did that.

I think they fell in love. The first interview was the first time a reporter was assigned to do a story about the First Lady on Inauguration Day in 1933. Things were so busy and so harried. Eleanor Roosevelt was being interrupted so much that they finally went into one of the back rooms of Eleanor Roosevelt's own bedroom–sitting room—which, by the way, was the Lincoln Bedroom—and went into the bathroom and she did this interview.

She was very important to Eleanor Roosevelt. She is the one who recommended that Eleanor Roosevelt have press conferences for women journalists only. She's the one who said, "Why are you writing all these ten-, twenty-page letters to me? The whole country wants to know how you spend your day." That became the origins of Eleanor Roosevelt's widely syndicated column, "My Day."

So, Lorena Hickok had a great impact on Eleanor Roosevelt's life, enabling her to become yet a more public person. But in her own life, she quit the Associated Press because Eleanor Roosevelt had two children who were getting divorced the first year that they were in the White House, and there was a lot of scandal going on. Rather than report the stories that she knew, and rather than have a divided allegiance and divided loyalty, Lorena Hickok quit her job and got other work. Eleanor Roosevelt helped her to get in the various New Deal agencies. But she was never fulfilled or happy after she quit her work. It's something that many women do for their great loves, but it's always a disaster to do it. . . . I think their intimate friendship lasted for about six years, and their friendship lasted until Eleanor Roosevelt died in 1962.

WASHINGTON WAS A HAUNTED TOWN for Eleanor Roosevelt. That's the town in which her uncle Theodore Roosevelt was president and she first discovered her own love for politics. . . . That's the town where she felt her Aunt Edith, Theodore Roosevelt's wife, had become absolutely a shadow, a veil—the White House, she felt, had destroyed her personality—so she worried about becoming First Lady. Washington was the town where people knew about FDR's affair with Lucy Mercer. Everybody knew but Eleanor Roosevelt. Her gossipy cousin, the famous Alice Roosevelt Longworth, had actually had FDR and Lucy Mercer to dinner parties in very public ways during the height of their affair. When

Eleanor Roosevelt found out about it and found out about how many people knew, she was devastated. Washington was just not her favorite place.

The low point in her life was the period from 1918 to about 1920 when she discovered the Lucy Mercer affair, she had no work of her own and they were still in Washington. By 1920, she came back to New York and she met with these wonderful political activist women, particularly a woman named Esther Lape, who nobody has written about but is one of the great heroes of American reform politics . . . and Elizabeth Read, who was a great international lawyer and who was Eleanor Roosevelt's financial adviser and lawyer. She wrote a great textbook of international law that was used at Harvard and Yale and law schools all over the country during the 1930s. Very interesting women. They helped to liberate Eleanor Roosevelt. She became involved in the League of Women Voters. She became involved in Democratic women's politics. She returned to that memory of what it was like to be an independent woman that she had acquired at school at Allenswood. . . .

ELEANOR'S POLITICAL LIFE EXPLODED after 1933. The Holocaust [was] very important, because FDR never wanted to do anything to make it easy for Jewish refugees or refugees from Hitler's Europe to get into the United States. Eleanor Roosevelt tried to get people in and to save lives. So you have a very interesting point-counterpoint: What did we know? When did we know it? There are these bitter questions that have lingered ever since World War II and the Holocaust.

The fact is that Eleanor Roosevelt knew what was going on in Europe virtually every day as early as August 1933. She and Carrie Chapman Catt, the great suffrage leader, organized a Christian women's protest against the atrocities against Jewish people in Hitler's Europe as early as August 1933. There are still historians who say, "We didn't know anything, and nothing could be done because the facts weren't available." My book is really going to blow that theory out of the water.

ONE OF THE THINGS THAT'S BEEN VERY INTERESTING—and I'm sort of sad about it—is that many members of the family are outraged that I suggest that Eleanor Roosevelt had a passionate life. While they say that they like the politics of the book, they are upset and offended at the thought that Eleanor Roosevelt had a private life. I find that very strange. . . .

I think Eleanor Roosevelt's goal was to live fully. She wrote a wonderful book at the age of seventy-six in 1960. It's called *You Learn by Living,* in which she defined her own life as an adventurer and she said, "I have lived my life as an adventurer, and my goal was to taste things as fully and as deeply as I could and to learn from every experience because there is not a single experience that you can't learn something from." That's an important thing for all of us.

Harry Truman

by
DAVID McCULLOUGH

Harry Truman (1884–1972), the thirty-third U.S. president, was born in Lamar, Missouri, and fought with the National Guard in France in World War I. After the war, he went to Kansas City, Missouri, to run a clothing store. Mr. Truman successfully ran for the U.S. Senate in 1934. In 1944, he was elected FDR's vice president. When President Roosevelt died the following April, Truman became president and was re-elected in 1948 after a close race against Thomas Dewey. Author David McCullough appeared on Booknotes *on July 19, 1992, to discuss* Truman: A Life, *published by Simon and Schuster in 1992.*

I T'S A BIG SUBJECT; it's a big life. The span, the arc of [Harry Truman's] life is a chronicle of American life in those years. He goes from what is essentially a Jeffersonian, Jacksonian agrarian America of farms and small towns, which he experiences directly as a boy growing up in a small town and as a farmer for eleven-some years, to a country, a nation that bestrides the world with power based primarily on industrial, technological, and scientific accomplishment.

He is a nineteenth-century man in all manner of speech, habit, thought, taste, everything, formed in that period before the First World War, yet he has to face the most momentous of all decisions of the twentieth century for which, theoretically, he's not prepared. But then we weren't prepared as a country either. To me, he is like Bunyan's pilgrim in *Pilgrim's Progress*. He has these various ordeals and complications and difficulties that he has to overcome . . . each one of which represents something that symbolizes the history of our country. This is a book about America for me. I wanted it to be as much a book about America as about Harry Truman. Truman liked to say, "I tried never to forget who I was, where I came from, and where I would go back to." It shows that he knew who he was, and he was proud of who he was. The return to Independence, Missouri, after he left the office of the presidency in 1953 was his way of letting his actions speak louder than his words.

When he got home, he found that living up to the idea wasn't as easy as he expected. While we all remember with affection the Harry Truman of Independence, Missouri, walking the same streets of the town he'd grown up in and just being citizen Truman, neighbor Truman once again, it wasn't all that easy for him. He missed Washington. He missed the stimulation and the pressure and the excitement of Washington.

In order to understand Truman, you have to understand life in Jackson County. He lived nearly seventy years of his life in Jackson County, Missouri. He lived to be almost ninety and spent twenty years in Washington as a senator and vice president and eventually president.

When Eisenhower took the oath [in 1953] and Truman walked down off the platform, he was right back down on ground level again as citizen Truman. He had no pension. He had no allowance for office space, no franking privileges, no Secret Service guards. His only income was his army pension, which was $119 a month. He got on a train. The new president, General Eisenhower, had loaned him the presidential parlor car,—the railroad car that had belonged to Franklin Roosevelt, the famous Magellan—to ride home to Independence. All the way across the country, he was greeted at one town after another by crowds that came down to the station to see him.

The last part of his life, in many ways, is as fulfilling and as happy and as interesting a part of his life as all of the rest of it. . . . The story of his retirement years was as appealing for me to write as almost anything in the book.

He had a new Chrysler. He loved to drive an automobile, which is interesting because it was one of the few recreations he had. He didn't know how to play any sports. He didn't play golf. He didn't play tennis. He didn't know how to dance. So driving an automobile and reading and walking were his primary recreation. He bought a new Chrysler, and, as he said, he wanted to give it a workout. So he and Bess decided that they would drive from Independence back to Washington in June 1953. Friends tried to persuade them from doing that, but they were determined. They set off in the car. It was an adventure in itself because every town they came to, people recognized him and there would be a great fuss.

The police would get very concerned that they were in town and worried about their safety. They worried if something happened to them that it would be the fault of the local police, so they would literally usher them out of town, as rapidly as possible. Mr. Truman liked to drive quite fast—above the speed limit. Bess, Mrs. Truman, didn't approve of that, so she would have him hold to the speed limit. As a consequence, they were often being passed. When people would pass them by, they'd look in the car and there was the former president of the United States and his wife driving along the highway. The cars would drop back and pass them again, just to see if their eyes were playing tricks on them. Truman turned to her and he said, "There goes our incognito."

When they arrived in Washington, many of the press corps who had covered him [in the White House] drove out to Maryland to pick him up. They heard that he was coming and waited for the car, and then they all followed him into town. He loved that. When he stopped at the Mayflower [Hotel] and got out with just his shirtsleeves on, the crowd all gathered around, traffic backed up, and it caused quite a commotion.

They then drove up to New York to see [their daughter] Margaret, who was living [there] and went to some shows. They went to see *Wonderful Town*, the Leonard Bernstein show, and went to restaurants just like anybody visiting New York. Again, causing great commotion. Taxicabs would pull over to the curb and drivers would jump out and say, "Hi, Harry. You're my man."

On the way back, on the Pennsylvania Turnpike, a state trooper pulled him over. Apparently he had been cutting people too close when he passed them. He said that the trooper just wanted to say hello to him and shake his hand. That was the last automobile trip they attempted. From then on, they would go by train or by plane, or by boat when they went to Europe.

Why wouldn't the government have a [presidential] pension? There were pensions for army officers and pensions for everybody else, but no pension for a president. He had very little money. He had to borrow some money, quite secretly, which Dean Acheson cosigned, to pay for the move back home. This is not well known. . . . When he got home, in order to provide himself some income, he undertook the writing of his autobiography, his memoirs, which no other president had ever done, except for Herbert Hoover. But Hoover's time in office was much briefer than was Truman's, and Truman's presidency covered far more tumultuous history than Hoover's had, so that to undertake that two-volume memoir was a very ambitious task.

[He received a $600,000 advance for his memoirs,] but by the time he paid all of his taxes and the rest, he wound up with not very much. What finally saved him financially—and, again, it's one of these great circles of the story—is the old family farm out at Grandview, which was sold to make way for a shopping center, a suburban sprawl. It turned out to be very valuable. Well, he'd been raised on the old Jeffersonian idea that the land was what mattered and in the long run it was the value of land that would see you through the hardest of times. The family had hung on to that farm through terrible times, through all kinds of depression and drought and all the rest because they felt this was what had real value. In the final analysis, it wasn't his political career, it wasn't his fame, it wasn't his memoirs or all of the other things that one would assume would give him security, but that land.

Then he built his library. There had been a previous presidential library—Franklin Roosevelt's library in Hyde Park—but it was established after Roosevelt had died in office. Truman was the first president to actually officiate over the establishment of his presidential library. There again, he was beginning something new.

One of the things I've tried to imply or to emphasize in the book is that Truman was at heart a very creative public figure. He was a creative president. He had been a builder all of his life. He'd built roads. He'd built courthouses when he got to Washington. When he became president, he built the famous Truman Balcony on the back of the White House, which caused a great flurry of criticism.

He is the one who entirely rebuilt the White House. The White House we have today is really the house that Harry built, except for the original outer shell, which was maintained. The entire interior is a reconstruction of the original house, and he took part in every detail of that reconstruction. He loved it. He loved building. He loved creating things. In a larger way, his presidency is marked by such creative and innovative acts as the Marshall Plan and the Truman Doctrine and NATO and The Point Four Program and so forth.

So to again be a builder in this last chapter of his life appealed to him tremendously. Building the library, having his office at the library, welcoming guests there, taking people around the library became his life, except for his travels when he went to Europe.

I'M SURE THERE IS SOME of [this biography] he wouldn't like because this is, after all, an honest attempt to see the complete man with his flaws and faults. I would hope that in sum, he would think I had understood him better than other people have. He was a much more complicated, complex, keenly intelligent, and thoughtful, considerate man than the stereotype Harry Truman portrait implies. He isn't James Whitmore playing *Give 'Em Hell, Harry.* He isn't just a kind of salty down-home Missouri Will Rogers. All of the people that I've interviewed, who knew him and worked with him and were in the White House with him, all say, "Please understand that this man was much more than met the eye."

The [Secret Service agents'] devotion to Harry Truman is a very compelling thing to listen to, and it's true of all the people that worked for him at all levels. I did not find a single person who knew him well, worked with him, who wanted to tell me what his terrible backstage temper was or what an ungrateful or difficult boss he was to work with. The closer people were to him, the more . . . they were devoted to him. In a way, I kept hoping I would find some people who really didn't like him, who had some skeletons to pull out of the closet, but that never happened.

The same people who were with him as Secret Service agents or as White House domestic staff in the mansion have said that they were by far the closest family that they have ever known in the White House. Though they don't want to be quoted by person, they all say that Truman was their favorite president. He was the first president in their memory ever to walk out to the kitchen to thank the chef or the cook for the dinner that night. They remembered Calvin Coolidge coming out once or twice, but they thought that was perhaps to see if anybody was filching food. Truman knew everybody by name on the staff, knew all about their families. This wasn't sort of a politician's device. It's just the way he was. The whole *Give 'Em Hell, Harry* [portrayal]—Harry Truman on the job, at the office, in the White House, with his people at the lowest level or the highest level never gave anyone hell. He never raised his voice. If anything, he's remembered for how considerate he was and for small favors and courtesies he would do.

WHEN [THE DEMOCRATS] ALL CONVENED in Chicago in 1944, it's one of the most dramatic stories in American political history. They know that their nominee for the presidency, Franklin Roosevelt, who's running for his fourth term, isn't going to survive. . . . He's a dying man. This is kept secret. It's a cover-up, as we would say, but for a very good reason. We were at war, and it was absolutely essential that neither our allies nor, to say the least, the enemy get the idea that this most powerful of all nations, powerful among the Allied nations, is being led by a dying man. But they know, therefore, that the vice presidency is worth everything. They're nominating two presidents. The irony of the story is that the man they nominate in the end, Truman, doesn't want to be nominated, whereas the other two, Henry Wallace and Jimmy Burns, are exceedingly ambitious and want it very much.

Henry Wallace was the vice president, and Roosevelt was playing a very tricky, manipulative game because he told both Wallace and Burns, "You're my man," in effect. "You go to Chicago, and you'll get the nomination. You're the man I want." But it was the political bosses who wanted Truman. One of the misconceptions about Truman is that he was an accidental president. He wasn't accidental at all. The political bosses, the big powers of the Democratic party, didn't want Wallace because they felt he was too left wing and too eccentric, and they didn't want Jimmy Burns, who had been a famous senator from South Carolina as well as a Supreme Court judge and one of Roosevelt's most important assistants at the White House. They didn't want him because he was too conservative and an avowed segregationist. They wanted Truman.

Roosevelt finally, under tremendous pressure from them, agreed, okay, it'll be Truman. . . . So Truman is very much the creation of the smoke-filled room, of the old boss system. One can't help to but feel, therefore, that the smoke-filled room wasn't an entirely bad way to go about the business of picking presidents and vice presidents. The bosses knew what they were doing because we were extremely fortunate as a nation that Harry Truman was there to replace Franklin Roosevelt in 1945. Even though he had not been told much, and even though on paper—by a conventional sum—his background would seem to be inadequate for the presidency, he had in many ways been superbly prepared for the presidency because of his life experience. He had been through what so much of the country had been through. He knew from firsthand personal experience so much of what American life was about then.

ONE OF THE MOST DRAMATIC moments in the whole story is when Truman, the evening of Roosevelt's death, is summoned from the White House by the press secretary, Steve Early, when Truman was having a drink with Sam Rayburn in what was euphemistically known as the "Board of Education." It was Rayburn's hideaway beneath the House side where they would meet for a drink after work every day. Truman, on getting the message from Early that he was to come at once to the White House, left Rayburn's office and ran back to his own office, his vice president's office, on the Senate side. . . .

Truman said later that he did not think. It didn't occur to him that the president was dead. He thought the president had come back from Warm Springs secretly and wanted to confer with him about something. But if he didn't think that the president was dead, why was he running? And if he did know the president was dead, what did he think he was running toward and what was he running away from? If it were a movie or a film, you could almost see a freeze frame on that moment where he's running down the hall. Of course, by then he's president of the United States, and he's running alone. . . .

He had to have known even if he wasn't admitting it to himself. He had to have known subconsciously. It must have been a dreadful time for him. Then he arrives at the White House. He goes up to family quarters, and he steps off the elevator. Mrs. Roosevelt comes forward and puts her hand on his arm and says to him very softly, "Harry, the president is dead." I feel that that's a very revealing moment about Harry Truman when you think of how he might have responded. At first he couldn't say anything. But when he was able to speak, he said to her, "Is there anything I can do for you?" Then, of course, she says to him, "No, Harry. Is there anything we can do for you? You're the one in trouble now."

He was a character on an odyssey who was in trouble of one kind or another much of his life—thrust in the jobs that he doesn't seem up to, but then he has to rise up to the occasion, whether it's to run the family farm when his father died, or whether it's to be an officer of an artillery battery in World War I, or whether it's to be a senator emerging from the shadow, the stigma of his Pendergast organization background. He always has to get out of the hole, so to speak. But this is the biggest hole he's ever in when he's suddenly president because Franklin Roosevelt had told him nothing. Most people know that he had been told nothing by the president about the atomic bomb, but that was only part of it. He was told nothing about anything by Roosevelt, which was not only, in my view, irresponsible on Roosevelt's part, but unkind. So when Mrs. Roosevelt says, "You're the one that is in trouble now," she knew what she was talking about.

IMAGINE, THE PRESIDENT of the United States sitting down every night writing, "Dear Mama and Mary Jane," from Potsdam [in 1945], where he's meeting with Churchill and Stalin for the first time. He's never been on the world stage before, let alone on the world stage with such figures as Churchill and Stalin. He had no small experience with stage fright. But he acquitted himself very well at Potsdam. Several of the people who were with him thought he did better overall than Roosevelt would have done.

Truman's affection, his devotion to Bess, is a very major part of his life. It's a very touching aspect of the story, and it's entirely true. . . . His courtship of her is one of the great stories that I know of, of pre–World War I middle America—this young fellow out on the farm who's in love with the daughter of a prominent, by the terms of Independence, well-to-do family. It's an uphill struggle. The family does not want her to marry him. It's his first campaign, and he pursues her. He doesn't let defeat discourage him. He's cheerful. He's devoted. He's loyal to her. He seems always to want to please her in the letters. He seems to be asking her always, "How am I measuring up?"

WHEN TRUMAN WENT OUT IN 1948, which in many ways is the ultimate expression of what he represents, and campaigned across the country in the so-called Whistle Stop Campaign, stopping the train at all the little towns along the way for twenty-two thousand miles, brutal—a physically shattering experience for lots of people who were on the train with him who . . . remember it vividly—he spoke to the people directly. He spoke spontaneously. He spoke complete sentences. His Latin teachers would have been very proud of him.

You read those speeches today and you think, Wouldn't it be wonderful, wouldn't it be reassuring if someone were as direct with us as that man was every day, five, six, fifteen times a day at these little stops? Talking about problems, talking about solutions, talking about where he stood, and never whining, never blaming other people, never blaming his star, so to speak. [He had] dogged determination and the conviction that he was going to win, which was shared by nobody. None of the experts, none of the pollsters, none of the professional politicians thought he had a chance.

IF THERE WAS ONE STARTLING DISCOVERY I made, it was that he had a pop in the morning. . . . Apparently it was his way of getting the engine going. He would go for his walk, which was a good vigorous two-mile fast walk or more than two miles, come back and do some sitting-up exercises and have a rub-down, and then have a drink. When I was first told this by the [White House] assistant head usher, J. B. West, I thought, Well, no, that couldn't be. But it was confirmed by two or three other accounts as well.

HE WAS A LIFELONG READER. I asked Margaret one day, "What would be your father's idea of heaven?" She said, "Oh, that's easy. It would be a good comfortable armchair and a good reading lamp and a stack of new history and biography that he wanted to read." He once said that all readers can't be leaders, but all leaders must be readers, and particularly history and biography.

His sense of history is one of the crucial aspects of him as a president. It meant that he knew that what mattered in the long run was the judgment of history, the judgment of the country in the long run. He could ride out the sinking polls or the calls for his impeachment, say, when he fired General MacArthur. . . . He knew that in the long run, he would be judged to have done the right thing, to have upheld civilian control of the military.

HE WAS VERY STUBBORN [IN DEATH], holding on long after he should have died in the hospital. I think he was sustained by what was then considered to be miraculous modern medicine longer than he should have been. He was a model patient. He never complained. It was a complete breakdown of the whole system—the heart, the lungs, the intestines, everything. [Bess] lived almost ten more years.

I WOULD NOT ONLY VOTE FOR HIM, I'd go out and work hard to see that he was elected. He wasn't perfect. He did make mistakes. His loyalty program was a serious mistake, and he made other mistakes. But he reminds us of what a man in that job can be and what he can do. It wasn't just that he made decisions. He accomplished things.

George Patton

---

by
CARLO D'ESTE

George Patton (1885–1945), a graduate of West Point, became one of America's most renowned generals. During World War II, he led the Third Army in Europe. Carlo D'Este, a retired U.S. Army lieutenant colonel, came to our studios on January 28, 1996, to talk about Patton: A Genius for War *(Harper-Collins, 1995).*

ONE OF THE ACHIEVEMENTS of this man was that as a second lieutenant of cavalry, barely out of West Point, the army appointed him the first-ever Master of the Sword. He was the army's best swordsman. He knew more about swordsmanship, which was part of cavalry routine, than anyone else in the army. Here he was, a young man, a student out at the cavalry school at Fort Riley, Kansas, and he's teaching men who have been in the army for many, many years the elements and rudiments of swordsmanship.

HE FOUGHT IN WORLD WAR I and had a terrific record. World War I is one of the great untold stories of Patton's life. He was a tremendous success, headed up the Allied Expeditionary Force Tank Corps, built it up from scratch. This was the American element that went to Europe to fight with the French and the British against the Germans.

Patton went to France with Pershing in 1917 when it was determined that we were going to have a Tank Corps. The British had introduced tanks to the battlefield for the first time, and we believed that this was something that we had to have. . . . Patton, who from December 1917 to November 1918 went from captain to full colonel as the head of this tremendous organization, ended up a war hero. Yet he considered himself a total failure. He thought he hadn't fulfilled his destiny, even though he was almost killed. He was badly wounded in the Meuse-Argonne on the twenty-sixth of September, 1918. He came out of the war believing that he had yet to fulfill his destiny. He had yet to do what he believed God had actually put him on this earth to do. [Yet] there were no other wars in prospect during this dismal period.

It was the worst period of his life. He suffered from depression. I think that he may well have suffered from what we now call post-traumatic stress disorder. He went through a midlife crisis. When he was fifty years old, he refused to get out of bed, and it took his wife Beatrice to literally coax him.

[HE WAS DYSLEXIC AND] one of the byproducts of this, and the one that's least addressed, is low self-esteem. There are many examples, particularly in his early life, of low self-esteem, which, in a way, acted to fuel Patton's desire to succeed. He felt he wasn't good enough on many occasions. They have a saying with dyslexics that most of them are smart but feel dumb.

PATTON BELIEVED that he had lived previous lives: He died on the plains of Troy, and he marched with Caesar's terrible Tenth Legion. . . . He was with Napoleon coming out of Moscow. He had been a Viking warrior and almost came back from the dead.

He believed this and was dead serious about it. Interestingly enough, in his previous lives, he never seemed to have appeared as a general, or as the commander. He was always an ordinary soldier—a centurion, a legionnaire, a warrior of some sort. He believed that part of his ability as a commander and as a soldier was based on what he had learned in these previous lives. Whether or not you or I or anyone else believes in reincarnation is totally immaterial. The point was that he believed in it. He always felt that these experiences were something that guided him through his command.

A classic example was when the Third Army went into Normandy [in 1944]. As one of his guidelines for the deployment of Third Army, Patton used a book called *The Norman Conquest,* which was about what William the Conqueror, who had fought in Normandy and Brittany, had done and what roads he had used. His logic, which was pretty astounding, went like this: In the days of William the Conqueror, they were only able to use roads that were passable and that his armies could cross. These were mainly secondary roads.

Patton said, "If they were good enough for William the Conqueror, they're good enough for us. They'll still be there, and the Germans won't be booby-trapping and mining them the way they always did. . . ." He based his campaign and what he was going to do on the road net. He used to say, "If the study of mankind is man, the study of war is the road net." This was part of this genius that he had for being able to take history and turn it to his own advantage.

TWO SLAPPING INCIDENTS that took place toward the latter part of the Sicily campaign were the defining moments of General George Patton's military career. On August 3 and on August 5, [1943] . . . Patton, as was his custom, visited two army field hospitals where there were wounded. He would do this almost daily, visit the wounded, pin on Purple Hearts, and generally commiserate with his troops. It was something that he did throughout his entire military career.

[These two times] he found soldiers that he believed were malingerers—who were in the hospital for no visible reason. He completely lost his composure to the point where both soldiers were slapped and cuffed around.

Patton ordered them out of the hospital, stormed out, and later said to U.S. general Omar Bradley that he had just made men out of a couple of yellow bellies. Patton was simply unable to understand that soldiers have different breaking points. He thought all soldiers had to live up to a high standard. In Patton's mind, bravery was the highest virtue that a soldier could have; cowardice was the deadliest sin. To him, it was worse than almost anything else to see a soldier act in what he believed was a cowardly fashion. He mistakenly thought both of these soldiers had [mental] problems. One was recovering from malaria or something, and another one had had dysentery.

He was unable to conceive, in this moment of irrational anger, that something more serious had been going on. This was triggered partly by two things: one, he was under tremendous stress toward the end of the Sicily campaign to conclude the campaign. He was in a so-called race with British general Bernard Montgomery not only to conclude the campaign but to beat the British into Messina. He'd also been under the gun from the Allied commander, General Dwight D. Eisenhower. There was an unfortunate friendly fire incident early in the Sicily campaign when the 504th Airborne Regiment was mistakenly fired upon as they came into Sicily and eighty-four or eighty-five people died. Eisenhower blamed him for this. The pressures on Patton up to this point were great.

The correspondents found out about [the slapping incidents] immediately. There was something of an uproar within the press corps. Some believed it was just Patton being Patton. Others believed it was a serious offense, and that Patton should be relieved. Several of them went to Algiers to Eisenhower's headquarters, went to see Bedell Smith, who was Eisenhower's chief of staff, and demanded that Patton be fired.

Eisenhower said to them, "Look, I can't stop you from filing your reports and from stating what happened, but, I beg you, in the name of Allied unity, I need this man. I can't win the war without Patton. If this thing becomes public, he's probably going to get relieved, and I may have to send him home. I'd ask you, as a gentleman's agreement, to keep this in confidence." And they did.

The only reason it became public was that someone tipped off columnist Drew Pearson, who was a national icon, in those days. These incidents occurred in August. In November, Drew Pearson blew the whistle on this on his national Sunday-night radio program. That's how the world found out about it. There was a predictable uproar in Congress. *The Washington Post,* for example, had an editorial demanding that Patton be fired. It was ironic. A year later [1944], during the Battle of the Bulge, they were saying just the opposite; that we were so lucky to have him. . . . The problem was that it cost Patton, in my opinion, the ground command for the Allied invasion of Europe.

IN THE BATTLE OF THE BULGE, the Germans launched a massive counteroffensive in the Ardennes on December 16. The Ardennes Forest is near the border between Luxembourg and France and Germany up around Aachen. It's one of the densest, most difficult areas to fight over anywhere in western Europe. The forests are deep. The road net is sparse. It's rugged country. What made it even worse in December of 1944 was it was the worst winter in almost fifty years. There were terrible snows. The cold was often six below zero.

It was Hitler's last gamble. He launched a massive counteroffensive with two Panzer armies and an infantry army in an attempt to drive through an area where the Allies were very weak; they only had a few divisions there. The idea was to drive this wedge, perhaps get the Allies to sue for peace. In Hitler's wildest dreams, he had this vision that these German Panzers were going to drive all the way to Antwerp, Belgium, and cut off the Allied logistics supply. Patton's Third Army was in Lorraine. The German counteroffensive caught the Allies flat-footed. There's no other way to describe it.

In the first few hours, no one really knew what to do. On the morning of the nineteenth of December, 1944, Eisenhower summoned all of his senior Allied commanders to a little French casern at Verdun. The purpose of this meeting was to figure out what the Allied response was going to be. Out of all these senior generals, Patton was the only one who came with a plan to counter what had happened. He didn't come with one plan. He came with three plans. Two weeks before the Germans launched this counteroffensive, he and his intelligence officer had already pretty well sussed out that there was a major problem brewing.

He came to the meeting, and Eisenhower said to him, "George, what can you do?" Patton said, "I can attack in forty-eight hours with three divisions." Eisenhower just looked at him and he scoffed. He said, "Come on, George, get serious. I want to know what you can do." Patton said, "I mean it. This is what I can do." He said, "I have three different plans. There are three different possible avenues of approach," depending on what he was going to be asked to do. He said, "All I have to do is pick up that telephone over there and give a code word and they're going to be on the way." And they did.

[HE DIED ON DECEMBER 21,] 1945. He had just recently been relieved as the commander of the Third Army. . . . His friendship with Eisenhower was on the rocks. He was put in command of a paper army. . . . He was burnt out, tired. . . . He was ready to go home. He was going to resign his commission, and he wasn't coming back to Europe. On the ninth, his chief of staff, to help cheer him up, said, "Look, let's go hunting. . . ." They jumped in his Cadillac touring car. They had a jeep behind them with a hunting dog in it, and they took off down the road. They came into the outskirts of Mannheim on one of the national highways, and the whole area was filled with wreckage, with bombed-out buildings and everything.

Patton was so inquisitive. He was always looking around, commenting, making statements to his chief of staff about how awful the damage was. He was sitting forward in the backseat of the Cadillac when a two-and-a-half-ton truck cut right in front of them. There was what amounted to a fender-bender accident, where the Cadillac slammed into the right front of this truck. Patton was thrown forward, because he wasn't prepared for this accident; hit his head up on the ceiling and on the glass partition, and was instantly paralyzed from the neck down. His doctor later said the only reason he lived eleven days, until the twenty-first, was that he was in such superb physical condition. It was a tragedy because here he was, ready to go home, ready to resign and on the day before, a freak accident literally takes his life. His chief of staff was cut up, but he wasn't seriously hurt. The driver was barely scratched.

GEORGE PATTON WAS A HERO. To whole generations of Americans, he represented some very old-fashioned virtues. It may sound corny, perhaps, in this day and age, but he seriously believed in the West Point creed of "Duty, honor, and country." Patriotism was one of the strongest words in his vocabulary. He believed that a citizen had a duty to serve his country in a time of crisis, in a time of war.

Dwight Eisenhower

by
JOHN S. D. EISENHOWER
HAROLD STASSEN

John S. D. Eisenhower, son of Dwight Eisenhower (1890–1969), appeared on Booknotes *on April 19, 1998, to discuss his book* Agent of Destiny: The Life and Times of General Winfield Scott *(Free Press, 1997). He told our viewers a little bit about his father, our thirty-fourth president. In 1990, former Minnesota governor and one-time Eisenhower cabinet member Harold Stassen, who himself sought the Republican nomination for president nine times, co-wrote with Marshall Houts a 1990 biography of Dwight Eisenhower. Governor Stassen appeared on* Booknotes *on October 14, 1990, to discuss* Eisenhower, *published by Merrill/Magnus Publishing.*

John S. D. Eisenhower

Agent of Destiny: The Life and Times of General Winfield Scott

I WAS BORN INTO THE MILITARY. My dad being an army officer, I was just born to it. I was raised in a military manner, and it was a given that army brats went to West Point, so I went to West Point in 1941. Being in the military has been my life.

After going to Fort Benning for infantry school, we were sent to Europe, and I reached Europe in the very last months of the war. I had a strange job as a tactical liaison officer, a vertical liaison officer with the First Army. I was a very junior operations officer.

I visited with my dad, General Dwight Eisenhower, for two weeks just after graduation while the rest of my classmates were on leave. I graduated West Point on D-Day, actually, June 6, 1944. That night I boarded the *Queen Mary* in the New York Port of Embarkation. The ship took seven days to reach Europe, and I had no word whatsoever during those seven days how the invasion was going. When I landed there on the thirteenth of June, I spent the next seventeen days with Dad. Quite an experience.

During the war when I was in Europe, I did have some mobility, so I was able to drop in every now and then and get a bath and say hello. But I never worked with him—we all worked under him.

The big thing I remember was that we visited Normandy twice; my father's headquarters were still in London. First, we visited [Field Marshal Bernard] Montgomery and [General Omar] Bradley, just before the Saint-Lô breakthrough. Here were all these generals sitting around under the trees, handling the war in a very professional manner; they were not excited. That was quite an experience that day under the trees, watching these generals talking over what they were going to do next.

The most dramatic thing that happened—when I look back on it, it's miraculous—was that a storm hit when we were trying to get to Normandy the second time—June 19, 1944. If D-Day had been deferred from the sixth of June, this was the day that the invasion would have been launched. This was the worst storm to hit the channel in fifty years; it tied up all the shipping. It wrecked the mulberries on Omaha Beach.

Buzz bombs [were hitting Normandy]; the guards' chapel was hit; one of his best friends was killed. Dramatic times. I was with him at the telegraph cottage when one piece of news came in. He just took it sitting down. He said, "Pour me a scotch." That was the only sign of emotion he really showed.

Harold Stassen

Eisenhower: Turning the World Toward Peace

PEOPLE STARTED SAYING I ought to write a book for the centennial of Dwight Eisenhower's birth. He was born October 14, 1890. I had been delaying, and thinking about it, and then Marshall Houts, a law-school fraternity brother, said he'd help me. . . . I went down to the Abilene library and was pleased to find that they have declassified a great amount of the National Security Council's secret minutes. I knew that all the big decisions revolved around the National Security Council. Those minutes used to come out [classified as] "top secret" on each page. Then we'd turn them in as soon as we reviewed them. Now, after over thirty years, they have extensively declassified them. That meant I really could write about those things.

I first got to know Eisenhower very well when he was president of Columbia University and I was president of the University of Pennsylvania. Then he was called back into service by President Truman. He had been the general commanding our victorious forces in World War II and then had come out to be president of Columbia. Then, when he was in Paris pulling NATO together, the movement got going that he ought to be president. I worked with him through the campaign. When he was starting his administration, he said I should come down to Washington with him.

LITERALLY, I NEVER RAN for president. I ran only for the Republican nomination. . . . My only real major campaign was back in 1948. We had a lot of delegates, and we were serious. That's the one that Dewey won and went on to be defeated. In 1952, it was the Stassen delegates who clinched Eisenhower's first ballot nomination, at the Chicago convention. That was a part of our whole plan. The key man in all that was a young lawyer in Minnesota who was my chairman, named Warren Burger. There have been nine different times, over a long span of years, in which my name was in some Republican primary somewhere.

FOR PRESIDENT EISENHOWER, I was what was called his director of foreign operations. At that time, all foreign assistance, all defense assistance, all educational assistance, all operations of a foreign nature were under my special organization, called the Foreign Operations Administration. John Foster Dulles was secretary of state, so we were very often together. As a matter of fact, we traveled to many countries together.

Dulles was brilliant, unique. His family had been in foreign policy since way back. He had very strong opinions. For President Eisenhower to decide that he would have a summit and would propose his Open Skies policy to the Soviet Union, he had to overrule Secretary Dulles. That was a very tense thing. . . . There were difficult issues, but I always respected Dulles.

Joseph Stalin died three months into Eisenhower's administration, in March of 1953. There were a number of changes in the leadership of the Soviet Union. . . . Eisenhower decided it would be good to have the first peacetime summit. . . . Eisenhower decided, and he at one meeting said to Secretary Dulles, "I'm going to instruct you to prepare for a summit." He very rarely used that kind of language.

General Jimmy Doolittle should get the major credit for Eisenhower's Open Skies policy. When the president asked me to work on this special assignment— What do we do in the space atomic age for policy?—I pulled together the best people I could think of. One of them was General Jimmy Doolittle. Another one was Ed Teller, the father of the H-bomb, and Doctor Ernest Lawrence, the Nobel Prize–winning physicist, and Harold Moulton, the head of Brookings Institution. Jimmy Doolittle spoke up about the importance of opening up so that nations would not fear a surprise attack. He said, "That is a crucial thing." This became a very important part [of our recommendation] to Eisenhower.

IN 1955, JUST THE SOVIET UNION and the U.S. had the bomb. The British were just beginning to get close to it. In this early period—that is, from 1950— the Korean War was going on. Chinese Communists came down with great strength across the Yalu, hundreds of thousands of them, backed by the Soviet

Union's military supply. They hit the MacArthur forces and drove them back into the middle of Korea, in the middle of that war. From that time on there was great tension, great concern; schoolteachers were teaching their children how to [hide] under desks if there was an air-raid siren.

In the middle of that period, Eisenhower said, "If I'm elected president, I will go to Korea." They would try to question him: "Then what will you do?" He said, "I'll go and find out what I ought to do, then I'll tell you about it."

We didn't ask General Douglas MacArthur to campaign in 1952. If he had campaigned, it would increase the issue for General Eisenhower—"If you're president, will you do what MacArthur says you should do in Korea?" Eisenhower didn't want to be in that box; he wanted to leave himself complete flexibility. What he finally did in Korea was not what anybody urged. He didn't let Truman tie him in to the Truman policy; he didn't let MacArthur tie him in to the MacArthur views. He didn't let any of the media put him in a corner.

I don't believe that Eisenhower ever said to the media in a press conference "No comment." He used to say, "If I say 'No comment,' they'll dig all over this town for leaks and they'll get the wrong kind of information. If it's a sensitive subject, instead of saying 'No comment,' I'll talk all around it. I won't say anything and give them any real information, but I'll cover the answer that way."

They used to think he was bumbling around, that he was using a lot of odd syntax, but that was his unique technique of how to respond to the media when he didn't want to talk about the subject.

HIS PRESS SECRETARY, James Hagerty, was a brilliant man who was with *The New York Times* for years. Jim Hagerty kept a remarkable diary for a while [but it's not complete], and nobody knows why he didn't keep it all the time, or whether he lost part of it, or the family lost part of it. Eisenhower had the very first TV press conference. This is what Jim Hagerty worked out with him— that he would go in, have a press conference, and let the TV cameras cover it and report it directly. Up to that time, they used to have a press conference with the president and then they'd have to clear whether or not they could report what he said.

EISENHOWER HAD A GREAT SENSE of humor, which he wasn't given credit for. Other times he had what we called his "command view." You could tell when he really meant that something should be done, period. Other times, he would be more relaxed. I find that historians are beginning, as they get into these secret files, to lift their appraisals of him. They tended to say, "When he got such marvelous results, he was just lucky." That also tended to be the media reaction. They're now learning that he had real policies and in handling crisis situations, nobody had his kind of a record.

First of all, he brought the Korean War to a close in six months—a war that no one had been able to close. From that time on, during a series of crises, there were a number of times he showed force, without a single American soldier being killed or killing anybody else. He enunciated a very important thing. He said, "At the end of a war, if you're a complete victor, you can impose an unconditional surrender. [However,] in a negotiation without war, you cannot have an unconditional surrender—it's just not realistic. If you're going to get a settlement diplomatically, you've got to work on it and have in mind that each side has got to be flexible."

He always said, "Try to get in position without shooting." Then he would put people to work immediately to work out the kind of flexibility, the kind of compromises that would resolve the situation and let history work out the competition. . . . You have to have in mind that he went through things with people who were saying, "You must force the unification of Germany. You've got to go in there with force, and unless you force that unification, there's going to be a terrible war over the division of Germany." He would say, "The forces of history have to decide that one."

Sometimes advisors were saying, "You've got to fight Communist China sometime; it's better we start bombing them now, while we're strong. You've got to let us go in and bomb them." And he would say, "No. Let the forces of history and competition between forces [decide this]." In Korea, when some wanted to drive north with all our weapons . . . he said, "No. Let the systems compete. You have got to go through history. We don't want to start expanding the shooting."

EISENHOWER WAS BORN IN DENISON, TEXAS, in 1890. At the age of two he moved to Abilene, Kansas, then at the age of twenty came up to West Point. A boyhood pal from Abilene went to Annapolis at the same time and these two young fellows left [the service academies] together. This was a lifelong friendship with Swede Hazlett, who became a naval officer. . . . He had a lot of good personal friends, but he also had a very strong rule that he would not let a personal friend try to use that to get special privilege from the government.

He came up right through the ranks. He'd seen Congress, he'd seen local governments, and he'd seen governments in other countries. He had a very strong conviction that the one thing that could undermine a free society and make it go wrong would be the greed of human beings. You had to always safeguard against greed. He'd grill that into Charlie Wilson [secretary of defense] and myself. The record will show that we established systems so nobody could, on a single signature, go wrong.

"Greed, greed, greed, that's the real plague of mankind. Think of it. If you could change man's greed, all the rest of his problems would go away." He kept re-emphasizing it. If you look back at the records, Charlie Wilson and I ran clean organizations. There were no scandals in defense or in foreign operations in those years, and part of it was this backup from Eisenhower. He always said, "Don't let anybody impose on you and watch out for greed."

[MARTIN DURKIN, EISENHOWER'S LABOR SECRETARY] was the head of the plumbers' union and a member of the AFL/CIO executive council. He had worked for Adlai Stevenson against Eisenhower, but Eisenhower accepted the view that labor ought to be represented by a leader from organized labor. Tragically, Durkin got a brain tumor and became very ill. He had a series of operations, and he didn't live very long, but it was a significant chapter [in Eisenhower's presidency]. We tried to aid the development of independent labor unions in other countries of the world, a forerunner of Solidarity in Poland, way back at that time. Martin Durkin was a marvelous fellow. That illness, the brain tumor, was a very sad business.

EISENHOWER WAS VERY SENSITIVE—having been a lifelong military man—about diplomacy or about anything in politics. He listened to those who knew that field and then would be very deliberate about overruling them when he was working in either diplomacy or politics.

He may be one of the most important presidents in history in working for peace. I think as they review him, historians are beginning to say that. As a matter of fact, they're changing their views. Anyone who wrote a book about President Eisenhower more than five years ago ought to go back now and see the files that have opened up and then reappraise what they criticized about Eisenhower.

Charles Coughlin

---

by
DONALD WARREN

Father Charles Coughlin (1891–1979) was born in Ontario, Canada, and later became an American citizen. He was the pastor of the Shrine of the Little Flower in Royal Oak, Michigan, a Detroit suburb. At the height of his appeal in the 1930s, an estimated thirty million people listened to his weekly broadcasts. Donald Warren researched Coughlin's life for twenty years. Mr. Warren appeared on Booknotes *on September 8, 1996, to discuss his book* Radio Priest: Charles Coughlin, The Father of Hate Radio, *published by The Free Press in 1996.*

[FATHER CHARLES COUGHLIN WAS] on the radio weekly, beginning in the fall of 1926, urged on by a group of his friends and [radio station] WJR's owner to try it out. . . . He was on at least once a week, although not in the summer. His season would begin in the fall and run through to the spring. . . . [The program] would begin with organ music, a very religious theme; the announcer would introduce him; he would give a sermon, which would be religiously focused, but then very quickly turn to a controversial political matter of the day.

I remember arranging an interview with Bill Paley at CBS. CBS had put Coughlin on for one year. It was a national contract in 1930. It had been arranged because one of the advertisers on CBS was the owner of station WJR in Detroit. . . . Coughlin gave a bitter attack on the Versailles treaty that caused tremendous controversy. As a result of that, CBS tried to get out of the contract, and it was terminated.

I thought it would be important to try to pick up on the details of that story. . . . I recall going up to CBS offices in New York and passing a number of secretaries in the inner sanctum. When I sat down, Paley was very gracious. He welcomed me. Then I said, "I am here to talk with you about Father Coughlin." At that point his face changed in demeanor. He said, "I have to ask you to leave. This is a subject I cannot and do not wish to talk about." And so rather unceremoniously I was escorted out. I think that reflected some of the still prevailing power that Charles Coughlin had in the mid 1980s and up to the present day, for those who had been involved with him in some way.

HE WAS A PIONEER in using radio for—let's call it activation of the audience, to get them to respond, to take action on the issues of the day. Some of those actions we would call hateful. I feel that there's a connection between his activities back in the 1930s and what we've seen emerge recently.

I would say in the early 1930s, [he had] an estimate of thirty million to forty million [listeners]. . . . Later on, by the late 1930s, he was down to five million to ten million, and at the very end, probably no more than about a million and a half to three million. . . . [Early on,] if you went to many of the neighborhoods in the major cities . . . you could simply walk down the street and hear his voice reverberating. This was very common in many of the neighborhoods in New York and Boston. People were listening in groups, they were listening at the local barbershop, they were listening in homes. And of course, he had his newspaper as well, so he was reaching an audience that made up the majority of the country at one point.

THROUGHOUT A GOOD PART of his career, he had the view that Jewish international bankers were undermining capitalism and that Jewish radicals were bringing communism to our shores as well as to Europe. . . . [For a Catholic priest] there was a real contradiction there. It was something that partly was reflected in the network of people that he associated with, all of whom shared these views. The church itself had condemned anti-Semitism, but it was part of the popular culture in the 1930s. And while the church condemned it officially, unofficially it was not unusual for Catholic priests . . . to carry a rather significant set of ideas about the Jews and their inordinate influence in society.

I WAS GIVEN AN ADDRESS that Coughlin made, the tape and the transcript. I was fascinated to read one paragraph. What Charles Coughlin said was that "the middle class is being ground under in twin threats from above and below." This is very contemporary—a lot of people are feeling this way in our country—and Charles Coughlin was the first to identify this kind of populist politics.

Charles Coughlin presented a kind of distinct politics that combined left and right, a concern with the elite exploiting the middle class, a concern with ethnic minorities sometimes seeming to gain power and with the middle class more or less squeezed in the middle. I call these middle-American radical politics. . . . The George Wallace movement of the 1970s had an antecedent in Charles Coughlin.

CHARLES COUGHLIN BUILT his national reputation on attacking Herbert Hoover, condemning his policies and his insensitivity to the concerns of the

Depression. He was the first political figure that Charles Coughlin used as a stepping stone to his own national fame. Ironically, Hoover's attitude toward World War II brought them back together by the end of the 1930s. They had similar views on the need to avoid any entanglements in Europe. But certainly at first they were bitter enemies. Hoover tried to find out how Coughlin was being supported and funded. There were attempts to take him off the radio during the time that Hoover was president. This was the first example of an attempt to curb Coughlin.

[He came] to center stage with Franklin Roosevelt. . . . He was tremendously popular by this time, 1932. A meeting was arranged, and Coughlin agreed that he would support Roosevelt's campaign. He was invited as one of those persons to give a supportive speech [at the 1932 Democratic convention]. He coined one of his marvelous phrases. He, in that speech, said, "My friends, it is either Roosevelt or ruin." Later he would change that to say "Roosevelt and ruin." But it was the kind of talk that helped Roosevelt gain supporters among those who saw Charles Coughlin and him as forming a kind of partnership

[He and Joe Kennedy, Sr.,] were buddies, comrades often. They exchanged jokes with each other. They met frequently. They fell out around New Deal politics. Joe Kennedy ended up having to try to cool down Charles Coughlin's passions and to try to do something about his opposition to many of the New Deal programs and policies.

Kennedy called Coughlin in Royal Oak and said, "The boss would like to see you." So Coughlin took the train to the Roosevelts' home, and Kennedy picked him up at the railroad station. They both drove to meet with the president. What was interesting was the timing. This was early September of 1935 and Huey Long had been shot and was dying in the hospital.

Huey Long was this marvelous political figure from Louisiana. He and Coughlin probably only met once or twice, but their politics were seen as quite similar. And their coming together to form a third party was a very serious concern to the Democratic party.

When Father Coughlin sent a call out to talented people to work with him on a third party . . . [architect] Philip Johnson was one of those who answered the call. He helped organize rallies. There was this huge, fantastic rally in Chicago, where the motorcycle police of the Chicago Police Department led the way to Soldiers Field, and Coughlin gave one of these rousing addresses. Philip Johnson helped set that up and organize it; he worked as a party activist. . . . His attitude was that we needed a strong leader, like Hitler. He thought Coughlin was that leader, but he found out that Coughlin did not have the political will. He felt that Coughlin was not genuine and not committed. For example, during the 1930s, Coughlin was compared to Kate Smith, who had this marvelous voice. But she was just that, a voice, and didn't have any other credibility in terms of politics. Philip Johnson began to think that

Charles Coughlin was just a voice without any real commitment. Disappointed, he left him.

[COUGHLIN WAS SILENCED for twenty-five years by the Catholic church in a] complicated process. There are some myths about it. It was really a combination of his own actions and the church. He had begun to have contacts with Nazi Germany. He had made contacts before with Fascist Italy. He had written letters to Benito Mussolini offering his help for Mussolini's economic policies. By the end of the 1930s there were examples of his staff who'd made contact with the German government. His closest aide, Louis Ward, had actually been working on behalf of the Japanese government as a paid agent of a foreign power.

The church was just appalled by what he was doing. . . . There were several fiery meetings between the attorney for Charles Coughlin and the bishop. Coughlin in these meetings threatened to pull millions of his followers out of the church. But he was afraid that he might have to go to jail. And, he warned . . . that "if I go to jail, you would have to testify. . . ."

An elaborate arrangement was worked out, a private understanding that if Charles Coughlin would withdraw from any kind of political activity, he could continue on at the shrine [in Detroit]. There would be no civil punishment; there would be no ecclesiastical punishment, but he would no longer be able to speak on directly political matters. He could not organize movements and could not be part of any political activity. In May of 1942, he signed this agreement. And until he died in 1979, the next thirty-seven years, he was not active in the way that he was before.

HE WAS RETIRED and still at his shrine in the 1950s. He was very concerned with the pigeons who were sitting atop that magnificent structure. He asked the groundskeeper if it was possible to get rid of the pigeons that were besmirching the edifice. . . . He ordered the groundskeeper to take a rifle and start shooting at those pigeons. The sheriff of the county came over and told him, "You can't be shooting up there because the bullets are landing out on Woodward Avenue in the traffic."

I heard him give a midnight mass in 1958. Memorable. I'll never forget his appearance. Tremendously theatrical. . . . I can remember the exact words, as a matter of fact. In 1958 he declared that "I predict by the end of the next year that blood will be running in the streets of Moscow, that the people will rise up against their leaders." Not quite accurate, but the power—I shall never forget the power of his presentation.

That wonderful voice simply exuded confidence and power at a time when many people were feeling confused and feeling that they didn't count anymore. The society was becoming a mass society, and change was happening so rapidly. They did not feel they were able to express themselves, and Coughlin could do it.

J. Edgar Hoover

by
CARTHA D. "DEKE" DeLOACH

J. Edgar Hoover was appointed director of the Federal Bureau of Investigation by President Coolidge in 1924 and served as director for every president from Coolidge to Nixon. Cartha D. "Deke" DeLoach, the author of Hoover's FBI: The Inside Story by Hoover's Trusted Lieutenant *(Regnery, 1995), was an FBI agent for more than twenty-eight years. When he retired in 1970, he was the third-ranking official in the agency. On August 20, 1995, Mr. DeLoach appeared on* Booknotes *to discuss the life of J. Edgar Hoover (1895–1972).*

[J. Edgar Hoover died on] May 2, 1972. His job was director of the FBI. He died on the job. He was 77 years of age. I was in Indianapolis, Indiana, presiding over a meeting, and I got a call from Dick Kleindienst, who was attorney general. He swore me to secrecy and then indicated that Mr. Hoover had died. I was shocked. I was distressed. Frankly, he'd been in the job so long that I thought he was going to stay in it forever. As a matter of fact, he told me once, "I will never leave this job," and he never did.

Hoover ran the FBI from 1919, when he became acting director—he became director in 1924—until 1972. I worked for him almost twenty-nine years. My formal title was assistant to the director. At times when he was out of town, I served as acting director of the FBI.

J. Edgar Hoover was a very complex man. He was formal, austere, aloof. He was a perfectionist. He was probably the best public relations toe-dancer in Washington insofar as realizing the importance of something and taking advantage of it. He could properly be called the father of modern-day law enforcement. Why? Because he, himself, advocated and promoted the centralization of fingerprinting by police all throughout the world—the free world, that is.

He raised the standards of law enforcement, giving law enforcement officers something to be proud of in handling their position. The National Crime Information Center, which is a great boon for law enforcement, has saved many lives—through the recording of stolen goods and stolen automobiles, stolen jewelry and paintings and the listing of fugitives throughout the United States. The FBI laboratory, the training of police—he brought all this about. It may not have been his idea to start out with, but nevertheless he capitalized on it and brought it about for use by all of law enforcement.

I WANTED TO COMBAT the distortions of history—the ludicrous charges that have been raised that J. Edgar Hoover was a homosexual and a transvestite. I lived with the man, as far as having an office next to his for fifteen years. I traveled with him. I've stayed in the same suite with him on occasion. I was in his home; he was in my home on very infrequent occasions. I knew the man. I knew he was not a homosexual, as did all of his people who worked for him. I knew that he was not a transvestite. He was a deeply religious, aloof, formal individual who was greatly charged by his rearing, by his mother, who was a formal, deeply religious person.

In light of the society of that particular day, back in the 1960s and 1970s, the director of the FBI, who was charged with some of the gravest security and espionage problems of the nation, would be totally subject to blackmail and many other things if he had been a homosexual or transvestite.

CLYDE TOLSON WAS THE ASSOCIATE DIRECTOR of the FBI. . . . Let me preface my remarks this way: Every man needs a close friend, somebody he can trust, somebody who's loyal to him, whether it's his wife, his son, his daughter. Hoover had no family after his mother died, so he needed a friend, an ally. Clyde Tolson was that ally. The basic wrong was that Clyde Tolson showed slavish obedience to J. Edgar Hoover when he should, at times, [have] disagreed with him for the good of the organization.

If the boss, meaning Mr. Hoover, said something, Clyde Tolson said, "This is what we've got to do." I can remember many times when the executive's conference voted 11 to 0, unanimously, for a specific matter. It was sent into Hoover and Hoover would say, "No, I disagree." Tolson would call us back together and say, "Obviously, we were wrong. Hoover is the director. He is right, and, therefore, we've got to do it over again."

HOOVER WAS A MAN that had an ego. He was vain to some extent. He loved luxuries. He would dress in sartorial splendor, even though his surroundings—his office and his home—didn't express splendor in the least. . . . He was very vain in wanting to dress the best he could and insisting that agents also have a proper dress code. He was vain insofar as weight is concerned. I recall one situation where he was dressing to go to a state dinner at the White House. He found out that his trousers wouldn't fit him—his waist had extended a couple of inches. So he had to buy new trousers right away to go to that state dinner.

The following day he put in an order that all agents should adhere to the Metropolitan Life Insurance standards concerning weight. Now many agents, particularly former football players, had gained a little weight since entering the FBI, and they had a tough time getting it off. But the weight control program saved many lives and I think it was a good thing regardless.

One day, he marched three of us, the top executives of the FBI, down to the nurse's quarters, the health room on the fourth floor, and he weighed us in. I was three pounds overweight. Another executive was twelve pounds overweight. One was ten pounds overweight. So he constantly dubbed us "The Dreadnoughts" and we were known as that for a long time. Vanity was one of his faults and he had a lot of vanity.

SID RICHARDSON AND CLINT MURCHISON were friends of Hoover. They were multimillionaires from Texas. They owned the New York Central Railroad for a time. They owned many other things, particularly land in Texas.

They would go on vacations and Hoover would meet them at the Hotel Del Charro in San Diego. He would also meet them in other places. They paid his bills from time to time. They paid his dinner bills. They paid his hotel bills from time to time. He thought that he was uncorruptible, particularly in his later years. It was wrong for him to allow this to be done, but he knew in his own mind that they would never ask him for any favors, and they never did. . . . Back then it wasn't considered totally wrong. In today's life, yes, it is. But as director of the FBI, that should not have been done.

Mr. Hoover did not like the syndicated columnist Jack Anderson because Anderson had printed a column about Hoover accepting favors from Richardson and Murchison in Texas. Mr. Hoover was infuriated about it. At a Women's Press Club cocktail party that he went to—not an interview, but strictly a social matter—the women asked him his opinion concerning Jack Anderson. He said, "I think he's a garbage-picking so-and-so." Jack didn't like that, so he had Hoover's garbage checked and found out that he drank Jack Daniel's, that he loved peppermint ice cream, and so on—nothing derogatory.

IN 1964, MIRIAM OTTENBERG of the *Evening Star,* Sarah McClendon, and other notable women reporters and writers . . . tried every way in the world to gain a meeting with J. Edgar Hoover. He turned them down until finally he couldn't turn them down anymore. He had to allow these women to see him and to allow them to question him.

Well, we worked for several days—working up what he was going to say—facts, figures, fugitives caught, automobiles recovered, etc., etc., but they were bored. They didn't like those statistics. They could have gotten those in writing from the annual report or from Hoover's testimony before Congress.

Hoover, sensing that they were bored, decided to give them some startling information. He said, "I have information that Dr. Martin Luther King is the most notorious liar in the country." [Assistant Director] Bob Wick, who was with me at the time . . . rolled his eyes and looked at me.

I looked a little startled. I passed Director Hoover a note saying, "Don't you want to keep this off the record?" He took the note and he balled it up and threw it in the trash. I passed him another note later on, saying, "Don't you think that remarks concerning King should not leave this room?" He threw that away. The third time I passed him a note towards the conclusion of the press interview, he looked at me and said, "No." He told the women, "De-Loach just told me to keep the remarks concerning Dr. King off the record." He said, "I refuse to do so. You may print them as I have given them to you."

Well, the women left the room like the roof was falling in. They couldn't wait to get to telephones. That started the feud all over again with Dr. King. It had quieted down considerably, but it had started up again as a result of that meeting and it was a public-relations fiasco.

The big allegation today is that Hoover harassed Dr. King by placing a wiretap on him. The wiretap was ordered by Attorney General Robert F. Kennedy. Burke Marshall, who was the assistant attorney general in charge of the civil rights division at that particular time, stated that the wiretap was placed because Bobby Kennedy didn't know what else to do.

Dr. King had been warned by President Kennedy in the Rose Garden about association with [two men who had suspected Communist party liaisons] . . . Bobby Kennedy had talked to him. But Dr. King knew the facts involved there and obviously felt that he needed these men or disbelieved the allegations concerning their Communist connections, because he kept them on regardless.

I have never seen anything [proving] that Dr. King, himself, was a member of the Communist party. I feel that, in my own opinion, Dr. King was somewhat naïve politically or else he needed these men to the extent that he kept them on.

An assistant FBI director who followed William C. Sullivan in office found proof later on that Sullivan—without approval from me, from Clyde Tolson, or from Hoover—had an employee on his staff take tape and a letter to Coretta King, Mrs. King. Hoover didn't know about that; Hoover had no knowledge whatsoever of that. It concerned sexual escapades that occurred in a hotel in Washington, D.C. Sullivan had no authority to do that and no right to do it, and it shouldn't have been done. It was a sickening act on his part.

THE ALLEGATION HAS BEEN MADE time and again that he had secret files for the purposes of blackmailing members of Congress. That's totally preposterous. We had, behind Helen Gandy's desk, his secretary for over forty-five years, two file cabinets. One of the file cabinets had two and a half drawers of files. Some of those files concerned John F. Kennedy, Eleanor Roosevelt; they concerned an undersecretary of state who had committed a homosexual act; and they concerned Richard Nixon and various other notables.

Why did we have them there? Simply because we didn't want young GS-2 clerks coming in from the boondocks and making a beeline right away for those files to satisfy their curiosity and then possibly going out and advising Mom or Dad or someone else, "I have had a chance to look at the file of this great personality." So we would take the top files of notables and put them behind Helen Gandy's desk. They were not secret files. I could look at them; any individual on a top level in the FBI could look at them if they had a legitimate reason for doing so.

There have been so many distortions of history—ludicrous yellow journalism—by people who wanted to make a fast buck by spreading arrogant rumors that were totally false, innuendo, which you'll find throughout the book and which I combat. I wanted the book to have believability so, consequently, I indicated [the FBI's] faults and J. Edgar Hoover's faults. But the book had to be written so that I feel that my children, my grandchildren, other people's children and grandchildren can go to the college and university libraries and find something besides garbage on the shelves concerning the FBI of our era and about J. Edgar Hoover.

Elijah Muhammad

---

by
CLAUDE ANDREW CLEGG III

Elijah Muhammad (1897–1975) was born Elijah Poole in rural Georgia, the son of former slaves. He became one of the early leaders of the Nation of Islam. Biographer Claude Andrew Clegg III appeared on Booknotes *on March 30, 1997, to discuss* An Original Man: The Life and Times of Elijah Muhammad, *published in 1997 by St. Martin's Press.*

MALCOLM X ALWAYS attributed in his writings and his speeches everything that he had become to one Honorable Elijah Muhammad. In Malcolm X's autobiography and much of the literature, Muhammad appears to be a background figure, even in his own organization. When I went to look for books on Elijah Muhammad, they weren't there. No biographies, nothing but newspaper articles. There was no biography to follow up on his life . . . so I devoted my graduate training at the University of Michigan to pursuing his life.

Very little [is known] about Elijah Muhammad. Everyone knows something about his disciple, Malcolm X. Louis Farrakhan is often in the newspaper or on television, so they know about him. People know about Muhammad Ali, the boxer, who was also a follower of Elijah Muhammad, but they know very little about Elijah Muhammad. It's surprising, given how long he lived and his kind of sustained impact on the African-American community.

His significance primarily is his impact on the racial consciousness of African-Americans. He made blackness, he made the heritage of African-Americans respectable, even to African-Americans during this century. . . .

Also, he pushed economics, or the economic initiative of his organization. It's very important as far as his significance is concerned. The real magic of the Nation of Islam was to mobilize largely lower-class people to pool their resources together to go into business. That was the real phenomenon behind the Nation of Islam.

IT WAS A VERY HARD LIFE for Elijah Muhammad, growing up in early twentieth century Georgia. At this time lynchings, mob murder of people, was a very horrifying pattern of life. . . . The family was very poor. They were share-croppers most of the time, although his father was also a minister. It was a large family. Elijah had at least twelve other siblings. . . . His educational experience was meager. At best, he perhaps made it to the eighth grade. He was unfortunate enough to see the aftermath of two lynchings. Also, he was unfortunate enough to not have some of the skills that were required to be gainfully and stably employed at any particular place. He held a few jobs in Georgia. He worked on the railroad; that's the last job he worked on in Georgia. By the First World War with the boll weevil plight that destroyed the cotton crop, the increased demand for industrial labor in northern and midwestern centers because of the war, and the racial discrimination and other things going on in the South, he was pulled away from Georgia.

He moved when he was about twenty-five, twenty-six to Detroit, Michigan; moved to Chicago; stayed for a few weeks in Milwaukee when he went on the run from a number of his organizational enemies. He wandered along the East Coast for a while between 1935 and 1942 and eventually came back to Chicago. Again, he was imprisoned in Milan, Michigan. He settled in Chicago. He also lived in Phoenix for a while because the climate was healthier for his bronchial asthma.

ELIJAH CONSIDERED BLACK PEOPLE—people of African descent—as original people, as the first people on the earth, as the creators of the universe and all of the natural wonders.

The Fruit of Islam were all of the males in the Nation of Islam. They were believed to be the best of humanity, the best of the world, the original men, lords of the universe, kind of divine individuals; all blacks were believed to be divine individuals by the organization. The Fruit of Islam were the cream of the crop, as far as the earth is concerned. They were the protectors of the women; they were the ones who spoke up for the race; they were the ones who guarded Muhammad and his ministers at the rallies, etc. They were supposed to epitomize what black manhood was supposed to be.

In the theology of the Nation of Islam, whites are described as devils and as being inherently evil. According to prophecy, whites were created by a black scientist named Yacub. They would be destroyed at the end of the twentieth century by a mother plane—a kind of spaceship—that would rain bombs on America and put the black man back on his throne, which he was believed to have sat on for trillions of years before the creation of the white man. Elijah didn't think very much of whites.

He got the image of the mother plane from his teacher Fard Muhammad. As far as the origins of that particular belief, it goes back to the 1920s and the 1930s. American culture was fascinated with the possibility of a Martian invasion, and that there was life on Mars. In the radio adaptation of H. G. Wells's

War of the Worlds in the late 1930s, the realism was so legendary that listeners believed there was actually life on Mars, that we might be under attack some day by Martians. Elijah Muhammad also ties it allegorically to passages in the Bible such as the Book of Ezekiel, in which he describes a wheel-shaped or some circular object that he apparently sees in the sky or is revealed to him in the heavens.

Fard Muhammad was Elijah Muhammad's spiritual teacher. In the Nation of Islam theology, he is God-in-person or Allah-in-person. It's very hard to conclusively sketch out Fard's background before he appears in Detroit in 1930. FBI and police records give a rather unflattering view of Fard Muhammad as a petty criminal out in California for a while who gets involved in narcotics, goes to prison in San Quentin for three years, and then arrives in Detroit to teach a peculiar kind of Islam to African-Americans there. That's the FBI-LAPD version of him. It's a bit credible, looking at the sources, but I haven't been able to conclusively prove that that is, in fact, his background. Some say that he came from Saudi Arabia; others say that he was Turkish. Fard Muhammad would say that he came from the Koresh tribe in Saudi Arabia, same tribe that the prophet Muhammad was from, and that he was sent to teach African-Americans about Islam or to save them before the judgment.

Over time, Elijah Muhammad and Fard invented him as God. Over time he went from Master Fard Muhammad to a Christlike figure, then to a prophetic figure, and then to God. It's a process in which you had stages of deification of this individual by Elijah Muhammad.

Fard virtually disappeared in 1934. Even the FBI lost track of him in 1934, which is amazing considering their interest in the organization. I've heard rumors that he recently died in California under an assumed name back in 1992. . . . According to the Nation of Islam, he was born in 1877. If he died in 1992, he would have been 115 years old, which is conceivable but highly unlikely.

ELIJAH WENT TO JAIL once during the early 1930s for contributing to the delinquency of a minor. He wouldn't let his children go to the regular public schools. He said he wanted them to go to the University of Islam, which is a grade school, to be taught by Muslim instructors. . . . He also went to jail in 1942 in Washington for refusing to obey his Selective Service orders to register for the draft. And he then went to prison in 1943.

THE HEIGHT OF Elijah Muhammad's power was probably the 1960s, from about 1962 through the 1970s. When we talk about power, we have to talk about it on different levels. The economic empire of the Nation of Islam was most significant during the late 1960s and the early 1970s. When Elijah Muhammad died in 1975, the organization had assets in excess of $40 million, which was sizable for that time. As far as popularity, as far as being in the media, as far as the public consciousness of the organization, the height was the early 1960s. That's when most of the press and the few books that were published came out.

Elijah lived very extravagantly by the 1960s in a nineteen-bedroom mansion in Chicago. He also had properties in Phoenix and a number of the organization's businesses were in his name. By the 1970s, he was building a mansion rumored to cost $1 million.

Most of his followers could cope with that. Some wanted their leader to live well. Elijah Muhammad was fond of saying that he drove a Cadillac not because he had a fancy for expensive, luxurious cars, but because he didn't want anyone to say that Islam had made him poor. Many of the followers desired to see their leader doing well, and perhaps that was a gauge of how the Nation was doing. If the leader did well, perhaps that would bring blessings on the rest of the following.

MALCOLM X FIRST HEARD of Elijah Muhammad when he was in prison for larceny back in the late 1940s. His brother Reginald was already in the organization, and Malcolm heard through his brother, who visited him in prison in Massachusetts, about this Elijah Muhammad, the Nation of Islam, and these teachings. His brother more or less coached him, coached Malcolm, in the teachings of Elijah Muhammad.

Elijah Muhammad eventually started sending literature and now and then a five-dollar bill to Malcolm in prison. And Malcolm, over time, became steeped in the teachings of Elijah Muhammad. By the time he was released in 1952, he was ready to devote the rest of his life, or at least most of it, to the ministry of Elijah Muhammad.

The X was bestowed upon him by Elijah Muhammad himself. The X symbolizes two things. First of all . . . the X represents the lost name that African-Americans can't know, the ancestral name from Africa. It also represents the persons as an ex-smoker, ex-drinker, ex-prostitute, ex-drug addict. It has that twofold meaning.

FBI DIRECTOR J. EDGAR HOOVER was very important as far as checking the activism of the Nation of Islam. After Elijah Muhammad went to prison during the 1940s for draft evasion, we saw the Nation of Islam becoming more and more conservative. Hoover's FBI and its censorship of the Nation of Islam and its activism had the effect of making the organization much more conservative, much more nonconfrontational, much less political over time. Hoover's FBI was instrumental in keeping the Nation of Islam out of politics, keeping it out of some of the earlier protest activities that they were involved in during the thirties and the forties and serving as a stone wall between the Nation of Islam and more activist-formed protests.

Those around him—family members, some top advisers—always knew there were things that Elijah Muhammad indulged in that the rank and file of the organization were forbidden from indulging in. The FBI knew. They kept constant surveillance on his life, so they knew exactly what things went on behind closed doors in his Chicago mansion headquarters. The press really didn't get a sense of his frailties, besides labeling him as a black supremist, a racist, until around 1964, when news of his relationships with a number of young women in the Nation of Islam became public knowledge. Some of the financial mismanagement that took place in Chicago came to public light by 1964 also. So by the mid-1960s, it was apparent that everything was not perfect.

OVER TIME there were doctrinal differences between Malcolm X and Elijah Muhammad. Malcolm was much more political in his nationalism, Elijah more religious. Malcolm wanted the Nation of Islam to become more involved in the civil rights movement, protest more, and become involved in international anti-colonial struggles. Elijah was more or less happy with the economic strivings of the Nation of Islam and waiting on Allah to settle the score between the races. There were ideological rifts between the two men.

As part of their battle against each other, Malcolm X brought out all the dirty linen in regard to Elijah Muhammad: the women, some of the financial malfeasance, and other things, some of the use of violence. . . . He went to the press and gave them an inside scoop.

Did Elijah order the killing of Malcolm X? Malcolm thought so. There were a few others who were followers of Malcolm X who thought so. There were those—apparently they were insiders in the Chicago headquarters—who called Malcolm in and said the order had been given. This was as early as July of 1964. I have seen nothing that independently confirms that there was an order, whether it was written or by telephone or whatever, that Elijah Muhammad said, "Go out and kill this man," or that he was responsible for the assassination of Malcolm X, which took place in February of 1965.

ELIJAH DIED IN CHICAGO in the hospital, battling heart disease. He was a sick man by February of 1975. He had a decades-long bout with bronchial asthma. He had high blood pressure. He had diabetes. There are a number of different elements that converged to take him to the hospital in late January of 1975, but eventually his heart failed. He died on the twenty-fifth of February, 1975.

Elijah's biggest legacy, his biggest significance, is that he makes blackness respectable among African-Americans. He sold black people to themselves. He rejuvenated people's sense of pride and self-esteem and their pride in their racial and cultural heritage. He also created the economic initiative of the Nation of Islam: that is, largely lower-class people pooling their resources together to buy a major newspaper, a printing press, farmland, grocery stores, jets, a bank.

Also of significance is a moral significance, although there are contradictions in his life as far as his own behavior is concerned. The moral message of the Nation of Islam [is] "Don't beat your wife. Don't smoke. Don't drink. Don't eat pork. Don't do drugs. Clean up your neighborhoods. Hold a steady job. Don't get on welfare." That moral message was appealing to people who had been prostitutes or who had been drug addicts or who had been on the margins of society, who had never lived within moral boundaries. The Nation of Islam created a structure for those individuals. Finally, he introduced African-Americans to an alternative religious vision outside of Christianity. If Elijah Muhammad had never existed, I don't think that Islam would be the kind of force it is in some American cities and urban areas today.

Amelia Earhart

by
SUSAN BUTLER

Amelia Earhart (1897–1937) made history in 1928 when she became the first woman to fly the Atlantic as a passenger. She then set out to make solo flights across the Atlantic and Pacific oceans. In 1937 her plane was lost when she attempted to fly around the world. On December 14, 1997, author Susan Butler, whose mother was a pioneering pilot, appeared on Booknotes *to discuss* East to the Dawn: The Life of Amelia Earhart *(Addison-Wesley, 1997).*

SHE WAS THE MOST FAMOUS WOMAN in America. She was probably the most famous woman in the world during her lifetime. She was catapulted to fame because she was the first woman to fly the Atlantic when it seemed as if nobody could fly the Atlantic without dropping into the sea. She went on to become a fine flier. She spent her life on the lecture circuit, in the public eye, deliberately, and then she wrote three books. I don't think there's anybody in our present-day scene who could possibly be all the things she was at the time.

She was five foot eight; she weighed 118 pounds. She was skinny. She was very good-looking, except she had thick ankles. She hated her ankles. She was obsessed even when she was famous with her ankles—which is one of the reasons why she always wore pants—because they showed off the best of her figure and hid the worst. She had absolutely beautiful hands, long, tapering fingers, that her husband was in love with.

There were two great loves in her life: one she married—and that was George Palmer Putnam [in 1931]—and one she didn't—that was Eugene Vidal. George Palmer Putnam was a publisher, an extrovert, an entrepreneur who was famous in his own right. He was the publisher who snared Lindbergh, which was the greatest publishing coup of that era; it put him on the map. He also published all the other explorers and adventurers. He was in love with the great outdoors and adventurers. When he kind of stumbled onto Amelia Earhart, he was just totally bowled over because she was everything. She was his dream woman.

Eugene Vidal is the father of [writer] Gore Vidal. He was the [other] great love of Amelia's life. He was also the head of the Bureau of Air Commerce—the highest civilian post in aviation.

George was married to Dorothy Binney Putnam, who by all accounts was quite a woman in her own right. . . . She and Amelia were fast friends; in fact, Amelia dedicated her first book to her. . . . Dorothy Binney Putnam had other male interests, and it became obvious that George Palmer Putnam was simply mesmerized with Amelia, so they got divorced. Amelia was not too happy about having anything to do with a divorce, but he overcame all her objections, and eventually they got married. He had to propose to her a number of times, by his own admission, before she agreed.

[On] the morning of the wedding, [she gave him this letter]:

Dear G.P.,
There are some things which should be writ before we are married, things we have talked over before—most of them. You must know again my reluctance to marry, my feeling that I shatter thereby chances in work which means so much to me. I feel the move just now as foolish as anything I could do. I know there may be compensations, but I have no heart to look ahead. In our life to-gether, I shall not hold you to any medieval code of faithfulness to me, nor shall I consider myself bound to you similarly. If we can be honest I think the difficulties which arise may be best avoided. . . .

Please let us not interfere with the other's work or play, nor let the world see our private joys or disagreements. In this connection, I may have to keep some place where I can go to be myself now and then, for I cannot guarantee to endure all the confinements of even an attractive cage. . . .

AFTER LINDBERGH—Lindbergh was in May of 1927—eighteen planes took off from both sides of the Atlantic. Three made it. Most of the people died. . . . It was like climbing Mount Everest. It was the most exciting thing that could happen.

Putnam had been given the job of finding a woman to fly the Atlantic in place of Amy Guest, who bought an airplane and planned to be the first woman to fly the Atlantic. . . . She was from a wealthy family, and she was fifty-five, headstrong, very intelligent. Her family didn't know what she was about. She kept it quite quiet. . . . When her family found out about it, they, not too surprisingly, hit the roof.

They talked her out of it, and she, stubborn lady, said, "Well, okay. I won't do it, but then the project has to continue. I want my place taken by an American woman who will be a credit to her sex and a credit to her country, she has to be somebody educated, a flier, and a wonderful person."

Earhart was a social worker at Denison House in Boston. She flew in her spare time. She had been in the papers a couple of times because she was a pilot, and she had done a publicity stunt for Denison House. She was just a local celebrity. She was not well known at all.

They asked her down to New York, and they interviewed her. She was perfect and everybody fell in love with her. . . . She was just going to ride in the plane. There were two pilots and she was just going to be the passenger. She hoped to actually get her hands on the controls, but she never did.

But she was more than just a passenger. Whether or not they had originally planned to do this, I don't know, but by the time the plane took off, they had given her authority to run the project. She was in control. . . .

While she was on the plane, she was keeping a log. She landed in Burry Port, Wales, and when she got to London, she handed in a finished story, which was published in the papers the next day.

It shows the world's mindset at the time: Nobody paid any attention to [the crew] Wilmer Stultz and Lou Gordon. She was continually saying, "Look, I was just a passenger. I didn't do anything." Later she said, "I was just a sack of potatoes." She was always with her arms around them, trying to push them forward. It stunned the world that a woman had been able to do this, that she hadn't passed out, that she hadn't died. It just seemed too incredible to believe.

SHE USED TO WEAR men's underwear. . . . It was more comfortable. Women didn't wear slacks; they didn't wear pants, and so they wore silk things that didn't work well under pants. Gene Vidal bought her Jockey briefs that worked better.

She decided she was going to design wearable women's clothes. She was sick of clothes that weren't wearable, and she thought it would be a good business enterprise. She loved getting into new businesses. She was always trying different things. . . . At that point, women's shirts were blouses, so she designed shirts that had long enough tails so that if [a women] stood on her head . . . the [tails] would stay tucked in. She used parachute silk for the blouses. She did very wearable clothes.

SHE ALWAYS WANTED . . . WOMEN TO BE THE BEST that they could be. She wanted them to lose their sense of inferiority. She was always trying to enhance women's self-esteem. She was offered a job to be on the faculty of Purdue, to be a consultant for women's careers. Of course, she was a huge hit. The girls just adored her. I think it was probably very satisfying for her, and I think it would have taken more and more of her time.

She was the first vice president of [the airline that became Northeast Airlines]. Four of them sat around their house in Rye—Sam Solomon, Amelia Earhart, Gene Vidal and Paul Collins—and they each threw in ten thousand dollars and started Northeast Airlines.

ELEANOR ROOSEVELT FIRST MET Amelia [in 1932]. She wanted to learn how to fly, and she wanted Amelia to arrange it. So Amelia got her a student pilot's license. Everything was going on absolutely beautifully. Then Eleanor told Franklin, and Franklin said, "Forget it."

IT HAD ALWAYS BOTHERED Amelia that she hadn't flown the [cross-Atlantic] plane herself, that she was so much in the public eye and everybody attributed things to her that she thought she hadn't earned. She had a very serious side, although she didn't let it show all that much. She wanted to earn her spurs. She felt she hadn't. So she decided [to fly] the Lindbergh trail.

Every woman flier wanted to do what Lindbergh had done and be the first woman to solo the Atlantic. Nobody had flown the Atlantic alone after Lindbergh—man or woman. But women, particularly, were on the Lindbergh trail. There were quite a few American women who had planes and were trying. On May 20, 1932 . . . exactly five years to the day after Lindbergh's [historic flight], she took off from Harbour Grace, Newfoundland, and spanned the Atlantic. It took 14½ hours. Although her plan was to land at Le Bourget and the American ambassador and everybody else had gone out to wait for her, she didn't make France because the winds went against her. She was also having all kinds of instrument problems. [She landed in Culmore in northwestern Ireland.] . . .

In 1935, she flew from Hawaii to Oakland, California, in a Vega. That was the first solo flight over that piece of water. . . . Later in 1935, she flew to Mexico City, which is quite high—it's 7,500 feet. . . . The air is thinner; it's hard to load up enough gasoline. Then she flew from Mexico City to Newark Airport and that was a first. She went into the record books again.

SHE WANTED TO GO AROUND the world at the world's waistline, twenty-seven thousand miles around the equator, [with] no time constraints. It had never been done. It was a huge undertaking. She hoped to do all kinds of experiments while she was doing this trip. She wanted to [test] fatigue factors. She had all kinds of general things that she was hoping to figure out.

It's very difficult to organize a trip of that magnitude. . . . She had to have gasoline shipped to various places around the world and get permission from every country that she flew over. Basically, Eugene Vidal organized the trip for her. He put the Department of Commerce at her [disposal]. He assigned an ex–navy pilot who worked for the Department of Commerce by the name of Bill Miller to Amelia to run interference.

SHE HAD HELPED GENE VIDAL get the job [as head of Commerce] and helped him keep the job. Washington being Washington, there were some senators who thought they had a better man for the job and they were pressuring Franklin Roosevelt to fire Eugene Vidal. At one point, Roosevelt actually issued an order saying that he was going to fire Vidal and put in someone else.

It was just before the 1936 election, Franklin Roosevelt's second-term election. Amelia Earhart sent a blistering telegram to Eleanor Roosevelt saying that if Franklin fired Gene Vidal, she wasn't going to campaign [for him]. . . . Within forty-eight hours, Franklin Roosevelt was having lunch with Eugene Vidal's boss at the Department of Commerce. He had changed his mind.

SHE TOOK OFF FROM MIAMI on June 1, 1937, in the Electra. Just herself and Fred Noonan. Their . . . first stop was San Juan, Puerto Rico. Then they went down to South America—Venezuela—and then across to Africa. They flew across Africa [to] Pakistan and India.

They'd had minor difficulties. There'd been a couple of short circuits . . . in the equipment. They'd had . . . several [problems] when they were in Bandung, Indonesia. . . . [The world was following her trip.] She was a syndicated columnist for the *Herald Tribune* and every time she wrote a dispatch, it was on the front page of the *Herald Tribune*.

In the end, nobody can know the details [of her disappearance] for sure. . . . Certainly . . . something went wrong. Navigation in those years was not as exact as it is now. There was probably an equipment failure. She was not communicating with the people she was supposed to on Howland Island. The plane was circling; she was definitely circling. They were going north and south—they thought they had gone far enough east and west. And somewhere, somehow, the plane ran out of gas, and they crashed into the sea.

The world's reaction was stunned amazement because she had never had a problem before. They couldn't believe it. Her navigator was supposed to have been a good navigator. He *was* a good navigator. Later, speculation has always centered on the fact that he might have been drinking because he had an alcoholic past. However, Amelia was much too smart to have taken off with a pilot that wasn't in shape. She was just too intelligent to do something like that.

Armand Hammer

by
EDWARD JAY EPSTEIN

Armand Hammer (1898–1990) was born the son of Julius Hammer, a Russian immigrant who was a founding member of the American Communist party. Armand Hammer became a premier industrialist and CEO of Occidental Petroleum. Edward Jay Epstein appeared on Booknotes *on January 5, 1997, to discuss* Dossier: The Secret History of Armand Hammer, *published by Random House in 1996.*

WHEN HAMMER DIED in 1990, he was the chairman of Occidental Petroleum. It was his company, even though he only owned 1 percent of the stock. He ran it like a personal fiefdom. He was involved in a number of philanthropic causes like the war against cancer. He was building a major monument to himself called the Armand Hammer Museum in Los Angeles. He had oil concessions around the world. He was a major industrialist.

WHEN HE WAS TWENTY YEARS OLD, his father, who was helping to found the Communist party in America, was put in prison for doing an abortion where a woman died. The whole family was disgraced. The family lost its money. They moved into a hotel. For the rest of Armand Hammer's life, he wanted to reconstruct a reputation for himself as a great man. Money didn't mean that much to Hammer. Power meant something, but it was a means to the end. The end for Hammer was honor and the Nobel Peace Prize. If he had achieved it, it would have given him this great honor. His entire life was really about this prize that he aimed for.

[Later on] he told his mistress that he had actually performed the abortion that day. . . . Because Armand wasn't even a doctor—he was a medical student—he would have gone to prison. His father, being a legitimate doctor, thought that he could get away with it. Doctors who performed abortions, if it was to save a patient's life, were allowed to do them. His father probably would have gotten away with it if it wasn't for his political background. . . . His father took the blame for Hammer and then unexpectedly went to Sing Sing, a prison in New York, for three and a half years. . . . Of course, we'll never know whether Hammer simply was taking [responsibility] for something his father did or whether he was telling the truth.

ARMAND IS A PLAY on the words *arm and hammer,* which was the symbol of the Socialist Workers party. His father was a true idealist . . . [who] believed in communism. . . . At the age of twenty-three, in 1921 . . . his father called him up to Sing Sing and said, "Now you're going to have to do something for me. The day you graduate medical school, you're going on a boat and you're going to go to Russia." It was very hard to get in. They were just finishing their revolution.

He was one of the first Americans [allowed] into Russia. . . . There were an enormous number of contacts because his father had been the unofficial ambassador of the Soviet Union and Lenin in New York. . . . His father's connections guaranteed him he would see Lenin. When he met with Lenin in November 1921, Lenin saw a young man who was smart and who was willing. As Hammer later said on one of the tapes I have, he would have jumped out of the window if Lenin had said to do it. Lenin used Hammer as an opportunity. [He] wrote a letter to Stalin some months later saying, "Armand Hammer will be our path to American business."

He first [went to the Soviet Union] in 1921 and left in 1930. During that period, he traveled back to America for [occasional] trips. . . . When his father got out of prison, he joined him in Moscow while the elder brother, Harry, remained an American and ran the New York side of the business. The business, basically, was a money laundry. It was an export-import business where the Russians would give them certain commodities at a fictitious price to guarantee them . . . a profit when they sold the commodities in America or Europe. Because it really belonged to the Soviet government, Hammer would then deliver part of the profit to a designated Soviet agent or a Soviet propaganda group. He was acting as a major money laundry for the Lenin government. He was exactly what Lenin said he was going to be. He was a path to America.

For ten years, the Soviets kept daily records on Armand Hammer in Moscow—his letters, his telephone communications, all the little businesses he set up, his accounting, money he borrowed from the banks. I got all this. So I was able to see on a day-to-day basis what Hammer had done in Russia.

OLGA WAS A GYPSY DANCER, a cabaret singer. He met her on the Russian Riviera in the Crimea when he was twenty-five years old. His brother had just gotten married, and he decided to take a wife. . . . He was married to her for about five or six years, but after he brought her back to America, he separated from her in all but name.

IN THE 1930S, he began to see that you could get political power. One of the men he eventually turned to was Jimmy Roosevelt, the son of FDR. . . . Hammer recognized the Roosevelt name and started to back him. Then Roosevelt became a congressman and introduced him to Senator Albert Gore, Sr.

Hammer went into partnership with Gore in a number of different cattle deals. . . . I don't know if there was anything wrong with the relationship. Hammer was a great liar. He would invent his past all the time; he was charming . . . and for all I know, he convinced Gore that he was totally legitimate. . . . After Senator Gore resigned from the Senate, in the late 1960s, he joined Occidental's coal company, Island Creek Coal, and Hammer made him chairman of the board. Gore . . . was a business associate almost his entire life, at least as an oil man.

WHEN HAMMER SET UP his corporation, Occidental Petroleum, he did it at a relatively late age, in his late fifties.

He basically had one oil concession, which was the basis of his entire oil company and which was in Libya. That oil concession probably was worth $4 billion or $5 billion. . . . With that money they bought other oil concessions, and they eventually merged with Iowa Beef, the largest beef processing company in America, and then bought some other companies. . . . He built a very large corporation.

Hammer had a huge corporation, but he only owned 1 percent of the stock. So he had to control the board of directors. When Hammer would appoint someone as a director of his corporation, he would ask him to sign an undated letter of resignation, which he would then keep in his desk drawer. If this person, this director, ever disagreed with Hammer or, more to the point, ever opposed him, Hammer could simply say, "You've just resigned," and replace him with someone else.

He was a man who wasn't moved by any sort of passion or emotion. He was totally focused on himself. He was focused on his plan and his advancement. People that worked for him were just steps on the ladder; he just moved them up or down as was necessary.

HILARY GIBSON . . . STARTED OUT as a journalist who met Hammer in 1974 in Los Angeles, interviewing him for *Aviations* magazine, an airline magazine. Her name [then] was Martha Kaufman, and she was very attractive and intelligent. Hammer liked her, and they began an affair. It went on for years. She eventually worked for the Armand Hammer Foundation. Then Frances Hammer, his third wife, found out about their liaison and demanded that Hammer do something about it.

Rather than give up his mistress or leave his wife, he found a solution that was typical [for him]. . . . He had his mistress totally change her identity, change her hair, change her appearance, wear a wig, and change her name from Martha Kaufman to Hilary Gibson. Then he told his wife he fired Martha Kaufman.

You just don't believe that your [spouse] is capable of such a grand deception. But the same kinds of deception that he applied in his marital affairs, he applied in his business affairs. It was the same thing to him. He would find a solution. And the solution had nothing to do with truth or ethics. It was whatever served his purpose.

He believed you could buy anything in this world. He set his sights on [the Nobel Peace Prize in 1980–81]. He had terrific focus. He would decide to do something and map [it] out, like a military campaign. . . . He realized that he needed to be nominated, which could be done by a number of parliamentarians around the world. He wanted Prince Charles to nominate him. He began cultivating Prince Charles by giving money to his favorite philanthropies and even building a college for him. . . . He began cultivating people in the Nobel Prize Foundation. He determined that the Peace Prize is given by basically a small number—five or six ex-legislators from the Norwegian parliament. He began approaching them. . . .

He had pleaded guilty to a misdemeanor having to do with violating American election laws, and he tried to get a pardon from George Bush so he'd be eligible for the prize. . . .

He had given money to the Nixon campaign after the [1972] election. This money, it turned out, was used to pay off the Watergate burglars that were in prison. The special prosecutor was very interested in why cash was donated after the election. Hammer orchestrated a cover-up where other people lied and said that they had loaned the money and that it hadn't come from Hammer. The FBI was able to penetrate this entire cover-up. When that collapsed, Hammer had the choice of either being prosecuted for obstruction of justice—that is for arranging a cover-up—or because he was old and said he was infirm, to plead guilty to a misdemeanor of simply giving the money. He pleaded guilty to the misdemeanor.

He thought he could get the pardon, and with the pardon it would facilitate him being considered for the Nobel Prize. . . . He needed a reason to get it, and he was going to try to settle the war in Afghanistan, acting on instructions of Brezhnev in Moscow, seeing Chirac in Paris, seeing Begin in Israel, seeing Jimmy Carter in Washington—shuttling back and forth.

He got Begin from Israel to nominate him. . . . He had helped Begin by supplying doctors to Israel and by helping him with his medical problems. Begin had no compunctions about nominating him. After all, it's just a letter. . . .

After Hammer died I went to Sweden and spoke to the president of the Nobel Foundation. I asked him how close Hammer had come. [To my amazement] he said, "Hammer was on a short list." "Well, how short?" "There were two people, Hammer and the Dalai Lama." The Dalai Lama won, but Hammer had almost achieved this remarkable accomplishment. It's remarkable given the fact that he was in no way deserving of a Peace Prize.

WHEN I RESEARCHED the book, . . . when I got the tapes and began to listen to Hammer, in his own voice, discussing bribes and things like that, I said, "Wow." . . . I had always had a picture of business like I read about it in *Forbes* or *Business Week,* presumably how it's taught in business school: You get up early in the morning, you work hard, you have imaginative ideas, you do things differently than other people, and you make money. With Hammer, what he really brought back from Russia was his education. That's what made him a wealthy man. It wasn't an education in literature or mathematics. It was an education in bribery, in compromise, in blackmail and how to approach a government figure and get him to give you a concession. . . . He was truly Lenin's first capitalist. He learned how to apply the principles of conspiracy to Western capitalism very successfully.

F. A. Hayek

by
ROBERT BARTLEY
MILTON FRIEDMAN
SEYMOUR MARTIN LIPSET
R. EMMETT TYRELL

Austrian economist F. A. Hayek (1899–1992) wrote The Road to Serfdom *in 1944. Because it became a seminal work that influenced economic thinking for the rest of this century, we assembled the comments of several* Booknotes *authors about Hayek: R. Emmett Tyrell,* The Conservative Crack-up *(Simon and Schuster, 1992); Robert Bartley,* The Seven Fat Years and How to Do It Again *(The Free Press, 1992); Seymour Martin Lipset,* American Exceptionalism *(Norton, 1996); and Milton Friedman, who in 1994 wrote an introduction to the University of Chicago's fiftieth-anniversary publication of Hayek's book.*

R. Emmett Tyrell

The Conservative Crack-Up

FRIEDRICH HAYEK WAS AN AUSTRIAN free-market economist. He wrote *The Road to Serfdom* right after World War II, in which he argued that Nazism was not an aberration. It was what collectivist, socialist society would lead to—Nazism, communism, and totalitarianism. [He believed] you can't have political freedom without economic freedom. Hayek was the founder of the economic thinking of modern American conservatism.

It's interesting that in Prague . . . in free Prague, in free Warsaw, in free Budapest, young men and women and old men and women whose fingers were broken by Communist truncheons for expressing their belief in freedom—those people are now in power all over Eastern Europe. They treat Hayek as a kind of founding father. They talk to people like me from the United States when we visit Prague and Budapest as though we read Hayek every morning. They think he is a formidable force and, of course, their appraisal is correct.

Robert Bartley

The Seven Fat Years and How to Do It Again

HAYEK WAS A VERY FAMOUS Austrian economist who died in 1992. He was a very elderly man. He was a contemporary and a critic of [British economist John Maynard] Keynes. Then he was more or less forgotten for a great many years. Well, "more or less forgotten" is not quite correct because he wrote a very famous book called *The Road to Serfdom.* He wasn't viewed in the forefront of modern economics during the Keynesian era. But Keynesianism collapsed during the 1970s, when you had this simultaneous inflation and unemployment that the Keynesian formulation doesn't allow. . . . Hayek said, "What will have to be explained by history is how a whole generation of economists woke up bewildered because they couldn't understand things that had been fairly widely understood before the Keynesian revolution." . . . This perception gradually spread around the world, and lo and behold, very late in his life, Hayek was given a Nobel Prize for economics.

Seymour Martin Lipset

American Exceptionalism: A Double-Edged Sword

FRIEDRICH HAYEK, who's one of the gods of the Reagan-Friedman ideology, would knock your head off if you called him a conservative. He was an Austrian. Conservatives there are people who believe in the emperor, believe in state church, believe in a strong state. Hayek was a liberal.

The original meaning of liberalism, not just in the United States and Europe, was anti-statist, anti-monarchic, and anti-mercantilist. Liberals were for a free society in which people were not only free socially and free politically, but were also free economically to do anything they wanted, without any restrictions on them by the state. The conservatives in Europe and in Canada believed in a monarchy and a strong state, in mercantilism and hierarchy. So the difference between the left and the right was that the left was anti-state, anti-monarchy, anti-hierarchy, and for separation of church and state; the conservatives were for a strong state. The right was for a strong state; the left was for a weak state.

That was relatively true in the United States, though our right was never like the European right. The point that has been made by many people is that we never really had conservatism in America. What we call conservatism, Europeans always called liberalism.

Milton Friedman

Introduction to F. A. Hayek's *Road to Serfdom*

FRITZ [FRIEDRICH] HAYEK was an economist. He was born in Vienna and started his professional career there. In the late 1920s, some people at the London School of Economics were greatly impressed with [a] book he had written and with his work. . . . At a relatively young age, he became a professor there, spending the 1930s and most of the 1940s at the London School of Economics. Early in the 1950s, he left London and came to the University of Chicago, where he was a professor for about ten years. Then he went back to Germany. He essentially retired to the University of Freiburg in Germany. . . .

He has published an enormous list of books and articles. *The Road to Serfdom* . . . was a manifesto and a call to arms to prevent the accumulation of a totalitarian state. One of the interesting things about that book is to whom it's dedicated. It's dedicated "to the socialists of all parties," because the thesis of the book was that socialism was paving the way toward totalitarianism and that Socialist Russia, at the time, was not different from Nazi Germany. Indeed, it was National Socialism—that's where "Nazi" comes from. This was a manifesto and had a very unexpected effect.

It was turned down by several publishers in the United States before the University of Chicago published it. Both in Britain and the United States, it created something of a sensation. It was a bestseller. *Reader's Digest* published a condensation of it and distributed six hundred thousand copies. You had a big argument arising about people who were damning it as reactionary against all the good things of the world, and people who were praising it and showing what the real status was.

It's a book well worth reading by anybody because there's a very subtle analysis of why it is that well-meaning people who intend only to improve the lot of their fellows tend to favor courses of action that have exactly the opposite effect. From my point of view, the most interesting chapter in that book is one labeled "Why the Worst Get on Top." It's another example of the famous statement of Lord Acton that "power corrupts and absolute power corrupts absolutely."

THE REASON THEY ASKED ME to write the introduction to the fiftieth anniversary of Hayek's *Road to Serfdom* was very clear. Hayek and I had been associated for a very long time, in particular in an organization called the Mont Pelerin Society, which he founded. The charter meeting was in 1947 in Switzerland. When I came back from the meeting, Hans Morgenthau, who was a professor of political science at the University of Chicago when I was there, asked me where I had been. I told him that I had been to a meeting called by Hayek to try and bring together the believers in a free, open society and enable them to have some interchange. He said, "Oh, a meeting of the veterans of the wars of the nineteenth century!" I thought that was a wonderful description of the Mont Pelerin Society.

Hayek and I worked together in the Mont Pelerin Society, and we fostered essentially the same set of ideas. His *Road to Serfdom,* which was published fifty years ago, was an amazing event when it came out. It's very hard to remember now what the attitude was in 1944–45. Throughout the Western world, the movement was toward centralization, planning, government control. That movement had started already before World War II. It started with the Fabian Society back in the late nineteenth century with George Bernard Shaw, [British intellectuals Beatrice and Sidney] Webb, and so on. But the war itself, and the fact that in war you do have to have an enormous amount of government control, greatly strengthened the idea that after the war what you needed was to have a rational, planned, organized, centralized society. You had to get rid of the wastes of competition. That was the atmosphere. Those of us who didn't agree, believed in what we would call a "liberal society," a free society— nineteenth-century liberalism. There were quite a number of us in the United States and in Britain, but in the rest of the world they were very isolated. Hayek's idea was to bring them together and enable them to get comfort and encouragement from one another without having to look around to see who was trying to stab them in the back, which was the situation in their home countries.

I WROTE AN INTRODUCTION to a German edition on the twenty-fifth anniversary. My introduction here is primarily the same one. It's just as applicable now as it was then. The troublesome thing is that everybody is persuaded that socialism is a failure, and yet in practice we keep moving down the Socialist road. When Hayek's book was published in 1944—or let's take not 1944, but take 1946 or 1950, just after the end of the war   government was much smaller in the United States than it is today. If I remember the numbers, government spending at all levels, for federal, state, and local, was about 25 percent of the national income. Today it's 45 percent.

The big problem with government, as Hayek points out, is that once you start doing something, you establish vested interests, and it's extremely difficult to stop and turn that around. Look at our school system. How is it our school system is worse today than it was fifty years ago? Look at the welfare state. We've spent trillions of dollars without any success. . . . I've said if an experiment in private enterprise is unsuccessful, people lose money and they have to close it down. If an experiment in government is unsuccessful, it's always expanded.

The story Hayek and I want to tell is a . . . more sophisticated and complicated story, that somehow or other there exists this subtle system in which, without any individual trying to control it, people seeking to promote their own interests will also promote the well-being of the country—Adam Smith's invisible hand. Now that's a very sophisticated story.

I'm not a conservative. I have never been a conservative. Hayek was not a conservative. The book that follows this one in Hayek's list was *The Constitu-*

tion of Liberty, a great book, and he has an appendix to it entitled "Why I Am Not a Conservative." We are radicals. We want to get to the root of things. We are liberals in the true meaning of that term—concerned with freedom. We are not liberals in the current distorted sense of the term—people who are liberal with other people's money.

Over the years, I've asked people who shifted from a belief in central government and socialism—what today goes by the name of "liberalism"—what led them to shift, what led them to an understanding that that was a wrong road. Over and over again, the answer has been *The Road to Serfdom.*

1900s

You're really, as a biographer in a sense, one part 1940s detective
with your Speed Graphic camera up over the transom catching
people in various revealing states in the next room. You're also
one part paramedic, doing artificial respiration on people who
have disappeared from the scene.

—Peter Collier

Ernie Pyle

by
JAMES TOBIN

James Tobin appeared on Booknotes *on August 10, 1997, to discuss* Ernie
Pyle's War: America's Eyewitness to World War II, *published by the Free
Press in 1997. Ernie Pyle (1900–45) was a journalist who won the 1944
Pulitzer Prize for his coverage of GIs serving on the front lines in World War
II. The 1945 movie* The Story of G. I. Joe, *was based on Mr. Pyle's life. By
the time of his death from a sniper's bullet in the Pacific theater, his column
was appearing in four hundred daily and three hundred weekly newspapers.*

ERNIE PYLE WAS THE MOST FAMOUS war correspondent of World War II.
He started out as just one war correspondent among many and became a kind
of folk hero. He was identified with the war effort and with the fighting men
of World War II in a way that no other reporter ever has been.

Pyle was a working newspaperman in the 1920s and 1930s, a good one, but
one who never reached any particular kind of acclaim or fame, until he went
out on the road in 1935 for the Scripps-Howard newspapers. [Pyle] became one
of only a very small handful of roving reporters. He wrote a six-day-a-week column based on the stuff that he saw wherever he . . . traveled around the U.S.

Pyle was a troubled guy . . . depressive, drank too much. His great difficulty
was a very sad marriage. He was married to a woman who was bright, witty, a
wonderful woman in many ways, Geraldine—Jerry—but she had just terrific
emotional problems and was alcoholic and suicidal. Their relationship became
more and more difficult as she tried to recover. . . . The recovery didn't happen,
and so ultimately they divorced in early 1942. To escape this problem and try
and shock her back into a sense of sanity, he decided it was best to go overseas.

HIS GREAT FAME began in the spring of 1943. He had, at that point, been in
North Africa for a number of months, but it was when the infantry campaign
really picked up in North Africa, when the warm weather came and the spring
campaign really began [that] he started to write these dispatches home. Quickly,
people started to realize that this guy was covering the war in a way that nobody
else was. He suddenly became this "must-read" figure.

Then he covered the Sicilian campaign that summer and that sense of "My God, you've got to see what this guy is writing" really picked up. . . . It's because he was offering a realistic, and at the same time affectionate, view of what the average soldiers were going through in combat, and [also] when they were not in combat, when they were sitting around in rest camps, when they were waiting to go into battle, recovering. . . . It was a view of the soldiers folks weren't getting anywhere else.

He's remembered for taking people to the emotional experience of being in combat, of making battle come to life. It's assumed that he was typing columns right there in the foxholes. In fact, he was almost never right at the fighting front, he was normally just to the rear, in a safer area. He would say that when he was at the front, especially when he'd been there a long time, he would become numb to the experience of combat and to the terrible scenes he was witnessing. It was only when he came back and spent time thinking about it, bringing it back to his memory, that he was able to re-create these scenes.

A GUY WROTE TO ME who was the son of a woman named Moran Livingstone with whom Ernie had a long love affair during the war. . . . I knew that Ernie had had an affair during the war, but I wasn't positive with whom and the son said, "Yeah, she was the one." He sent me back an envelope, a full file of Ernie's love letters to her, the originals.

They met just before the war. She was married to a guy named Barney Livingstone, who was the head of the AP bureau in Albuquerque, which is where the Pyles made their home. They ran in the same social circle; they developed a close friendship and, I think, had a mutual crush on each other. After Ernie was divorced, that's when the affair began and [it] became more intense after his remarriage.

Ernie was just the kind of guy who didn't keep secrets from his best friends, and he was constantly making fun of himself for his impotence. But it was what a psychiatrist would call selective impotence. He was not able to have a sexual relationship with his wife after a certain time but then overcame it with Moran Livingstone.

HIS CLOSEST CALL in Italy . . . was in Anzio, a very narrow beachhead—there was no rear in Anzio. They were constantly under shell fire. At a villa on the waterfront, where the press had their headquarters, Pyle was sleeping upstairs and a big stick of bombs hit right next to the building. He had just gotten out of bed and gone over to the window when the bomb hit; the wall collapsed right onto the bed where he had been only a few seconds earlier. That was a real close call and shook him up very badly.

WHEN HE WAS COVERING the invasion of Normandy, he wrote a famous couple of columns about walking on Omaha Beach, writing about the little things that he saw at his feet, the personal debris that soldiers had left behind, whether dead or still alive. He wrote those columns right away. He spent a day on the beachhead and quickly went back to the ship and composed these columns, so that's pretty firsthand, shortly after the event:

> I took a walk along the historic coast of Normandy in the country of France. It was a lovely day for strolling along the seashore. Men were sleeping on the sand, some of them sleeping forever. Men were floating in the water, but they didn't know they were in the water, for they were dead.
>
> The water was full of squishy little jellyfish about the size of your hand. Millions of them. In the center, each of them had a green design exactly like a four-leaf clover, the good-luck emblem. Sure. Hell yes.
>
> I walked for a mile and a half along the water's edge of our many-miled invasion beach. You wanted to walk slowly, for the detail on that beach was infinite. The wreckage was vast and startling. The awful waste and destruction of war, even aside from the human life, has always been one of the outstanding features to those who are in it. Anything and everything is expendable, and we did expend on our beachhead in Normandy during those first few hours.

He went in the second day, June 7. He had hooked up with General Omar Bradley, who was in charge of the ground forces in the invasion. . . . Bradley invited him to go on his ship—that was the kind of invitation you didn't turn down lightly. But he did turn it down, ultimately, and went ashore with low-level GIs. He actually went onto the beachhead with Bradley's staff. So he was right there on Omaha Beach, but it was the day after the worst of the fighting.

HE HAD HOPED TO GO all the way through the end of the war in Europe. After the invasion, he was with infantry and then came under the bombardment at the so-called Saint-Lô breakout. This is when Bradley coordinated a huge effort to break out of the Normandy beachhead, which had been very difficult to do, and the Allies had failed to do a couple of times.

There was an absolutely horrific artillery bombardment and mistakes were made by the air force, which involved American bombs falling on American troops. Ernie was in that and American bombs [were] falling all around him. That was an experience that shook him very deeply. He continued for a number of weeks but really lost his steam. He said in a column, "I had been pushed down into a flat, black depression."

He stuck it out through Paris and then decided he had to leave; he went home for a rest. He didn't get a rest because by that point, his fame was such that he was being constantly hounded for appearances—the real celebrity-whirlwind type of thing. He decided at that point that he did feel an obligation to go over to the Pacific.

Could he have stayed home? I think the answer is no. He had become so much a symbol of the war effort that to stay home would have been unbearable to him. He said, "I couldn't have lived with my conscience if I had stayed home." Certainly, he had done as much as anybody could expect him to do. He felt that he had to go, and so he did.

It's a long trip to get to the Pacific. He reached Guam about the end of January 1945. One of the first things he did was go on a long carrier trip . . . on board the U.S.S. *Cabot,* which was a so-called baby flattop, one of the smaller aircraft carriers. It was a long cruise, which he found unbelievably peaceful and easy to take.

He got in trouble with a lot of the guys over in the Pacific because he said that their war was paradise. . . . The guys over there were disappointed to hear him say that and criticized him for it.

It was partly to convince himself that he was doing justice to the Pacific side that he went in on the invasion of Okinawa, which involved him in the campaign called Ie Shima, a little island off Okinawa, which is where he was killed.

On the seventeenth of April, he went ashore with the army, the Seventy-seventh Division, and spent an afternoon and a night on shore. Then he caught a ride with a colonel who was crossing the island to set up a new command post. Their jeep was fired upon by a Japanese machine gunner. Ernie and the others jumped out of the jeep, got into a ditch at the side of the road. A minute later, Ernie raised his head up to get a look at what had happened to the other guys. He was hit in the head and killed. . . . His body just laid there for several hours, and a number of guys finally came and retrieved it and pulled him back.

ERNIE DIDN'T SET OUT to be a cheerleader for the GI. He set out to tell what he was seeing, and because of a natural gift for empathy, he saw that these soldiers were going through a very great ordeal that people at home needed to understand.

Adlai Stevenson

---

by
JEAN BAKER
PORTER MCKEEVER

Adlai Stevenson II (1900–65), who captured the Democratic presidential nomination in 1952 and 1956 and dominated liberal politics in postwar America, was the best-known member of an Illinois political dynasty. Historian and biographer Jean Baker tells the story of four generations of the Stevenson family in her 1996 Norton book, The Stevensons: A Biography of An American Family *which she recounted in an April 7, 1996, Booknotes interview. On August 6, 1989 viewers heard a personal view of Adlai Stevenson from Porter McKeever, a friend, UN colleague, and political aide. His book,* Adlai Stevenson: His Life and Legacy, *was published that year by William Morrow and Company.*

Jean Baker

The Stevensons: A Biography of an American Family

THE STEVENSONS CAME ORIGINALLY from the lowlands of Scotland. Life got pretty dour and tough over there so then they went to Ireland. They were part of this big migration that came to the United States in the eighteenth century, came into Pennsylvania and then worked its way by means of the Great Philadelphia Wagon Road down into the South. Each generation moved on. This is a really American story, this Scots-Irish migration.

In a critical decision for the Stevensons when they were living in Kentucky, they chose to move into the free state of Illinois. Their family history would have been entirely different had they stayed in the South, or even gone farther west into slave-holding states.

They moved to the town of Bloomington, Illinois, and stayed there for generations. Buffie Stevenson Ives maintained the old family house until she died, and it is an important part of the Stevensons' story. It's certainly something that Adlai Stevenson II depended on. He always talked about how in

Illinois, quiet reason abounded, there was less of the passion that he felt on the East Coast.

RECENTLY, THE STEVENSONS opened some private papers. In the process of doing that, they've afforded historians a longitudinal look so that you can begin with a family that's living in North Carolina and trace them all the way up to 1996. But you're not only looking at their public lives, you're also looking at their private lives. I'm convinced that the feminists have it right, that the personal is the political and the political is personal. If you're really going to understand public figures, you've got to know what their backgrounds are, what their personalities are, and what their personal turmoils are.

Adlai Ewing Stevenson IV lives in Illinois. I don't think that he has much interest in entering politics. This is one of the themes of the book, that we look at the Stevenson family—always, for generations, so interested in public life— and what we see now is a family, like many, many Americans, less interested in party politics and more interested in other aspects of life.

Porter McKeever

Adlai Stevenson: His Life and Legacy

TO ME, ADLAI STEVENSON II was someone who could be serious without being solemn. He made important issues fun to be around, exciting to be around, and even inspiring to be around. I was around him from the early days of the U.N., when he was in the Preparatory Commission in London and through two sessions of the General Assembly. Then when he went out to Illinois, those of us at the U.N. were so delighted we had someone . . . in the isolationist Midwest who would talk about the United Nations and be a positive spokesman for international affairs that we kept feeding him material all the time.

He was a president of the Council on Foreign Relations, and it was his chairmanship of the council that brought him to national attention. Particularly in the days leading up to World War II, because that led to his becoming the head in Chicago of the Committee [to Defend America by Aiding] the Allies—the William Allen White committees, as they were known in those days. This was the leading internationalist organization in the country at that time. Of course, in the area of the *Chicago Tribune,* it was a matter of great public controversy; that brought him into national and even international limelight during that period.

Edward Stettinius was appointed the chairman of our delegation to establish the U.N.—the so-called Preparatory Commission. Stettinius quickly came down with gallstones, and Adlai succeeded him to the chairmanship. He was in charge of our delegation during the whole period when the formation of the various organs of the United Nations and Security Council, etc., were being decided. It was a very influential period. He served two years with General Assembly delegations, and then he didn't hold appointive office again until Kennedy appointed him ambassador [in 1961].

HE WAS BORN in Bloomington, Illinois. He came out of a family with a long history of public affairs and public service. As a matter of fact, one of his ancestors was in command of the expedition to take Fort Duquesne and was killed on the way there. His lieutenant, named George Washington, took over. Then others of his family moved west through the Cumberland Gap and grew up in the same area where Abraham Lincoln was born. His grandfather was vice president under Grover Cleveland. His father was secretary of state of Illinois. So Adlai said he grew up with a bad case of hereditary politics. Although he didn't think of politics early in his life, he always was imbued with public service. But it wasn't until after World War II that he decided to get involved with what he then called "combat politics." General George Marshall was one of those who was rather instrumental in persuading him to go for elective office.

HE WENT TO PRINCETON. His main activity was working on the Princeton University newspaper. Those were the F. Scott Fitzgerald days—there was a whole range of humanistic studies and no one took scholarship terribly seriously. . . . It was a fairly distinguished class but, the fellow who was voted in their senior class most likely to be a politician wound up as a stockbroker. Adlai was not given any kind of a label as a politician, and he was the only one who wound up as a politician.

He was elected to public office only once, as governor of Illinois in 1948. He served four years. He wanted to serve another four years, but the presidential nomination in 1952 came to him quite unusually, almost uniquely in our history, as a genuine draft.

He tried to avoid it. Avoiding it is what led President Truman to call him indecisive. He wasn't indecisive. He was very decisive about not wanting it; he wanted another four years as governor. He did want to run in 1956, which made it difficult for him to cut it off completely in 1952. But he really wanted four more years as governor. He was a reform governor, and he knew that it would take four more years to make the reforms really stick.

But he became the Democratic presidential nominee in 1952 and again in 1956. Both times he ran against Eisenhower and nobody could defeat Eisenhower. Adlai knew he couldn't defeat Eisenhower. . . .

That election of 1956 occurred in the week that the Russians invaded Hungary, and the British and French and Israelis invaded Egypt. There was a war going on and, quite naturally, the public flocked to the leadership of an established military figure.

Once you're nominated, your job is to keep up the morale of your associates, and he kept up a brave front all through the campaign. But I had talked to him enough about it before he was nominated to know that he not only thought he couldn't win the 1952 election, but he had a real question in his mind—at the beginning, at least—as to whether he should win. He himself thought it was time for a change; he thought that the country probably needed the father figure that Eisenhower then represented. It wasn't until he got into the campaign and he was a little outraged by some of the things that happened during it that he got really gung-ho to put up a big fight.

John Brademas, who was the Democratic whip of the House for a long time, was Adlai's director of research in the 1956 campaign. John later became president of NYU. He said that during the 1956 campaign, which was quite chaotic, it was sometimes difficult to get Adlai's attention. They could always get it by going to him and saying, "Now, Governor, this will lose you votes, but it's important." He would say, "Tell me more!" This was characteristic of him. I think because he knew he couldn't win, he approached the campaign almost entirely as a instrument for educating the public on important issues.

He never got credit for it, but most of the legislative agenda—particularly in the social field—of both Kennedy and Johnson grew out of the position papers in the 1956 campaign. Federal aid to education; what is now known as Medicare; housing for the elderly; a whole range of issues and policies that we now just take for granted.

THERE'S A PULITZER PRIZE–WINNING PHOTOGRAPH of Adlai with a hole in his shoe. It tells you an awful lot about Adlai, because he was a terrific penny pincher. He would have made Calvin Coolidge look like a spendthrift if he'd ever gotten to the White House. He was careful with money because it was drilled into him as a child. One of his grandparents kept, like the elder Rockefeller did, an account of every cent that was spent. He grew up feeling that money had to be accounted for, and he was particularly meticulous about the people's money.

ADLAI STEVENSON AND HARRY TRUMAN got along with difficulty. Truman never could understand how a man would be reluctant to accept the nomination as presidential candidate, and this lack of understanding led to a lot of problems. Also, Adlai's style was quite different. Truman was decisive. He made his decisions and stuck by them. Adlai's training was as a lawyer, and he would examine several sides of a question before he'd make up his mind. To President Truman that was being indecisive.

ADLAI'S WIFE was Ellen Borden Stevenson. Her father was one of the richest men in Chicago. Her mother was one of the leading social queens of Chicago at that period. She was a bright, attractive, lovely, talented young lady. It wasn't until years later that her illness was diagnosed. It was persecutory paranoia, and it became progressively more serious and wound up being terribly destructive. It was a very sad episode in everybody's life.

She divorced him in 1949. The more famous Adlai became and the more attention that was paid to him, the more difficult it became for her. In their early married life she was the sun around which everybody revolved. Later on when Adlai became prominent, she was not that central figure, and it was terrible on her psyche.

Alicia Patterson, who with her husband Harry F. Guggenheim was the founder and publisher of *Newsday*, was a niece of Colonel McCormick who owned the *Chicago Tribune* and her father was the publisher of the New York *Daily News*—was the other love in Adlai Stevenson's life. Later on, he had a lot of good lady friends. But I think the only really serious ones were his wife and subsequently Alicia.

His relationship with Eleanor Roosevelt was very intimate. I refer to it as almost a spiritual relationship. It was so intense and lovely and mutually rewarding. At one point, Adlai was asked if the rumors were true that he was going to marry her. And he said of this woman who was sixteen years older than he: "She's much too young to consider me."

He had a lot of good lady friends. Most of them were rich and most of them were married. I think one of the main reasons was that he never looked down on women, even in his college days and post-college days. Women commented on the fact that Adlai was one of the few young men of their acquaintance who took them seriously, who, at a dance, would want to sit down and talk about serious affairs in an engaging and entertaining fashion and would listen to their opinions. They were not used to that and they liked him for it. All of his life he gave women a respect and interest that they weren't used to getting.

For a long time he never gave up being in love with Ellen, his wife. He really held on to that for a long time. I think the only other person he would have considered was Alicia. She was a very difficult, temperamental, strong-minded lady, and she would scare him off from time to time. In the last years of his life, he was enamored with the idea of marriage. He was in love with the idea of being married, but the minute it became imminent, he got a little frightened of it. He didn't want to change his way of life, and none of these "romances" ever came to fruition.

HIS RELATIONSHIP WITH HIS SONS was very good. And it got closer as the years went on because Ellen in her paranoia would not let Adlai be in touch with her, so that any efforts he made to help her out, he had to do through the boys.

ADLAI'S MOTHER was a very strong, domineering woman, and a protective mother. That was one of his struggles in life, to get out from under the protectiveness of his mother. When they would go away to camp in the summertime, she'd get a hotel very nearby. Even when he was in Princeton two different years, she took a house on the Princeton campus, which, Adlai said in one letter, was the cruelest thing that could be done to a young man. On the other hand, she also was terribly important in a positive way. She brought music into the household; she brought literature into the household. Part of Adlai's phenomenal capacity to remember things grew out of sitting at his mother's knee and hearing her read stories, literature, Shakespeare, history. More than any person I've ever heard of, he was able to learn through his ears.

His father, Adlai Stevenson, had less influence on him. They had a good relationship when he was secretary of state and just before that. They traveled a lot together around Illinois, particularly when his father was running for political office. But the poor man was afflicted with bad health. He had an accident with a gun when Adlai was young, which gave him what we'd probably now call cancer of the bone in the shoulder, which was terribly painful and caused him to have fits of anger.

STEVENSON WOULD BE SICKENED by [today's political environment]. Yet he was sophisticated enough to know that this often goes with the territory. He moved into a situation as governor that was profoundly corrupt; at that time it was believed that the governor's office got 10 percent off the top of every contract that was negotiated by the state of Illinois. At one point, when Adlai thanked the leader of the Senate for getting a piece of legislation through, the leader said, "I appreciate your thanks, Governor, but that bill cost me fifty thousand dollars." Everything was being bought and paid for in Illinois in those days. Adlai got rid of most of that, so he was aware of the real world and willing to fight it.

Jean Baker

The Stevensons: A Biography of an American Family

HE DIED A SORT of noble death. Here he was on a soft London day, walking along the street with Marietta Tree. He suddenly dropped behind, paled, and said to her this ancient Stevenson motto, "Keep your head up high," and crashed to the ground, dead of a coronary at exactly sixty-five years of age. This, it seems to me, might be a proper lifetime for a man who was born in 1900. There is a certain irony about his death because he was walking with some secret material and his briefcase sprang open and all of the pink slips were flying around in the London breeze and here lay Adlai Stevenson dead on the pavement. [His death was] a great shock to numbers of Americans who respected him a great deal.

Whittaker Chambers

---

by
SAM TANENHAUS

Whittaker Chambers (1901–61) was a member of the Communist party for thirteen years who later turned against the party. Mr. Chambers testified before Richard Nixon's House Un-American Activities Committee on August 3, 1948, accusing former State Department official Alger Hiss of being a Communist. The Hiss case so polarized the country that it continues to be debated today. Author Sam Tanenhaus appeared on C-SPAN for a special two-part Booknotes *on February 23 and March 2, 1997, to discuss his book,* Whittaker Chambers: A Biography, *published that year by Random House.*

I COMBED THROUGH THE EVENTS of [1948], and one leapt out at me: the Hiss case. It was the O. J. Simpson case of 1948 and of the cold war era. I saw very quickly that the story had been missed by all but a very few. The story was not Alger Hiss, although I originally thought it was; the story was Whittaker Chambers. Chambers, the man who recanted, the one who'd traveled that path and recoiled in horror when he saw what it led to and then, in a very public way, denounced himself and all he had done and came before the nation to make a confession about the reality of his experience and the political experience of his generation.

Chambers was the most remarkable of the era's figures, because he'd written a great book about it, *Witness,* which in 1952, when it was published, was regarded instantly as a classic. [It was] probably the best book ever written about communism by an ex-Communist who was now an anti-Communist.

Witness is one of the great American autobiographies. One of the things that fascinated me early was Chambers's literary acquaintances. Here was a man who, in his early twenties, seemed destined for great literary promise. He had the talent of Dos Passos, of a major writer, if not of one of the very greatest writers. He might not have been a Faulkner or a Hemingway, but he was born to write, and those in a good position to know these things were convinced of it. . . . Here was a man with these enormous literary gifts who turned his back on them in order to serve a cause that would bring him no glory and possibly extinction.

HE WAS BORN Jay Vivian Chambers, and his father Jay was a commercial artist. . . . He was born in Philadelphia but raised on Long Island on the South Shore, about twenty miles east of New York City. He changed his name right before he went to college. The name had always been a burden to him because he was known as Vivian. . . . On his college application to Columbia, he called himself Whittaker Chambers. Whittaker was his mother's maiden name.

[HIS POOR TEETH ARE NOTEWORTHY] because they seemed to make him, from a very early age, different from the people around him. His acquaintance Lionel Trilling was astonished by Chambers's teeth when he met Chambers at Columbia. Trilling writes in an essay that Chambers looked like he belonged to the proletariat. He looked like the kind of student radical who should be throwing a canister into the coach of the Russian czar. . . . Chambers was very proud of that.

Later, when he became a successful journalist, long after he'd left the party, he had his teeth fixed. And that was an emblem, to himself and others, that he had become a bourgeois, more ordinary man. And then, later, during the Hiss case, when it was not clear as yet whether Alger Hiss recognized his accuser, he partly identified Chambers by his terrible teeth.

HE ENTERED THE PARTY in the very beginning of 1925. He broke with it briefly from about 1929 to 1931 and then became a spy and went underground in 1932. So he spent a total of thirteen years as a Communist.

One of the things he liked about communism was the romance of it: conspiracy, changing names, changing accents. Sometimes he would speak as if he really came from Germany or Russia. He was a gifted linguist. This was easy for him to do. He spoke German, according to the wife of his friend James Agee, the great writer, with perfect inflection.

In 1931, Chambers became the hottest literary Bolshevik in New York. After having had a falling out with the Communist party, he won himself back into its graces by writing several quite ingenious short stories about the Communist movement. They were published in *The New Masses,* the party's monthly literary magazine. He later became its editor.

He worked at *Time* from 1939 until the Hiss case broke in 1948. He resigned shortly after he produced the so-called Pumpkin Papers, the incident that proved he had been an espionage agent. He was then forced to resign from *Time,* not by the company, but by his own understanding that he had misled it. He'd misled his friends, Henry Luce and others, who knew he'd been a Communist, but not a spy.

THE HOUSE UN-AMERICAN ACTIVITIES COMMITTEE was originally formed in 1938 as a subcommittee on un-American activities, chaired by Martin

Dies, interestingly, a Texas Democrat. The idea was to pursue subversion, both Communist and Fascist. There was a fair amount of Nazi agitation in the country at that point and this committee promised to look even-handedly into both.

The Hiss case began in Washington, D.C., when Chambers was summoned [to testify]. He received a subpoena at his office in *Time*. He knew it was coming. President Truman had reconvened Congress for a special session, the famous "turnip session," in the summer of 1948 in order to pass legislation that Congress had not passed, but really as a publicity stunt for his upcoming presidential campaign.

And the Congress, controlled by Republicans as a result of the 1946 elections, decided to pay Truman back by holding hearings into Communist subversion, an issue that had been very big for several years, since—and especially after—the war. A witness named Elizabeth Bentley, who had been a [Communist] courier, as Chambers had been, with Washington contacts, first testified. In order to back up her testimony, the congressional committee subpoenaed Chambers, who had previously asked to be spared a summons.

Chambers appeared on August third, testified for about an hour. None of those he named refuted his testimony but for two: Alger Hiss and his younger brother, Donald Hiss, who had also been a State Department official but had left government to work for a Washington law firm.

Both Hisses denied Chambers's testimony. Alger asked to be given equal time to appear before the committee himself, almost unprecedented among witnesses accused of communism. Hiss, at this point, had been, for a year and a half, the president of the Carnegie Endowment for International Peace. So when the story broke, Whittaker Chambers, the senior editor of *Time* magazine, one of the best-known journalists in America—another myth is that he was obscure; he was not—had accused the president of the Carnegie Endowment of having been an ex-Communist, and it was explosive. It seemed to summon up all the fears and anxieties of that era.

Nixon got into it after Alger Hiss made his first appearance before the committee—two days after Chambers had testified, August 5, 1948. Hiss gave a dazzling performance and members of the committee were ready to drop the investigation. He made a much more impressive appearance than Chambers had. Chambers spoke very well, but he was not a handsome man. He'd been up the night before. His suit was rumpled; his suits were always rumpled. He was a reluctant witness. He didn't meet his questioners' eyes. He was articulate but seemed detached as he spoke. Hiss came before the committee very forthrightly, denied everything, or seemed to, in the most forthright manner. So the committee felt embarrassed and thought they had better drop the investigation.

Richard Nixon, who had been virtually silent during both Chambers's testimony and Hiss's, had been rubbed the wrong way by Hiss. He took an instant dislike to him. Also, Nixon was familiar with the basics of Chambers's story. Nixon had come to Washington as an anti-Communist when he was a freshman congressman in 1946. He was then thirty-three years old and had defeated a very popular New Deal incumbent who held a seat on HUAC. Nixon took a seat on the committee, quickly establishing himself as the most reasoned, nonpartisan, and effective of the interrogators. For one reason, he was the only lawyer, so he knew how to question a witness; he knew how to weigh testimony. . . . Nixon . . . told the committee that he would volunteer to head a subcommittee that would look further into the investigation and would oversee it himself. And it was one of the great political moves in modern history. It got him to the presidency.

THE CAUCUS ROOM of the House of Representatives, August 25, 1948: This is the famous confrontation day when Whittaker Chambers and Alger Hiss were brought together for the first time publicly to make statements and answer allegations. They had been brought together privately about a week and a half before. This was the first great televised congressional hearing in American history.

It was a great novelty then to see television. This hearing attracted a very large audience, but I don't think the number has ever been calculated.

Chambers and Hiss testified for a total of nine hours, Hiss for seven of them. Chambers then was summoned at the last portion of the hearing. His relationship with Alger Hiss was the crux of the inquiry—not centered much on communism, interestingly enough. It was really about whether the two had been friends.

One of the long-standing myths of the Hiss case, one Chambers himself invented or perpetuated and even the leading scholars of the case have accepted, is that Chambers never mentioned the name Alger Hiss until he went before the public session of the committee, and that was not true.

[AFTER THE HEARING,] HISS LODGED his slander suit against Chambers, challenging Chambers to repeat his testimony outside a hearing room where he was protected by immunity, and Chambers did so on *Meet the Press*.

The very first question Chambers was asked was, "Are you willing to say, clear of the immunity protection of a congressional committee, that Alger Hiss was a Communist?" and Chambers said, "Alger Hiss was a Communist and may be one now."

In the slander trial, Chambers was deposed at great length by Hiss's attorneys. While being deposed, Chambers suffered a torment of conscience. He did not know whether he should produce the documentation [the Pumpkin Papers] he had. He had put it away ten years before as a life preserver, he called it, against possible recrimination by his ex-Communist comrades. He then brought some of those documents into the deposition and said, "Here is evidence that proves Alger Hiss had been a Communist before." When Chambers, in early December, produced the Pumpkin Papers, the microfilm documents turned the tables on Hiss. All parties agreed to suspend the slander trial pending the outcome of the grand jury, which was hastily reconvened in New York, to investigate the question of Hiss having been a Communist.

Alger Hiss came very close to winning early on, to having persuaded his listeners—not only the congressional committee but reporters, journalists, and interested parties—that he had been slandered by Chambers.

TRUMAN INITIALLY PORTRAYED all this as a partisan witch-hunt and, to a limited degree, he was correct, because . . . the FBI had conducted a thorough investigation. There were grand jury hearings in 1946 and 1947, and Hiss had testified at these and there had been no indictments of government employees. So he said, "This is old news." "It's a red herring" became the famous phrase.

But the Justice Department suspected that there might be trouble with Hiss. He'd been investigated before. In fact, the State Department security office had recommended his dismissal as early as 1945. They got the indictment on December 15, the very last day a grand jury sat in 1948. He was indicted on two counts of perjury, for first having denied he had known Chambers in 1936 and 1937, which had been the crux of the HUAC questioning, and secondly and more importantly, for denying he had given classified, confidential State Department documents to Chambers.

[THE FIRST OF TWO TRIALS began in May 1949. Justice Felix] Frankfurter and Justice Stanley Reed were the first two Supreme Court justices ever to give testimony in a criminal trial. Hiss had been Felix Frankfurter's protégé . . . at Harvard Law School. Hiss had studied with him, been one of his favorite pupils, and had kept up with him through the years. Stanley Reed had been the solicitor general when Hiss, in 1936, briefly went to the State Department to help write the department's defense of New Deal programs, which were being challenged as unconstitutional.

[Nonetheless, Hiss was convicted on January 21, 1950]. He spent forty-four months in jail. He had been sentenced to five years in Lewisburg Penitentiary . . . in Pennsylvania. He was a model prisoner. There is quite a fine piece by the journalist Murray Kempton, who said Alger Hiss was a great con, and by that he meant convict, I think, not con man. Maybe he meant both. In prison, he wrote briefs for fellow inmates. He instructed them in the legal process. He worked in the library. When he left the prison in 1954, there was applause. The prisoners crowded against the bars and clapped.

IT HAS BEEN PROVEN that Hiss was a Communist as definitively as it could be without a membership card surfacing, which he never would have had because he was an underground agent. Whatever doubts I had were dispelled as soon as I read the HUAC testimony, because it's very clear by the second session that Hiss is not only lying but lying in a way to protect himself against a future charge of perjury.

CHAMBERS'S RELATIONSHIP WITH McCARTHY was very interesting and complicated. . . . Joseph McCarthy, born in 1909, was a junior senator from Wisconsin in 1950 after the Hiss guilty verdict was achieved. And fifteen days later, he gave a speech in which he declared there were as many as 205 active Communists still working in the State Department . . . causing a great furor. There had been two trials and Hiss, after the first, received a hung jury. The vote was 8 to 4 to convict. In the second trial, he was found guilty of two counts of perjury, which really meant espionage, because he had perjured himself in denying he had passed confidential papers to Chambers.

After Hiss's conviction, there was a great outcry, and conservatives pointed not only to Hiss but to his wide support among Truman administration officials, including Secretary of State Dean Acheson, a friend of Hiss's, as evidence that Communists were still being sheltered by the Democrats in power. McCarthy with great, but ghastly, demagogic skills was able to make that the great frightening crusade of the early 1950s.

IN 1950, CHAMBERS WAS ON HIS FARM writing *Witness*. This is one of the extraordinary things about Chambers. I can't think of another man, another American, who could be meeting with Joseph McCarthy one day and the next writing one of the great literary classics of the century. To combine those features in a single mind or soul is almost beyond comprehension.

Whittaker had a very difficult and tumultuous life . . . [his] bisexuality [was] something that was exploited very cruelly during the Hiss case at a time when there were only rumors and very vicious rumors at that. But eventually Chambers himself, in an act of great courage, told the FBI that he had had a brief period of homosexual activity. This emerged in the 1970s when the FBI released documents under the Freedom of Information Act. . . . It was something a reader should know about, not only because it tells us something about Whittaker Chambers, but it also explains the great pressures he labored under during the Hiss case, because he knew very early that this would be brought up and used against him in some way.

What surprised me about Whittaker Chambers was how fair-minded he could be. Chambers has been reviled for his treatment of his colleagues and of the news while at *Time* magazine. What I discovered was, he was right in almost everything he said and treated those around him with great personal consideration. He was a very warm and humorous man.

WILLIAM F. BUCKLEY was Chambers's closest friend in the last years of Chambers's life and had edited a marvelous series of letters called *Odyssey of a Friend,* which was the very voluminous correspondence Chambers sent him from 1954 until his death in 1961. Chambers was bedridden in his last years. This is something even people who know a fair amount about him don't realize. I learned it simply because I had to prepare a chronology for my book and I calculated what he was doing in any given month. He was on his back a lot of the time. He got well up over two hundred pounds in his last years. He stopped worrying about his health. However, he was enormously strong. If you'd looked at his forearms, you'd see he was very powerful. One of his *Time* colleagues said, "He was fat, but it was hard fat." He worked his farm as well as he could despite his ailments. . . .

He died in 1961 of prolonged heart ailments. He was sixty years old. He had his first heart trouble as early as the 1940s, when he was working at *Time* magazine, and there were recurrent bouts.

PEOPLE HAVE THE IMPRESSION that once he left the Communist party, he instantly became a conservative. That's not quite right. He became an anti-Communist, as many others did. But his move to the right was rather more gradual than that, and in his last years, he found himself distancing himself from what was then the dominant strain of American conservatism: the McCarthy wing of the Republican party and also the conservative tenets of *The National Review.* He found himself increasingly concerned about that. And so, in a sense, Chambers himself arrived at a kind of liberalism, but never a secular kind.

I HAVE ENORMOUS ADMIRATION and sympathy for Chambers. What I remind people, especially conservative friends, is that Chambers himself, at one point, was one of the most radical men in America. It's impossible to understand him . . . unless one has real sympathy for the progressivist or liberal political outlook that he himself embraced fervently for a number of years.

Chambers was a very religious man. Even when he was a Communist, he was a kind of religious man. That is, he sought great answers and absolute answers, final solutions to important questions. . . . That made Chambers appealing to me because he embodied so many of those different sides. But he was never happy. He wanted one answer. If it wasn't communism, it had to be anti-communism. If it wasn't anti-communism, it had to be Quakerism. [He wanted] something very powerful that he could invest all his being in.

Strom Thurmond

by
NADINE COHODAS

Once the Democratic governor of South Carolina, Strom Thurmond (b. 1902) has been a United States senator since 1954, setting the record for U.S. Senate service. In 1964, he switched to the Republican party. Nadine Cohodas, formerly a reporter for Congressional Quarterly, *is the author of* Strom Thurmond and the Politics of Southern Change *(Simon and Schuster, 1993). She appeared on* Booknotes *on April 4, 1993, to discuss the senator's long political career.*

PEOPLE TAKE [STROM THURMOND] SERIOUSLY down in South Carolina. They have learned over a long period of time that if he says, "I am ready to go," you better get out of the way or be prepared.

I can sum my book up in two sentences, two themes: to show the power of race to shape politics but also the power of laws to shape behavior. It seems to me that Senator Thurmond's very long career illustrates that.

Senator Thurmond . . . is a man who loves politics—who lives, sleeps, eats, and breathes it. He ran for his first office when he was twenty-six years old, becoming a superintendent of the Edgefield County schools, state senator, judge, governor, United States senator. His entire life has been out among people as a politician. I don't use that word pejoratively, but as in listening to people, talking to people, feeding off of that [interaction].

I've always thought that Senator Thurmond is ideological, with strong views, but he is primarily a legislator. This is somebody who, if he wants to get something done, listens to where the other side is. You can do business with him. . . . Look at Senator Thurmond's elections in South Carolina—extraordinarily large margins. Even after the 1965 Voting Rights Act, when you have blacks finally voting in a state with the second largest black population . . . Senator Thurmond won, with one exception, with over 60 percent of the vote.

RIGHT BEFORE HIS MARRIAGE to his first wife, Jean Crouch, who was twenty, twenty-one years his junior, he did a famous headstand for her. She had just graduated from college. He had seen her and found her attractive and invited her to work in the governor's mansion. A romance blossomed. They announced their engagement, to a lot of titters. To show, as the photo caption in *Life* magazine said, that he was plenty vigorous and virile, he stood on his head. He was just a few months shy of his forty-seventh birthday. They had no children. She died, tragically, very young in 1960—in her early thirties—of a brain tumor. A painful experience for him, from all that I can gather.

Her father was a very longtime Democratic party official in Barnwell County, South Carolina. Senator Thurmond had gone to see him and noticed the picture on the wall and said, "Who is that lovely-looking girl?" He said, "That's my daughter." Later, when he was governor, he went to Winthrop College, where she happened to be a student, and saw her again. That reminded him of the picture, as his telling of it goes. He invited her to come to the governor's mansion to work after graduation. It was one of those chances—seeing a picture, seeing the person, being governor, having a job to offer.

There is a little story about her that's rather poignant, about not fully understanding what she was getting into. After they were married, they came back and had an open house at the governor's mansion. After an hour and a half, she had to excuse herself and go upstairs because her hand had swollen from shaking hands. This was not an experienced politician.

Another thing that was rather poignant: In writing [to] her parents that she wanted to marry then-Governor Thurmond, she said that she knew that he would take very good care of her, and they would be very happy. He would be through being governor in just a few years, and then they could move on. I don't think she fully realized that this was a man as much in love with politics as with other things and that there was a long political career ahead of him.

He was governor one term: elected 1946 and served until 1950. He was actually a very progressive governor, in terms of moving toward a reorganization of government agencies. The most important thing that happened during those years as governor was . . . his inexorable journey from a brand-new governor of a relatively small state to someone who was going to be the focal point, the mouthpiece, for the states' rights Democrats.

His inaugural address was quite striking. It was one of the longest ones ever given because of the detail, the things that he set out that he wanted to do. He had been interested in education as a state senator and repeated that theme as governor. He said directly in his inaugural speech that we must have more money to educate our Negro children, which was the term then. I think that is noteworthy for a couple of things: first, his interest in education; second, his clearly addressing the separate-but-equal concept and making some acknowledgment that equal was not equal. . . . He deserves some credit for that.

There is one other story related to this whole theme of race and politics: Within a month of his taking office, there was the most brutal lynching in

South Carolina in years. A man named Willie Earle was thought to have killed a cabdriver. Some of this cabdriver's friends came to the jail, overpowered everybody. They took Earle out and killed him in such a brutal manner that he was able to be identified only because somebody knew that he had some money in his pocket and they found these torn bills in his pocket.

Governor Thurmond issued a statement in the strongest terms condemning the act and dispatched a special prosecutor up to Greenville, S.C., to help the local authorities try the case. The men were tried, but the jury—all men, all white—found all the defendants, some of whom had even admitted taking part in this event, not guilty. Governor Thurmond said, in response to letters, "We did the best we could, but at least we've shown that lynching will not be tolerated." He received a lot of acclaim for that from the North.

[IN 1954, HE WON ELECTION to the Senate by write-in—the first and only time in history.] By this time, he had been out of office for a couple of years; he'd finished his gubernatorial term in 1950. He ran for the Senate against Olin Johnston—the only head-to-head race he ever lost—and was a very successful lawyer in Aiken. But he kept speaking to civic groups, and people certainly knew that Strom Thurmond was around. . . . He finally announced that he was going to be a write-in candidate. . . . It was a handsome victory. . . .

HIS ACTUAL, OFFICIAL SWITCH to a Republican was 1964, to support Barry Goldwater. It was really the end point of something that began in 1948, when he emerged as the leader of the states' rights Democrats and said, like so many southerners, "We're the [true] Democrats." . . . I believe he supported Eisenhower in 1956 and was very cagey about what he was going to do in 1960. He certainly spoke harshly about the [Democrats'] platform in 1960.

HE RAN FOR PRESIDENT in 1948. They called themselves the States' Rights Democrats. His vice presidential running mate was Fielding Wright. . . . He won four states and, I believe, [thirty-nine] electoral votes. The senator said that in all the elections that he's been in, he thought that was very important. It pulled four states out of the traditional Democratic allotment. And it let the South know for the first time since the days after Reconstruction . . . that if you didn't vote straight Democratic the sky was not going to fall.

IN 1957, IN THE MIDST OF WORK on a civil rights bill, he gave the longest filibuster speech in Senate history. Eisenhower was president. Lyndon Johnson was majority leader. Richard Russell of Georgia was the senior tactician for the southern senators. They were not very happy about a civil rights bill, but . . . they thought something was going to be enacted and they should try to make it as little harmful to the South as possible.

Senator Thurmond was particularly concerned about the jury trial provisions and whether somebody would be entitled to a jury trial if he were found liable for violating someone's civil rights. . . . Senator Thurmond quietly told Russell on his own that he was going to have to oppose it. . . . [His aide, Harry Dent,] began to think something was up when he saw the senator gathering papers to take reading material to the floor in the early evening.

Earlier in the day the senator went to the steam room for a long time to completely dehydrate himself so that he would not have to go to the bathroom and, therefore, give up the floor. He put a bunch of malted milk balls in one pocket and some throat lozenges in another and went out to the floor. He had been brought dinner by his wife . . . who went upstairs in the family gallery to watch. Coincidentally, Clarence Mitchell, who was then one of the senior people with the NAACP in Washington . . . also sat in the gallery as he began speaking at 8:54 P.M. on August 28, 1957.

He began by reading every state statute that covered voting in an effort to say we don't need a federal voting rights law. . . . He got a couple of acceptable breaks when somebody asked permission to put something in the record, and he could yield for that purpose. This went on until 9:12 the next night, August 29, when he walked off the floor.

Harry Dent had gone to see the Senate doctor. He was worried about Thurmond, and the doctor sent a message back and said, "You tell him if he doesn't get off the floor, I'm going to come and carry him off." Dent had brought a bucket right inside the cloakroom in case Thurmond needed to relieve himself right away, but he just brushed Dent aside and talked to reporters. There is a wonderful picture of Jean Thurmond waiting for the senator, and the gloss is so clear you can see the stubble on his cheeks. . . .

[During the filibuster] the senator would ask Harry Dent periodically, "Are you hearing anything?" "Go check, are there any phone calls coming in; are there any telegrams?" He was hoping that when people knew that he was out there—southerners—they would start pressuring their own senators and he might get some support. . . . [However,] it was not at all well received by his southern colleagues.

It was fascinating to me when Senator Thurmond and I went over that incident; he told me about this with the same degree of detail and emotion as though it had been yesterday. He got angry all over again that his southern colleagues would not come out and join him because he was convinced they could have stopped it.

HE MARRIED HIS SECOND WIFE, NANCY, not too long after the 1968 presidential election that brought Richard Nixon to the White House. . . . His decision to marry Nancy Moore was not at all popular with the people closest to him. His closest aides, Harry Dent and Fred Buzhardt, begged and pleaded with him that it was just the worst thing in the world to do. He said, "All right. Go and talk to Nancy and if she says that she won't, well, then it's all right with me." They worked on her, and she said, "But I love him, and I want to marry him." Later when I was talking to the senator about that, he said, "I knew she wouldn't say no. . . ." By that time the senator was nearly sixty-eight years old and Nancy Moore was about twenty-two and a half—a forty-four-year age difference. . . . It just was not a very smart political thing to do.

But, as history has shown, it has not turned out to be that [problematic] at all. Indeed, in 1978, having a young, attractive wife and four very cute children who ran around the state in the Strom [campaign] truck with T-shirts that said "Vote for my daddy" was a wonderful thing to blunt [challenger] Pug Ravenel's appeal. . . .

SENATOR THURMOND was born at the turn of the century into a social system that was already set and was only going to be hardened, that said blacks do not become lawyers who might represent white people; they certainly don't become judges; they don't become doctors who serve the white population; they don't become college presidents, anything like that. Yet here he was, many years later, embracing a black man, Clarence Thomas, for a seat on the United States Supreme Court.

I had covered Senator Thurmond since 1979. I had seen this man, whom I had identified, like so many others, as this old segregationist, the Dixiecrat candidate who holds the record for the longest filibuster against the civil rights bill. He had given a speech right after he was going to become the Judiciary chairman, saying, "We're going to have a voting rights act; it's got to be a national act," which is a euphemism for saying "We're going to gut the thing." Yet, he turned out to be such a completely different kind of chairman; [he even] supported the Martin Luther King holiday.

There is a terrific story in Senator Thurmond's life because, in one political career, you have the old South and you have the new South. There is no other senator—I'll even go as far [as to say no other] member of Congress—whom you can look at in quite the same way.

Clare Boothe Luce

by
SYLVIA JUKES MORRIS

Clare Boothe Luce (1903–87) wrote Broadway hits, a book on the fall of France during World War II, was an editor at Vanity Fair, *and, in 1942, became a U.S. congresswoman, representing Fairfield County, Connecticut. Her husband, Henry Luce, was the founder of* Time *magazine. Sylvia Jukes Morris appeared on* Booknotes *on July 27, 1997, to discuss* Rage for Fame: The Ascent of Clare Boothe Luce *(Random House, 1997).*

ONE DAY I WAS READING CLARE'S YEARBOOK from when she was a child at St. Mary's School in Garden City, [N.Y.]. She was about fourteen years old, and in the yearbook, there was a picture of her, and underneath she had written, "A rage for fame attends both great and small" . . . I did some research and I found it was from an eighteenth-century English poet. It was an ode, and the last two lines were "A rage for fame attends both great and small; Better be damned than not be named at all." I realized that from a small girl, she had . . . wanted to be famous. I thought that *Rage for Fame* was just a perfect title [for my book] because her whole life . . . was to that end.

She became a celebrity because she was such an achiever. Playwright, . . . foreign correspondent, reporter, . . . congresswoman . . . and novelist, too. She wrote a series of short stories that read like a novel, but they're actually interrelated stories called *Stuffed Shirts*. That was her first published book. She wrote a serious work of history . . . called *Europe in the Spring*. She wrote three big Broadway plays, every single one a hit and every one made into a movie. *The Women* came first, then one called *Kiss the Boys Goodbye*, 1938, and then in 1939, a play called *Margin for Error*, which had Otto Preminger playing a Nazi consul who was protected by a Jewish New York policeman.

SHE HAD VERY LITTLE EDUCATION. . . . She left school at sixteen and married, at twenty, a very wealthy Fifth Avenue millionaire and found that he drank a lot. They had one child. After six years of marriage, she was divorced. She found herself extremely restless, bored, even depressed and went to a psychiatrist for a while. That didn't seem to fix it. She met Condé Nast at a dinner party one night and asked him for a job on *Vogue* or *Vanity Fair* or [another] one of his magazines. He said, "Oh, no, you society women—I'll give you a job, and then come winter you'll be off to Palm Beach."

But she wouldn't take no for an answer. She simply took herself down to the Graybar Building, which housed *Vogue* in those days, found an empty desk, sat down, and began to write captions for *Vogue* articles. At the end of the week, when the pay man came around with the paychecks, there wasn't anything for her. She said, "Oh, well, when the editor gets back from Europe"—she was seeing the French collections in Paris—"I'm sure I'll be put on the list." When the editor came back and saw her sitting there, she thought Condé Nast had hired her. Nast saw her there and he thought the editor had hired her. That's how she got the job with *Vogue*.

She became a feature writer. Right next door to *Vogue* were the offices of *Vanity Fair,* and the editor-in-chief was a man called Frank Crowninshield, an extremely cultivated Bostonian. He used to go snooping in the *Vogue* offices looking for talent for his own magazine. That's how he found Dorothy Parker. He quickly sniffed out Clare Luce—Clare Brokaw in those days— and lured her away. She started to work for him. She learned a great deal from her then managing editor, a man called Donald Freeman, who was just a little younger than she was. He fell madly in love with her, and he taught her all he knew. She began to write stories of her own, as well as doing editing chores. When he was killed in a car crash—maybe a suicide over love for her, we're not quite sure—she became managing editor. She got the job in *Vogue* late 1929, moved to *Vanity Fair* at the end of that year. By late 1932, she was managing editor.

It's extraordinary. In her usual way, she mastered a job very quickly and then got quickly bored and wanted to move on to something new. She loved to learn. After about eighteen months as managing editor, she took a leave of absence and said she wanted to try her hand at writing plays. She went south and stayed at a resort . . . called The Cloister in Georgia. Eugene O'Neill lived just along the beach from the hotel. She got herself a dinner invitation so she could compare herself with the great dramatist to see if he really was smarter. I don't think she found herself wanting, and so [she] stayed down there for about three months writing plays.

When she went back to New York, she still didn't have a finished work, so she took a job as . . . a travel writer with Hearst and other syndicated newspapers and worked on that for a few months until she met Henry Luce.

Henry Luce was the publisher then of *Time* and *Fortune* magazines. They met at a dinner party. He was extremely rude to her on their first encounter. He had a very quick conversation about picture magazines, which were still not a big thing here, but they were in Europe. He was thinking of emulating them. She, while at *Vanity Fair,* had tried to make *Vanity Fair* into a picture magazine, but Condé Nast had lost a lot of money in the Crash; he didn't have the finances. She still had the idea that it would be a great thing to do. She talked to Luce about it. Suddenly he took out his pocket watch, looked at it, said it was time to go, snapped it shut, clicked his heels, and walked away. She thought he was the rudest man. He picked her brains and just left her standing.

When they met the next time . . . it was to celebrate *Anything Goes,* [Cole Porter's] new musical. . . . She saw him coming across the room carrying champagne glasses—one was for his wife. She said, "Oh, Mr. Luce, is one of those for me?" At that moment, the lights went down because the floor show was coming on. She said, "Why don't you sit down." He sat down, and they talked and talked and talked intensely. He invited her down to the lobby—this was the Waldorf-Astoria Hotel. He admitted that he'd fallen in love. It was a *coup de foudre*—a stroke of lightning. She was now the one woman in his life. He would call on her next Thursday afternoon to see what they were going to do about it.

He was married with two small children. At first, he wanted to have a little experiment: They would see each other quietly for a year, but he didn't want any scandal because he didn't want to disturb his little ménage. He didn't want any scandals attached to his magazines, either. But Clare didn't want that. She said, "I don't think that's appropriate for us. We're both well-known figures in New York society, and there's no way we could keep it secret anyway. I think you should go away and take care of your affairs. Meanwhile, I'll go to Europe for several months. If you resolve that you still want to marry, then come to me."

We're talking now about 1934–35. They actually married at the end of 1935. He was not yet quite as powerful as he later became in the 1950s, but he certainly was getting that way. . . . *Time* magazine . . . was widely circulated and read and was a real opinion-maker.

His magazine editors didn't care for [the relationship] because they were very possessive of him. He'd always been hard-working and collegial with them—rolling up his sleeves with them to put the magazines to bed. Suddenly he's married to this enchanting, brilliant woman, with whom he was totally besotted. He would want to take the five o'clock train home to Connecticut every night so he could be with her and [he wanted to] take long vacations with her. At one point, two of his editors took them both out to dinner and said, "Harry, you used to be here till ten o'clock at night on the magazines. Now you want to be home on the five o'clock train. There's no way you can run your magazines this way." She, who had hoped that they were going to offer her a job on one of the magazines at this dinner party, fled the room in tears, saying, "He could edit all his magazines with one hand tied behind his back." She rushed off and decided she was going to be a playwright, took herself off to the Greenbrier Hotel in West Virginia, and wrote *The Women* in three days, which was her biggest Broadway hit.

[SHE WAS ELECTED TO CONGRESS] twice, [representing] Fairfield County, Connecticut, for the Republican party. It was wartime, and she was a good deal more liberal in her voting than people now give her credit for. She was very pro GI Bill; she was pro liberalizing the immigration laws. She was much more Democratic in her way of thinking in those days than she subsequently became. She later became the great anti-Communist that she's now known for and a big fiscal conservative.

She was appointed by [President Dwight] Eisenhower as ambassador to Italy in 1953. She was the first woman to have a major diplomatic post of that kind. There had been women ambassadors but only to minor posts. . . .

She always kept up her journalistic career. She was a war correspondent for *Life* magazine before she went to Congress. She always kept her hand at writing political columns for the rest of her life. . . . She was, I think, the most admired woman in America next to Eleanor Roosevelt and the most admired in the world next to Eleanor and the queen of England.

RANDOLPH CHURCHILL WAS A SMALL FLING; he was much younger than she was. They met in the summer of 1934 when she went to stay one weekend at his father's country house in Kent, when she was having an affair with the financier Bernard Baruch. He called her in Paris and said, "Mr. Churchill invites you to join us for the weekend." The person who met her at the station was Randolph Churchill. He then was about twenty-two years old and like an Adonis; he was a stunning man and also had a romantic turn of mind, as she did.

One day she started to tell me about that weekend at Churchill's country house. She went to bed that night. She was just on the point of falling asleep when her bedroom door opened and somebody came in in the dark. She heard him crossing the room; he tripped over the coal scuttle. She put on the light quickly and she said, "Well, it was Bernard Baruch, and I was expecting Randolph. . . ."

The Bernard Baruch affair didn't go on, but the friendship was lifelong until he died in his nineties. They were always friends. Bernard Baruch was a so-called speculator. He was a man who knew Wall Street and who became something of an adviser on economics to Presidents Wilson, Roosevelt, Hoover, and various others. She fell in love with him because he was much older. She'd lost her father when she was very young, so he was something of a father figure as well as a mentor. He taught her about politics and economics. He was not attainable. Anybody who was not attainable for Clare became the one that was most desired. Although they had a small fling in the early 1930s, it didn't go on for long because he was so much older than she was. He was married, and he had grown children. He was not in love with her either. He said to a mutual friend who passed the word on that although he was fond of Clare his heart was not involved. That was devastating to her.

There's no actual documentary evidence of an affair with Joseph Kennedy. . . . He had so many with other women. She did, in one of her diary entries, when she was staying in a Paris hotel, once write that he was in her room all morning. She kept meeting him on transatlantic crossings when she was alone, without Harry Luce. She saw him in Rome and in London many, many times when Harry wasn't there. It's probably correct to say that there was something of a short fling.

Sir Charles was General Charles Willoughby, who was an intelligence chief to General Douglas MacArthur in the Philippines. Clare was always interested in military men—particularly if they had anything to do with spying. Since he was the intelligence chief, she was incredibly drawn to him. He was also rather taciturn—the strong, silent type—and tall and striking looking. She said to me that he was the one man that she might have liked to run away with. It turned out that Willoughby never came back after the end of the war. . . .

Condé Nast . . . was [also] in love with Clare. Clare said that Nast wanted to divorce his wife and marry her, but she was not interested in Condé Nast. She was not attracted to him at all. . . . She saw him frequently and socialized with him a lot. He was madly attracted to her, but she simply wasn't attracted to him. His wife was apparently sapphic; she went both ways, and she did make a pass at Clare.

I FIRST MET CLARE IN THE FALL of 1980 in Washington. It was really a strange meeting because I had already conceived the idea of doing a biography of her. This invitation came from a hostess in Washington. I was in New York at the time. I said, "Well, it's a long way to come for a dinner party. Who's coming?" My hostess said, "Oh, Clare Luce." I had just had the idea of the biography. I thought, Well, should I go and meet this person because I may not like her or I may like her too much and—either way, it's not a good frame of mind to write a biography. You have to like, but not to be in love with, [your subject]. . . . [I went there and] the hostess said, "She won't take any notice of you because she's only interested in men." She sat at my table, and I was across from her. She sat next to the military historian Alistair Horne. . . . The whole evening, she just concentrated on talking to him about military things because that was one of her loves. Then at the end of the evening, I was standing at the top of the staircase. . . . She put her hands on my shoulder and I thought she'd mistaken me for the hostess. She said, "Oh, good night, you sweet thing," and then just swept out. Shortly after that I wrote to her and asked her if I could do the book.

I LIKED HER A LOT, and I admired her very much. She had this incredible sense of humor. Sometimes she would be a bit of a monologist. At dinner parties she'd get a little boring with her political views, but she was so funny. . . . She had this redeeming humor.

[She died in October of 1987 of brain cancer.] When I picked up the phone and the secretary said, "Sylvia, Clare died last night," I had that feeling you sometimes have when your heart goes . . . thud. It was a real thud. I rushed over to the apartment straight away and was at all the funeral services and went down to the burial, at her southern plantation in South Carolina, which is now a Trappist monastery. She's buried there under the great live oaks by the Cooper River. [For] the next three months or so . . . I kept dreaming about her a lot.

I had strange dreams, and one was particularly weird. . . . She was a stripper in a vaudeville show wearing a bright blue spangled dress. It was a Technicolor dream, which is strange, because I think most people dream in black and white. Although she actually didn't take off her clothes, I knew it was a strip show. But it was an old Clare; it was an old face with a sort of blond wig and very long black eyelashes and a deep gash of a red mouth. I realized that what this dream symbolized was that I was going to expose Clare in my writings. I was going to write about her most intimate life. It was very troubling. . . . I was grieving, and the grieving wouldn't end; it just went on and on. For several months, I dreamt about her constantly. I suppose it was because I loved her; I'd come to love her, even though I tried to distance myself from her.

Thurgood Marshall

by
HUNTER CLARK AND MICHAEL DAVIS
JUAN WILLIAMS

The great-grandson of a slave, Thurgood Marshall became a counsel for the National Association for the Advancement of Colored People in 1938. His most famous case was Brown v. Board of Education *(1954), which overturned* Plessy v. Ferguson *(1896) and its "separate but equal" ruling that legalized segregation. In 1968, he became the first African-American to serve on the Supreme Court. On January 3, 1993, Hunter Clark and Michael Davis appeared on* Booknotes *to talk about their book* Thurgood Marshall: Warrior at the Bar, Rebel on the Bench *(The Carol Publishing Group, 1992), and on October 11, 1998, Juan Williams discussed* Thurgood Marshall: American Revolutionary *(Times Books, 1998).*

Hunter Clark and Michael Davis

Thurgood Marshall: Warrior at the Bar, Rebel on the Bench

BROWN V. BOARD OF EDUCATION was probably Thurgood Marshall's most important achievement as a lawyer. Certainly, as a case, it stands as perhaps the most significant legal opinion of the twentieth century, in terms of its social impact.

To put it in context, the NAACP began a litigation strategy during the 1920s designed to challenge the separate but equal doctrine. . . . Their initial goal was to show that African-Americans were being accorded separate treatment, [yet] not equal. The purpose of the strategy was to force equality of treatment, the idea being that most states would probably decide that it was easier to integrate their schools or their public accommodations than to set up a wholly separate but equal school system for blacks—or a system of public accommodations for blacks.

Thurgood Marshall was the lawyer [who argued *Brown v. Board of Education* for the NAACP]. Black and white media started referring to him as "Mr. Civil Rights." When the headlines were written and when the newscasts went out, it wasn't the name of NAACP President Roy Wilkins that was foremost in the minds of Americans when they thought about the NAACP. It was Thurgood Marshall [their chief lawyer].

Thurgood Marshall had argued in his brief [for *Brown*] that the only reason segregation had ever been imposed was because of a belief in the inferiority of African-Americans. When Earl Warren called together the justices to consider *Brown,* he said very simply to them, "I agree with Thurgood Marshall that segregation was imposed out of a belief that blacks are inferior. If anyone here believes that, they should be willing to say it openly, to write it straightforwardly. But if no one is willing to do that, I think we have a unanimous decision." The Supreme Court unanimously sided with the NAACP and said that segregation had no place in public education under the Constitution.

Juan Williams

Thurgood Marshall: American Revolutionary

THURGOOD MARSHALL WAS BORN in 1908 in Baltimore and died in 1993. . . . At the time that he was ready to go to law school right after graduating from Lincoln University in Oxford, Pennsylvania, the University of Maryland Law School was not accepting any applicant who was black. Marshall needed the opportunity to go to his state law school because his family didn't have much money. He was a middle-class black kid in the city of Baltimore. His father had been a Pullman car porter and then a steward at the Gibson Island Country Club off the Chesapeake Bay. His mother was a schoolteacher. They had another son who had just gone through college and who'd had a difficult time paying the tuition bill for college because Thurgood's father had become ill. . . . The parents had thought that Aubrey was the star of the family and Thurgood wasn't as serious a student. But here came Thurgood who wanted to go to law school. The ideal would have been for Thurgood to go just down the street; the University of Maryland Law School being in Baltimore. . . . But they weren't accepting blacks, so he applied instead to Howard University Law School; he would get on a train about 5:00 A.M. every morning from Baltimore, ride to Washington, D.C. to attend classes, and not get back home till after midnight.

Howard turned out to be a wonderful thing, a godsend, in that Charlie Houston [was on the Howard Law School faculty]. . . . Houston had such a wide network of connections. [Thurgood] was already doing some work for the NAACP. . . . Houston had Marshall help him on a criminal case in Virginia where a man was charged with the murder of a white woman, then ran away to Boston. . . . Marshall was there to help as the case was argued. He [gained] the experience of what it was like to be a lawyer, to feel . . . the thrill and to connect with the idea that this was about more than just winning cases. This was about changing the sociology of America with regard to race.

[Thurgood Marshall graduated from Howard in 1933. From] 1933 to about 1938, he was in Baltimore . . . in private practice. But much of his work was taken up with NAACP affairs. Houston was up in New York running the NAACP's legal office as a one-man show. He was relying on Marshall oftentimes to do work for him. Marshall came into a relationship with a man named Carl Murphy, who was the head of the *Afro-American* in Baltimore. Mr. Carl, as he was called, was a real bantam rooster of a character and very much a man who was involved in trying to improve race relations in Maryland. [He] began to use . . . Marshall's legal skills to work on the race issue in that state. So Marshall began, almost from the time that he got out of law school, finding that this was his calling. People who were trying to create a strong NAACP chapter in Baltimore were making use of him and Houston was making use of him from New York for national issues. He began to pester Houston from early on "Please, can I come up and join your staff?" The NAACP at first didn't have the money. But by 1938, the decision was made to bring Marshall on board.

MARSHALL FIRST MARRIED right at the end of his college years. This was an interesting time in his life. He'd been a frat boy, out for a good time. He had a transforming experience during those college years, meeting Langston Hughes, the writer, and becoming engaged in critical arguments about whether or not the faculty at Lincoln should be all white. . . . Marshall at first was dismissive of this. . . . [Then] he had an incident where he went down to a movie house on a Saturday afternoon and tried to sit down in the mezzanine area instead of up in the balcony, where colored were supposed to sit. He was rousted and run back to campus. He started to [think], "This isn't right." Langston Hughes was [soon] knocking at the door. "What happened to you? You paid your money, didn't get to see your western movie?" Marshall began to change. He [became] racially conscious for the first time. He was not content with the segregation he had seen practiced.

His consciousness was being raised at the moment . . . when he had a terrible accident. He was coming back from a trip and was running to catch up with a truck and landed on the hitch of the truck and severely damaged a testicle; it had to be removed. It had a tremendous impact on his life and on his thinking. Suddenly he was in the mood to settle down. His first marriage was to Vivian Burey, a woman who was a coed at the University of Pennsylvania. He was married to her in his senior year at Lincoln, from which he was graduated in 1930.

They were married until right after *Brown* in 1954. She died of cancer, a horrible death in which she wasted away. He tried to be with her as much as he could. . . . His life with her was interesting in that he was on the road a great deal. He was [at that point] lead lawyer for the NAACP and had to travel all over the country. They didn't have children, which was a great frustration to him, partly tied to the fact that he wanted evidence that he could father a child. Having lost a testicle, it was very important to him. . . . She had several miscarriages, and it lent a chill to the relationship, although she was a great supporter of his. But more and more, he found himself on the road and away from home.

HE WAS ON THE SECOND CIRCUIT from 1961 until he became solicitor general in 1965. The story here was the difficulty in getting confirmed. . . . At first, Robert Kennedy, the attorney general, did not want to take the risk of appointing Thurgood Marshall to an appeals level court. He was more content to say, "Okay, Thurgood Marshall has earned some spurs. People know who he is. He's 'Mr. Civil Rights' in much of black America, and he is *the* black lawyer. But we don't want to offend southern senators or anybody who might remember his work for the NAACP, especially with the Brown case, which had caused such a political stir. So, we'll give him a district court job."

Marshall refused. Marshall said "I don't want a district court job. It's an appeals court job or nothing"; he even had a meeting with Kennedy in which he said, "You may not believe it, but I'm used to nothing. I know how to live with nothing. So it's nothing or the Second Circuit." . . . Finally Robert Kennedy got turned around, and Marshall was nominated for the Second Circuit seat, but the opposition of those southern senators was very real. You had people, including Senator [James] Eastland and others, who stopped Marshall from getting confirmed to that court for a year. There was a real question as to whether or not he was going to make it. Every kind of charge was brought up against him: ties to communists and that he was stirring up trouble for no reason by trying to get black people to take part in these lawsuits with the NAACP. All of the grudges that some of these southern politicians held against the NAACP were played out in those hearings.

HE HAD LOTS OF FIGHTS with Bobby Kennedy, even when he was solicitor general of the United States and Bobby Kennedy was a . . . senator from New York and looking to run for president. Bobby Kennedy was a threat to . . . Lyndon Johnson, the president who appointed Marshall as solicitor general and then to the Supreme Court. [Marshall] looked at Bobby Kennedy as a spoiled brat, someone who didn't come to the table as a great believer in civil rights. [He saw him as] more of a hardball politician who was always looking for his advantage and seeing if the civil rights issue was playing for or against him or his brother. [Marshall didn't think Kennedy] looked at the issue as one of a moral, important choice for all Americans to treat each other [well], regardless of race.

I discovered in the Johnson Archives at the University of Texas in Austin that there are notes—right from the start, even before Marshall was [appointed] Solicitor General—in Lady Bird Johnson's diary [where] she says that Lyndon has a plan to make Thurgood Marshall the first black Supreme Court justice, but wants to see how he does as solicitor general. . . . Ramsey Clark, who was an intimate of the president, and [Johnson] were sailing on the Potomac. . . . Johnson was lying down on the bed. When [Clark] mentioned Thurgood Marshall's name, Johnson sat straight up and bumped his head on the ship's floor and said, "He's going on the Supreme Court." So right from the start, Johnson had this in mind.

MONROE DOWLING WAS MARSHALL'S VERY GOOD FRIEND for many years. Dowling, who was a graduate of Harvard as an accountant, worked for Rockefeller, worked for the mob, a very interesting character. [Dowling said,] "Marshall would get drunk and get out of the house and get onto the street. In his drunkenness, he would accost women, any woman. . . . One of these days, we thought, he was going to grab some woman, and her husband was going to kill him." Dowling recalled one episode in which [Marshall's second wife] Sissy and a friend had to drag Marshall into the house after he grabbed a woman. "With whiskey, he could not discriminate," [Dowling said.]

Dowling [told me] with sadness that Marshall's life, as he came onto the Court, and even from the time he was solicitor general, became more circumscribed, as he was more isolated here in Washington. . . . His life became very tight and closed off, and he began to drink more. People talk about his three-martini lunches even as solicitor general. The way that he would let off steam increasingly was with the liquor. Monroe Dowling says that these incidents would happen with women on the streets. They would cause great tension to the point where, according to Monroe Dowling, Sissy Marshall's decision to move the family out to suburban Virginia, to Lake Barcroft, was tied into the fact that there would be fewer neighbors directly adjacent to hear all the little episodes and to report on what was going on; they would have more privacy and the boys would have more green space to run around.

HE WAS ON THE COURT from 1967 to 1991. He was waiting [to retire] until Clarence Thomas was confirmed. He had announced . . . his retirement, but he had not quit the Court. So even if Thomas had not been confirmed in those tumultuous hearings, Marshall would have been able to stay on for a little longer.

[JUSTICE ANTONIN] SCALIA AND MARSHALL were on the opposite sides of many issues, including the key race issue of our time, affirmative action. . . . Scalia said the weight of Marshall's presence, just by being there, was sufficient to change the nature of the discourse between the justices in their private conference. For some years during the eighties, as Marshall became a member of the minority and the conservative majority grew on that Court, Marshall became really angry. He would have outbursts in the conference and give them hell. This was an opportunity for Scalia and others to say he was carrying on, [to say that] he was ranting and raving about race issues because he felt they weren't giving him enough consideration and that they should have been listening to him and doing what he said. But Scalia understood Marshall's ranting; he understood and appreciated what Thurgood Marshall had been through, that the changes he had been able to craft in the nature of the law on race in American society had been substantial. He respected Marshall.

ONE OF THE REASONS I WROTE THIS BOOK is I think lots of people didn't quite understand or perceive clearly who Thurgood Marshall was. Part of this had to do with the fact that [in his second marriage] he was married to a Filipino woman, an American woman, but of Filipino ancestry. . . . Marshall in the interviews that I had with him basically said, "Who cares? What's the big deal?" But I think it added to the sense that Marshall was not a black nationalist, not a black power person. Lots of people lost track of him during those Supreme Court years. They saw him as an aloof, distant figure in a black robe. He had gotten heavy. He was curmudgeonly. He could be cantankerous. And he wasn't one of the people that was out front giving speeches. He wasn't the charismatic leader.

I CAN'T CLAIM to have studied every lawyer in this century. But if you do a quick survey in your mind, if you think about who has changed the legal landscape in the country, you'd have to put Marshall up there. In Washington, D.C., Marshall felt greatly underappreciated by the legal community. There were people who argued at the time of his confirmation, first, to the Second Circuit in the early sixties and then to the Supreme Court, that he wasn't that great a lawyer, that he wasn't a brilliant legal mind. But what he did, nonetheless, was . . . gather strings together in legal thought and legal argument and make the presentation. Most people in the legal fraternity will say he was an outstanding advocate. He could stand before that Supreme Court and argue like no other. He was before the Court as an advocate thirty-two times, and won twenty-nine of those cases. Before the Court, in terms of his solicitor general work, [he was] outstanding. He was there nineteen times and won fourteen of those cases. If you look at this record on the Second Circuit, he was never reversed by the Supreme Court.

What you see is that Thurgood Marshall was a winner. This is someone who was shifting the terms on which people were thinking and arguing about legal issues. When you consider that the greatest political and social problem that the United States has faced in this century has been race relations, Marshall stands as a titan, a giant in terms of how he has restructured the terms on which we consider and argue and think about race in America.

Lyndon Baines Johnson

by
ROBERT CARO

Pulitzer Prize–winning biographer Robert Caro is working on a multi-volume biography of Lyndon Johnson (1908–73), who was sworn in as our thirty-sixth president in 1963, following the assassination of John Kennedy. Mr. Johnson won election in his own right in 1964 but declined to run in 1968—the height of the Vietnam War. Means of Ascent: The Years of Lyndon Johnson *(Knopf, 1990), Mr. Caro's second volume, details Lyndon Johnson in the 1940s as he sought the Senate and lost, made his fortune, then battled for the Senate again, this time successfully. His perspectives on LBJ were offered to* Booknotes *viewers on April 29, 1990.*

WHEN I STARTED THIS PROJECT, there were already seventeen biographies of Lyndon Johnson. I felt that his youth and his early years I would hardly have to do any work on, because I thought they had been covered over and over again. But when I went to Texas, I started finding out that most of the stories that we knew about him, the anecdotes that we knew about him, were a legend that he had created about his life and it wasn't really the truth. So I had to start all over.

I was a reporter on *Newsday.* . . . I never conceived of writing books just on the lives of famous men. I had no interest in that at all. What I wanted to do was explain how political power worked. I knew I wanted to do [a biography] on Lyndon Johnson, because I felt he understood national power better than any other president in our time.

What got my attention was when Lyndon Johnson was in the Senate. With Johnson, everyone said, "No one ever dominated the Senate of the United States like Lyndon Johnson." He controlled it as Senate majority leader. So I said, "Well, if no one else did it, [perhaps] I can find out how he did it and show how he used power and how he obtained this power"—That was what first got me interested.

MY FIRST VOLUME ON JOHNSON starts before his life, because I wanted to show what life in rural Texas was like and [explain] his ancestors, which I thought was such an important part of his life. It takes him up to the age of thirty-two, when he gets his first national power. At the end of that book, he tries for the Senate—that's the last scene, in 1941—and loses to this Texas campaigner, "Pass-the-Biscuits Pappy" O'Daniel, with his hillbilly band. He has national power, but he can't move up to the Senate.

The second book focuses on only seven years of his life. It's after that defeat, when he's stuck in the House of Representatives, which he really dislikes, and he cannot find a way to advance himself politically. These are his seven years in the wilderness. It's when he turns to making money with a radio station, and he is consumed with his need to try to move up to the Senate, on what he always envisioned as his road to the presidency. . . . In 1948, he decides to take one last chance and run for the Senate. He says if he loses, he will leave politics forever.

The next volume takes him from being sworn in to the Senate, through his rise to power in the Senate, his majority leadership, running for president against Jack Kennedy, losing, and being the vice president. It ends with the [Kennedy] assassination, with him being sworn in on the plane in Dallas. The last volume will be the presidency. I'm determined to try to do the presidency in one book, because it's one story, really.

JOHNSON WON THE 1948 SENATE ELECTION by eighty-seven votes out of about a million votes that were cast. The election was stolen. I proved it. It's not actually that hard to prove—it's just that nobody apparently did it [before]. There are more than a thousand pages of court transcripts. Hearings were held on this at the time, and more than a thousand pages of testimony were taken. . . . Luis Salas, who was the election judge in the crucial precinct, Box 13, in Jim Wells County, testified to the opposite of all the other people. I found Mr. Salas in Houston in 1986. He was then quite old but clear of mind. I asked him about the discrepancy between his testimony and everybody else's. He said, "Well that's simple, Robert. I lied under oath." He then took me in great detail through the story of what happened in Box 13. This time his story simply corroborated what everybody else had said, [proving that Johnson had stolen the election].

Johnson was a man who had to win. I see in this election a man who had to win. He had kidney stones during this campaign. Kidney stones are a particularly agonizing pain, and this was a terrible attack. His fever was 105 degrees, and the doctors told him, "You must get to a hospital, you're risking the loss of kidney function. You're risking the loss of your life." He wouldn't stop campaigning. He was driving back and forth across Texas, lying in the back of the car between stops, gagging and retching, perspiration pouring off him. Every time they pulled into a town, he'd get on a clean shirt, big smile, and he'd bound out. He'd shake every hand and give the speech. . . . He simply had to win.

TEXAS IS SO DIFFERENT. . . . I had never seen Johnson City. I had no idea of the loneliness and the emptiness of the Hill Country. . . . Out of Austin . . . towards Johnson City . . . about forty-two or forty-three miles, you come to the top of what they call Round Mountain. It's just really a high hill, but from it you can see this vast valley in front of you, maybe thirty miles long and maybe fifteen or twenty miles across. In this whole area, you couldn't see one sign of human habitation.

I remember Sam Houston Johnson, Lyndon's brother, telling me how he and Lyndon used to sit—one corner of the Johnson ranch abutted a road—and they'd sit on the fence there at that corner all day, hoping for one person to drive by so they'd have somebody new to talk to. . . . There was an old postmistress in Johnson City named Stella Glidden, and she said to me once, "You're a city boy, you don't understand the land. Unless you understand the land, you're never gonna understand Lyndon Johnson." . . . I came to realize that she was telling me something—that it was the struggle to survive in a land where survival was hard that shaped a lot of Johnson's characteristics.

WITH JOHNSON THERE'S ALWAYS TWO SIDES—the bright side and the dark side. . . . His fight to bring electricity [to the Texas Hill Country]—which seemed impossible, because there was no source of hydroelectric power for hundreds of miles in some places—was a noble example of the use of the powers of government to help people, to do something they couldn't do themselves. No matter how ingenious or determined [the local people] were, they were never going to get electricity. Johnson did this for them.

There were more bright sides in the period of time covered by the first volume. Then, he was doing things that were going to emerge [as themes] in his presidency. We see his compassion for the Mexican-American kids when he was a schoolteacher. He taught Mexican-American children down in Canutillo. No teacher had ever cared if they learned or not. This teacher cared. He worked with them ceaselessly beyond anything that was expected of him. Later, we see that compassion in the civil rights legislation, when he was majority leader and president. And we see in him, helping his constituents with rural electrification, this great gift that Lyndon Johnson had for mobilizing the powers of government to help the dispossessed.

WITH LYNDON JOHNSON, [what was] very striking to me was learning how he betrayed House Speaker Sam Rayburn. Rayburn loved Lyndon Johnson. We can call it a father-son relationship, as a cliché, but Rayburn was his great patron. When Johnson came to Washington, age twenty-three, twenty-four, he was an assistant to another congressman. Rayburn was then the mighty majority leader—a grim, fierce-visaged man that everyone was afraid to approach, with immense power.

But Rayburn was a very lonely man. He had no family, no wife, no children. He once wrote to his sister, "God, what I would give for a towheaded boy to take fishing." But he didn't have one. When Lyndon and Lady Bird came to Washington, Lyndon's father, who had known Sam Rayburn, [connected them]. Mr. Sam, as they called him, used to come and spend Sundays, have Sunday breakfast and then stay around the Johnsons' little apartment. He was very fond of both Lyndon and Lady Bird. Once, when Johnson was still a young assistant, he got pneumonia, which was very serious back in those days. Mrs. Johnson was back in Texas on a vacation, and Rayburn sat next to Johnson's bed all night in the hospital, in a straight-backed wooden chair. . . . He smoked all night. But he was so afraid of making a movement and disturbing Lyndon that he didn't want to get up and brush the ashes away. So when Lyndon Johnson woke up in the morning, Sam Rayburn was sitting there with his lapels covered with this cigarette ash. As soon as he saw that Lyndon Johnson was awake, Johnson recalled, Rayburn leaned over him and said, "Lyndon, don't worry about anything. If you need anything, call on me."

And shortly Johnson did call on Rayburn. Rayburn got his career started. [By] now, it was 1939; John Nance Garner and Franklin Roosevelt had split. Garner was always Roosevelt's man in Texas. Someone was going to be Roosevelt's man in Texas, the dispenser of the New Deal power and patronage in Texas. Rayburn, who was the majority leader, was the logical choice, but Johnson wanted that job. To get it, he persuaded Roosevelt, falsely, that Rayburn was his enemy.

THE STORY OF LADY BIRD JOHNSON'S TRANSFORMATION . . . is one of the most wonderful stories that I ever heard. She had this painful public shyness, where she couldn't bear to speak in public. When she was in high school, she told me that if she finished first or second in the class and would have to give a speech as valedictorian at her graduation, she prayed that she would get smallpox. I wrote, "She would rather risk the scars than speak in public."

She married Lyndon Johnson. She could not campaign for him, make speeches for him. More than that, she didn't participate in the political part of his life at all. I asked her why not, and she said, "Well, I didn't want to be part of absolutely everything." Suddenly, he went off to navy service on the West Coast, and in one instant, it seemed like, he had to say to her, "Now, you have to run the [congressional] office for me."

She had to go in, having done nothing like this, and be, in effect, the congressman for the Tenth District of Texas. . . . One of her secretaries told me how Mrs. Johnson would sit in her husband's big chair, behind his big desk, and her hand would be reaching out for the telephone, but she couldn't bear to make the call. She'd have to call a cabinet official or some high government official, and she couldn't bear to make it. But she always made the call. . . . Her story of how she turned herself into the Lady Bird Johnson that we know today—with her poise and graciousness and dignity—I said, "I'm going to tell this in full."

[HE HAD A MISTRESS NAMED ALICE.] During the war, when he was out on the coast, she visited him, and later wrote jokingly to a friend who gave me the letter, "Let's corroborate on a biography on Lyndon. I can write the chapter on his war service in Hollywood, where the Hollywood photographers were trying to teach him which is the best side of his face."

It was not a short affair. It was very important in his life. When he came to Washington, he was a young, awkward, gawky congressman. He didn't know how to dress. He had long arms, the wrists stuck out of his shirt. She taught him how to dress. She had a very elegant salon. She had a wonderful estate in the Virginia hunt country, and she also was very astute politically. There was a time in Johnson's early career where he had a problem with his chief financial backer, Herman Brown, of [Texas contracting firm] Brown and Root. Brown was a man nobody crossed, and Johnson and he were on a collision course. It was Alice Glass who devised the compromise . . . which really saved his career in that sense.

His entire character emerged, in some ways, in his dealings with Alice Glass. When he went to the Pacific, he couldn't decide whether to file for the Senate or file for Congress—and it was her opinion he wanted.

THIS VOLUME, *Means of Ascent,* raises the great question of the connection between means and ends. Many of the ends of Lyndon Johnson's life were noble. Heroic advances. We wouldn't have a lot of the civil rights legislation we have today if Lyndon Johnson hadn't pushed it through. . . . However, that's not to say his presidency was a triumphant presidency, because it divided the country, it caused the credibility gap. It had a lot of dark sides. But, whatever the ends are, good and bad, they wouldn't be possible if it weren't for the means by which he got to a position to reach those ends.

Lyndon Johnson, as we saw as president, did not take kindly to criticism. However, [if he could read] all four [of my] books, he would likely feel that I gave him—both in the bright sense, as well as the dark sense—his place in history. I wrote in the introduction to this book that it was Abraham Lincoln who struck the chains from black Americans, but it was Lyndon Johnson who took them by the hand, led them into the voting booth, drew democracy's curtain behind them, and made them once and for all and forever a part of American political life.

Joseph and Stewart Alsop

by
ROBERT MERRY

A Washington journalist himself, Robert Merry tackled the lives of two well-known Washington writers of an earlier generation—brothers Joseph (1910–89) and Stewart (1914–74) Alsop. Merry's resulting work, Taking on the World: Joseph and Stewart Alsop, Guardians of the American Century, *was published in 1996 by Viking. From their base in Georgetown and from the postwar years until the Vietnam War, the aristocratic Alsop brothers sought to influence policy through their widely distributed columns. Mr. Merry told their story on* Booknotes *on March 24, 1996.*

I STUMBLED ACROSS THE ALSOP PAPERS at the Library of Congress. Stewart, when he was writing a very wonderful column in *Newsweek* magazine in the late 1960s, early 1970s, was just about my journalistic hero when I was in college and in the army. So I knew a lot about the Alsops. I had written about them, and I had reviewed their books over the years. But Stewart had died in 1974, [and] Joe retired in 1975, so they were not very current for a long time. Once I discovered the Alsop papers, which is a treasure trove of historical gems, it occurred to me that what we have here is a real window on the history of America from about 1935 to 1975. That's what it turned out to be.

When they were writing the column together, they appeared in two hundred newspapers with a combined circulation of about twenty million. This was in the mid-1950s to 1960. The column broke up in 1958. They were writing regularly for *The Saturday Evening Post*—which had a circulation of six million and probably twenty million readers. They had a huge circulation for those days. That was before television had gained the kind of stature and status and reach that it has now.

In the later years of their lives, Stewart Alsop emerges as the greater journalist. But for most of their lives, Stewart lived in the shadow of Joe. Joe brought his brother, Stewart, into the column-writing business. He insisted that he be the senior columnist while Stewart was the junior columnist. Stewart ultimately chafed under that. It was etched into their relationship in a 55–45 split of the proceeds of their column writing and magazine writing together. He split with Joe in 1958 after twelve years and became a magazine writer of some note for the next decade.

JOE DIED IN 1989. He was born in 1910, so he was about seventy-nine. . . . He was most influential, by far, in the early 1960s and during the Kennedy and Johnson administrations. He had reached his pinnacle. He was very close to the Kennedys, both Jack and Jackie Kennedy. His friendship with Jackie Kennedy was a loving friendship; they had a lot of affection for each other. And he was very close to Lyndon Johnson. I tell a funny story about Lyndon Johnson from when Joe was a rising young columnist in Washington and Lyndon Johnson was a rising young congressman. Because of his connection with Sam Rayburn, Lyndon Johnson would get invited down to the White House for strategy sessions and he would slip a lot of good information to Joe. . . .

After doing that for a while, Johnson felt like he should get a quid pro quo and so he unabashedly asked Joe to write a column about what a great congressman he was. Well, Joe didn't think that it would be quite appropriate to use his national column to promote Johnson, but he didn't want to make him angry. So he went to a syndicate and asked, "Do you think it would be all right if I wrote a column about Lyndon Johnson just for the Texas newspapers?" He did that, and it was sent down to the Texas newspapers. Johnson was mollified and felt that he had [been] done a good turn.

By the time Johnson became president, they went back a long, long ways. They spoke a lot. Joe and his wife, Susan Mary, were invited to the White House through those years for very intimate dinners, both under the Kennedys and under the Johnsons. He had immense access—tremendous access—throughout the government in those years. I would say that that was his point of greatest influence.

JOE AND STEWART WERE BORN in Avon, Connecticut, in the family farmhouse not too far from Hartford. It became a suburb of Hartford years later. Joe was born in 1910 and Stewart was born in 1914. The guts of the story begins at their life. It explains what life is like in a small Yankee town in the Northeast around the turn of the century.

The Alsops were Anglophiles. In fact, their whole class of people was the old Anglo-Saxon class leading America. They were charter members of that class of Americans, the Anglophiles. It was drummed into their heads at prep school, at Groton and further, at Princeton and Yale. It went so far that [when] Stewart, after Pearl Harbor, couldn't get a combat job in the U.S. forces because of high blood pressure, he joined the British army and became a platoon leader, a lieutenant, in the British Rifle Corps. He fought in the Italian campaign, went to North Africa, and later parachuted behind the lines in France right after

D-Day to help the French Resistance, [to] help the Allies move forward in the Continent.

Stewart befriended [Winston Churchill's son] Randolph, and Joe did, too. In fact, Stewart wrote a marvelous little essay about a lunch he had in Chartwell [the Churchill home outside of London] in which Winston Churchill was having lunch and Randolph invited Stewart. He thought it would maybe be twelve or fifteen people and it turned out to be just Winston Churchill and Randolph Churchill and Stewart. . . . It was typical of the Alsops. They always managed to get in the company of the high and the mighty throughout the world.

[BY ABOUT 1937,] Joe weighed probably over 250 pounds and was five foot nine. . . . He was working as a young columnist and magazine writer for *The Saturday Evening Post*—working endless hours, socializing endlessly, drinking quite a little bit socially. He always was a rather heavy drinker, not to excess until perhaps his later life, but always a heavy social drinker. Then he began having rather serious heart trouble. The doctor said that if he didn't lose a significant amount of that weight he wasn't sure that he'd last the year.

His mother, who by the way was the first cousin of Eleanor Roosevelt and the niece of Teddy Roosevelt, went into a panic at that. She paid for Joe to go to Johns Hopkins University Hospital for a brand-new nutritional and dietary regimen. In two to three months, he lost fifty pounds. He never gained it back, but he always had a difficult time with his weight and he always would go to health spas at least once or twice a year.

GROTON PLAYED A HUGE ROLE in their lives. Groton is the academic foundry where the nation's elite sent its sons to be forged into models of upper-crust gentility. Groton was founded by Endicott Peabody, who had gone to school in England at Cheltenham. He and all these people were total Anglophiles and he modeled his school on the English boarding-school model—the English public schools, they call them. The interesting thing about Groton is that Joe and Stewart both hated the place. And yet they never questioned its significance in molding and shaping them as they grew into manhood. That was typical of that time. Years later, in the next generation, Stewart's children hated Groton and Stewart's reaction initially was, "Well, you're supposed to hate prep school. You're supposed to hate boarding school." But the children disliked it so much and wouldn't accept it, unlike the older generation, that they pulled one of their sons out of Groton and let him move on to another school.

Joe hated Groton for a number of reasons. The things that Groton prized, Joe didn't have. Groton prized athletic ability; Joe had none. Groton prized a rote, unimaginative intelligence; Joe was a man of highly imaginative intelligence and artistic temperament. Joe was also a fat young man, which wasn't highly prized at Groton. So he was a very unhappy person at Groton and didn't have many friends for a good part of that time. He wrote years later that it was the only time in his life when he ever significantly considered taking his own life.

He went on to Harvard, where he discovered that people didn't care that much about whether you were an athlete or not. His intellectual bent and his ability to be amusing caught on with his peers, and so he created himself there. He began to redefine himself into a Dr. Johnson character. And it seemed to work. People were very highly amused. The more they were amused, the more he played it up, and the more he played it up, the more he was amusing. By the time he got through his first year at Harvard, he had really transformed himself into a flamboyant man with elaborate mannerisms and an ersatz British accent with long vowels and clipped consonants. That was the role he played for himself throughout the rest of his life.

STEWART ALSOP MET HIS WIFE PATRICIA when he served as a young lieutenant in the British army in London. She was very young, twelve years his junior, and she was working for British intelligence, although he didn't know that at the time. She was undercover or she had a cover. She was eighteen when they were married. He was thirty. I believe they married in 1944.

It was tough for Patricia. Her new family was extremely well connected and important and hobnobbed with famous people. She was this young woman who didn't have much in the way of those kinds of experiences, and she was expected to move right in.

In fact, Joe's first dinner party after he moved back into his house in Georgetown included the French ambassador, a Supreme Court justice, and a couple of senators. Joe asked Tish to act as hostess. She said she would, although, no doubt, she was very nervous about it. At one point she thought that the dinner was over and so she rose to do as she had been instructed—to lead the women to their separate conversation, which was conventional in those days. Joe shrieked at her, "Darling, we haven't had dessert yet!" She had to slink back to the table. It was not easy coming into the Alsop family in those days, especially if you were somebody like Tish Alsop.

THE SUNDAY-NIGHT PARTIES have taken on almost a legendary tone. They didn't last as long as a lot of people think. It was in the immediate postwar period. It was not started by the Alsops, although they became a very significant part of them early on. The people who started it were Frank Wisner, who was a CIA operative, and his wife Polly, who was quite wealthy. Some other couples got together—I think it might have been Tracey Barnes, also of the CIA. They soon invited the Alsops.

These were all relatively young people, and they liked to entertain, but they had young children. So on Sunday evening one of them would act as the host and hostess. One of the homes would be the locus of this evening, and it would be a potluck. Different people would bring different parts of the meal, there would be plenty of alcohol, and everyone who was part of the group would be allowed to invite a source, or somebody that they dealt with in the government. They became quite raucous. Joe rechristened them the "Sunday Night Drunk." The Sunday night supper was quite an institution. It lasted from about 1947 until the early 1950s, and then they petered out.

I DON'T BELIEVE THERE IS ANYBODY in journalism today like the Alsops. First, you have to remember that in those days, print was king; it was the monarch of journalism. If you were a columnist, then you were at the pinnacle of the monarchy, essentially. Today journalism is all fragmented. There are all kinds of broadcast outlets. There are various kinds of print media outlets. There are now new media and online distribution. Nobody can command that much of a corner of the whole journalistic façade that somebody could in the Alsops' days. . . . Number two, they were part and parcel of the connected families of America. They had an entrée that was natural and automatic that doesn't exist today. You would have to be a real grasper and somebody who was a real climber today to have the kind of access that to the Alsops was just a natural, normal part of everyday life.

STEWART OBSERVED WHAT WE MIGHT CALL journalistic niceties more assiduously than Joe did. Stewart didn't believe in getting too close to sources. He played tennis with the Kennedys, and he would have dinner with them, but he didn't allow himself to become close friends with them. Stewart angered the Kennedys on a number of occasions and actually had his access cut off. Joe, on the other hand, was very close and fostered an ongoing friendship with both Jack and Jackie Kennedy.

Joe Alsop was always in controversy with people. The biggest example of that was Lyndon Johnson. He was close to Lyndon Johnson and was invited over for intimate little dinners of maybe six or eight people quite frequently in the early years of the Johnson administration. But in 1964, there was one thing that Lyndon Johnson did not want to do, and that was to get embroiled in Vietnam before the election. Joe felt that things were going sour in Vietnam in a very big way. He began writing a series of columns almost endlessly on the fearful challenge and the lack of resolve that the president seemed to be showing in the face of this fearsome challenge. Johnson was getting increasingly angry. Ultimately, Johnson just cut him off.

I TRIED TO HANDLE [Joseph Alsop's personal story] quite sensitively. Joe was homosexual. He lived in the closet of a secret life through most of his life. He had a couple of episodes that were somewhat threatening as a result of that. One famous episode occurred in Moscow, where he had a homosexual encounter with a young man, and it was all captured by KGB—actually, NKGB, the predecessor of the KGB—photographers. His room was rigged, and they attempted to turn him into an agent of influence. Basically [they said], "We're going to blackmail you unless you give us a lot of information about what's going on in Washington." Joe was pretty foolish to get himself into that kind of a situation in Moscow, but he handled it from that moment quite well. He was totally arrogant, as was his wont, to these operatives of the Soviet intelligence. He went immediately to the U.S. embassy, where the ambassador was his very good friend, Chip Bohlen. . . . Chip and his friend, Frank Wisner of the CIA, and others rallied around and got him out of the country. Basically, he managed to escape that episode. And there's no evidence that he ever succumbed to the pressures that were put upon him.

Joe's wife Susan Mary told me that she did not know he was a homosexual throughout their longtime, very close friendship. When he wrote to her to propose to her, he revealed to her that he was homosexual. He did indicate to her that what he was proposing was a platonic marriage, but that he didn't see any reason why it couldn't be a very happy and loving relationship. She initially, delicately and sensitively, declined the proposal, but some months later . . . she decided that she would marry Joe, and they were married in the early weeks of 1961.

THE GREATEST CHALLENGE AND TEST of their careers was Vietnam. Joe failed the test, and Stewart passed the test with flying colors. This is not a question of whether they believed in the war or supported the war. Both of them did. But Stewart understood what was going on in Vietnam in a way that Joe did not. So, in my view, Stewart emerges as a journalist of real immense proportion in American postwar journalistic history.

[STEWART BATTLED LEUKEMIA FOR THREE YEARS.] Joe would go [to visit him] all the time. He would take him soup and martinis. They loved martinis, especially Stewart. The friendship of the brothers was probably never more tender than it was during those years. They had a stormy relationship, but the love between them was really quite something to behold. Joe was a very difficult guy to get along with. Especially when they were writing the column together, there were a lot of frictions within the family. They argued endlessly on political matters. It was just part of their lives. They loved it.

Joe Alsop got cranky in the end. He knew he was cranky, even before he retired. There was a touching letter he wrote to Scotty Reston, who was another one of the giants of postwar American journalism. He lamented that their controversies had seemed to interfere with their friendship. He said, "As soon as I retire, I'm never again going to discuss politics." That lasted about a week and a half. The world was changing on him, and he didn't like a lot of the changes that he saw.

Ronald Reagan

by
LOU CANNON
HAYNES JOHNSON
EDMUND MORRIS

Prior to entering politics, our fortieth president, Ronald Reagan (b. 1911), was a sportscaster, movie star, and union leader. In 1966, he was elected governor of California, serving two terms. He captured the Republican presidential nomination in 1980 and defeated the incumbent, Jimmy Carter. Biographer Edmund Morris has spent thirteen years creating Dutch: A Memoir of Ronald Reagan, *scheduled for publication by Random House in 1999. Two other views come from 1991 books by veteran political reporters: Haynes Johnson's* Sleepwalking Through History: America in the Reagan Years, *published by Norton, and Lou Cannon's* President Reagan: The Role of a Lifetime, *published by Simon and Schuster.*

Lou Cannon

President Reagan: Role of a Lifetime

THE FAVORITE MOMENT I EVER HAD in an interview [with Ronald Reagan] was personal. We were talking about his father, and Ronald Reagan, like a lot of us, romanticizes his boyhood. Everything was wonderful. But he was talking about his dad's drinking. By this time Reagan was a young man working as a sports announcer in Des Moines, and his father apparently had been drinking kind of heavily. . . . He wrote his father a letter and said that he wanted him to stop drinking because he, Ronald Reagan, had this problem, too. Reagan said this was a lie. . . . Sixty years later, it still troubled him that he did it. It was a noble lie, if there is such a thing. His father never replied, and he never knew what impact, if any, that lie had on him. The reason that that sticks with me is that Ronald Reagan rarely told you anything about himself.

I CALL THIS THE THIRD BOOK in an unintended trilogy. I never set out to write three books about him, but I found that there was more to Ronald Reagan than the surface, that beneath the surface you had a rather complicated character who wasn't quite what either his fans or his critics thought. He was a little sharper than his critics thought. He knew more, he saw further. But he had great gaps in his knowledge and great lapses that his fans didn't see. My effort was to try to get beyond this and get some kind of a coherent whole.

RONALD REAGAN IS A PERSON who values the performance and who thinks of himself as a performer. After he was elected governor, he was asked what kind of a governor he would make. He said, "I don't know. I've never played a governor." When he left the White House, he was asked how acting had helped him be president and he said, "I don't understand how anybody could do this job without having been an actor." So Ronald Reagan didn't run away from the fact that he was an actor. He was proud of it.

THERE ARE A LOT OF . . . moments in the Reagan presidency that are worth something. One was him standing in Berlin saying, "Mr. Gorbachev, tear down that wall," which still gives me goose bumps. Another was in Red Square . . . he and Gorbachev walking together. Even though they both had their own propaganda impulses for this meeting, it was a signal to the world, this Cold War is really over.

Another darker one was that speech in November of 1986, . . . where he's explaining what happened—or thinks he is—in the Iran-Contra affair, and he was so unbelievable. You see a different kind of Ronald Reagan. . . . People who had always trusted Reagan said, "This guy's lying to me." That was a new experience for Ronald Reagan.

RONALD REAGAN WAS MUCH BRIGHTER than people like to say he was. . . . I quote an authority on intelligence in the book as saying that Ronald Reagan made sense of the world narratively. He was not a good analyst. He didn't have a high intelligence in the way scientists and lawyers do—analytical, logical intelligence—but he had a great understanding of people and of the power of storytelling. Stories move us. Ronald Reagan knew that.

Haynes Johnson

Sleepwalking Through History: America in the Reagan Years

RONALD REAGAN WAS ELECTED TWICE, overwhelmingly. The country had every reason to understand fully what Mr. Reagan represented, what he stood for. He didn't practice deceit in terms of telling the public what he wanted to do: He was going to cut the taxes; he was going to redistribute the wealth; he was going to disband government regulation—all those things *and* rebuild the defense establishment, and he accomplished those things. If I'm angry at anything, it's at all of us, because there was a heavy consequence to [his policies.]

The country was in a mood and, in fact, had a desperate need to want to celebrate a sense of success and stability. I came to Washington in 1957. I've watched . . . presidents starting with John Kennedy, every single one was destroyed, or disgraced, or driven from office. . . . We began to lose a sense of faith and hope.

We also went through the Vietnam period. We went through Watergate. We went through a sense of America's decline internationally. Here came Mr. Reagan, who said, "It's morning in America again. Don't take those gloom-and-doomers and all the rest." I think the country wanted to believe that desperately, and they suspended judgment in the hope that it would be true.

I believe one of the reasons Reagan was so successful and had such a strong hold on the country was because he survived that assassin's bullet. . . . That elevated him instantly to a place he didn't have before in people's affections. It made him almost a mythic figure. If you believed that the president [could] survive, then the country was going to survive. It seemed to break the stream of bad luck.

I WAS GOING TO TRY TO WRITE a sociopolitical history of the eighties. A friend at Berkeley called me up and said, "You've got to come out here. We have a treasure that has barely been tapped into. The University of California system did oral history interviews of all the particulars in the Reagan governorship years." That covers eight years, long before he ran for president. They interviewed Reagan himself. All these [interviews] were done and checked by the people themselves for accuracy. All of these interviews were done before 1980. I found it fascinating that many of the people became big players in the Reagan administration.

I was able to go through boxes and boxes of these transcripts. I found them eerie, because what I was reading of that period was like seeing the future. The past was prologue in that sense. The attitudes, the values, the political methods, all of the questions about deficit spending, problems with the administration, problems with the press and the rest—all were foreshadowed in those interviews.

[The group included] Edwin Meese, Michael Deaver, William French Smith, [and] Reagan himself. I think the ones that particularly struck me as most interesting were the interviews with the so-called Kitchen Cabinet in California. These were the people, very wealthy Californians, who set out to make Ronald Reagan, first, governor of California and then, president of the United

States. They bankrolled his campaigns; they formed the committees for him; they helped pick the personnel; they staffed the administration in Sacramento; and then they did the same thing in Washington.

RONALD REAGAN WAS AN INATTENTIVE PRESIDENT. There's no question about this. I'm not being polemic here—the testimony of all of his aides, his Cabinet officers [reflects this notion]. There were people in his Cabinet who never had a single serious meeting with him —not one—alone. He would come into the White House or to these briefings and he would have 3-by-5 cards, carefully written out with what he was going to say. He would read the cards, then he'd leave and the meetings would transpire. The portrait that comes across of Mr. Reagan in that sense is what Clark Clifford said: "He was an amiable dunce." I happen to think he was much more than that. I think that in the things that he cared about, he was fully involved; he knew what he was doing. He was a strong, bold, even risk-taking president, like during Iran-Contra.

I have no question in my mind from the basis of my own interviews with virtually everyone on [Congress' Iran-Contra investigation] committee and with the investigator, that Reagan was fully knowledgeable of what was happening and fully knew, too, that he might be impeached. He was willing to take that great risk because he believed. He was a strong president in that sense.

REAGAN WAS SOMETHING ON TELEVISION. Reagan filled that camera. He was like a canvas himself . . . You could see the flag waving in the background, almost like he was old Uncle Sam. He was jaunty and he had that wonderful engaging smile and people responded. Even if you didn't like Ronald Reagan or didn't think he was very smart or thought he did a lot of damage, you still had to admire the way in which he handled himself.

THE RELATIONSHIP BETWEEN THE PRESS and Reagan was very complicated, because Reagan was the first president to use television as an instrument of power. I don't mean naively that he was the first ever to try to do it—John Kennedy did it and all presidents since. But he was a master at it, and everything that he did in his White House was staged for the cameras. But the truth is, he was inaccessible [to the press]. Nobody saw him. He would do these set things and he'd be marvelous, then he'd disappear.

THERE IS A WONDERFUL STORY about the Reagan years. As he got on the helicopter after George Bush's inaugural to take his last fly-over of the capital, [he was captured by the cameras] saluting. It looks so wonderfully "Reaganesque." Now, they scripted that in advance. All the cameras were there. It was the last act, and it was part of the stage. The salute was arranged, the cameras were told in advance that the two presidents would salute each other, the incoming, outgoing, and it would be the final photo opportunity. And it worked.

What [the American people] saw in Ronald Reagan was an overwhelming hunger for someone that was strong, that you could believe in, that you hoped [with whom] the last act was going to be successful and powerful.

Edmund Morris

Dutch: A Memoir of Ronald Reagan

A BIOGRAPHER'S CONSTANT PROBLEM is to come to terms with his subject's own self-image, particularly when that subject is a public man and the image, the picture on the monitor, is more or less identical with what the public perceives. I am not suggesting that Ronald Reagan, the inner man, is essentially different than the outer. In a very large sense, what you saw was what you got. Yet, the more I talked to him and interviewed him, the more I realized that what we saw is only what he wanted us to see. From a biographical point of view that was not very much, but from a political point of view it was plenty. Biographers like to know everything that they can. I found that like most natural leaders he held himself aloof. As Charles de Gaulle once said, "You have to cultivate mystery . . ." Reagan certainly understood the value of cultivating mystery. He was an impenetrable man and a perpetual frustration for those who tried to articulate things about him.

[THE DESIRE TO WRITE REAGAN'S BIOGRAPHY] sort of snuck up on me. I was preoccupied with [writing a second volume on] Theodore Roosevelt. Reagan was elected in 1980 and became president in 1981. He was given a copy of my biography on TR, and he read it during his first year. All presidents, as you can imagine, are curious about their predecessors, which is why, I guess, Reagan was interested in reading about TR. After he read it, I began to get subtle intimations from the White House that if I wanted to write his biography, the president wouldn't object. In retrospect, this was an invitation for me to start making advances. But frankly, I didn't find Reagan very interesting in those days. He was obviously attractive and popular. He had a large electoral victory. But I found him bland and rather boring. I was involved in the second volume on Theodore Roosevelt, which described TR's presidency, [and so] I was preoccupied with this enormously large personality; I didn't have any room for Reagan's. So I didn't do anything about it. It was only as time went by and the Reagan presidency got more dramatic, and more important, that I realized that I had missed a real historical opportunity. It was in 1985 that the Reagan presidency got seriously dramatic, particularly with the Bitburg crisis in the spring;

Reagan was plunged, for the first time in his presidency, into a genuinely large political crisis, a moral crisis. I realized I was very sorry that I hadn't become his biographer because I would have loved to have been there at Bergen-Belsen and seen Reagan confront the Holocaust as directly as he did. It was then that I decided to make my belated pitch to become his biographer. From then on, it was remarkably easy. They said yes, and I signed on.

By going to Tampico, Illinois, I learned more about Ronald Reagan than I could have learned in a year of studying books, just by [seeing] the physical environment he was born in. I walked out into the corn. It is a one-horse town, a one-block town in the middle of Middle America. There is nothing there except one main street where he was born and the corn stretching in all directions, a flat, circular horizon, a great blue sky, a windmill or two lazily rotating. I stood in the corn thinking, "This is the environment little 'Dutch' Reagan was born into."

Reagan was an intuitively brilliant man, but he almost entirely lacked speculation. That's why so many people thought he was stupid, because Reagan would never explain why he had a particular policy or attitude. He never questioned his own decisions. He seemed to arrive at them almost by thinking with the back of his head instead of the front of it. . . . Because Reagan was so private, so opaque, so hard to get answers from when you asked him things about his mental processes, a lot of people walked away thinking he was stupid. If he was stupid, he was an amazingly successful fool.

The role that Nancy Reagan played in his presidency is less than meets the eye. She protected him. I don't think he would have become president without her. She is a doctor's daughter. She knew what his weakness was. He was a sucker for liking everybody. Presidents who indiscriminately like everybody who comes through the door [run into trouble,] because a lot of people who come through the door are predatory. Nancy Reagan had the instinct to spot predators a mile off. She protected him against that kind of thing. [But,] she had very little influence on policy. She wasn't particularly interested in policy and in some of the fundamental issues that Reagan cared about.

He was very close to death [after the assassination attempt in March of 1981], much closer than we realized. He lost well over 30 percent of his blood supply. It got to be such an emergency that instead of injecting blood, they had to rip open an artery and literally slosh it in, as with a bucket. For a while there, we very nearly lost him. We all know how he recovered from it and with what grace he recovered. It is also well known that as he was recovering, he developed a sense that he had been spared. Reagan had a very simple and profound religious faith expressed largely in terms of conventional Christian church clichés, but it was sincere nevertheless. He felt he had been spared to do good work for God's own country, and by God, he was going to do it for the rest of his term.

I CERTAINLY NEVER SAW ANY SIGNS of dementia whatsoever [during his presidency.] I saw him getting old and tired toward the end. I saw him being poleaxed by Iran-Contra for a few weeks. Iran-Contra, at its worst, coincided with his prostate condition. He had an operation in December of 1986 and was out of shape for six weeks. He was at his worst then, very abstracted by his political crisis and also by his medical condition. But mentally, he had amazing powers of recovery. In fact, when Howard Baker came in [as chief-of-staff], there was some doubt in the Baker team's mind; [they were concerned] that Reagan might be past it—might be incapacitated in office. So they made a point of meeting the president in the Cabinet Room on their first day in the White House. I was there that Monday morning. They arranged their chairs so they could sit and scrutinize the president very carefully to see if there was something seriously wrong. In came Ronald Reagan, quite unsuspecting, and performed brilliantly. Howard Baker has gone on television to confirm this. He says that Reagan was astonishing and there was absolutely nothing wrong. However, he did start getting old in the last couple of years. He began to switch off at times.

ALZHEIMER'S HAPPENED VERY SUDDENLY after he had that accident where he fell off a horse in Mexico, in early 1990. He came down on his head from fifteen feet in the air. Within weeks, I noticed that he was getting strange. . . . The predisposition [to get Alzheimer's] has to be there, and Reagan had it in his system. His mother and his brother had it. But the trauma seems to have precipitated it. It was so noticeable, and so sudden, that there is no question that before that fall, he had all his marbles.

I DON'T SPEAK MUCH ABOUT HIS CURRENT LIFE ANYMORE. Since he announced he had Alzheimer's in that shattering letter to the American people, I think he is entitled to his privacy. The last time I saw him was after he wrote his letter and took his formal farewell. I stopped seeing him because it was extremely distressing, to be honest. Secondly, I didn't want to start getting emotionally involved and protective.

REAGAN'S STOCK HAS RISEN TO AN EXTRAORDINARY EXTENT. Ten years have gone by [since his presidency]; nostalgia is beginning to set in. The world has irrevocably changed since he was president. A lot of the changes can be traced back to his reign. The temporary reason for the nostalgia is pretty obvious to all of us. And that is, whatever you thought of him politically, he had dignity. Dignity and decency. In the words of [former French President François] Mitterrand, he had *la notion de l'Etat*. He personified the dignity of the American state. That dignity has been grotesquely compromised in recent years. People are nostalgic for that sort of past and it is a dignity that Reagan exuded wherever he went.

Thomas P. "Tip" O'Neill

by
GARY HYMEL

Thomas P. "Tip" O'Neill (1912–94) was a member of the U.S. House of Representatives for thirty-four years. He served as Speaker of the House from 1977 until his retirement in 1987. In 1994, he gathered his political wisdom into All Politics is Local, and Other Rules of the Game *(Times Books). Speaker O'Neill died shortly after its publication, so we asked his co-author and longtime aide Gary Hymel to visit* Booknotes *on January 23, 1994, and reflect on Tip O'Neill's life.*

I WORKED FOR TIP O'NEILL for eight years. For two years, I was his administrative assistant as majority leader. Then he was elected Speaker, and I was administrative assistant to [him] for six years. Some people would call him Mr. Speaker, but he didn't change any going from just a congressman to becoming the Speaker.

From the day I met Tip O'Neill to the day he died, he was the same person. I can say that without fear. He was open and unpretentious. Tip O'Neill never made me mad. He certainly made me laugh a lot but never mad.

Tip O'Neill was a great storyteller. Probably more than any politician I've ever known, he entertained audiences or was able to defuse a lot of tough arguments, tense situations, by telling a story. It's a lost art; not many people know these stories today. But when Tip was being brought up, the person who could tell a story—and I think it's got something to do with his Irish heritage—was the fellow who succeeded.

His [literary] agent, a fellow named Jay Acton from New York City, got this idea. . . . He had heard all these stories that Tip had told over the years—so why not put them on paper for posterity? He suggested the form of Strunk and White, *The Elements of Style,* a book that high school and college students have been required to buy. . . . *The Elements of Style* would state a principle of grammar and then illustrate it with an example. Jay Acton said, "Why don't we have political principles listed and illustrate each of them with a Tip O'Neill story?"

If any politician would read that book and adhere to the principles Tip lays out, he would be successful, because Tip talks about some awfully important things to politics—loyalty, integrity, telling the truth, remembering the folks back home, and not getting above your raising, staying humble, being unpretentious—all those things that the nuns and Tip's father and the priests at Boston College taught him. He never forgot them; he lived them. It's easy to say those kinds of things, but Tip O'Neill lived that for eighty-one years. That's what made him a special person.

It often struck me, Why would anybody on the House floor change his mind on a vote because Tip asked him? That was Tip's job as a leader. He had to go to members and in some way build 218 votes on the floor. If he couldn't do that, there's no sense being there. So what it is, is compromise. You have to go to a person who's already made up his or her mind about something and say, "Look, we need you to change your mind, and we need you to vote with us to make a majority." Why would anybody do that? Why wouldn't they say, "The heck with you, I've already made up my mind."

I think it was because Tip O'Neill was a person everybody liked. He told stories; that was the basis of his popularity. People liked to be around him to hear these stories. He didn't use them to teach a lesson; he didn't use them to make judgments or moralize. He told them because they were good stories. They initially liked him because he was a good person to be around, telling these stories. Then they got to trust him, and in most cases it turned into love. They really loved the guy.

He had no personal agenda. He didn't care about headlines, press conferences, sound bites on television. He didn't meet with his staff every morning at eight o'clock and plot how he was going to be on the six o'clock news. . . . You rarely saw him on those Sunday talk shows, because it interfered with his golf schedule or his getting back home. He went home every weekend. One time, I remember, he agreed to do one of these press shows on Sunday morning, but he made them tape it. They said, "We'll make an exception, and we'll tape it, but on one condition: If something big happens in the world, then you've got to come back." He taped the show on a Thursday; he goes off to the Cape for his golfing weekend and that weekend all hell broke loose in Cyprus. They called him up and said, "You've got to come back." He came back on Saturday night. He was fuming. We had to prepare him for the show. The next morning he went on, and he was just steaming because it interrupted his weekend.

He was aware of the press. He loved reporters, and he held a press conference every day, fifteen minutes before the House went in session. The Speaker still does that; it's traditional. Tip enjoyed the camaraderie and the give-and-take with reporters. . . . He wasn't a person who sought publicity. Other congressmen and other politicians knew that and knew that Tip wasn't looking to get his name in the paper. When Tip asked them to do something—change their vote or help—it was because it was good for the country or good for the party. It wasn't necessarily good for Tip O'Neill. They knew it wasn't his ego asking them, that it was [based] on the merits. That's why he could greatly influence them.

TIP LOST HIS FIRST ELECTION. He didn't do very well in his own area. His father, who was superintendent of sewers of the city of Cambridge, [Massachusetts,] told him, "Never forget, all politics is local." Tip took that as his word. . . . You've got to take care of your local folks if you intend to stay in office. Tip took it a little step further. He said what he meant by it was that you keep your local people informed about everything you're doing. [Keep them informed] about every decision that you have to make—the tough ones—and get back to your constituents. Don't hide out in Washington; let them know what you're doing; let them know what the problems are when you have a tough vote. You may not vote like they would intend, but they will let you, in effect, get away with it. They will excuse you voting for some national or international thing. Because you have shown that you care about them, you've done your work for them.

ONE TIME THE *MONA LISA* WAS ON EXHIBIT at the National Gallery of Art. The director had run into Tip somewhere and said, "If you want to see the *Mona Lisa,* we've got these tremendous lines, but about fifteen minutes before we open, bring your office staff over." This was typical of Tip. How many congressmen would take their office staff, pile in a couple of cars, and drive down to the National Gallery? They walked past this big line. Well, they got booed roundly. It taught Tip a lesson. He put that in the book—it's bad politics to buck a line.

ONE STORY THAT HE LOVED to tell . . . was the story of the old Irishman who wanted to buy a house. He went to the local bank, and there was a Yankee in charge of the bank as was the case in those times. He asked for a loan. The old banker said, "Well, your credit rating is pretty good; you've got a savings account here, so we will probably loan you the two thousand dollars you need for the house. However, I have one more test you have to pass. I want you to look at me—I have one glass eye—and tell me which is the glass eye." So the old Irishman looks him in the eye, and he says, "The left eye is the glass eye." The Yankee banker says, "Okay, you get the loan. But tell me, how did you know that that was my glass eye?" The old Irishman says, "Because that was the one with the warmth in it."

TIP WATCHED TELEVISION a lot, so he knew the time had come for television [in the House]. It was seven years ahead of the Senate, and he was somewhat proud of that. Now there were a lot of people who didn't want television in the House. They raised the specter of members using television for their own personal gain. He knew there was going to be some abuse. The theory was, though, that it would be self-enforcing; if anybody did that, he would lower himself in the esteem of his colleagues. I think [self-enforcement] happens somewhat, but there were some instances where it was abused. I remember one time somebody wanted to cut off the debate and continue the next day and not go late at night. Some member went to the Republican leaders, and the Republican leaders came to Tip and said, "Can we keep going a little while longer? One of the congressmen has alerted everybody back home that he is going to be on television and make a speech." It got Tip angry that we would be inconveniencing the other members just for this one member, so he said, "No, the heck with it. We knock it off right now."

There were times when you'd see a member with a blue shirt and a red tie . . . and you'd know he'd told everybody, "Watch me on TV. I'm going to make a speech." [Tip] thought that that would take care of itself, and I think it generally has.

TIP WASN'T TOO BIG for remembering names in the entertainment field. He knew the names of politicians, which counted, but when it came to the entertainment world, particularly popular music, which wasn't his music, he wasn't too hip. Also movie stars. . . . Tip came back from a trip to Denver one time. He told us that he had been walking through the Denver airport and this fellow stopped him. He said, "Speaker Tip O'Neill, you don't know who I am, do you?" Tip said, "Look, I'm on C-SPAN all the time. I'm a popular figure and everybody recognizes me. I've got this white shock of hair, the cauliflower ears, and this bulbous nose. I'm easily recognizable. But I don't know who you are." The guy says, "I had lunch with you last week in your office with my wife." Tip says to us, "The guy said, 'My name is Richard Roquefort.'" We all looked at him kind of funny—who the heck is Richard Roquefort? Then somebody in the staff remembered, "You mean Robert Redford?" He said, "Yes, that was his name."

The other story was at a mini-convention in Memphis, a Democratic convention. Joe [Moakley, a representative from Massachusetts,] was talking to Warren Beatty. Tip walked up, and Joe introduced him to Warren Beatty. Tip said, "Gee, Mr. Beatty, you're good-looking enough to be a movie star." Joe said, "Don't you know who that was?" Tip said, "Beatty—Clyde Beatty?" Joe said, "No, Clyde Beatty was the lion tamer." Tip wasn't too big on entertainment figures, I would say.

TIP O'NEILL'S HUGS are an interesting story too. . . . [There was] a tough debate against the Republicans and it looked like [Tip and another representative] would never speak again, but then they walked off the floor, arms around each other. He often said that foreign parliamentarians could never understand that. What is at work here, and Tip often talked about this, is when you have a two-year term and you have annual authorization and annual appropriations, you have these fights all the time. The difference between the Democrats and

Republicans probably is that the Democrats want to do more, want to spend more money than the Republicans do. So they have these economic fights. They're not fights over morals or even principles. They're fights on how much to do for people. So you do your best, but you don't take it personally. I think that's what Tip O'Neill was about: You don't take it personally.

HE FELT THAT THE HOUSE is where the real work of the Congress is done— the appropriations bills, the authorization, the plotting, the slugging through amendments, where the real [legislative] fashioning goes on. It only takes the name of a senator to get a [news] story, whereas a House member has to work a lot harder at it. You know what House members say . . . when a House member gets elected to the Senate: "That will improve the intellectual level of both bodies." I think he believed that.

I NEVER TALKED ABOUT DEATH with Tip O'Neill. I guess the feeling was he would go on forever. He had all these things wrong with him, and he used to complain about them. I would call up and say, "Tip, how are you feeling?" because I was genuinely interested in knowing. He would tell me, but it wasn't anything new because these things had bothered him for decades. He was a guy who didn't take doctors' instructions too seriously but kept going. It was an inspiration to anybody who has something wrong with them. The thing that really clobbered him was that colostomy. He went in the hospital, and they told him he'd have to have a colostomy. He'd have to wear that bag the rest of his life. It really depressed him.

A friend of his, a golfing partner, came to see him in the hospital. Tip was going on about how depressed he was about the bag. This guy stood up and dropped his pants and showed Tip that he had a bag. He said, "Tip, you never knew that, and I've been wearing this bag for twenty-five years and playing golf and living a normal life." It really inspired Tip. From then on, he just plunged ahead.

WE DON'T HAVE TIP WITH US any longer, but . . . he lives on through this book. The principles that he lived by and the ideas that he had are in this book, and it's a chance [for him] to keep going.

I hope [people] take away from the book a picture of Tip O'Neill and what he stood for. Politicians are held in low esteem today. All the polls show that. Tip certainly took a lot of criticism, and the Congress would be down, but what Tip said [was] that the pendulum swings in politics. . . . The lesson is, if you're in there for the long haul and you do what's right, then you'll survive and your ideas will too. That's what Tip did.

PREVIOUS PAGE: A statue of Eleanor Roosevelt stands above Blanche Wiesen Cook in Riverside Park in New York City. The sculpture was crafted by Penelope Jencks and was dedicated by Hillary Clinton on October 5, 1996. (*All photos courtesy Brian Lamb*)

ABOVE: Robert Merry stands in the living room of Joseph Alsop's former Georgetown house. Here the Alsops entertained journalists, presidents, and many other Washington notables.

'Good evening. Mr. and Mrs. America and all the ships at sea. Let's go to press!'

—Walter Winchell, NBC

Ernie Pyle

On April 18, 1945, soldiers plant a sign on the Pacific island of Ie Shima: "At this spot the 77th Infantry Division lost a buddy." Killed there by a Japanese sniper was Ernest Taylor Pyle (1900–1945), who wrote about GIs, their socks and field rations, their letters home, their deaths. Pyle's Scripps-Howard column has real-people appeal. Says President Truman: "No man in this war has so well told the story."

Bourke-White

Margaret Bourke-White (1904–1971) ...th" in her work, "how it looks, how it ... Life magazine's first cover, a New Deal ...d War II, as the first woman to fly on ...she takes photos from bombers. She ... leaders, liberated concentration camp ...own torpedoed ship.

John Hersey

...e New Yorker fills ar ...1945 with this literary ...ort on the atomic bomb ...roshima.

Edward R. Murr...

THE WORLD GOES TO WAR

Ernie Pyle
State Historic Site

James Tobin stands next to the Ernie Pyle exhibit at the Newseum in Rossyln, Virginia. Pyle is one of more than 500 journalists featured here. INSET: The Ernie Pyle House in Dana, Indiana.

ABOVE: David Hackett Fischer stands on Old Battle Road in Concord, Massachusetts. Paul Revere took this road on his midnight ride.

OPPOSITE: Carol Reardon, a Civil War author and professor at Penn State, sits on the wall that Confederate soldiers unsuccessfully attempted to take in Pickett's Charge. Next to her is Dr. John Splaine, a professor at the University of Maryland and C-SPAN history consultant.

ABOVE: David Levering Lewis in his New York City apartment. On the desk is a miniature of *Winged Victory*—a favorite sculpture of W.E.B. Du Bois.

OPPOSITE: Ron Chernow stands nose to nose with the bust of John D. Rockefeller at the National Portrait Gallery in Washington, D.C.

ABOVE: Nadine Cohodas in C-SPAN's studio control room. On screen is Senator Strom Thurmond presiding over the Senate.

OPPOSITE: Representative John Lewis in his congressional office on Capitol Hill.

ON THIS SITE WAS BURIED
THOMAS PAINE
1737 · · · 1809
AUTHOR OF
COMMON SENSE
THE PAMPHLET THAT STIRRED
THE AMERICAN COLONIES TO INDEPENDENCE

JOHN ADAMS said:
"Without the pen of Paine the sword of
Washington would have been wielded in vain"
AND
"History is to ascribe the American Revolution to Thomas Paine"

DONATED BY ROWENA STURMAN IN THE
150TH YEAR OF THE AMERICAN REPUBLIC

OPPOSITE: Jon Katz in front of the Thomas Paine's cottage in New Rochelle, New York. The house is run by the Huguenot Historical Society and is the site of Paine's original grave. In his book *Virtuous Reality*, Jon Katz tells us how some of Paine's bones were dug from this grave and carted off to Europe.

ABOVE: Charles Fecher in the Mencken room at the Enoch Pratt Free Library in Baltimore. A portrait of journalist H. L. Mencken hangs on the wall behind him.

OPPOSITE: President George Bush, C-SPAN staffer Carol Hellwig, and Brent Scowcroft in C-SPAN's *Booknotes* studio.

ABOVE: John S.D. Eisenhower stands next to a bust of General Winfield Scott on display at the National Portrait Gallery in Washington, D.C.

Frank McCourt in a classroom at Stuyvesant High School in lower Manhattan. He spent thirty-two years there teaching English.

Richard Nixon

by
MONICA CROWLEY
RICHARD NIXON
BRUCE OUDES
TOM WICKER

Our thirty-seventh president, Richard Nixon (1913–94), had a long political career that took him from the U.S. House and Senate to the vice presidency under Dwight Eisenhower. He lost his first bid for the White House against JFK in 1960 but was successful in 1968 and again in 1972, only to resign from office under the weight of the Watergate scandal. Mr. Nixon gave a two-part interview to Booknotes *on February 23 and March 1, 1992, upon the publication of his 1992 book,* Seize the Moment *(Simon and Schuster). Other views of Richard Nixon come from journalist Tom Wicker, who appeared on* Booknotes *on April 7, 1991, to discuss* One of Us *(Random House, 1991); Bruce Oudes, who came to* Booknotes *on April 16, 1989, to talk about* From: The President—Richard Nixon's Secret Files *(Harper and Row, 1989); and Monica Crowley, who came to* Booknotes *on September 29, 1996, after publishing* Nixon off the Record *(Random House, 1996).*

Richard Nixon

Seize the Moment: America's Challenge in a One-Superpower World

I LIKE THE FACT that I went to undergraduate school at a small school, and then went to a top-flight graduate school where the competition was as high as it could be. What is most important is that an individual who wants to develop all of his abilities can't do it unless he has to compete. . . .

Competition . . . I think you're born with it. . . . I don't relish the battle, the personal battle of personalities. But the running for a post, the competing in a great cause, that to me has always been very fascinating. I like to read about it; I like to think about it; and when the occasion allows, I like to compete. . . . I do best when the odds are great. . . .

[Leading the investigation into Alger Hiss] was quite an experience for a freshman Congressman. That was a time when we didn't have the huge staffs. This will be hard to believe, but I was the only lawyer on the House Un-American Activities Committee, which investigated that case. We had no lawyers on our staff. It was a staff of only five people. We had a brilliant chief investigator, Bob Stripling, who was really better than a lawyer. Yet we were able to expose Hiss for what he really was. He had lied when he said he didn't know Whittaker Chambers; he had lied with regard to turning over documents to a Soviet Communist agent. Yet we were able to do that when we were up against the Justice Department, the administration, up against one of the greatest law firms of the country with scores and scores of people. You don't need huge staffs, such as the staffs that have investigated the Iran-Contra thing, in order to do a good job of investigation. Smaller staff, overworked, does far better than a huge staff where a lot of people are spending most of their time cutting each other up.

LEADERSHIP HAS TO COME from the top. It has to come from the secretary himself, or in the case of the administration on a national policy, it has to come from the president. If it doesn't come from there, it will not come up from the bureaucracy, although those in the bureaucracy can be very effective in implementing a policy, once they know what is to be done. It isn't a question of their being disloyal. They're not disloyal to the country; they're not disloyal to their president. But the point is that they simply don't have the capability—they have never developed it—to lead.

TELEVISION HAS ENORMOUS POWER. I'm the expert in that. I was saved by television when I made my fund speech in 1952. People say I lost because of television in 1960 in the debates with Jack Kennedy. In 1968, again, I won with television. My "silent majority" speech saved our policy in Vietnam so that we were able to go ahead and finally reach a peace agreement. But as far as television's concerned, it is certainly a mixed blessing in politics, if it is a blessing at all. . . . The fact that somebody is good on television should not be the deciding factor in determining whether he's going to be elected to public office.

If I had survived into the second term, I would have spent more time in press conferences. It was very difficult in the first term apart from the Watergate period. During the war, a president can't be as available to the press as he otherwise would be. I think it's important with the press that the relationship be one of not trying to win them by having them to dinners and all that sort of thing. They're not going to be bought off by that kind of bribery. The way to deal with them is straightforward in press conferences and don't play favorites. It's very important not to play favorites.

The Hiss case particularly was very difficult for the media. They all thought he was innocent, and if they didn't think he was innocent, they didn't want him exposed—one individual said it would be a reflection on the foreign policy of the Roosevelt administration, which was not my goal at all. So with that it was difficult. Not that I didn't have many friends in the media, but media people, while they try to be objective—many of them do—they also have strong convictions. Frankly, they generally are not particularly enamored with conservatives, as I am, even though I'm probably more reasonable than some of the conservatives that they go after.

THE LEGACY OF WATERGATE and Vietnam fortunately is now past us. . . . Vietnam was not a military defeat for the United States. It fell because the Congress didn't provide the assistance to the South Vietnamese, who were our allies, that the Soviets and the Chinese were providing to the North Vietnamese. But it was an enormous defeat for the American spirit, because a country that we had supported . . . came under Communist domination.

Right after Vietnam, the general conventional wisdom in this country was that the United States couldn't do anything well because we had lost in Vietnam to this Third World power. That was wrong, just as it was wrong to assume after we had won in the Persian Gulf that we could do anything. . . . Then to carry the syndrome a little further, after the collapse of communism in Russia and Eastern Europe, there's nothing left to do. These are all instant evaluations that are incorrect. The world remains the same. The United States still could play a major role after Vietnam because we had not suffered a military defeat; we should have played the role. For a while we did not, and it cost us dearly.

[AS FOR FOREIGN POLICY,] . . . what happens in Russia is the most important thing. Let me describe why that is so important—because Yeltsin must not fail. Historically speaking, it was about 170 years ago that the Battle of Waterloo was fought. After that battle, Wellington said, "It was a very close-run thing." But Napoleon's defeat at Waterloo and Wellington's victory affected the course of history in Europe for a century. Today, what happens in Russia, whether freedom survives and wins, will affect the course of history for the whole twenty-first century. If he fails, if Russia reverts to authoritarianism or dictatorship—it won't go back to communism, but dictators could be on the sidelines—then it means that the forces of freedom in the world will have an enormous setback. Take China. As China sees what happens in Russia, these tough, hard-line leaders in China at the present time would be delighted to see Yeltsin fail. If he does not fail, the pressure then will be irresistible on them—that they, too, will have to have political reforms to go along with their economic reforms.

To say that because communism has collapsed in the Soviet Union there's nothing left to do assumes that is all the problems we had. People will be surprised by this, but since the end of World War II, there have been 140 wars. Eight million more people have been killed in those wars than were killed in all of World War I, which used to be called the big one. Most of those wars would have been fought had there been no conflict between the Soviet Union and the free world and the United States. That has not changed. That is why the United States must continue to maintain adequate military forces, because what happened in the Gulf, affecting our vital interests, can happen in other places as well.

The title of my book comes out of a recollection that I had of my visit to China. On that occasion, in a toast that I gave there in the Great Hall of the People, I quoted from a poem that Mao Tse-tung had written in which he said, "Seize the day, seize the hour, because many things urgently remain to be done." Mao Tse-tung was talking about seizing the day and seizing the hour in order to serve the interests of communism. At the present time we must also recognize a sense of urgency. We should seize the moment, not for communism, but for the victory of freedom, and that is what this book is all about. Communism as an idea has been defeated all over the world except for China and a few other smaller countries like Vietnam, Laos, and Cambodia. But freedom has not yet won. It has not won in the sense that it has not yet proved itself. Until it proves itself, there's always a chance we will revert or some of the countries will revert to an authoritarian leadership.

THE AMERICAN PEOPLE ARE SOMETIMES for the underdog. Maybe I'm gaining a little [popularity] from that. Also, the American people like so-called celebrities, whether they're celebrities for good reasons or bad reasons, and maybe I benefit from that. But I would say what means the most to me is when somebody comes up to me, as one did just recently, and said, "I just want to thank you." He said, "Because of what you did, I got home from Vietnam." That makes it all worthwhile.

Tom Wicker

One of Us: Richard Nixon and the American Dream

THERE WERE THE TWO OF US, alone in this echoing corridor in the Capitol. As we walked towards each other, I was inescapable, but he never even noticed that I was coming along. He'd never notice anybody who was coming along. I would have thought that a political figure—one who was already talked about as the next president—would have had a glad hand for a voter. I would have thought that the man would have had a more confident air about him. I had learned by then, although I was a newcomer in Washington at the time, that most congressmen parade the halls with an entourage of staff and so forth. But there he was, all alone, hands shoved down his pockets, shoulders slumped, a rather despondent look on his face. His head was down, and he never noticed that I or anyone was passing.

Ultimately I decided that I would try to write about him and see if perhaps I could understand this elusive and strange, even bizarre, man. Dr. Arthur Burns—who worked with him in the Eisenhower administration and then was appointed chairman of the Federal Reserve by Richard Nixon—knew him well, liked him. Dr. Arthur Burns said to me in an interview, "You will never understand Richard Nixon." I don't think I have, and I'm not sure the readers will, but I hope that perhaps my book gives some insight into this man.

THE TITLE OF MY BOOK is *One of Us,* and the publisher was puzzled by that. A lot of people have been. But I maintain that Richard Nixon is one of us because in all of our character there's good and there's bad. Depending on circumstance, depending on events, depending on pressures, the good dominates or the bad dominates—not necessarily all the time, but as things happen. Richard Nixon is one of us in that sense. Sometimes the well-known dark side of his character has dominated and sometimes what Lincoln called "the better angels of our nature" have dominated.

In 1960, Kennedy won that election—if he did—by either 118,000 or 113,000 votes out of well over 60 million cast. . . . That's virtually a dead heat. . . . The evidence suggests to me that Richard Nixon believed that election had been stolen from him. A lot of [Republicans] certainly did believe this. . . . Nixon had made it clear that he was not going to challenge the election. I don't think that he could have sustained a challenge. I don't think he could have won, had the results reversed, or anything of that sort. But had he raised the challenge, had he called for a recount, had he pushed for some kind of a reversal of the election, it would have clouded the legitimacy of President Kennedy at the time he was taking office. It could have led to some terrible political imbroglio like that of 1876. I believe Richard Nixon thought that election had been stolen from him and decided not to challenge because it would tear the country apart. I think it would have.

[DURING WATERGATE,] WHEN FINALLY in June of 1974 the Supreme Court ruled that those [White House] tapes had to be turned over, that they were evidence or possible evidence in a criminal case, Nixon in fact turned over the tapes. You may say, "Well, what could he do? The Supreme Court had told him he had to." That is true. There's no question of that. But what could he do? He was president of the United States; he still had a great deal of political support in the country. He had some support, still, in Congress, although not enough. He was commander-in-chief of the armed forces. I think there's a lot Richard Nixon could have done in 1974 had he said, "I simply refuse to turn over those tapes, Supreme Court or no Supreme Court."

He could have done all of that if he were the evil figure that many people thought then and still think that he is. He would have done that if he had been the conniving figure that many people think he is. He would have done that, and it would have been a terrible crisis in this country. He did not do that. Once again, knowing that it was his own destruction, he turned over the tapes. Now, you may say—many people do and I do myself—"What's so great about that? He's only obeying the law." Granted. What I am saying is that if Nixon were the terrible, really evil person that so many people think, he might not have done that. The fact that he . . . spared the country the torments it would have caused, that seems to me to be a mark in his favor, even though I understand how many people resent marks in his favor.

Bruce Oudes

From: *The President—Richard Nixon's Secret Files*

IN HIS INTERVIEW with NBC in April of 1988, Nixon suggested at one point that he probably had been too rough on the press. It was quite an admission. And it was true. It was a carrot-and-stick technique that Nixon used on the press. It was Nixon who created the improved conditions at the White House for reporters. There was a lot of courting of the press. But by the same token, Nixon really used more of a stick than had ever been used before in the press. . . . One of the most amazing discoveries that I made was that . . . tricks were used against the political opposition during the 1972 campaign. . . .

The dirty-trick procedure specifically was the use of disinformation—propaganda against the press. Network anchors like Dan Rather, John Chancellor, or Walter Cronkite would say something that was not particularly appreciated in the White House. The White House would then get out a suggested letter or telephone call memo, which would go over to the Republican National Committee. Then the Republican National Committee would contact its friends around the country. These people would contact NBC, CBS, ABC and express their opinion on a given subject without telling NBC, CBS, ABC that they were doing so upon the explicit instructions of the White House. Many of these people didn't know it was the White House that was doing it. They thought it was the Republican National Committee. . . . It's really a lack of civility in the relationship between press and politician for politicians to use that technique on a systematic basis. . . .

The technique, in and of itself, is the kind of thing that on an informal basis we would use almost every day. . . . But when, as was the case in the Nixon administration, the president orders, as he did in the summer of 1969, a specific program on an organized basis to do this sort of thing regularly and routinely on a large scale and to do it to the press, it goes over the boundary line of propriety and civility.

Monica Crowley

Nixon off the Record: His Candid Commentary on People and Politics

NIXON ALWAYS CLAIMED that he never watched television, and of course he did. He liked to watch the news. He watched sporting events. He used to watch football and baseball quite avidly. But he never admitted to watching mindless entertainment. . . . I was usually about five minutes late for our meetings at the residence in the afternoon, so he normally expected me to be late. One day in particular I was five minutes early. I was walking up the stairs, and before I could clear the stairs to the third floor, I heard the television going. Then I heard canned laughter coming out of that television, and I realized that he was watching something that was meant to amuse. I was very surprised by this. I looked at him, and he had his shoes off and his feet were stockinged, up on the ottoman, crossed, and he had the remote control in his hand, and he was laughing.

He was just enjoying the show and the moment so much. I observed him for a couple of moments because I really wanted him to have those few extra minutes when he didn't have to be "on" and he didn't have to be the serious Richard Nixon that he presented to me most of the time. I enjoyed seeing that. But then I cleared my voice, and I cleared the top of the stairs. He looked at me, and he was horrified that he had been caught in the act of watching television, *The Dick Van Dyke Show* no less. He tried to simultaneously shut the TV off with the remote control and jam his feet into his shoes, and he dropped the remote control. It was a big, chaotic scene. He said, "Well"—because he was red-faced—"you caught me. You caught me watching the tube."

NIXON ALWAYS SAID THAT HIS PROBLEMS with the media or his disagreements with the media stemmed from the Alger Hiss case. He said when he exposed Alger Hiss, he exposed the press. He said the worst thing that you can do to a member of the press is prove that they are wrong. He said, "That's what I did with Alger Hiss, and they never forgave me for it."

NIXON WAS VERY SKEPTICAL about the polling process in America. He described to me an incident in 1960, when he was running against Jack Kennedy. He said that the pollsters had a poll in October that showed him a couple of points behind Kennedy. They ran another poll a couple of days before the election that showed them neck and neck, and he said, "They never published that poll because they wanted to keep the winning momentum on Kennedy's side." That gave him a very bitter taste of the whole polling process.

He usually referred to himself and Kennedy as "the candidates" whenever he talked about 1960. He never said, "Well, I did this and Kennedy did that."

He said, "Well, the candidates did that." It was in the third person, which I thought was very interesting. He considered Kennedy a formidable political challenger. He thought that he had had a fairly cordial relationship with him, a constructive relationship with him, when they were in the Congress together. He did think, though, that Kennedy had been a reckless president, not only reckless in his personal life, but reckless with the national security of the country.

USUALLY, THE OUTGOING and the incoming president meet, and they talk once about whatever issues are on the table. But Nixon and Lyndon Johnson met several times. He said, "We had so much to talk about. We had the war in Vietnam; we had the Russians and nuclear disarmament, all of these great issues to talk about." Nixon said, "But the first time I got to the White House, one of the first things Lyndon Johnson did was take me up to the family residence. He took me into the president's bedroom, and he got down on all fours. He was on his hands and knees." This was the outgoing president of the United States showing the incoming president of the United States underneath the bed. He said Johnson lifted the bedspread, and he swished his hand underneath the bed. Johnson was referring to the listening devices that Kennedy had installed under the beds. He said, "Dick, they're voice-activated."

OBVIOUSLY, [MANY PRESIDENTS HAD] a great political problem in dealing with Richard Nixon. This was a Republican president who had been driven from office. They did not want to publicly acknowledge the association that they had with Richard Nixon. Even though Reagan and Bush consulted with Nixon on a fairly regular basis, although not as regularly as Bill Clinton, they never did it publicly. They never put a picture out when he visited the White House. They used to invite Nixon at night so that the press couldn't actually see him entering the White House. Even though Nixon understood that, because he was a political animal, it wounded him to a certain extent.

NIXON'S STROKE CAME OUT OF THE BLUE, totally unexpected. Nixon was an extremely disciplined person. He ate spartan diets, and he exercised on a daily basis. He used to take three-mile walks every day, rain or shine, freezing cold, stifling heat. He took very good care of himself because he dreaded the entire aging process. He hated everything associated with mortality and death. He fought it with every fiber of his being.

I remember Nixon being particularly pensive on that last afternoon. In fact, we sat out on the deck. Normally, we would have our meetings in his library in the residence, but he insisted that we sit out that day. It was a nice, warm spring day. He wanted to take advantage of it, and he was quieter than usual. I'm not a medical person, I don't mean to speculate, but it may have been that there were some things going on in his body that even he wasn't aware of, but he seemed quieter than usual.

I LIKED HIM VERY MUCH, and I admired him very much. He was a good man. He really was a good person, and he was very good to me. I think that Nixon's greatest flaw was his impatience. He was very impatient with himself. He was very impatient with those around him. He was very impatient with history. He was always trying to nudge history forward so that he would have a more favorable rating, so that his mistakes would be put in context with his accomplishments—that ultimately, those mistakes would pale in comparison to what he had accomplished for this country. [He hoped that] eventually he would emerge as a great president, particularly when his presidency would be put up against other presidencies.

Gerald Ford

by
JAMES CANNON

Gerald Ford (b. 1913) became the thirty-eighth president of the United States in 1974. Mr. Ford served in the U.S. House from 1949 to 1973, representing Grand Rapids, Michigan, rising to minority leader. He was appointed vice president after Spiro Agnew resigned in 1973, and he became president following the resignation of Richard Nixon. Shortly after Mr. Nixon resigned, President Ford granted him a full pardon. Mr. Ford ran for the presidency in his own right in 1976 but was defeated by Democrat Jimmy Carter. Author James Cannon was our guest on Booknotes *on April 17, 1994, for his book* Time and Chance: Gerald Ford's Appointment with History *(Harper-Collins, 1994).*

THIS IS A CLASSICAL STORY of good versus evil. What this story is about is what Richard Nixon did to put this country in such a state of constitutional peril and how this rather solid but honest man came to the rescue and ended— a little raggedly—but ended the national nightmare that Watergate had been.

I worked for Jerry Ford in the White House for two years. When I first thought of doing this book, I went out to see President Ford to tell him of my plans. His immediate reaction was, "I thought nobody would ever ask." I said, "There may be a lot of things that I find out that won't be very advantageous to you. I wouldn't want this to cost us our friendship." He said, "Don't you worry about that. I know more about the mistakes I made than anyone else, and I'll tell you what they were." He then opened his files; he opened his diaries; he opened the then-closed parts of his library to me. He made available to me about a million and a half words of oral history that he had done in 1977, when he was preparing to write his own autobiography. I would estimate only 10 or 15 percent of that had ever been used.

HE SAID VERY LITTLE about his growing up. But I realized, after about a year or year and a half of research into this book, that the significance of Ford's growing up is that he was taught, trained, and educated in an environment of all the old-fashioned virtues that families in America seemed to have in the 1920s and 1930s more significantly than they have today.

They were trained to be honest, to tell the truth, to work hard, to study hard. Their report cards were examined. Their parents were very assiduous about what they did in school and after. Ford grew up in a time . . . in a family and in a place, Grand Rapids, Michigan, where honesty and integrity were highly prized. I felt it was essential to understand the presidency of Ford, indeed to understand how it was that he got to be president. I had to show how this boy grew up into the person he was, so that when the time came to find someone to replace Richard Nixon, they turned to a man who had the degree of integrity and credibility that Ford did. Nobody disliked him. Everybody trusted him.

IN ORDER TO TELL THE STORY of how Ford became president, I had to tell the story of Watergate. Without Watergate, he would not have become president. I had to tell the story of [former vice president Spiro] Agnew. Without Agnew's being forced from office, Ford would never have become president.

Watergate was such a powerful story, in and of itself, that the Agnew story seemed almost a sidebar. In essence, it was dramatic in and of itself, but it was in the shadow of Watergate and never seemed as consequential as it actually was.

Agnew was never Nixon's first choice for vice president. In particular, in 1972, Nixon wanted to dump him from the ticket and replace him with [treasury secretary John] Connally. But that was politically unfeasible, as John Mitchell, his campaign manager, and others argued. Nixon came to the conclusion, "Okay, we'll make sure that Agnew is not the nominee in 1976. We'll make sure that John Connally is."

Immediately after the election of 1972, Nixon made the first moves to make certain that Agnew was not going to be his political successor. The notes of their conversations are in the Nixon papers over in the Nixon archives. . . . At this point, the only true evidence is that it was more or less coincidence that Nixon wanted to get rid of Agnew and that weeks later Agnew was first investigated for income-tax problems.

They found it out by pursuing a series of reports in Maryland that it had been common practice in Maryland for payments to be made by contractors who received . . . public contracts. They'd gone back over time, and they found that some of these contractors had indeed made cash payments. In pursuing them, they found out that Agnew had, as county executive of Baltimore County and as governor of Maryland . . . taken bribes and that these bribes had continued even after Agnew became vice president.

The Twenty-fifth Amendment, fortuitously, was in place when Agnew resigned. When Kennedy was assassinated, Johnson became president. For a period of more than a year the Speaker of the House, who was the next in line of succession, was John McCormack. John was quite old then, and there was considerable concern about whether he could function as president if, indeed, something should happen to Lyndon Johnson.

Senator Birch Bayh and a number of others thought it was a good idea to have a process created, where if there was no vice president, then the president would nominate a candidate for vice president, and the House and the Senate would separately confirm him. Usually it's only the Senate that confirms a nominee, but deliberately they included the House because they wanted all the members of the House to have a chance to weigh in on so important a matter. So the Twenty-fifth Amendment, which was passed in the late 1960s, was fortuitously in operation when Agnew left office.

Agnew resigned because of the abundance of evidence against him and because, very frankly . . . Agnew was scared that Al Haig, then chief of staff, would have him killed if he didn't resign—physically [kill him]. This was the import of Agnew's concern, and so he has written in his book that finally he decided he had no choice, that he knew what might happen to someone who resisted the president. He felt that the only course he had was to resign. And he did. He pleaded no contest to one tax charge, but Agnew has never admitted that he took a bribe.

It's interesting there was never any animosity between Agnew and Ford. On the day that Agnew resigned [October 10, 1973,] when Ford got home that night, he had a message that Agnew had called. He called him back, and they talked for a few minutes; Agnew congratulated Ford. Ford told Agnew that he was sorry it turned out that way.

ONE OF THE MOST FASCINATING THINGS about my research into this book was the degree to which Nixon consciously and deliberately lied. He made a conscious decision to lie at Camp David the day he fired [Chief of Staff Bob] Haldeman and [Presidential Assistant for Domestic Affairs John] Ehrlichman. He said—and he's written this in his book—"I either had the choice to tell the truth and risk being taken out of the presidency or to lie, and I decided to do the latter."

Ford found out that Nixon had lied to him on August 1, 1974—the afternoon when Al Haig came in alone, having insisted that the meeting be one-on-one, and told then–Vice President Ford that he had seen the transcript of the smoking-gun tapes. There was no question but there was evidence against Nixon that would force him from office. It was at that point that Haig told Ford, and for the first time Ford understood it. It had been a long course for him. He had been friends with Nixon for twenty-five years, and Nixon had told him more than once that he had nothing to do with Watergate. Ford is not only a man who can be trusted, he does trust. And he trusted Nixon. He believed Nixon. He believed what Nixon told him, that he had nothing to do with Watergate, until that afternoon when Haig came over and revealed the truth to him.

THE STORY OF THE PARDON is in two parts. The first part of the story must begin with Al Haig coming over to tell Vice President Ford that there's evidence against Nixon that may force him out of office. At the same time, he presents six options, as he calls them. The sixth option—which is in writing, which is very important—suggests that Nixon will resign if Ford will agree to pardon him.

Ford did not turn down that option—that sixth option—right away. He was cautious. He was careful. He told Haig he wanted to think about it and get back to him. He did talk later that afternoon with Bob Hartmann. Bob Hartmann was his speechwriter and senior political counselor. And Hartmann was outraged and said so—that this was a terrible thing for Haig to have presented; that it was unthinkable that this should be done. But Ford did not yet agree. He talked that night with Betty Ford, who was concerned also, but she said finally, "I'll go along with whatever you think is the best thing to do."

Then Friday, August the second, was the day when Ford was finally convinced by [adviser] Bryce Harlow that this was unthinkable. The net message was that "Mr. Vice President, your own presidency will be tainted if you do this. You cannot do this." Ford said, "Well, what do you want me to do?" Harlow said, "Right now don't call Nixon." He said, "That would be the worst possible thing you could do. But call Haig and tell him that none of this is to be regarded as a deal." Ford called Haig on the telephone and said, "Al, no deal."

What happened next is that once Nixon found out that there was no deal, he told his staff and his speechwriter that he was going to stick it out, he was going to force the impeachment and force a trial in the Senate. And he did plan to do that. We're now on Saturday and Sunday. He planned over the weekend to stick it out. But on Monday, the smoking-gun tape was revealed.

It was an audiotape. What it came down to is that on this tape, in three instances on June twenty-third of 1972, six days after Watergate . . . Nixon told his chief of staff, Haldeman, to have the CIA stop the FBI investigation of Watergate. That was obstruction of justice, a clear-cut case of it. Once it was revealed, Nixon lost all of his final support on the House Judiciary Committee.

Ford was not absolutely sure of becoming president. Haig told him not to be absolutely sure of it until he heard it from Nixon himself. He heard it from Nixon himself on Thursday, August 8, the day before Nixon actually resigned.

[Ford became president the next day, the ninth of August, 1974.] Nixon's pardon was granted about five weeks later. The pardon was granted because Ford, who went in wanting to solve every problem and put this behind him— and indeed he said in his inaugural address, "The long national nightmare has ended"—thought it was over.

He realized also that there was no way to put this behind him unless something drastic happened. [The pardon] was a result of his thinking over the problem and what ought to be done about it. Essentially Ford was convinced that the most important thing for the country was to get on with governing: to address the serious economic problems we were having, to address serious foreign policy problems. We would have to get on with that and get off the subject of Watergate. The only way, he felt, that we could get off the subject was for him to pardon Richard Nixon. . . . He felt it was the most important thing for the country. He did not believe this country should be put through the agony and the international humiliation of putting a former president in the dock. There was no question about Nixon's guilt. There was no question—people understood his guilt. Not only had the special prosecutor found the evidence—and that evidence is in the National Archives—[but] there was enough evidence there to put Nixon in prison for thirty years. The evidence turned up by the House Judiciary Committee, under Peter Rodino, was exhaustive, extensive, and is a matter of record in the congressional files.

Two or three days after Ford granted the pardon, Nixon called him and apologized for all the problems that the pardon had caused. He said that maybe he ought to just decline to accept the pardon. Ford, who took very careful notes on this telephone conversation, said, "No, no. The damage is done. We'll let it stand as it is." Ford felt, correctly, that for Nixon to say he wouldn't accept the pardon wouldn't help anything; it would just make the whole problem worse.

FORD IS A FORGIVING MAN, but he could not [forgive], and I don't believe he has forgiven Nixon for deceiving him and deceiving the American people on what had actually happened in Watergate. In the first place, Richard Nixon left such an appalling impression on the country as a consequence of Watergate and his long delay in telling anything like the truth about Watergate. People wanted a change. They had a change in Ford, and they liked that change. But politically, the pardon damaged Ford and reminded voters and others in the country that we'd had a very bad time in the second term of Richard Nixon.

Robert McNamara

by
DEBORAH SHAPLEY
ROBERT MCNAMARA
PAUL HENDRICKSON

Robert McNamara (b. 1916) oversaw America's deepening involvement in Vietnam as secretary of defense for presidents John F. Kennedy and Lyndon Johnson. Many of the authors interviewed on Booknotes *have written about Robert McNamara. For this chapter, we drew upon Mr. McNamara's own 1995 memoir,* In Retrospect *(Times Books), as well as Deborah Shapley's 1993 book,* Promise and Power *(Little, Brown), and Paul Hendrickson's* The Living and the Dead *(Knopf, 1996). Mr. McNamara came to our studio on April 23, 1995, Deborah Shapley on March 21, 1993, and Paul Hendrickson on October 27, 1996.*

Deborah Shapley

Promise and Power:
The Life and Times of Robert McNamara

YOU HAVE TO REMEMBER that Robert McNamara stood for a quintessentially rational approach to our defense policy. He maintained that through analytic techniques he was going to find the objective answers: What size force is best? How much is enough? What is right for the nuclear forces? This idea that everybody agrees that there are certain problems that can be solved rationally—[President] Kennedy even said, "Some problems are so complicated, we have to allow for experts to work on them and wait until they tell us what the answer is" . . . that gets back to the riddle of McNamara. How could he be such a remarkable analytic mind, so intellectual, so curious, and so wonderfully intentioned and be associated with this [Vietnam] tragedy?

What McNamara was saying for the first time, in quotes that he released to me, is that what he and Kennedy intended was to pull out "even if the South Vietnamese were to be defeated." Of course, a lot of [former] Kennedy advisers claim this, too. They want to believe John Kennedy would have handled this thing more wisely than Lyndon Johnson did. It's very subjective, and we really need something hard. So at the moment I don't believe him.

IN EFFECT, LYNDON JOHNSON did fire Robert McNamara. He was becoming a liability. He was becoming very emotional and very out of sync with the other advisers. In 1967, the Johnson administration was dug in; the wagons were drawn. [White House adviser] Walt Rostow and [Secretary of State] Dean Rusk and Lyndon Johnson himself were shooting through the wagons at the Indians out there, including the media and everybody else. If you read the minutes of [some of the meetings at the time] . . . you feel this sense of entrapment. Meanwhile, McNamara was becoming progressively more open in his wish to stop the bombing.

On November 1, 1967, he laid on the president a memorandum recommending a bombing halt, saying he thought it would lead to negotiations with North Vietnam and that that was the course to follow. He was recommending a whole bunch of things that were so far out of line with what the advisers' circle wanted that Johnson, at that moment, picked up the phone and told the Treasury to start McNamara's move out [of the administration and] into the World Bank. So the World Bank was, in a sense, not dumped on him, but laid on him. It was not against his will. He was interested in it as a possibility, but he went out of his way to create no record that he wanted out. If word that he wanted out were to get out, then the Washington media would have a heyday: "McNamara seeks to leave office."

So they played a game with each other—Johnson not telling McNamara, [and] McNamara not wanting to say anything in the open to Johnson. Two close men that were cheek by jowl day after day, month after month, year after year, unable to talk to each other about the major thing that was going to divide them.

MCNAMARA WAS BORN in Oakland, California, and educated in the public schools there. He came from a very modest background. I stress the absence of money in the household, the extreme frugality, the optimizing of the shopping, and the mathematical element of the housekeeping, which is true in many households. It stamped him with this idea that he had to conserve money and be frugal—money was important. These are all American attitudes; it's a classic American story. But it also sends a message to a boy to make money, because money is power; money will get you out of there; to be frugal; allocate resources; don't spend too much. All of these things came to be the McNamara trademark at the Department of Defense. He tried to fight the war with a certain amount of frugality, not giving the military everything they asked for. That was an attitude stamped on him in childhood.

He met his wife Margaret in Berkeley at the campus while they were both there. He fell in love with her later when he had returned home to work right after business school. She was a charming and wonderful person who, in a sense, had all the qualities that he lacked. She had a lot of warmth, a lot of ability to sense where people were at, and a lot of ability to relate to them very quickly. They were like two halves of one coin, their friends often say.

She is a thread throughout the entire book because her influence on him as a balancing factor was tremendous during his lifetime. She died in 1981, and I think that was a very big blow. I quote a friend as saying that her death was a bigger blow to him than Vietnam because she was such a force for balance and stability. He's a very driven person, and a lot of these people who get as far as he does can't contain their ambition and aggression and drive. If McNamara were here, he'd be in constant movement. He is very restless. When he gets impatient, he starts pulling his socks up. He was a hyperactive type, and she calmed him down and had a very measuring effect on him.

HE WAS AT FORD MOTOR COMPANY for fourteen years. He was president for only a few months. He was secretary of defense for seven years. After that, he was at the World Bank for thirteen years, leaving in 1981. Since then, he has had an office [awarded to him by] the Corning company because he's on their board. He writes and gives speeches. . . . He has avoided Vietnam like the plague.

He has become a citizen of the planet—zinging around, on and off airplanes, compulsive travel. I compare him to the Flying Dutchman because the Flying Dutchman dared nature in the legend. He was cursed by God for having tried to sail around the Cape of Good Hope against the storm and was cursed to sail forever because he had been too bold. There's a lot of hubris in McNamara. In a way, all of this global travel has such a restless air, as though there's no place he can come to rest because he's still so controversial in his own country. I won't say he doesn't have a home in the United States, because he's very well respected by people in the arms-control community and the international banking community. But, in a sense, he doesn't have a home, I think, until he comes to terms with us.

He is a pivotal figure in the weakening and decline of America, despite the many virtues of the American century he embodies. I wouldn't have had to write this except that Vietnam itself was so pivotal. Had any of his mistakes been on a lesser scale—[nothing] ever came up to hit him the way Vietnam did. Vietnam is . . . unique. It's a watershed event. It's like World War I for Great Britain. . . . Vietnam did weaken us—our morale, our economy, our civic spirit, our trust of public institutions.

Robert McNamara

In Retrospect: The Tragedy and Lessons of Vietnam

I BELIEVED [Vietnam was a failure] in 1966. That's when I first had the idea for the Pentagon Papers. I thought then, This is a failure; we're not achieving our objective. Scholars should, and I hope will wish to, review what happened: How did we get in this damn mess? I knew enough about government to know it isn't that people consciously destroy documents; that isn't the problem. But in a government as large as ours, the documents get misplaced, they get lost; they're not brought together. So I started the Pentagon Papers to bring these things together.

I'm not going to say whether I favored John F. Kennedy or Lyndon Johnson. Let me put it this way. I loved and respected and admired both of them. They were totally different people. Johnson was a paradoxical figure. At the end, I got so emotional when I left. . . . I say to this day, I don't know if I quit or I was fired. On my ideals, you don't quit. If your president wants you, you stay. It was certainly not my intention to quit. Frankly, I don't think I did. I was with Kay Graham, the former publisher of *The Washington Post* and I made this statement to her. She said, "Bob, you're crazy! Of course you were fired." Now, I don't think I was.

I WAS BORN IN SAN FRANCISCO, and I grew up there. My earliest memory is of a city exploding with joy. The date was November 11, 1918, Armistice Day. I was two years old. The city was celebrating the end of World War I, which we'd won. More fundamentally, it was celebrating the belief that that was a war to end all wars. That was President Woodrow Wilson's view. That was the view of many Americans. We were totally wrong! This is the bloodiest century in history. We, the human race, will have killed 160 million other human beings.

My father was Irish. Many, if not most, of my uncles and aunts, his sisters and brothers on my father's side, were born in Ireland. My father was much older than my mother. His father and mother and many of his sisters and brothers—it was a rather large family—had been forced out of Ireland by the potato famine. The potato famine, as I recall, was 1845–48. They came in the 1850s to Massachusetts, and then the full family went to California. My father crossed the Isthmus of Panama on his way to California on muleback in 1863. He never went beyond the eighth grade. My mother never went beyond high school. This was one of the reasons I was expected to achieve. I was expected to learn, to take advantage of the opportunities that were open to me—ones that they hadn't had an opportunity to take advantage of, and this was a tremendous stimulus to me.

Money has never been a motivating factor for me. People say I'm wealthy, and in the sense that my children are well educated, that I have a nice house, sure. But, in the sense of wealthy, no way. It never mattered to my children. . . . When I was president of Ford Motor Company, we lived in a house that cost around fifty thousand dollars. Marg and I talked after I'd said to President Kennedy that I wasn't qualified and I couldn't possibly accept his offer to be secretary of defense. He kept pressing me. I went home one weekend. We talked about it, and we brought in the children. We said, "Now, this is what we're considering, and if we do it, we'll be going from"—in today's dollars what would have been, I suppose, $2.5 million a year down to what then, in those dollars, was $25,000. It's hard for people to believe that the cabinet officers' salary was $25,000. My children could care less. Marg didn't care.

I'VE LIVED IN WASHINGTON thirty-five years. I've been in public life in various ways, to different degrees for thirty-five years. I'm familiar with it. I understand this [mixed reaction to my book]. Some of the people that were working with me on the book didn't expect it. They thought I was wrong in saying that there was going to be a tremendous controversy stirred up by it. I thought there would be. I'm pleased in one sense. People stop me on the street and they say, "For the first time, I'm beginning to understand what happened." . . . I'm not arguing [that it is] a great book; that's not my point. What I'm arguing is the subject. [Vietnam] lies below our conscience. We need to surface it; we need to understand it, and we need to avoid it in the future.

THERE ARE STILL OPEN WOUNDS relating to Vietnam. One of my hopes was . . . that the book would help close wounds rather than open them. I knew there were open wounds, but I hope it will close them, and it may.

Paul Hendrickson

The Living and the Dead: Robert McNamara and the Five Lives of a Lost War

MR. MCNAMARA REPRESENTS a postwar, technocratic, hubristic fable. He was an extraordinarily impressive person, almost a new Adam, who abused his [public] trust. He knows he did and has spent the rest of his life paying for it.

Mr. McNamara ceased believing that the Vietnam War could be won militarily, and he stayed on to prosecute it for another two years and four months. He was not the secretary of state. He was not the counselor to the president. He was the man who was in charge of America's military forces. He ceased believing that it could be won on the battlefield and he did not resign his office. I feel, in sum, that . . . he [should have] resigned his office at the point at which he began to believe it could not be won militarily. . . . The consequences of this are profound, because young eighteen-year-old boys were continuing to go into the tall elephant grass and would not come out again. . . . If he had resigned at the point at which he ceased believing, when he lost faith, I believe that today there would be something known as the McNamara Prize, and that prize would be coveted around the world by men and women of conscience.

Mr. McNamara struggled within himself. I would like to stress that point. People who see him as the Tin Man without a conscience, without a heart, are way off. He tried to alter his fatal mistakes. He tried to cap the war. He tried to do an awful damn lot, but he did not resign. So the question "Is he moral?" cannot be answered in a yes or no. In his book *In Retrospect,* I do not find moral anguish. I do not find moral grief. I find a man saying on, essentially, the first page, "We were wrong." But when you read his book, you begin asking yourself, Well, wait a minute. What is he saying we were wrong about? It seems he is saying we were wrong strategically, we were wrong geopolitically, we were wrong globally. Where is anguish—the moral anguish—for lives lost needlessly?

WHAT HAPPENED in Dean Rusk's dining room—that's a great moment. . . . That's one of the moments where [he was] outed. Like murder, truth will out. On February 27, 1968, two days before he left office—it was a leap year, so he left office on February 29, 1968. On February 27, 1968, he was at a private luncheon in Dean Rusk's dining room with the Secretary of State. There were six or seven other key figures in the room. They were there to say good-bye to McNamara, to have a little farewell luncheon, but also to have some discussions about Vietnam and especially about the Tet offensive, which was taking place during this point. Mr. McNamara was just getting set to leave. . . . There was lots of gloom in the room because the Tet offensive was seeming to change everything about the war. Mr. McNamara got up, and he lost control. He said, "The goddamn war has done nothing. We've overrun them. We've carpet-bombed the place. We've done more bombing than we did in all of Germany in the last year of World War II. And what's it done? It's done a goddamned nothing, a goddamned nothing."

I talked to [some] of the participants who were in that room. These people were looking at their shoe tops—a man named Harry McPherson, who was an LBJ aide; [another White House aide] named Joe Califano; [and then–Secretary of Defense] Clark Clifford, [who] wrote about it in his own book and talked about the barely suppressed sobs. It poured out, all of his anger—I don't think "anger" is strong enough—all of his incredible rage about the way the war had turned out for him, for America. He was leaving in disgrace. He was leaving broken, and it just flooded out.

Katharine Graham

by
KATHARINE GRAHAM

Katharine Graham (b. 1917) won a Pulitzer Prize for her 1997 memoir Personal History *(Knopf). Mrs. Graham is chairman of the executive committee of* The Washington Post Company, *which owns* The Washington Post *and other media holdings. Mrs. Graham and the* Post's *history are linked: Her father, Eugene Meyer, purchased the newspaper, her husband Phil Graham grew it, and—after Mr. Graham's suicide—Kay Graham, as publisher, shepherded it through Vietnam and Watergate. Mrs. Graham came to C-SPAN on February 16, 1997, to talk about her life.*

I DON'T SUPPOSE that I meant to tell everything to everybody. But once I sat down to write my story, I tended to be frank and open. I wanted to be very truthful. I wrote it the way I saw it, and the way the research [went]. I told it the best I could.

I am chairman of the executive committee of The Washington Post Company. . . . We're at about $1.6 billion in annual revenues, and the company holds mainly *The Washington Post.* We have a small newspaper, the *Everett Herald,* and half of the *International Herald Tribune.* Then we have *Newsweek,* and we have six television stations and a million and a half cable connections. We also have Digital Ink, which is our electronic media, and a *Washington Post* Web-site.

[My father bought the *Post*] in 1933. He had just gotten out of the government, been out about three weeks. He'd been governor of the Federal Reserve Board, and he had started the Reconstruction Finance Corporation under Hoover. He stayed as Federal Reserve chairman for a little while under Roosevelt. Then he resigned because he didn't like Roosevelt's monetary policies. . . . The *Post* came up for auction three weeks later on the steps of the building, and he bought it anonymously. . . .

The *Post* was fifth in the field of five [Washington papers]. It had circulation of fifty thousand in a pretty broken-down building. . . . He was a businessman. He thought he knew how to turn around businesses, but he had never had any newspaper experience. He encountered the most horrendous difficulties in fighting his way up. But he did a terrific job starting with nothing.

[MY PARENTS MET] in 1908; they met in a museum in New York City. My father had picked up a friend, and they were driving downtown in an old car that he called a Stanley Steamer. He picked up this friend whom he didn't know very well or like very much and said that he would like to give him a ride, but he was going to stop off at a Japanese print show. They did that, and they saw my mother walking around the show. My father said to his friend, "That's the woman I'm going to marry." The friend said, "Well, then you have to speak to her." My father said, "No, no, that would spoil everything. One of us is going to meet her, and whoever meets her first will call the other one." About two weeks later, the friend called my father and said, "Guess what?" [My father] said, "You've met the girl." And [his friend] said, "Damn you, I have, and I've arranged that we're all going to have dinner." . . . That was on Lincoln's birthday, and they were married two years later on Lincoln's birthday.

I WENT TO VASSAR for two years and for two years to the University of Chicago. I had proudly gone off and gotten myself a job. I'd used my labor-relations professor, Paul Douglas, who later became a senator and who knew the publisher of the then *Chicago Times,* the afternoon tabloid. I went down there and asked the publisher for a job. He said he would take me, but if I wasn't any good, then I shouldn't think he was going to keep me. I said, "That would be fine. I'd love a tryout." Then I went home and my father asked me to go out to San Francisco with him on a train trip he was taking. . . . I said, "Fine." I'd never seen San Francisco. And I stayed there. . . . I said [to my father], "I love this town and if I will swallow my pride, give up my job in Chicago, will you help me find a job here?" And he did.

After school, in 1939, my father came out and suggested that I come back from San Francisco and work on the *Post.* . . . [My first job at the *Post*] was low person on the editorial page. I edited letters to the editor; I made up the page; and I wrote a few editorials of no great moment.

[I MET MY HUSBAND PHIL GRAHAM] that year that I came back. I was surprised because when I'd left Washington to go to college, it was still a very Republican town, and it was kind of stuffy. . . . When I got back, the New Deal had come and [Washington had] grown up. It was prewar, and the town was just full of attractive young men. It was not the town I remembered, and I was simply thrilled.

I met him in a house where two of the people who worked on the *Post* were living. There were twelve bachelors in this house, and he was one of the twelve. . . . I actually met him one night when we'd all gone to a restaurant and were coming back. . . . I leaned out the window because the tail end of the party was coming in. Unfortunately, the screen fell out, onto his head. He was startled and looked up, and I looked at him.

I met a girl that night when I went to the bathroom, and she said she went to law school. I said, "How marvelous. I could never do that. Tell me about it. How do you do it?" She said, "Well, I'm engaged to Phil Graham, and he comes by and picks me up. We talk things over and that helps a lot." . . . Then they broke up, and he went out with a friend of mine named Alice Barry. She [asked if I knew Phil] and I said no, I didn't. She said, "You should. He's just the greatest here." Then about New Year's, my sister gave a party and invited everybody from the house. . . . He was at the party, and we first got to know each other that way. This developed rather quickly because the third time we went out together, he discussed marriage. I said this was a little hasty . . . but I was really intrigued by the idea. I said we had to be very deliberate and wait a month. We hardly did wait a month, and we were married . . . June 5, 1940.

I lost our first baby, which was tremendously traumatic. [The baby] was born full term, but it was in Washington at the beginning of the war, and the hospitals were very busy. It was an accidental thing in the hospital; it shouldn't have happened. Phil went in the army right afterwards, so it was pretty devastating.

We had four [children]. My oldest is Elizabeth Weymouth, who is a journalist and writes for the *Post* on foreign affairs, but other things, too. [She's] known as Lally. And Donald, who is chief executive officer of the company. William, called Bill, who has an investment partnership in Los Angeles, but who lives on the Vineyard in the summer and lives next door to me with his children. I love that. And Steven, who is married and lives in New York and is getting a postgraduate degree in literature and is in teaching. He has been in the theater and has produced . . . experimental theater.

MY FATHER . . . HAD INVESTED heavily of both financial resources and energy and effort in building up the *Post*. It was very discouraging because they were losing money every year. He was making progress of great kinds, both in circulation and, to some extent, in advertising, but it just looked terribly discouraging. He wanted to make sure that he had a successor in place, that there was some point to all this work. My brother was a psychiatrist and was interested in medicine, and so he asked Phil if he'd be interested. We had long talks about it, and I said he had to decide, and he did, finally. . . .

He became publisher when he was not quite thirty-one. . . . He went on the *Post* right after he got back [from the army] and we had terminal leave. It was January of 1946. Six months later, my father was offered [a position as] president of the World Bank by President Truman. He said to Phil, "I won't leave if you don't want me to, but this is my first love," because that was the kind of thing he'd done for the government. My father thought somebody ought to start this World Bank. Phil said no, that was all right, he should do what he wanted to do. So my father . . . named Phil publisher [and] he took up the struggle. From 1947 to 1954, he, too, had the same really difficult time.

PHIL WAS HEAVILY INVOLVED in politics and involved with Lyndon Johnson and involved with [the civil rights movement in] Little Rock. . . . I tell a story about desegregation of the swimming pools in Washington. . . . [He] made a deal with the Interior Department that if he quieted the story of a riot that had taken place about swimming pools, that they would desegregate them. That was using the paper and influencing the news. That's unacceptable these days; [today,] you have to influence events by giving people information by which they can make decisions. . . .

I ADORED OUR LIFE. I liked being what I called the chief operating officer. I did everything at home. I kept the houses running; I took care of the children. I made the decisions about summers. I bought and sold houses and moved. I did everything that most families share because he was working so hard, and I was trying to take the pressure off by doing everything at home. I was interested in our life; I was interested in meeting the people we met. I adored the family.

PHIL WAS SUBJECT to manic depressive illness before lithium [was available]. I think it was being experimented with, but it certainly wasn't being used. He went to a psychiatrist who didn't believe in drugs or any kind of electric shock or anything. Phil himself didn't [believe in it, either] because of the psychiatrists and because he naively thought [the treatment] left you not as human as you had been, that it affected your mind.

He essentially suffered from untreated manic depression. At the end, he went off with a young woman, a researcher at *Newsweek* whom he met and very quickly . . . took up with. After some hesitations and backs and forths, he left with her and said that . . . he wanted a divorce. He was going to keep the paper and he was going to marry her. . . .

We had successfully hidden his illness, which had started getting serious in 1957, and from then on the cycles were getting closer and worse. But people didn't know about it until this very public event happened. I even said to one friend, "You know, he's ill," and she said, "Don't say that. Everybody says that when their husband leaves them." [Yet] I knew this was part of it. He got depressed in the summer of that year, in July 1963, and came . . . home and asked the girl to go back home. He came back to us, but he was so ill and so depressed. I had seen him through two of these depressions, and I just felt unequal to doing it again. He was asked to—and voluntarily did—go to a hospital, from which he succeeded in getting a day off, during which he killed himself.

[Phil is buried right across the street from where I live.] It's a perfectly beautiful cemetery across the street, Oak Hill, and . . . it's a very old cemetery. [Phil] got interested in having a plot there for us. It was kind of like getting into a club or something. Our great friends, the Bruces, and the John Walkers and the Achesons and people we knew all had these plots there. He made jokes about this and said we should be sandwiched in there somewhere. One day he came home from a school meeting and said, "Well, I've got this plot because I've become acquainted with somebody on the St. Albans school board, and we can get in." It became a family joke, and he even made lugubrious jokes about "You can just wheel me across the street." With what happened it's appalling, but [at the time, I] never thought of it as a reality.

[AFTER MY HUSBAND SHOT HIMSELF,] I went away for a month and came back and went to work, but that wasn't to say I took over the *Post*. I went to work to learn the issues. I didn't really see myself as taking over the *Post*, but I did go to work right away. Gradually I learned that you couldn't sit there studying the thing. I was encouraged by some of the executives and mainly by Frederick Beebe, whom Phil had made the chairman, who had been our corporate lawyer. He said, "You have to come to work." I was happy to do that, because I cared a great deal about the company and about the *Post*. . . . It'd been part of my whole life, and I knew what had gone into making it as successful as it was, which was still competitive. Gradually, I worked with Frederick and worked as president of the company. I became publisher when John Sweeterman, who had been made publisher by Phil, left. Then [Frederick] died ten years later just after we'd gone public. So then I did take over the company.

[THE YEARS 1971 THROUGH 1976 WERE TURBULENT ONES] because we rapidly went through the Pentagon Papers and Watergate, and just as I thought things had calmed down, we went through a very violent pressmen's strike in 1975. Those were three really cosmic events that happened and in public, so to speak.

I made a lot of speeches defending us during Watergate. I guess that's when I started really speaking the most. I was trying to explain that we were reporting a story, that we weren't after the administration, and that it wasn't our intention to do them in. We were following the footsteps of the story. I started speaking quite a lot that year.

[When I first got to the *Post* and was in charge, I was petrified about public speaking.] Couldn't open my mouth. I had to practice in front of the children the first year I was working at the paper. I was asked to go down and say "Merry Christmas" at the company lunch. My children are hilarious, they keep telling this story. I practiced making this speech saying "Merry Christmas" in front of the children, because I'd never said anything in public.

[IN MY BOOK,] I TRY TO EXPLAIN the power of a newspaper or a magazine or television stations. For instance, the *Post* has the power to inform people, and where they play a story matters, probably. If they cover it well, it matters. Because you're talking to the government as well as people in Washington. . . . Sometimes people think I run downstairs and talk to editors. I never see stories before they get in the papers. I have the power to pick an editor or a publisher that will do the job well, and that is my general mode of thought. But after that, they have autonomy. . . . People envision me as making or breaking people or influencing events directly. It sounds like goody two-shoes, but I have more responsibility than power.

John F. Kennedy

by

MICHAEL BESCHLOSS
RICHARD REEVES

John F. Kennedy (1917–63) was our thirty-fifth president. Historian Michael Beschloss describes the three years of John F. Kennedy's administration as The Crisis Years *(HarperCollins, 1991) because of the ongoing tensions between the U.S. and the Soviet Union. He appeared on* Booknotes *on July 14, 1991. Then, on December 12, 1993,* Booknotes *viewers heard about Richard Reeves's day-by-day narrative of life inside the Kennedy White House,* President Kennedy *(Simon and Schuster, 1993). Mr. Reeves, a columnist and political scientist, wrote the book to coincide with the thirtieth anniversary of Kennedy's 1963 assassination.*

Michael Beschloss

The Crisis Years: Kennedy and Khrushchev, 1960–63

IN 1960, WHEN JOHN KENNEDY ran for president, over and over again he said, "The United States is in imminent danger of falling into second place behind the Russians." Now that the cold war is over and we have a lot more information, we know that the Soviet Union in 1960 was actually a fourth-rate economic power, second-rate military power, had one-eighteenth the number of nuclear weapons that we had. Given all that, when Kennedy came into power in 1961, he couldn't very well just say, "Sorry, folks, what I said during the campaign is now inoperative." He had to act on the assumption that not only was the Soviet Union an equal, but perhaps in danger of becoming a superior, and that was one of the reasons why these three years, 1960 to 1963, were so dangerous. . . .

The argument I make is that 1960 to 1963 was a period that was absolutely unique. These were the only years in all of our experience when Americans felt an imminent danger of dying in a nuclear war.

[MANY PEOPLE THINK THAT] Nikita Khrushchev, for sinister reasons we couldn't understand, out of the blue, moved missiles into Cuba. John Kennedy demanded that he take them out. The missiles went out, and that was the end of it. What I found from my Soviet interviews was that the reality was a little bit more complex. The people who were around Khrushchev say that in early 1962, Khrushchev was very worried about something named Operation Mongoose. This was thirty-three different covert operations managed by the CIA against Cuba—sabotage, poisoning of sugar exports, shooting from motorboats, and also efforts to assassinate Fidel Castro. Castro and Khrushchev thought that Operation Mongoose was the forerunner to an American invasion of Cuba with full U.S. military force, probably in the fall of 1962. It turns out that Castro and Khrushchev put their heads together, asking the question "What can we possibly do that will thwart this American invasion of Cuba?" The answer that they came up with was to put in nuclear missiles.

During the Cuban missile crisis, October of 1962, the Joint Chiefs of Staff had resolved if an American plane were downed in Cuba during that crisis, we would automatically bomb the Soviet missile sites. It took John Kennedy to stand up against the Joint Chiefs and say no. Had he not stood up, those sites would have been bombed, and Russians would have been killed. Nikita Khrushchev would have been under enormous pressure to retaliate against the United States.

[KENNEDY WAS] . . . someone who was a tremendous crisis manager. You have to remember that, given the fact that 1961 and 1962 and 1963 were so dangerous, especially over Berlin and Cuba, if it were not for John Kennedy's very careful management of those crises, you might have seen two hundred million human beings die. He also was probably the most, or one of the most, intelligent presidents of this century. At the same time, on the down side, I don't rate him very high on crisis avoidance. . . . These crises did not have to happen. Simply because that many people did not die does not mean that we can entirely forgive either Kennedy or Khrushchev for keeping the world on the brink for three years.

Richard Reeves

President Kennedy: Profile of Power

I WOULD PUT [John Fitzgerald Kennedy] very high [on the list of presidents]. I would probably put him toward the bottom of the top ten, maybe the top of the next round. . . . He had enormous impact as a cultural figure—almost as an artist in the sense that he made us see things differently. He made us see ourselves and our country differently. There was a role-model effect of his coming along when the country first got very rich and when technology made it enormously richer in a short period of time, jet planes being the best example, because they democratized travel. . . .

People looked for a role model at that time as to how we were supposed to act now that we were these rich people. . . . He set a tone—both favorable and unfavorable—culturally, which was don't wait your turn, just go out and do it. Now I think everybody does do that; a lot of institutions have suffered fairly and unfairly because of that.

As to his presidential decisions, I would say that he had two big good ones and one big bad one, and they were linked in a certain way. . . . He was the man who decided, alone really, that the United States government would be on the side of the minority in the period of civil rights. . . . Up to that point, the government had tried to stay neutral.

He handled Europe, in the end, quite well. He did it in ways we didn't really understand at the time. The Berlin Wall—for all the celebration of its coming down—going up probably prevented a confrontation between the Soviets and the Americans in Berlin in that period. He went into Vietnam for all the wrong reasons. [He] left the country in a terrible position there because at the time he died we had just overthrown, with him signing off on it, a legitimate government in South Vietnam because it wouldn't take orders from us.

KENNEDY WAS A FURNACE in the sense that if you got near him you melted into him. He was a lovely, likable guy to most people. But the people who served him were not that different than the court that served Haile Selassie—if they got too close to the sun, as it were.

George Thomas was a black man; he was his valet. . . . Arthur Krock . . . was the bureau chief of *The New York Times* in Washington for years, decades; he was also a columnist—not a daily columnist; I think it was three columns a week. He had great power. He was very close to Kennedy's father. When Jack Kennedy was elected to Congress in 1946, Joe Kennedy asked Krock if his son could borrow [Krock's valet] George Thomas to take care of him: [John] Kennedy was not the kind of guy who knew how to take clothes to the cleaners or that kind of thing. Kennedy lived a very Scott Fitzgerald kind of life. There were always people to clean up the messes. . . . He changed clothes five times a day from the skin out.

He was forever questioning people about how much money they made, what they did with it, because he had never . . . worked for a living. His salaries were from the government—the navy and the presidency—and he donated those to charity. Krock delivered George Thomas to that operation. Krock also edited Kennedy's first book, *Why England Slept.*

Both of Kennedy's books were knockoffs of Winston Churchill books. There was a certain controversy: Did he write his own books? He probably did, but they were written first by Winston Churchill, the same books. Winston Churchill did a book on British leadership at the turn of the century that was exactly the same as *Profiles in Courage;* some of the sentences were exactly the same. *Why England Slept,* which was Kennedy's college thesis, was taken from, and often repeated, Winston Churchill's book *While England Slept.*

I would consider it plagiarism, but I'm a professional writer. I don't think that . . . the general public considers that sort of thing to be plagiarism.

[His books] were both bestsellers. *Profiles in Courage* won a Pulitzer Prize, which was an intellectual ornament that Kennedy very badly wanted. I don't know that he was an intellectual, but he certainly was at ease with ideas. . . . He intended to write his memoirs, and I think that he thought he would do it pretty well. It was a thing he thought was worthwhile in his life, which he considered a pursuit of excellence, although other people—me among them—might characterize it as a race against boredom.

He was a politician. He couldn't stand to be alone. He couldn't stand silence. And he structured his life with as much stimulation as possible.

I WOULD VOTE FOR HIM for president today, but he would not be president today. His health problems would have become public. They were just too severe and too debilitating to make it possible. . . . The man was in constant pain, [took] every drug known to man, including injections with amphetamines. Dr. Max Jacobson, later to be known as "Dr. Feelgood," traveled secretly with Kennedy to keep him up with corticosteroids. These things all had side effects, including depression. Increased sexual desire was one side effect.

All of that would have come out, including the fact that he was lying about Addison's disease, a terminal disease that he kept in check by stashing medication in safety deposit boxes around the world. He was the first Addisonian to ever survive traumatic surgery. . . . The disease is a withering away of the adrenal glands, and when they're gone, you die. But the cortisone could substitute, they found during the war. His operation, without his name on it, was so famous among doctors that his entire medical history was in *The Journal of the American Medical Association* in 1957, without his name. It just said, "the thirty-seven-year-old man," but today, the press would have found it.

HE LIED VERY EASILY. Lying in America bothers me. To an enormous extent I think that it is undermining both to the democracy and the Republic. People are not being punished for lying. In that time you were punished more for lying, but he was facile at it. One of the reasons Khrushchev beat up on him so badly was that Kennedy had told people that he had studied at the London School of Economics under Harold Laski. But he had never been there. Everyone thought that here was a real scholar on Marxism and on communism, but he knew almost nothing about it. It was the reason that Khrushchev was able to tie him in knots at the Vienna summit in June of 1961. Kennedy was sitting there defending colonialism and imperialism in the military dictatorships. . . .

Because he went in and tried to defend the status quo against a trained dialectician . . . he was eaten alive. He walked out of that room and said, "We have to go into Vietnam. We have to confront them because they think I'm too weak and foolish."

PROBABLY THE SINGLE THING that is most unbelievable that I was able to dig out because of Averell Harriman's papers—he had recorded the conversations—is that Kennedy tried to get Khrushchev to consider a joint American-Soviet air strike [against] China to destroy their nuclear capability. It literally was lined up. It was going to be done like a firing squad; that is, neither the Russian crew nor the American crew would know that they had the real weapon. One weapon would be a dud, one weapon would be real, as they do on a firing squad so every man can think he didn't fire the fatal shot if he wanted to. Khrushchev turned him down.

KENNEDY WOULD PICK UP PHONES and call reporters. . . . He would bully reporters and threaten them and scream at them. . . .

[When he was on the cover of *Gentlemen's Quarterly* magazine,] Kennedy was incredibly upset. John Kennedy spent hours on [his press coverage] every day; he was extraordinarily interested in what was said about him, and he had also been a newspaper reporter, working for Hearst. *GQ* was a men's fashion magazine, and they had a picture of Kennedy on it. Kennedy didn't like that because the Kennedys were pretty homophobic, and they considered *GQ* a magazine for homosexuals. . . .

That didn't bother him as much as the fact that *Time* magazine then said he had posed for exclusive photographs for *GQ*, which was not true. They had used file photographs of some sort. What Kennedy was mad at was the fact that people thought he was posing for, as Bobby said, this "fag rag. . . ."

[He] built up this gigantic staffing of the White House. He made the White House the center of action to the point that there was no point in being out at the Agricultural Department—everything was going to come through the White House, the way the White House wanted it. Suddenly you had this centralization of media control.

There was a wonderful generational match that worked for the [press during the Kennedy administration]. After all, their generation was now taking over power. You get some of that with Clinton too, but the way the press in the country was structured then . . . was a very personal operation. If a reporter messed with the president of the United States, particularly this president of the United States, Henry Luce was going to get a phone call about [magazine] postal rates. So we didn't have the access, and the spontaneity, and all of that that we now have. The information is out and about before anyone can try to block it these days.

MY MAJOR TAKE on [John Kennedy's womanizing] was: One, people who live that kind of life have to lie all the time. Part of his facility as a liar comes from covering up clandestine affairs of some sort. [Two,] it was incredibly corrupting. . . . I think that to him it was like tennis, in a way, and it took less time than scheduling tennis games. But the logistics were a heck of a lot more complicated, so that everyone up to Dean Rusk [Kennedy's secretary of state] had to run these operations with helicopters and cars and whatever to get women here and there. Then they'd be with Kennedy for twelve minutes, or something, and they were gone.

Many of these people were proud to do this because they felt it was a rite of initiation—that they had been brought in, they were closer. That corruption of his own people and breaking them essentially was what I found interesting and significant about the womanizing. . . . It had to do with lying and with the corruption of other people, where it was important. We're talking about Daisy Buchanan, in a way, in *The Great Gatsby*—this rich boy who does whatever he wants. There are people there to clean up the mess, whether it involves paying off people or whatever it takes. That John Kennedy, at least to me, is pretty unattractive.

[To research Kennedy's affairs] . . . I started with airplane logs and coming-and-going logs, beginning with the inauguration, when [actress] Angie Dickinson was with him during the inaugural after Mrs. Kennedy went home. . . . The whole idea of my book was [to report] what it was like to be president, what a president does, how it feels—only forty-one people have known. I did not want to get myself drowned by what was, in some ways, the least interesting part of his life and a relatively small part, although it would be foolish to ignore it or to pretend it didn't happen.

BOBBY KENNEDY WAS JACK'S POLITICAL WIFE. A man or a woman needs someone they can turn to whom they trust completely and know they have no other ax to grind but their own interest. Usually that's a husband or wife. Jacqueline Kennedy had no interest whatever in any of those things, and Bobby served that function for his brother. . . .

[Jackie Kennedy] . . . was thirty-four years old when [her husband was assassinated]. She was our [country's] Princess Di; it was a very similar story in many ways. She was also a very bright woman, and she got the choice of facing history as the princess of this wonderful golden period or as a young wife who is being deceived by a lusty and sometimes pretty nasty husband. I think she made an intelligent choice. Why should she wallow in that stuff?

Kennedy was a lot of [things], and these existed in combination. . . . Jacqueline Kennedy, to a large extent, orchestrated [the idea of Camelot]. Camelot was never mentioned while Kennedy was alive. Mrs. Kennedy brought that to [reporter] Teddy White in doing a posthumous portrait of him in *Life* magazine. [Kennedy] was a hell of a guy. Every person I talked to said they thought he was the most charming human being they ever met. [He] lit up a room and there was incredible pleasure just being in his company. Paul Fay's book [about him] was called *The Pleasure of His Company*. He was all of those things—and that got him to the White House. He charmed his way.

Fannie Lou Hamer

by
KAY MILLS

Fannie Lou Hamer (1917–77) was a Mississippi sharecropper's daughter who rose to national prominence in the civil rights movement, giving a memorable address during the 1964 Democratic National Convention. Her story was told by journalist Kay Mills in This Little Light of Mine: The Life of Fannie Lou Hamer, *which was published in 1993 by Dutton. Kay Mills appeared on* Booknotes *on February 28, 1993.*

I WOULD LIKE TO THINK that a lot of people do know Fannie Lou Hamer. If someone followed the [civil rights] movement at all or was part of it, they know Fannie Lou Hamer. . . . If they don't know who she was, one reason why is that she died in 1977 when the movement was at its ebb. She didn't have someone like Coretta Scott King, [the wife of] Martin Luther King, to burnish her memory. . . . Another reason is that a lot of the women in the movement have not gotten their due because, frankly, it has been the men who've written history. . . .

I remember [when I met her] that she filled up a room. That's the main thing. . . . I met her in 1973. I had gone to Mississippi to do a set of stories on the civil rights movement and what became of it. I specifically chose Mississippi because . . . so much of the violence occurred there, and I wanted to meet her. I had seen her testify at the 1964 Democratic convention. . . . I went to her house on a very hot, steamy July day. She wasn't well. She was frustrated, she was angry, but she spent an enormous amount of time with me. *Charisma* is an overused word, but it applied to her. When I left that day, I came back to Washington—that's where I was working then—and I had lunch. I remember it was at the Peking Restaurant in Washington, with Lawrence Guyot, one of the people who had been in jail with her. I told him how incredibly dazzled I had been by her, and he said, "Why don't you write a book about her?" That's when the idea was born.

FANNIE LOU HAMER was born in 1917, the youngest of twenty children of a Mississippi sharecropper. She died in March of 1977 in a hospital not more than twenty miles from where she'd lived most of her adult life. She was born in Montgomery County, Mississippi. . . . When she was two years old, her family moved into the Delta, right outside Ruleville. . . . She lived the rest of her life outside or in Ruleville, Mississippi, which is in Sunflower County.

Dirt poor is about the most concise way of summing up [her life]. She was the child of sharecroppers—a farmer who rents the land or uses the land of a white plantation owner. The sharecroppers might be white or black, but they were mainly black. They would rent the land; the plantation owner would advance them seed and money to get through the summer. The sharecropper would plant the crop, chop the cotton, which meant weeding the crop, and then at the end of the season they'd weigh the crop and figure out what share— that's where the term came from—the worker got. Well, things managed to get subtracted a lot from what the worker got and so it really was a modern-day form of slavery.

At about six years old, she started picking cotton herself. She had only a sixth-grade education. She was very smart, but she had to go to work after the sixth grade. In fact, that's almost false to say that she had a sixth-grade education because the children of sharecroppers could only go to school when they weren't working in the fields, so that would be about four months of the year. They didn't have very good teachers; they didn't have books. . . . Mississippi basically wanted to keep an uneducated work force to pick the cotton. So she was poor, and they never had enough to eat; she didn't have shoes to go to school. . . .

She, in the summer of 1962, was forty-four years old, wanted to vote, had never been able to vote because after Reconstruction in Mississippi, the state Democratic party systematically disenfranchised—barred from voting—the black population. Because if they voted, then they would share power; they would want better schools; they would want roads paved; they would want indoor plumbing. They would want to share in the system, and the plantation owners didn't want them to share in the system. She wanted to vote. She knew that the system was wrong, but she didn't know anything to do about it until the summer of 1962, when the young people from the Student Nonviolent Coordinating Committee [SNCC] came to Sunflower County.

This was a group that was formed after the student sit-ins started in 1960— lunch counter sit-ins that started in Greensboro, North Carolina, and spread across the South. . . . Originally Dr. King wanted them to be a student branch of the Southern Christian Leadership Conference, the group that he headed. But the students wanted independence; they wanted to do things their own way.

It was the late summer of 1962, after the Student Nonviolent Coordinating Committee people had come to Sunflower County. They held a meeting. They told people what they could do if they would register to vote. It made perfect sense to Fannie Lou Hamer. . . . It was on a Monday night, and they said,

"Who will go down with us to the courthouse on Friday to register?" She put up her hand. And when she put up her hand that night, she certainly changed her personal history. She changed a lot of the history for the people who worked with her and lived around her. They made the drive to Indianola [Mississippi]. They tried to register. There was a literacy test, and it was geared for prospective black voters to fail, no matter how smart you were. They would always catch you on something. If you didn't fail that part, they'd make you interpret a section of the state constitution. You know the state constitutions: they're incredibly complicated. She failed the test. When she got back home that night, [she was] thrown off the plantation. . . . The man who threw her off the plantation really threw her into the arms of the civil rights movement. . . .

The following summer, she'd gone to several meetings to learn how to train people to vote—citizenship education, they called it. She'd been in Charleston, South Carolina. She was on her way home, and that's when she and half a dozen other people who were on a bus—[at] the Winona bus station—were arrested.

The charge was something trumped up, like disturbing the peace. I always like to say they were disturbing the peace of Mississippi. But they were taken to this little brick jail and booked.

They put the people in the cells—I think June [Johnson, who was only 15 at the time,] was probably the first one that they hit with their fists—hit her in the mouth, beat her. . . .

These were policemen [who were beating them]. It was the sheriff, highway patrolmen, and the chief of police. Then Annell Ponder, who was in charge of the group, was brought out of her cell. They kept trying to make her say, "Yes, sir." She wouldn't do it. She'd say, "Yes." It was not that she was impolite; she was not going to be humiliated, not going to be subjected to their indignities.

Then they took Mrs. Hamer out of her cell, took her to what they call the bullpen, which is where they kept the male prisoners. They had two black inmates then that they [told] would be beaten or worse if they didn't beat Mrs. Hamer. They made Fannie Lou Hamer—at that point, a forty-five-year-old stout, short woman who walked with a limp—they made her lie down on the cot and then one beat her with a blackjack until he got tired. Then the other one beat her with a blackjack, at the order of the law officers.

She was left with permanent kidney damage. She was black and blue. June said if you'd ever seen a snake's skin, it was like that after she was beaten. She couldn't sit down for several days. They took her back to her cell, where I think she promptly passed out. One of the women who was in the cell with her said that she ran a fever that night. She had been brutally beaten. They sang to keep their spirits up. They weren't given proper food. They were in jail for about three or four days. One of the SNCC workers, Lawrence Guyot, came to try to get them out of jail. He was thrown in jail and beaten. . . .

Julian Bond [a SNCC worker and now the chairman of the NAACP] was at work in Atlanta. He called the FBI. There were a lot of calls coming into this little jail. Finally, on about the third or fourth day, Andrew Young [a SNCC worker who went on to become mayor of Atlanta] arrived with bail money. They got [the group] out of jail. When they got out of jail, Mrs. Hamer and the rest were told that while they had been in jail, Medgar Evers, who was the NAACP director in Jackson, Mississippi, had been shot and killed in the driveway of his home.

There was a trial [of the law officers] the following December. It was right after John Kennedy had been assassinated, so there was no press coverage—none. . . . The trial lasted three or four days, [with an] all-white jury in Oxford, Mississippi. . . . Women didn't serve on juries at that point in Mississippi, another whole story. The jury deliberated a little over an hour and acquitted all the law officers.

This was one of many cases that made the people working in Mississippi decide that they needed help. They weren't getting protection—black people were dying, were being jailed and beaten, and it seemed that nobody cared. That's when they brought the college students down to Mississippi for the summer of 1964 and challenged the all-white Democratic party delegation to the 1964 convention. . . .

[They testified before the Credentials Committee at the 1964 convention.] They lost, but they won. Mrs. Hamer was the star witness. Their attorney was Joseph Rauh, who was active in the Democratic party and a national committeeman from the District of Columbia. He knew a good witness when he saw one. He had heard Fannie Lou Hamer's story. He put her on the stand and while she was on the stand in front of the credentials committee, telling what it was like to try to vote, try to be a first-class citizen, Lyndon Johnson called a press conference in the White House to try to bump them off the air. [But] it was played on tape or on film that night over and over, so everybody saw her testimony. This is the first time I ever heard of Fannie Lou Hamer. [I] was watching this testimony on television. She talked about going to try to vote. She talked about being beaten, described it in great detail. She talked about having shots fired into the house. She talked about the threats that she had gotten. And then, finally, she said, "If the Mississippi Freedom Democratic party isn't seated, then I question America." It was pretty powerful stuff. She argued against a compromise that Hubert Humphrey proposed. What they said they would do is give the Mississippians who'd come up—there were sixty-eight of them—they would give them two at-large seats, and they would tell the Democratic parties all over the country that hereafter, no one could discriminate. They said anyone who will sign a loyalty oath to the party's nomination can be seated, knowing very well that the regular Democrats wouldn't sign a loyalty oath. But at any rate, Mrs. Hamer argued against the compromise because, she said, "We didn't come all this way for no two seats, because all of us is tired." . . . It was voted on. It did become the rule of the party, and it did start opening up the party to diversity.

JAMES O. EASTLAND was the senator from Mississippi; he was chairman of the Senate Judiciary Committee. It fascinated me—he was also from Sunflower County. Here you had these two giants of that time, James O. Eastland and Fannie Lou Hamer, who lived ten miles apart in Sunflower County and worlds apart. He had gone to several colleges. He had been elected to the state legislature when he was in his twenties. He had been elected to the U.S. Senate in 1942. . . . He had a plantation; he had power. Fannie Lou Hamer, roughly the same age, sixth-grade education, couldn't vote until she was forty-four or forty-five years old, lived in a house with no working indoor plumbing. It was fascinating to me that these two people were in the same county.

She kept talking about Eastland this and Eastland that, and then I finally realized—I think that was the spur that helped goad her to do even more than she did. She knew of Eastland's power over people. She meant it when she said she was opposing him. She wanted to bring Jim Eastland down. Ultimately, the work that she did [succeeded]. In 1978, he chose not to run because he wouldn't have been re-elected. Enough blacks had been registered by that time.

[SHE DIED IN] 1977. Her life was one of very great frustration in her last three or four years. She wasn't well. She had hypertension. She had a nervous breakdown at one point. I'm sure from overwork, but she kept on going. It was extraordinary. She had very poor health care. She developed breast cancer and had surgery for that in 1976, but she stayed active. She helped bring low-cost housing to her home town; she sued the local school system, helped save the job of the black principal in the high school there. Her dream was a farm co-op that would help people produce their own food so they could have some independence from "the man"—as she put it—from the plantation owner.

She stayed active. Five months before she died she went to Jackson for a demonstration about cuts in Medicare, and she wasn't well. She found Mississippi was resisting the full enforcement of the Voting Rights Act. This frustrated her enormously. She felt somewhat abandoned, that things were moving on without her. I get sad when I think that she didn't live to see the changes that have happened today. I have to tell this story: I was in Ruleville, Mississippi, very recently, speaking at the public library that thirty years ago she couldn't use—at the invitation of the librarian from Sunflower County. And the new state senator, a black man named Willie Simmons, stood up. . . . Simmons is the first black senator from Sunflower County. He stood up and said, "I am living Fannie Lou Hamer's dream." That was a pretty powerful moment.

"THIS LITTLE LIGHT OF MINE" was her theme song. That was what she sang in any number of the mass meetings to get people fired up to go out and confront the police dogs or the voter registrars. . . . If people were scared, she'd sing it to calm their fears. . . . "This Little Light of Mine" really summed her up. She was a little light. She was actually a pretty big light, and she shone that light on a lot of the dark places in the American soul.

George Wallace

by
STEPHEN LESHER

George Wallace (1919–98) was first elected governor of Alabama in 1962. Governor Wallace ran for president in 1968 on the American Independent party ticket, receiving over nine million votes. He served three more terms as governor, from 1971 to 1979 and 1983 to 1987. In 1972, he was shot and paralyzed while campaigning in Maryland. Author Stephen Lesher appeared on Booknotes *on February 27, 1994, to talk about* George Wallace: American Populist *(Addison-Wesley, 1994).*

I THINK THE FIRST IMAGE and the lasting image that you have of George Wallace is a feisty little bantam rooster, jutting his chin out, curling his lip, and saying to the federal government, "Thou shall not pass. You shall not put black people into the University of Alabama or into our schools."

He was a man who, nonetheless, had this populist agenda that went beyond race and identified very strongly with the issues that today are getting a lot of attention . . . [such as getting] tough on crime, tough on welfare, taxing the super-rich . . . and talking about the need for young people who are not bound for college to get educational support. There is a still, small voice that kept whispering in my ear . . . , "They're all saying now what I was saying back then."

Wallace said those words to me in one of our interviews. . . . In my view, every successful presidency, every successful presidential campaign, starting with Nixon's in 1968, was based on, as a defining issue, an issue that first was identified and articulated and popularized by George Wallace, and his issues that are now quite mainstream.

HE WAS BORN in the little town of Clio, Alabama, in Barbour County, which is in southeast Alabama. It was one of the most violent counties during the period of Reconstruction in Alabama. He grew up with that tradition of incipient dislike, if not downright hatred, for the North, the sense that the North had imposed poverty and ignorance on the South during and following the

Civil War. He grew up, and he read books that I read, textbooks in school, which talked about the sins of carpetbaggers and scalawags. A great deal of hyperbole, but that's what he learned in school as a kid. So he had that built-in resentment that most southerners, deep southerners, anyway, had for the North during that time.

He had a law degree from the University of Alabama. He never really practiced law. . . . He got it because it was a ticket to politics. Everything George Wallace did was politics. He [always] remembered . . . the name of the girl in third grade who nominated him for class president. He could tell you . . . [how every precinct] in Barbour County voted in every one of his elections, whether for president of the United States or for the state legislature. . . . He knew what his vote totals were in every statewide race. He couldn't give you state-by-state in the presidential elections, but he could come pretty close in round figures. It was just always his life. It was second nature.

He was a state legislator and was considered one of the most farsighted state legislators in the state—voted so by the press at the time—for introducing and getting through education-advancement bills, building trade schools for both white and blacks separately. . . . He then became a judge in his home county of Barbour County, Alabama, where he got a reputation as being extremely solicitous of blacks who were seeking redress in his court. There is a very well known civil rights leader from Selma, Alabama, an attorney named J. L. Chestnut, who wrote a book not too many years ago in which he recalled being in Judge Wallace's court. They were seeking some redress from a large white-owned, white-run southern company. The attorney kept referring to Chestnut and his clients as "those people," rather pejoratively: "those people" want this, "those people" say that. According to Chestnut, Wallace stopped him and directed him. "From now on," he said, "when you refer to Mr. Chestnut and you refer to his clients, you will call them by name or not refer to them at all." Chestnut went on to say that that was the first time a white man in Alabama had called him "Mister."

I'M A NEW YORKER, but I got my first newspaper job in Montgomery, Alabama, and coincidentally and fortuitously, I became a reporter in Montgomery just a few months before Mrs. Rosa Parks refused to give up her seat on a bus in Montgomery to a white man. I was the police reporter, and because I was the police reporter, I got to cover the whole Montgomery bus boycott from its inception until the U.S. Supreme Court outlawed inter-city segregation on inter-city transportation.

I was in Montgomery about a year and a half. I then went to the newspaper in Columbus, Georgia, which is right on the Alabama border. I continued covering some Alabama politics, including Wallace's first run for governor in 1958, which he lost to John Patterson. He lost it because by those standards, at that time, he was considered too moderate on the issue of segregation. He ran again four years later, and he became a little more strident at that time.

HE WAS GOVERNOR four times. His [first] wife, Lurleen, was elected for what would have been a fifth Wallace term except she died about halfway through her term. I'd say he ran the state for four and a half terms altogether. He ran for president in 1964, 1968, 1972, and 1976. . . .

His second wife, Cornelia, was with George when he was shot in 1972 in Maryland and stayed with him on through 1978, when they finally split in a rather acrimonious divorce. [His third wife,] Miss Lisa Taylor, was a country-western singer who, as a nineteen-year-old, . . . entertained at Wallace political rallies. She said she always loved him. After she was divorced and after Wallace's divorce from Cornelia, she began, according to the governor, pursuing him. They married before he decided to run for governor the last time. She couldn't stand public life, and when he did run for governor, finally, in 1982, she moved out of the mansion after about a year into the little house that he still owned . . . but didn't get a divorce until after he finally left office. Then they got a divorce in 1987.

A HUGE VOTING RIGHTS DEMONSTRATION had been going on for months, centering on Selma, Alabama which had the harshest anti-voting regulations toward blacks of any county in the state. . . . They kept blacks from voting more stringently than anywhere in the state of Alabama and probably in the entire South. They had this tough sheriff, Jim Clark. Brutal would be the only way to fairly describe him in his behavior toward black demonstrators.

Martin Luther King used it to try to push [President Lyndon] Johnson into submitting a voting rights bill to Congress. Johnson didn't want to do it for about a year. They had just gone through riots, and they had just gone through internal difficulties in Congress over the latest civil rights bill in 1964. Johnson wanted to wait a year. They mounted the famous march led by John Lewis, now a congressman, and some of King's aides. They went to march over a bridge toward Montgomery to take their complaints directly to Governor Wallace. They were met by state troopers and by local police on horseback. "Bloody Sunday" ensued where people were pushed, beaten, knocked down, run over by horses. The pictures made international news and spurred the president to much more quickly introduce and send to Congress a voting rights bill with his famous speech in which he said . . . , "We shall overcome," taking the words of the anthem that was part of the whole modern civil rights movement.

[When Wallace described] . . . his meeting with Lyndon Johnson in 1965 during the Selma crisis . . . [he] never claimed to get the better of it. He just maintained that the descriptions of the meeting by some of the president's assistants who were in and out of the meeting . . . which were highly unfavorable to Wallace, were not true. But in the course of our conversation he started telling me how President Johnson would say, "Now, George, we don't want the press to think we've been talking just about the niggers for these last three and a half hours," then suddenly Wallace stopped.

He said, "Turn off the tape." He didn't want me to use that term. He said, "I don't think Johnson meant it pejoratively. I think he was trying to impress me with being one of the boys. . . ." But I wanted to use the quote because I wanted to depict that conversation as best and as honestly as I could. I knew people who knew President Johnson, and this was not something that sounded unusual.

I PICKED UP WALLACE AGAIN in 1970, covering his gubernatorial campaign. I remember his wife had died in 1968, midway through her term. Wallace went on to run for president that year, but he needed to be governor again if he was going to have a platform to run for president in 1972. It was a breathlessly close race against the man who had been Lurleen's lieutenant governor. He did win it in a run-off. He then went on to run in 1972 for president with both triumph and tragedy. . . . He was shot in Laurel, Maryland, in May of that year.

[The gunman, Arthur Bremer also] stalked President Nixon, but he couldn't get to him. He switched to Wallace, which to me adds to the validity of the concept that he acted alone and there was no conspiracy. The reason Wallace was thinking about a conspiracy is some reporting that Seymour Hersh did with . . . people who were going through the Nixon tapes. . . . Nixon did say on these tapes [that] right after the shooting of George Wallace . . . he immediately summoned Chuck Colson, his aide in the White House, and said, "Let's get somebody into that guy," meaning Bremer's apartment, "and plant some McGovern literature so they'll think that a liberal did the shooting" . . . Colson confirmed this with Hersh; Colson went out and got Howard Hunt. Hunt had his bags packed, his ticket bought, when [Hunt] learned that the FBI had already sealed the apartment off.

IN 1976 WALLACE WAS TRYING AGAIN for president. He went to Florida, which had been the scene of one of his great triumphs in 1972. He was making some headway. He had a lead, it was a narrow one over Jimmy Carter. He was being lifted into a plane when one of the people tripped, fell on top of him, and splintered his leg. The whole country saw that he was a crippled man, not powerful and strong enough to run for president, much less carry the office. That's why he decided later in 1978 not to seek the Senate seat that he probably, according to the polls, could have won at that time.

[I decided to write this book] just before Wallace announced that he would not run again. I began making inquiries of his staff and of the governor himself, to see if he would be cooperative in doing a book. I felt that his career was

winding down, and I sensed that so many of the issues that had been so prominently identified with him were now going mainstream that I wanted to tell
that story. The second part of what changed was that in 1982 he had been
elected to his final term as governor because of winning a . . . large majority of
the black vote in Alabama. Here was the symbol, the icon, of racism and segregation in our country who won office because he won the support of the
black voters of Alabama. How did this come to pass? I wanted to look into that
story.

[Today, both] black and white [people are his fans]. I am getting used to that
by now. . . . Wallace was asked to come to Tuskegee, Alabama, to the National
Black Mayors Conference. He was no longer governor, but they asked him to
come there to say hello to the group. He went up on stage. He welcomed them
to Alabama, said a few words about what great things they were doing for their
cities, and he got a standing ovation. The mayor of Tuskegee told a reporter
who was there . . . , "You know, in the South we have the ability to forgive each
other, and when we see that a man has made the kind of changes that George
Wallace has, we can love him. People in the North," he said, "don't understand
that."

Betty Friedan

by
BETTY FRIEDAN

Betty Friedan (b. 1921) appeared on Booknotes *on November 28, 1993, to discuss her book* The Fountain of Age *(Simon and Schuster, 1993). In 1963, Ms. Friedan's first book,* The Feminine Mystique, *became a worldwide bestseller and helped create the women's liberation movement. In 1966, Betty Friedan helped found the National Organization for Women, serving as its first president.*

[THE FEMININE MYSTIQUE WAS PUBLISHED in] 1963. I wrote it for the five years [prior to] that. It's assigned in colleges and in classes. It's on these lists of the ten books through all time that have shaped history. It's assigned in college courses in American history or sociology. So young people are reading it. I'm amazed they still find it so applicable, because we have changed so much since that book in breaking through the feminine mystique.

What intrigues me is that women of all ages still stop me, if they run into me in the airport or the street: "It changed my life, you know." They tell me where they were when they read it: . . . "I was in the hospital having my third child." "I was doing this, I was doing that," because it really did have this effect of putting into words what they'd been groping and yearning for. It enabled them to take steps to change their life.

[*The Feminine Mystique* sold] millions, in about twenty countries. I have no idea how many [sold], but years ago they were saying three million, so it must be a lot more than that now.

I was technically a housewife in Rockland County, suburban New York, with three kids [when I wrote the book]. I had been freelancing for women's magazines after I'd been fired from a newspaper job for being pregnant with my second child. What I later called the "feminine mystique" was filling me full of guilt for working, even though my husband had been in the theater and then started in advertising [and] we needed my paycheck. But I'd been feeling so guilty. Now I was fired and you couldn't look for a job with your belly out to here, pregnant—not in those years. Well, not now, either.

I was a housewife, but I couldn't quite get rid of the itch to do something. I was freelancing for magazines, mainly the women's magazines, like secret drinking in the morning, because none of the other mothers in that suburb were working then. . . . And after about five years of writing according to this limited image that was supposed to be the image of the American woman, [defined] solely in terms of her husband, children, home, nothing else, I got restive about it. I began [my work on feminism] through the happenstance of doing the fifteenth reunion questionnaire of my Smith College alumni [association].

[People] were saying, "Education is making women frustrated in their role as women; too much education." I had valued my education, and I thought I was going to disprove [this theory] with this questionnaire of Smith 1942. Instead, [the survey] raised more questions than it answered. Then, when the magazines I wrote for, one after the other, either turned down or rewrote [my resulting article] to say the opposite, I took it back. I knew I'd have to write the book *The Feminine Mystique.*

Every chapter I'd finish, I thought, Gee, I must be crazy, because it went against everything that was accepted as both the conventional and sophisticated truth about women.

But [did I have] the idea that it would have the impact it did? They say [my book] really started the consciousness part of the women's movement and led to the modern women's movement. In my gut, I knew it was very important, but I didn't have the confidence I later acquired. It was such a mystery to me that I was able to write that book. [But], of course, the experiences and the skills and my training as a psychologist, a journalist, the life I lived, enabled me to write *The Feminine Mystique* . . . helping to give the vision of the women's movement.

I GREW UP IN PEORIA, ILLINOIS. My father, who was a brilliant man, . . . was an immigrant with no higher education, though he read philosophy every night after dinner. . . . He sent his youngest brother to Harvard Law School and was inordinately proud of all my intellectual accomplishments.

My mother grew up in Peoria and went to the local college, Bradley. She had been the women's page editor of the newspaper there, but she had to quit that when she married my father and started having kids. She couldn't wait for me to get into junior high school to get me to try out for the paper. I edited the college paper at Smith. That was one of the most fun things in my life. She insisted that I get a good education; my father said to me on his deathbed, "Don't come back here." In other words, "Go beyond."

My father died too young. He was in his early sixties, and he had that . . . male . . . inability to express the pain you may be feeling. He endured the anti-Semitism of a Middle West small town at that time and the pressures of the Depression.

My mother lived till she was ninety. It was my mother's frustrations that gave me the psychological motivation for the women's movement. But my mother, at the age of seventy-odd [years], after burying her third husband, got herself licensed as a duplicate bridge manager. She'd always been a brilliant card player. She lived in Leisure World in Laguna Hills, California. She would toodle around, running these duplicate bridge tournaments into her eighties, with the prodigious feats of memory that required.

If I was coming out to California and I knew I'd be on TV, I'd say, "Oh, God, I've got to go see Mother." It terrifies me to drive in California because I can't stand the freeways, so it's not easy to get from L.A. to Laguna Hills. I'd call her up and I'd say, "Mother, I'm going to be in L.A. in two weeks. Can we meet?" "Darling," she would say, "I'm so busy. Why didn't you let me know longer in advance?" She was no pathetic old lady.

[TODAY] I HAVE AN APARTMENT in New York and feel more rooted. I have a little old house in Sag Harbor, an old whaling town on the Sound. That's where my kids bring my grandkids. Then four months of the year I teach in Los Angeles at the University of Southern California. In the fall, I'm a visiting professor at New York University. So, for months of the year, I live in different places.

The family ties of my children with each other and with their father and with me are very strong. I like that. . . . On the wall of my kitchen in Sag Harbor, there are some Hebrew letters from a song—Hebrew songs that pass from generation to generation. . . . That kitchen is where we all get together, and I have this long dining table that will hold the fourteen of us, when we're all in residence. And so, from generation to generation.

I THINK, FINALLY, WHAT EVOLVES [in us] is a sense of the affirmation of your whole life as you've lived it . . . and then some great sense of the meaning of that life, that your life is a part of the continuum that will live after you, through your children, through your grandchildren, but also through your human generativity, that's not just biological.

For me, [my generativity] has been the women's movement and . . . the social and political causes that make the world better. [These all] somehow are a part of my morality. The last ten years' task of breaking through the mystique of age, the fountain of age . . . [has allowed me to make a contribution]. My sense is, even from what's already happening, that there are implications here for revolutionary social change. I can't predict what form it will take, any more than I could have predicted the women's movement after writing *The Feminine Mystique*. I think it will happen, and I'm open to what happens. I'll follow the leads where they go.

Henry Kissinger

by
WALTER ISAACSON

Henry Kissinger (b. 1923), a German-born Jewish émigré, became interna-tionally known as Richard Nixon's national security advisor and then secre-tary of state, overseeing the ceasefire in Vietnam, détente with the Soviets, and the opening to China. He was awarded the Nobel Peace Prize in 1973. In 1992, journalist Walter Isaacson published Kissinger: A Biography *with Simon and Schuster. His* Booknotes *interview aired on September 27, 1992.*

MOST OF THE JEWS FROM FÜRTH, when they escaped right before the Nazi Holocaust, came to Washington Heights, which is in Manhattan. They all set-tled within a four- or five-block area. Paula Kissinger, Henry's mother, [lived for many years] in the apartment there.

Henry Kissinger emigrated to America [in 1938] from Germany. He joined the U.S. Army, the Eighty-fourth Infantry Division, and went back to Ger-many as part of the Counter-Intelligence Corps of that division, during the oc-cupation of Germany right at the end of World War II. . . .

KISSINGER WENT TO HARVARD. He wrote his undergraduate thesis on Kant and then on Metternich. Then he wrote about Bismarck and Napoleon and Lord Castlereagh, the British foreign minister, all these nineteenth-century statesmen. He was very interested and believed in the role that personality plays in affecting history, because one great school of historical thought in the past generation has downplayed the role that people and personalities play and played up economic forces or other things.

During the Middle East shuttles, Kissinger said, "When I was a professor, I thought great forces shaped history. Now that I'm up close to it, I see what a difference personalities make." I was always interested in the personalities of history, Kissinger being [a] larger-than-life personality.

KISSINGER'S . . . philosophy of the world . . . is one of understanding bal-ances of power, realizing that power rather than sentiment or morality or human rights determines the way the world works, and understanding that America has certain interests and you have to pursue those interests in the world, sometimes with a cold and calculating sense of realism.

[Today,] . . . his consulting firm, Kissinger Associates, serves as a sort of private national security adviser and secretary of state to about thirty major corporations around the world. . . . Each of them pays about $250,000 a year retainer, plus $100,000 per month for a project fee if there's a special project they want either Dr. Kissinger or the two or three main associates he has in the firm to do for them. Plus, Dr. Kissinger makes money on boards of directors; he makes money for his speaking fees; he charges up to $35,000 a speech. It all adds up to quite lucrative post-government work. . . . If you look at the spectrum of influence peddling in Washington, it's not a very honorable tradition, but it's an old tradition in Washington. . . .

I do think that it does present some conflicts of interest when a guy goes . . . out of government and appears to be cashing in on the connections he made. For that matter, in Kissinger's case, he's somebody who . . . was paid by ABC and then NBC as a commentator, [later] on the board of CBS, appears on CBS, writes a newspaper column. When he's writing, say, a newspaper column or appearing on the news, saying, "We shouldn't impose sanctions on China" after the Tiananmen Square massacre, it would have helped if he would have said, "By the way, I represent ARCO, which is doing an oil and gas exploration business in China. I represent H. J. Heinz, which is trying to open a baby food factory in China. I've formed a group called China Ventures with Coca-Cola," which is another client. . . . He could say—and . . . it would be truthful if he [did]—"My opinions about China aren't influenced because I have these clients there."

HE IS A BRILLIANT MAN. I know that my book has been interpreted as being critical of him, and he certainly thinks it's far too critical of him, but I hope I also put on display his ability to understand linkages in foreign policy. For example, how something you do in China might affect the relationships you have in Malaysia. Or how dealings in the Middle East might affect your ability to do similar dealings in Eastern Europe.

HE DOESN'T LIKE TO GIVE UP the perks that he had when he was secretary of state. There are certain people who, as soon as they leave office, retire back into that semi-obscurity that is the luxury of people who have already been famous. They get to go into restaurants unnoticed, they fly commercial, that sort of thing. Henry Kissinger does not like to fly commercial. He does not like to enter restaurants unnoticed. So among other things, if he's going to do something in Indonesia, he's going to want to borrow the corporate jet. He's going to want to be flown around.

He has three or four security guards at all times, which helps. Not only does he have to worry about his own security somewhat, but anybody who enters a meeting with three security guards, two preceding and then one coming after, enters with a bit of a splash. You notice that Henry Kissinger has arrived, and in Manhattan, it means you don't have to wait at the bar for a table at a fancy restaurant if your security guards are coming in with you. He likes to travel with all the pomp and circumstance that is befitting a secretary of state. I think that adds to his aura.

One thing that people ask me when we talk about Kissinger is "Why is it, fifteen years after he left office, he's still a larger-than-life personality? . . . [why is it that] when he speaks, he still commands a great awe as well as animosity?" He arouses strong emotions, unlike, say, Cyrus Vance or Edmund Muskie, or other people who have been secretary of state. The reason is he works at it. He works at keeping his celebrity aura, at keeping his image high. . . . He tends to his celebrity.

He has learned one of the true secrets of the media age, because all of us know that if you're powerful, it translates into celebrity. But he realizes it works the other way: If you keep your celebrity or if you're a celebrity, it translates into power because people are more interested in what you say if you're a celebrity. You can command a higher speaking fee. You can command a higher consulting fee. And when you arrive in Indonesia or India or Egypt or Morocco, it's more likely that the prime minister or the king is going to want to call you in and have you in for lunch if you're a big celebrity.

INTERVIEWING RICHARD NIXON was the most interesting bit of [my research]. . . . You could tell this ambivalence he felt towards Kissinger. He . . . admired Kissinger's mind enormously but was very wary of Kissinger's personality and very jealous of the acclaim Henry Kissinger got for things that Nixon felt should go to Nixon. Nixon's sentences about Kissinger would have spin on them, if you know what I mean. He would say, "Well, I'm not one to say that Henry Kissinger is paranoid, but . . ."

Nixon and Kissinger used to sit in that room that's the hideaway office across the street from the White House in the Executive Office Building. Nixon would sit there with his feet propped up; he'd take a yellow legal pad and make little notes. He would spend hours just ruminating about the world. One of Nixon's strengths, as well as his weaknesses, was that he loved to circle around a subject for hours and take different angles on it. Of course, that was bugged, that room, and the White House tapes caught him in that room many times. I guess he forgot the tapes were on. . . .

They would sit in that room for hours just figuring out what would happen—what would China do if we did this with the Soviet Union? How would the North Vietnamese react? Or how would Moscow react if we started bombing Hanoi right before the summit in Moscow? They were sort of conspirators as they sat there in that room and figured out foreign policy. Also, [they were] very secretive. As they sat in that room, they cut out the State Department, they cut out the Defense Department from all their deliberations. If you look at the opening to China, it was done without the State Department even knowing; it was Kissinger's secret trip. If you look at the Paris peace talks on Vietnam, Kissinger was handling those secretly behind the backs of the State Department, which was conducting the . . . official negotiations. The State Department didn't even know that Kissinger was doing this.

Likewise with the arms-control talks with the Soviet Union, and likewise with the secret bombing of Cambodia. You would have Nixon and Kissinger sitting in the office there, making all of these plans and keeping the rest of the government in the dark.

NIXON AND KISSINGER [were together as Nixon made the decision to resign]. . . . They talked for about an hour in the Lincoln Sitting Room. Nixon was going to resign the presidency the next day. Nixon asked Kissinger to kneel down and pray with him. They did, and they prayed, and Nixon cried. Kissinger told him that he would be remembered better by history than by his contemporaries. Drenched with sweat, his shirt soaked, Kissinger went back to his office in the West Wing of the White House. . . .

He . . . started to retell the tale [to aides Brent Scowcroft and Lawrence Eagleburger], and then the private phone line from the president rang on Kissinger's phone. . . . Nixon said to Kissinger, "Please don't tell them what just happened. Don't tell them I was weak. Don't tell them I cried." And Kissinger said, "If I ever speak of this scene, I will speak of it in terms of respect." By the way, Kissinger does speak of Nixon in terms of respect about this scene.

WHENEVER YOU HAVE PEOPLE . . . talk about conspiracy theories . . . Henry Kissinger and Nelson Rockefeller and David Rockefeller are always sort of at the center of it. The Council on Foreign Relations is really just a discussion group and club in New York City founded about seventy, seventy-five years ago to discuss foreign affairs. It's largely funded by the old-boy establishment network of the foreign policy elite in the East Coast, partly John McCloy and the Rockefellers. It's not an insidious institution. It's a perfectly respectable place. I guess its only drawback is it's occasionally quite boring if people drone on. But it's not . . . the heart of some conspiracy to control the world. . . .

Henry Kissinger got his start there, to some extent. He was a graduate student at Harvard, about to become an assistant professor at Harvard. He took some time off, went to the Council on Foreign Relations to run one of their study groups . . . on nuclear weapons and foreign policy. . . . He wrote a book on it, nuclear weapons and foreign policy, that was published by the Council on

Foreign Relations, became a bestseller. It helped redefine our thinking about nuclear weapons and how they affect the conduct of foreign policy. After that, he became associated with the Rockefellers and worked for Nelson Rockefeller. . . .

KISSINGER BECAME our first celebrity statesman or celebrity diplomat. He realized that in order to be popular in the Nixon administration—not popular with President Nixon, who hated this, but be popular with the press—he had to be on the Georgetown party circuit. . . . He was the most eagerly sought dinner guest in Georgetown. All the Georgetown social circuit, including Katharine Graham, Joseph Kraft, Joseph Alsop, the Bradens, that crowd—he was the toast of their dinner tables.

It helped him form good relationships with newspaper columnists, TV commentators, as well as the real opinion makers, because that is the way a lot of the wheels are greased in Washington. People may want to leak a little something about how a particular person in government is not doing very well. . . . The way to do it is to tell the tale at a dinner party, and within maybe six hours, it's spread all over Washington. Kissinger was a master at going to the dinner parties, cultivating the commentators, and getting good press as a result.

He loved dealing with the press, and most of the time he would talk not for quotation—in other words, he wouldn't talk on the record. Instead of just talking off the record, which means the stuff can't be used, he was the one who perfected the notion of having different grades, such as he would talk on background, which meant whatever he said could be used, but it couldn't be directly quoted to Henry Kissinger. That's how the phrase "a senior administration official" . . . was often used when Kissinger said something.

He'd sometimes talk on deep background, which meant nothing could be really quoted at all. The reporter could use the information but not attribute it in any way. He had all those rules; every now and then it would get too complicated. . . . As one reporter said, he played the press like a fiddle. He was so interesting, so expansive, so great at explaining foreign policy, that reporters naturally gravitated towards him as a source.

THERE ARE PEOPLE who tell the tales, and, sure, he had an enormous temper. He was very thin-skinned. Les Gelb, who became a columnist for *The New York Times* [and later head of the Council on Foreign Relations] but who was a student of Kissinger's at Harvard, . . . said that Kissinger was the typical product of an authoritarian background—Kissinger being from Nazi Germany. He said he was devious with his peers, obsequious to his superiors, and domineering towards his subordinates. That's the aspect of Kissinger's personality I found very unattractive.

He was always playing people off against each other, denigrating people, talking about people behind their backs. He wasn't necessarily outright duplicitous, saying one thing to one side and one thing to the other side—but he came close. He would allow one side to believe—the doves or the liberals— that he agreed with them, and then he'd go talk to conservatives and hawks. . . .

He was charming. He was brilliant. He was powerful, and a lot of people didn't [put up with it]. They got very mad at him. He made a lot of enemies. He was the most venerated and most respected secretary of state in many ways, but he was also the most hated secretary of state . . . but he didn't get away with it. Somebody once said he was not that masterful a liar because if he was more masterful, he wouldn't have such a reputation for being one. He kept getting caught at it.

The foreign policy he was able to develop—an opening towards the Soviet Union, balancing it off with China, allowing America to have a new diplomatic role in the Middle East—helped preserve America's role in the world and its influence in the world after Vietnam. There was a great sense of retreat after Vietnam, almost a neo-isolationism. He helped preserve our influence in the world. That was important, because it helped us stand up to the Soviet threat, stand up to the spread of communism. He gets some of the credit—and who knows how historians will apportion all of the credit—for letting the internal contradictions of the Soviet system work themselves out and allow communism to collapse.

His legacy in the long run was not as lasting as it could have been—and in many ways [was] detrimental. He had a feel for power in this world, but he didn't have a feel for the strength that comes from the openness and the values of our system. If anything won the cold war, it was an appreciation around the world for American values, for individual rights, for the openness of our system—all sorts of things that Kissinger, with his secretive diplomacy, did not fully appreciate. The structures were masterful, but in some ways, they were built on a foundation of bricks without straw.

Jimmy Carter

---

by
JIMMY CARTER

James Earl "Jimmy" Carter (b. 1924) served as governor of Georgia before campaigning as a Washington outsider to win the 1976 Democratic nomination for president. He narrowly defeated incumbent Gerald Ford to become the thirty-ninth president of the United States. He lost his bid for re-election in 1980. Mr. Carter appeared on Booknotes *on February 19, 1995, to discuss his volume of poetry,* Always a Reckoning and Other Poems *(Times Books, 1995), in which he wrote of both his private and political life.*

> *There always seemed to be a need*
> *for a reckoning in early days.*
> *What came in equaled what went out*
> *like oscillating ocean waves.*
> —*Jimmy Carter*

THIS IS FROM A POEM about my father, and how he ran our farm. Everything had to balance. There was no possibility in his mind to have anything on the farm, as I said in the poem, that you couldn't plow or that didn't give milk or you couldn't get eggs from or you couldn't find a rabbit or a quail. It meant that my father required a reckoning from all of us who worked on the farm. I think it's applicable to life in general. When you put an investment in something, you get back a dividend. It's like an ocean wave going in and out.

I've been amazed at how much self-revelation comes from a poem. I start writing a poem about things that I want to treat superficially in a way, and before I know it, I've explored the inner depths of my soul and my consciousness and my memory and revealing things that otherwise I would never have told anyone.

PLAINS, GEORGIA, IS NOW and always has been the center of my life. Even when I was in the navy, there was a magnet pulling me back to Plains. . . . My ancestors and Rosalynn's, who were born in the 1700s, were buried there. We've got the same land that's been in our family since 1832. . . . I doubt that very many people in this modern, fast-changing, technical, mobile world have that intensity of attraction to a small town, where a husband and a wife both are from there and feel compelled, pleasantly, to go back.

I USED TO WALK DOWN the railroad track about two miles and a half to Plains and sell twenty bags of peanuts for a total of one dollar and walk back home.

In the first place, as a five-, six-, seven-, eight-year-old boy, omnipresent on the Plains streets every day, the adults learned just to ignore my presence. They would say things and do things as though I was not there. Some of the men would talk about their sexual exploits. Some of the ones that were more— I would say—disreputable or whatever, would brag about going down to Albany, Georgia, thirty-five miles away, to a whorehouse and having sex with whores, some of whom were white, some of whom were black. The same men would be the ones most likely to be mentioned as members of the Ku Klux Klan. This was an unpleasant facet of Plains city life. At that time, Plains had about five hundred people total population. So far as I know, all that has gone away. Except the physical town is there, and it's a little bit larger, as a matter of fact, in total population than it was back then.

RACHEL CLARK WAS A VERY SMALL queen-like black woman [who] was our next-door neighbor. She had an extraordinary impact on my life. She was a friend.

She died recently. She was ninety-two years old and died within the last few years. But she had a lot of impact on me. She would take me fishing. She would teach me how to pick cotton more rapidly, and she would help me in my row if I was getting behind. She was a philosopher. She was so competent.

There was something special about her. People from all around . . . knew about Rachel Clark. She could pick more cotton in a day than anyone else. She could hoe cotton or peanuts or corn better than anyone. She could stack more peanuts for curing than anyone else. She was just a superb person.

When I went home from the White House, one of the first things I always did was to kiss my mother and then I'd go and find Rachel and share experiences. She always had some advice for me.

DADDY DIED IN 1953. He had cancer. He was fifty-nine years old. He was a member of the state legislature and a very fine, very stern disciplinarian who was honored in his community and who, I think, loved me very much—he was quite reticent about indicating his affection—and who has always been one of my heroes.

I was a naval officer for eleven years, and I was a very stern disciplinarian [at home, too]. When I told my three boys to do something, they did it. If they didn't, they suffered the consequences. Then we waited about fifteen years, and my daughter Amy came along, but I never was that stern with Amy. My rationalization is that she didn't really need to be chastised. In another poem I wrote, "I want to be part of my father's world." I realized when I was an adult and had sons of my own and was at my father's bedside during his death that there was a surprising parallel between my father's relationship to me, which I resented very much on occasion, and my relationship with my sons. I saw that my father had implanted in me not only habits and attitudes but also genetic material that mirrored himself in me. I wrote one of my most difficult poems about that.

ALL OF MY FAMILY HAS DIED OF CANCER. They all smoked cigarettes; they all died with cancer: my father, my mother, my two sisters, and my brother— all of them. I'm the last one left.

There is a poem about my sister Gloria Carter Spann, who was an avid motorcyclist and a hostess for a bunch of rough motorcycle drivers who would stop at her house on the way to Daytona every year. When my sister died, the bikers came into Plains and stayed with her at her bedside for several days before her death. During her funeral, they formed a motorcycle cortege in front. There were thirty-seven motorcycles. One Harley Davidson had to be in front, and then thirty-six behind it. And on her tombstone in Plains there is an inscription: "She rides in Harley heaven." She was very deeply committed to cycling.

My family passed away one at a time. My father first, back in 1953. And then my mother lived to be in her early eighties. My brothers and sisters all died fairly young. It was a very sobering experience. Strangely enough, they all had pancreatic cancer. One out of 1,500 people die with pancreatic cancer, so it's beyond the realm of mathematical probability that everybody in a family would die with it. But now the American Cancer Society is doing a special study on our family to see if there is not a familial inherited trait that causes the incidence of pancreatic cancer. Every three or four months, I have a special test run on my body to see if I am becoming afflicted with pancreatic cancer.

My wife and some of my staff [have discussed my funeral], because they work out very complete [presidential] funeral ceremony plans in advance. We've really inherited what President Ford has [planned]. There are some things that you have to decide before a person's demise . . . so that you can handle that in an orderly fashion. There are a lot of plans that have to be made.

I haven't been participating in it. I've let my wife be the ultimate judge on what should be done. There's a professional staff associated, I think, with the Marine Corps who know the history of presidential funerals and processions and the display of the body and how much is done within the Capitol building and how much is done in different places.

BEGINNING ABOUT FIVE YEARS AGO, I studied textbooks about poetry and the different kinds of poetry and meter and whether they rhymed or not, all sorts of poetry books that analyzed what famous poets were saying and the words they chose. My favorite poet of all time is Dylan Thomas, but I don't have any ability or inclination to try to emulate his poetry.

When I was president, I went over to London for the economic summit conference. Since Dylan Thomas had always been my hero in poetry, I wanted to go to Laugharne in Wales to visit his homeplace. The prime minister asked me to go to Newcastle upon Tyne instead, so I had to skip my visit to Wales. I've been since. While president, I went to Westminster Abbey, and I asked the archbishop, with a group of White House reporters following me around, where Dylan Thomas's stone was.

He said, "We couldn't have Dylan Thomas commemorated here; you know he was a drunkard." I said, "Well, look, there's Lord Byron, who was gay. There's Edgar Allen Poe, who was a drug addict. You got other people here. Why not Dylan Thomas? I think he's the greatest poet of this century." I went back to the White House, and I wrote a letter to the screening committee, or whatever you call it, at Westminster Abbey, and told them I thought Dylan Thomas should be included. It was almost four years later before they finally accepted Dylan Thomas to be honored in the Poet's Corner in Westminster Abbey.

Later a group of people came from Wales over to Georgia and brought me a replica of the Dylan Thomas stone that's in the floor at Westminster Abbey. Caitlin, Dylan Thomas's wife, read the news reports from that trip to Westminster Abbey and wrote me a nice letter thanking me for mentioning her husband.

POLITICS IS HARD. It's a brutal environment, but also gratifying. I was most gratified when I won the election to be president and when I was elected governor. By far my most difficult election was when I ran for the state senate the first time. I wrote an entire book about this called *Turning Point.*

ONE TIME DURING THE CAMPAIGN . . . I was making [what I thought was] a funny statement. I said, "It's not good for us to judge people." I think I said it in a church. I said, "But I know how to judge people. I learned how to judge people when I was eight years old. I used to sell boiled peanuts in Plains, and I very quickly learned how to judge everybody in town: The good people were the ones that bought boiled peanuts from me, and the bad people didn't." It was a joke. But later, two psychiatrists got hold of that quote and just psychoanalyzed me as being twisted or depraved or thinking that I could judge people by whether they did me favors. I'm sure that when psychiatrists get hold of this, or psychopoliticians or whatever they call themselves, get hold of this series of poems, they're going to have a field day.

CERTAINLY WITH ADVANCING AGE, I've become a lot more mellow in my attitude towards others. I would think that most people would say that I have a gentle approach to other folks now.

In a final mediation or negotiation, you have to be extremely tough. You have to know exactly how far you can go and go no further. You have to use the maximum degree of persuasion to induce a recalcitrant party to accept your proposal. You have to be tough.

THERE IS A VERY SIMPLE POEM about our going to the roof of the White House one night. My youngest son was an amateur astronomer. He wanted us to look at a constellation. We were aggravated because we couldn't see the stars very clearly because of the Washington city lights, and all of a sudden we heard this primeval sound coming from the north. There was a beautiful flight of geese going over Washington, and the city lights were being reflected from their breasts. It was one of the most memorable and beautiful sights I've ever seen.

HISTORICALLY, I'D LIKE TO BE REMEMBERED for things that we did that contributed to peace and human rights. I'd like people to understand that I have been honest and truthful, that I've loved the simpler things of life. I'd like to be remembered as a good grandfather—we have nine grandchildren. Those are a wide range of things I'd like to be remembered for. I was an outstanding farmer at one time. I produced the best seed peanuts in this country, perhaps in the world. I was very proud of that. I was a good submarine officer. In the different phases in my life, I've wanted to be remembered for different things.

George Bush

by
GEORGE BUSH
FITZHUGH GREEN

George Bush (b. 1924) had been president for one year when Fitzhugh Green appeared on Booknotes *on January 21, 1990, to discuss his book* George Bush: An Intimate Portrait *(Hippocrene Books, 1989). On October 4, 1998 George Bush and Brent Scowcroft discussed their book* A World Transformed *(Knopf, 1998). From that interview, we drew some of Mr. Bush's observations of himself. Son of a U.S. senator, George Bush began his own public career in the U.S. House of Representatives. Bush later served as ambassador to China, chairman of the Republican National Committee, and director of the CIA. After serving two terms as Ronald Reagan's vice president, Mr. Bush was elected the forty-first president of the United States in 1988. He lost his bid for re-election in 1992 and retired to private life in Texas.*

George Bush (and Brent Scowcroft)

A World Transformed

THE FIRST TIME I went into the Oval Office, I was a tourist; my dad was in the Senate and I got to stick my head in there. Then I was in the Oval Office again as a junior member of Congress. . . . [When I was President] we tried to treat the Oval Office with respect; I'd wear a necktie in there. I would go over late at night, sometimes, and maybe not be as formal. But there is something about that room that makes whoever goes in there have a certain awe. And there is also something that made us—and I am not just talking just about me, I am talking about our team, our cabinet, the wonderful people that surrounded me—treat it with respect. It was a given.

[As a former president,] I didn't want to be a constant critic of my successor; he beat me fair and square. Even today if I got into the hurly-burly in Washington, somebody would say, "Hey, this is the guy who lost; now he is trying to get even or . . . say I told you so." I have tried to stay out of all that. I think its better for me to say, "I had my chance. We did the best we could; I tried to conduct myself with honor. Now its somebody else's turn. And after him there will be someone else."

I FELT WHETHER I WAS PRESIDENT or not that personal relations are important. It is not that if someone likes you or someone knows you they are going to change their policy toward the United States of America. But I believe and I tried to practice this while I was vice president and long before that—that you have a better chance of succeeding if you know a person, know his heartbeat, know about the family and are interested in those things. . . . I first learned that at the United Nations, which is a huge political forum. I believed and practiced it there and tried to do that for the rest of my life. I don't think you can overdo it. Now, if you let your friendship with a foreign leader color the objectivity of your judgment, you are making a big mistake. But you get a break, the guy is going to give you the benefit of the doubt, if you know the person and he knows you are not trying to blindside him; not trying to set him up.

I DON'T THINK I ATTACKED the press much. I remember writing one publisher on one subject in the four years I was president, that's all. [The best example of the press hurting American diplomacy]—and I don't mean to single him out because he was recently under fire—was [CNN's] Peter Arnett broadcasting from Baghdad [during the Gulf War]. That caused us a great deal of problems, and it caused Saddam Hussein great joy. I am sorry; I know he differs with me on this, but that's how strongly I feel about it.

[I ONCE ASKED RONALD REAGAN how he kept his emotions in check,] and it was a great lesson because I remember this superb speech he gave in Normandy [for the fortieth anniversary of D-Day]. I said to him in one of our weekly luncheons, "How do you do this?" He said, "I say the words over and over again." And he did. It works. I have tried it. . . . If you say it over and over again, it becomes less personal. Yet the way that Reagan delivered that Normandy speech, you would never have guessed he had conditioned himself to get through it. When I think about emotional moments, I think about the Berlin Wall. Some people thought I should have been standing around jubilantly, dancing with kids, beating myself on the chest, saying, "We did it; we won." It was that kind of emotion that I didn't want to try to demonstrate. [House Democratic Leader] Dick Gephardt and [then Democratic leader] Senator George Mitchell said, "The president doesn't get it. He doesn't understand the emotion we feel. He should go and show these German kids, by dancing on the wall, how we feel." [It was] the dumbest possible thing I could have done because who knows how Gorbachev's legions right there in the GDR or Hungary might have reacted.

I GOT PRETTY DARNED CLOSE, . . . emotionally close to Mikhail Gorbachev. . . . I remember my last talk with him while he was in office. It was Christmas or New Year's Eve. . . . I first met him when I was vice president—the day he assumed office. I was the guy in those days who went to a lot of funerals—I was the vice president. I cabled back to Ronald Reagan, "This man is different—much more open, much more frank, much less inclined to turn to his aides to tell him what to say; much less programmed." It was a very revealing first meeting. I thought he was different and nothing to the day he left convinced me that he was not different.

[THE MOST IMPORTANT MOMENT in my presidency was] the fall of the Berlin Wall because we had worked very hard with Helmut Kohl, worked with the Allies to try and bring them along and not to stand in Kohl's way. We worked with the Russians to be sure that they understood where Helmut wanted to go. We were determined that Germany was going to be reunited, be free and stay in NATO, aligned with the West. When the wall came down, that started the final chapter. It's such a strong symbol and that's what I remember most.

Fitzhugh Green

George Bush: An Intimate Portrait

I'VE HAD DEALINGS with George Bush or his family since I was a little boy. We grew up in a town next to where Barbara Pierce, his wife, lived and were friends with her, and her sister and her brothers. Largely because of her, I began to see [George] when he started coming to Washington. I worked for the father-in-law of his brother, Prescott Bush, Jr., as aide to an admiral; he was an admiral in the Second World War. So I've been aware of the family directly and indirectly for well over fifty years.

GEORGE BUSH'S GREAT-UNCLE was called "Poppy"—George Herbert Walker. . . . When they named George, George Herbert Walker Bush, they called him "Little Poppy," and then it got to be "Poppy." When he got into the navy and into college, he just didn't answer to it anymore.

He did get rid of "Poppy," but he never got rid of "preppy." He went down to Texas clearly to get away from being a carbon copy of his dad. Of course, his dad wasn't from New England either, but he'd gone to a prep school there and he was a New England politician and a very strong personality. George Bush is a very strong, hard-driving individual himself and clearly wanted to cut his own furrows, so he went down to Texas and started his life all over again. There are a million stories about how he keeps trying to be a Texan when he really isn't. He once told Lyndon Johnson, "My Lord, I spent more time in Texas since 1948 than you did." But he has never really shaken the fact that he's not a Texan. I say that he's 100 percent American, but an ersatz Texan.

[HIS FATHER] PRESCOTT BUSH had a great deal of influence on George Bush. It's interesting that when I interviewed Barbara Bush for this book, she said, "Well, everybody says that, but the real strong influence was his mother." That could well be in terms of deep moral strength and so forth. But there's no question that his father was a very imposing man.

When Prescott Bush was a senator, George Bush was already in Texas. George Bush went to Texas in 1948. His father became a senator in 1952 and stayed there for a couple of terms. His father was a Republican. They didn't have right-wing and left-wing Republicans and Democrats in those days. Much as he was an eastern businessman, I'd think you'd call him a moderate Republican. I think he would agree, if he were here today, with his son's positions on politics.

GEORGE BUSH IS A VERY MORAL PERSON, a very hardworking fellow, a very joyful fellow, a very athletic, fun-loving, family-loving—he's a typical heart-of-America type of American. He has had advantages that other people don't have, but he lives a simple life and cares about people. One of his people in the White House told me that he wrote as many as forty private notes to friends and contacts around the country every day. He's that careful with the jobs he does. He's always been a bear of a worker, and when he gets involved with something, he's involved all the way to the marrow. He gradually began to see that, if you're going to be in politics, you can do the most if you get to the top, just as it is in any walk of life. He didn't make a big announcement anytime, but it began to come through in the 1970s that [the presidency] was where he ought to be going. He went at it hammer and tong.

He was considered shallow and not even very powerful. They called him "The Wimp" during the campaign. But the man works all the time and he's very bright at what he does. He studied what they call a "dismal science," economics, at Yale. He got through Yale in two and a half years; he made Phi Beta Kappa, and he also won the top prize in economics while he was there.

He was also, all the way through his various careers, a very quick study. . . . This is a much brighter man than the image of him. The other side of him that I don't think has come through too well is how tough he is and how, physically, he's a very brave man, as he proved in the war on numerous occasions. Morally and managerially, he's a very tough fellow, and he's tough without being mean. . . . This fellow is the opposite of mean. He's very giving. They used to call him "Have Half" when he was a kid because he was so generous with whatever he had in terms of food or clothes or baseball bats or whatever. If he had half a piece of pie left, he'd say, "Have half of mine."

It was hard to get people to tell anecdotes about the president because he doesn't really lend himself to anecdotes. He's not a fellow who tries to be like his father and command the room. This is probably the biggest difficulty he had in becoming a successful politician. Until he actually started to run for office, he was one of these people whom nature had smiled on. He was handsome; he was always a good athlete. He was a good-looking fellow, physically, and in all respects. Being a good athlete and being bright, people just naturally made him a leader wherever he was. The mantle was laid on him. Suddenly, a lifetime of never asking for anything for himself, changed. He had to start saying, whenever he'd meet somebody, "I want you to vote for me." It didn't set well with him.

WHAT YOU DON'T SEE in the press coverage of Barbara Bush is how beautifully organized she is and how strong she is. You see her as this person who jokes about her age and about her white hair and so forth. When I interviewed her, I realized this isn't just Barbara Pierce grown up—this is a person who could run a corporation, in the very best sense of the word. She arrived for our interview at the vice president's house exactly one minute ahead of time. She left exactly on the half-hour of when we were supposed to complete it. During the period that we talked, I was impressed by the fact that she valued the time that we were spending together. She was totally aware of all the things that were going on, good, bad, and indifferent, about his campaign. If I suddenly inherited General Motors, I'd like to have her run it.

GEORGE BUSH DECIDED TO JOIN the navy on Pearl Harbor Day, when he was only seventeen. . . . As soon as he was eighteen, which was in June of 1942, he became the youngest pilot in the navy. I've talked to people who served with him. He was known as a hard-charger. He was an eager beaver without being a pain in the neck about it. He was gutsy. He was on the job and became an excellent pilot and a leader among the people in his squadron.

As a businessman, he started out working for one of his father's friends; curiously, though, because he was trying to get away from his father. . . . He started out on a very low-level basis. He was painting and maintaining and keeping records of oil-drilling machinery. Gradually, he worked up to where he was in the sales end. He was a very good salesman. Eventually, he went into business on his own. . . . Apparently he made a pretty good amount of money, but he got interested in politics before he made a great deal of money. He sold his interests in Zapata Off-Shore, which he formed. . . . When he started to get active in Texas politics, he figured that he couldn't do both.

When he got to Congress, he had learned specifically from his father and was very punctilious about staying on top of the casework—the individual relationships back in his district, the Seventh District, Harris County in Houston. He was busy supporting legislation, but you don't initiate much when you're a freshman congressman. He was a freshman in 1968.

He ran for the Senate at the beginning and the end of that stage of his political career. He ran for the Senate in 1964 and was defeated, but he did very well. Then he ran in 1970 and was defeated again. He thought he was going to be running against Ralph Yarborough, and he figured he could beat Yarborough, who was then senator. What he didn't realize was that Yarborough was in trouble. . . . Yarborough was defeated by Lloyd Bentsen in a Democrat primary. So Bush ran against Bentsen, and Bentsen beat him.

[HE WAS APPOINTED AS AMBASSADOR to the United Nations in 1971.] He left a mark at the U.N. He fought hard to sell the two-China policy. Those were the days when there were a lot of people in public life back here in Washington and in the country who felt that, since Chiang Kai-shek had been our ally in World War II . . . we ought to stick with him. The policy that Bush was asked to sell was "Let's have a two-China policy; we'll have them both in the U.N." What he didn't realize was that, behind his back and without telling him, which is unconscionable, President Nixon and Henry Kissinger were secretly negotiating with the Chinese on the mainland. When this became known, the people who were willing to vote for the two-China policy . . . felt that they didn't have to stick with their votes. They lost the vote. Then China was admitted because of the negotiations of Kissinger and Nixon.

[After the U.N., President Nixon made him Republican National Committee chairman.] It was a little bit like being made captain of the *Titanic* after the ship had struck the iceberg. It was the time of Watergate. In many ways, this was his finest time. I saw him make a speech in Rhode Island when the president was clearly implicated in the bad things of Watergate, and the Republican party was under fire everywhere in the country. He got up and told five hundred or six hundred Rhode Islanders, "Now is the time that we should fight for the party. It is not the party that's bad. It is some people in the party who have behaved badly. This is when we've got to keep this party going." He was not asking for votes for himself. . . . He was fighting for something he believed in. He remained loyal to the president right up till the end. Finally, when he saw that the president was in trouble because of his own poor judgment on some of those matters, he was the fellow who wrote him a letter and said, "Mr. President, it's time for you to resign."

PRESIDENT FORD SAID [TO HIM], "You can have anything you want. You can be in London or Paris." He said, "You've done a good job for the Republican party. What would you like?" To make a long story short, he said, "I'll take China." The president thought he was kidding, but he obviously [wasn't]. This was one of those decisions where he wanted to stretch out and not do what everybody else did. [His experience in China] reinforced the basic premise that he saw in all dealings of business and politics, which is that decisions are made on personal relationships.

He was in China for less than two years. He was invited back to take over the CIA. It's hard to learn a lot about what happens at the CIA except that he was very popular there. It was in terrible trouble. It was clear that if he took the CIA job, it was going to hurt any chance he ever had of getting ahead as a political power. Although you need the CIA, there are a lot of people who think if you get into that you can't be really all good anymore; the CIA is a terrible thing because it's sneaky—it's full of secrets and so forth. This is the unexpressed paranoia that this country has. People don't like to have propaganda or intelligence agencies, but you need both. He realized that, and he thought it was a chance to serve. He took it even though he realized that it might hurt him.

As vice president under Ronald Reagan, George Bush was a hardworking, crafty fellow who kept his own counsel. He learned very soon after he became vice president that, if he said anything—even in a cabinet meeting—that was at all controversial, it was going to get in the paper. He realized that the fellow who has his own agenda and pursues it as vice president is not going to succeed. His own agenda by that time clearly was that he wanted to be president.

It's commonly felt that a leader of a country should have a vision for the country. I think that Bush had a vision, but it was based on the principles by which he was running his own life. . . . In other words, a vision where mankind is more important than power; where people must be respected and cared for, both in this country and the rest of the world; and where this country's got to be strong if it's going to be a strong pursuer of the moral concepts that he learned as a boy. He wants America to succeed, and the way he went about it was to try to lead it the way he led his own life—quietly, with a great deal of hard work and prudence, but with a desire to surprise people sometimes.

William F. Buckley, Jr.

---

by
WILLIAM F. BUCKLEY, JR.

William F. Buckley, Jr. (b. 1925), founder of The National Review, *has been a leading voice in conservative politics since the 1950s.* Booknotes *aired a conversation with Mr. Buckley on October 24, 1993, about his book* Happy Days Were Here Again: Reflections of a Libertarian Journalist, *which was published that year by Random House.*

U P UNTIL AGE SIX I spoke only Spanish. . . . Then I went to my first school in Paris, where, of course, they spoke French. Then at age seven I went to London, and that's where I learned English for the first time. Now what ought I to sound like? . . . Nobody who's British thinks I have a British accent. Occasionally people would say to me, in Minnesota, "Where are you from?" I say, "I'm from Connecticut." And they say, "Well, maybe that's how they speak in Connecticut." But there's nothing cultivated in my accent, as my family and friends would tell you.

My father was in the oil business, and he had a very large family. He was bilingual himself, and he had a family staff who spoke French or Spanish. [There were ten children in the family. My brother James] was a senator from New York. He was beaten by [Pat] Moynihan in 1976.

I ran once for mayor of New York. I didn't run thinking that I would win. I ran under the Conservative label. Up until then, the most they had gotten was 1½ percent [of the vote], I got 13 percent. My joke, made for the benefit of the people who teased me about coming dangerously close to winning, is if I were to run again, my campaign slogan would be "Voting by invitation only."

I HAVE AUTHORED more than thirty-five books. The book that sold the best was the second of my four sailing books, called *Atlantic High*. Then the mystery books all came in somewhere, you know, between seventy-five and one hundred [thousand in sales], except the very last one, which came out shortly after the end of the cold war and suffered. I was a casualty of the end of the cold war. Most of the books I've written have been on the bestseller list.

I AM NO LONGER THE EDITOR of *National Review,* but I'm the president of the board and the owner. . . . I lecture a lot, so I keep busy. I live in Stamford, Connecticut. [I spend most of my time] there and on boats, and traveling around. . . .

The *National Review* doesn't make a profit. I don't know of any journal of opinion that ever made money, perhaps with the exception of *The New Republic,* when it was the house organ of the Progressive Citizens of America, which was then a fellow traveling outfit designed to make Henry Wallace president of the United States. Journals of opinion tend not to make money. But we're doing better than ever before. . . . [I've kept it going] through an annual fund appeal, plus directing a certain amount of my own income in its direction.

SOMETHING CALLED THE FUSION MOVEMENT was encouraged by me and by *National Review* during the late 1950s. The idea was to point out to the straight libertarians and to the conservatives how much they had in common and how effective the symbiosis would be between them. From time to time I stress the fact that I'm conservative and, every now and then, that I'm a libertarian. There's a certain amount of libertarian [views expressed] in most of what I write . . . a certain amount that is oriented to "Does this augment or diminish human liberty?"

I ONCE HAD AN EXCHANGE with [author] James Baldwin, in which he was defending the littering of the streets on the grounds that it was a form of protest against the city [of New York] for not paying close enough attention. And I said, "Look, it isn't very helpful to use that as a means of protesting. Should I throw my garbage out into the street when [then candidate for mayor] John Lindsay walks down, since I don't think he'd make a good mayor?" It was just sort of a rhetorical joust-about.

I came to terms very early with the proposition that a minority in a democracy lives by the rules of the majority. Even if I wanted to see the post office privatized, I am not going to protest it by not using the facilities of the post office. On this I agree 100 percent with [economist] Milton Friedman. . . . His answer [is to] . . . continue criticizing that aspect of [society] that you think is wrong on how it's run. But to fail to participate in it is a failure to live by the verdict of a majority that runs a republic in which you are a participant—and whose rules you agreed to abide by unless they become tyrannical.

ADAM SMITH SAID THAT THE STATE can legitimately [only] do certain things, and those are a very short list: it can look after the common defense and be the custodian of monuments. So I asked myself the question: Does the authority of Adam Smith attach itself to a state enterprise that makes the music of dead musicians available?

I had specifically in mind something that happens in Switzerland, [where] for about buck a month or whatever it is, [a state-supported service allows you to] plug your telephone line into six channels. One of those channels . . . has nothing but classical music day and night. It is simply a marvelous amenity. So, I [am] trying to manipulate conservative orthodoxy in such a way as to suggest that a monument need not only be something chiseled in marble, sitting in the middle of a park, but might also be keeping alive a musician and providing the wonderful amenity of access to him cheaply.

I SUPPOSE WHAT BRINGS [ME] THE MOST and the easiest pleasure is sailing. I sail a lot. I've done it since I was thirteen years old. It is, to me, a marvelous form of recreation. . . . I [also] used to ride [horses] a lot when I was a boy, but I don't do that anymore. . . . [As for music,] there is nothing for me as difficult as trying to master a piece of music on the harpsichord, in part because I have very bad fingers. They don't behave well, and they are insufficiently disciplined.

I THINK IT'S A TERRIBLE SIN to bore people. I'm easily bored myself. I'm perfectly prepared to admit that if I attended a lecture by Immanuel Kant, I might very well go to sleep. But that's my fault, not his. So under the circumstances, when I write, I do make an effort to please the reader in the same way that a pianist at a dive, a *boîte,* wants to use chords that please the listener. If you sit down to play a musical repertoire and limit yourself to a dominant or subdominant and a tonic, you're never going to give music the kind of variety that makes it so special.

By the same token, it seems to me that if you deny yourself the hard work and the pleasure of using language exploitatively, you shouldn't be writing professionally.

I really don't like to write. It's terribly hard work. That may be one reason why I have managed to develop the facility to write quickly. If I had the same kind of languorous pleasure in writing that, say, Eudora Welty has, who just gets up with a light in the eye, thinking, "My God, this is a day in which I write," then I could answer a question [about writing] with a greater sense of hedonism. George Will once said to me, ". . . When I wake up in the morning, the first question I subconsciously ask myself is, Is this a day in which I have to write a column? If the answer is affirmative, I wake up bright and happy." It happens exactly the reverse with me.

A lot of us do things for the after-pleasure of it, even weeding your garden— the after-pleasure of seeing the roses and the grass come up, or practicing your scales for the after-pleasure of helping to develop your technique. As Whittaker

Chambers once put it to me, "I like to have written." That's a nice feeling—to have written—in part because it is so onerous.

WHITTAKER CHAMBERS, DURING THE PERIOD where we were very close friends, which is about seven years, wrote me such beautiful letters that they were published as a book. He kept saying things that were very arresting both in what he said and in the way that he said it.

Whittaker Chambers was the *Time* magazine senior editor who, in sworn testimony, named people he had known while working as a secret intelligence agent for the Soviet Union, one of whom was Alger Hiss. There ensued the greatest ongoing division in American cultural history on the question of who was lying. The evidence is pretty overwhelming that the person who was lying was Alger Hiss. . . . [Whittaker and I] became friends in 1954. He became, formally, a senior editor of *National Review,* though he came up [to our editorial offices in New York] very infrequently. He died at a very young age, sixty, of a heart attack.

He had an enormous impact when his book, *Witness,* was [published]. . . . The first chapter was a letter to his children in which he said, "When I left the Soviet Union, left the Communist cause to join the cause of the West, I couldn't help but feel that perhaps I was leaving the winning side to join the losing side. . . ." They serialized that first chapter of his book, "A Letter to My Children," in *The Saturday Evening Post* and sold five hundred thousand more copies than normal. It had a huge impact on everybody who read it. From that moment on, he became something of an American legend and probably still is.

I graduated from college in 1950. The Hiss-Chambers drama was a very significant episode when I was in school. Liberals tended to assume that Hiss was correct because of his pedigree—it was so formidable. He had gone to Johns Hopkins, then he had gone to the Harvard Law School, then he had clerked in the Supreme Court, with the famous Jewish liberal [Justice Felix] Frankfurter. . . . Dean Acheson testified to the nobility of his character. All this time he was piping out secrets to the Soviet Union with his wife, Priscilla Hiss. He was a tremendous blow to the liberal establishment. This shining legacy of the New Deal was a traitor. . . . Some people are still hypnotized with the subject—like the "grassy knollers" on JFK. It's more fun to believe that there was a conspiracy beneath the conspiracy.

MY PROGRAM [*FIRING LINE*] HAS BEEN GOING ON [since 1966]. It's the longest-running program with the same host in America. I have had [only] one complaint in those . . . years from my guests, that I didn't give them all the time they wanted, in the way that they wanted, to say what they wanted to say. That's not bad.

I often have [guests] who are not widely known—philosophers or poets or whatever—and I feel an obligation to acquaint the listener with them. . . .

Sometimes one has a guest [on the program] whom one feels one ought to have on—because he is on to something important that we want to talk about. But he might be an awfully boring human being; after one hour, you're sweatily glad that it's over. By contrast . . . [former British prime minister] Harold Macmillan, at the end of forty-two minutes, said, "I say, aren't we through yet?" And I said, "No. We have seventeen more minutes to go." . . . Whereupon he told some more marvelous stories about what he said to Churchill, what Churchill said to Hitler, and so on. That interview was a sheer joy.

YOU CAN DISAGREE very pointedly with somebody and still have an enormous bond of friendship. Curiously, this is absolutely routine in England. The editor of *The New Statesman* and *The Nation* might be the godfather of the new child of the editor of *The Tablet*. There, it's not considered unusual for a member of the Labour party and a member of the Conservative party to be very close friends.

So I don't think that it's unusual to have somebody [as a friend] with whom you disagree. In the first place, I don't spend all my time talking politics. . . . It's not the kind of thing that interests me that much. There are other things to talk about.

Martin Luther King, Jr.

by
TAYLOR BRANCH

Born in Atlanta, the son of a Baptist minister, Martin Luther King, Jr. (1929–68), became prominent in the civil rights movement in the 1950s and 1960s. He was assassinated in Memphis in 1968. Historian Taylor Branch, who won the Pulitzer Prize for his first King volume, appeared on Booknotes *on April 12, 1998, to discuss his second volume,* Pillar of Fire: America in the King Years, 1963–65 *(Simon and Schuster, 1998).*

MARTIN LUTHER KING got a Nobel Peace Prize in 1964, largely on the strength of world recognition for the huge breakthrough in Birmingham [Alabama] that spread the demonstrations across the country and got the civil rights bill introduced by President Kennedy. Then he gave the "I Have a Dream" speech and had the political skill to work with President Johnson to get it passed in 1964. The Nobel Prize was essentially in recognition for that series of events that changed American politics forever, and changed the legal standard for equal citizenship in America.

THE YEAR OF THE *BROWN* decision, [1954,] is the year that the Supreme Court unanimously said that racial segregation and separation is in conflict with the American Constitution, [thus] renewing the challenge of the Civil War period about slavery being in conflict with the premise of equal citizenship. . . . 1968 is when the movement built on that premise largely dissolved. It's the same year Dr. King was killed.

If you study this period . . . you see how parochial, how limited [people were], how much violence there was, how unaccustomed a lot of white people were even to meeting somebody from a different denomination or a different section of the country. The ads in the newspapers were divided not only by race, but by sex: "Help wanted, female." Jobs for women were secretaries and teachers. We've lifted up a whole new reality, not to minimize the severe problems that still are here. What is lacking in our dialogue [today] is universal voices talking about what we have in common in America, speaking across these lines, which is what we had [back then].

This movement has lifted American values all around the world, [causing] miracles in South Africa; singing "We Shall Overcome" when the Berlin Wall went down; forming the model for the Tiananmen Square demonstration. We have a lot to be proud of as far as the way we have lifted up our objective relations, stretched ourselves to not just be a white Protestant country. . . .

THIS WAS A PERIOD, 1963 [through] 1965 . . . where everything was happening at once. Freedom Summer, and Vietnam, and Malcolm X, all these things were happening at once.

[King] was killed at thirty-nine. He never reached his fortieth birthday. So in this period, 1963 to 1965, he was thirty-four to thirty-six years old, a very young man, boyish-looking, well educated, had his wife, Coretta, and four children, who were quite young. . . . Dexter, the youngest, was just an infant during this period. This was the period when Dr. King was most political. . . . He was getting drawn into other people's movements because he was an orator, and he would help out.

The bus boycott wasn't his idea. The Freedom Rides and the sit-ins certainly weren't his idea; he would get called into these meetings. But by 1963, he was frightened that the South was hardened against segregation and that the zeitgeist—the moment in history—might fade without implanting something that would resist that retrograde trend. So, he took huge risks. He said, "I'm gonna have my own movement. I'm gonna risk everything": first, in Birmingham, to try to crack segregation, and then later in Selma, after the long year of 1964, when he was lobbying and submitting to jail in St. Augustine to try to keep pressure on for passage of the 1964 Civil Rights Act. . . . Here you see not just the spiritual or prophetic side of King . . . but a consciously political King, trying to maneuver with the president and maneuver between the parties, use the media, use the press, and deal with a divided movement, his rivals and allies. . . . This is King at the zenith of the movement's political impact on America, when the race issue has the country's full attention.

A LOT OF DR. KING'S SERMONS are preserved. Unfortunately, much of the broadcast sources are not . . . and that's sad, because television footage of Birmingham awakened me as a kid. Today, it's hard to find it. You can't go in the library and look up film from that period. . . . A lot of that stuff has disintegrated. Occasionally people would make tapes of mass meetings, which are a great institution. They were the engine of the civil rights movement. When they had a meeting in a church, it would be part religious ceremony, part rally, part information, because they didn't have newspapers of their own.

I AM THE FIRST PERSON to write about King's distressing personal ego conflict with Ralph Abernathy. . . . [Civil rights leader] Andy Young told me that he thought that the estrangement with Abernathy over money—Abernathy wanted half the money from the Nobel Peace Prize—really choked the relationship. Andy said that he thought that this was more painful to Dr. King than anything [FBI director] J. Edgar Hoover might do to him.

King and Abernathy were very close. [They kept] no secrets from one another. But there was an undercurrent of jealousy from Abernathy because he had been with Dr. King all along. Abernathy had an amazing hold over audiences. He was a very comic and gifted preacher, but he resented Dr. King's sophistication. He was starved for status, as many black people were during that period, to the point that he created incidents. It became a burden for Dr. King. At the Nobel Peace Prize ceremony, Abernathy refused to get in the second limousine, according to protocol, when all of the Nobel officials were lined up. It mortified not only Dr. King but a lot of the people with him.

Ralph Abernathy was one of the first people close to Dr. King to acknowledge that King had had extramarital affairs, which is an object of denial among many of the people around him. Since then, there have been lots of others who've acknowledged this. A woman even wrote a book about her relationship with Dr. King. So the fact that there were extramarital affairs is no longer as sensitive, but coming from Abernathy, it was seen as a betrayal.

King had a number of long-term affairs with people very loyal to him, over a period of years, on the road. . . . I've talked to a number of those people and my main question is, How did he reconcile this with his career? He wrestled with it. He preached about it in a general [way, saying] that evil is something very close to you. You can't overcome it by trying to stamp it out, by trying to repress it. You overcome it by dedicating yourself to something higher. He was constantly using the analogy of Ulysses and the Sirens, that it didn't work to stuff wax in your ears to try to repress evil; you had to sing a sweeter music.

There was a part of him that was always reproaching himself for [not] being able to give up women—especially once he knew that it could hurt the movement, that blackmail could severely damage people who really believed in him and that they would be disillusioned. In many respects, his sermons sound like he's almost punishing himself to do penance by taking greater risks. I have never tried to argue that there's no relationship between one's private life and one's public life, but I think it's very complicated [to define] exactly what that relationship is. In many respects, there are a lot of signs that he used his private failings and regarded them as such to drive his public mission.

J. Edgar Hoover versus Robert F. Kennedy: that's a Shakespearean wrestling match. There's no way of simplifying that. Hoover was a skilled bureaucrat. He was also to some degree a bully, in that he would try to get his way, and he was a gossip. People who really stood up to him could back him off. Bobby Kennedy never did. This was a younger, not mature, Bobby Kennedy who felt heavily the burden of having to defend his brother, President Jack Kennedy, who was vulnerable because he was having affairs with people in the Mafia and even an East German woman. Bobby Kennedy had to have Hoover's help to protect his brother; it compromised him by creating this three- or four-way dance he was doing to try to protect the Kennedys' political position in the South and the alliance with Martin Luther King. It was like riding on razors. Ultimately, I believe that Hoover, without ever saying "You've got to do this for that"—he was far too skilled a bureaucrat for that—would say, "Okay, I'll help you over here; I'll keep down the scandal against your brother. But I'm very concerned about Martin Luther King, and we need a wiretap." Ultimately, [Attorney General] Robert Kennedy signed that wiretap [order], knowing that he was surrendering with it any pretense of controlling J. Edgar Hoover. It was a very complex political wrestling match.

They used the wiretaps primarily for advance notice of King's travel plans. "Hello, I'm flying to Chicago. I'll be in the such-and-such hotel. I'm flying to New York." They put the taps on his home . . . in Atlanta. They put the taps on his offices, both in Atlanta and in New York. Hoover, being a bureaucrat, included a clever phrase in [the order, which said,] "Permission to mount technical surveillance"—that is, wiretaps—"on Dr. King's home office and any home to which he may move." They interpreted that to mean a hotel room. Anyplace he went, there was blanket authority [to wiretap]. They used that advanced knowledge to have agents go in and implant microphones in the walls of the hotel, for which Bobby Kennedy didn't give authority. Hoover just assumed he had that authority. It was one of the embarrassments of American law. They would use those taps to intercept not just what he said on the phone, but what he would say when he was . . . in bed or when he was arguing. They used the intercepts, essentially, to do anything they could, either to poison people's opinion of King or to poison politicians against one another. . . . In other words, Hoover's job was basically to ingratiate himself with [Lyndon] Johnson to punish Bobby Kennedy, whom Hoover didn't like, and to punish King whenever he could.

A lot of the time, [people in the movement] thought the hostile things being done to them by police were being done by segregationist police forces. Once they became aware that it was the FBI, they had these meetings . . . [to ask Dr. King,] "What are our vulnerabilities here?" Dr. King said, "It's not [about] money." In fact, when he died, he was only worth about twenty thousand dollars. He died intestate. He never had much money. He raised an enormous amount of money but gave it away. He said, "It's not communism. I take people for what they are. I'm far too spiritual to be a Communist leader. I reject communism. But I am vulnerable—there may be a few things on women." . . . Some of his staff actually knew this very well. But it was painful for him to admit to some of the aides who were not privy to his private life that he was vulnerable on this.

His infidelity never became a public issue. . . . It was a private poison; it was used mostly for blackmail behind the scenes. It never became a public issue. Hoover's agents offered the material from the King buggings all over the place, but only under the condition that the FBI could never be identified as the source. In that day and age, nobody wanted to take that leap into people's private lives without . . . a source. Nowadays, maybe we would figure out a way to get around that. But in those days, it meant that the political maneuvering around these sex issues was confined to propaganda. J. Edgar Hoover would send his agents to a university: "We hear you're thinking of giving an honorary doctorate to Dr. King. Let us whisper in your ear." And they'd spike [the degree]. He would send them to the Vatican, to the pope [, telling them]: "Don't see Martin Luther King."

A sample of the intercepted buggings of Dr. King's private life [was delivered to him,] together with an extremely hostile, anonymous note saying, "You are a fraud, and you are evil. We will expose you before the world if you don't take a certain act within thirty-five days"—in other words, before he accepted the Nobel Prize. It meant that Dr. King was to kill himself. It became known as "the suicide package" because it was warning him that he was under threat of exposure. That's when they figured out it was the FBI, because they could tell that the tapes, which were garbled, . . . were [from] different cities. They knew that no police agency would have access to a whole bunch of different cities. They knew it was the FBI, that it was essentially your own government telling you to commit suicide. . . .

I have some FBI characters in the book who are heroes, like Joe Sullivan, the man who solved several of the cases down in St. Augustine, Florida. It's one of the unsung stories of this period. He was the model for Inspector Erskine on the long-running *FBI* series. He was a no-nonsense cop. Most FBI agents don't go in with an ambition to do political work, which means listening to earphones and planning propaganda and prying into people's private lives. They go in to solve cases. So you have a delicious or a painful conflict running in this era: You have the most spectacular political misuses of the FBI going on at the same time the FBI is trying to solve new kinds of crime. [They were] confronting the Klan in the South at the same time they were almost, at will, committing these crimes all through this 1963 to 1965 period. So in the same institution, you have . . . new kinds of heroes and old kinds of corruptions.

SELMA IN FEBRUARY 1965: Dr. King came out of jail in there . . . and his aides said, "You can't just come out of jail. You have to have a purpose for coming out of jail." He said, "I'm tired. I'm depressed. I've been in jail." He won

the Nobel Prize and he's still in jail in Selma on the right to vote. The aides simply told Dr. King, "You've gotta say you had a purpose. Let's say that you're
coming out of jail to meet with the president." That infuriated Lyndon Johnson, because he said, "Nobody invites themself [to the White House] in the
middle of a controversy. I'm trying to run the country." But, on the other hand,
he didn't want to say, "I won't meet with Martin Luther King," partly because
he shared the goal of getting a voting rights bill. What they worked out was an
ego salve. They said that Dr. King was officially coming up to meet with the
vice president [Hubert Humphrey], but they planned to have the president
spontaneously call and say, "Since you're here, why don't you come over and
talk to me?" It was a way of dancing around the egos and the political sensitiv-
ities on the race issue in this period.

THERE WAS A TREMENDOUS DRIVE from Dr. King to go onward and not to
rest on his laurels. To some degree, it was because of the guilt that he had. Lots
of people wanted him to go to honorary dinners and bask in the Nobel Prize
and never do anything else. But within three weeks, he said, "I've got to go
back to the valley." He was jailed in Selma, and yet he went back down to seek
the right to vote. This strong drive in him really dominated the latter part of
his life . . . which ultimately ended up with him being assassinated in the campaign among garbage workers in Memphis.

Dr. King is my favorite among the civil rights leaders. I admire him more
now than I did when I started [this project. Before I began my research] I knew
he was part of this movement that had affected me and I admired him, but I
used to think maybe he was just a Baptist preacher who had gotten carried
away with turning the other cheek.

Ross Perot

by
CAROLYN BARTA

Texas industrialist Ross Perot (b. 1930) twice ran as an independent presidential candidate, garnering 19 percent of the vote in 1992. Carolyn Barta, a Texas journalist, appeared on Booknotes *on January 16, 1994, to discuss her book* Perot and His People: Disrupting the Balance of Political Power *(The Summit Group, 1993).*

I LIVE IN DALLAS, and I've been a journalist in Dallas for twenty-eight years. Ross Perot has been right there in my backyard, so I guess I knew what a fascinating character he was. I've also covered politics, and it seemed to me that he had the potential to change American politics; that he was tapping a chord out there that politicians in recent years had not tapped. I just sensed that there was something going on in American politics that ought to be paid attention to.

When I first met him I was covering city hall in Dallas, and he came in for a zoning change on a piece of property to build EDS. I was covering that, and at the time he—in an indication of the kind of guy he would become, or already was—threatened the city of Dallas that "if you don't let me have my zoning change for EDS to build my campus right here, I'll move out of Dallas and move to the suburbs."

I was aware of his work and did some coverage when he was appointed to head a statewide task force on public education reform in Texas. . . . He also served as head of a statewide task force on drugs in Texas. From time to time, his name would come up. People would say, "Ross Perot ought to run for Senate" or "He ought to run for governor" or this or that. He would always say, "No, I'm not temperamentally suited for politics. I don't want to be in elected office; I want to be behind the scenes."

HE WENT UP TO NASHVILLE to do a talk-radio show, and some business leaders had a little reception for him there. This was in February of 1992. It was not long before the *Larry King Live* show. He said something to the effect that you've got to get in the ring. "If you get in the ring, put some skin in the game.

I might do it." It was published in *The Tennessean,* but nobody else picked up on it. John Jay Hooker, who has been a businessman and had run for office in Tennessee, talked to Perot after that. They talked about national venues where Perot could go to get this message out—that he would be available [to run for president] if people wanted him to do it.

It was no coincidence that [he announced his interest in the presidency] on *Larry King Live.* I think they had decided that it would be *Larry King Live.* That was where he would throw his hat in the ring, and in so doing, he would appeal to a different segment of the populace, people who watch these talk shows. He had already decided that was where the future of communication was, in electronic media, not in newspapers. He didn't want to go to *The Wall Street Journal* or to the *Los Angeles Times* or *The New York Times* or have just a regular press conference to do it. He wanted to do it a different way. So they decided that he would go on *Larry King Live.* I was told it was [John] Siegen-thaler [chairman emeritus of *The Tennessean*] who called *Larry King Live* and said, "If you press him, he will—he might—announce on your show." That's exactly what happened.

A lot of people thought . . . he had his apparatus all in place, ready to run a campaign. That was not true. He said then that he did not anticipate the reaction that he would get. He said, "Nothing will come of it. I said it, yes. I did it, but nothing will come of it." Then the phone started ringing off the hook. That's when they started setting up the campaign apparatus.

After his *Larry King Live* announcement, people were calling Dallas to find out how they could call Perot. The calls continued to come in and eventually . . . after a week or two, Perot said, "Look, we've got to do something about these calls." He called in six people who were part of his business staff and said, "Do what you can to set up a phone bank to handle these incoming calls." Very quickly thereafter, that team of six volunteers started coming in. They started answering the phones and they started feeding the information back out. It just went from there.

EARLY IN THE 1992 PRESIDENTIAL CAMPAIGN . . . I went out to do a col-umn on the Perot petition drive. It was probably early April and I started talk-ing to people who were trying to circulate the petitions. I was struck with the passion of the people who were involved in this movement. I went out to talk with [Perot press spokeswoman] Sharon Holman about writing this book. I was also interested because I knew that Perot had this mastery of high technol-ogy, and he was talking about using the communications revolution [to ad-vance his campaign]. He had his own money; he could put whatever money he wanted to into it. It seemed like a unique combination of factors, and I thought it would make a book.

I went out to talk to Sharon Holman about it, and she said, "Fax me a list of everybody you want to interview, and I will get it over to Mr. Perot." So I sent her a list of everybody I wanted to interview—mostly they were . . . leaders in the campaign. She called back and said, "Mr. Perot said no to all of your interview requests. He said to tell you to go out and talk to the volunteers."

I later said that Sharon Holman did me a real favor because I went out and started talking to volunteers and spent three months talking with people around the country who were interested in this Perot phenomenon. That really is the guts of the story.

PEROT IS AN INTERESTING GUY, a fascinating guy. He is in the tradition of larger-than-life, mythical Texas politicians I had grown up with and known and followed and covered. In some ways, he's a lot like LBJ in that he wants to have control and to be powerful. He also draws his sustenance from the people. Unlike LBJ, who felt that government should do for people what they can't do for themselves, Perot feels that government should get out of the way and let the people do what they do best. I think that it would be a mistake for him to be president. I don't think he'll ever be president. I don't think he wants to be president; I think he wanted to shake up the system. I think he wanted to wake people up to what has been going on in Washington. He wanted to get them involved, and I think he wanted to beat George Bush. Those were his goals in 1992.

I suspect that he and George Bush had some personal differences. One had to do with a mission that Perot wanted to do to get the rest of the [Vietnam] MIAs home. This was when Bush was vice president. Bush wouldn't go to bat for him, wouldn't help him with it. He also thought that Bush was more involved in the Iran-Contra [scandal] than he let on. He thought that Bush was not up to the job of being president, that he was smarter and more capable than Bush. Whether or not he wanted to be [president], Perot thought he ought to be because he thought he was a better guy.

THE BIG PROBLEM with [his campaign was political consultant Ed] Rollins. Rollins came in; he brought thirty or forty professionals in with him. The professionals took over the campaign. It was no longer the unconventional campaign that Perot said he wanted in the beginning. It became the kind of campaign that Perot said . . . he abhorred, that he wasn't going to run, with all the manipulation and the spin. That was a problem. And then, Perot didn't get along with Rollins at all. It was the clash of the giant egos.

When Rollins came in, he was the one who had a driver. He was the one who had aides who would fetch his cleaning and do this and do that. That's not Perot's style. Perot drives his own car. He sits in line in the barbershop to get his eight-dollar haircut.

Tensions developed within the campaign. You would have thought tensions would have developed because you have one Democrat consultant, then you have one Republican consultant. But the tensions were really between the volunteers and the professionals. The volunteers who were working in the phone bank there in Dallas resented the fact that all these professionals had come in, and they were behind locked doors doing God knows what. While they were trying to keep up the grassroots movement, you had these professionals trying to put together a slicker professional campaign.

Not long after the professionals came on board, things started breaking down. The height of Perot mania was about early June at the time of the 1992 California primary. The exit polls in California said that if Perot had been on the ballot, he would have won. . . . . About that time, the press was also starting to focus on Perot's business dealings, on his family, on anything that they could find because he didn't have a political record to focus on. He was beginning to take some hits in the media. . . . All of a sudden things start just sliding downhill. About late June of 1992, things really started falling apart.

Rollins wanted to use Hal Riney, who had produced the "Morning in America" ads for Ronald Reagan. Once again, that just wasn't Perot's style. Perot had already decided that what he wanted to do was just be Ross Perot in front of the cameras with his pie charts and his graphs; he didn't want that slick "Morning in America" style advertising campaign. Plus he didn't want to spend his money doing that.

EARLY ON [IN THE CAMPAIGN], he could pick up the phone and call almost any network show and get on because he was a good draw. He commanded an audience, so I think [the networks] did love him early on—until they started wanting more specifics and he was not more forthcoming. Some of the shows ridiculed him from the very beginning. Some of the Sunday-morning talk shows did not treat him as well as, say, talk TV, the Larry King show, the call-in shows, and so forth.

As one reporter from *Newsweek* said to me, "The press resented the fact that he had not gone through the primary system." They had not had the opportunity to ask him questions that they normally would ask of candidates. A reporter from *Newsweek* said to me, "There was a collective feeling among the press that we had to put him through a primary." So that was what we did.

Perot went ballistic. He never envisioned he would have the kind of press scrutiny that he got. [His senior aide] Tom Luce never envisioned it. At one point in June, there were eleven *New York Times* reporters in Dallas working on stories on Perot. He never envisioned that they would be looking at his family, that they would be looking at all of his business dealings like they did. A lot of people have said he was thin-skinned, and I guess he was. He could not take it when the media started tearing down the image he had spent a lifetime developing. The way he sees himself and the way the media was picturing him were totally different. . . . That was one of the main reasons, if not *the* reason, that he got out of the race in July—he could not take the ruination of this image that he had spent a lifetime developing.

I don't think there was one story [that caused him to quit the race]. There were many stories that bothered him. Then there was the threat of more stories, and, of course, therein came the threat of stories that his daughter's wedding was going to be disrupted. [Then there was] the fact that the campaign had become the kind of campaign that he didn't want to run—those were all factors in the decision that he made to get out.

A STAFFER WHO HAD KNOWN PEROT for a long time and watched him over the years said that Perot has a way of exhausting personal relationships. He has a way of exhausting people because he demands so much, he wants so much, and he takes so much from people. [His volunteers] got so emotionally involved in the work. . . . Perot got out of the race in July and left all of these people holding the bag. These people had put their lives on hold. Many of them were working sixteen-hour days for no pay to get this guy on the ballot and to make him president. When he just, like that, got out without so much as a howdy-do, these people . . . felt loss . . . and anger.

THE MAIN THING I LEARNED was that there was such a deep-seated alienation of people from their government. It was something that other politicians were not aware of or were not paying attention to. Over the process of the campaign, Perot was repeatedly called crazy. Well, he wasn't crazy at all because he was prescient enough to recognize the alienation that was out there of the people from their government. They were tired of being taken for granted, of being treated condescendingly, and it was an opportunity for them to get involved. People who had felt powerless to affect [the system appreciated] the fact that he was finding new ways to communicate with people, that he was utilizing the communications revolution in new and different ways. The fact that he was energizing people to get involved in politics, was a good thing. That was the main contribution of Perot in the 1992 campaign: He empowered a lot of people who had felt they had been left out of the process. Those people are still out there today.

Frank McCourt

FRANK MCCOURT

On August 31, 1997, Frank McCourt (b. 1930) appeared on Booknotes *to discuss his bestselling memoir,* Angela's Ashes *(Scribner, 1996). His tales of growing up in the slums of Limerick create a story not only of family relationships, but of politics and religion. As a young man, McCourt left Ireland to return to his birthplace, New York, where he taught high school English for nearly thirty years.*

I ALWAYS WANTED to be a writer, but I didn't know that I wanted to write about this lane in Limerick, this slum. Because anybody that comes from those circumstances doesn't want to write about it. You're ashamed of it. You don't have any self-esteem. . . . In social circles, I started talking about growing up in Limerick, and I suppose some of the stuff I told them was amusing. They'd laugh because poverty is so absurd . . . and they'd say, "You should write this. When are you going to write about it?" I'd been hearing this for years. . . . But there was no more insistent voice than the little voice in my head: "Write the damn book."

I'd tried it over the years. . . . I was imitating everybody—[Sean] O'Casey and [James] Joyce and Henry [James] . . . and Evelyn Waugh—imagine me writing like Evelyn Waugh. I tried to be a smart-ass, upper-class British writer. None of it worked until eventually I found my own way.

I write in the morning, like my father. I have a lot of his early morning habits. . . . Some days I just want to put a pin through my brain because it's so difficult. But on certain good days I would write nine or ten pages. . . . If it's coming, it's coming; I stay with it. I'm not like Anthony Trollope who used to write three thousand words every single morning before he got on his horse and inspected post offices. I couldn't do that.

THE BOOK STARTS with my mother and father meeting. . . . This was . . . 1929 to 1949, so that's twenty years. I was born in 1930 in New York and taken to Ireland in 1934. I left again in 1949. It's mainly the story of me and my family from our arrival in Ireland to my leaving in 1949.

I'm not sure if I was born in Brooklyn or Manhattan. Mother would never tell me. She always shied away from that . . . because I was conceived beyond the sheets. I was the cause of sin. She used to say, "Frankie was the cause of marriage." It was a shotgun wedding, and I was what appeared five months after their wedding. . . . One of my friends told me I was a bastard, and there was no way of getting around that. He said I was doomed. It was a sin that could not be washed away with the baptism of water. I'm doomed . . . because I'm a bastard.

My mother had six children in five and a half years—including twins. Three of them died—Margaret, the little girl, and the twins—in that five and a half years. . . . Margaret died in Brooklyn and the twins died in Ireland. They died of bronchial pneumonia, or something like that—something preventable. The death of the little girl [Margaret] drove my father crazy because he was mad about her. I know that. I remember the kind of attention he'd pay her which he didn't pay us. He was very good to us. He was a very kind gentleman when he was sober. My mother went into a deep depression. Now if the death of the little girl drove them into a depression and drove him to the bottle, you can imagine what it was like when the twins died in Ireland:

There's a knock at the door, Mr. MacAdorey. Och, Malachy, for God's sake it's three in the morning. You have the whole house woke with the singing.

Och, Dan, I'm only teaching the boys to die for Ireland.

You can teach them to die for Ireland in the daytime, Malachy.

'Tis urgent, Dan, 'tis urgent.

I know, Malachy, but they're only children. Babies. You go to bed now like a dacent man.

Bed, Dan! What am I to do in bed? Her little face is there day and night, her curly black hair and her lovely blue eyes. Oh, Jesus, Dan, what will I do? Was it the hunger that killed her, Dan?

Of course not. Your missus was nursing her. God took her. He has his reasons.

One more song, Dan, before we go to bed.

Good night, Malachy.

Come on, boys. Sing.

> *Because he loved the motherland,*
> *Because he loved the green*
> *He goes to meet a martyr's fate*
> *With proud and joyous mien;*
> *True to the last, oh! true to the last*
> *He treads the upward way;*
> *Young Roddy McCorley goes to die*
> *On the bridge at Toome today.*

You'll die for Ireland, won't you, boys?

We will, Dad.

And we'll all meet your little sister in heaven, won't we, boys?

We will, Dad.

That [scene] takes place in Brooklyn after my sister died. She was twenty-one days old when she died. He went demented. It was a habit of his to get us up because he was a frustrated patriot. He was born in the wrong time. I think he would have been very happy if he had fought the English and been caught and hanged. He would have died singing "Roddy McCorley" or "Kevin Barry." But this was his way of continuing the excitement that he felt when he was fighting in "the Troubles" in Ireland.

My mother was appalled. Everybody was appalled, but we enjoyed it. . . . We'd sing. This was a connection with my father—any excuse for making a connection with him was wonderful. I feel sorry for my father's wasted life. If it wasn't for the drink, he would have been the perfect father. I'll remember what he had in his head, the stories, the legends, his sensitivity to Irish history, his yearning . . . for a part in the struggle.

I think towards the end my father stopped drinking—maybe in the last few years in Belfast. He had the pension. He didn't go out that much anymore. He drank his tea. [Toward the end] I never saw him. If I did see him, it was kind of a formal conversation. It was very hard to get into an intimate conversation with him. If I were to look at this from the outside, I would have said to myself, "Well, why didn't you go back and talk to him?" But I had a feeling that there was no point in it—that he wouldn't come through. He was so blocked-in everywhere. He'd say, "Well, how's your mother?" And "How's your brothers?" That was it. Then he'd look out the window, and he'd drink his tea. There was no getting through to him.

"The dole" is unemployment; my father was always on the dole. Most of the so-called working men were on the dole. You'd get about nineteen shillings, which was about three dollars a week in American terms in those days. It was not enough to keep a family going.

He'd go down—all the men would go down—on Thursday morning to what they call the Labour Exchange to get their money, unlike in America, [where] if you're going on unemployment, you only have to send in a statement once a week or something like that. But you had to appear at the Labour Exchange every morning in case there might be work. Everybody used to laugh—there was never going to be any work. And you'd sign. This was to make sure that you weren't working.

You would get your money on Thursday. . . . It was a big day. You'd see women clustered at both ends of this open-ended lane in Limerick. Women waiting for

the men, to head them off before they went to the pubs. My father was very conscious of his dignity. He didn't want my mother there at all. He wanted to be able
to go to the Labour Exchange, get his money, and then go home, which he did
often. But often, he went to the pubs. He would just drink the whole damn
thing. My mother threatened him. She said she was going to go down to the
Labour Exchange and get the money from the man, the clerk, which she did. He
was shamed forever because a woman came into the Labour Exchange and took
the man's dole. That's not what a woman was supposed to do. Well, she wanted
to make sure her children were fed. That's what a woman is supposed to do.

He lost his dignity. He left for England in the end of 1941. He went off to
work in the factories in Coventry. Once or twice he sent a few pounds. It wasn't
enough; it was just a gesture. I don't know, maybe somebody persuaded him to
send the money back. But he left us to starve.

I remember waiting for the telegram boy. The telegram boys on Saturdays
used to deliver the telegrams to the families whose fathers were in England.
Most of the families like the Meagers or the Downes across from us would get
their telegrams. Solid, steady men sending their money home from England.
We'd wait all day on Saturday. We'd hope and hope and hope. You could hear
the Angelus [prayer bells] always ringing in Ireland—six o'clock in the morning, noon, and six o'clock in the evening. But you knew—*bong, bong, bong*—
when the Angelus rung in the evening and the telegram hadn't been delivered,
that was it: You're going to face another week of starvation. . . .

You just never felt satisfied, and you never had a full feeling. We used to
make up fantasies. There was a bush that grew in Limerick out in the country—a little green leaf and a little red berry bush—which was really inedible.
We used to call that bread and cheese. We'd eat these leaves and little berries
and imagine they were bread and cheese. I thought sometimes, "Some day I'm
going to have a big bread and cheese sandwich." That was my dream.

One time, my mother did get some money. She got a job as a charwoman.
She got some potatoes and a bit of corned beef and jelly and custard. We had
this on a Sunday. She said, "We're not going to eat all of this today. Now we'll
save some for tomorrow." There were about four potatoes left over—boiled
potatoes and some of the jelly and custard. . . . She put it in the windowsill.
She had a little curtain like a larder.

I came home on Monday from school. There was nobody in the house. I
went over and looked. I said, "I'll eat one potato or a half." I couldn't stop eating. . . . I ate the four potatoes and all the jelly and custard. And boy, did she
kill me. She knocked me around the place that night. My brother hated me. It
was the biggest crime I ever committed.

THERE IS A NATIONAL CHARACTERISTIC of the Irish—this poetic, mercur-
ial, flamboyant race. We don't go around saying, "I love you." The word *love*

was something that was reserved for God or babies. "I love you, darling"—you talk [that way] to babies or maybe horses that win, but not for personal relationships. I used to think when I was a kid, when people said "I love you" that that was only for something on the screen at the Lyric Cinema. We never heard it. I never heard a mother saying, "I love you," to her child.

My brother Malachy once had an experience. He was nine. I think this may have changed the course of his life somehow, emotionally. He was in the kitchen. He was nine years old. He said to my mother—he was overwhelmed for some reason—"Mam, I love you." She looked at him. Later on, he's there at the kitchen fiddling around and her friend Bridey Hannon comes in from next door. My mother says, "Bridey, do you know what he just said to me?" "What, Angela?" "He told me he loved me." The two of them had a good laugh, and I think Malachy sank through the floor. So you had to be careful about telling people you loved them.

I HAVE NO TIME FOR INSTITUTIONAL CATHOLICISM. I know individual priests and nuns who are doing, literally, God's work, but the church has to catch up. With what, I don't know, but it's dying.

My father wanted me to be an altar boy and made me learn the Latin, made me learn all the responses. He knew the Mass backwards and forwards, the priest part and the boys' parts. He trained me, and I memorized all the Latin. He made me kneel on the kitchen floor in Limerick and speak Latin. He took me around the corner then to St. Joseph's Church and the sacristan there, who took care of the church, just looked at me and said, "We don't have room for him. . . ." My history is a history of having doors shut in my face.

I CAME TO AMERICA permanently in 1949. Oh, boy, that is another story of thievery. I worked in the [Limerick] post office delivering telegrams. Then I worked in Easons Wholesale News Agents, which is like the Irish Barnes and Noble. In the meantime, I got a job with this old woman, writing. She was a moneylender, a loan shark—Mrs. Finucane. . . . I was delivering a telegram. She said, "Are you in any way smart?" "Well," I said, "I can read and write." She said, "Half the people above the lunatic asylum can read and write. Can you write a letter?" [I said,] "Of course I can write a letter."

She hired me to write threatening letters to dilatory customers. I was to threaten them that if they didn't pay up they'd go to jail. I threatened with all kinds of things. I let my imagination run wild. I was very successful. She'd pay me threepence for each letter and sixpence if it was successful. I suppose Irish money was much more powerful than it is now; it would be [worth] about maybe thirty cents for each letter and then ninety cents if it was successful. . . .

Everyone said it was a horrible thing. Who would write a letter like that to their own class of people? A person like that should have their fingernails pulled out and be boiled in oil. . . . I was listening to all of this and I felt awful that I had to write these threatening letters. I felt so powerful, at the same time, that my letters were so effective.

But I made money—I was putting it away in the post office savings account—even to the extent where she'd give me money for stamps to mail those letters, and I would keep the money for the stamps and stick the letters under doors. All of this was going into the post office for my fare to America.

Well, she died. She used to send me out on Friday nights to the pub for a bottle of sherry, and [one night] when I came back, she was dead in the chair. She had her purse [with her], and I stole from her purse. . . . Her purse had dropped to the floor. I averted my eyes from her because I was terrified. But still the main thing in my life was to get to America. I think I would have robbed somebody's grave to go there. I had to get out of Ireland. I didn't report her death. I just walked away. Nobody knew. I used to go in the back door. Nobody knew who I was. So I got the fare to America.

I taught [in New York for] a total of close to thirty years—including substitute teaching. . . . I stood in front of those classes for over twenty-seven years talking, exhorting, evoking, and learning, mostly. . . .

MONGRIE GRAVEYARD IS WHERE we took my mother's ashes to be sprinkled. It's an old medieval abbey outside Limerick. She died in New York [in December of 1981], and we had her cremated. We took her back there. She used to say, "I want to be buried with my own people in Mongrie." She was a large woman. . . . I said, "Do you know the cost of transporting your body to Ireland?" We cremated her . . . and took her back with five or six days of grief and celebration.

It was a very strange occasion because . . . our wives were there and a group of friends. . . . I remember mostly our awkwardness. . . . Usually we're not caught short for words. But I think my brother Malachy and I felt a bit awkward on this occasion because we simply didn't know what to do. Usually you have a priest taking care of it. . . . We sprinkled the ashes. I'm the oldest son, so I was the chief mourner, I suppose, so I just started saying, "Hail Mary, full of grace, the Lord is with thee." And that was it. We blessed ourselves and climbed back over that gate again because [the graveyard is] a national shrine now and you can't get in. . . .

I HAVEN'T HAD TIME TO REFLECT on [my fame since my book was published]. I know people who are public because I used to hang around the Lion's Head Bar in New York. I knew Pete Hamill and people like that who'd been public for years and years and years. I'd see them come and go and I'd be on the periphery of that crowd. I was what they called in America "only a teacher." Only a teacher. They were journalists and writers and poets. I'm only a teacher. I was always on the periphery. In a sense, I was like my father, an outsider.

Now people look at me—oh, they look at me. It's like Ralph Ellison's book, *Invisible Man.* People don't see you until you write a book. I taught for twenty-seven years and nobody paid me a scrap of attention, then I write a book about slum life and I'm an expert on everything.

Rosa Lee Cunningham

by
LEON DASH

Rosa Lee Cunningham (1936–95) grew up in Washington, D.C., on the fringes of Capitol Hill, had her first child at fourteen—followed by seven more—and spent the last few years of her life addicted to heroin. Leon Dash was a staff reporter for The Washington Post *when he followed Rosa Lee and her family for four years. The result was a Pulitzer Prize–winning series that grew into his book* Rosa Lee: A Mother and Her Family in Urban America *(Basic Books, 1996). On November 10, 1996, Leon Dash discussed Rosa Lee's life on* Booknotes.

I'M A REPORTER with *The Washington Post* on the investigative desk. Rosa Lee Cunningham was a woman that I met in a D.C. jail in January 1988 and who I followed until her death from AIDS in July 1995. . . . I was interested in what's happening with the American underclass. I had read studies by the Urban Institute which said that the underclass has tripled in size in the United States since 1970. I was interested in the reasons . . . why this poverty—a very deep and distressful poverty, as well as criminal deviancy—was [moving] from one generation to the next. So I went into the D.C. jail, literally, in the summer of 1987 and interviewed, over an eighteen-month period, twenty men and twenty women inmates who fit the profile the Urban Institute had established of what constitutes an underclass family. In that process I also met Rosa Lee Cunningham. [She] had just come out of the most harrowing withdrawal from drug addiction when I met her in January of 1988. She had gone into the jail that previous October. She had been arrested at the corners of Fourteenth and W Streets Northwest selling heroin while babysitting three of her grandchildren. She was selling the heroin both for her addiction and to get enough money to feed her three grandchildren. The mother of the three children, her youngest daughter, also . . . was in jail on a drug arrest.

My first interview with Rosa Lee lasted over nine days, just to put her life together. She was then fifty-one. [We covered] . . . from her earliest childhood memory up to that point in her life, January of 1988. . . . She said to me, "I want you to tell my story, every part of it, because I'm hoping that other people who read it won't take the steps and take the path that I have taken." I said to her, "Well, I don't think the people who need to read your story for that reason will read this story. They'll be involved in their criminal lifestyles and their drug addictions and so on. They really won't be interested in reading your story." Her reaction was, "That's okay. You write it like I tell it." I said, "Fine. This is going to take some time." She said, "I don't care how much time it takes." . . .

When she came out in May of 1988, I began then to follow her outside prison. Over a period of time, she introduced me to all eight of her children and told them what I was doing and that she was participating, and she wanted them to participate. Initially, they were wary, but after a while, I just became to them a part of the family; a person who came in and out, regularly interacted with them, and chronicled their past and their present.

There were stolen goods passing in front of me, there were drug transactions going on around me. I watched them do drugs; I watched them smoke crack; I watched them shoot up with heroin. If I was going to be there, then I had to be part of all of that. . . .

Rosa Lee Cunningham was born in Washington, D.C., October 7, 1936. She was born a year after her parents and her grandparents arrived there. They were sharecroppers who came out of deep rural isolation in Northampton County in North Carolina, a section just north of the north bank of the Roanoke River. They had been on the Bishop and Powell plantation at least since they were emancipated as slaves in 1863. . . . The person that they were working for on the plantation lost the plantation because of the Depression. They ended up migrating to Washington looking for work and a better life.

She married when she was sixteen years old—she was pregnant with her third child—to a man named Alvin Cunningham. . . . Rosa Lee's mother told the man—he was then twenty-one—Albert Cunningham, that if he did not marry her, she would inform the police because Rosa Lee was underage. [In all,] she had eight children with six different men.

Rosa Lee lived in eighteen different places over her lifetime, twice in shelters for the homeless. She grew up in poverty—very deep poverty here in Washington—and never really got out of it. Her dwellings were either slum housing or public housing.

When [her daughter] Patty was eleven, Rosa Lee prostituted Patty. . . . A man who she knew as a regular customer came by and asked her, could he have sex with her daughter? Rosa Lee asked Patty would she be willing to have sex with this adult man. The man was in his forties and Patty was eleven years old. Patty agreed because her mother had asked her to. When Patty first told me about that, she felt that she was helping her mother bring income into the house because the man was willing to pay twice as much to have sex with her than to have sex with her mother. . . . it was somewhere between forty or fifty dollars to have sex with Patty; twenty to twenty-five dollars to have sex with Rosa Lee.

Patty had also, at this point, gone through three years of sexual abuse by two male relatives. She had been raped at age eight by a male relative who had continued to rape her. At the time the rapes began, he was fourteen; she was eight. Also, an adult male relative who was in his thirties raped Patty on a number of occasions.

ROSA LEE TAUGHT ALL OF HER CHILDREN to shoplift. Only two rejected that very early on as children, Alvin and Eric, the two sons who had never been involved in drugs or crime. . . . Alvin works as a stationmaster now on the [Washington] Metro rail system. . . . Eric works for the U.S. Park Service. Rosa Lee did a lot of stealing. She had her first sentence for stealing, nineteen days in a juvenile institution, when she was fifteen and pregnant with her second child. That did not stop her. She stole a lot. . . . [She went to jail,] both for stealing and for drug offenses, twelve times in her lifetime.

ROSA LEE HAD A LESBIAN RELATIONSHIP that began in 1972, when she moved into a federally subsidized apartment complex called Clifton Terrace. She met a young girl . . . who was eighteen years old, Lucky, and established a relationship. . . . Then Lucky moved in with her and her eight children and lived with her for three years. What I got out of that was Rosa Lee was very needy, emotionally needy. Any man or any woman who was willing to pay attention to her and give her the love and affection that she felt was missing in her life was welcome.

SHE GOT AIDS EITHER THROUGH PROSTITUTION or sharing needles with four of her children. Four of her eight children were drug-addicted, two daughters and two sons, in terms of intravenous drug abuse. One of the daughters also was involved in prostitution. The oldest son was involved in male prostitution—Bobby, who died of AIDS in 1994. She shared needles with all of them. . . .

She entered the hospital on April 18, and this is significant. It's the same day that there was a funeral for her fifteen-year-old grandson. He had been killed on April 11 in a drug shoot-out . . . that grew out of rivalry between two groups of boys, called crews, over the drug trade. . . .

That morning, I went to the funeral, Rico's funeral. . . . There wasn't a dry eye in the place. It was a very painful funeral. Everyone was upset, as you can imagine. I was upset. I had known this boy since he was eight, when he was a gregarious, open child. I had watched the transition into the criminal lifestyle he was involved in, and there wasn't anything to do to stop it. He wasn't listening to anyone. Now he was dead, and here he was in this casket.

When I went around the funeral home, I was looking for Rosa Lee. Someone told me, "Rosa Lee went into the hospital at four o'clock this morning, suffering from pneumonia. An ambulance took her." This was her about eighteenth hospitalization since I had known her for both AIDS-related illnesses and drug overdoses. I wasn't alarmed. . . . I had seen her just a couple of days before, and she seemed strong and healthy and as feisty as ever.

I went, after the funeral . . . to the office. By that time, the office was abuzz with a rumor that myself and Lucian Perkins had won a Pulitzer [for the eight-part series on Rosa Lee that had run in *The Washington Post* in September 1994]. . . . I felt ambivalent about the whole thing because I'd just come from Rico's funeral. . . . It was an odd day for me.

Right after all the celebration died down, I left and went over to Howard University Hospital and went up to the receptionist and said, "Which room is Rosa Lee Cunningham in?" The receptionist looked it up, said, "Oh, she's in intensive care." In intensive care? She had never been in intensive care. . . . She never left the hospital alive. . . . July 7, at seven-thirty in the morning, her son Eric called me at home and said, "Mama died at two-thirty this morning." . . . I went to the funeral July 15.

WHEN I TALK WITH COLLEAGUES and friends, a lot of people who were in my social circle, everyone assumes that middle-class values are universal. They're not. The middle class dominates American life and American culture, but our values are not universal—as is particularly shown with Rosa Lee's family. Her family lived by a different code, a different value system, a value system that said anything is acceptable for survival—even prostituting an eleven-year-old girl.

Lee Harvey Oswald

***

by
NORMAN MAILER

Lee Harvey Oswald (1939–63) was the accused assassin of President John F. Kennedy. He was murdered himself by Dallas nightclub owner Jack Ruby while in police custody. As a young man, Mr. Oswald defected to the Soviet Union, living in Minsk from 1959 to 1962. In this biography, Oswald's Tale: An American Mystery *(Random House, 1995), Norman Mailer focuses on Mr. Oswald's childhood and his years spent in the Soviet Union. Mr. Mailer appeared on* Booknotes *on June 25, 1995.*

I HAVE BEEN OBSESSED with Lee Harvey Oswald for more than thirty years. Had he [shot Kennedy]? Hadn't he done it? Was he part of a conspiracy?

I was very impressed with John F. Kennedy. For one thing, I realized that he was a man of many faces. When I saw him . . . I saw four or five faces on him. . . . At one point he looked like a professor—a comfortable . . . man of forty-five, even of fifty: he was gray at the edges; he had a gentle, intellectual face. Ten minutes later he could look like a movie star under the sun speaking to a press conference. His face kept changing.

When he was shot . . . I was in a restaurant with [writer] Norm Podhoretz, who used to be a great friend in the old days. We were on the middle East Side, East Fifties, in Manhattan. . . . The news came in, and I was very cynical. I was bitter at Kennedy at that point, for whatever reason. I said, "That shot just singed his scalp. He's not really hurt. He's just letting us all wait for an hour or two so we realize we love him and need him, but in fact there's nothing going on." An hour later he was dead. I realized that I had a great deal to learn about a great many things. You learn that over and over again, but that day I learned it dramatically.

THIS BOOK IS . . . AN INFORMAL BIOGRAPHY of Lee Harvey Oswald that starts in the middle [of his life]. The first half is about him at the age of nineteen, going into Russia and leaving Russia at the age of twenty-two. It's got a lot of new material about Oswald in Russia living in Minsk, getting married, having children there, trying to get along in the Soviet system, becoming disillusioned. . . .

[Oswald arrived in Russia on October 16, 1959, and] got to Minsk, [about 450 miles from Moscow]. He had arrived in Moscow as a tourist on a deluxe ticket. There was always a great mystery made about how he got into Russia; I think that mystery was overexaggerated, because in those days if you landed in Finland and you were willing to buy a deluxe ticket to get into Moscow, the Russian embassy in Finland would send you on quickly. They liked the idea of tourists coming in, giving dollars, and moving on. So he landed in Moscow.

He announced on the first or second day he was there to his tourist guide, whose name was Rimma, that he wished to become a Soviet citizen. He wanted to give up his American citizenship to become a Soviet citizen. She was very taken with this. She was intensely patriotic, as most young tourist girls were in those days, and she loved the idea. She said she would help him.

They quickly got nowhere. On the fifth day he was told he'd have to go home. Nobody was going to take him in, because to the Russians this [request] was extremely odd and unpleasant. The KGB was immediately brought in and they were asking, "Who is this man? Why is he coming? He's an ex-marine, and he wants to live among us. There's something wrong here."

In the beginning, I didn't believe that they could have been that indifferent and that cautious, but what you come to understand is that in Russia the key thing was not to make a mistake. If you were going to do your job, do it in such a way that you make no serious mistakes. Slowly, you'll get promoted over the years. Don't do anything bold because it could get you in terrible trouble; it could boomerang. They had the memory of all the Stalin years, after all. You never wanted to be someone who could be noticed. So, the idea that someone would give Oswald permission to stay in the country or give him citizenship, that had to go up to the very top.

There wasn't time to get it up to the very top in the first five days. . . . They ignored him. Then they decided "We'll send him back. Let him start in America and get admission here and all that, do it properly from the Russian embassy in Washington." At that point he made a suicide attempt.

The suicide attempt, we discovered as we interviewed the doctors, was a superficial attempt, a phony suicide attempt. He slashed one wrist, but he didn't slash it very deeply, not deeply enough to kill himself. They were not going to send back somebody who had just tried to commit suicide; it would have been a scandal in the international press, since America already had been full of notices about how this marine had defected. . . . They put him in a hotel in Moscow—the Metropole—and waited to decide what to do with him.

Months went by and before long . . . he went over to the American embassy and turned in his passport. He said that he wanted to take up Russian citizenship. That made the Russians even more suspicious, because they had bugs

planted in all the walls. He was yelling at the consul, Richard Snyder, "I want
to turn in my passport. I want to become a Russian citizen." Their attitude was
"Why is he yelling? If he knows anything at all, particularly if he's a CIA man,
he knows that we have bugs in the wall. Why is he doing all this to get our attention? It makes no sense at all." A man who seriously wanted to become a
Russian citizen would speak quietly at this point; he wouldn't yell. Yelling is a
way of indicating he's false. So given these permutations for the KGB, they just
debated and debated: "What do we do with him? It's possible he's sincere. . . ."
Don't forget, this is still 1959, early 1960. In those days, they had much more
optimism about what was going to happen to their system.

They felt that things would improve, and they'd end up with a fine system;
eventually the whole world might be Communist. In those days, they didn't see
themselves as a hopeless, dwindling empire. They thought it would be terrible
if they didn't accept him, if he was sincere; but if he was not sincere, what
should they do with him? . . .

They said, ". . . From our point of view, we don't want to take any overt action. We are tempted to, but we won't. So we just observe him. The next question is where do we observe him? Moscow's a dangerous city. . . . He can get
into trouble. We can have a scandal. He can commit suicide. . . . Let's send him
to Minsk. That's a quiet city where the level of living is pretty good for us."

"We have very good KGB [in Minsk] because they're used to doing all sorts
of border investigations with English spies coming in, American spies coming
in, people crossing the border in various ways. . . . We'll send him there, and
we'll observe him in Minsk." They did; for the next two years, they observed
him, and often were bored with him. He led a very quiet life. But occasionally
they had great shocks because at one point he married a young girl, Marina,
who was the niece . . . of a colonel in the MVD, which is to the KGB roughly
what the FBI is to the CIA.

Marina was a year younger than him, and at that point when they got married he was twenty-one going on twenty-two. They were married in April of
1961. His birthday was in October, so he was not yet twenty-two.

She had extraordinary blue eyes, absolutely beautiful; they looked like dia-
monds. That was always her feature. She was a very good-looking young girl,
quite attractive. . . . She's had a tough life, so you might say [today that] some
of that shows. She's very small, thin, suffused with big guilt, as Russians are.

OSWALD USED HIS WITS [to get out of Russia]. He was very resourceful. . . .
He had to fight the Russian bureaucracy and the American State Department
bureaucracy. He finally ended up making it so uncomfortable and so unpleasant for each bureaucracy that each one said, "Let's get rid of this problem." The
only way to solve certain impasses with a bureaucracy is that you become so intolerable that the people of the bureaucracy say, "Isn't there some way we can

pass this indigestible morsel through our system?" He succeeded in doing that in both places. People always think that it was very mysterious that he got out and came back, but in fact it wasn't. He just wore out two bureaucracies. . . .

PRESIDENT KENNEDY WAS ASSASSINATED when Oswald was twenty-four years old. There are two halves to the conclusion. Originally, I was going to do a book about Oswald in Minsk—in fact, that was the working title—but by the time I finished . . . I felt that I'd learned a lot about him. I had some sense of what he was like in a room. He was like a character in a novel to me, but I had no idea at all about whether he was innocent or guilty. . . . He seems innocent because most of the Russians saw him as rather passive and gentle, particularly the ones in Minsk—not a fellow to do big things.

After the assassination, very few of the Russians believed he'd done it, maybe a third of them at most. Most of them felt it was an American plot and that they used him because he had lived in the Soviet Union.

I felt unsatisfied with what I'd learned and I thought I'd write a hundred-page epilogue about coming back to America. That hundred-page epilogue became a four-hundred-page second volume. As I got into it, I discovered the Warren Commission report had endless uses . . . what accumulated [was] a huge amount of material. There's very little interpretation; very few leads were followed up. I speak of its value as an investigative force as equal to a dead whale decomposing on a beach. But there was wonderful material in the Warren report. You could go through and find all kinds of short stories and extraordinary little moments.

THE CONCLUSION I REACH is that he probably did it. I felt there was a 75-percent certainty that it was a lone gunman, but I hedge about it with a great many qualifications, the first of which was that if I'd been a lawyer I could have gotten him off. Any good lawyer could have gotten him off, because there was so much confusion in the evidence. It's so very hard to be able to state definitively that he did it.

There's an awful lot of evidence that would have him doing it, but there's an awful lot that wouldn't. There are always the great questions: How did he get from the sixth floor to the second floor without breathing heavily in sixty seconds? How could he, who was a bad shot, have shot so successfully and skillfully? How could that magic bullet have done what it did? These questions, I don't pretend to answer. If I'd been a lawyer, as I say, I could have used those questions to win over a jury. I felt finally that he did it because it was the logic of his life, but you have to read the book to know what I'm talking about.

I WANT PEOPLE TO THINK about the cold war and what a tragicomedy it was as personified by the life of this one man who really attempted to deal with the cold war. He went over to the Soviet Union in protest of what was going on in America. He got dissatisfied with the Soviet Union. He came back to America. Now he was dissatisfied with both countries. He lived at the bottom, and he saw the ironies of both countries and the way that there was just no need for that cold war. They were both horrible systems as far as he was concerned. I want people to ponder that.

John Lewis

by
JOHN LEWIS

John Lewis (b. 1940) became involved in the civil rights movement while he was in college, chairing the Student Nonviolent Coordinating Committee (SNCC), taking part in the "Freedom Rides" and addressing the 1963 civil rights March on Washington. On July 12, 1998, John Lewis, now a member of Congress who represents Georgia's Fifth District, appeared on Booknotes *to talk about* Walking with the Wind: A Memoir of the Movement, *published in 1998 by Simon and Schuster.*

I GREW UP IN SOUTHEAST ALABAMA on a farm in an area called Carter's Quarters, in the heart of Pike County, near a little place called Troy. One day a bad storm came up, and I was in this old tin-roof house and the wind started blowing. My aunt suggested that we clasp hands. We started walking with the wind. One part of the house would lift up, and we'd try to hold it down with our tiny bodies—my first cousins and my aunt. The other side would blow and try to lift up, and we would move to that side. In America, during the past few years, the wind has been blowing. I think I've been walking with the wind, trying to hold the American house together, keep it from being divided, keep it from coming apart.

THE CIVIL RIGHTS MOVEMENT . . . started in 1955 when Rosa Parks took a seat on a bus in Montgomery, Alabama, and refused to get up and give her seat to a white gentleman. She was arrested and went to jail. Martin Luther King, Jr., emerged as a leader [of the movement].

I remember that week so well when the bus boycott started. I was fifteen years old, in the tenth grade. What Martin Luther King, Jr., and the people in Montgomery did inspired me to find a way to get involved in the civil rights movement. It gave me a way out. It taught me how to stand up to segregation and racial discrimination. I wanted to meet Dr. King.

A few years later when I finished high school, I wrote Dr. King a letter. Dr. King wrote me back and invited me to come to Montgomery. . . . I boarded a bus and traveled from Troy to Montgomery. A young black lawyer who had been a lawyer for Rosa Parks and Dr. King met me at the Greyhound bus station and drove me to the First Baptist Church in Montgomery, which was pastored by Reverend Ralph Abernathy. They ushered me into the pastor's study and introduced me to Martin Luther King, Jr. That was my entrance into the civil rights movement.

When I first met him I was scared. I was nervous to be standing in the presence of Martin Luther King, Jr. When he said to me, "Are you John Lewis, the boy from Troy?" I said, "Yes, I'm John Robert Lewis." I gave my whole name. From that moment on, we hit if off very well.

I WENT TO SCHOOL in Nashville, traveling there by Greyhound bus, in September 1957. I was seventeen years old when I left Pike County. I had an uncle who saw that I wanted to get an education—I was the first one in my family to go to college. This uncle bought me a footlocker and gave me a hundred-dollar bill.

I went to a little school called American Baptist Theological Seminary, the college of the Bible. I was studying to become a minister. It was a big city, the biggest place I ever lived. I had my own bed for the first time and my own room for the first time. As a child, with six brothers and three sisters, I had to share a bed with my brothers, many of us in the same room. But going off to school, I had a degree of independence. I was on my own. I think I grew up overnight.

In 1957, the South was still a very segregated place. When I traveled to Montgomery or to Birmingham or to Nashville or to Atlanta I saw signs that said "White Men," "Colored Men." "White Women," "Colored Women." "White Waiting," "Colored Waiting." Segregation was the order of the day. There was a tremendous amount of fear in the South during those years.

This was the period of Little Rock Central High [in Arkansas]. This was after the Montgomery bus boycott. You couldn't go into a store and buy something like a book or buy clothing and then go to the lunch counter or go to a restaurant. You couldn't go into some drugstores and get a prescription filled or buy toothpaste or soap and then try to take a seat at a lunch counter. You would be denied service. You would be arrested. You would be jailed.

WHEN I GOT ARRESTED the first time back in 1960, I had been told over and over again, "Don't get in trouble. Don't go to jail. Don't break the law." That's what my grandfather and my great-grandfather, my mother, my father told me. It was not the thing to do. But when I was arrested and went to jail for the first time, I felt free. I felt liberated.

Forty days is the longest period I spent in jail. To be exact, it was thirty-seven days. That was in Mississippi. Parchman Farm, the state penitentiary of

Mississippi. I will never forget what happened in Parchman Farm during the Freedom Ride [a cross-country campaign to end segregation of bus terminals].

We were arrested in Jackson at the Greyhound bus station. We tried to use the so-called white waiting room, the so-called white restroom facilities, the so-called white restaurant. It was May of 1961. There was a police captain there. He became known as Captain Ray. The moment that you started in, Captain Ray would say, "Move on." Before you could even move, he would say, "You're under arrest." He literally put us in a paddy wagon and took us to jail. We filled the city jail in Jackson. We filled the Hinds County jail in Jackson. When all of these facilities became full, they decided to take us to Parchman Farm.

A guy told us . . . to sing our freedom songs. He said, "We have niggers here that will eat you up." He was talking about black justice. He said, "They will eat you. They will beat you up." He brought us into a long hall and told us to take off our clothes. We stood there with all our clothing off. These guys had their rifles drawn on us . . . but I wasn't afraid. I was really concerned about what was about to happen. They led us in twos to take showers. If you had a beard, mustache, any facial hair, you had to cut it off. There were no mirrors for you to look in; you just had a razor. While you were standing there, taking your shower, the guy still had this rifle drawn on you.

They led us, after the shower was over, in twos into a cell with a bunk bed, a commode, and a tiny face bowl. We stayed there nude for, maybe, two hours. Then they brought us pairs of [state-issued] undershorts and T-shirts. That's what we kept on our entire stay there.

They flooded the cells with water; they cut off the air conditioner. It was very, very hot. You're talking about May and June in Mississippi.

They tried to dehumanize us. They tried to destroy our sense of dignity and self-worth. They tried to send a message to other people who were joining the Freedom Ride from all across the country. They wanted that message to get out—for other people not to come to Mississippi.

DURING THE HEIGHT of the movement, I was beaten two times. [Once was during] these Freedom Rides in May of 1961, at the Greyhound bus station in Montgomery. I was hit in the head and left lying, bleeding and unconscious, at the bus station.

The next occurred on March 7, 1965, when we attempted to march from Selma to Montgomery to dramatize to the nation that people wanted the right to register and vote. I was one of the leaders of that effort. We walked through the streets of Selma in an orderly, peaceful, nonviolent fashion. It was a silent march; no one saying a word. We got to the apex of the bridge crossing the Alabama River. We saw a sea of Alabama state troopers in blue. And we continued to walk.

We came within hearing distance of the state troopers and a man identified himself, saying, "I'm Major John Cloud of the Alabama State Troopers. This is an unlawful march, and it will not be allowed to continue. I give you three minutes to disperse and return to your church." We continued to walk. After about a minute and a half, Major Cloud said, "Troopers, advance." You saw these men putting on their gas masks. They came forward, beating us with nightsticks and bullwhips, using tear gas. That Sunday became known as "Bloody Sunday." I had a concussion and was hospitalized.

IN THE FAMOUS 1963 March on Washington . . . I tried to prepare a speech that represented the feelings, the attitudes of the people in the organization that I represented—the Student Nonviolent Coordinating Committee—and the people that we were working with all across the South.

The original idea of the March on Washington was not to support a particular piece of civil rights legislation; it was a march for jobs and freedom. President Kennedy had proposed a piece of legislation that said if you had a sixth-grade education, you should be considered literate and be able to register to vote. Those of us in the Student Nonviolent Coordinating Committee felt that it was too little; that it just didn't go far enough. We felt that the only qualifications for being able to register to vote in the South should be age and residence.

In that March on Washington speech, I said, "One man, one vote is the African cry. It is ours, too. It must be ours." I went on to say that there was not anything in that proposed legislation that would protect people involved in peaceful nonviolent protests. I tried to suggest that the party of [John] Kennedy was the party of [James] Eastland. This was a reference to Senator Eastland, who was the chair of the Judiciary Committee from the state of Mississippi. I said the party of Nelson Rockefeller was the party of Barry Goldwater. Where was our party?

I was twenty-three years old on that day—August 28, 1963—when I delivered the speech at the steps of the Lincoln Memorial. [Later,] we left the Lincoln Memorial and went to the White House and had a meeting with President Kennedy. That was my last time seeing President Kennedy alive. He invited us all in, and we had tea and cookies and orange juice with him. He stood and congratulated each one of us. He was very, very pleased that the march went off so well.

The Student Nonviolent Coordinating Committee I chaired at the time was very involved. These were young people, black and white young people, working all across the South—some of the bravest and most courageous young men and women. They were literally putting their bodies on the line.

It was very integrated. I used to think that during those early years of SNCC the only real and true integration that existed in America was within the movement itself. It was the essence of what Martin Luther King, Jr., would call "the beloved community on interracial democracy."

We didn't think about race and color during those early years. These were people, black and white, that were willing . . . to go to jail together. Some of the young people died together. During the Mississippi Summer Project in 1964, three young men—Andy Goodman, Mickey Schwerner, and James Chaney—were working to get people to register to vote. They went out to investigate the burning of a black church that was being used for a voter registration workshop. These three young men were arrested, taken to jail, taken out of jail later that night, beaten, shot, and killed. When someone is struggling and going to jail with you, dying with you, you don't think about race. You forget about race. That was what was so beautiful about those days, when things were so simple.

I FIRST MET BOBBY KENNEDY in the spring of 1963 [when] he was attorney general. Bobby Kennedy was an unbelievable person as attorney general. I got to know him very well. . . . I remember him saying to me once in July of 1963, "John, I now understand. These young people, the students, have educated me. They have taught me a lesson." This man really did believe. He became convinced and committed. He believed deeply in his soul, in his gut, in the causes of civil rights and social justice.

In March of 1968, when he announced that he would seek the Democratic nomination for the presidency, I sent him a telegram. I was in Jackson, Mississippi, and said, "Senator Kennedy, I want to help. I want to volunteer. I want to be part of your campaign." He asked some of his people to call me and they invited me to go to Indianapolis. I went there to work on voter registration, organizing mass rallies on behalf of the Kennedy campaign.

I was with Bobby Kennedy the night of April 4, 1968, when we heard that Dr. King had been shot. . . . Robert Kennedy came and spoke to the crowd we had organized and said that Dr. King had been assassinated. I will never forget that evening.

Robert Kennedy . . . said, "I have some bad news tonight. Martin Luther King, Jr., was assassinated in Memphis, Tennessee." People cried. Some people dropped to their knees. Robert Kennedy went on. . . . He urged people not to turn to violence, not to get lost in a sea of despair. We left the rally and went back to the local hotel, where we all went to his room. He laid across the bed. We were all sitting down. We all cried there together.

I said to myself during the week leading up to Dr. King's funeral, "Well, we still have Bobby Kennedy." . . . I went to Atlanta for the funeral and then got very much involved in the campaign. I went out to Oregon, campaigned for Kennedy, introduced him at a college rally out there. Then I went on to California. I just knew he was going to win the Democratic nomination. We saw hundreds and thousands of people filling the streets of Los Angeles, [watching] the motorcade, pulling for Robert Kennedy.

When Bobby Kennedy was shot, I was in his room on the fifth floor of the Ambassador Hotel. I had spoken with him just a few minutes earlier. He joked with me that evening: "John, you let me down tonight. More Mexican-American voters turned out and voted for me than Negroes." He suggested that we wait for him and that he would be back in fifteen minutes.

I was in his room with Teddy White, the writer, and several other media people, members of his family, and others. We saw the announcement—it was a bulletin saying that Senator Kennedy had been shot. We all dropped to our knees. I cried, like so many other people.

I wanted to get out of L.A. that night. I just wanted to leave, to get to Atlanta. The next morning, I boarded a plane and flew from Los Angeles to Atlanta. I cried all the way. This was June 6, and as we flew across the mountains in Colorado, I could still see the snow on the mountains.

A day or so later, the family invited me to come to New York for the funeral. I went there the night before and stood as one of the honor guards with Reverend Abernathy. . . . After the funeral, I boarded the funeral train and traveled from New York. All along the way, you saw people with handmade signs saying "We love you, Bobby." "Good-bye, Bobby." Hundreds and thousands of people. In some way, I didn't want that train to stop in Washington. I wanted it to keep on going. But we knew this was the end. Bobby Kennedy represented so much hope and optimism, the same way that Martin Luther King, Jr., did.

IN 1986, THERE WAS AN OPEN SEAT in Georgia's Fifth Congressional District. [State senator and fellow activist] Julian Bond and I both wanted to go to Congress. I remember very well, back in October 1985, we had lunch together at a local restaurant in Atlanta. Julian called me "Mr. Chairman" because I had been chair of the Student Nonviolent Coordinating Committee. He said, "Mr. Chairman, what are you going to do?" I said, "I'm running for Congress." I said, "Senator, what are you going to do?" He said, "I'm running for Congress." I think it was the shortest lunch we ever had together.

In the first election, the primary, he received 47 percent of the vote, and I got only 35 percent. There were several other candidates. We had a runoff. In three weeks, I went up seventeen points, and he went up one point. I got out there and I worked. He is very good. The mistake that Julian made was he challenged me to debate him. He was already the front-runner and this put me on the same level with him. . . . I think the people in the district saw me out there working day in and day out. I won 52 percent and he got 48 percent.

I BELIEVE IN NONVIOLENCE as a way of life, not just as a means, not just as a technique. . . . When you accept nonviolence as a way of life, then everything that you do and everything that you say is governed by that principle. When I speak of revolution, I'm talking about a revolution of values, a revolution of ideas. That revolution must take place in the hearts, in the minds, in the souls of people—not a revolution in the streets.

I believe you cannot separate means and ends. If you're striving to create the beloved community, an open society, then the method must be one of love, of peace.

I believe the great majority of the people of the world want to live in a world community at peace with itself. I think it is the desire of humankind not to go down that violent path. We're seeing what violence will do. There have been too many killings. It leads to chaos, not to the essence of community, not to the building of a house that is together.

Newt Gingrich

by
ELEANOR CLIFT AND TOM BRAZAITIS
NEWT GINGRICH

A former history professor from Georgia, Newt Gingrich (b. 1943) was first elected to the House of Representatives in 1978. He led a group of members called "The Conservative Opportunity Society" and helped Republicans win control of the House for the first time in forty years. In January 1995, he was elected House Speaker, a position he held for four years. He resigned following disappointing GOP returns in the 1998 election. On July 23, 1995, Mr. Gingrich was a Booknotes *guest, discussing his book* To Renew America *(Harper-Collins, 1995). Reporters Eleanor Clift and Tom Brazaitis appeared on August 25, 1996, to discuss* War Without Bloodshed *(Scribner, 1996), which chronicled Newt Gingrich's rise to power.*

Eleanor Clift and Tom Brazaitis

War Without Bloodshed: The Art of Politics

WAR WITHOUT BLOODSHED came to us from Newt Gingrich, the Speaker of the House. . . . He got it from Chairman Mao Tse-tung, who said, "Politics is war without bloodshed and war is politics with bloodshed." Some people would say the way Newt Gingrich practices politics there's plenty of bloodshed, but it's metaphorical blood.

I remember in early 1994, March, we took a walk with him at six in the morning around the Washington monuments, and it was Tom who asked him how he was preparing to take over the minority leadership of his party. He stopped and said, "Minority leadership?" He said, "That's like preparing to be vice president. I'm going to be Speaker." And we thought, "Of course. Sure, buddy." But he turned out to be right. What we do [in our book] is chart his seventeen-year rise to power, and how he accomplished that.

WHEN NEWT GINGRICH was first running for Congress, one of the stops he made was to come to Washington, to meet with [conservative activist] Paul Weyrich, to try to persuade him to help finance his congressional campaign, to use his influence. Weyrich gave him a lot of advice, including "If you want to make a name for yourself, go after some of the big-name Democrats and throw some mud." He didn't say it in those exact terms, but that's what it amounted to. Newt Gingrich went after Speaker Jim Wright. It was there that he earned his reputation as a tough customer in Washington. So Weyrich's advice was good.

THERE'S ONE THING that separated Gingrich from the other Republicans who had been in the minority a long time. After all, with over forty years [of Republican minority status] you can serve a lot of time. You can be there twenty of those forty years and get used to the minority. Well, he wasn't used to it, and he wasn't about to get used to it. So he kept telling them, "Don't think like losers. Don't get up in the morning and look in the mirror and say, 'I'm a loser.' "

Just a few months after Gingrich had been in Washington, he called all the leaders of the party together and chewed them out for not thinking like winners. He said at one point, "I wish I'd brought the movie *Patton* along, so I could screen it so you can see what a real army is like."

They came to Newt's office, which was kind of unusual, and they had to take out all the furniture that he had in there and put in suitable furniture for a meeting. These leaders, reluctantly as I recall, showed up late, as a way to show Gingrich—"Well, we're here, but we're not all that persuaded." But it wasn't long before he did start to persuade people. He got the younger members of Congress and some of the more aggressive ones to be the core of his team. However, he never did quite win over [Republican House leader] Bob Michel and the older gentry of the Republican party.

ANYBODY WHO HAS DEALT with Newt Gingrich over the years understands that he throws out a million ideas, but his follow-through is not great. . . . This goes back to the early 1980s, soon after Gingrich arrived in Washington in 1978. . . . He was just full of ideas about how to take over the House and so forth. He would throw all these ideas out. But you can only marshal the troops to do so much. Paul Weyrich and others got tired of him getting them to march up the hill, and then nobody knew what to do next. We saw a little bit of that in Newt Gingrich's approach after taking over the Congress. Plan A was great: Get the president to cave on the budget. However, when plan A didn't work, [Newt Gingrich had] no plan B.

Newt Gingrich

To Renew America

EVERY ONCE IN A WHILE, you'll see somebody making some reference to me being a typical [southern conservative], based on my roots. [But] I'm an army brat—born in Pennsylvania—and I grew up all over the world, so I find interesting the assumptions people project onto you about how things must work.

I was first exposed to politics when I was a kid going to see African movies on a summer afternoon. When I came out of the matinee, there was a sign next to the theater that said "City Hall." I was all pumped up about seeing animals and seeing these great African films, and I thought, We ought to have a zoo. So for some reason—I think this is partly my grandmother, who was a very devout Lutheran and pounded away at this idea of having to do your duty—I walked through the alley and went to city hall. . . . I went upstairs to the Parks Department, which is where I was sent by the receptionist. I think I was nine at the time, maybe ten. The head of the Parks Department was gone. I got to see the civil servant who was his deputy, who was in his early sixties. It turned out he had dated my grandmother, so he took me in and showed me . . . the records from before World War II when they had a zoo in Harrisburg. He talked to me about what they fed the lions. . . . It was a wonderful adventure for a little kid. He said, "What you have to do is you come back next Tuesday and come to the city council meeting and tell them why we need a zoo."

He called my mother and said he was sending me home in a cab and not to worry about the fact that I hadn't been on the bus. This was a much simpler and safer world, obviously. I went home and my mother said, "Well, if you need to go back"—my mother was very supportive of this stuff—"to city council, I guess you have to go to city council."

The following Tuesday, I came wandering in. I remember vividly the couple ahead of me complaining about garbage being dumped near their house. Then it was my turn. I got up and I talked about why Harrisburg needed a zoo. The local reporter had nothing to write that day, so the next day, here was this nice article about me talking [to the city council]. If you're a little kid, and here's this whole article about what you just did at the city council, you're hooked. There was no turning back—at least in terms of some form of public life and public involvement.

I LOST [MY FIRST TWO] CONGRESSIONAL BIDS: in 1974 and 1976. I won in 1978. In December of 1978, I had not even been sworn in when Guy [Vander-Jagt, chairman of the National Republican Congressional Committee,] made me chairman of its planning committee. I helped . . . plan the 1980 campaign. So, very early in my career, I was already being allowed to be involved directly in designing national campaigns. Guy was just always fabulously supportive. I would not have been elected Speaker without Guy VanderJagt's help.

TOM MURPHY IS A VERY POWERFUL, very successful politician who spent twenty-six years as Speaker [of the Georgia House]—so far, the longest-serving Speaker in the country. In December of 1978 . . . Murphy gave me advice that, ultimately, helped me become Speaker [of the U.S. House]. He told me how he became Speaker; how he sat on the back rail and he helped people. When people needed an amendment written, he helped them write it. When they needed somebody to help them speak for something, he—over the years—consciously helped. Then when there was a vacancy, he was the natural person to rise.

I often thought all through the 1980s of Murphy's advice, which he gave to a freshman congressman as an act of generosity. But, because I was a partisan Republican and he was a partisan Democrat, it really got to him that I was his congressman. . . . It drove him nuts. He gradually went to work on trying to beat me. He recruited candidates, raised money. Finally, he gerrymandered my district. It was a very sincere effort. I don't think it was a major part of his career, but he paid a fair amount of attention to trying to knock me out.

ONE THING I'VE LEARNED [about Washington] is that there is a press corps that is probably a couple thousand people who go to each other's cocktail parties, hang out with each other, have lunch with each other, talk with each other, ride on the press bus with each other. Over time, they shape their own collective views. There have been all sorts of studies of this. They consistently vote to the left of Clinton. They are consistently far more liberal than the country at large. Their values are far more left [-leaning] than the country at large.

If you want to get a lot of press coverage—if you're a Republican—[I learned that you should] attack another Republican and you'll be described instantly by all sorts of elite media as a wise, sophisticated, thoughtful person. Whereas if you stay with the party, you'll remain anonymous. So in the short run, there's a certain payoff in the media to being willing to break with your party.

JOE GAYLORD IS A REMARKABLE STUDENT of American politics. . . . [He was the director of the National Republican Campaign Committee] and was in charge of designing the 1984, 1986, and 1988 campaigns. . . . He is one of my closest personal friends. In June of 1994, he wrote a paper [estimating the outcome of the November congressional elections]. . . . In September we got on an airplane. We were going to have a planning meeting. I said, "Are we planning for Speaker or for minority leader?" He said very bluntly, "You better be planning for Speaker because that's what you're going to be." The other two people on the plane—Steve Hanser and my chief of staff, Dan Meyer—we all three stared at him because he said it so flatly. . . . And we said, "Okay, smart aleck."

ABOUT TWO O'CLOCK IN THE MORNING [on election night, 1994], we all had enormous adrenaline, as you can imagine. We had just won control [of the House for the first time since 1954]. . . . About twenty-five of us sat around and chatted for an hour. I said, "What do you think of what you've seen so far?" The number-one concern that four or five people raised from having watched me do interviews that night was . . . "Don't get lured into this idea that you now have to grow into being acceptable to the Georgetown set." "We want you. You were elected because the country wants a more conservative Congress. Make sure you stick with what you believe in. . . ."

The job of Speaker of the House, teacher, leader of the revolution, writer—that's a different job than the job of back-bench, bomb-throwing Republican whip. So what does the Speaker's job require? It's not about "How should Newt do a better hairdo?" but "What does the new job require?" And "How can you learn the new job?" I think that is what matters.

To HAVE MY MOTHER, father, my wife, my mother-in-law, and all of our various relatives and our nieces and nephews [in the House gallery on my first day as Speaker]—I don't think I had ever, at a human level, had a notion of what it would be like to stand there. Somehow, being Speaker was an abstract [concept]; it would be a good thing to do and you knew other guys did it. But to stand at the center of the House chamber and realize it was you was much more powerful, much more emotional. I don't think I'd ever, inside myself, realized what it would be like to actually be in that position.

THE GREAT DEPRESSION, under Hoover and Franklin Roosevelt, left us with a centralized bureaucracy dominated by Washington. But I wouldn't criticize all the programs Roosevelt brought in. Social Security's been an enormous success in its own right. There are other things he did that were amazing. If you went back and looked at [his administration], you'd say, "Yeah. We should do that." The creation of the national park in Tennessee; the creation of the Tennessee Valley Authority. There are areas of activist behavior. Things that were right in the 1930s may be wrong in the 1990s, but if you take what he tried to accomplish between saving democracy at home and then saving democracy abroad in World War II, I think he is the most remarkable politician of the twentieth century.

That doesn't mean I wouldn't have, in many ways, opposed him in that period as a Republican. It doesn't mean I wouldn't have raised questions. But anybody who wants to study how a democracy achieves things ought to start with FDR, because he is the most sophisticated, most complex leader that we had in this century. He accomplished a great deal. You don't have to agree with all of it to say, "Boy, that was a great accomplishment." He was truly a remarkable figure.

WHAT [REPUBLICANS] DO that is helpful is shrink the size of government. We're going to have a smaller government. We're going to have less money to give away. There is going to be less pork out there. So at least at the margins, we begin to create an environment where you have more money in your take-home pay, you get less money from the bureaucrat, and I, as a politician, have less to give you. That puts me in an odd position—[columnist] George Will described it as "negative ambition." He said, "These guys all have this negative ambition of giving up power so that people back home have to do more on their own." That's different from a liberal Democrat standpoint, in which building a big bureaucracy to give away goodies was a legitimate use of government.

ANY OF US WHO HAVE BECOME SUCCESSFUL and have large institutions that depend on us have to learn some new habits. You can't be the same person. . . . It's a different job. Eisenhower learned a great thing. Fox Conner, who had been John Pershing's chief of staff in Europe in World War I, taught Eisenhower in the 1920s: "Always take your job seriously—never yourself." It's a wonderful admonition to people who are growing and trying to do things.

Bill Clinton

by
DAVID MARANISS
ROGER SIMON

The accounts of two veteran political journalists make up this view of Bill Clinton (b. 1946), forty-second president of the United States. The story of Mr. Clinton's early years through his 1991 announcement for the presidency comes from Pulitzer Prize–winning journalist David Maraniss whose First in His Class *was published by Simon and Schuster in 1995. Mr. Maraniss was interviewed on* Booknotes *on May 7, 1995. On February 2, 1998, a later view of Bill Clinton was offered by columnist Roger Simon, who analyzed the 1996 presidential campaign in* Show Time *(Times Books, 1998).*

David Maraniss

First in His Class

BILL CLINTON'S EARLY CHILDHOOD . . . is probably the least known part of his life and the part I had the most frustration trying to recreate—starting with his birth and up through his first ten years, dealing first with a young man without a father and then an alcoholic stepfather. . . . I really don't know what it was like for young Bill Clinton to be in that household.

Essentially, he had two mothers. His own mother, Virginia, had left Hope [Arkansas] when he was less than two to go down to New Orleans to study to be a nurse-anesthetist. He lived with his "Mammaw" Cassidy, who was a very rigid character. Bill Clinton is such a contrast of people; he has a certain discipline, and yet he's very undisciplined. His discipline comes from that grandmother, who would wake him at a specific hour, whether he was ready to awake himself or not, and fed him constantly on a pattern. So he had two mothers, one mother who was sort of rebelling against the life in Hope and wanted to get away from it, and this grandmother who was teaching him the discipline of that time and place.

His grandparents didn't have a lot of money, but they weren't poor by Hope's standards. They certainly weren't rich. His grandfather never cared about money, but he did run a store and live in a nice white house. Roger Clinton, his stepfather, was terrible with money and was always losing it—wasting it on alcohol and women and gambling. Roger Clinton's brother, Raymond Clinton, was a wealthy auto dealer in Hot Springs and belonged to a country club. Young Bill Clinton had a car in high school and played golf at a country club. So I wouldn't say that's poverty. I think there's a little bit of myth there.

VIRGINIA'S . . . FIRST HUSBAND, Bill Blythe, . . . is Bill Clinton's biological father, most likely. It's a very sensitive subject. But in the book you'll notice that the time when Bill Blythe got out of the military in World War II does not quite correspond with the point where Virginia, Bill's mother, always claimed that he got out of the military. So there's some question about when Bill Clinton was conceived.

Bill Blythe had been married at least four times before he met Virginia Cassidy. She knew about none of those marriages. It's possible that there were one or two others. It was hard for me to trace them out throughout the small courthouses of the South, but there are several others.

Virginia married Bill Blythe, and she married Roger Clinton, then she married Jeff Dwire, and then she married Dick Kelley. She'd been married to four men, but five times. She married Roger Clinton twice. Roger Clinton married Virginia when Bill Clinton, President Clinton, was four years old. They divorced when President Clinton was fifteen, but only for three months. Then Virginia felt sorry for him. She didn't love him anymore; he was an alcoholic who had abused her. The divorce records are full of [incidents]. One time he took her high heels and beat her on the head with the heels. It was not a comfortable marriage, but she remarried him after only three months of divorce because she felt sorry for him.

BILL CLINTON LEFT ARKANSAS when he was seventeen years old, went to the East Coast, and was away for nine years, dealing with a totally different culture. He was the southern Baptist at Georgetown [university, which was] full of upper-middle-class Catholic kids from the East Coast. The sons and daughters of presidents of El Salvador and Saudi Arabia and the Philippines were in his class. Unlike so many of the kids of that era who would try to forget their pasts, Clinton used that past almost as a defense mechanism. Rather than being embarrassed about coming from a small town, he played it up.

He was awarded a Rhodes Scholarship during the Vietnam War. . . . About half of the thirty-two Rhodes Scholars went to England their first year with sort of unofficial but clear deferments that they didn't deserve. [President] Johnson had just eliminated graduate school deferments, but most of the local draft boards considered these guys local heroes, and they didn't want them to get drafted right when they'd won this great prestigious honor. . . . Finally, in the spring of his first year, Clinton got his draft notice. He went back to Arkansas that summer of 1969 in agony trying to figure out what to do.

He didn't want to fight in Vietnam. He was against the war. Who knows whether he was afraid of dying, but I think most young men are. There's a whole mixture of feelings he was going through. He wanted to be in politics. He believed in the established way. He was trying to figure it out, and he eventually manipulated his way into an ROTC post that he never served in and went back to England feeling guilty.

In 1974, at the age of . . . twenty-seven, he ran for Congress in Fayetteville, Arkansas. He had just moved back from Yale Law School to be an assistant professor at the University of Arkansas in Fayetteville. [He ran] against John Paul Hammerschmidt. [It was] his first race, which he did well in but lost.

IN ALMOST EVERY ERA of his life, there's at least one story that has become mythologized. Sometimes it's totally innocuous, and it's just probably bad memories. . . . Sometimes there was definite psychological or political reason for the mythologizing. For instance . . . one of the myths that Bill Clinton would tell was about how he accidentally got his job as a professor at the University of Arkansas. He says he was just driving back from Yale Law School and stopped at the side of the road on the interstate, called the dean, and got the job.

In fact, he had tried to get the job for many months and had gone through the normal patterns of using friends and contacts to get that job. That myth was established by Clinton because he was going back to a place that all his Yale Law School friends thought he was crazy to go to. . . . The reason was that he was going back to run for Congress. He had worked so hard to get hired as a professor when he had not much interest in being a professor. That's why he would create this myth that it was just sort of a fluke.

His whole life has a measure of calculation in it that he has tried to diminish for a lot of reasons, one of which is that raw political ambition in America is often seen as a bad thing. You would never say that about someone who wanted to grow up and become the best ice skater in the world or the best pianist, but if you wanted to become president at an early age, people would see that as a negative. So, he always wanted to couch that, even though he had that burning desire in him.

Part of the way to temper that [ambition] was to make it look like a lot of those things happened by accident. . . . His handshake with John Kennedy in 1963 [is depicted as] the iconic transfer of ambition from a president to a future president. . . . That was no accident, that handshake. He was the one on the bus ride who kept asking the chaperon whether they could get pictures taken, and once the bus got to the White House, he race-walked his way to the best position in line to get the handshake. So there was always that calculation.

[THROUGHOUT HIS VARIOUS POLITICAL CAMPAIGNS, Bill Clinton relied on a political consultant named Dick] Morris. Morris is the one who told Clinton to apologize to the people of Arkansas for his first term as governor—which proved to be very effective—saying that he understood that he'd made mistakes, almost like the prodigal son saying, "Let me back." It worked very effectively. It was a technique, a humble admission that Clinton and Hillary remembered for the future and used again and again over the years.

The public apology happened in 1981, when he was preparing to run again [for governor] in 1982. They taped a TV spot where Clinton essentially said, "I'm sorry. I learned my lessons. It will never happen again." At that point Clinton was the youngest ex-governor in American history. He was depressed and fit the ironic description of the Rhodes Scholar, which is a bright young man with a future behind him. Morris pulled him out of it and told him, "Apologize. Go forward."

Betsey Wright came down to Little Rock about a week or two after Bill Clinton was defeated in 1980. She lived in the governor's mansion for a while, piecing back together all of the detritus of his life, of his political career. She put into computers all of the thousands of note cards he had of his key political allies and contributors. Then, when he won re-election, she became his chief of staff from 1983 through 1990. Her relationship with Clinton is one of the most interesting that I encountered. There was a real sisterly-brotherly, love-hate relationship going on there. She is both fiercely loyal to him and yet is angry at him all the time.

There's a scene in the book where Betsey Wright and Bill Clinton meet at her house. They go over a list of women who might be problematic for him if he were to run for president in 1988. When the book came out, she issued what I call a nondenial denial [about this incident], saying that David Maraniss might have misrepresented her, "misinterpreted what I had told him." But I hadn't; she knows I didn't. It was very clear to me and my editors at *The Washington Post*. . . . We have documents about it.

CLINTON'S RELATIONSHIP with Hillary Rodham Clinton is . . . always changing. It was built on a shared passion for policy and politics and books and ideas and intellectual life and also a sense of humor. When he married Hillary, he told his friends that he was going for brains over glamour. She knew what she was getting into when she married him in the sense of his enormous appetite for life, and it's added several tumultuous parts to their marriage. It's a pragmatic, political partnership with some extra spice to it as well.

To understand their relationship now, you have to understand that it has gone through three stages, basically: They met at Yale Law School. From that point in the early 1970s until 1980, when he was defeated as governor—although they saw that they could get to their ultimate goal together—they were really leading independent lives. . . . She was building up her own life and career, first as a law professor and then as a lawyer and working in Children's Defense Fund issues.

Then he got beat, and she came to the realization that he could only recover with her more profound help. From then on, she was his key financial person, his key political advisor, his pro bono lawyer on ethical issues, and his main policy person. She was the head of the task force on education reform, which was successful and made his name in Arkansas. It established his career for the 1980s and helped him become a national figure. They carried that policy partnership into the White House almost without even thinking twice about it.

HE TOLD THE PEOPLE when he ran for governor in 1990 that if he were elected, he'd serve out four years. Someone asked him that question at a political forum: "Will you serve out your term if you're elected?" In classic Clinton style, without even thinking, he said, "You bet." Just like that. Then he had to live with those two words and break them.

There's a joke in Arkansas that they voted for him to get rid of him. That's not it, obviously. But most of them think that Clinton is always asking for forgiveness of one sort or another . . . They knew all along that his goal was to be president. By the time he made that decision, people in Arkansas knew him so well that those who were for him were for him no matter what, and those who were against him hated his guts and didn't care. There were no undecideds about Bill Clinton in Arkansas by that time.

WHATEVER ANYONE THINKS of Bill Clinton's presidency or his ideology, his life is a great American story. It's a narrative that I thought revealed a lot about ambition, the clash between ambition and idealism, coming out of nowhere, that part of America, dealing with a troubled family, rising out of Arkansas from the point where he shook John Kennedy's hand in 1963 to actually living in the White House himself.

The number-one question about Bill Clinton . . . is "What does this guy really believe the most?" In a general way, I can say that he went into politics to do good. His life and career have been [a] clash between idealism and ambition.

Roger Simon

Show Time: The American Political Circus and the Race for the White House

WHEN AIR FORCE ONE WOULD LAND and the doorway would open and they would roll up the wheels, Bill Clinton, before every event, would suck in his gut, button his jacket, turn to [top aide] Harold Ickes and say, "It's show time." That's how he approached the [1996] campaign.

This is a book about seduction, the seduction of a nation, the seduction of a people. That's what political campaigns are, and that's what Bill Clinton's political campaign was. He is a master at beguiling people, at seducing people. There is a book, coincidentally enough, on the president's past flirtations and accusations of sexual improprieties called *In Character,* which at the time I didn't think would be of any great particular importance. Now it's obviously the focus of what we're all looking at in regards to [Clinton's] presidency.

Bill Clinton in 1992 denied having an affair with Gennifer Flowers. It is now [in February of 1998] reported that in a sealed deposition, he admits to it. If that is so, then I think a lot of people, especially people in the press, are going to feel betrayed. A high value is placed on candidates telling the truth.

On the other hand, Bill Clinton is never going to be impeached for lying to the American people. It's not a crime. And if you believe the poll numbers, I think perhaps a high degree of public cynicism feeds into it, showing that a lot of people just really aren't too upset by [the stories of infidelity].

IT'S HARD TO TAKE any small piece [of the 1996 campaign] and say Bill Clinton won because he stood close to [his Republican opponent] Bob Dole; Bill Clinton won because he had orange Mylar [balloons]. Obviously, Bill Clinton won for a lot of reasons. Maybe people liked his positions better. Positions and policies are important. But it is impossible just to say . . . only policy counts, only positions count. The press is really wrong to concentrate on the process. Bob Dole was that kind of candidate. He had all sorts of policies and positions, and he could not sell them to the American people. Heck, he couldn't even explain them coherently to the American people.

A political campaign is about selling a product: the person running for president, running for governor, running for senator. The skills that people have in selling entertainment, products, and presidents are all the same. The key players that Bill Clinton has always surrounded himself with are people who not just understand politics, but people who understand salesmanship, image, and theatrics.

If there's one of the points of the book, it's that no one gets to run for president on his terms. The terms you run on are the terms set by the American people, and that means what the American people are receptive to. If you can't get them to listen and you can't sell yourself, then you're probably not going to win.

BILL CLINTON'S GENUINELY FAVORITE ACTIVITY . . . is to work the rope line after a speech. He likes the speech, but he loves the rope line. The rope line is sometimes literally a rope; sometimes it's a barrier, what the White House calls "bicycle stands" of metal barriers. [They are there] simply to keep people back so they can't get too close to the president of the United States. After almost every speech, Bill Clinton climbs down from the stage, walks along the rope line, and shakes the hands of people—not just the people in the first row, but in the second and third rows. He reaches his hands out into them. The Secret Service hates that because it opens up his body. It's a very vulnerable and unnatural thing to do in a crowd, to open yourself up like that. He lives for that. He loves touching the people. He loves talking to the people, even for a few seconds.

But it's fascinating to see him. [I was with him] on Air Force One. It was after a regular speech in Ohio, and what was fascinating to the president was all the neat stuff that people gave him at the University of Ohio. They gave him sweatshirts and sweatpants. One woman on one stop gave him an entire suit of clothes. He gets beer mugs and stuff. Perhaps it's because he grew up in middle-class circumstances, he really likes to get neat stuff. [The gifts were] what he was showing me.

DURING THE CAMPAIGN, they had [staff meetings] frequently; now they're down to once a week. The top staff, both political, policy, and White House staff of the president, would gather in this room with very ornate French furniture, and a portable screen would be set up. The president would be shown his latest poll numbers. No president in history has polled as much as Bill Clinton. He really wants to see those polls. He believes in those polls.

THE CLINTONS . . . DON'T LIKE THE PRESS. They see themselves as having won—the president sees himself as having won—his first election in spite of the press. The press has always been an enemy to him.

Bob Woodward's book came out during the campaign, called *The Choice* . . . Hillary was quoted about having "séances"—I think he didn't quite use that word—with the ghost of Eleanor Roosevelt. That information clearly came from people close to the First Lady. When she read that book, she felt that she couldn't trust anyone anymore in the White House.

It did two things: It isolated her even further from people who were around who probably liked her a lot. She picked her own staff, and not all of them are leakers. So it tended to isolate her even further. But it probably also tended to bring the president and the First Lady closer together. By the time the [1996] campaign ended, they felt they were the only two people that could be trusted.

AT A CERTAIN TIME PERIOD in American history, the press no longer wrote about the personal life of the presidents. When we first started out as a republic, the press was vile. It would write anything. Some people may think we've come full circle. Then there was a period of greater responsibility, and the press decided that, generally speaking, a president's personal life did not count.

We [have] come to believe that everything in a person's background and character now affects what they do. The press learned a lesson from Watergate, too; the lesson is that character counts. It's not only what these people say as president and do as president, but it's who they are and who they were before they got in the office.

This is the double-edged sword of what Bill Clinton has done: He has sold himself relentlessly to the American people as a friend, as an acquaintance. It's called "the Oprah effect" in the White House. He's someone Americans feel they know because all candidates now, in the current era—all campaigns— want to sell candidates as people just like you and me, not on a high pedestal, but ordinary folks. The difficulty—and the reason it's a double-edged sword— is that if you do anything to betray the trust of the American people, they feel that it's not just a politician who's done something wrong, but a family acquaintance who's betrayed their trust.

Anita Hill

by
ANITA HILL

Anita Hill (b. 1956) was a law professor at the University of Oklahoma when she was called to testify at the confirmation hearing for U.S. Supreme Court nominee Clarence Thomas. Ms. Hill's testimony before the Senate Judiciary Committee on October 11, 1991, provoked a national debate about sexual harassment in the workplace. Her account of the proceedings, Speaking Truth to Power *(Doubleday, 1997), was the subject of* Booknotes *on November 23, 1997.*

OCTOBER 11, 1991, WAS THE DATE of my testimony [before the Senate Judiciary Committee, which was considering Clarence Thomas's Supreme Court nomination]. A lot of people say to me, "Oh, I watched you testify." For some reason they think that my testimony lasted at least two or three days and maybe the whole hearing took weeks, but . . . I was only there one day and that was on a Friday. The hearings wrapped up by Sunday night. It was very short in terms of time span . . . but it clearly had a larger impact.

The vote was 52 to 48 . . . in favor of Clarence Thomas's confirmation. That happened on October 15. [Senators Chuck Robb, Alan Dixon, and David Boren—and Richard Shelby, who's now a Republican—are the only four Democrats who voted] . . . for Clarence Thomas.

If those four individuals had voted against the confirmation, it would not have happened. Senator [Robert] Packwood was one of the Republicans who voted against the confirmation. Mr. Dixon, from the Chicago area, I think lost his seat because of his vote in favor of the confirmation.

I WROTE THIS BOOK because I looked at the situation that I found myself in in Washington, D.C., in trying to tell my story—the truth about my experience—to a hostile but very powerful organization in the Senate Judiciary Committee. I looked at attempting to help the media understand . . . and thought that [a book] was a good way to express what my experience had been. As I have shared the title [*Speaking Truth to Power*] with other people, I have found that they feel the same way, not only about my experiences, but what they experience when they make complaints about this kind of behavior.

There are EEOC guidelines that define [sexual harassment]. There are two forms of it: There is a quid pro quo sexual harassment, which is defined by someone requiring sexual demands in return for keeping a job or getting a promotion. That is, if you give me these sexual favors or perform these sexual favors, then you will get promoted, you will get hired, you will get raises; if you don't, then you will be fired or dismissed or demoted. There's [also] hostile environment sexual harassment. A hostile environment forum is the creation of an environment that is so rife with sexual innuendo that it creates a hostile workplace for the individual who is the target. It can be innuendo, it can be insults, it can be jokes, and it can go into the level of touching and sexual assault. So it's a broad range of behavior.

I suppose we've all experienced jokes that make us uncomfortable . . . the innuendos or suggestions, but I had never experienced anything like what I experienced with Clarence Thomas. There's another thing that I do have to say, too, about the hearings, and that is that when I went to Washington, what I thought I was doing was providing information about the character and fitness of the individual. I did not see my role as going to Washington, D.C., to file a complaint about sexual harassment. The tables were turned on me and it became "Unless she can support her claim of sexual harassment, then we cannot recognize what she has to say." It put a really improper burden on me.

The standard should have been whether or not I had credible evidence that went to the character and fitness of this particular nominee. When I provided that credible evidence—as long as it went to the character and fitness and as long as it was relevant—I maintained that whether it came to the level of a complaint, a legal complaint for sexual harassment, was not the issue. The issue was the character and fitness of this individual for [the Supreme Court of the United States].

AFTER THE HEARINGS, in an article that both he and his wife participated in, he made a statement that he was not evolving [beyond his stressful confirmation process]. His wife stated that she felt that he'd been badly treated, and that he owed nobody. I think that that was an expression of closed-mindedness and bitterness. I tend to think that [his bitterness] has not been overcome, that you see some of that seeping through his [court] opinions. That's unfortunate. . . . He is a person; he's entitled to some humanity. But at the same time his office needs to be bigger than that. The Supreme Court needs to be bigger than that.

I'M SURE THERE WERE SOME SYMPATHETIC PEOPLE within the media, but that was not what I was faced with when I had the barrage of reporters camped out across the street in my neighbors' yards. That was not what I experienced when I returned to my home after being in a hotel—returned to my home at five o'clock in the morning—to be practically ambushed by someone with a camera and lights. [They] stuck a mike in my face, demanding some kind of a statement from me. At that point, there may have been sympathy, but I did not feel it. . . . I felt that if there had been real sympathy that they would've realized the intrusion on my life. They would've handled it with a lot more sensitivity.

Shortly after the hearing, in particular, there was a concerted effort by many individuals to educate people . . . to look at [sexual harassment] as a workplace issue. That was not what the media was going for at the time of the hearing. They were going for the Washington political scandal angle, and that was what they pursued. They pursued me as part of that, instead of looking at this as an issue involving how people interact with each other in the workplace. That's changed, and I'm thankful for that, but that has been a part of the evolution.

I WAS BORN IN A SMALL COMMUNITY called Lone Tree, Oklahoma. I was actually physically born in Okmulgee, but I was only in the doctor's office long enough to be born, and then my mom brought me back that same day to Lone Tree, which is a very small community.

It's a rural community in eastern Oklahoma. It's a farm community. It's not an incorporated town. It's a very isolated area. My family's home was nearly the only place that you could see. If you stood in our front yard, you couldn't see another house. That's where I grew up.

My parents were both farmers. We worked the farm. I guess it was made a little bit easier by thirteen children, my brothers and sisters. But they're both farmers and have been all their lives.

I'm the youngest of the thirteen [children], which is great. Ten [of my brothers and sisters] graduated from segregated schools. . . . I went to an integrated school, [but] it wasn't integrated because of the decision by the Supreme Court in *Brown v. The Board of Education.* The integration of my school, in . . . the early 1960s, took place because it was a tiny rural school that was threatened to be closed. Rather than close the school, just to get the number of pupils they would need to keep it open, they opened it up to integration.

I always loved books, even from first grade, when I first learned to read. One of the great benefits of having so many older brothers and sisters who are in school is that they teach you how to read early on. You get involved with books through their schoolwork even before you start school. I used to love the library in our school even though it wasn't very sophisticated and it wasn't very extensive. But I'd spend time reading and I'd get through with my classwork early so that I could read the books that were there.

I went to college at Oklahoma State University. I studied psychology . . . [but] it was a toss-up: I wanted to go into the hard sciences, but at the time, because I had come from this rural background and didn't have the extensive science courses . . . —also I think because I was female and black—there was not a lot of support for that decision. I went into social science, and I enjoyed that as well. It wasn't until later that I became convinced that I was going to go to law school, that I actually could accomplish that.

I attended Yale Law School. . . . I came to Washington in the fall of 1980. I studied for the bar and passed the bar in the fall of 1980. . . . My first job was with a law firm. I had been a summer clerk at the firm and liked the people there, liked the atmosphere at the firm. I thought I could do some good work there.

After thinking that was what I wanted to do, I got there and worked a year. The work was interesting and challenging, but it wasn't something that I could feel personally connected with. Having grown up and come of age in the civil rights era, I knew that these were issues that I cared about and that I wanted to do work in. I made a switch after a year at the firm . . . to government. I worked at the Office for Civil Rights at the Department of Education, was hired by Clarence Thomas.

He was introduced to me by someone who worked at the law firm that had hired me. They had been friends and both had gone to Yale Law School. It was in the home of this friend, Gil Hardy, this mutual friend, that I met Clarence Thomas.

Thomas . . . seemed a little bit rough around the edges. . . . But Gil assured me that he was also a very solid person; that he would do a good job when he got an appointment with the government, which is what he was hoping to have happen at the time that I met him.

I am somewhere on the left politically. But at the same time, I was assured that even though Clarence Thomas worked at the time for a Republican senator and this was a Republican administration, that my ideas and my work could be valued.

I BEGAN THE BOOK with some questions that had come up from time to time from people who had a sincere interest in understanding what had happened during the [Clarence Thomas] hearings. People asked, "How did you get through it?" People . . . understand that the hearings failed, but they wanted to know, expressly, How did it fail? What went wrong? What might have been done right?

I started trying to answer those questions. Eventually, it came back to my family when I looked at that question about how I got through it. It came back to my family and some of their struggles in the past and present. I knew I had to write about my family in order for people to really understand me, what I care about, who I am, and certainly who I was in 1991.

The second part was a little harder. I had press clippings . . . I had a transcript of the hearing. I sat down and immersed myself in the hearings, revisited the hearings, because I wanted that part of the book to be real, as it happened. I wanted to almost re-experience it so that I could tell people what it was like. That was hard. Very hard.

[Telling my story is] about keeping this from happening again . . . Senator Paul Simon, at the time of the hearing, suggested that somebody [should] help us do better. Somebody [should] advise us on how this could have been handled better. I sat down and thought about it.

One of the things I thought of was here I was, a private citizen coming into Washington, D.C., facing a process that I didn't understand and didn't know how to navigate very well. It wasn't made easier for me. I thought, If there is another citizen with information that's relevant to the process, they shouldn't have to face the kind of roadblocks that I had to face.

I watched parts of [the videotaped hearing]. I saw . . . how painful it was. . . . It's written all over my face during some of the worst parts of the testimony. I was struggling so hard to help people understand what had happened. It was so hurtful to me to have my parents in the room, to feel helpless to protect them against it. . . .

RECENTLY . . . I WAS IN THE AIRPORT in Oklahoma City and I saw a person in the airport who looked an awful lot like [Senator] Arlen Specter [a Republican on the Judiciary Committee who was a strong critic of Anita Hill]. I thought, This can't be happening because Arlen Specter is not going to be in Oklahoma City. It was Arlen Specter. . . . It was the first I'd ever talked to him.

We were both a little shocked. He recovered more quickly than I did. . . . Then it was almost bizarre because he began to talk with me. He asked me if I was on a book tour and told me that he was at the university for a reunion. . . . It was as though we were having a conversation between acquaintances, that, but for me, it was as though those six years didn't matter. When someone has called you, accused you, of flat-out perjury on national TV, especially when they have no basis for it . . . I could not just jump into a conversation with him as though we had just been civil acquaintances . . . It was at that point I realized that he had no sense of how my life had been impacted by his behavior. He was that out of touch with the reality of my experience. For him, I think it was another political episode. For me, it was about my life. I don't think he got that at all.

In some ways, this experience has been very difficult. In some ways, it has been rewarding and fulfilling. It's hard to be viewed so disparately. Some people see me as a heroine, and other people see me as the worst villain. . . . There are people who feel that I lied and tried to ruin Clarence Thomas. Writing this book was helpful because it helped me bring some kind of closure to it and put it in perspective. It's been hard, but it's also been rewarding because I've seen potential that I did not know I had. . . . I would never have lived those potentials had it not been for those hearings. So it's a mixed bag.

Complete List of C-SPAN *Booknotes*
(1989–1999)

SEPTEMBER 14, 1988
Pre-*Booknotes* Interview
with Neil Sheehan
*A Bright Shining Lie: John Paul
Vann and America in Vietnam*
Publisher: Random House

1. APRIL 2, 1989
Zbigniew Brzezinski
*Grand Failure: The Birth and
Death of Communism in the
Twentieth Century*
Publisher: Macmillan

2. APRIL 9, 1989
Judy Shelton
*The Coming Soviet Crash:
Gorbachev's Desperate Pursuit of
Credit in Western Financial
Markets*
Publisher: The Free Press

3. APRIL 16, 1989
Bruce Oudes
*From: The President—Richard
Nixon's Secret Files*
Publisher: Harper & Row

4. APRIL 23, 1989
Susan Moeller
*Shooting War: Photography
and the American Experience
of Combat*
Publisher: Basic Books

5. APRIL 30, 1989
Henry Brandon
*Special Relationships: A Foreign
Correspondent's Memoirs*
Publisher: Atheneum

6. MAY 7, 1989
Colonel David Hackworth (with
Julie Sherman)

*About Face: The Odyssey of an
American Warrior*
Publisher: Simon & Schuster

7. MAY 14, 1989
James Fallows
*More Like Us: Making America
Great Again*
Publisher: Houghton Mifflin

8. MAY 21, 1989
Gregory Fossedal
*The Democratic Imperative:
Exporting the American Revolution*
Publisher: Basic Books

9. MAY 28, 1989
Stanley Karnow
*In Our Image: America's Empire
in the Philippines*
Publisher: Random House

10. JUNE 4, 1989
James MacGregor Burns
The Crosswinds of Freedom
Publisher: Knopf

11. JUNE 11, 1989
Robert Christopher
*Crashing the Gates: The
De-WASPing of America's Power
Elite*
Publisher: Simon & Schuster

12. JUNE 18, 1989
Sen. Robert Byrd
The Senate: 1789–1989
Publisher: Government Printing
Office

13. JUNE 25, 1989
Elizabeth Colton
*The Jackson Phenomenon: The
Man, The Power, The Message*
Publisher: Doubleday

14. JULY 2, 1989
Nathaniel Branden
*Judgment Day: My Years with
Ayn Rand*
Publisher: Houghton Mifflin

15. JULY 9, 1989
Roger Kennedy
*Orders From France: The Ameri-
cans and the French in a Revolu-
tionary World (1780–1820)*
Publisher: Knopf

16. JULY 14, 1989
(BASTILLE DAY SPECIAL)
Simon Schama
*Citizens: A Chronicle of the
French Revolution*
Publisher: Knopf

17. JULY 16, 1989
George Wilson
*Mud Soldiers: Life Inside the
New American Army*
Publisher: Scribner

18. JULY 23, 1989
Jeanne Simon
*Codename: Scarlett—Life on the
Campaign Trail by the Wife of a
Presidential Candidate*
Publisher: The Continuum
Publishing Company

19. JULY 30, 1989
Michael Kaufman
*Mad Dreams, Saving Graces—
Poland: A Nation in Conspiracy*
Publisher: Random House

20. AUGUST 6, 1989
Porter McKeever
*Adlai Stevenson: His Life and
Legacy*
Publisher: Morrow

21. AUGUST 13, 1989
Gary Paul Gates and Bob Schieffer
The Acting President
Publisher: E. P. Dutton

22. AUGUST 20, 1989
Bruce Murray
Journey Into Space—The First Thirty Years of Space Exploration
Publisher: Norton

23. AUGUST 27, 1989
Jack Germond and Jules Witcover
Whose Broad Stripes and Bright Stars—The Trivial Pursuit of the Presidency 1988
Publisher: Warner Books

24. SEPTEMBER 3, 1989
Walter Laquer
The Long Road to Freedom: Russia and Glasnost
Publisher: Scribner

25. SEPTEMBER 10, 1989
Thomas Friedman
From Beirut to Jerusalem
Publisher: Farrar, Straus & Giroux

26. SEPTEMBER 17, 1989
Gen. Ariel Sharon
Warrior: An Autobiography
Publisher: Simon & Schuster

27. SEPTEMBER 24, 1989
George Gilder
Microcosm: The Quantum Revolution in Economics and Technology
Publisher: Simon & Schuster

28. OCTOBER 1, 1989
Mort Rosenblum
Back Home: A Foreign Correspondent Rediscovers America
Publisher: Morrow

29. OCTOBER 8, 1989
Barbara Ehrenreich
Fear of Falling: The Inner Life of the Middle Class
Publisher: Pantheon

30. OCTOBER 15, 1989
Harrison Salisbury
Tiananmen Diary: Thirteen Days in June
Publisher: Little, Brown

31. OCTOBER 22, 1989
Kenneth Adelman
The Great Universal Embrace: Arms Summitry—A Skeptic's Account
Publisher: Simon & Schuster

32. OCTOBER 29, 1989
Rev. Ralph David Abernathy
And the Walls Came Tumbling Down
Publisher: Harper & Row

33. NOVEMBER 5, 1989
Vassily Aksyonov
Say Cheese: Soviets and the Media
Publisher: Random House

34. NOVEMBER 12, 1989
Felix Rodriguez
(and John Weisman)
Shadow Warrior: The CIA Hero of a Hundred Unknown Battles
Publisher: Simon & Schuster

35. NOVEMBER 19, 1989
Robin Wright
In the Name of God: The Khomeini Decade
Publisher: Simon & Schuster

36. NOVEMBER 26, 1989
Peter Hennessy
Whitehall
Publisher: The Free Press

37. DECEMBER 3, 1989
Clifford Stoll
The Cuckoo's Egg: Tracking a Spy Through the Maze of Computer Espionage
Publisher: Doubleday

38. DECEMBER 10, 1989
Arthur Grace
Choose Me: Portraits of a Presidential Race
Publisher: University Press of New England

39. DECEMBER 17, 1989
James Reston, Jr.
The Lone Star: The Life of John Connally
Publisher: Harper & Row

40. DECEMBER 24, 1989
Richard Rhodes
Farm: A Year in the Life of an American Farmer
Publisher: Simon & Schuster

41. DECEMBER 31, 1989
William Lutz
Doublespeak: From "Revenue Enhancement" to "Terminal Living"—How Government, Business, Advertisers and Others Use Language to Deceive You
Publisher: Harper & Row

42. JANUARY 7, 1990
Sig Mickelson
From Whistle Stop to Sound Bite: Four Decades of Politics and Television
Publisher: Praeger

43. JANUARY 14, 1990
John Barry
The Ambition and the Power—The Fall of Jim Wright: A True Story of Washington
Publisher: Viking

44. JANUARY 21, 1990
Fitzhugh Green
George Bush: An Intimate Portrait
Publisher: Hippocrene Books

45. JANUARY 28, 1990
Charles A. Fecher
The Diary of H. L. Mencken
Publisher: Knopf

46. FEBRUARY 4, 1990
Jim Mann
Beijing Jeep: The Short, Unhappy Romance of American Business in China
Publisher: Simon & Schuster

47. FEBRUARY 11, 1990
David Burnham
A Law Unto Itself: Power, Politics and the IRS
Publisher: Random House

48. FEBRUARY 18, 1990
Peggy Noonan
What I Saw at the Revolution: A Political Life in the Reagan Era
Publisher: Random House

49. FEBRUARY 25, 1990
Michael Fumento
The Myth of Heterosexual AIDS
Publisher: Basic Books

50. FEBRUARY 27, 1990
Hedley Donovan
Right Places, Right Times: Forty Years in Journalism Not Counting My Paper Route
Publisher: Henry Holt

51. MARCH 4, 1990
Richard Barnet

The Rockets' Red Glare: When America Goes to War—The Presidents and the People
Publisher: Simon & Schuster

52. MARCH 11, 1990
Frederick Kempe
Divorcing the Dictator: America's Bungled Affair with Noriega
Publisher: Putnam

53. MARCH 18, 1990
(Neil Livingstone and)
David Halevy
Inside the PLO
Publisher: Morrow

54. MARCH 25, 1990
James Abourezk
Advise and Dissent: Memoirs of South Dakota and the U.S. Senate
Publisher: Lawrence Hill Books

55. APRIL 1, 1990
Fred Graham
Happy Talk: Confessions of a TV Newsman
Publisher: Norton

56. APRIL 9, 1990
Leonard Sussman
Power, the Press & the Technology of Freedom: The Coming Age of ISDN
Publisher: Freedom House

57. APRIL 15, 1990
Helmut Schmidt
Men and Powers: A Political Retrospective
Publisher: Random House

58. APRIL 22, 1990
Michael Barone
Our Country: The Shaping of America from Roosevelt to Reagan
Publisher: The Free Press

59. APRIL 29, 1990
Robert Caro
Means of Ascent: The Years of Lyndon Johnson
Publisher: Knopf

60. MAY 6, 1990
Morley Safer
Flashbacks on Returning to Vietnam
Publisher: Random House

61. MAY 13, 1990
Brian Duffy and
Steven Emerson

The Fall of Pan Am 103: Inside the Lockerbie Investigation
Publisher: Putnam

62. MAY 20, 1990
Allister Sparks
The Mind of South Africa
Publisher: Knopf

63. MAY 27, 1990
Bette Bao Lord
Legacies: A Chinese Mosaic
Publisher: Knopf

64. JUNE 3, 1990
Dusko Doder
Gorbachev: Heretic in the Kremlin
Publisher: Viking

65. JUNE 10, 1990
Thomas Sowell
Preferential Policies: An International Perspective
Publisher: Morrow

66. JUNE 17, 1990
Judith Miller
One, By One, By One: Facing the Holocaust
Publisher: Simon & Schuster

67. JUNE 24, 1990
Kevin Phillips
The Politics of Rich and Poor: Wealth and the Electorate in the Reagan Aftermath
Publisher: Random House

68. JULY 1, 1990
Chris Ogden
Maggie: An Intimate Portrait of a Woman in Power
Publisher: Random House

69. JULY 8, 1990
Denton Watson
Lion in the Lobby: Clarence Mitchell, Jr.'s Struggle for the Passage of Civil Rights Laws
Publisher: Morrow

70. JULY 15, 1990
Caspar Weinberger
Fighting for Peace: Seven Critical Years in the Pentagon
Publisher: Warner Books

71. JULY 22, 1990
Teresa Odendahl
Charity Begins at Home: Generosity and Self-Interest Among the Philanthropic Elite
Publisher: Basic Books

72. JULY 29, 1990
Michael Shapiro
In the Shadow of the Sun: A Korean Year of Love and Sorrow
Publisher: Atlantic Monthly Press

73. AUGUST 5, 1990
Dan Raviv and Yossi Mellman
Every Spy a Prince: The Complete History of Israel's Intelligence Community
Publisher: Houghton Mifflin

74. AUGUST 12, 1990
Roger Kimball
Tenured Radicals: How Politics Has Corrupted Our Higher Education
Publisher: Harper & Row

75. AUGUST 19, 1990
Tad Szulc
Then and Now: How the World Has Changed Since World War II
Publisher: Morrow

76. AUGUST 26, 1990
Christopher Wren
The End of the Line: The Failure of Communism in the Soviet Union and China
Publisher: Simon & Schuster

77. SEPTEMBER 2, 1990
Lee Edwards
Missionary for Freedom: The Life and Times of Walter Judd
Publisher: Paragon House

78. SEPTEMBER 9, 1990
Sen. Robert Dole
Historical Almanac of the United States Senate
Publisher: Government Printing Office

79. SEPTEMBER 16, 1990
M. L. Farber
Outrage: The Story Behind the Tawana Brawley Hoax
Publisher: Bantam Books

80. SEPTEMBER 23, 1990
Janette Dates
Split Image: African Americans in the Mass Media
Publisher: Howard University Press

81. OCTOBER 14, 1990
Harold Stassen
Eisenhower: Turning the World Toward Peace
Publisher: Merrill/Magnus

82. OCTOBER 21, 1990
Tim Weiner
*Blank Check: The Pentagon's
Black Budget*
Publisher: Warner Books

83. OCTOBER 28, 1990
Pat Choate
*Agents of Influence: How Japan's
Lobbyists in the United States
Manipulate America's Political
and Economic System*
Publisher: Knopf

84. NOVEMBER 4, 1990
Paul Taylor
*See How They Run: Electing a
President in an Age of Mediaocracy*
Publisher: Knopf

85. NOVEMBER 11, 1990
Blaine Harden
*Africa: Dispatches from a Fragile
Continent*
Publisher: Norton

86. NOVEMBER 18, 1990
Jean Edward Smith
Lucius D. Clay: An American Life
Publisher: Henry Holt

87. NOVEMBER 25, 1990
Martin Mayer
*The Greatest-Ever Bank Robbery:
The Collapse of the Savings and
Loan Industry*
Publisher: Scribner

88. DECEMBER 2, 1990
Carol Barkalow
(with Andrea Raals)
*In the Men's House: An Inside
Account of Life in the Army by
One of West Point's First Female
Graduates*
Publisher: Poseidon Press

89. DECEMBER 9, 1990
Sally Bedell Smith
*In All His Glory: The Life of
William S. Paley: The Legendary
Tycoon and His Brilliant Circle*
Publisher: Simon & Schuster

90. DECEMBER 16, 1990
Shen Tong
*Almost a Revolution: The Story of
a Chinese Student's Journey from
Boyhood to Leadership in Tianan-
men Square*
Publisher: Houghton Mifflin

91. DECEMBER 23, 1990
John and Janet Wallach

Arafat: In the Eyes of the Beholder
Publisher: Lyle Stuart

92. DECEMBER 30, 1990
Garry Wills
*Under God: Religion and Ameri-
can Politics*
Publisher: Simon & Schuster

93. JANUARY 6, 1991
Ben Wattenberg
*The First Universal Nation: Lead-
ing Indicators and Ideas About the
Surge of America in the 1990s*
Publisher: The Free Press

94. JANUARY 13, 1991
Daniel Roos
*The Machine That Changed the
World*
Publisher: Macmillan

95. JANUARY 27, 1991
Daniel Yergin
*The Prize: The Epic Quest for Oil,
Money and Power*
Publisher: Simon & Schuster

96. FEBRUARY 3, 1991
Carl Rowan
Breaking Barriers: A Memoir
Publisher: Little, Brown

97. FEBRUARY 10, 1991
Theodore Hesburgh
(with Jerry Reedy)
*God, Country, Notre Dame: The
Autobiography of Theodore M.
Hesburgh*
Publisher: Doubleday

98. FEBRUARY 17, 1991
Ronald Brownstein
*The Power and the Glitter:
The Hollywood-Washington
Connection*
Publisher: Pantheon

99. FEBRUARY 24, 1991
Robert Kuttner
*The End of Laissez-Faire: Nation-
al Purpose and the Global Econo-
my After the Cold War*
Publisher: Knopf

100. MARCH 3, 1991
Haynes Johnson
*Sleepwalking Through History:
America in the Reagan Years*
Publisher: Norton

101. MARCH 10, 1991
Georgie Anne Geyer

*Guerrilla Prince: The Untold
Story of Fidel Castro*
Publisher: Little, Brown

102. MARCH 17, 1991
Leonard Goldenson
(with Marvin Wolf)
*Beating the Odds: The Untold
Story Behind the Rise of ABC: The
Stars, Struggles and Egos That
Transformed Network Television*
Publisher: Scribner

103. MARCH 24, 1991
Richard Brookhiser
*The Way of the WASP: How It
Made America and How It Can
Save It . . . So to Speak*
Publisher: The Free Press

104. MARCH 31, 1991
Dayton Duncan
*Grass Roots: One Year in the
Life of the New Hampshire
Presidential Primary*
Publisher: Penguin

105. APRIL 7, 1991
Tom Wicker
*One of Us: Richard Nixon and
the American Dream*
Publisher: Random House

106. APRIL 14, 1991
William Strauss and Neil Howe
*Generations: The History of Amer-
ica's Future, 1584–2069*
Publisher: Morrow

107. APRIL 21, 1991
Robert Shogun
*The Riddle of Power: Presidential
Leadership from Truman to Bush*
Publisher: Dutton

108. APRIL 28, 1991
Caroline Kennedy and
Ellen Alderman
*In Our Defense: The Bill of Rights
in Action*
Publisher: Morrow

109. MAY 5, 1991
Nick Lemann
*The Promised Land: The Great
Black Migration and How It
Changed America*
Publisher: Knopf

110. MAY 12, 1991 (PART ONE)
Lou Cannon
*President Reagan: Role of a
Lifetime*
Publisher: Simon & Schuster

III. MAY 19, 1991 (PART TWO)
Lou Cannon
President Reagan: Role of a Lifetime
Publisher: Simon & Schuster

112. MAY 26, 1991
Robert Reich
The Work of Nations
Publisher: Knopf

113. JUNE 2, 1991
Robert Kaiser
Why Gorbachev Happened: His Triumphs & His Failure
Publisher: Simon & Schuster

114. JUNE 9, 1991
George Friedman &
Meredith LeBard
The Coming War with Japan
Publisher: St. Martin's Press

115. JUNE 16, 1991
Dixy Lee Ray
Trashing the Planet: How Science Can Help Us Deal with Acid Rain, Depletion of the Ozone, and Nuclear Waste Among Other Things
Publisher: Regnery

116. JUNE 23, 1991
Bob Woodward
The Commanders
Publisher: Simon & Schuster

117. JUNE 30, 1991
Roger Gittines
Consequences: John G. Tower—A Personal and Political Memoir
Publisher: Little, Brown

118. JULY 7, 1991
Donald Ritchie
Press Gallery: Congress and the Washington Correspondents
Publisher: Harvard University Press

119. JULY 14, 1991
Michael Beschloss
The Crisis Years: Kennedy and Khrushchev, 1960–1963
Publisher: HarperCollins

120. JULY 21, 1991
Alan Ehrenhalt
The United States of Ambition: Politicians, Power and the Pursuit of Office
Publisher: Random House

121. JULY 28, 1991
Clark Clifford

Counsel to the President: A Memoir
Publisher: Random House

122. AUGUST 4, 1991
Elaine Sciolino
The Outlaw State: Saddam Hussein's Quest for Power and the Gulf Crisis
Publisher: John Wiley & Sons

123. AUGUST 11, 1991
Len Colodny and Robert Gettlin
Silent Coup: The Removal of a President
Publisher: St. Martin's Press

124. AUGUST 18, 1991
Liz Trotta
Fighting for Air: In the Trenches with Television News
Publisher: Simon & Schuster

125. AUGUST 25, 1991
E. J. Dionne, Jr.
Why Americans Hate Politics
Publisher: Simon & Schuster

126. SEPTEMBER 1, 1991
Andrew and Leslie Cockburn
Dangerous Liaison: The Inside Story of the U.S.-Israeli Covert Relationship
Publisher: HarperCollins

127. SEPTEMBER 8, 1991
Liva Baker
The Justice from Beacon Hill
Publisher: HarperCollins

128. SEPTEMBER 15, 1991
Reuven Frank
Out of Thin Air: The Brief Wonderful Life of Network News
Publisher: Simon & Schuster

129. SEPTEMBER 22, 1991
Robert Dallek
Lone Star Rising: Lyndon Johnson and His Times 1908–1960
Publisher: Oxford University Press

130. SEPTEMBER 29, 1991
Stephen Carter
Reflections of an Affirmative Action Baby
Publisher: Basic Books

131. OCTOBER 6, 1991
Ken Auletta
Three Blind Mice: How the TV Networks Lost Their Way
Publisher: Random House

[October 13, 1991: Preempted by U.S. Senate]

132. OCTOBER 20, 1991
Anthony Lewis
Make No Law: The Sullivan Case and the First Amendment
Publisher: Random House

133. OCTOBER 27, 1991
Don Oberdorfer
The Turn: From the Cold War to a New Era—The United States and the Soviet Union, 1983–1990
Publisher: Simon & Schuster

134. NOVEMBER 3, 1991
Larry Sabato
Feeding Frenzy: How Attack Journalism Has Transformed American Politics
Publisher: The Free Press

135. NOVEMBER 10, 1991
Tina Rosenberg
Children of Cain: Violence and the Violent in Latin America
Publisher: Morrow

136. NOVEMBER 17, 1991
Suzanne Garment
Scandal: The Culture of Mistrust in American Politics
Publisher: Times Books

137. NOVEMBER 24, 1991
James Stewart
Den of Thieves
Publisher: Simon & Schuster

138. DECEMBER 1, 1991
Gary Sick
October Surprise: America's Hostages in Iran and the Election of Ronald Reagan
Publisher: Times Books

139. DECEMBER 8, 1991
James Reston
Deadline: A Memoir
Publisher: Random House

140. DECEMBER 15, 1991
Thomas Byrne Edsall and
Mary Edsall
Chain Reaction: The Impact of Race, Rights and Taxes on American Politics
Publisher: Norton

141. DECEMBER 22, 1991
Martin Gilbert
Churchill: A Life
Publisher: Henry Holt

142. DECEMBER 29, 1991
Jimmy Breslin
Damon Runyan: A Life
Publisher: Ticknor & Fields

143. JANUARY 5, 1992
Charles Hamilton
Adam Clayton Powell, Jr.: The Political Biography of an American Dilemma
Publisher: Atheneum

144. JANUARY 12, 1992
August Heckscher
Woodrow Wilson: A Biography
Publisher: Scribner

145. JANUARY 26, 1992
Frederick Downs
No Longer Enemies, Not Yet Friends: An American Soldier Returns to Vietnam
Publisher: Norton

146. FEBRUARY 2, 1992
Robert Cwiklik
House Rules: A Freshman Congressman's Initiation to the Backslapping, Backpedaling, and Backstabbing Ways of Washington
Publisher: Villard Books

147. FEBRUARY 9, 1992
Francis Fukuyama
The End of History and the Last Man
Publisher: The Free Press

148. FEBRUARY 16, 1992
Sen. Al Gore
Earth in the Balance: Ecology and the Human Spirit
Publisher: Houghton Mifflin

149. FEBRUARY 23, 1992 (PART ONE)
Richard Nixon
Seize the Moment: America's Challenge in a One-Superpower World
Publisher: Simon & Schuster

150. MARCH 1, 1992 (PART TWO)
Richard Nixon
Seize the Moment: America's Challenge in a One-Superpower World
Publisher: Simon & Schuster

151. MARCH 8, 1992
Robert Massie
Dreadnought: Britain, Germany and the Coming of the Great War
Publisher: Random House

152. MARCH 22, 1992
Linda Chavez
Out of the Barrio: Toward a New Politics of Hispanic Assimilation
Publisher: Basic Books

153. MARCH 29, 1992
Nan Robertson
The Girls in the Balcony: Women, Men and The New York Times
Publisher: Random House

154. APRIL 5, 1992
Robert Remini
Henry Clay: Statesman for the Union
Publisher: Norton

155. APRIL 12, 1992
Orlando Patterson
Freedom in the Making of Western Culture
Publisher: Basic Books

156. APRIL 19, 1992
Paul Hollander
Anti-Americanism: Critiques at Home and Abroad, 1965–1990
Publisher: Oxford University Press

157. APRIL 26, 1992
Tinsley Yarbrough
John Marshall Harlan: Great Dissenter of the Warren Court
Publisher: Oxford University Press

158. MAY 3, 1992
Earl Black and Merle Black
The Vital South: How Presidents Are Elected
Publisher: Harvard University Press

159. MAY 10, 1992
David Moore
The Superpollsters: How They Measure and Manipulate Public Opinion in America
Publisher: Four Walls Eight Windows

160. MAY 17, 1992
Robert Bartley
The Seven Fat Years and How to Do it Again
Publisher: The Free Press

161. MAY 24, 1992
Lewis Puller, Jr.

Fortunate Son: The Autobiography of Lewis Puller, Jr.
Publisher: Grove Weidenfeld

162. MAY 31, 1992
Lester Thurow
Head to Head: The Coming Economic Battle Among Japan, Europe and America
Publisher: Morrow

163. JUNE 7, 1992
R. Emmett Tyrell, Jr.
The Conservative Crack-Up
Publisher: Simon & Schuster

164. JUNE 14, 1992
William Lee Miller
The Business of May Next: James Madison and the Founding
Publisher: The University Press of Virginia

165. JUNE 21, 1992
John Jackley
Hill Rat: Blowing the Lid off Congress
Publisher: Regnery

166. JUNE 28, 1992
David Savage
Turning Right: The Making of the Rehnquist Supreme Court
Publisher: John Wiley & Sons

167. JULY 5, 1992
William Rehnquist
Grand Inquests: The Historic Impeachments of Justice Samuel Chase and President Andrew Johnson
Publisher: Morrow

168. JULY 12, 1992
Jeffrey Bell
Populism and Elitism: Politics in the Age of Equality
Publisher: Regnery

169. JULY 19, 1992
David McCullough
Truman
Publisher: Simon & Schuster

170. JULY 26, 1992
Richard Ben Cramer
What It Takes: The Way to the White House
Publisher: Random House

171. AUGUST 2, 1992
Gilbert Fite
Richard B. Russell, Jr.: Senator from Georgia

Publisher: University of North Carolina Press

172. AUGUST 9, 1992
Robert Donovan and Ray Scherer
Unsilent Revolution: Television News and American Public Life
Publisher: Cambridge University Press

173. AUGUST 16, 1992
Martin Anderson
Impostors in the Temple: American Intellectuals Are Destroying Our Universities and Cheating Our Students of Their Future
Publisher: Simon & Schuster

174. AUGUST 23, 1992
Mickey Kaus
The End of Equality
Publisher: Basic Books

175. AUGUST 30, 1992
Neil Postman
Technopoly: The Surrender of Culture to Technology
Publisher: Knopf

176. SEPTEMBER 6, 1992
Terry Eastland
Energy in the Executive: The Case for a Strong Presidency
Publisher: The Free Press

177. SEPTEMBER 13, 1992
James Billington
Russia Transformed: Breakthrough to Hope
Publisher: The Free Press

178. SEPTEMBER 20, 1992
Paul Simon
Advise and Consent: Clarence Thomas, Robert Bork and the Intriguing History of the Supreme Court's Nomination Battles
Publisher: National Press Books

179. SEPTEMBER 27, 1992
Walter Isaacson
Kissinger: A Biography
Publisher: Simon & Schuster

[October 4, 1992: Preempted by U.S. House of Representatives]

[October 11, 1992: Preempted by Presidential Debate]

180. OCTOBER 18, 1992
George Will
Restoration: Congress, Term Limits and the Recovery of Deliberative Democracy
Publisher: The Free Press

181. OCTOBER 25, 1992
Susan Faludi
Backlash: The Undeclared War Against American Women
Publisher: Crown

182. NOVEMBER 8, 1992
Barbara Hinkley and Paul Brace
Follow the Leader: Opinion Polls and the Modern Presidents
Publisher: Basic Books

183. NOVEMBER 15, 1992
Derrick Bell
Faces at the Bottom of the Well: The Permanence of Racism
Publisher: Basic Books

184. NOVEMBER 22, 1992
Gen. Norman Schwartzkopf
It Doesn't Take a Hero
Publisher: Bantam Books

185. NOVEMBER 29, 1992
Charles Sykes
A Nation of Victims: The Decay of the American Character
Publisher: St. Martin's Press

186. DECEMBER 6, 1992
Daniel Boorstin
The Creators
Publisher: Random House

187. DECEMBER 13, 1992
Brian Kelly
Adventures in Porkland: How Washington Wastes Your Money and Why They Don't Stop
Publisher: Villard Books

188. DECEMBER 20, 1992
Eric Alterman
Sound & Fury: The Washington Punditocracy and the Collapse of American Politics
Publisher: HarperCollins

189. DECEMBER 27, 1992
Michael Medved
Hollywood vs. America: Popular Culture and the War on Traditional Values
Publisher: HarperCollins

190. JANUARY 3, 1993
Michael Davis and Hunter Clark
Thurgood Marshall: Warrior at the Bar, Rebel on the Bench
Publisher: The Carol Publishing Group

191. JANUARY 10, 1993
Jeffrey Birnbaum
The Lobbyists: How Influence Peddlers Get Their Way in Washington
Publisher: Times Books

192. JANUARY 17, 1993
P. F. Bentley
Clinton: Portrait of Victory
Publisher: Warner Books

193. JANUARY 24, 1993
Robert Gilbert
The Mortal Presidency: Illness and Anguish in the White House
Publisher: Basic Books

194. JANUARY 30, 1993
Benjamin Stein
License to Steal: The Untold Story of Michael Milken and the Conspiracy to Bilk the Nation
Publisher: Simon & Schuster

195. FEBRUARY 7, 1993
Jack Nelson
Terror in the Night: The Klan's Campaign Against the Jews
Publisher: Simon & Schuster

196. FEBRUARY 14, 1993
Nathan Miller
Theodore Roosevelt: A Life
Publisher: Morrow

197. FEBRUARY 21, 1993
Richard Norton Smith
Patriarch: George Washington and the New American Nation
Publisher: Houghton Mifflin

198. FEBRUARY 28, 1993
Kay Mills
This Little Light of Mine: The Life of Fannie Lou Hamer
Publisher: Dutton

199. MARCH 6, 1993
Alex Dragnich
Serbs and Croats: The Struggle in Yugoslavia
Publisher: Harcourt Brace Jovanovich

200. MARCH 13, 1993
Paul Kennedy
Preparing for the Twenty-first Century
Publisher: Random House

201. MARCH 21, 1993
Deborah Shapley
Promise and Power: The Life and Times of Robert McNamara
Publisher: Little, Brown

202. MARCH 28, 1993
Michael Kelly
Martyrs' Day: Chronicle of a Small War
Publisher: Random House

203. APRIL 4, 1993
Nadine Cohodas
Strom Thurmond & the Politics of Southern Change
Publisher: Simon & Schuster

204. APRIL 11, 1993
Blanche Wiesen Cook
Eleanor Roosevelt: Volume 1, 1884–1933
Publisher: Viking

205. APRIL 18, 1993
Douglas Brinkley
The Majic Bus: An American Odyssey
Publisher: Harcourt Brace

206. APRIL 25, 1993
Lisa Belkin
First, Do No Harm: The Dramatic Story of Real Doctors and Patients Making Impossible Choices at a Big-City Hospital
Publisher: Simon & Schuster

207. MAY 2, 1993
Marshall DeBruhl
Sword of San Jacinto: A Life of Sam Houston
Publisher: Random House

208. MAY 9, 1993
Charles Adams
For Good and Evil: The Impact of Taxes on the Course of Civilization
Publisher: Madison Books

209. MAY 16, 1993
Anna Quindlen
Thinking Out Loud: On the Personal, the Political, the Public and the Private
Publisher: Random House

210. MAY 23, 1993
George Ball
The Passionate Attachment: America's Involvement with Israel, 1947 to the Present
Publisher: Norton

211. MAY 30, 1993
Douglas Davis
The Five Myths of Television Power: Or, Why the Medium Is Not the Message
Publisher: Simon & Schuster

212. JUNE 6, 1993
J. Bowyer Bell
The Irish Troubles: A Generation of Violence, 1967–1992
Publisher: St. Martin's Press

213. JUNE 13, 1993
David Brock
The Real Anita Hill
Publisher: The Free Press

214. JUNE 20, 1993
Howard Kurtz
Media Circus: The Trouble with America's Newspapers
Publisher: Times Books

215. JUNE 27, 1993
George Shultz
Turmoil and Triumph: My Years as Secretary of State
Publisher: Scribner

216. JULY 4, 1993
Joel Krieger
The Oxford Companion to Politics of the World
Publisher: Oxford University Press

217. JULY 11, 1993
David Halberstam
The Fifties
Publisher: Villard Books

218. JULY 18, 1993
Molly Moore
A Woman at War: Storming Kuwait with the U.S. Marines
Publisher: Scribner

219. JULY 25, 1993
David Remnick
Lenin's Tomb: The Last Days of the Soviet Empire
Publisher: Random House

220. AUGUST 1, 1993
Alexander Brook
The Hard Way: The Odyssey of a Weekly Newspaper Editor
Publisher: Bridge Works

221. AUGUST 8, 1993
Tom Rosenstiel
Strange Bedfellows: How Television and the Presidential Candidates Changed American Politics, 1992
Publisher: Hyperion

222. AUGUST 15, 1993
Lewis Lapham
The Wish for Kings: Democracy at Bay
Publisher: Grove Press

223. AUGUST 22, 1993
Harold Holzer
The Lincoln-Douglas Debates
Publisher: HarperCollins

224. AUGUST 29, 1993
Peter Macdonald
Giap: The Victor in Vietnam
Publisher: Norton

225. SEPTEMBER 5, 1993
Joseph Ellis
Passionate Sage: The Character and Legacy of John Adams
Publisher: Norton

226. SEPTEMBER 12, 1993
Ronald Kessler
The FBI: Inside the World's Most Powerful Law Enforcement Agency
Publisher: Pocket Books

227. SEPTEMBER 19, 1993
Madeline Cartwright
For the Children: Lessons from a Visionary Principal
Publisher: Doubleday

228. SEPTEMBER 26, 1993
Malcolm Browne
Muddy Boots and Red Socks
Publisher: Times Books

229. OCTOBER 3, 1993
Peter Skerry
Mexican-Americans: The Ambivalent Minority
Publisher: The Free Press

230. OCTOBER 10, 1993
Alan Brinkley
The Unfinished Nation: A Concise History of the American People
Publisher: Knopf

231. OCTOBER 17, 1993
Christopher Hitchens
For the Sake of Argument
Publisher: Verso

232. OCTOBER 24, 1993
William F. Buckley, Jr.
Happy Days Were Here Again: Reflections of a Libertarian Journalist
Publisher: Random House

233. OCTOBER 31, 1993
Andrew Nagorski
The Birth of Freedom: Shaping Lives and Societies in the New Eastern Europe
Publisher: Simon & Schuster

234. NOVEMBER 7, 1993
Charles Mee
Playing God: Seven Fateful Moments When Great Men Met to Change the World
Publisher: Simon & Schuster

235. NOVEMBER 14, 1993
Herbert Block
Herblock: A Cartoonist's Life
Publisher: Macmillan

[November 21, 1993: Preempted by U.S. House of Representatives]

236. NOVEMBER 28, 1993
Betty Friedan
The Fountain of Age
Publisher: Simon & Schuster

237. DECEMBER 5, 1993
Margaret Thatcher
The Downing Street Years
Publisher: HarperCollins

238. DECEMBER 12, 1993
Richard Reeves
President Kennedy: Profile of Power
Publisher: Simon & Schuster

239. DECEMBER 19, 1993
John Podhoretz
Hell of a Ride: Backstage at the White House Follies, 1989–1993
Publisher: Simon & Schuster

240. DECEMBER 26, 1993
Willard Sterne Randall
Thomas Jefferson: A Life
Publisher: Henry Holt

241. JANUARY 2, 1994
David Levering Lewis

W. E. B. Du Bois (1868–1919): The Biography of a Race
Publisher: Henry Holt

242. JANUARY 9, 1994
William Bennett
The Book of Virtues: A Treasury of Great Moral Stories
Publisher: Simon & Schuster

243. JANUARY 16, 1994
Carolyn Barta
Perot and His People: Disrupting the Balance of Political Power
Publisher: The Summit Group

244. JANUARY 23, 1994
Gary Hymel (co-author with Tip O'Neill)
All Politics is Local and Other Rules of the Game
Publisher: Times Books

245. JANUARY 30, 1994
William Chafe
Never Stop Running: Allard Lowenstein and the Struggle to Save American Liberalism
Publisher: Basic Books

246. FEBRUARY 6, 1994
Stanley Weintraub
Disraeli: A Biography
Publisher: Dutton

247. FEBRUARY 13, 1994
Bill Emmott
Japanophobia: The Myth of the Invincible Japanese
Publisher: Times Books

248. FEBRUARY 20, 1994
Peter Arnett
Live from the Battlefield: From Vietnam to Baghdad, Thirty-five Years in the World's War Zones
Publisher: Simon & Schuster

249. FEBRUARY 27, 1994
Stephen Lesher
George Wallace: American Populist
Publisher: Addison-Wesley

250. MARCH 6, 1994
Nathan McCall
Makes Me Wanna Holler: A Young Black Man in America
Publisher: Random House

251. MARCH 13, 1994
Norman Ornstein
Debt and Taxes: How America Got into Its Budget Mess and

What to Do About It
Publisher: Times Books

252. MARCH 20, 1994
Clare Brandt
The Man in the Mirror: A Life of Benedict Arnold
Publisher: Random House

253. MARCH 27, 1994
John Corry
My Times: Adventures in the News Trade
Publisher: Putnam

254. APRIL 3, 1994
Andrew Young
A Way Out of No Way: The Spiritual Memoirs of Andrew Young
Publisher: Thomas Nelson Communications

[April 10, 1994 Booknotes Fifth Anniversary Special]

255. APRIL 17, 1994
James Cannon
Time and Chance: Gerald Ford's Appointment with History
Publisher: HarperCollins

[April 24, 1994: Encore Booknotes Richard Nixon (Part Two)

256. MAY 1, 1994
Howell Raines
Fly Fishing Through the Midlife Crisis
Publisher: Morrow

257. MAY 8, 1994
John Keegan
A History of Warfare
Publisher: Knopf

258. MAY 15, 1994
Forrest McDonald
The American Presidency: An Intellectual History
Publisher: University of Kansas Press

259. MAY 22, 1994
James McPherson
What They Fought For, 1861–1865
Publisher: Louisiana State University Press

260. MAY 29, 1994
Pete Hamill
A Drinking Life: A Memoir
Publisher: Little, Brown

261. JUNE 5, 1994
Stephen Ambrose
D-Day: June 6, 1944: The Climactic Battle of World War II
Publisher: Simon & Schuster

262. JUNE 12, 1994
Mark Neely
The Last Best Hope of Earth: Abraham Lincoln and the Promise of America
Publisher: Harvard University Press

263. JUNE 19, 1994
Sam Roberts
Who We Are: A Portrait of America
Publisher: Times Books

264. JUNE 26, 1994
Lani Guinier
The Tyranny of the Majority: Fundamental Fairness in Representative Democracy
Publisher: Martin Kessler Books

265. JULY 3, 1994
Murray Kempton
Rebellions, Perversities, and Main Events
Publisher: Times Books

266. JULY 10, 1994
Cal Thomas
The Things That Matter Most
Publisher: HarperCollins

267. JULY 17, 1994
David Hackett Fischer
Paul Revere's Ride
Publisher: Oxford University Press

268. JULY 24, 1994
Dan Quayle
Standing Firm
Publisher: HarperCollins

269. JULY 31, 1994
Colman McCarthy
All of One Peace: Essays on Nonviolence
Publisher: Rutgers University Press

270. AUGUST 7, 1994
Peter Collier
The Roosevelts: An American Saga
Publisher: Simon & Schuster

271. AUGUST 14, 1994
Merrill Peterson
Lincoln in American Memory
Publisher: Oxford University Press

272. AUGUST 21, 1994
Hugh Pearson
The Shadow of the Panther: Huey Newton and the Price of Black Power in America
Publisher: Addison-Wesley

273. AUGUST 28, 1994
John Leo
Two Steps Ahead of the Thought Police
Publisher: Simon & Schuster

274. SEPTEMBER 4, 1994
Paul Weaver
News and the Culture of Lying: How Journalism Really Works
Publisher: The Free Press

275. SEPTEMBER 11, 1994
Shelby Foote
Stars in Their Courses: The Gettysburg Campaign
Publisher: Modern Library

276. SEPTEMBER 18, 1994
Irving Bartlett
John C. Calhoun: A Biography
Publisher: Norton

277. SEPTEMBER 25, 1994
Ben Yagoda
Will Rogers: A Biography
Publisher: Knopf

278. OCTOBER 2, 1994
Harry Jaffe and Tom Sherwood
Dream City: Race, Power and the Decline of Washington, D.C.
Publisher: Simon & Schuster

279. OCTOBER 9, 1994
Henry Louis Gates, Jr.
Colored People: A Memoir
Publisher: Knopf

280. OCTOBER 16, 1994
Nicholas Kristof and Sheryl Wudunn
China Wakes: The Struggle for the Soul of a Rising Power
Publisher: Times Books

281. OCTOBER 23, 1994
Liz Carpenter
Unplanned Parenthood
Publisher: Random House

282. OCTOBER 30, 1994
David Frum
Dead Right
Publisher: Basic Books

283. NOVEMBER 6, 1994
Bill Thomas
Club Fed: Power, Money, Sex and Violence on Capitol Hill
Publisher: Scribner

284. NOVEMBER 13, 1994
John Kenneth Galbraith
A Journey Through Economic Time: A Firsthand View
Publisher: Houghton Mifflin

285. NOVEMBER 20, 1994
Milton Friedman
Introduction to F. A. Hayek's
Road to Serfdom
Publisher: University of Chicago Press

286. NOVEMBER 27, 1994
Melba Pattillo Beals
Warriors Don't Cry: A Searing Memoir of the Battle to Integrate Little Rock's Central High
Publisher: Pocket Books

287. DECEMBER 4, 1994
Charles Murray
The Bell Curve: Intelligence and Class Structure in American Life
Publisher: The Free Press

288. DECEMBER 11, 1994
Elizabeth Drew
On the Edge: The Clinton Presidency
Publisher: Simon & Schuster

289. DECEMBER 18, 1994
Peter Robinson
Snapshots from Hell: The Making of an MBA
Publisher: Warner Books

290. DECEMBER 25, 1994
Glenn Frankel
Beyond the Promised Land: Jews and Arabs on a Hard Road to a New Israel
Publisher: Simon & Schuster

291. JANUARY 1, 1995
Doris Kearns Goodwin
No Ordinary Time: Franklin and Eleanor Roosevelt: The Home Front in World War II
Publisher: Simon & Schuster

292. JANUARY 8, 1995
Robert Wright

The Moral Animal: Why We Are the Way We Are: The New Science of Evolutionary Psychology
Publisher: Pantheon

293. JANUARY 15, 1995
Anthony Cave Brown
Treason in the Blood: H. St. John Philby, Kim Philby, and the Spy Case of the Century
Publisher: Houghton Mifflin

294. JANUARY 22, 1995
Marvin Olasky
The Tragedy of American Compassion
Publisher: Regnery

295. JANUARY 29, 1995
Steven Waldman
The Bill: How the Adventures of Clinton's National Service Bill Reveal What is Corrupt, Comic, Cynical and Noble about Washington
Publisher: Viking

296. FEBRUARY 5, 1995
M. Stanton Evans
The Theme is Freedom: Religion, Politics and the American Tradition
Publisher: Regnery

297. FEBRUARY 12, 1995
Philip Howard
The Death of Common Sense: How Law is Suffocating America
Publisher: Random House

298. FEBRUARY 19, 1995
Jimmy Carter
Always a Reckoning and Other Poems
Publisher: Times Books

299. FEBRUARY 26, 1995
Alan Ryan
Introduction to de Tocqueville's
Democracy in America
Publisher: Knopf

300. MARCH 5, 1995
Lynn Sherr
Failure Is Impossible: Susan B. Anthony in Her Own Words
Publisher: Times Books

301. MARCH 12, 1995
Donald Kagan
On the Origins of War
Publisher: Doubleday

302. MARCH 19, 1995
Neil Baldwin
Edison: Inventing the Century
Publisher: Hyperion

303. MARCH 26, 1995
James Loewen
Lies My Teacher Told Me: Everything Your American History Textbook Got Wrong
Publisher: The New Press

304. APRIL 2, 1995
Gertrude Himmelfarb
The De-Moralization of Society: From Victorian Virtues to Modern Values
Publisher: Knopf

305. APRIL 9, 1995
Stanley Greenberg
Middle Class Dreams: The Politics and Power of the New American Majority
Publisher: Times Books

306. APRIL 16, 1995
Alvin and Heidi Toffler
Creating a New Civilization: The Politics of the Third Wave
Publisher: Turner Publishing, Inc.

307. APRIL 23, 1995
Robert McNamara
In Retrospect: The Tragedy and Lessons of Vietnam
Publisher: Times Books

308. APRIL 30, 1995
Michael Klare
Rogue States and Nuclear Outlaws: America's Search for a New Foreign Policy
Publisher: Farrar, Straus & Giroux

309. MAY 7, 1995
David Maraniss
First in His Class: A Biography of Bill Clinton
Publisher: Simon & Schuster

310. MAY 14, 1995
Tim Penny and Major Garrett
Common Cents
Publisher: Little, Brown

311. MAY 21, 1995
Linn Washington
Black Judges on Justice
Publisher: The New Press

312. MAY 28, 1995
John Niven
Salmon P. Chase: A Biography
Publisher: Oxford University Press

313. JUNE 4, 1995
Hanan Ashrawi
This Side of Peace
Publisher: Simon & Schuster

314. JUNE 11, 1995
Peter Brimelow
Alien Nation: Common Sense About America's Immigration Disaster
Publisher: Random House

315. JUNE 18, 1995
Yuri Shvets
Washington Station: My Life as a KGB Spy in America
Publisher: Simon & Schuster

316. JUNE 25, 1995
Norman Mailer
Oswald's Tale: An American Mystery
Publisher: Random House

317. JULY 2, 1995
Ari Hoogenboom
Rutherford B. Hayes: Warrior and President
Publisher: University Press of Kansas

318. JULY 9, 1995
DeWayne Wickham
Woodholme: A Black Man's Story of Growing Up Alone
Publisher: Farrar, Straus & Giroux

319. JULY 16, 1995
Armstrong Williams
Beyond Blame: How We Can Succeed by Breaking the Dependency Barrier
Publisher: The Free Press

320. JULY 23, 1995
Newt Gingrich
To Renew America
Publisher: HarperCollins

321. JULY 30, 1995
John Hockenberry
Moving Violations, A Memoir: War Zones, Wheelchairs, and Declarations of Independence
Publisher: Hyperion

322. AUGUST 6, 1995
Marc Fisher
After the Wall: Germany, the Germans and the Burdens of History
Publisher: Simon & Schuster

323. AUGUST 13, 1995
Robert D. Richardson, Jr.
Emerson—The Mind on Fire
Publisher: University of California Press

324. AUGUST 20, 1995
Cartha "Deke" DeLoach
Hoover's FBI: The Inside Story by Hoover's Trusted Lieutenant
Publisher: Regnery

325. AUGUST 27, 1995
Robert Timberg
The Nightingale's Song
Publisher: Simon & Schuster

326. SEPTEMBER 3, 1995
Robert Leckie
Okinawa: The Last Battle of World War II
Publisher: Viking

327. SEPTEMBER 10, 1995
Emory Thomas
Robert E. Lee: A Biography
Publisher: Norton

328. SEPTEMBER 17, 1995
Elsa Walsh
Divided Lives: The Public and Private Struggles of Three Accomplished Women
Publisher: Simon & Schuster

329. SEPTEMBER 24, 1995
Irving Kristol
Neoconservatism: The Autobiography of an Idea
Publisher: The Free Press

330. OCTOBER 1, 1995
Andrew Sullivan
Virtually Normal: An Argument About Homosexuality
Publisher: Knopf

331. OCTOBER 8, 1995
Susan Eisenhower
Breaking Free: A Memoir of Love
Publisher: Farrar, Straus & Giroux

332. OCTOBER 15, 1995
Nicholas Basbanes
A Gentle Madness: Bibliophiles,

Bibliomanes, and the Eternal Passion for Books
Publisher: Henry Holt

333. OCTOBER 22, 1995
David Fromkin
In the Time of Americans: The Generation That Changed America's Role in the World
Publisher: Knopf

334. OCTOBER 29, 1995
Ben Bradlee
A Good Life: Newspapering and Other Adventures
Publisher: Simon & Schuster

335. NOVEMBER 5, 1995
Marlin Fitzwater
Call the Briefing! Reagan and Bush, Sam and Helen: A Decade with Presidents and the Press
Publisher: Times Books

336. NOVEMBER 12, 1995
Pierre Salinger
P.S., A Memoir
Publisher: St. Martin's Press

337. NOVEMBER 19, 1995
bell hooks
Killing Rage: Ending Racism
Publisher: Henry Holt

338. NOVEMBER 26, 1995
Sanford Ungar
Fresh Blood: The New American Immigrants
Publisher: Simon & Schuster

339. DECEMBER 3, 1995
James Baker (with Thomas DeFrank)
The Politics of Diplomacy: Revolution, War and Peace, 1989–1992
Publisher: Putnam

340. DECEMBER 10, 1995
David Brinkley
A Memoir
Publisher: Knopf

341. DECEMBER 17, 1995
Evan Thomas
The Very Best Men—Four Who Dared: The Early Years of the CIA
Publisher: Simon & Schuster

342. DECEMBER 24, 1995
David Herbert Donald
Lincoln
Publisher: Simon & Schuster

343. DECEMBER 31, 1995
Charles Kuralt
Charles Kuralt's America
Publisher: Putnam

344. JANUARY 7, 1996
Colin Powell
My American Journey
Publisher: Random House

345. JANUARY 14, 1996
William Prochnau
Once upon a Distant War
Publisher: Times Books

346. JANUARY 21, 1996
Michael Kinsley
Big Babies
Publisher: Morrow

347. JANUARY 28, 1996
Carlo D'Este
Patton: A Genius for War
Publisher: HarperCollins

348. FEBRUARY 4, 1996
Dennis Prager
Think a Second Time
Publisher: HarperCollins

349. FEBRUARY 11, 1996
Lance Banning
The Sacred Fire of Liberty: James Madison and the Founding of the Federal Republic
Publisher: Cornell University Press

350. FEBRUARY 18, 1996
Dan Balz (with Ronald Brownstein)
Storming the Gates: Protest Politics and Republican Revival
Publisher: Little, Brown

351. FEBRUARY 25, 1996
H. W. Brands
The Reckless Decade: America in the 1890s
Publisher: St. Martin's Press

352. MARCH 3, 1996
Hillary Rodham Clinton
It Takes a Village: And Other Lessons Children Teach Us
Publisher: Simon & Schuster

353. MARCH 10, 1996
Johanna Neuman
Lights, Camera, War: Is Media Technology Driving International Politics?
Publisher: St. Martin's Press

354. MARCH 17, 1996
Clarence Page
Showing My Color: Impolite Essays on Race and Identity
Publisher: HarperCollins

355. MARCH 24, 1996
Robert Merry
Taking on the World: Joseph and Stewart Alsop, Guardians of the American Century
Publisher: Viking

356. MARCH 31, 1996
Fox Butterfield
All God's Children: The Bosket Family and the American Tradition of Violence
Publisher: Knopf

357. APRIL 7, 1996
Jean Baker
The Stevensons: A Biography of an American Family
Publisher: Norton

358. APRIL 14, 1996
Wayne Fields
Union of Words: A History of Presidential Eloquence
Publisher: The Free Press

359. APRIL 21, 1996
Robert Kaplan
The Ends of the Earth: A Journey at the Dawn of the 21st Century
Publisher: Simon & Schuster

360. APRIL 28, 1996
David Reynolds
Walt Whitman's America: A Cultural Biography
Publisher: Knopf

361. MAY 5, 1996
David Broder (with Haynes Johnson)
The System: The American Way of Politics at the Breaking Point
Publisher: Little, Brown

362. MAY 12, 1996
Stanley Crouch
The All-American Skin Game, or the Decoy of Race: The Long and Short of It, 1990–1994
Publisher: Pantheon Books

363. MAY 19, 1996
Michael Sandel
Democracy's Discontent: America in Search of a Public Philosophy
Publisher: Harvard University Press

364. MAY 26, 1996
Noa Ben Artzi-Pelossof
In the Name of Sorrow and Hope
Publisher: Knopf

365. JUNE 2, 1996
James Thomas Flexner
Maverick's Progress: An Autobiography
Publisher: Fordham University Press

366. JUNE 9, 1996
Christopher Matthews
Kennedy and Nixon: The Rivalry That Shaped Postwar America
Publisher: Simon & Schuster

367. JUNE 16, 1996
Albert Murray
Blue Devils of Nada: A Contemporary American Approach to Aesthetic Statement
Publisher: Pantheon

368. JUNE 23, 1996
Seymour Martin Lipset
American Exceptionalism: A Double-Edged Sword
Publisher: Norton

369. JUNE 30, 1996
Glenn Simpson (with Larry Sabato)
Dirty Little Secrets: The Persistence of Corruption in American Politics
Publisher: Times Books

370. JULY 7, 1996
Paul Greenberg
No Surprises: Two Decades of Clinton Watching
Publisher: Brassey's

371. JULY 14, 1996
Ted Sorensen
Why I Am a Democrat
Publisher: Henry Holt

372. JULY 21, 1996
Eleanor Randolph
Waking the Tempests: Ordinary Life in New Russia
Publisher: Simon & Schuster

373. JULY 28, 1996
James Lardner
Crusader: The Hell-Raising Police Career of Detective David Durk
Publisher: Random House

374. AUGUST 4, 1996
Denis Brian

Einstein: A Life
Publisher: John Wiley & Sons

[August 11 and August 18, 1996: Preempted by Reform Party Convention]

375. AUGUST 25, 1996
Eleanor Clift and Tom Brazaitis
War Without Bloodshed: The Art of Politics
Publisher: Scribner

376. SEPTEMBER 1, 1996
Drew Gilpin Faust
Mothers of Invention: Women of the Slaveholding South in the American Civil War
Publisher: University of North Carolina Press

377. SEPTEMBER 8, 1996
Donald Warren
Radio Priest: Charles Coughlin, the Father of Hate Radio
Publisher: The Free Press

378. SEPTEMBER 15, 1996
Lloyd Kramer
Lafayette in Two Worlds
Publisher: University of North Carolina Press

379. SEPTEMBER 22, 1996
Michael Elliott
The Day Before Yesterday: Reconsidering America's Past, Rediscovering the Present
Publisher: Simon & Schuster

380. SEPTEMBER 29, 1996
Monica Crowley
Nixon off the Record: His Candid Commentary on People and Politics
Publisher: Random House

[October 6, 1996: Preempted by Presidential Debate in Hartford, Ct]

381. OCTOBER 13, 1996
Louise Barnett
Touched by Fire: The Life, Death, and Mythic Afterlife of George Armstrong Custer
Publisher: Henry Holt

382. OCTOBER 20, 1996
David Friedman
Hidden Order: The Economics of Everyday Life
Publisher: HarperBusiness

383. OCTOBER 27, 1996
Paul Hendrickson
The Living and the Dead: Robert McNamara and Five Lives of a Lost War
Publisher: Knopf

384. NOVEMBER 3, 1996
Andrew Ferguson
Fools' Names, Fools' Faces
Publisher: Atlantic Monthly Press

385. NOVEMBER 10, 1996
Leon Dash
Rosa Lee: A Mother and Her Family in Urban America
Publisher: Basic Books

386. NOVEMBER 17, 1996
Conor Cruise O'Brien
The Long Affair: Thomas Jefferson and the French Revolution, 1785–1800
Publisher: University of Chicago Press

387. NOVEMBER 24, 1996
Mikhail Gorbachev
Memoirs
Publisher: Doubleday

388. DECEMBER 1, 1996
Robert Bork
Slouching Towards Gomorrah: Modern Liberalism and American Decline
Publisher: HarperCollins

389. DECEMBER 8, 1996
Nell Irvin Painter
Sojourner Truth: A Life, A Symbol
Publisher: Norton

390. DECEMBER 15, 1996
President Bill Clinton
Between Hope and History: Meeting America's Challenges for the 21st Century
Publisher: Times Books

391. DECEMBER 22, 1996
David Denby
Great Books: My Adventures with Homer, Rousseau, Woolf and Other Indestructible Writers of the Western World
Publisher: Simon & Schuster

392. DECEMBER 29, 1996
Stanley Wolpert
Nehru: A Tryst with Destiny
Publisher: Oxford University Press

393. JANUARY 5, 1997
Edward Jay Epstein
Dossier: The Secret History of Armand Hammer
Publisher: Random House

394. JANUARY 12, 1997
Robert Ferrell
The Strange Deaths of President Harding
Publisher: University of Missouri Press

395. JANUARY 19, 1997
Alfred Zacher
Trial & Triumph: Presidential Power in the Second Term
Publisher: Midpoint Trade Books

396. JANUARY 26, 1997
David Boaz
Libertarianism: A Primer
Publisher: The Free Press

397. FEBRUARY 2, 1997
Henry Grunwald
One Man's America: A Journalist's Search for the Heart of His Country
Publisher: Doubleday

398. FEBRUARY 9, 1997
John Brady
Bad Boy: The Life and Politics of Lee Atwater
Publisher: Addison-Wesley

399. FEBRUARY 16, 1997
Katharine Graham
Personal History
Publisher: Knopf

400. FEBRUARY 23, 1997 (PART ONE)
Sam Tanenhaus
Whittaker Chambers: A Biography
Publisher: Random House

401. MARCH 2, 1997 (PART TWO)
Sam Tanenhaus
Whittaker Chambers: A Biography
Publisher: Random House

402. MARCH 9, 1997
Sarah Gordon
Passage to Union: How the Railroads Transformed American Life, 1829–1929
Publisher: Ivan R. Dee

403. MARCH 16, 1997
John Fialka
War by Other Means: Economic Espionage in America
Publisher: Norton

404. MARCH 23, 1997
Jon Katz
Virtuous Reality: How America Surrendered Discussion of Moral Values to Opportunists, Nitwits and Blockheads like William Bennett
Publisher: Random House

405. MARCH 30, 1997
Claude Andrew Clegg III
An Original Man: The Life and Times of Elijah Muhammad
Publisher: St. Martin's Press

406. APRIL 6, 1997
Keith Richburg
Out of America: A Black Man Confronts Africa
Publisher: Basic Books

407. APRIL 13, 1997
David Horowitz
Radical Son: A Generational Odyssey
Publisher: The Free Press

408. APRIL 20, 1997
Leonard Garment
Crazy Rhythm: My Journey from Brooklyn, Jazz, and Wall Street to Nixon's White House, Watergate and Beyond
Publisher: Times Books

409. APRIL 27, 1997
Stephen Oates
The Approaching Fury: Voices of the Storm, 1820–1861
Publisher: HarperCollins

410. MAY 4, 1997
Christopher Buckley
Wry Martinis
Publisher: Random House

411. MAY 11, 1997
Richard Bernstein (with Ross Munro)
The Coming Conflict with China
Publisher: Knopf

412. MAY 18, 1997
Anne Matthews
Bright College Years: Inside the American Campus Today
Publisher: Simon & Schuster

413. MAY 25, 1997
Jane Holtz Kay
Asphalt Nation: How the Auto-mobile Took Over America, and How We Can Take It Back
Publisher: Crown Publishers

414. JUNE 1, 1997
Jill Krementz
The Writer's Desk
Publisher: Random House

415. JUNE 8, 1997
Pavel Palazchenko
My Years with Gorbachev and Shevardnadze: The Memoir of a Soviet Interpreter
Publisher: Penn State Press

416. JUNE 15, 1997
Walter McDougall
Promised Land, Crusader State: The American Encounter with the World Since 1776
Publisher: Houghton Mifflin

417. JUNE 22, 1997
James Humes
Confessions of a White House Ghostwriter: Five Presidents and Other Political Adventures
Publisher: Regnery

418. JUNE 29, 1997
Walter Cronkite
A Reporter's Life
Publisher: Knopf

419. JULY 6, 1997
Jack Rakove
Original Meanings: Politics and Ideas in the Making of the Constitution
Publisher: Knopf

420. JULY 13, 1997
Tom Clancy and Gen. Fred Franks (Ret.)
Into the Storm: A Study in Command
Publisher: Putnam

421. JULY 20, 1997
Robert Hughes
American Visions: The Epic History of Art in America
Publisher: Knopf

422. JULY 27, 1997
Sylvia Jukes Morris
Rage for Fame: The Ascent of Clare Boothe Luce
Publisher: Random House

423. AUGUST 3, 1997
LeAlan Jones (and Lloyd Newman)
Our America: Life and Death on the South Side of Chicago
Publisher: Scribner

424. AUGUST 10, 1997
James Tobin
Ernie Pyle's War: America's Eye-witness to World War II
Publisher: The Free Press

425. AUGUST 17, 1997
Pauline Maier
American Scripture: Making the Declaration of Independence
Publisher: Knopf

426. AUGUST 24, 1997
Peter Maas
Underboss: Sammy the Bull Gra-vano's Story of Life in the Mafia
Publisher: HarperCollins

427. AUGUST 31, 1997
Frank McCourt
Angela's Ashes: A Memoir
Publisher: Scribner

428. SEPTEMBER 7, 1997
Brian Burrell
The Words We Live By: The Creeds, Mottoes, and Pledges That Have Shaped America
Publisher: The Free Press

429. SEPTEMBER 14, 1997
John Toland
Captured by History: One Man's Vision of Our Tumultuous Century
Publisher: St. Martin's Press

430. SEPTEMBER 21, 1997
Peter Gomes
The Good Book: Reading the Bible with Mind and Heart
Publisher: Morrow

431. SEPTEMBER 28, 1997
John Berendt
Midnight in the Garden of Good and Evil: A Savannah Story
Publisher: Random House

432. OCTOBER 5, 1997
Howard Gardner
Extraordinary Minds: Portraits of Four Exceptional Individuals and an Examination of Our Own Extraordinariness
Publisher: Basic Books

433. OCTOBER 12, 1997
Geoffrey Perret
Ulysses S. Grant: Soldier and President
Publisher: Random House

434. OCTOBER 19, 1997
Nat Hentoff
Speaking Freely: A Memoir
Publisher: Knopf

435. OCTOBER 26, 1997
Alan Schom
Napoleon Bonaparte
Publisher: HarperCollins

436. NOVEMBER 2, 1997
Thomas West
Vindicating the Founders: Race, Sex, Class, and Justice in the Origins of America
Publisher: Rowman & Littlefield

[November 9, 1997: Preempted by coverage of the U.S. House of Representatives]

437. NOVEMBER 16, 1997
David Gelertner
Drawing Life: Surviving the Unabomber
Publisher: The Free Press

438. NOVEMBER 23, 1997
Anita Hill
Speaking Truth to Power
Publisher: Doubleday

439. NOVEMBER 30, 1997
Jeff Shesol
Mutual Contempt: Lyndon John-son, Robert Kennedy, and the Feud that Defined a Decade
Publisher: Norton

440. DECEMBER 7, 1997
Tim Russert
Meet the Press: Fifty Years of His-tory in the Making
Publisher: McGraw-Hill

441. DECEMBER 14, 1997
Susan Butler
East to the Dawn: The Life of Amelia Earhart
Publisher: Addison-Wesley

442. DECEMBER 21, 1997
Jim Hightower
There's Nothing in the Middle of the Road But Yellow Stripes and Dead Armadillos
Publisher: HarperCollins

473. JULY 26, 1998
Richard Holbrooke
To End a War
Publisher: Random House

474. AUGUST 2, 1998
F. Carolyn Graglia
Domestic Tranquility: A Brief Against Feminism
Publisher: Spence

475. AUGUST 9, 1998
Roy Reed
Faubus: The Life and Times of an American Prodigal
Publisher: University of Arkansas Press

476. AUGUST 16, 1998
Patricia O'Toole
Money and Morals in America
Publisher: Potter

477. AUGUST 23, 1998
Barbara Crossette
The Great Hill Stations of Asia
Publisher: Westview

478. AUGUST 30, 1998
Robert Sobel
Coolidge: An American Enigma
Publisher: Regnery

479. SEPTEMBER 6, 1998
Linda H. Davis
Badge of Courage: The Life of Stephen Crane
Publisher: Houghton Mifflin

480. SEPTEMBER 13, 1998
Arnold A. Rogow
A Fatal Friendship: Alexander Hamilton and Aaron Burr
Publisher: Hill and Wang

481. SEPTEMBER 20, 1998
Larry Tye
The Father of Spin: Edward L. Bernays & The Birth of Public Relations
Publisher: Crown Publishers

482. SEPTEMBER 27, 1998
Balint Vazsonyi
America's 30 Years War: Who Is Winning?
Publisher: Regnery

483. OCTOBER 4, 1998
George Bush and
Brent Scowcroft
A World Transformed
Publisher: Knopf

484. OCTOBER 11, 1998
Juan Williams
Thurgood Marshall: American Revolutionary
Publisher: Times Books

485. OCTOBER 18, 1998
Christopher Dickey
Summer of Deliverance: A Memoir of Father and Son
Publisher: Simon & Schuster

486. OCTOBER 25, 1998
Doroty Herrmann
Helen Keller: A Life
Publisher: Knopf

487. NOVEMBER 1, 1998
Charles Lewis
The Buying of the Congress: How Special Interests Have Stolen Your Right to Life, Liberty, and the Pursuit of Happiness
Publisher: Avon Books

488. NOVEMBER 8, 1998
Simon Winchester
The Professor and the Madman: A Tale of Murder, Insanity, and the Making of the Oxford English Dictionary
Publisher: HarperCollins

489. NOVEMBER 15, 1998
Eric Foner
The Story of American Freedom
Publisher: Norton

490. NOVEMBER 22, 1998
Philip Gourevitch
We wish to inform you that tomorrow we will be killed with our families: Stories from Rwanda
Publisher: Farrar, Straus & Giroux

491. NOVEMBER 29, 1998
Melissa Muller
Anne Frank: The Biography
Publisher: Metropolitan Books

492. DECEMBER 6, 1998
Shelby Steele
A Dream Deferred: The Second Betrayal of Black Freedom in America
Publisher: HarperCollins

493. DECEMBER 13, 1998
William Greider
Fortress America: The American Military and the Consequences of Peace
Publisher: PublicAffairs

494. DECEMBER 20, 1998
A. Scott Berg
Lindbergh
Publisher: Putnam

495. DECEMBER 27, 1998
Peter Jennings
The Century
Publisher: Doubleday

496. JANUARY 3, 1999
P. J. O'Rourke
Eat the Rich
Publisher: Grove Atlantic

497. JANUARY 10, 1999
John Morris
Get the Picture: A Personal History of Photojournalism
Publisher: Random House

498. JANUARY 17, 1999
Dava Sobel
Longitude: The True Story of a Lone Genius Who Solved the Greatest Scientific Problem of His Time
Publisher: Walker

499. JANUARY 24, 1999
Michael Ignatieff
Isaiah Berlin: A Life
Publisher: Metropolitan Books

500. JANUARY 31, 1999
Peter Kann and
Frances FitzGerald
Reporting Vietnam
Publisher: Library of America

Photo Notes

John S.D. Eisenhower, 11:30 A.M., March 18, 1998, National Portrait Gallery, Washington, D.C.

Sam Tanenhaus, 8 A.M., April 7, 1998, Chambers childhood home, Lynbrook, New York

David Reynolds, 2 P.M., April 7, 1998, Whitman house, Old Westbury, New York

Jon Katz, 9:30 A.M., April 8, 1998, Paine house, New Rochelle, New York

Neil Baldwin, 2:30 P.M., April 8, 1998, Edison laboratory, West Orange, New Jersey

Blanche Wiesen Cook, 11 A.M., April 9, 1998, Riverside Park, New York, New York

Edward Epstein, 12:30 P.M., April 9, 1998, Epstein residence, New York, New York

Monica Crowley, 12:30 P.M., April 10, 1998, former Nixon residence, Upper Saddle River, New Jersey

Carol Reardon, 3 P.M., April 27, 1998, Gettysburg battlefield, Gettysburg, Pennsylvania

Leon Dash, 8:30 A.M., April 29, 1998, New York Avenue, Washington, D.C.

Robert Merry, 12 noon, May 6, 1998, former Alsop residence, Washington, D.C.

Betty Friedan, 3:45 P.M., May 12, 1998, U.S. Capitol building, Washington, D.C.

Robert McNamara, 9 A.M., May 14, 1998, McNamara office, Washington, D.C.

Katherine Graham, 11 A.M., May 21, 1998, Graham residence, Washington, D.C.

Ron Chernow, 10:30 A.M., May 22, 1998, National Portrait Gallery, Washington, D.C.

Edmund Morris, 4 P.M., June 9, 1998, Morris residence, Washington, D.C.

Sylvia Morris, 4:30 P.M., June 9, 1998, Morris residence, Washington, D.C.

Robert Caro, 11 A.M., June 16, 1998, Caro office, New York, New York

Robert Bartley, 3 P.M., June 16, 1998, *Wall Street Journal* offices, New York, New York

David Levering Lewis, 9 A.M., June 18, 1998, Lewis residence, New York, New York

James Tobin, 4:30 P.M., June 22, 1998, Newseum, Arlington, Virginia

Frank McCourt, 3 P.M., June 18, 1998, Stuyvesant High School, New York, New York

Index

About the Author

BRIAN LAMB is the founding CEO of C-SPAN. He has been the host of C-SPAN's *Booknotes* since its inception in 1989, an experiment that quickly became an oasis of literary programming on television. He lives in Arlington, Virginia.